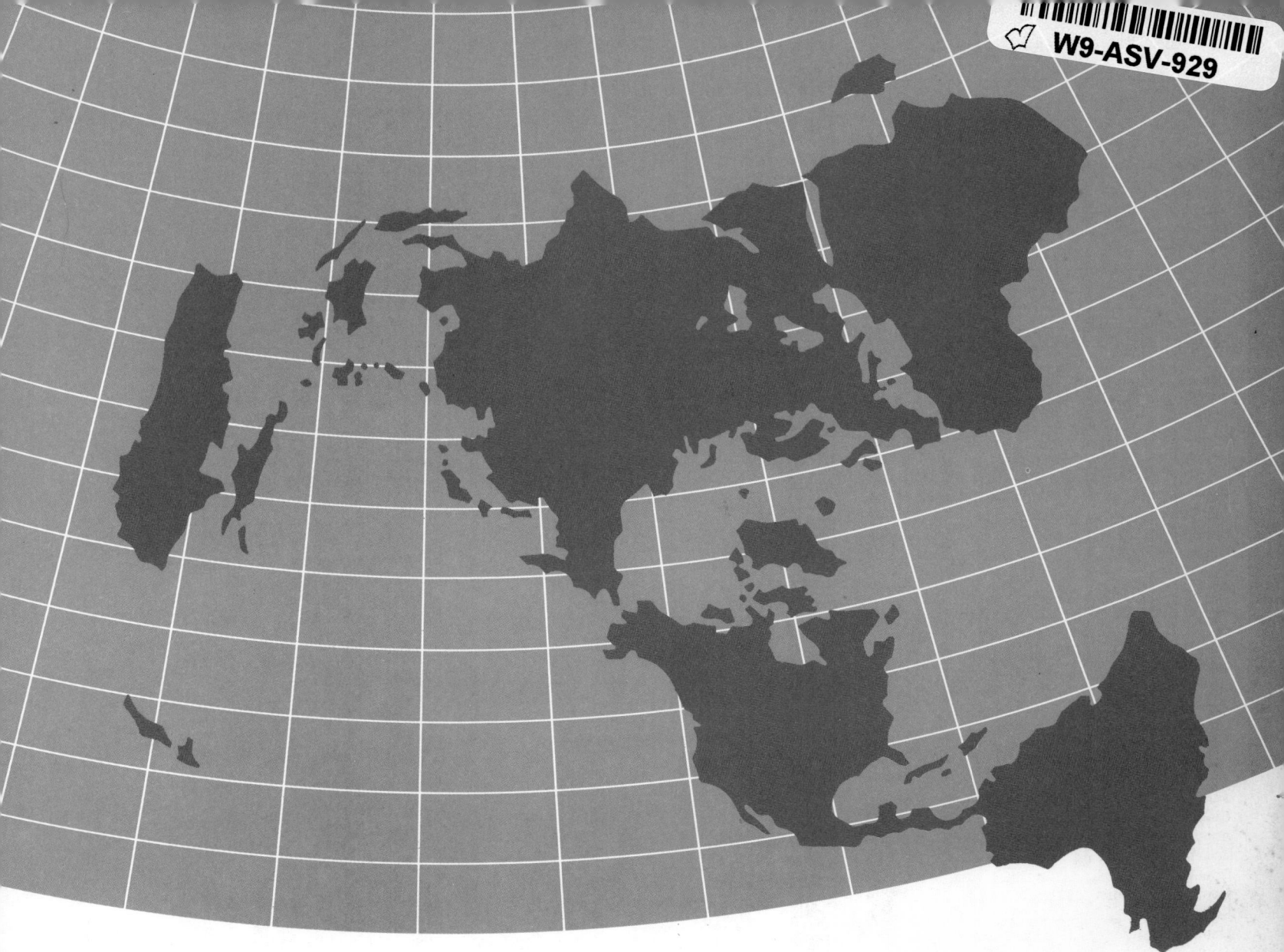

Rand McNally
World Atlas

Rand McNally & Company

Chicago / New York / San Francisco

Contents

The Political World in Maps

Maps and Atlases

Since ancient times, maps have played a unique role in presenting information about the world, and maps defining territory and ownership are almost as old as the human territorial instinct itself. Dating from the second and first millenia B.C., the rock-carving map of the Val Camonica, Italy, in figure 1 shows stepped square fields, paths, rivers, and houses. Elegant as well as useful maps have been produced by many cultures. In figure 2, the Mexican map of the Tepetlaoztoc Valley, drawn in 1583, marks hills with wavy lines and roads with footprints between parallel lines. The methods and materials used to create these maps were dependent upon the technology available, and their accuracy suffered considerably, whereas modern maps are highly accurate, benefiting from our ever-increasing technological knowledge. Satellite imagery, shown in figure 3, now furnishes current, highly precise material from which maps such as that in figure 4 may be created or updated.

In the 1500s Gerardus Mercator, a Flemish cartographer, coined the word *atlas* to describe

Using the Atlas

a collection of maps. The atlas is unique among reference publications because only it, with its maps, actually shows *where* things are located in the world. As a dictionary defines words, as an encyclopedia defines things, an atlas graphically defines the world. Only on a map can the countries, cities, roads, rivers, and lakes covering a vast area be simultaneously viewed in their relative locations. Routes between places can be traced, trips planned, boundaries of neighboring states and countries examined, distances between places measured, the meandering of streams and the sizes of lakes visualized—and remote places imagined.

This atlas brings together not only a variety of

maps but also an assortment of tables and other reference material, with topics ranging from the world's size and population to the countries' political status. To get the most out of the atlas, it is necessary to have a general idea of the arrangement of the information.

Sequence of the Maps

The world is made up of seven major landmasses: the continents of Europe, Asia, Africa, Australia, South America, North America, and Antarctica (figure 5). To allow for the inclusion of detail, each continent is broken down into a series of maps, and this grouping is arranged so that as consecutive pages are turned, a continuous and successive part of the continent is shown. Larger-scale maps are used for regions of greater detail (having many cities, for example) or for areas of global significance.

The continental sequence of the maps is as follows: Europe (traditionally first in atlases), Asia (connected to Europe and forming the Eurasian landmass), Africa, Australia and Oceania, South America, and North America.

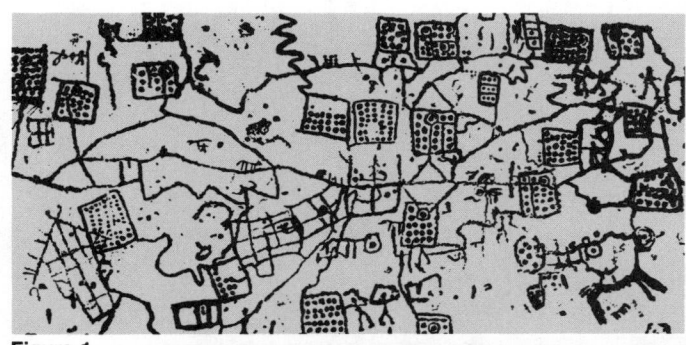

Figure 1

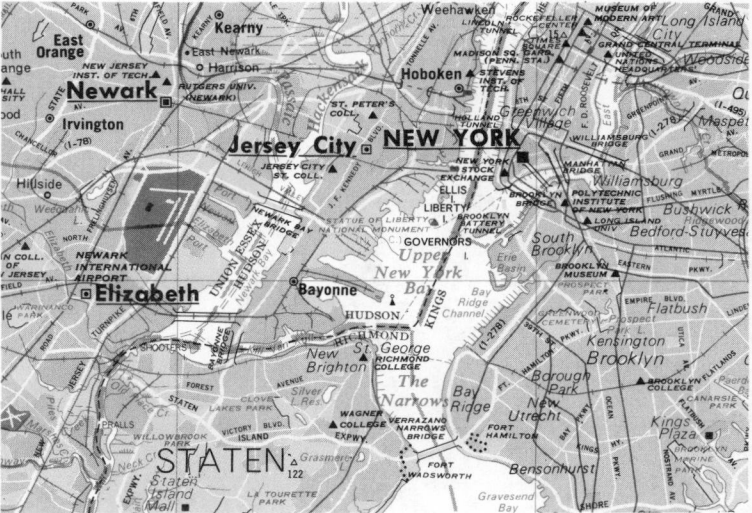

Figure 2

Figure 3

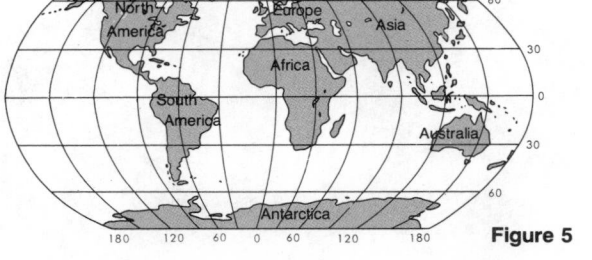

Figure 5

Figure 4

Getting the Information

An atlas can be used for many purposes, from planning a trip to finding hot spots in the news and supplementing world knowledge. But to realize the full potential of an atlas, the user must be able to:

1. Find places on the maps
2. Measure distances
3. Determine directions
4. Understand map symbols

Finding Places

One of the most common and important tasks facilitated by an atlas is finding the *location* of a place in the world. A river's name in a book, a city mentioned in the news, or a vacation spot may prompt your need to know where the place is located. The illustrations and text below explain how to find Benguela, Angola.

1. Look up the place-name in the index at the back of the atlas. Benguela, Angola, can be found on the map on page 24, and it can be located on the map by the letter-number key *C2* (figure 6).

Bay-Ber		155
Benewah, Idaho	B2	57
Benewah, co., Idaho	B2	57
Bengal, reg., Bngl., India	D8	20
Bengasi (Banghāzī), Libya	B2	23
Bengbu, China	E8	17
Bengkulu, Indon., ...	F2	19
Benguela, Ang.	C2	24
Benguela, dist., Ang.	C3	24
Benham, Ky.	D7	62
Ben Hill, co., Ga.	D3	55

Figure 6

2. Turn to the map of Central and Southern Africa on page 24. Note that the letters A through H and the numbers 1 through 10 appear in the margins of the maps.

3. To find Benguela on the map, place your left index finger on C and your right index finger on 2. Move your left finger across the map and your right finger down the map. Your fingers will meet in the area in which Benguela is located (figure 7).

Figure 7

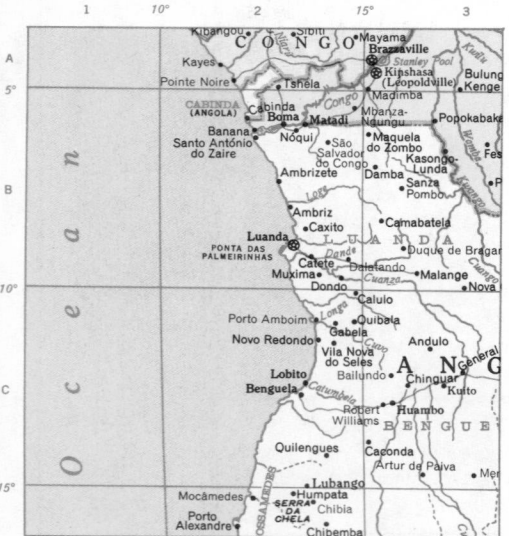

Measuring Distances

In planning trips, determining the distance between two places is essential, and an atlas can help in travel preparation. For instance, to determine the approximate distance between Paris and Rouen, France, follow these three steps:

1. Lay a slip of paper on the map on page 5 so that its edge touches the two cities. Adjust the paper so one corner touches Rouen. Mark the paper directly at the spot where Paris is located (figure 8).

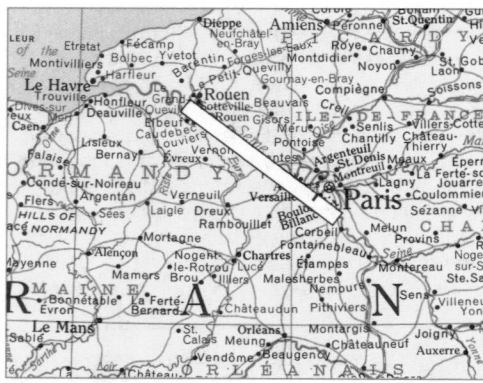

Figure 8

2. Place the paper along the scale of statute miles beneath the map. Position the corner at 0 and line up the edge of the paper along the scale. The pencil mark on the paper indicates Rouen is between 50 and 75 miles from Paris (figure 9).

Figure 9

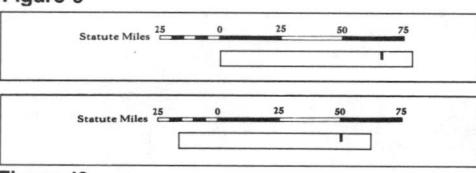

Figure 10

3. To find the exact distance, move the paper to the left so that the pencil mark is at 50 on the scale. The corner of the paper stands in the fourth 5-mile unit on the scale. This means that the two towns are 50 plus 15 plus 2, or 67 miles, apart (figure 10).

Determining Directions

Most of the maps in the atlas are drawn so that when oriented for normal reading north is at the top of the map, south is at the bottom, west is at the left, and east is at the right. Most maps have a series of lines drawn across them—the lines of latitude and longitude. Lines of latitude, or parallels of latitude, are drawn east and west.

Figure 11

Lines of longitude, or meridians of longitude, are drawn north and south (figure 11).

Parallels and meridians appear as either curved or straight lines. For example, in the section of the map of Europe in figure 12, the parallels of latitude appear as curved lines. The meridians of longitude are straight lines that come together toward the top of the map.

Figure 12

Latitude and longitude lines help locate places on maps. Parallels of latitude are numbered in degrees north and south of the *Equator*. Meridians of longitude are numbered in degrees east and west of a line called the *Prime Meridian,* running through Greenwich, England, near London. Any place on earth can be located by the latitude and longitude lines running through it.

To determine directions or locations on maps, you must use the parallels and meridians. For example, suppose you want to know which city is farther north, Bergen, Norway, or Stockholm, Sweden. The map in figure 12 shows that Stockholm is south of the 60° parallel of latitude and Bergen is north of it. This means that Bergen is farther north than Stockholm. By looking at the meridians of longitude, you can determine which city is farther east. Bergen is approximately 5° east of the 0° meridian (Prime Meridian), and Stockholm is almost 20° east of it. This means that Stockholm is farther east than Bergen.

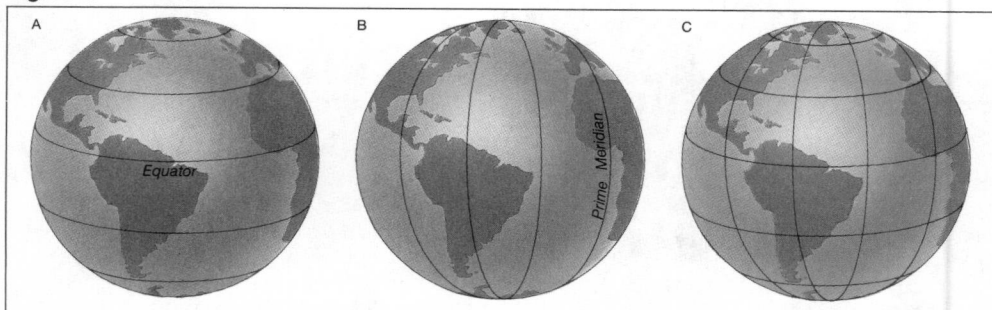

Global View
Europe

This global view centers on the western extension of Asia, the region the world knows as the continent of Europe. Often the two are linked together under the name Eurasia. This peninsula, or arm, of the great Asian landmass, itself is comprised of numerous peninsulas—those of Scandinavia, Iberia, Italy, and the Balkans—and many offshore islands, the most important group being the British Isles.

The thrust of this arm of Asia into the Atlantic Ocean, the North and Mediterranean seas provides a clear-cut western terminus. But the limits of Europe are not so clearly defined on its eastern flank where no natural barriers exist. For the sake of a "boundary" geographers have come to recognize the low Ural Mountains and the Ural River, the Caspian Sea, the Caucasus Mountains, and the Black Sea as the eastern and southeastern border.

From Europe's eastern limits, where the north to south dimension is approximately 2,500 miles, the irregularly shaped continent tapers toward the southwest and the surrounding bodies of water. Through Europe's history its miles of coastline encouraged contact with the other continents, and the seas became avenues of exchange for culture, politics, and technology with other regions of the world.

Internally Europe embraces a varied landscape comparable to no other region of its size in the world: In a total area of only 3,825,000 square miles are found extremes from zero winters and dry steppes in the east to year-round humid, mild climates in the west; extremes in elevation from the heights of the Alps to the below-sea-level Belgian and Netherlands coasts; and a variation in the distribution of inhabitants from the densely populated, industrialized northwest to the sparsely peopled areas in the agricultural south and east. Thirty-three independent nations, each with its own national, religious, cultural, and political heritage, add to this variegated landscape.

Because much of Europe is neither too hot or cold, or too high or low, a great extent of its land has been developed, aided by an impressive river-canal system, dominated by the Rhine and Danube. Its natural and cultural wealth has made possible an economic-social-political system which has long influenced the economic, political, and social structure of the rest of the world.

Today, because of its density of population, strategic location, politics, history, economic strength, and cultural tradition, Europe still may rightfully and strongly claim to be one of the hubs of the world.

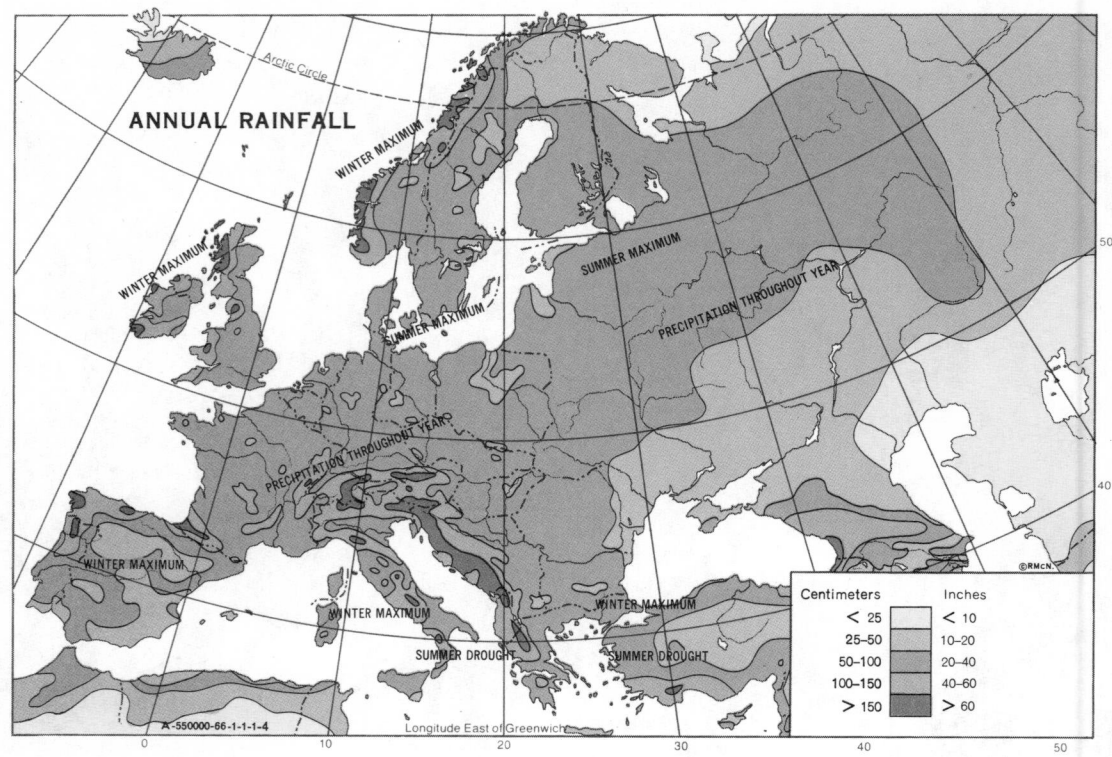

ANNUAL RAINFALL

WINTER MAXIMUM

WINTER MAXIMUM

SUMMER MAXIMUM

SUMMER MAXIMUM

PRECIPITATION THROUGHOUT YEAR

PRECIPITATION THROUGHOUT YEAR

WINTER MAXIMUM

WINTER MAXIMUM

WINTER MAXIMUM

SUMMER DROUGHT

SUMMER DROUGHT

Centimeters	Inches
< 25	< 10
25–50	10–20
50–100	20–40
100–150	40–60
> 150	> 60

A-550000-66-1-1-1-4   Longitude East of Greenwich   ©RMcN

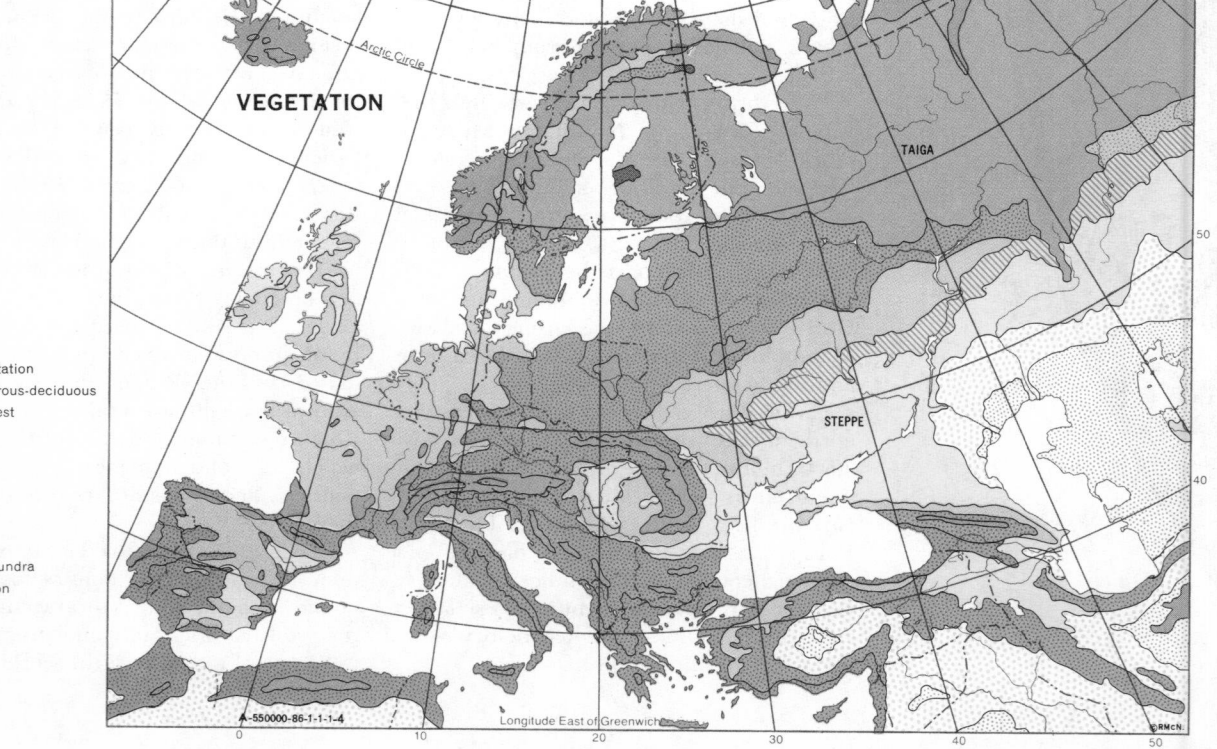

VEGETATION

TAIGA

STEPPE

VEGETATION

- Coniferous forest
- Mediterranean vegetation
- Mixed forest: coniferous-deciduous
- Semi-deciduous forest
- Deciduous forest
- Wooded steppe
- Grass (steppe)
- Short grass
- Desert shrub
- Heath and moor
- Alpine vegetation, tundra
- Little or no vegetation

A-550000-86-1-1-1-4   Longitude East of Greenwich   ©RMcN

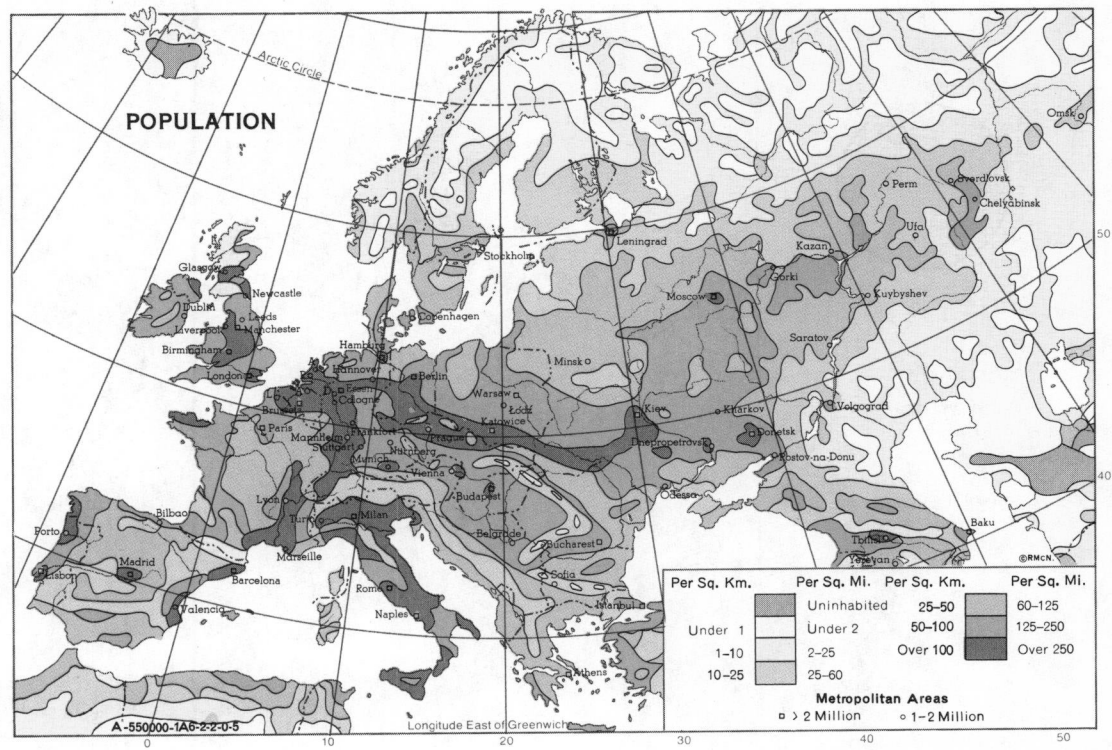

POPULATION

Per Sq. Km.	Per Sq. Mi.	Per Sq. Km.	Per Sq. Mi.
	Uninhabited	25–50	60–125
Under 1	Under 2	50–100	125–250
1–10	2–25	Over 100	Over 250
10–25	25–60		

Metropolitan Areas
□ > 2 Million   ○ 1–2 Million

A-550000-1A6-2-2-0-5   Longitude East of Greenwich

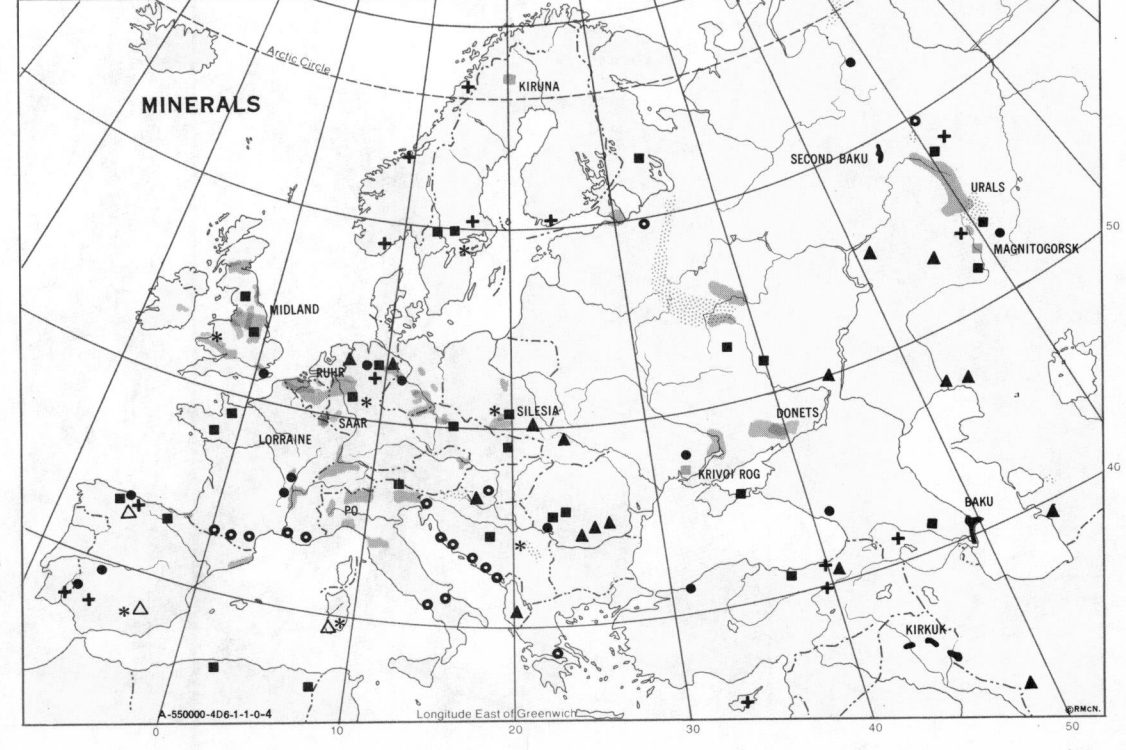

MINERALS

- Industrial areas
- Major coal deposits
- Major petroleum deposits
- Lignite deposits
- ▲ Minor petroleum deposits
- ● Minor coal deposits
- ■ Major iron ore
- ■ Minor iron ore
- ✳ Lead
- ⊙ Bauxite
- △ Zinc
- ✚ Copper

A-550000-4D6-1-1-0-4   Longitude East of Greenwich

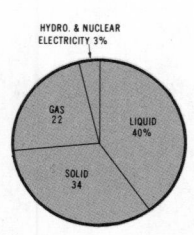

HYDRO. & NUCLEAR
ELECTRICITY 3%

GAS
22

LIQUID
40%

SOLID
34

Energy Consumption
3,699,305 metric tons
coal equivalent–1979

ENERGY

Energy Producing Plants

▽ Geothermal
• Hydroelectric
■ Nuclear

Mineral Fuel Deposits

• Uranium: major deposit
△ Natural Gas: major field
▲ Petroleum: major field
• Petroleum: minor field

Petroleum: major producing area

Coal: major bituminous and anthracite

Coal: minor bituminous and anthracite

Coal: lignite

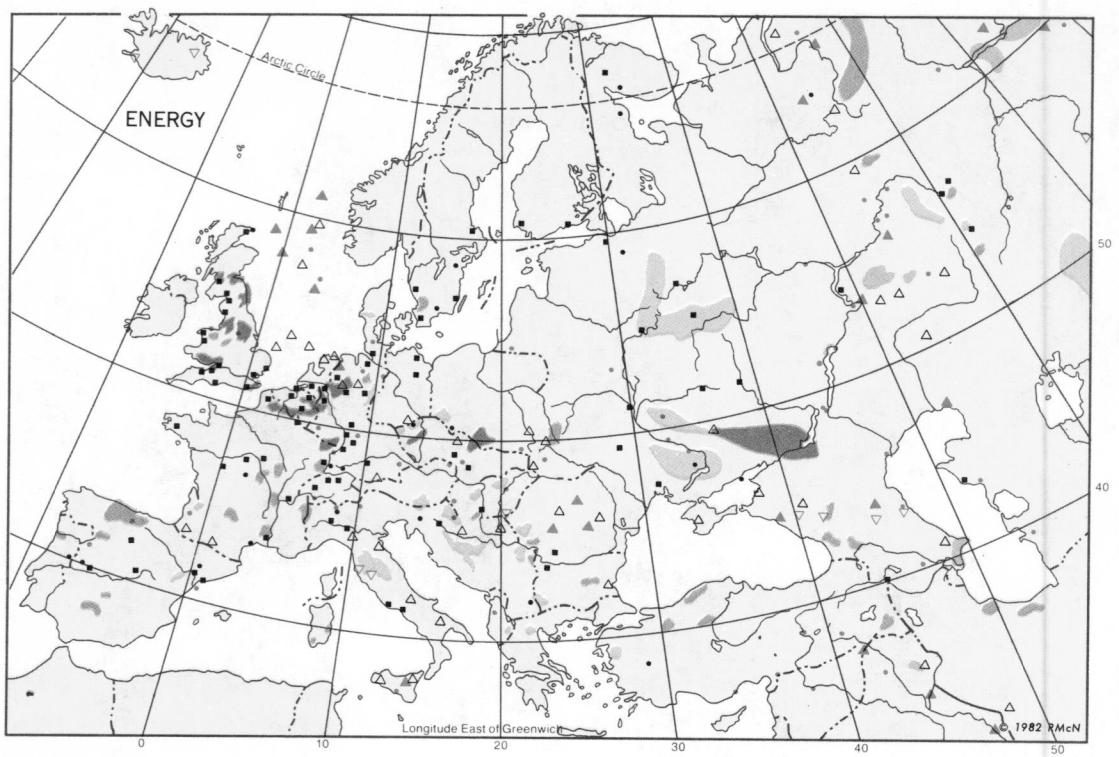

ENERGY

Longitude East of Greenwich

© 1982 RMcN

NATURAL HAZARDS

○ Volcanoes*
● Earthquakes*
● Major flood disasters*
━━ Tsunamis
─── Limit of iceberg drift

Temporary pack ice

Areas subject to desertification

*Twentieth Century occurrences

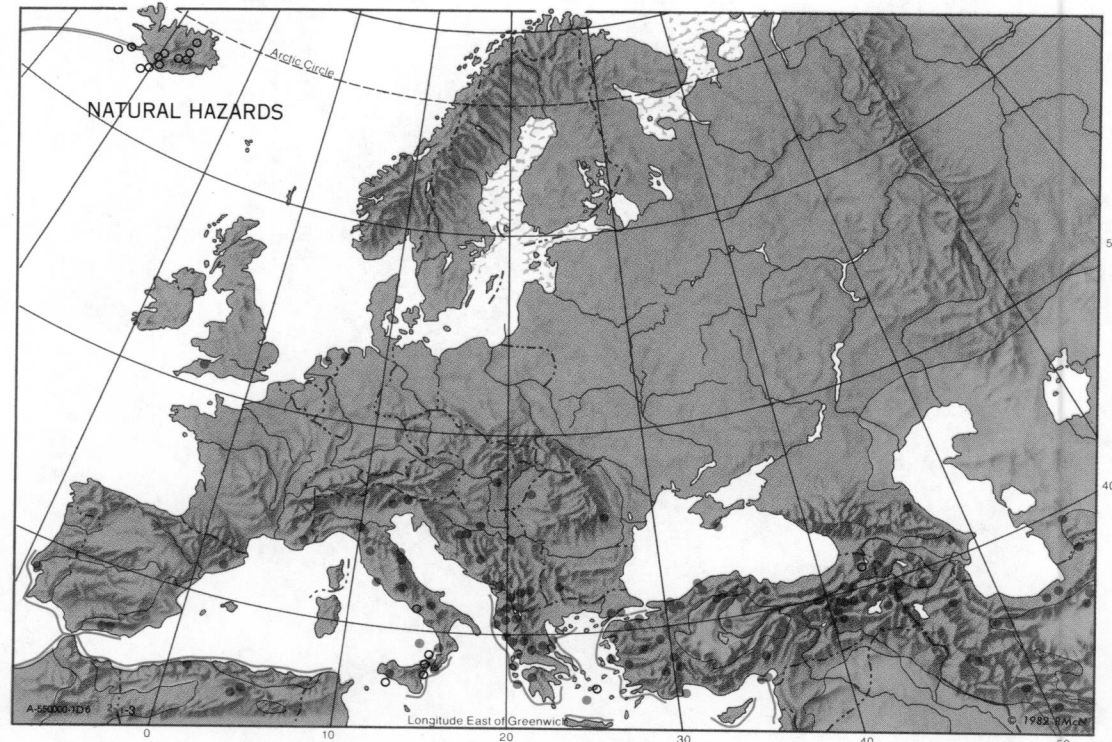

NATURAL HAZARDS

A-550000-1D6

Longitude East of Greenwich

© 1982 RMcN

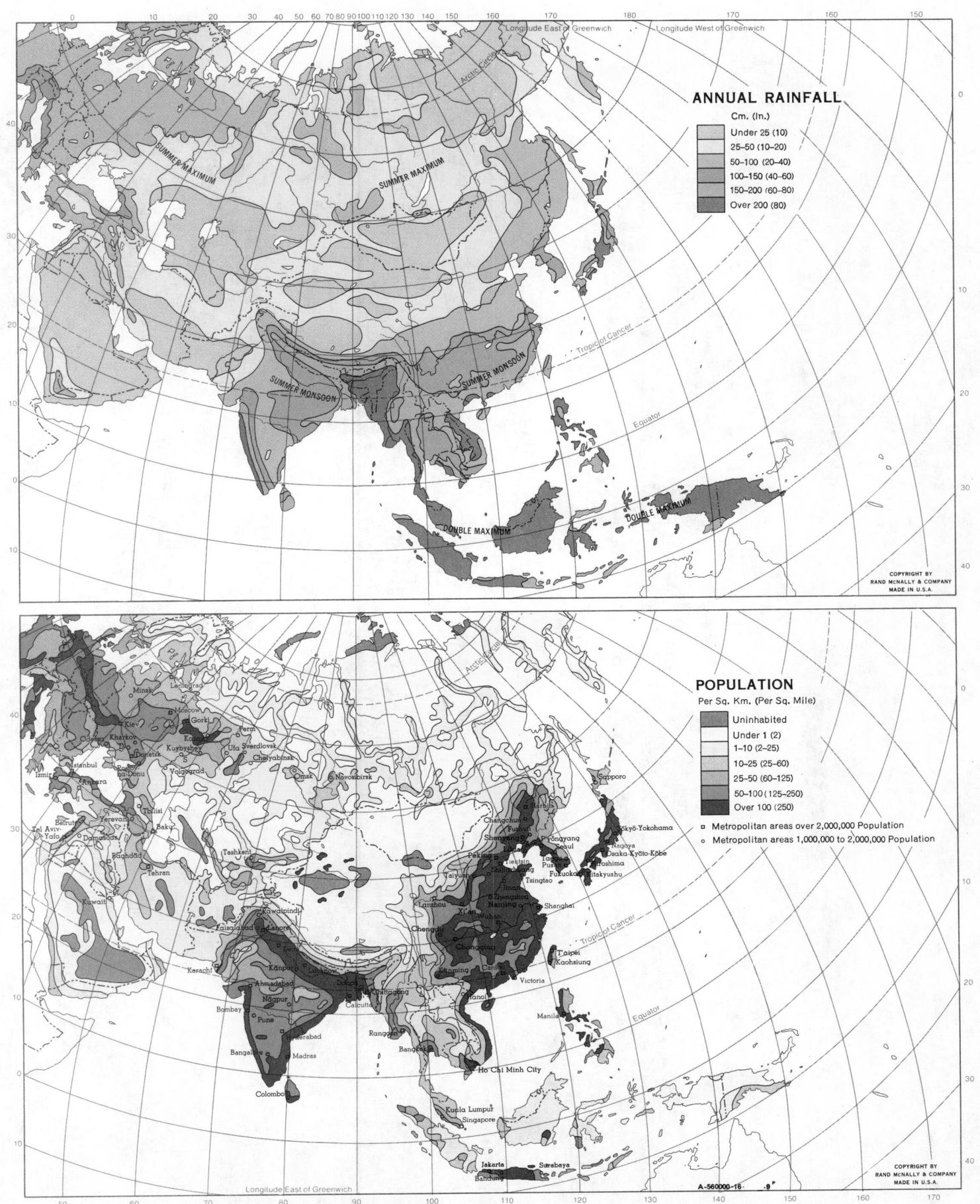

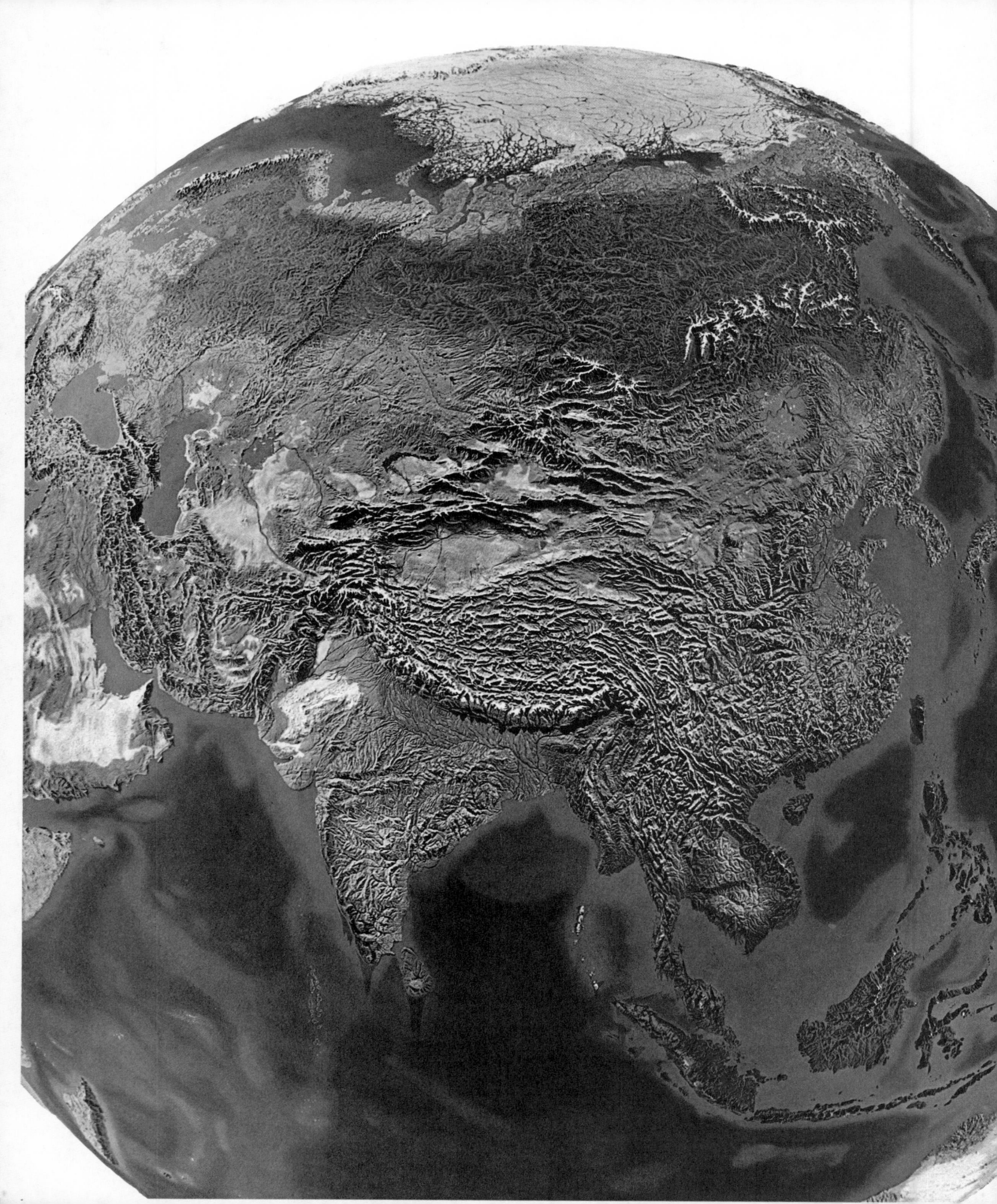

Global View
Asia

Asia, the massive giant of continents, spreads its 17,085,000 square miles from polar wastes to regions of tropical abundance, and from Oriental to Occidental hearthlands. Much of Asia's vastness, however, is occupied by deserts, steppes, and by frozen and near-frozen wastes. Rugged upland areas stretch from Turkey and Iran, through the two-mile-high Tibetan Plateau, to the Bering Strait, leaving only one-third of Asia suitable for human habitation. These barriers also separate the two dominant, sharply contrasting parts of Asia—the realm made up of Southwest, South, and Southeast Asia from that of "European" Asia.

Rimming the south and east coasts of the continent are the most densely populated regions of the world, each dominated by a life-giving river system—the Tigris-Euphrates, the Indus and Ganges, the Brahmaputra, the Irrawaddy and Salween, the Menam and Mekong, the Yangtze and Hwang Ho, as well as innumerable small river valleys, plains, and islands. Separated from one another by deserts, massifs, and seas these regions account for over one-half of the world's population.

The civilizations associated with this population (where rural densities frequently may exceed 1,000 people per square mile) were developed largely upon the strength of intensive agricultural systems. Today these

systems still occupy more than 60 percent of the populace, who manage only to win a bare subsistence. Changeover from subsistence agricultural economic systems to industrialized economies has been successful only in Japan and parts of the U.S.S.R.

North of the great Gobi Desert and the mountain barriers of the interior is the second Asia which, on almost every hand, differs from the southern portion of the continent. In the far north severe climatic elements send temperatures to −90°F., and permanently frozen ground impedes growth of vegetation. Only the scattered settlements next to the Trans-Siberian Railway give the area an indication of development. The activities of most of the populace are clearly directed toward Europe rather than Asia.

These two realms of the Asian continent do share two common characteristics. One is vast, yet generally inaccessible, natural resources—extensive forests, minerals, and hydroelectric potential—and the second is the drive to industrialize in order to "catch up" to the general material well-being of the Western World.

In the future, as the common characteristics, resources and drive, are developed, Asia's two realms may witness a change. A material way of life may result consistent with their heritage and historic contributions to the world.

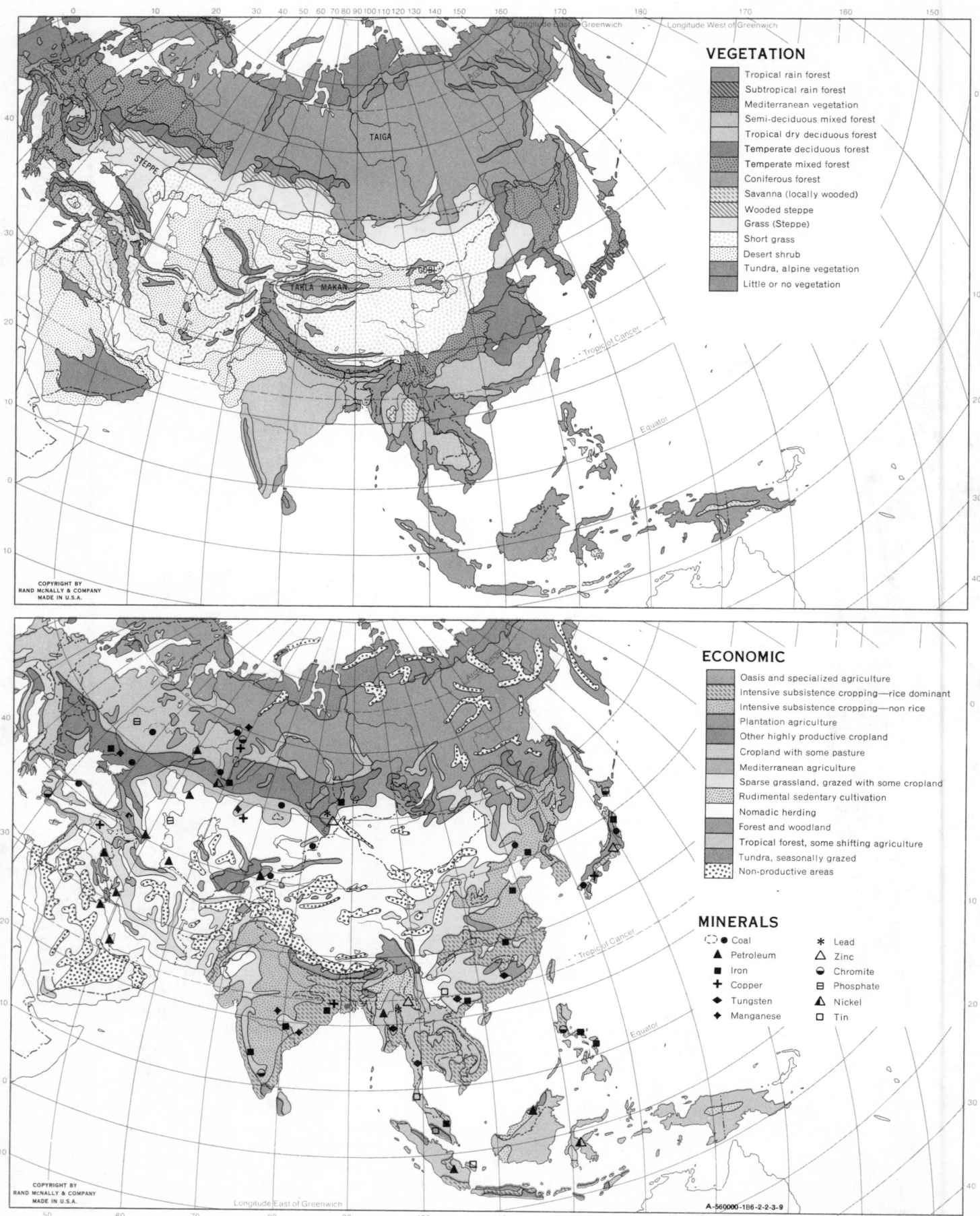

VEGETATION

- Tropical rain forest
- Subtropical rain forest
- Mediterranean vegetation
- Semi-deciduous mixed forest
- Tropical dry deciduous forest
- Temperate deciduous forest
- Temperate mixed forest
- Coniferous forest
- Savanna (locally wooded)
- Wooded steppe
- Grass (Steppe)
- Short grass
- Desert shrub
- Tundra, alpine vegetation
- Little or no vegetation

ECONOMIC

- Oasis and specialized agriculture
- Intensive subsistence cropping—rice dominant
- Intensive subsistence cropping—non rice
- Plantation agriculture
- Other highly productive cropland
- Cropland with some pasture
- Mediterranean agriculture
- Sparse grassland, grazed with some cropland
- Rudimental sedentary cultivation
- Nomadic herding
- Forest and woodland
- Tropical forest, some shifting agriculture
- Tundra, seasonally grazed
- Non-productive areas

MINERALS

- Coal
- ▲ Petroleum
- ■ Iron
- ✚ Copper
- ◆ Tungsten
- ◆ Manganese
- ✳ Lead
- △ Zinc
- ◖ Chromite
- ⊟ Phosphate
- ▲ Nickel
- ☐ Tin

A-560000-1B6-2-2-3-9

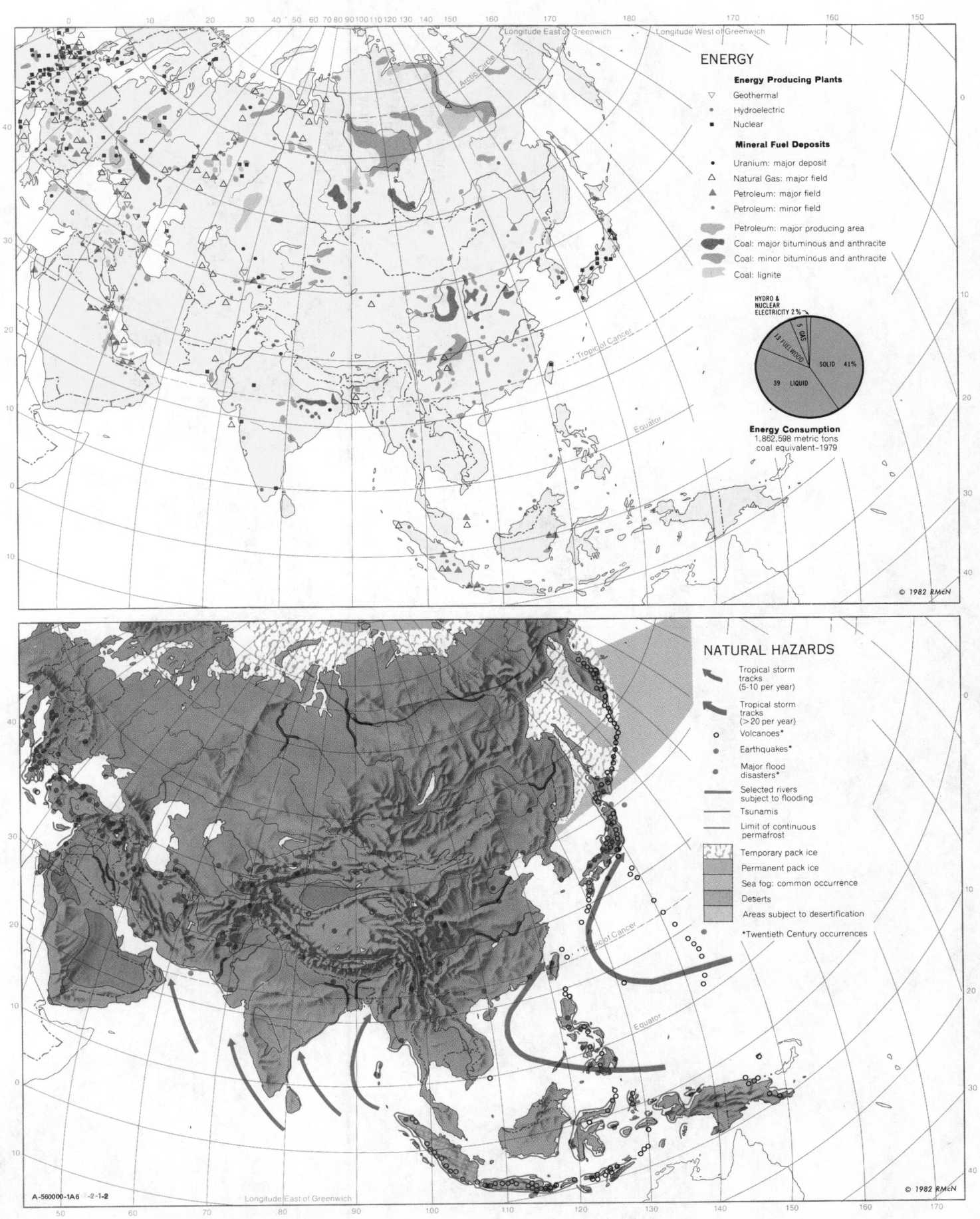

ENERGY

Energy Producing Plants
▽ Geothermal
• Hydroelectric
■ Nuclear

Mineral Fuel Deposits
• Uranium: major deposit
△ Natural Gas: major field
▲ Petroleum: major field
• Petroleum: minor field

Petroleum: major producing area
Coal: major bituminous and anthracite
Coal: minor bituminous and anthracite
Coal: lignite

HYDRO & NUCLEAR ELECTRICITY 2%
GAS 5
13 FUELWOOD
SOLID 41%
39 LIQUID

Energy Consumption
1,862,598 metric tons
coal equivalent–1979

© 1982 RMcN

NATURAL HAZARDS

Tropical storm tracks (5-10 per year)
Tropical storm tracks (>20 per year)
○ Volcanoes*
• Earthquakes*
• Major flood disasters*
Selected rivers subject to flooding
Tsunamis
Limit of continuous permafrost
Temporary pack ice
Permanent pack ice
Sea fog: common occurrence
Deserts
Areas subject to desertification

*Twentieth Century occurrences

A-560000-1A6   -2-1-2

Longitude East of Greenwich

© 1982 RMcN

Global View
Africa

For centuries most of Africa's 11,685,000 square miles was unknown to outsiders. Access by one available avenue, the Nile, was impeded by the cataracts above Aswan. Since much of the interior is upland or plateau, usually dropping off rather sharply near the coasts, most of Africa's great rivers have rapids or falls close to the seaboard and so have not provided convenient routes to the interior. Moreover, the coastline is very regular, with few of the natural harbors of the other continents.

Once penetrated, much of the interior proved inhospitable to man. In the north, the world's largest desert, the immense expanse of the Sahara, blocks Africa's north rim from the central and southern portions. Near the other end of Africa, the Kalahari Desert helps separate the pleasant southernmost portion from the rest of the continent. In the center, the vast Congo Basin, humid, thinly settled, and unattractive, runs from the Atlantic seaboard east to the foot of the rugged highlands of East Africa, marked by the Rift Valley, which can be identified by the string of elongated lakes.

Africa's most important internal boundary is the Sahara. North of it the Mediterranean coastal countries are Moslem in tradition and have had close connections with Europe and the Near East. South of the Sahara are the many rich and varied cultures of Negroid tribal Africa. Unlike in many ways though they are, Mediterranean and Black Africa have until recently shared a common history of domination by non-African colonial powers. As late as 1945 there were only four independent nations in the entire continent. Now, spurred by the forces of nationalism, one new nation after another has emerged.

Past developments in communications, transport, education, and agricultural and industrial techniques, though limited, have formed a legacy from the old colonial powers on which the new African nations can build. Resources of iron ore, gold, oil, copper, timber, and a host of other vital raw materials are available. And there are many areas where climate and soil conditions are conducive to commercial agriculture particularly for peanuts and cacao.

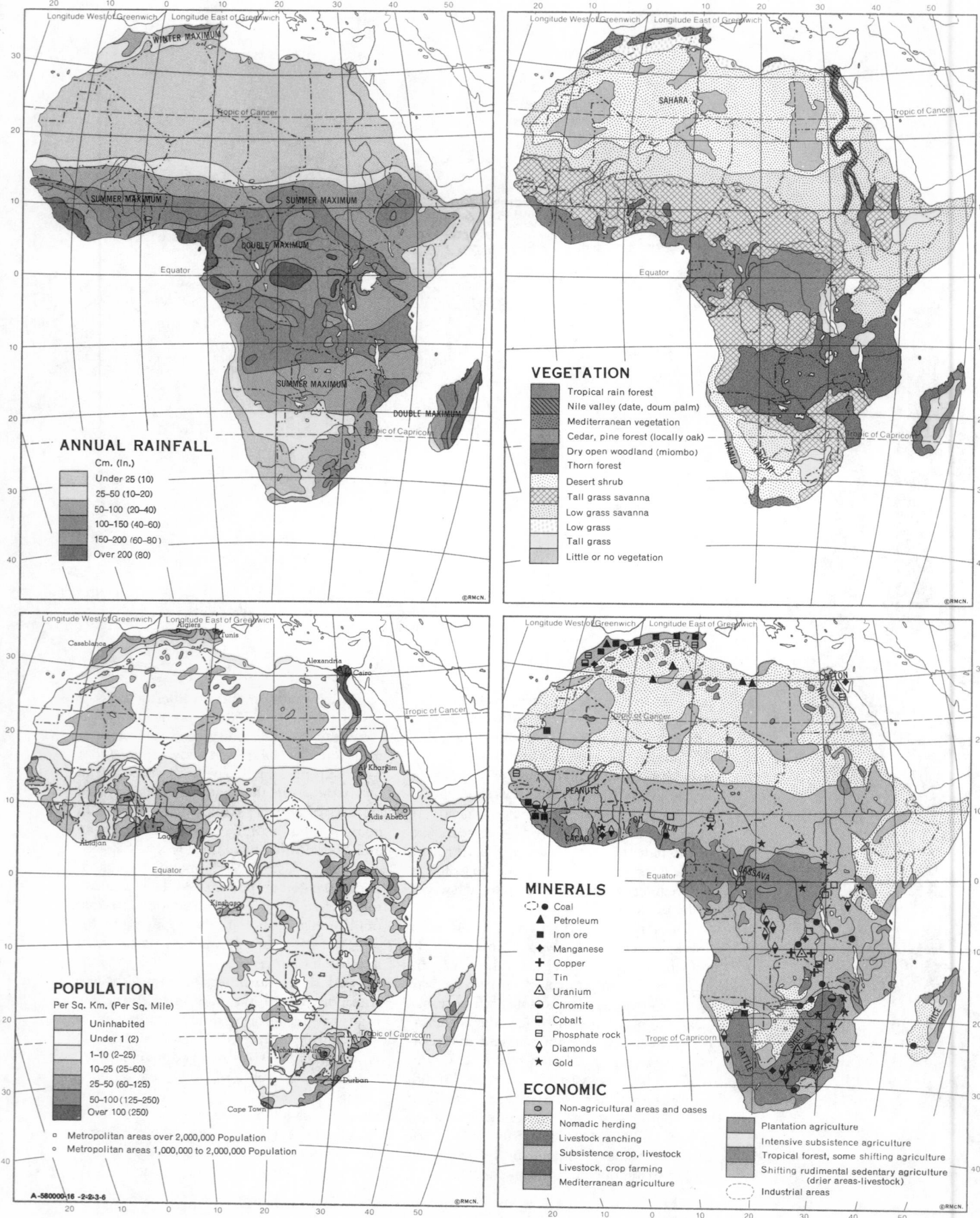

ANNUAL RAINFALL

Cm. (In.)

- Under 25 (10)
- 25–50 (10–20)
- 50–100 (20–40)
- 100–150 (40–60)
- 150–200 (60–80)
- Over 200 (80)

VEGETATION

- Tropical rain forest
- Nile valley (date, doum palm)
- Mediterranean vegetation
- Cedar, pine forest (locally oak)
- Dry open woodland (miombo)
- Thorn forest
- Desert shrub
- Tall grass savanna
- Low grass savanna
- Low grass
- Tall grass
- Little or no vegetation

POPULATION

Per Sq. Km. (Per Sq. Mile)

- Uninhabited
- Under 1 (2)
- 1–10 (2–25)
- 10–25 (25–60)
- 25–50 (60–125)
- 50–100 (125–250)
- Over 100 (250)

□ Metropolitan areas over 2,000,000 Population
○ Metropolitan areas 1,000,000 to 2,000,000 Population

A-580000-16 -2-2-3-6

MINERALS

- ● Coal
- ▲ Petroleum
- ■ Iron ore
- ◆ Manganese
- + Copper
- □ Tin
- △ Uranium
- ◒ Chromite
- ▣ Cobalt
- ▤ Phosphate rock
- ◊ Diamonds
- ★ Gold

ECONOMIC

- Non-agricultural areas and oases
- Nomadic herding
- Livestock ranching
- Subsistence crop, livestock
- Livestock, crop farming
- Mediterranean agriculture
- Plantation agriculture
- Intensive subsistence agriculture
- Tropical forest, some shifting agriculture
- Shifting rudimental sedentary agriculture (drier areas-livestock)
- Industrial areas

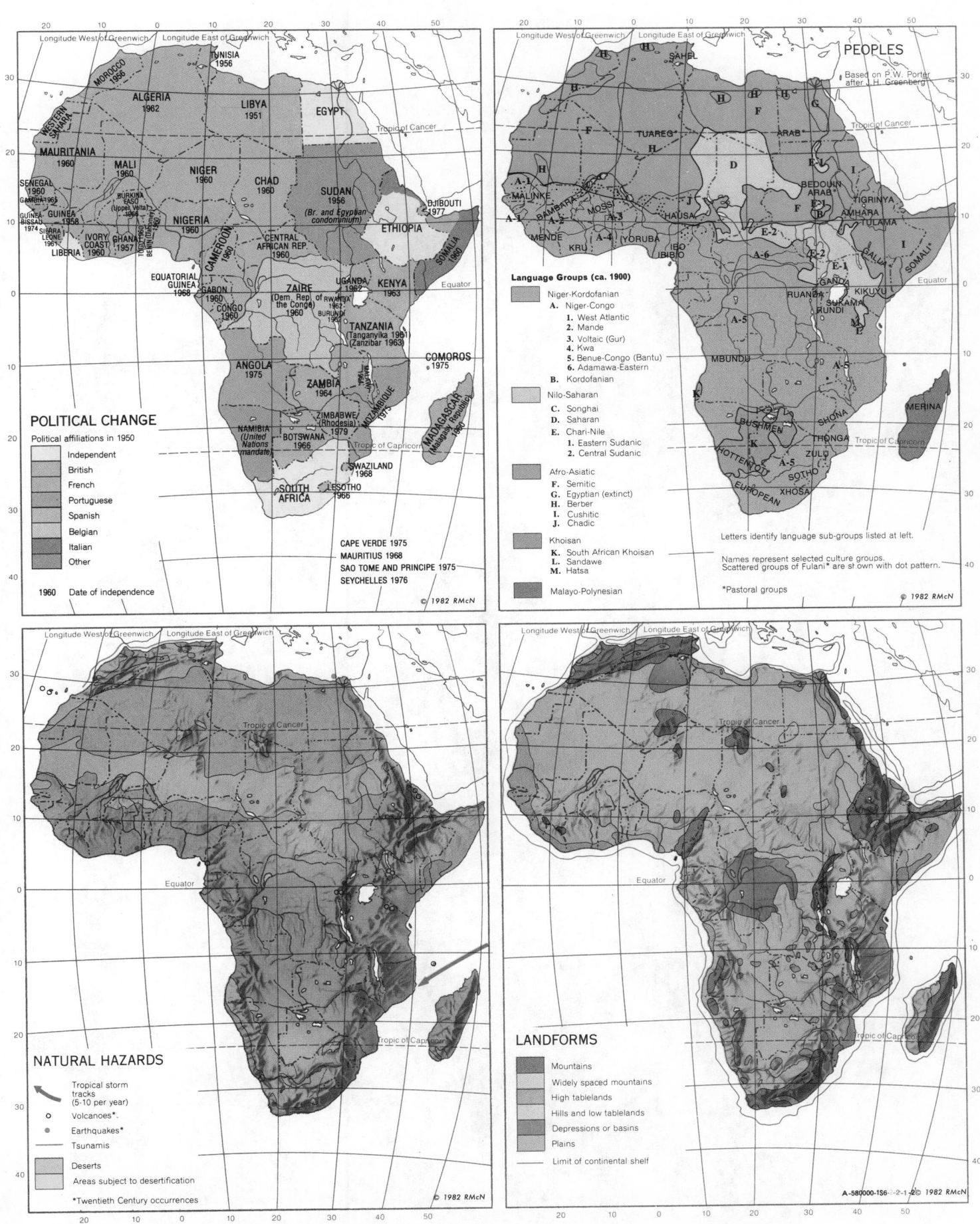

POLITICAL CHANGE

Political affiliations in 1950

- Independent
- British
- French
- Portuguese
- Spanish
- Belgian
- Italian
- Other

1960   Date of independence

CAPE VERDE 1975
MAURITIUS 1968
SAO TOME AND PRINCIPE 1975
SEYCHELLES 1976

© 1982 RMcN

PEOPLES

Based on P.W. Porter
after J. H. Greenberg

Language Groups (ca. 1900)

Niger-Kordofanian
  A. Niger-Congo
    1. West Atlantic
    2. Mande
    3. Voltaic (Gur)
    4. Kwa
    5. Benue-Congo (Bantu)
    6. Adamawa-Eastern
  B. Kordofanian

Nilo-Saharan
  C. Songhai
  D. Saharan
  E. Chari-Nile
    1. Eastern Sudanic
    2. Central Sudanic

Afro-Asiatic
  F. Semitic
  G. Egyptian (extinct)
  H. Berber
  I. Cushitic
  J. Chadic

Khoisan
  K. South African Khoisan
  L. Sandawe
  M. Hatsa

Malayo-Polynesian

Letters identify language sub-groups listed at left.

Names represent selected culture groups.
Scattered groups of Fulani* are shown with dot pattern.

*Pastoral groups

© 1982 RMcN

NATURAL HAZARDS

Tropical storm tracks (5-10 per year)

- ○ Volcanoes*.
- • Earthquakes*
- —— Tsunamis

Deserts

Areas subject to desertification

*Twentieth Century occurrences

© 1982 RMcN

LANDFORMS

- Mountains
- Widely spaced mountains
- High tablelands
- Hills and low tablelands
- Depressions or basins
- Plains
- —— Limit of continental shelf

A-580000-1S6---2-1-2© 1982 RMcN

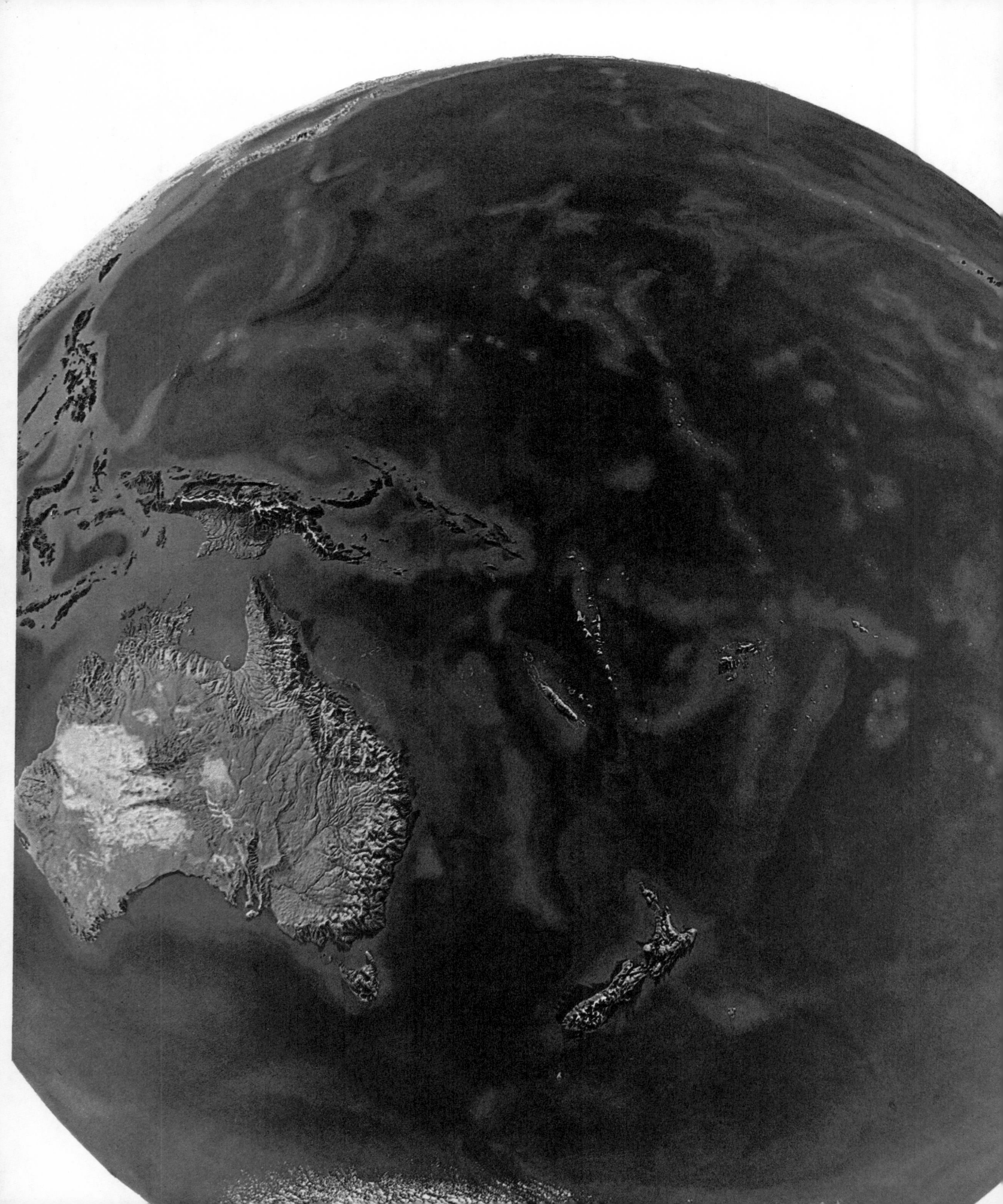

Australia, New Zealand, Oceania

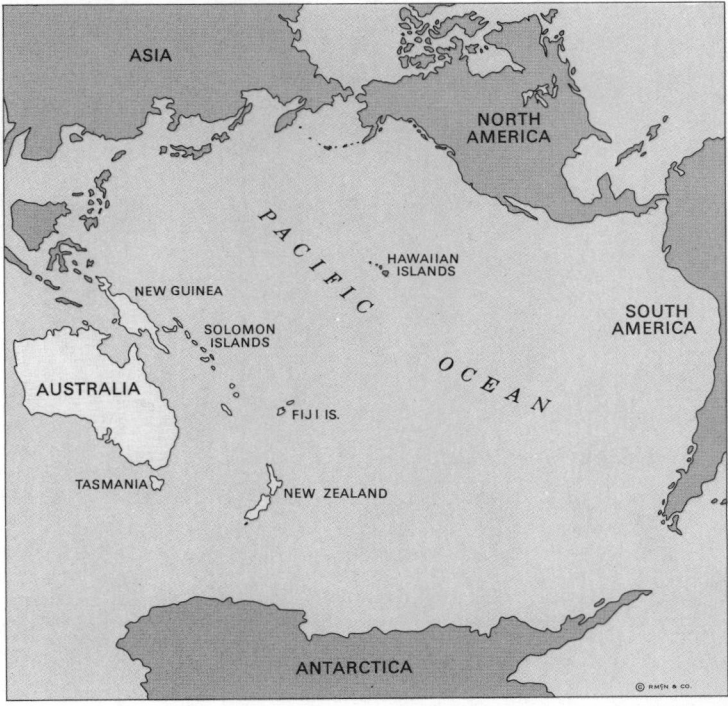

This region of the world is composed of the island continent of Australia, the substantial islands of New Zealand and New Guinea, clusters of smaller islands, and the many pinpoint atolls scattered throughout the expanse of the central and southern Pacific. Extreme isolation and their island nature are common characteristics held by these realms, but other similarities are few.

Australia's size compares with that of the forty-eight conterminous United States. Dry air masses sweep across the western interior from the west, creating the largest desert outside of the Sahara. Along the eastern coast higher temperatures and humidity have combined to produce climates conducive to a varied agricultural system, and therefore, the population is concentrated along this favorable coastal strip. The mountains of the east tend to isolate the population in a number of distinct clusters. Sydney, Melbourne, Brisbane, and Adelaide are the four principal centers, acting as chief exporters of the wool and wheat, and the importers, manufacturers, and distributors for the continent.

New Zealand, like Australia, is an enclave of a European settlement in the Pacific. Upon the vegetation of this climatically mild area the descendants of European settlers have established a thriving economy based upon the exportation of butter, beef, and mutton. The mountainous spine running the length of New Zealand provides some magnificent scenery and the gamut of climatic types.

New Guinea is closely related to both Indonesia and Melanesia, and so links Southeast Asia with Oceania. Although much larger, it typifies the larger islands of the Southwestern Pacific. Like New Guinea, these islands have a mountainous core and narrow, alluvial coastal plains. Upon the plains, under tropical heat and humidity, a variety of tropical agricultural products are raised and some of the islands, such as Fiji, have well developed commercial economies.

Unlike New Guinea and the larger islands are the speck-like atolls scattered throughout the central and southern Pacific. These South Sea Islands are famed for isolation, mild climate, and scenic beauty. But their size, limited resources, and small population, keep their economies at a subsistence level.

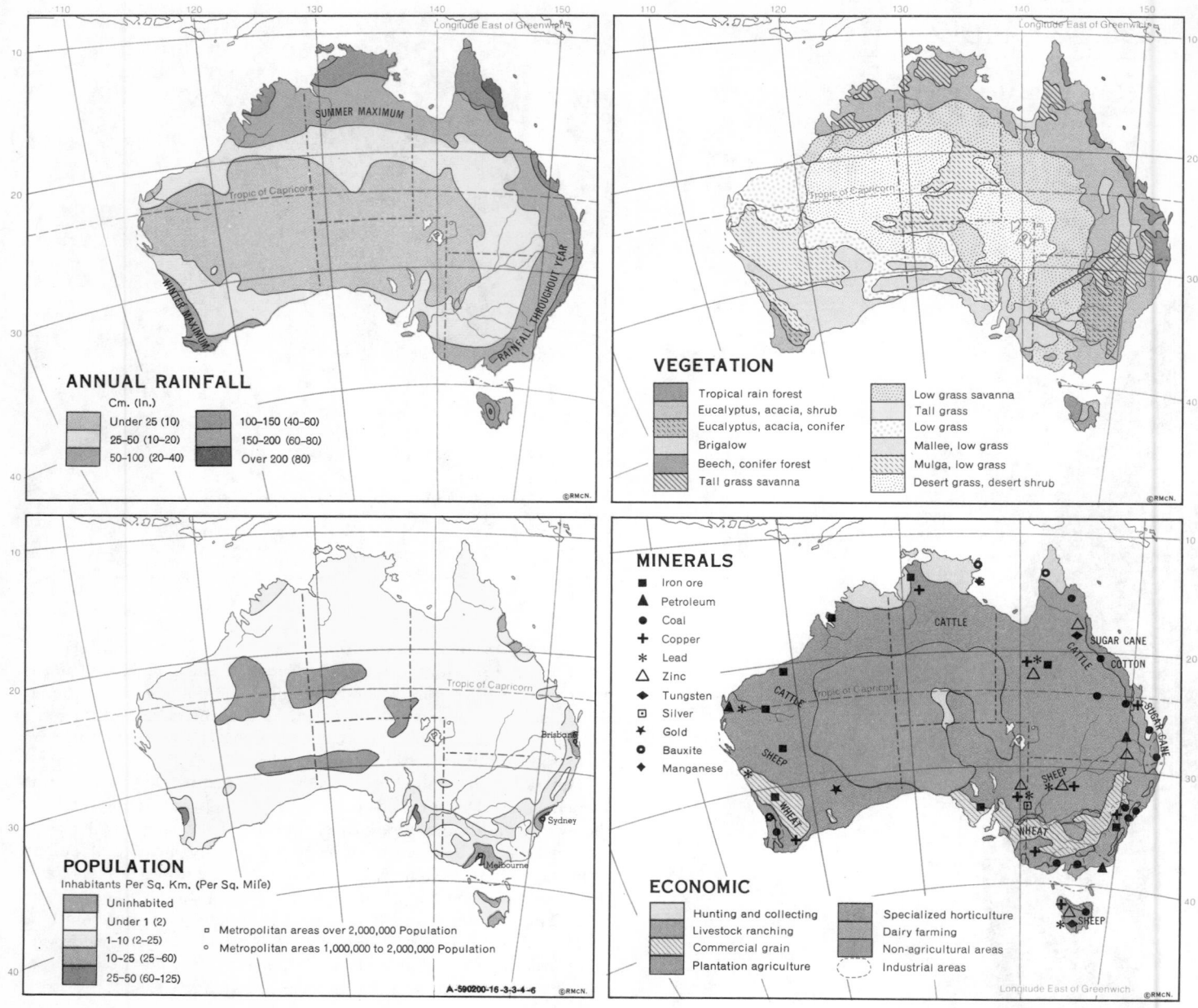

ANNUAL RAINFALL

Cm. (In.)

- Under 25 (10)
- 25–50 (10–20)
- 50–100 (20–40)
- 100–150 (40–60)
- 150–200 (60–80)
- Over 200 (80)

VEGETATION

- Tropical rain forest
- Eucalyptus, acacia, shrub
- Eucalyptus, acacia, conifer
- Brigalow
- Beech, conifer forest
- Tall grass savanna
- Low grass savanna
- Tall grass
- Low grass
- Mallee, low grass
- Mulga, low grass
- Desert grass, desert shrub

POPULATION

Inhabitants Per Sq. Km. (Per Sq. Mile)

- Uninhabited
- Under 1 (2)
- 1–10 (2–25)
- 10–25 (25–60)
- 25–50 (60–125)

□ Metropolitan areas over 2,000,000 Population
○ Metropolitan areas 1,000,000 to 2,000,000 Population

A-590200-16-3-3-4-6   ©RMcN.

MINERALS

- ■ Iron ore
- ▲ Petroleum
- ● Coal
- + Copper
- ✳ Lead
- △ Zinc
- ◆ Tungsten
- ⊡ Silver
- ✶ Gold
- ◉ Bauxite
- ◆ Manganese

ECONOMIC

- Hunting and collecting
- Livestock ranching
- Commercial grain
- Plantation agriculture
- Specialized horticulture
- Dairy farming
- Non-agricultural areas
- Industrial areas

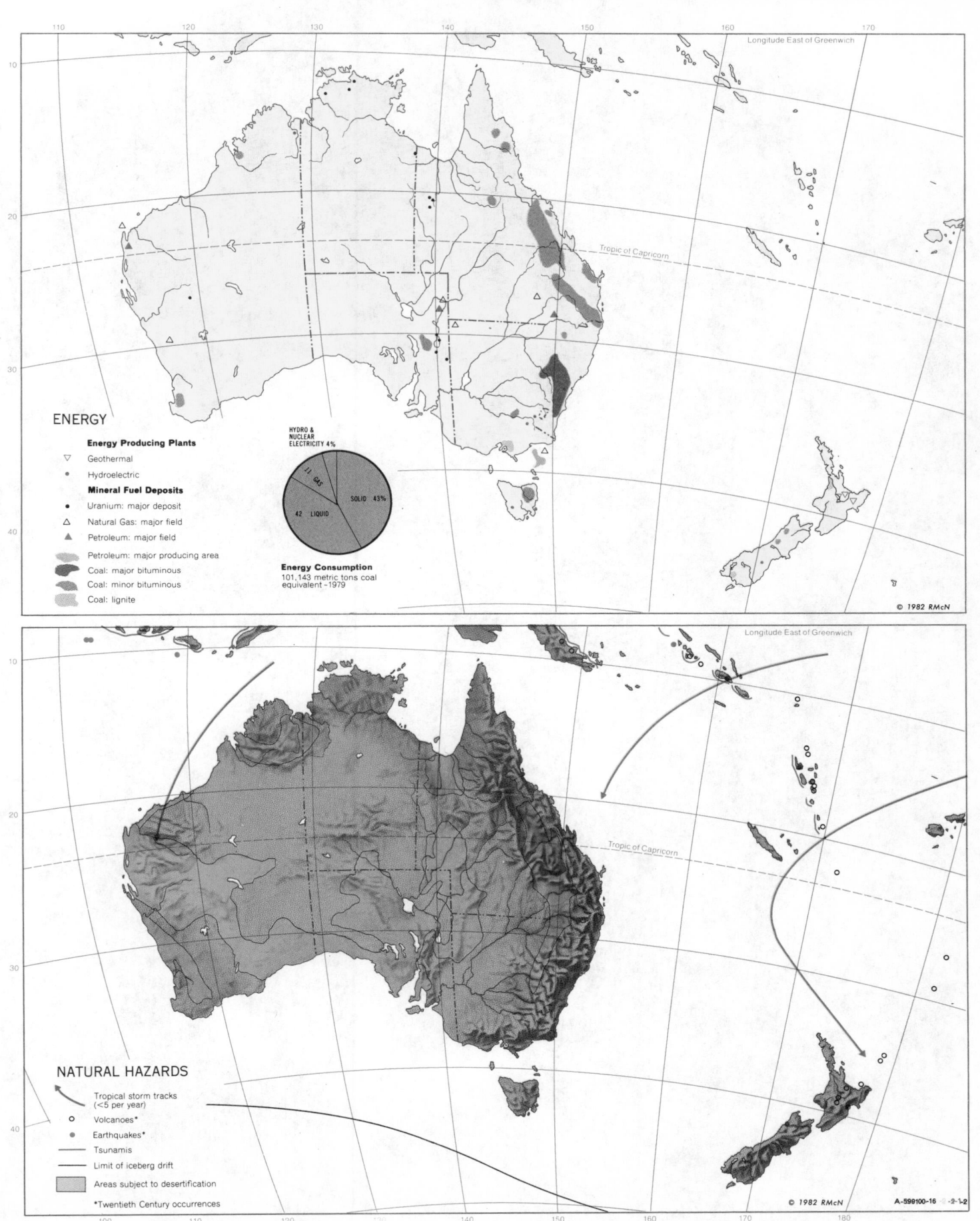

ENERGY

Energy Producing Plants

▽ Geothermal

• Hydroelectric

Mineral Fuel Deposits

• Uranium: major deposit

△ Natural Gas: major field

▲ Petroleum: major field

Petroleum: major producing area

Coal: major bituminous

Coal: minor bituminous

Coal: lignite

HYDRO &
NUCLEAR
ELECTRICITY 4%

11 GAS

SOLID 43%

42 LIQUID

Energy Consumption
101,143 metric tons coal
equivalent –1979

© 1982 RMcN

Longitude East of Greenwich

Tropic of Capricorn

NATURAL HAZARDS

↰ Tropical storm tracks
(<5 per year)

○ Volcanoes*

• Earthquakes*

—— Tsunamis

—— Limit of iceberg drift

Areas subject to desertification

*Twentieth Century occurrences

© 1982 RMcN   A-599100-16   -2-1-2

Longitude East of Greenwich

Tropic of Capricorn

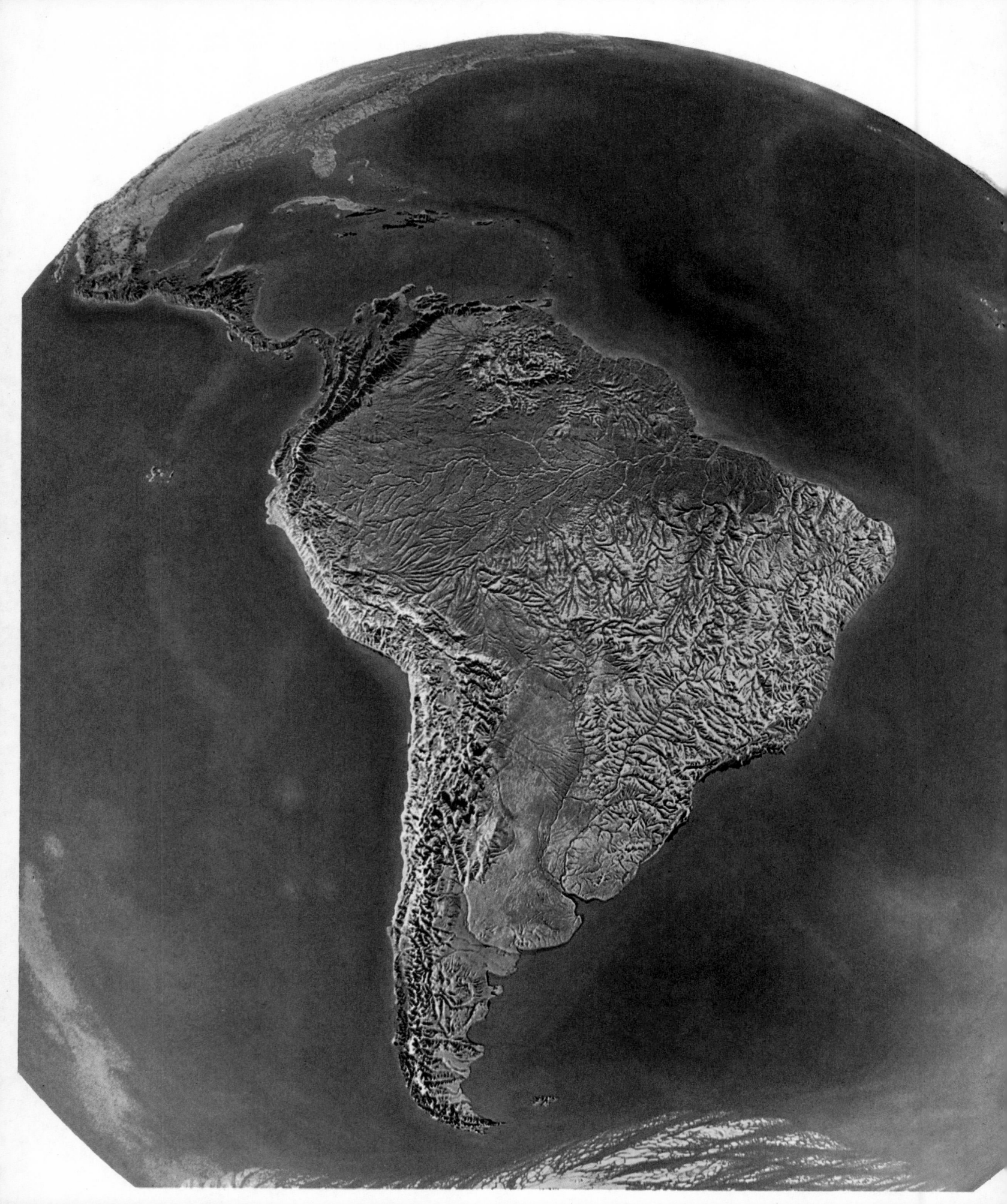

Global View
South America

Triangularly shaped South America is surrounded by water except at the narrow Isthmus of Panama. No great peninsulas extend into its seas or oceans, and its outlines are more regular than those of most other continents.

The Andes Mountains rise like a wall along the western shores, and this formidable chain runs the entire length of the continent, rising to altitudes of over 20,000 feet. It is the longest continuous mountain chain in the world.

The bulk of the continent slopes eastward from the eastern face of the Andes. From north to south, landforms include plains drained by the Orinoco and the eroded plateau areas of the Guiana and Brazilian highlands, the tropical lowlands of the Amazon Basin, savanna called the Gran Chaco, which is drained by the Paraná-Paraguay-Plata river systems, the pampas, and the plains of Patagonia.

The shape of the continent, its position astride the Equator, the water surrounding it, and the mountainous terrain have resulted in a variety of climates. The area east of the Andes from Venezuela to Northern Argentina, is dominated by moisture-laden air masses of the Atlantic. This two-thirds of the continent has a tropical or subtropical environment. Most of the remaining portion is under the influence of the relatively dry, cool Pacific air masses, which create the driest region in the world —the Atacama Desert of Chile. These cool Pacific air masses, too, on crossing the Andes in the narrow southern portion of the continent, create the Patagonian Desert of Argentina. In the higher altitudes of the mountain chain climates familiar to mid and upper latitudes are found.

Much of the interior of South America is still inaccessible, owing to extensive regions of mountains or jungle. Most of the settlement has been around the periphery of the continent. Spanish and Portuguese settlers, and later Germans and Italians, have developed highly specialized commercial economies in certain of the peripheral areas. Around Buenos Aires, São Paulo, Santiago, Bogotá economies based on agricultural products have been developed— wheat, beef, coffee, citrus fruit to name a few. Exported minerals—oil from Venezuela, tin from Bolivia, and copper from Chile— are economic mainstays of other countries.

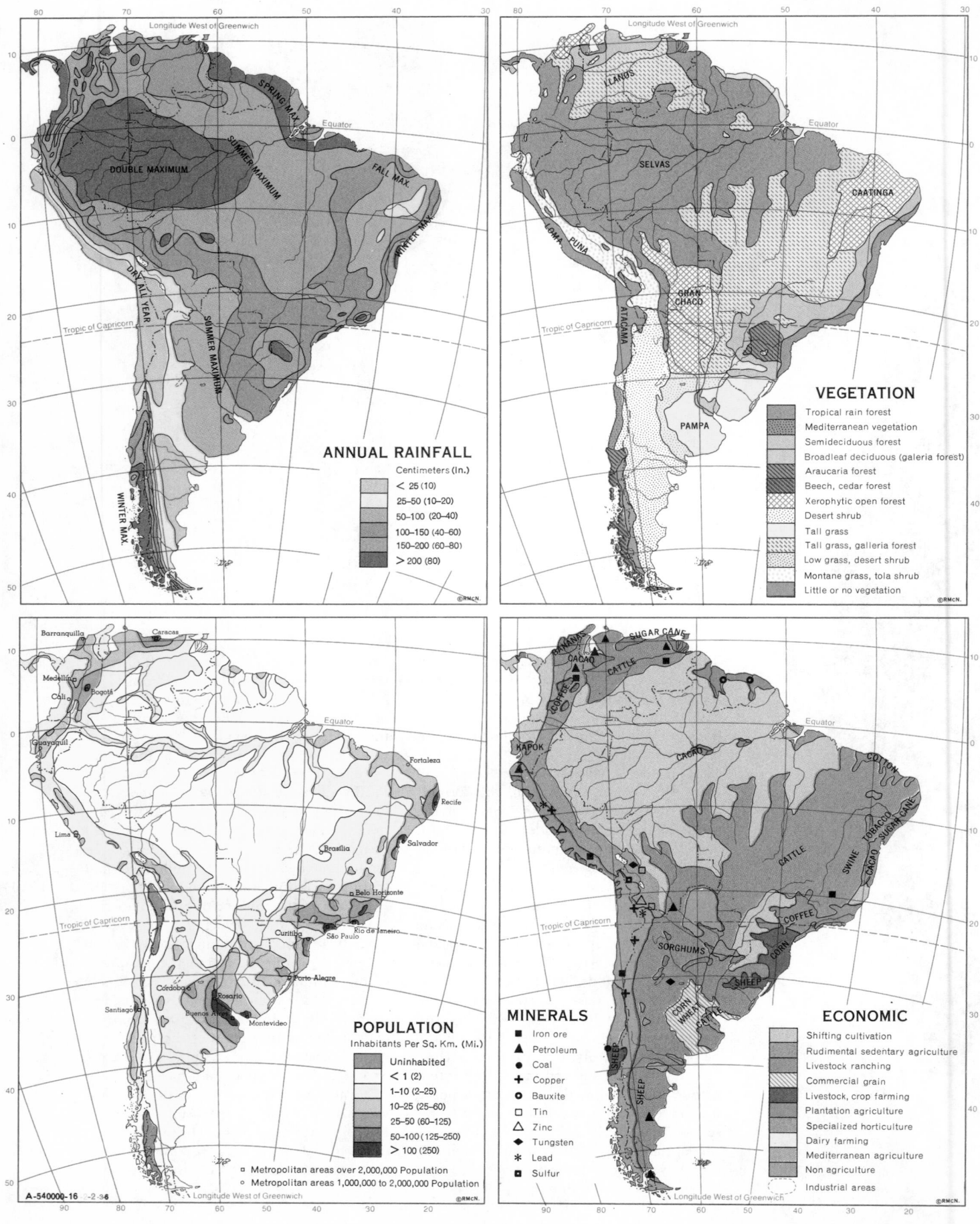

ANNUAL RAINFALL

Centimeters (In.)

	< 25 (10)
	25–50 (10–20)
	50–100 (20–40)
	100–150 (40–60)
	150–200 (60–80)
	> 200 (80)

VEGETATION

- Tropical rain forest
- Mediterranean vegetation
- Semideciduous forest
- Broadleaf deciduous (galeria forest)
- Araucaria forest
- Beech, cedar forest
- Xerophytic open forest
- Desert shrub
- Tall grass
- Tall grass, galleria forest
- Low grass, desert shrub
- Montane grass, tola shrub
- Little or no vegetation

POPULATION

Inhabitants Per Sq. Km. (Mi.)

	Uninhabited
	< 1 (2)
	1–10 (2–25)
	10–25 (25–60)
	25–50 (60–125)
	50–100 (125–250)
	> 100 (250)

- □ Metropolitan areas over 2,000,000 Population
- ○ Metropolitan areas 1,000,000 to 2,000,000 Population

A-540000-16 -2-3-6

MINERALS

- ■ Iron ore
- ▲ Petroleum
- ● Coal
- ✛ Copper
- ◉ Bauxite
- □ Tin
- △ Zinc
- ◆ Tungsten
- ✳ Lead
- ▪ Sulfur

ECONOMIC

- Shifting cultivation
- Rudimental sedentary agriculture
- Livestock ranching
- Commercial grain
- Livestock, crop farming
- Plantation agriculture
- Specialized horticulture
- Dairy farming
- Mediterranean agriculture
- Non agriculture
- Industrial areas

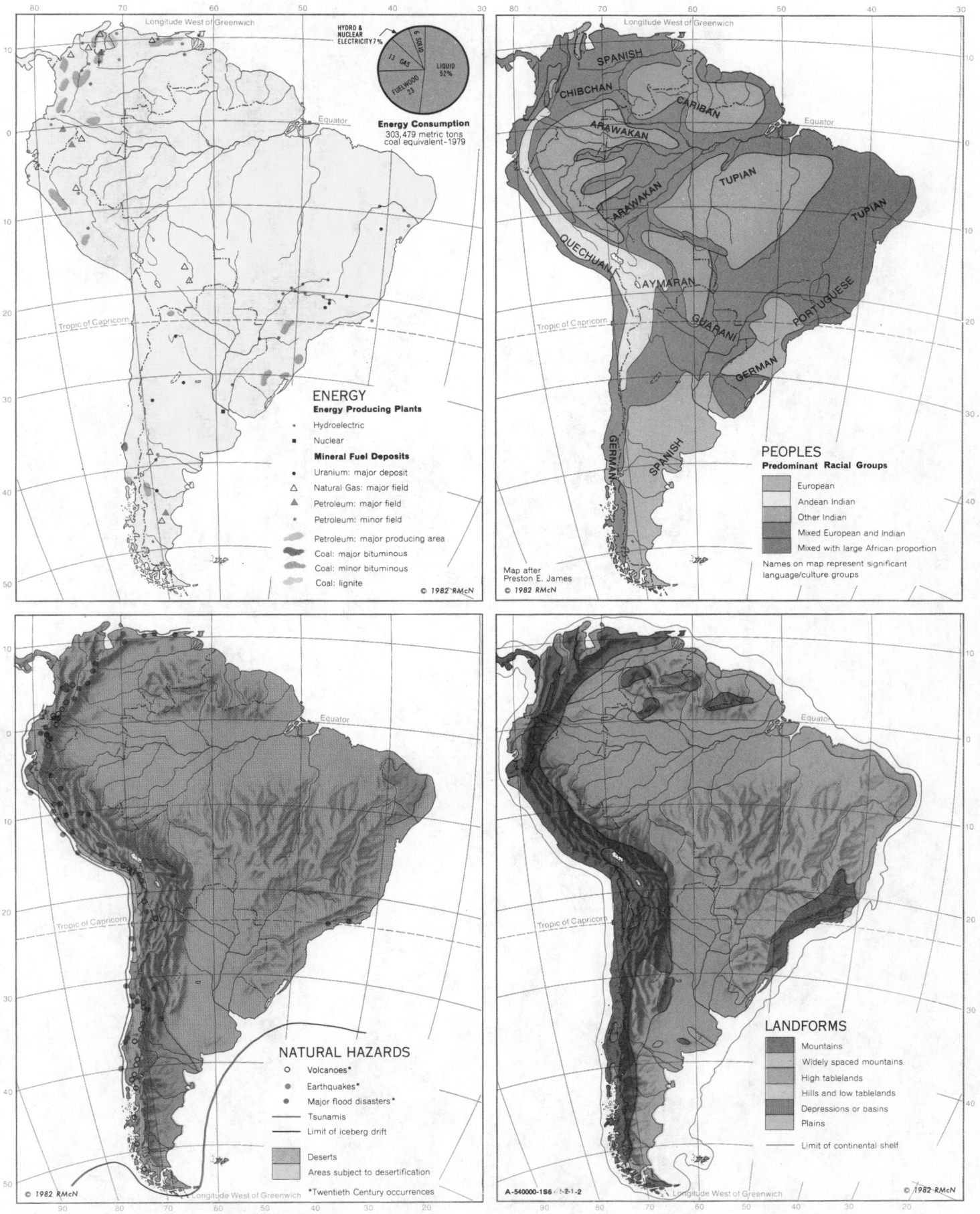

ENERGY
Energy Producing Plants

• Hydroelectric

■ Nuclear

Mineral Fuel Deposits

• Uranium: major deposit

△ Natural Gas: major field

▲ Petroleum: major field

• Petroleum: minor field

Petroleum: major producing area

Coal: major bituminous

Coal: minor bituminous

Coal: lignite

© 1982 RMcN

HYDRO & NUCLEAR ELECTRICITY 7%

6 SOLID
13 GAS
LIQUID 52%
FUELWOOD 23

Energy Consumption
303,479 metric tons
coal equivalent–1979

PEOPLES
Predominant Racial Groups

European

Andean Indian

Other Indian

Mixed European and Indian

Mixed with large African proportion

Names on map represent significant
language/culture groups

Map after
Preston E. James
© 1982 RMcN

SPANISH

CHIBCHAN

CARIBAN

ARAWAKAN

ARAWAKAN

TUPIAN

TUPIAN

QUECHUAN

AYMARAN

GUARANI

PORTUGUESE

GERMAN

GERMAN

SPANISH

NATURAL HAZARDS

○ Volcanoes*

● Earthquakes*

● Major flood disasters*

—— Tsunamis

—— Limit of iceberg drift

Deserts

Areas subject to desertification

*Twentieth Century occurrences

© 1982 RMcN

LANDFORMS

Mountains

Widely spaced mountains

High tablelands

Hills and low tablelands

Depressions or basins

Plains

—— Limit of continental shelf

A-540000-1S6 · 1-2-1-2

© 1982 RMcN

Equator

Tropic of Capricorn

Longitude West of Greenwich

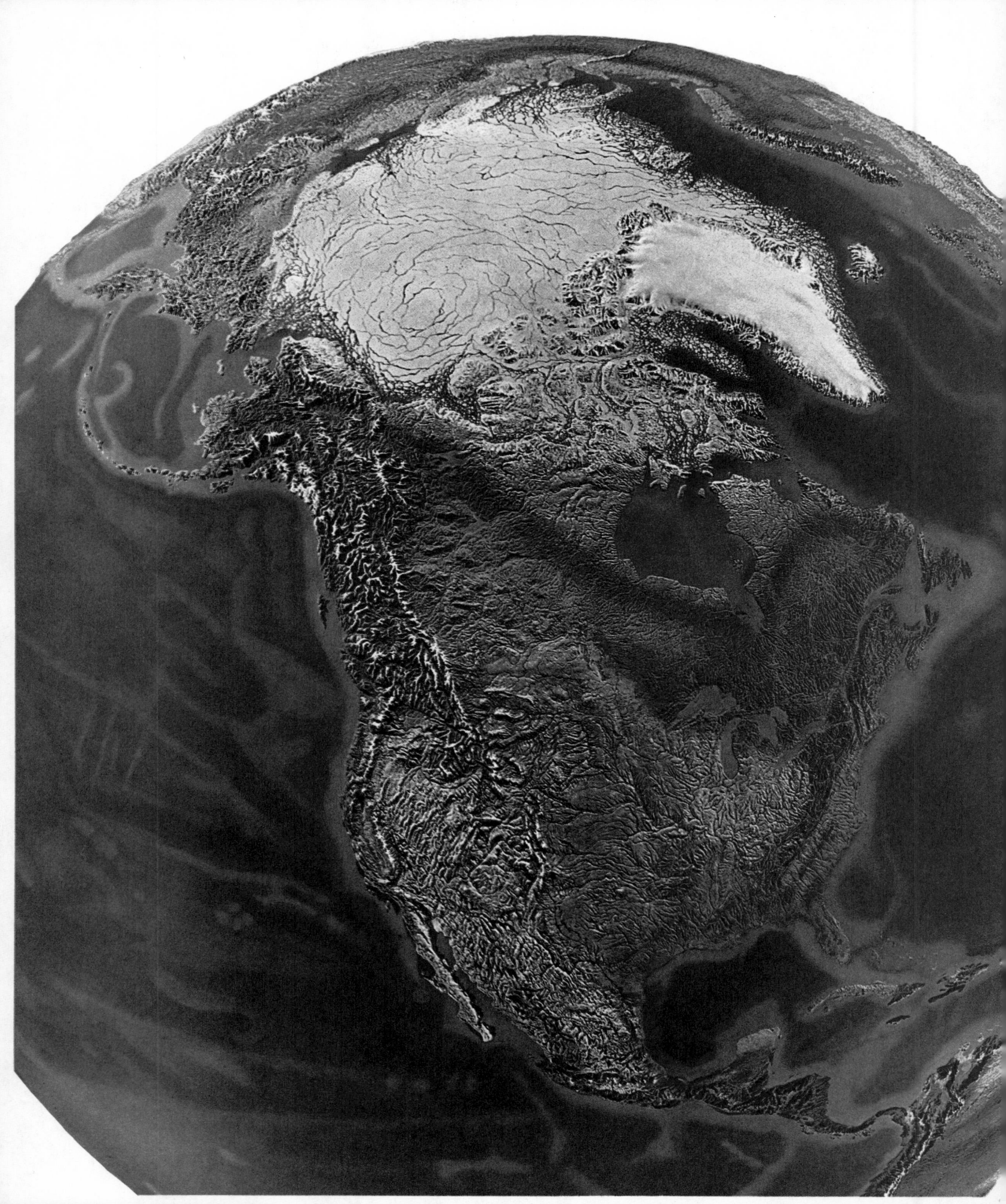

Global View
North America

Physically the North American continent extends from the ice-covered Arctic Ocean in the north to the tropical Isthmus of Panama in the south. North America, like Africa and South America, tapers from north to south. Canada, the United States, and Mexico occupy over 85 per cent of its total area of nearly 9,500,000 square miles. Central America, the West Indies, and Greenland make up the remainder.

Within this vast area, differences, rather than similarities, abound. All major types of climate can be found in North America ranging from the cold, perpetual ice cap of Greenland to the hot, moist tropical rain forests of Central America. Landforms vary from the towering chain of the Rocky Mountains, through the high plateau of Mexico, the relatively low Appalachian Highland, the featureless expanses of the Arctic tundra, the regularity of the Great Plains, and the fertile fields of the interior lowlands and coastal plains. Soils, vegetation, temperature, precipitation—all reflect the differences that can be expected over such an area.

Similarly, the development of agriculture and industry has varied considerably over the North American continent. Modern methods and the extensive use of machinery characterize agriculture in the flat to gently rolling areas of Midwestern United States and the Prairie Provinces of Canada. Stock-grazing is prevalent in the more arid areas of the continent. Agriculture in Middle America is characterized by the extensive use of hand labor. Here subtropical crops are important, for instance, bananas in Central America and sugar cane in the West Indies.

Early settlement, access to raw materials, a well developed transportation network, and a density of population providing both labor and markets have led to a heavy concentration of industrial development in the northeast quarter of the United States and the southeastern rim of Canada. Other industrial development has taken place in scattered locations in southern and western United States and in the largest cities of Middle America.

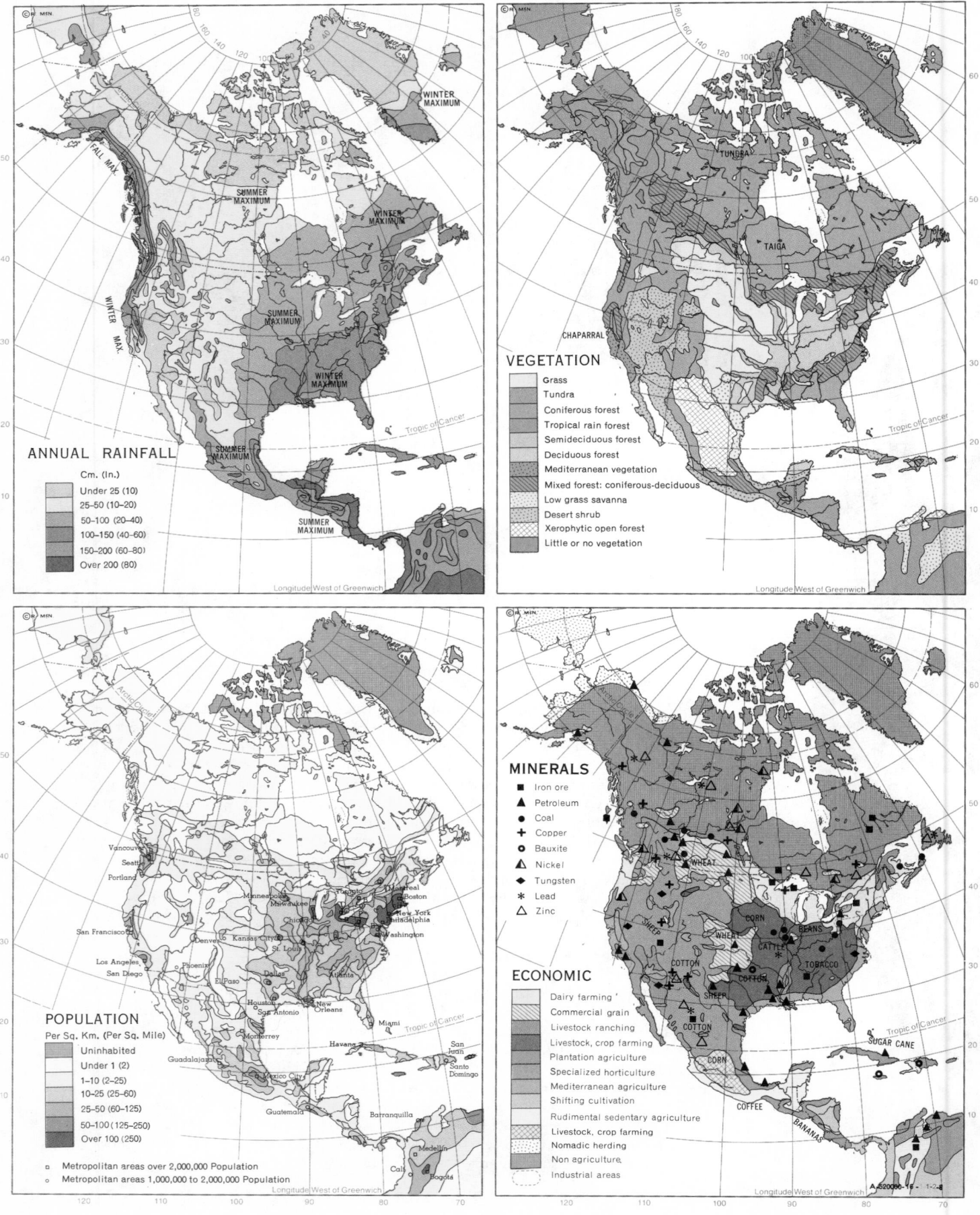

ANNUAL RAINFALL

Cm. (In.)

Under 25 (10)
25–50 (10–20)
50–100 (20–40)
100–150 (40–60)
150–200 (60–80)
Over 200 (80)

WINTER MAXIMUM
FALL MAX.
SUMMER MAXIMUM
WINTER MAXIMUM
WINTER MAX.
SUMMER MAXIMUM
WINTER MAXIMUM
SUMMER MAXIMUM
SUMMER MAXIMUM

VEGETATION

Grass
Tundra
Coniferous forest
Tropical rain forest
Semideciduous forest
Deciduous forest
Mediterranean vegetation
Mixed forest: coniferous-deciduous
Low grass savanna
Desert shrub
Xerophytic open forest
Little or no vegetation

TUNDRA
TAIGA
CHAPARRAL

POPULATION

Per Sq. Km. (Per Sq. Mile)

Uninhabited
Under 1 (2)
1–10 (2–25)
10–25 (25–60)
25–50 (60–125)
50–100 (125–250)
Over 100 (250)

□ Metropolitan areas over 2,000,000 Population
○ Metropolitan areas 1,000,000 to 2,000,000 Population

Vancouver
Seattle
Portland
San Francisco
Los Angeles
San Diego
Phoenix
El Paso
Denver
Kansas City
St. Louis
Minneapolis
Milwaukee
Chicago
Toronto
Montreal
Boston
New York
Philadelphia
Washington
Atlanta
Dallas
Houston
San Antonio
New Orleans
Miami
Monterrey
Guadalajara
Mexico City
Havana
San Juan
Santo Domingo
Guatemala
Barranquilla
Medellin
Cali
Bogotá

MINERALS

■ Iron ore
▲ Petroleum
● Coal
+ Copper
○ Bauxite
△ Nickel
◆ Tungsten
∗ Lead
△ Zinc

ECONOMIC

Dairy farming
Commercial grain
Livestock ranching
Livestock, crop farming
Plantation agriculture
Specialized horticulture
Mediterranean agriculture
Shifting cultivation
Rudimental sedentary agriculture
Livestock, crop farming
Nomadic herding
Non agriculture
Industrial areas

WHEAT
CORN
BEANS
WHEAT
CATTLE
TOBACCO
COTTON
SHEEP
COTTON
COTTON
SHEEP
CORN
SUGAR CANE
COFFEE
BANANAS

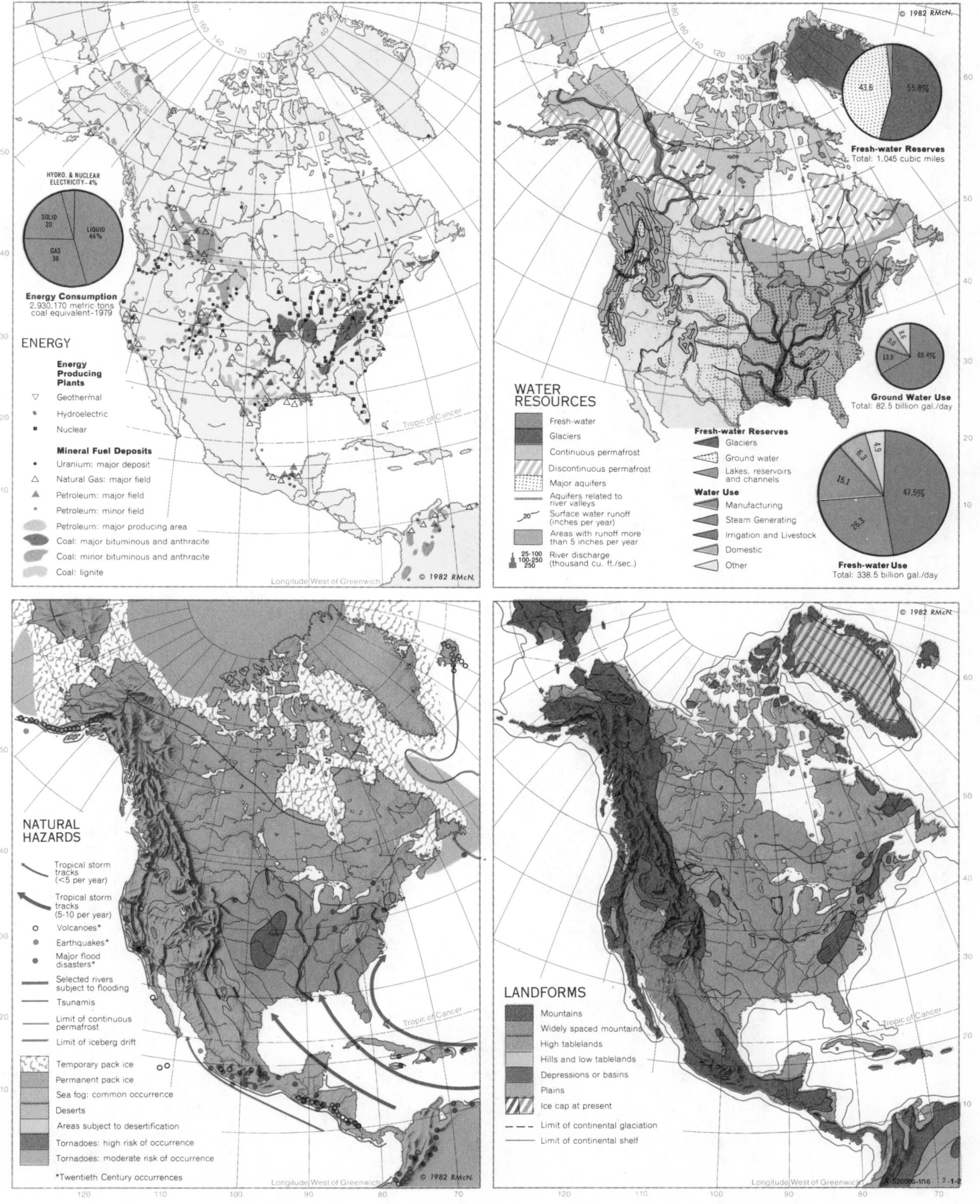

ENERGY

© 1982 RMcN.

HYDRO. & NUCLEAR ELECTRICITY–4%
SOLID 20
LIQUID 46%
GAS 30

Energy Consumption
2,930,170 metric tons
coal equivalent–1979

Energy Producing Plants
▽ Geothermal
• Hydroelectric
■ Nuclear

Mineral Fuel Deposits
• Uranium: major deposit
△ Natural Gas: major field
▲ Petroleum: major field
• Petroleum: minor field
   Petroleum: major producing area
   Coal: major bituminous and anthracite
   Coal: minor bituminous and anthracite
   Coal: lignite

Longitude West of Greenwich
© 1982 RMcN.

WATER RESOURCES

© 1982 RMcN.

Fresh-water Reserves
Total: 1,045 cubic miles
55.8% 43.8

Ground Water Use
Total: 82.5 billion gal./day
68.4% 13.9 8.0 8.6

Fresh-water Use
Total: 338.5 billion gal./day
47.5% 25.3 15.1 6.3 4.9

   Fresh-water
   Glaciers
   Continuous permafrost
   Discontinuous permafrost
   Major aquifers
   Aquifers related to river valleys
20 Surface water runoff (inches per year)
   Areas with runoff more than 5 inches per year
25-100
100-250
250 River discharge (thousand cu. ft./sec.)

Fresh-water Reserves
   Glaciers
   Ground water
   Lakes, reservoirs and channels

Water Use
   Manufacturing
   Steam Generating
   Irrigation and Livestock
   Domestic
   Other

NATURAL HAZARDS

→ Tropical storm tracks (<5 per year)
⇒ Tropical storm tracks (5-10 per year)
○ Volcanoes*
• Earthquakes*
• Major flood disasters*
   Selected rivers subject to flooding
   Tsunamis
   Limit of continuous permafrost
   Limit of iceberg drift

   Temporary pack ice
   Permanent pack ice
   Sea fog: common occurrence
   Deserts
   Areas subject to desertification
   Tornadoes: high risk of occurrence
   Tornadoes: moderate risk of occurrence

*Twentieth Century occurrences

© 1982 RMcN.
Longitude West of Greenwich

LANDFORMS

© 1982 RMcN.

   Mountains
   Widely spaced mountains
   High tablelands
   Hills and low tablelands
   Depressions or basins
   Plains
   Ice cap at present
- - - Limit of continental glaciation
   Limit of continental shelf

Longitude West of Greenwich

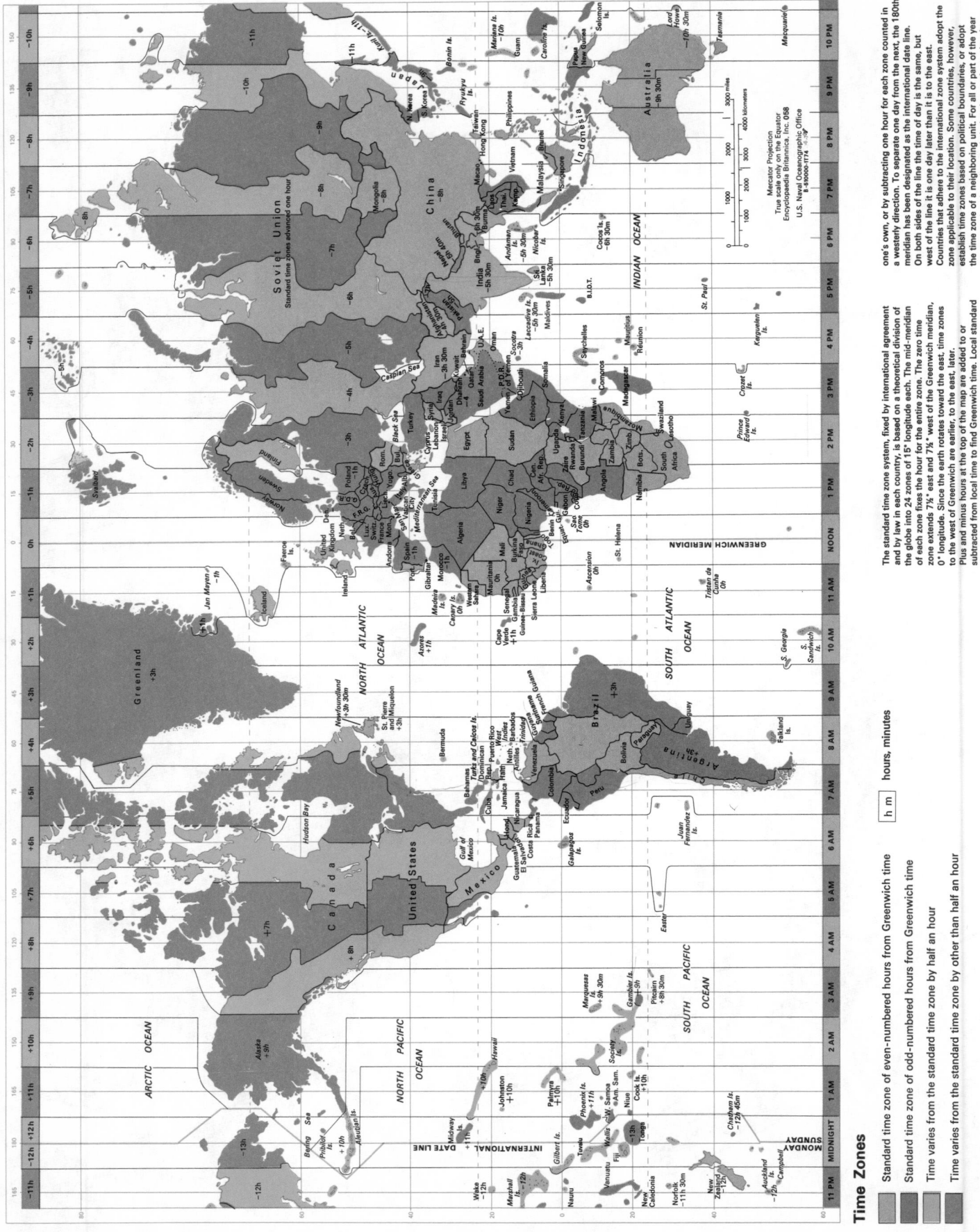

Time Zones

The standard time zone system, fixed by international agreement and by law in each country, is based on a theoretical division of the globe into 24 zones of 15° longitude each. The mid-meridian of each zone fixes the hour for the entire zone. The zero time zone extends 7½° east and 7½° west of the Greenwich meridian, 0° longitude. Since the earth rotates toward the east, time zones to the west of Greenwich are earlier, to the east, later.

Plus and minus hours at the top of the map are added to or subtracted from local time to find Greenwich time. Local standard time can be determined for any area in the world by adding one hour for each time zone counted in an easterly direction from

one's own, or by subtracting one hour for each zone counted in a westerly direction. To separate one day from the next, the 180th meridian has been designated as the international date line. On both sides of the line the time of day is the same, but west of the line it is one day later than it is to the east. Countries that adhere to the international zone system adopt the zone applicable to their location. Some countries, however, establish time zones based on political boundaries, or adopt the time zone of a neighboring unit. For all or part of the year some countries also advance their time by one hour, thereby utilizing more daylight hours each day.

| h m | hours, minutes |

Standard time zone of even-numbered hours from Greenwich time

Standard time zone of odd-numbered hours from Greenwich time

Time varies from the standard time zone by half an hour

Time varies from the standard time zone by other than half an hour

Mercator Projection
True scale only on the Equator
Encyclopaedia Britannica, Inc. 058
U.S. Naval Oceanographic Office
B-8?000-IT74

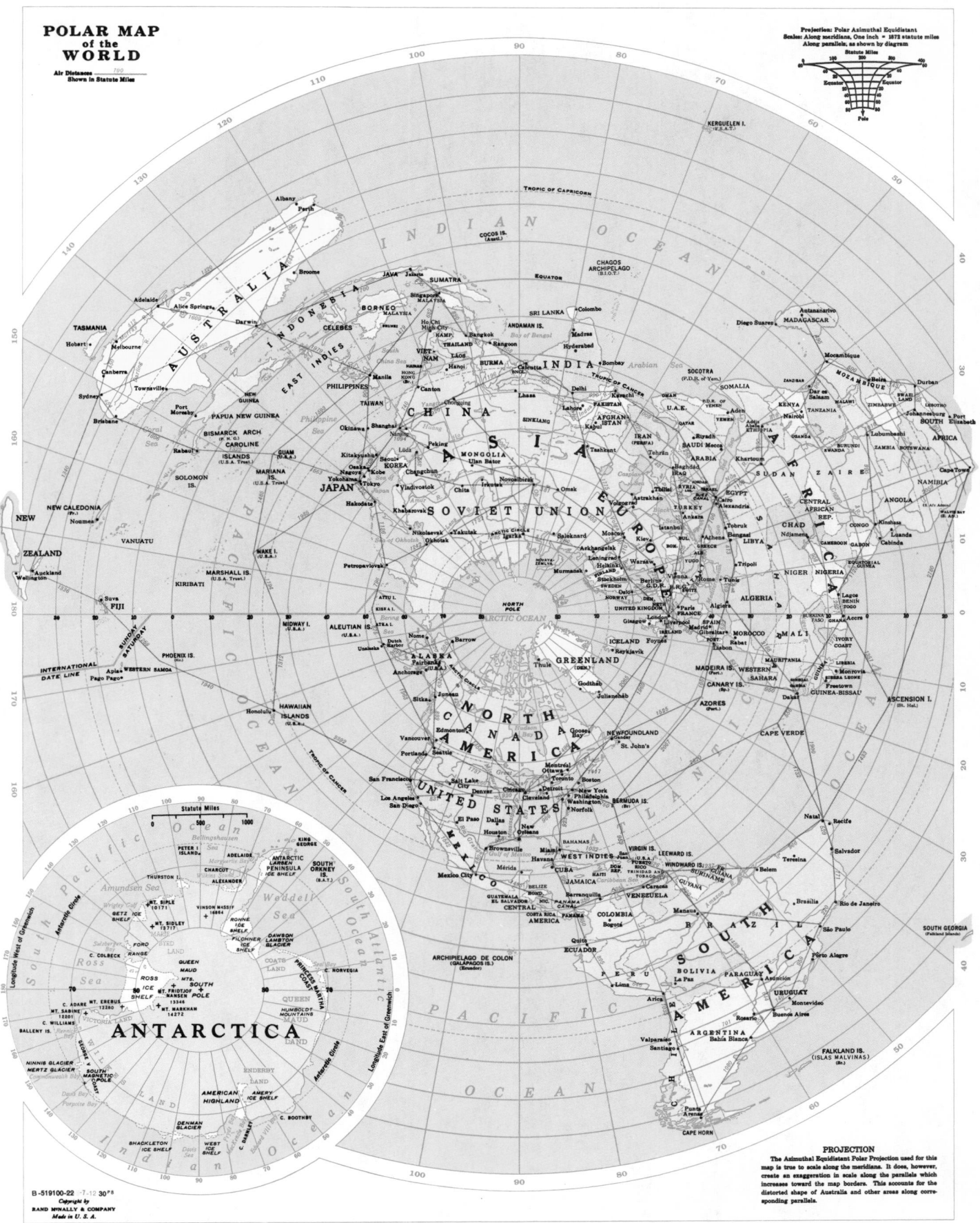

POLAR MAP
of the
WORLD

Air Distances
Shown in Statute Miles

Projection: Polar Azimuthal Equidistant
Scales: Along meridians, One inch = 1872 statute miles
Along parallels, as shown by diagram

Statute Miles

ANTARCTICA

Statute Miles

B-519100-22 -7-12 30°8

Copyright by
RAND McNALLY & COMPANY
Made in U.S.A.

PROJECTION

The Azimuthal Equidistant Polar Projection used for this
map is true to scale along the meridians. It does, however,
create an exaggeration in scale along the parallels which
increases toward the map borders. This accounts for the
distorted shape of Australia and other areas along corre-
sponding parallels.

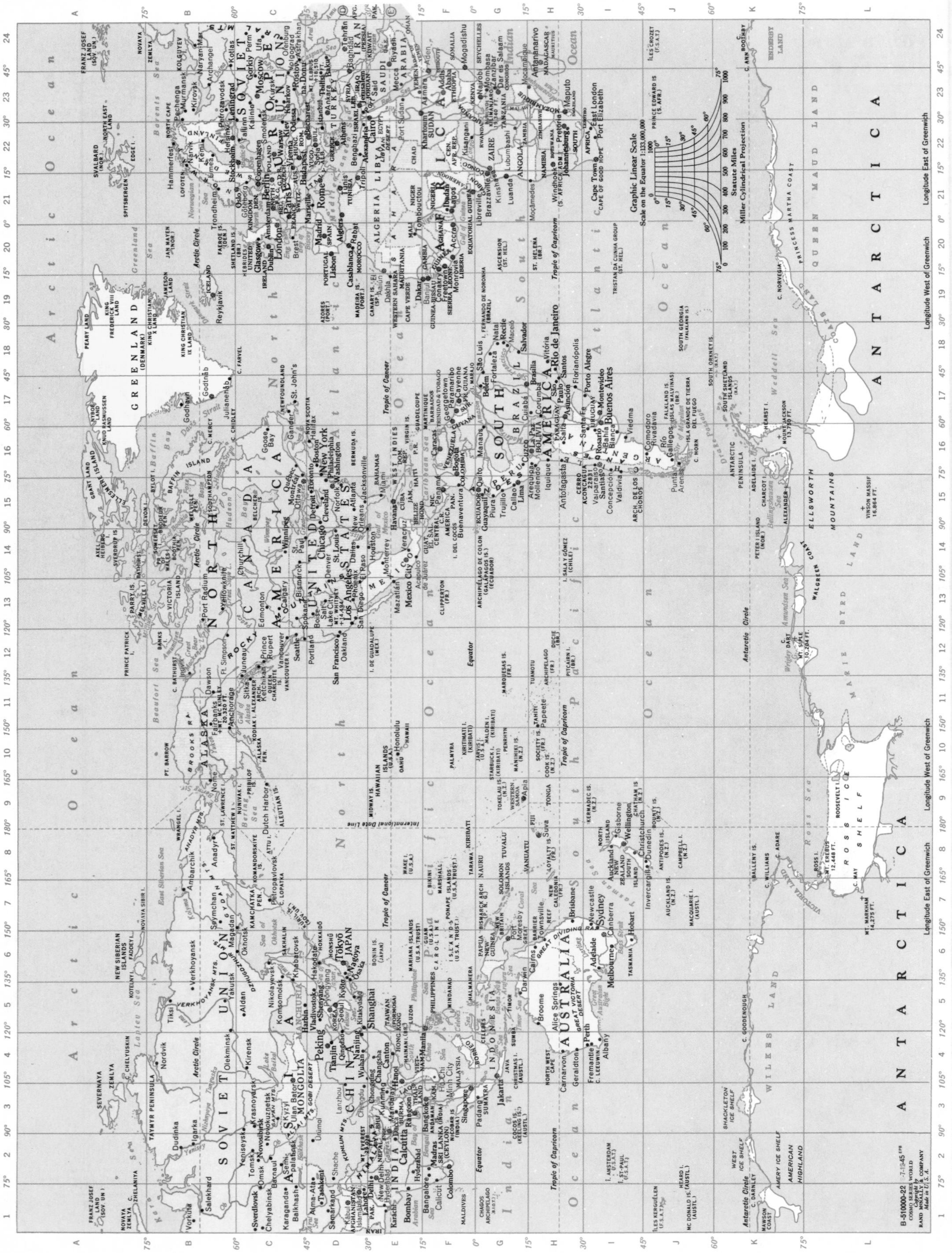

Graphic Linear Scale

Scale on the Equator 1:133,000,000

Statute Miles

Miller Cylindrical Projection

Longitude West of Greenwich

Longitude East of Greenwich

B-510000-22
COSMO SERIES® WORLD
RAND McNALLY & COMPANY
Made in U.S.A.

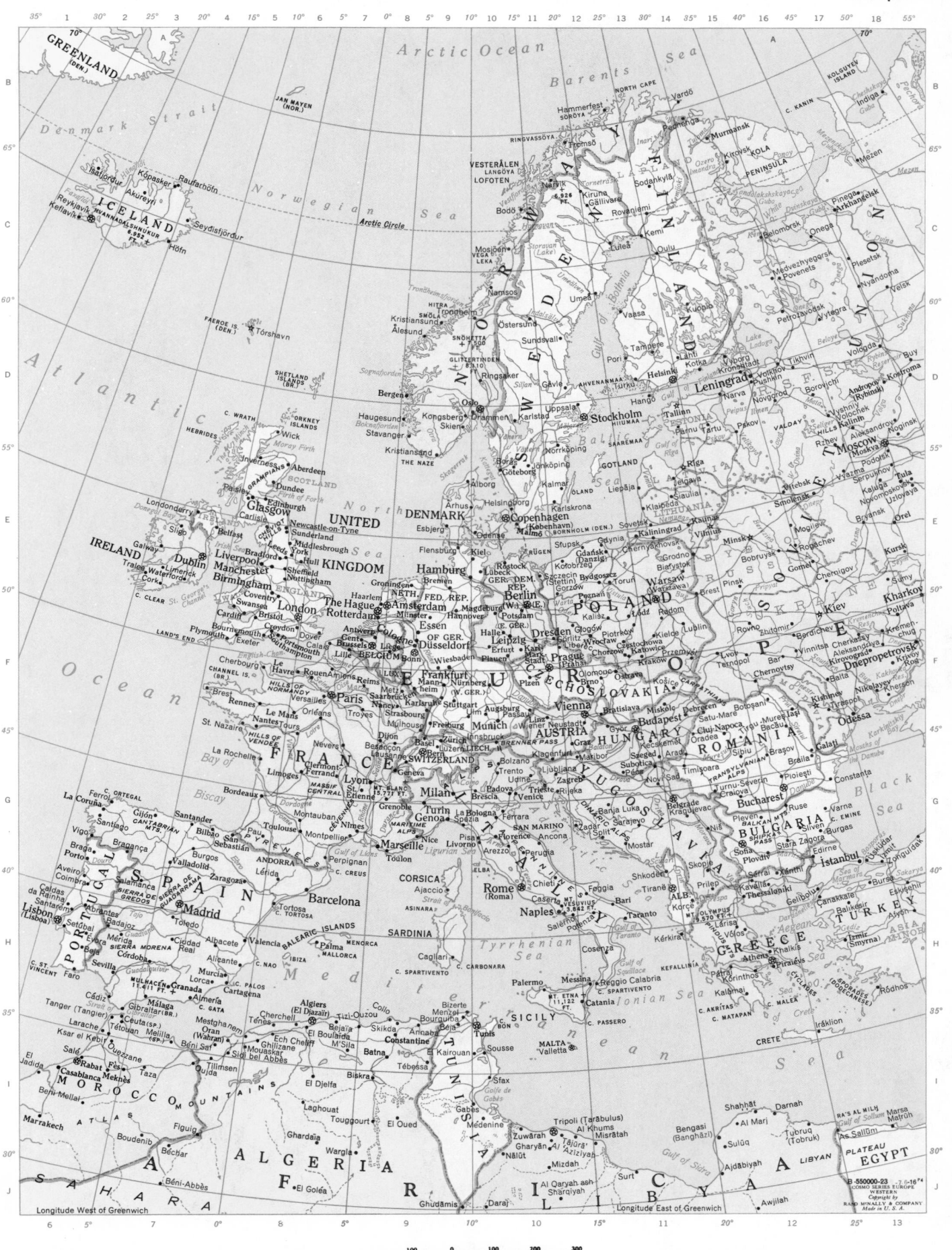

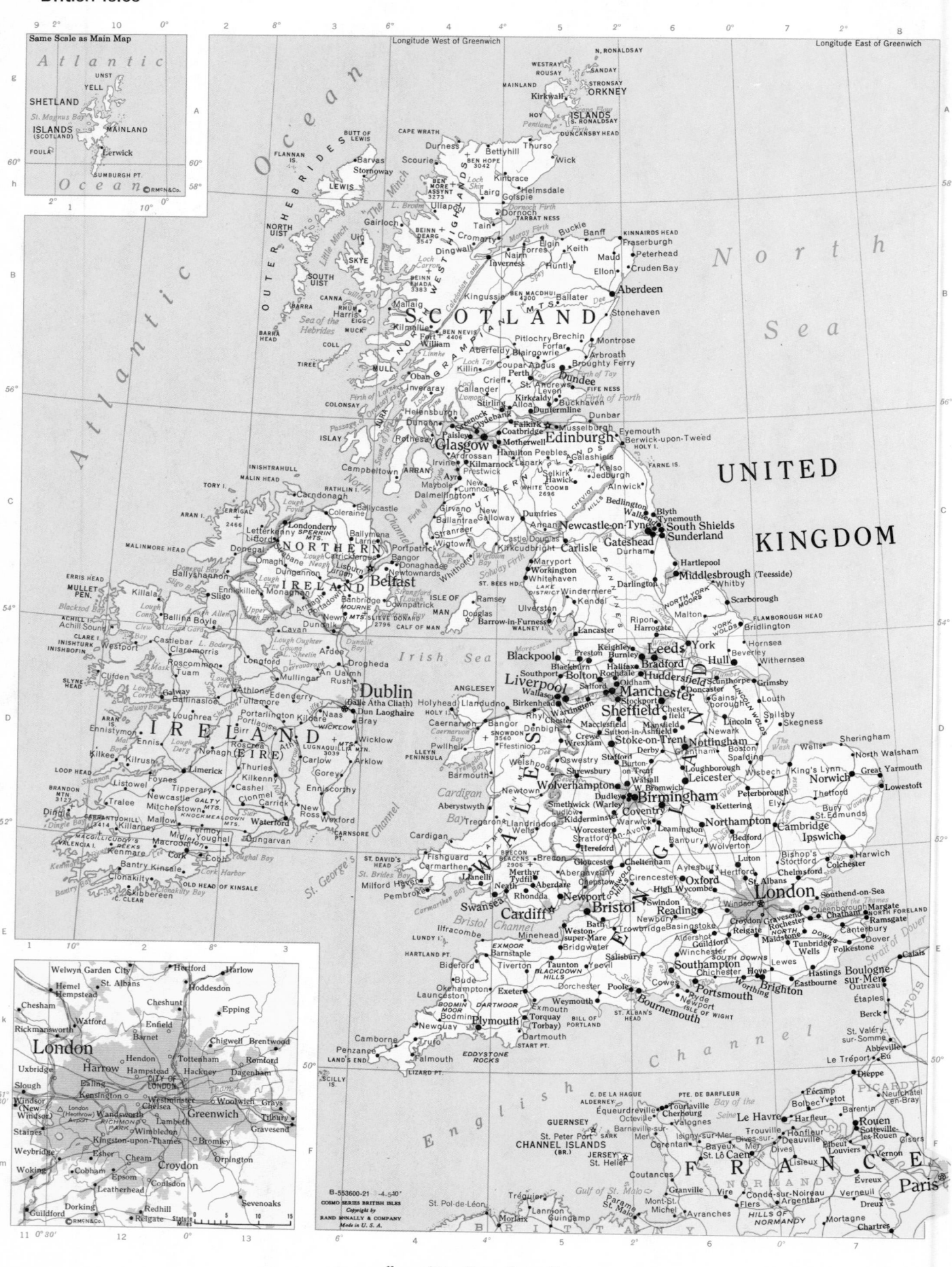

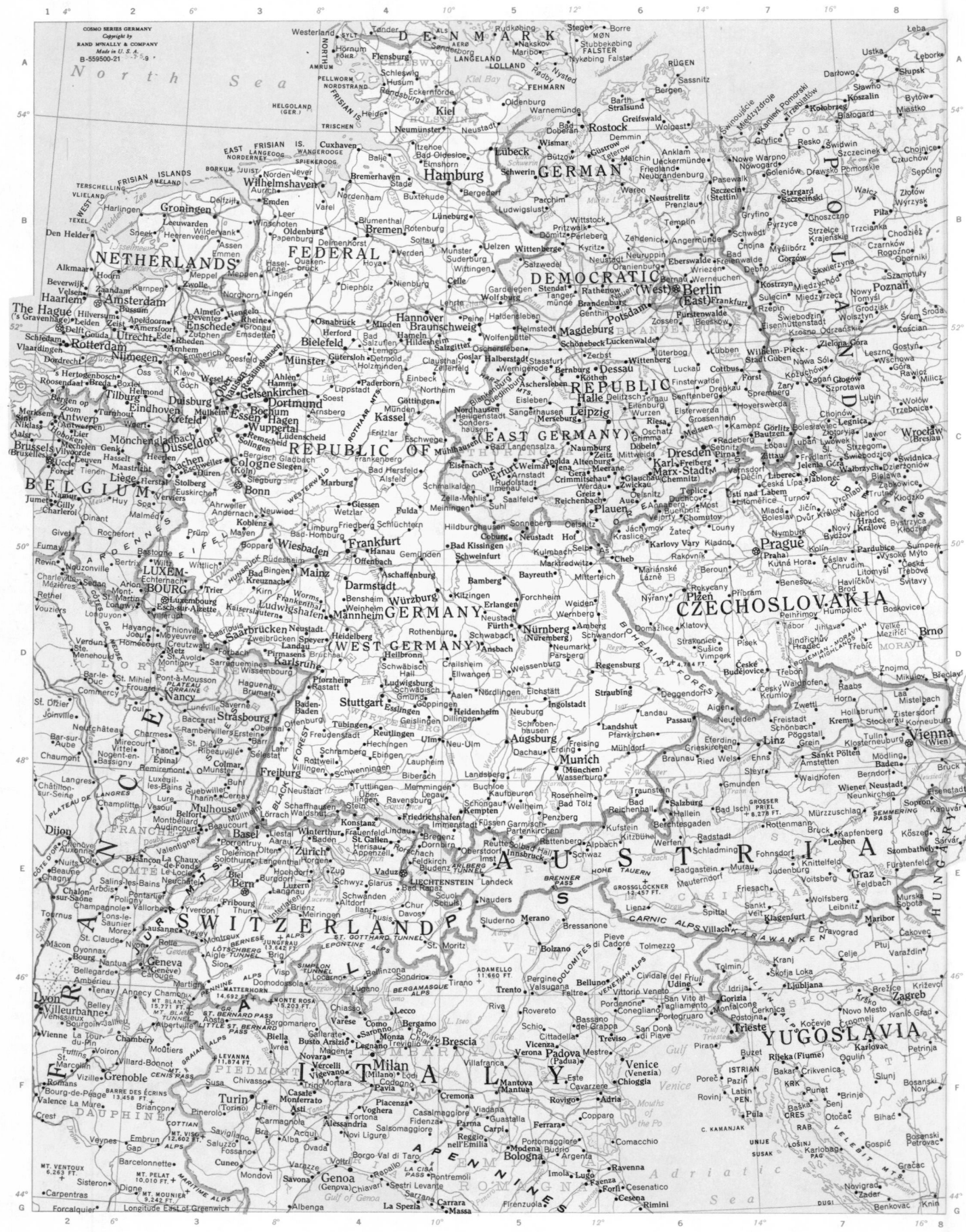

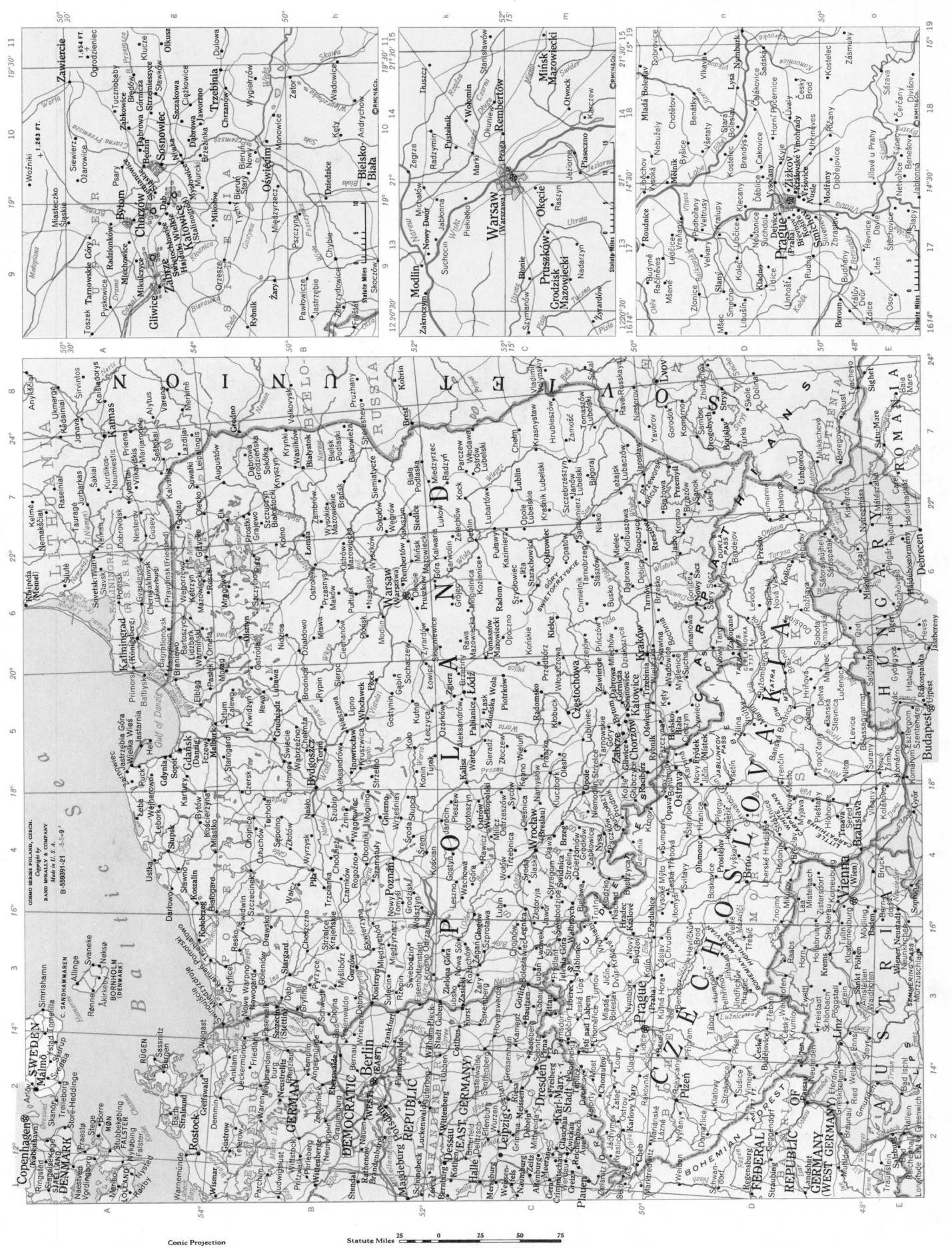

Conic Projection

Statute Miles 25 0 25 50 75

Kilometers 25 0 25 50 100

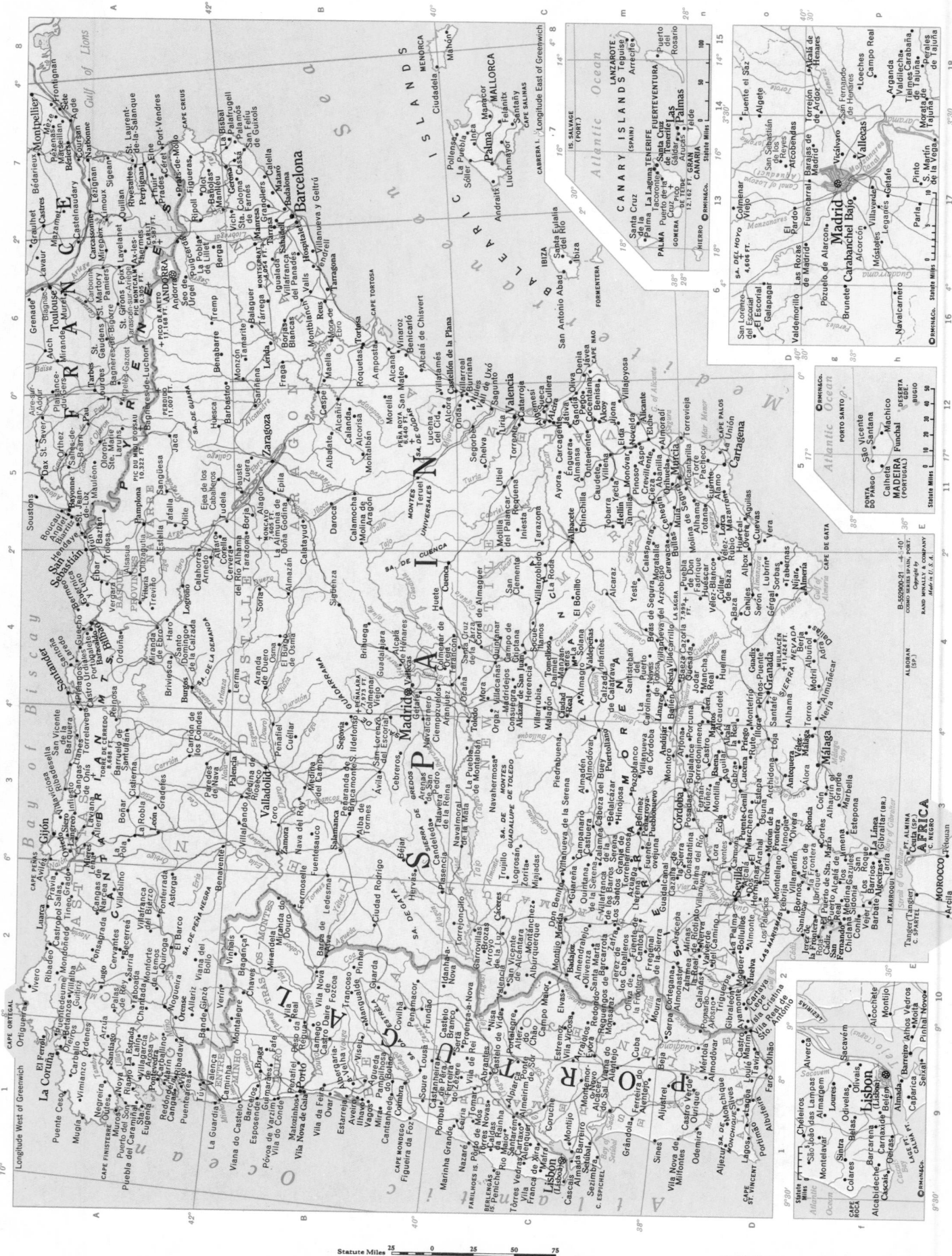

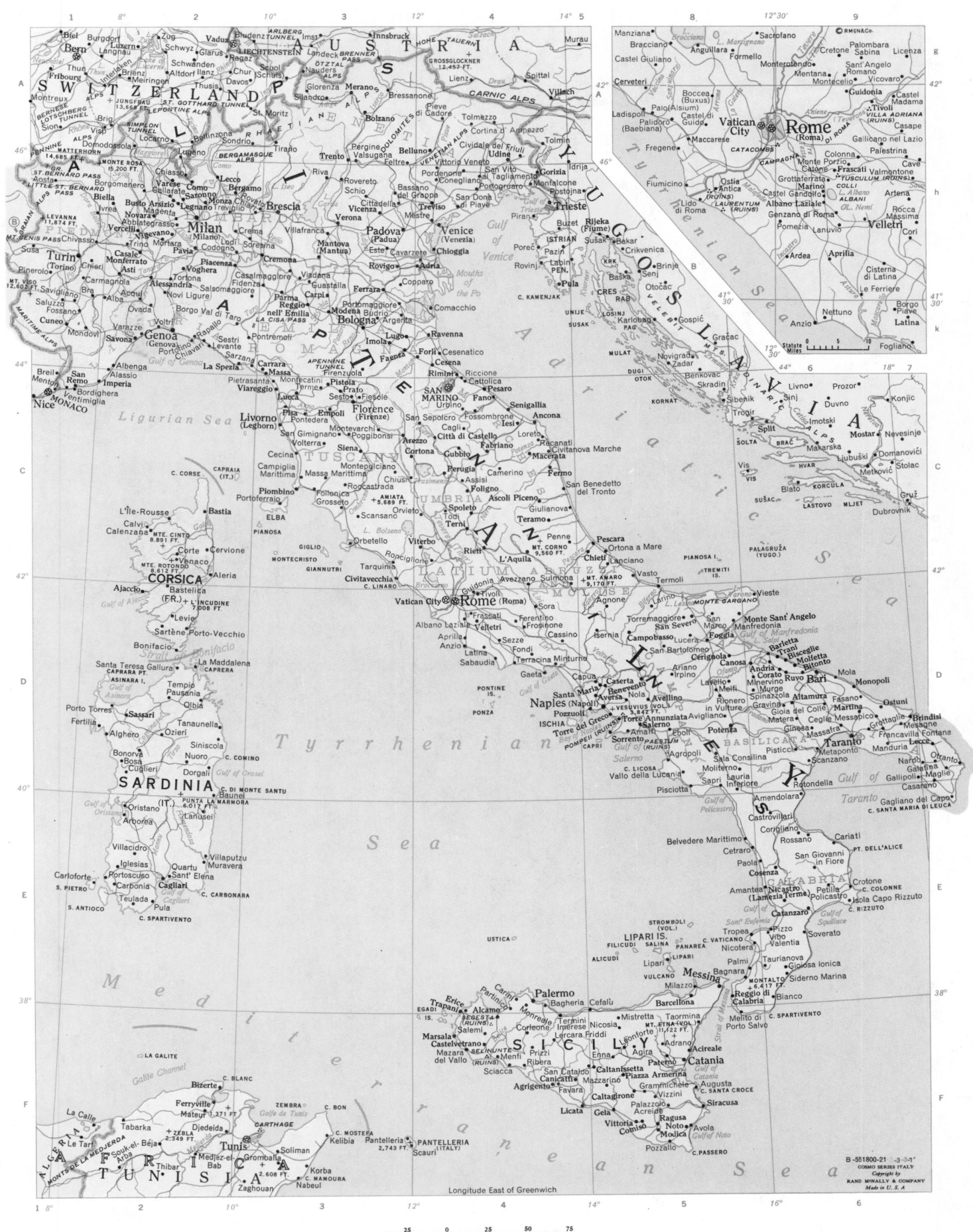

Conic Projection

Statute Miles
25   0   25   50   75

Kilometers
25 0 25 50 100

Longitude East of Greenwich

SOVIET UNION

CARPATHIAN

ROMANIA

TISZA

TRANSYLVANIAN ALPS

TRANSYLVANIA

WALACHIA

OLTENIA

HUNGARY

AUSTRIA

CZECHOSLOVAKIA

Vienna (Wien)

Budapest

YUGOSLAVIA

CROATIA

BOSNIA

HERCEGOVINA

MONTENEGRO

DINARIC ALPS

Belgrade (Beograd)

Bucharest (Bucureşti)

BULGARIA

Sofia (Sofiya)

MACEDONIA

ALBANIA

GREECE

TURKEY

Istanbul

Sea of Marmara

Black Sea

Adriatic Sea

Aegean Sea

ITALY

Naples (Napoli)

Taranto

Brindisi

Thessaloniki (Salonika)

Statute Miles 25 0 25 50 75
Kilometers 25 0 25 50 100

Conic Projection

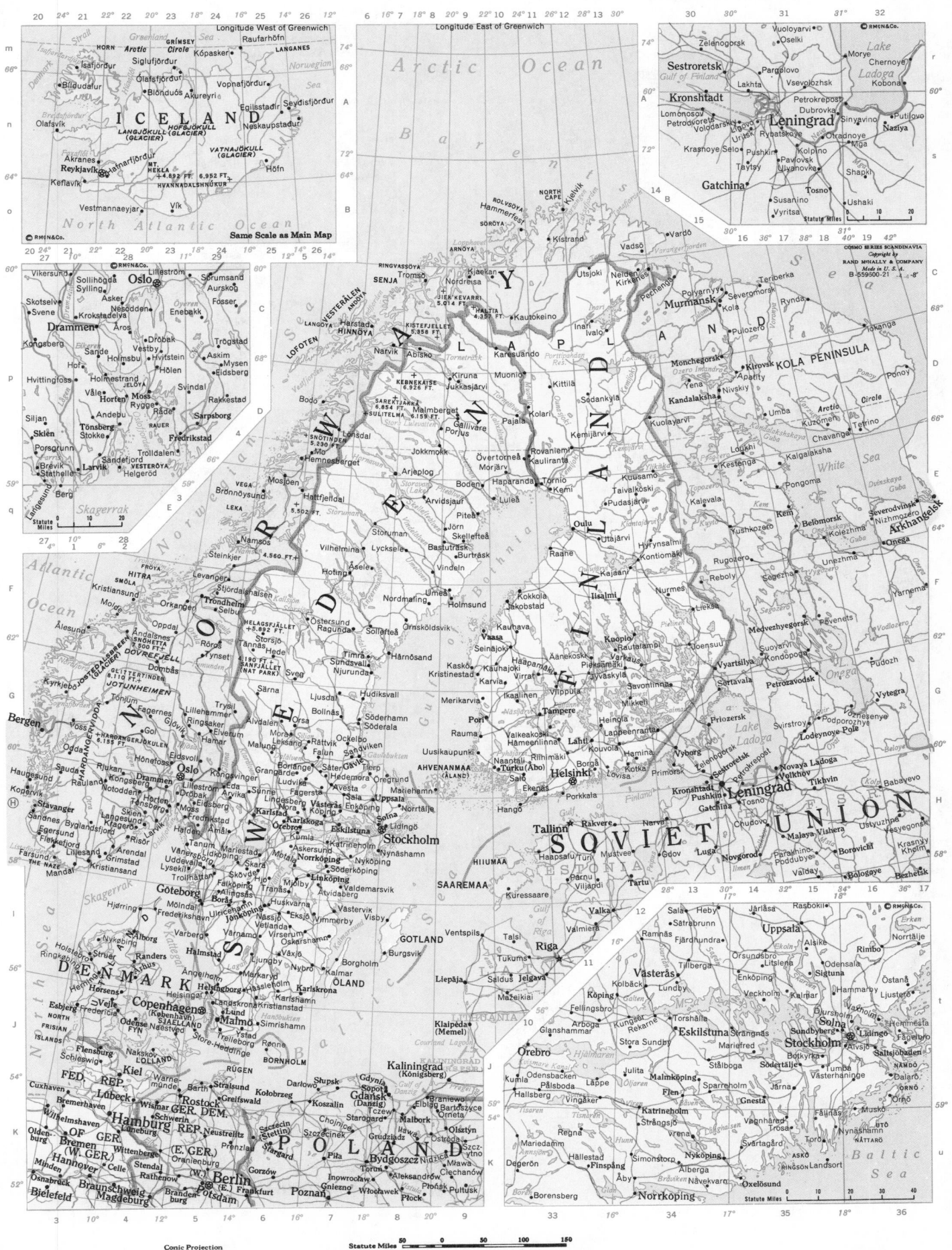

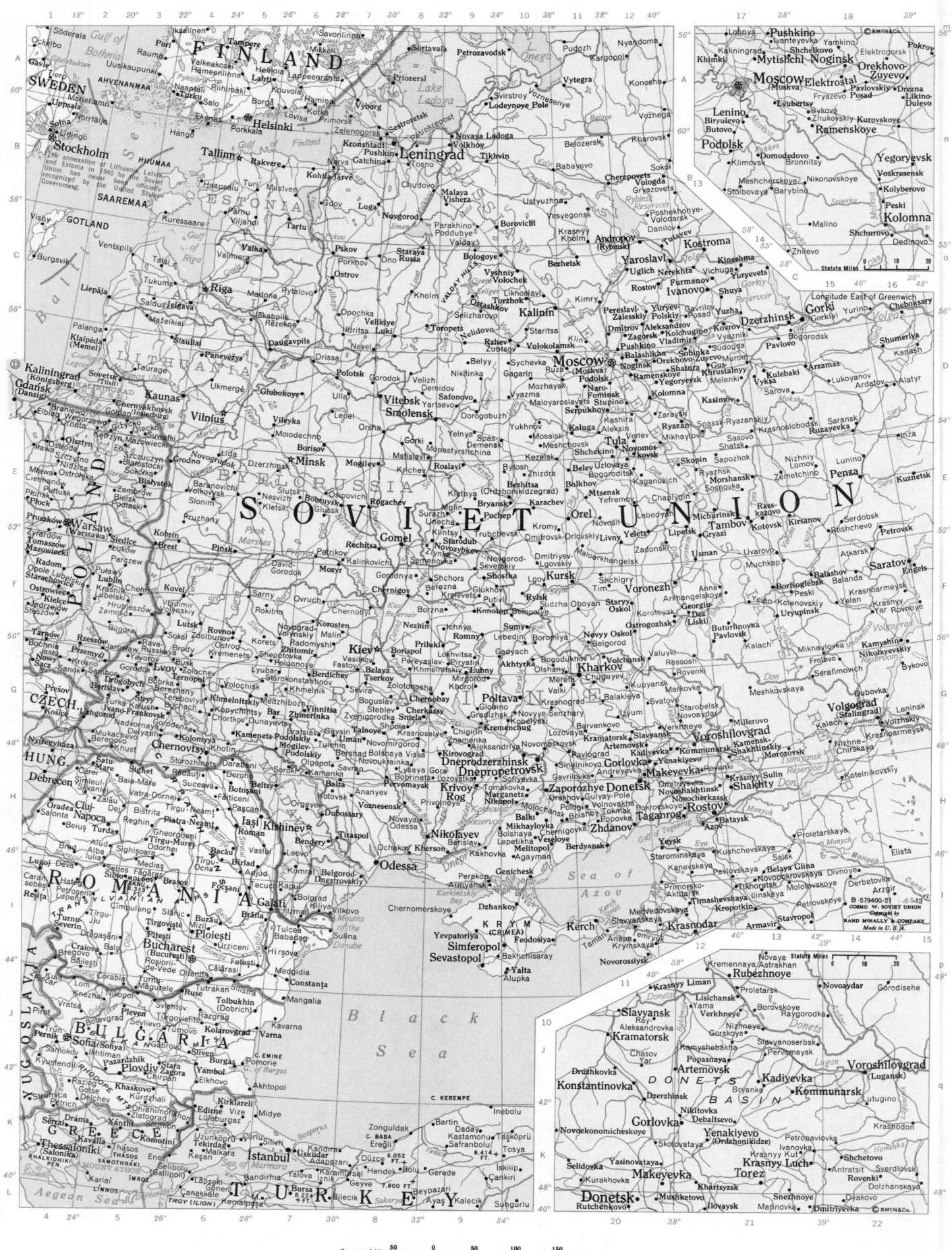

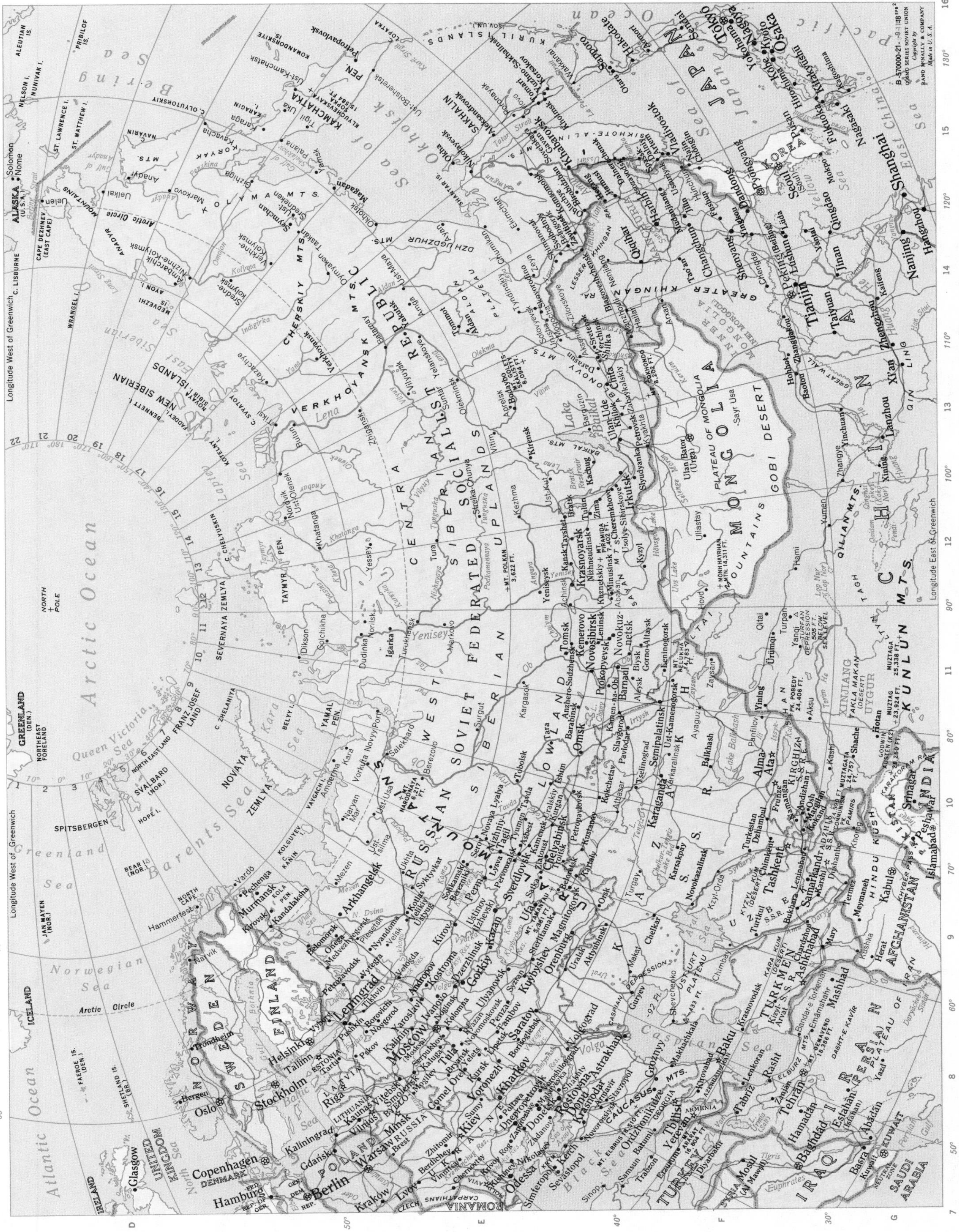

Lambert Azimuthal Equal Area Projection

Statute Miles
100 0 100 200 300 400 500

Kilometers
100 0 100 300 500 700

For Eastern Iraq, see map of Iran and Afghanistan.

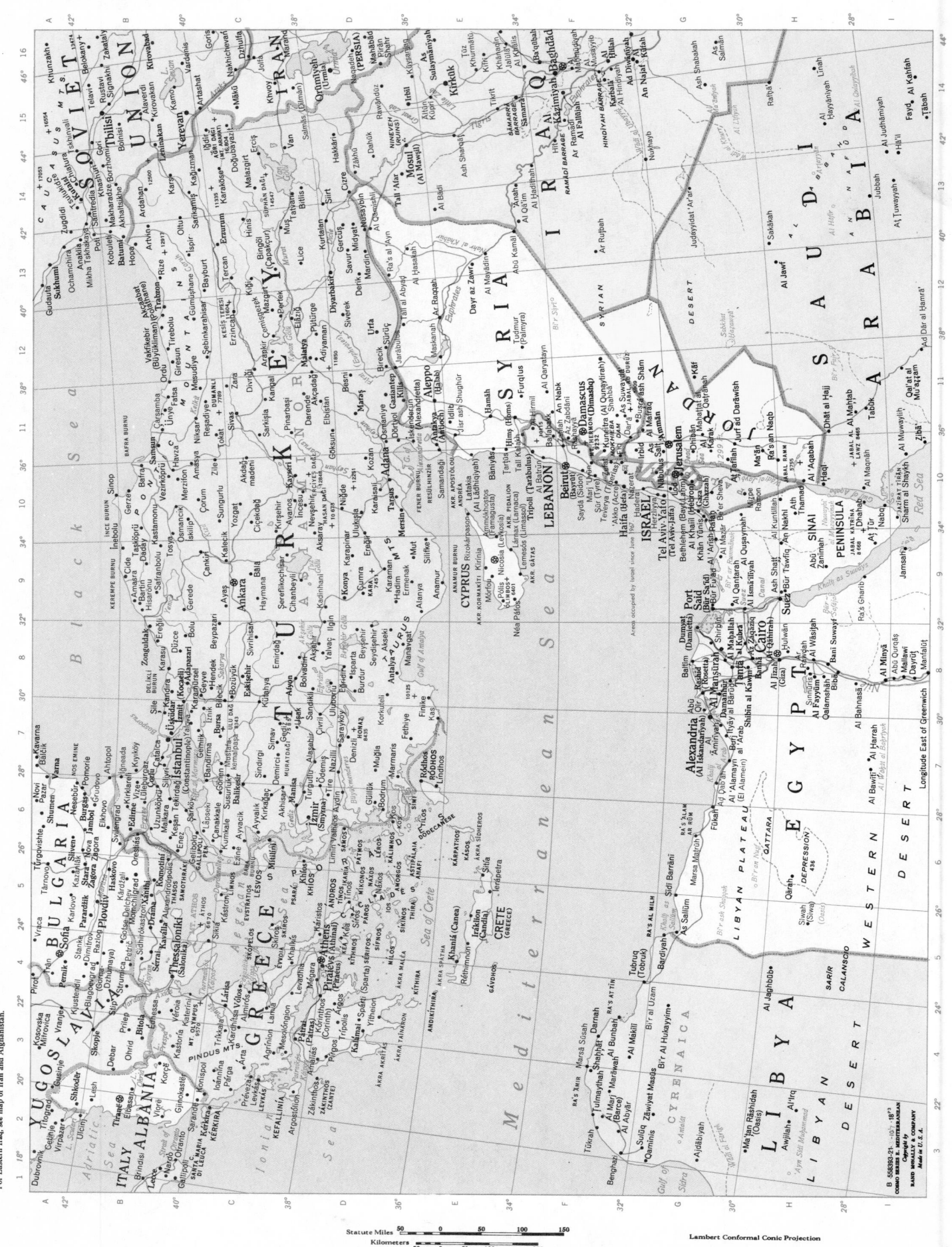

Statute Miles   50   0   50   100   150
Kilometers   50   0   50   100   200

Lambert Conformal Conic Projection

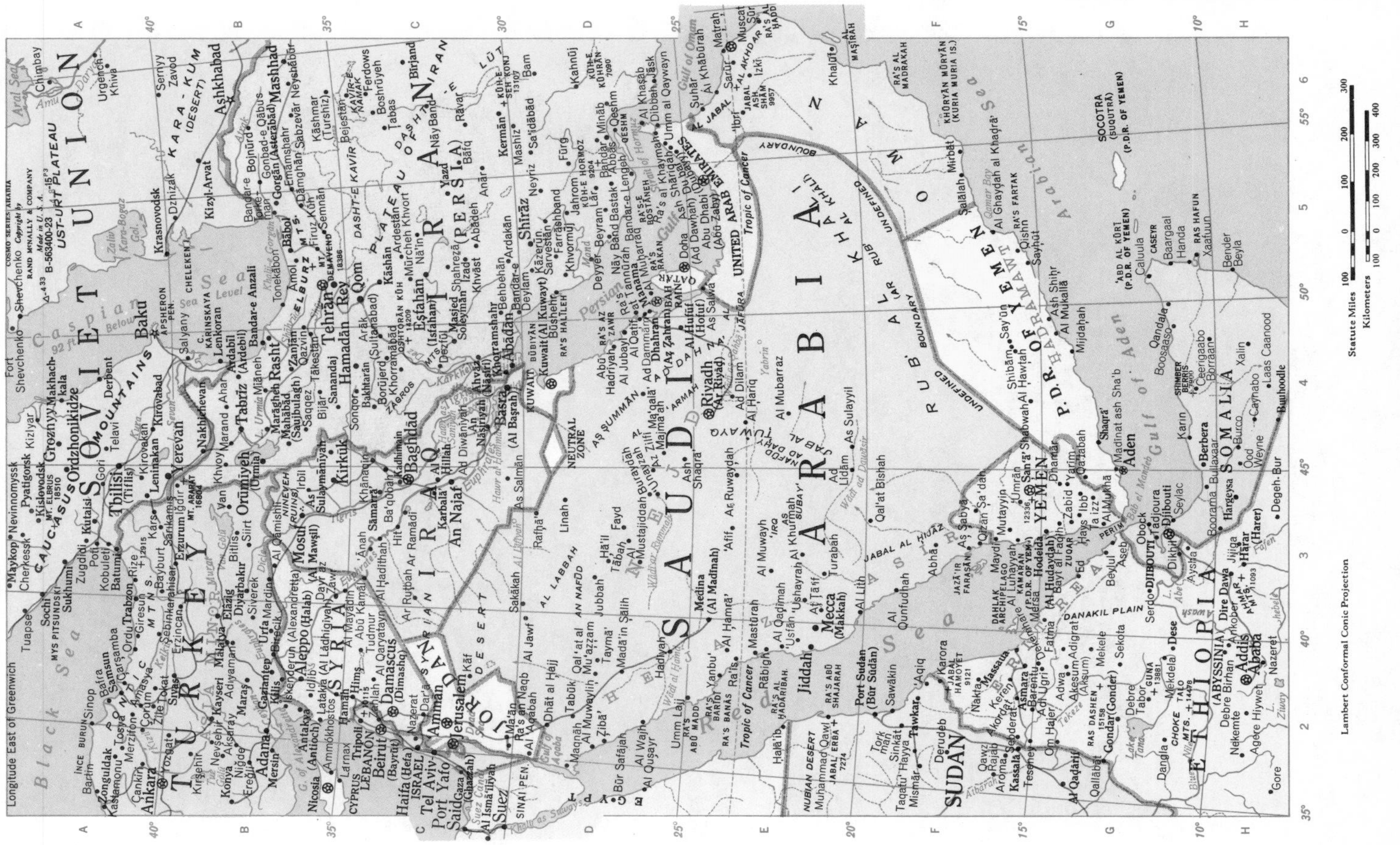

Longitude East of Greenwich

SOVIET UNION

TURKEY

SYRIA

IRAQ

IRAN

PERSIAN GULF

SAUDI ARABIA

JORDAN

ISRAEL

LEBANON

EGYPT

SUDAN

ETHIOPIA (ABYSSINIA)

YEMEN

P.D.R. OF YEMEN

SOMALIA

SINAI PENINSULA

Caspian Sea

Black Sea

Mediterranean Sea

Red Sea

Arabian Sea

Gulf of Aden

Gulf of Oman

Persian Gulf

RUB' AL KHALI

Tropic of Cancer

Lambert Conformal Conic Projection

Statute Miles

Kilometers

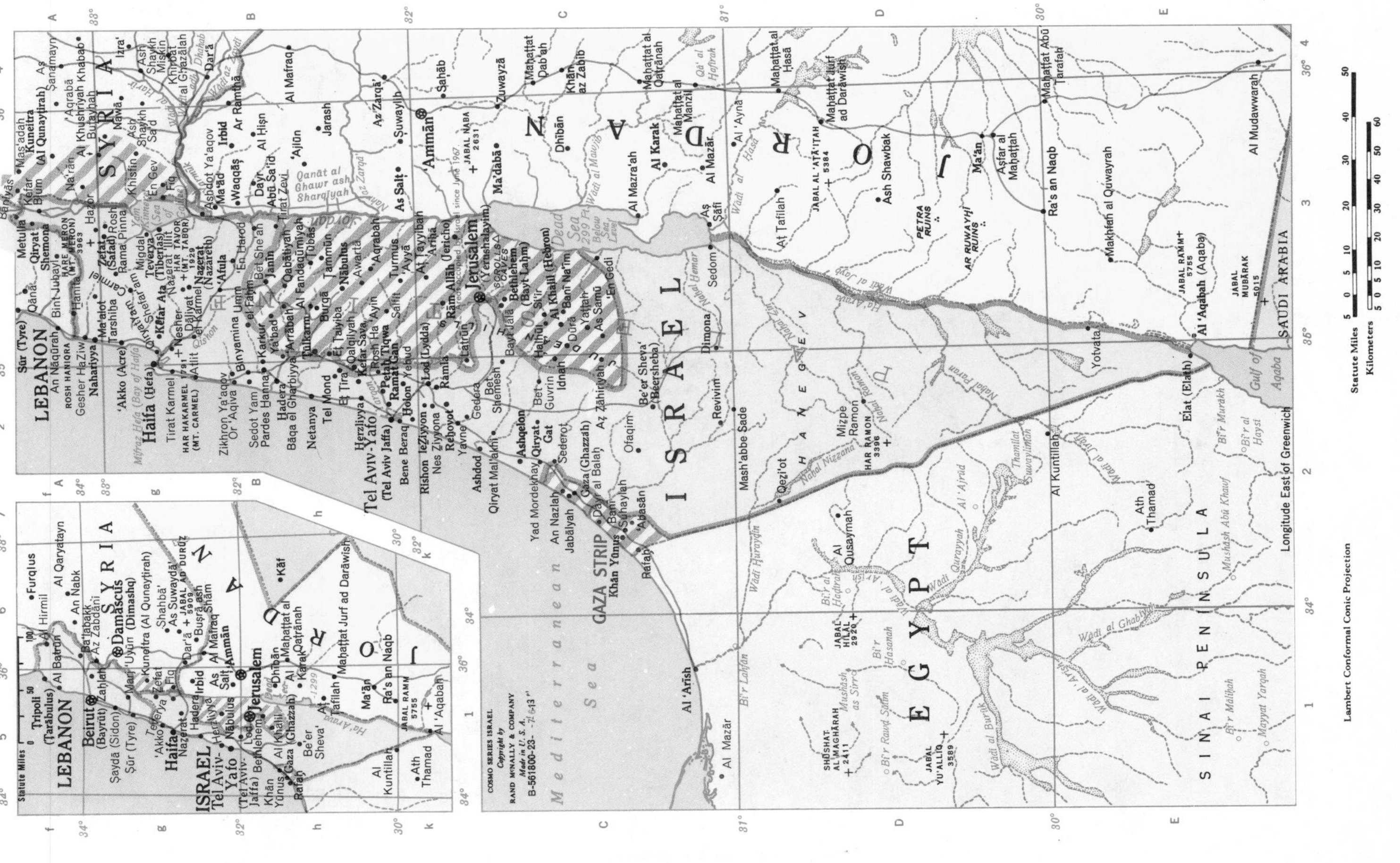

COSMO SERIES ISRAEL
RAND McNALLY & COMPANY
Copyright by
Made in U.S.A.
B-561800-23

GAZA STRIP

Gulf of Aqaba

NEGEV

Dead Sea

Sea of Galilee

Statute Miles 100 0 100   300   500   700   900

Kilometers 100 0 100   300   700   1100

Lambert Azimuthal Equal Area Projection

B-519695-21
Copyright by
RAND M$NALLY$ & COMPANY
COSMO SERIES EURASIA
Made in U.S.A.

Longitude West of Greenwich

Longitude East of Greenwich

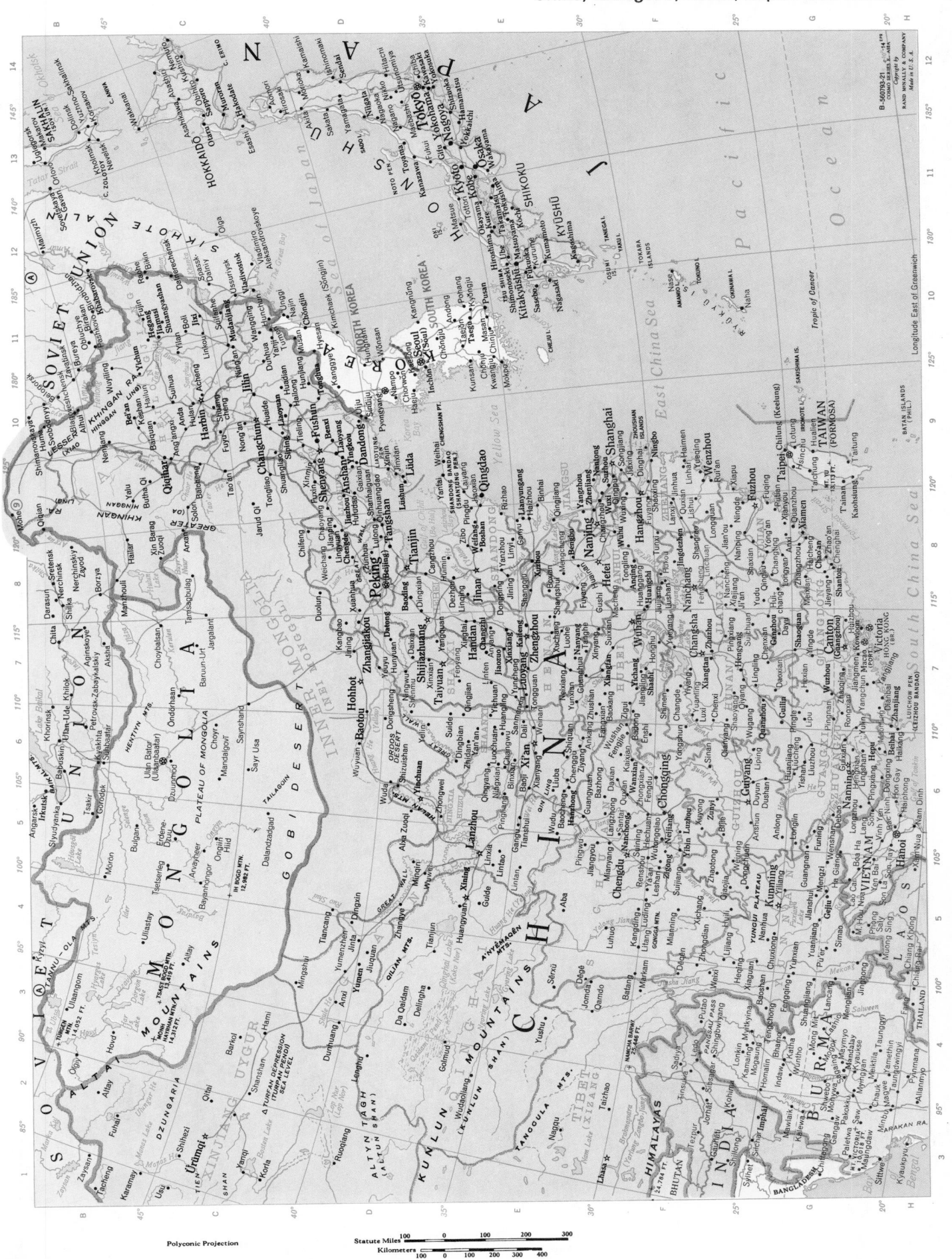

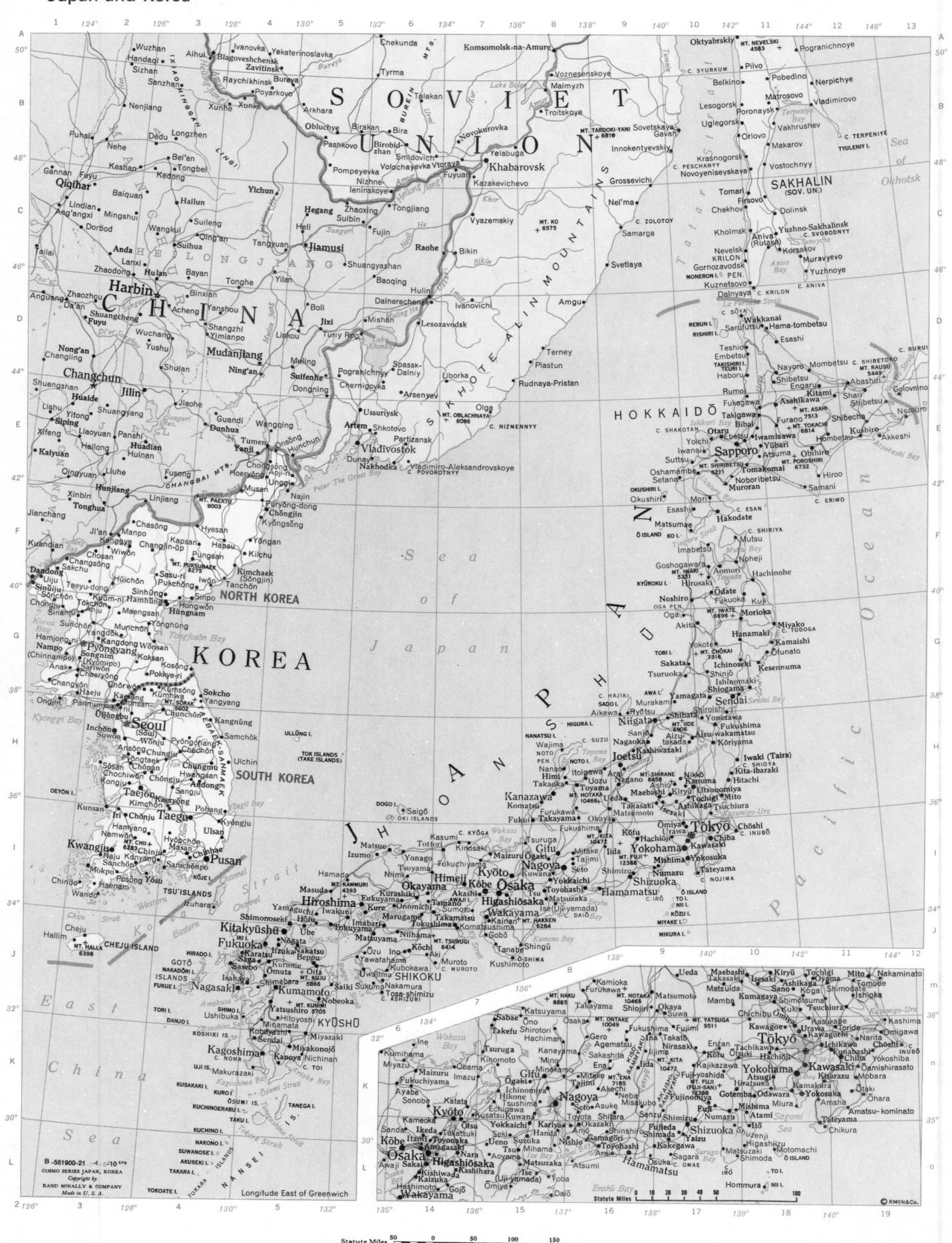

Longitude East of Greenwich

Statute Miles

Kilometers

Lambert Conformal Conic Projection

© RM&N&Co.

Polyconic Projection

Statute Miles
100   0   100   200   300

Kilometers
100 0 100 200 300 400

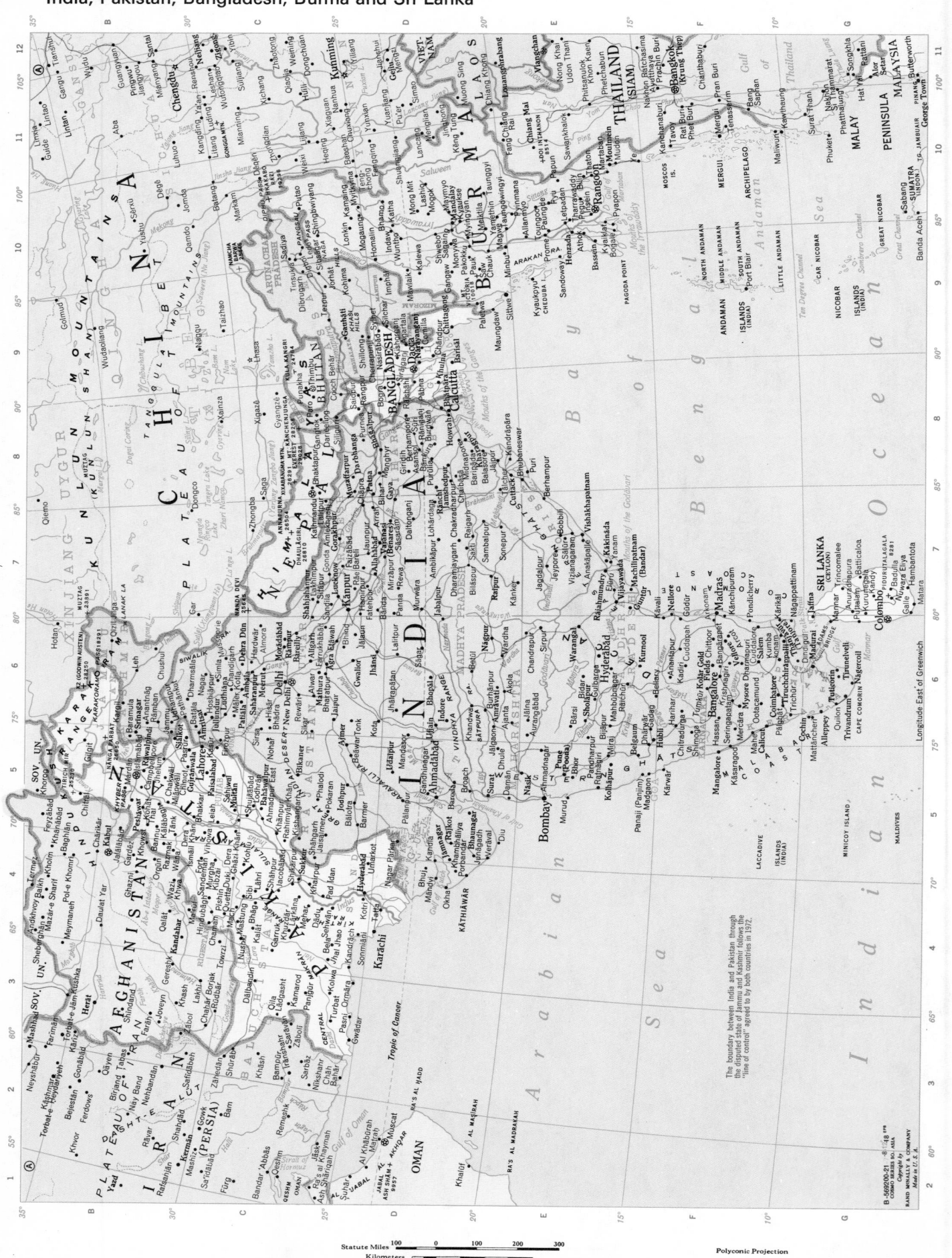

The boundary between India and Pakistan through the disputed state of Jammu and Kashmir follows the "line of control" agreed to by both countries in 1972.

Statute Miles   100   0   100   200   300
Kilometers   100   0   100   200   300   400

Polyconic Projection

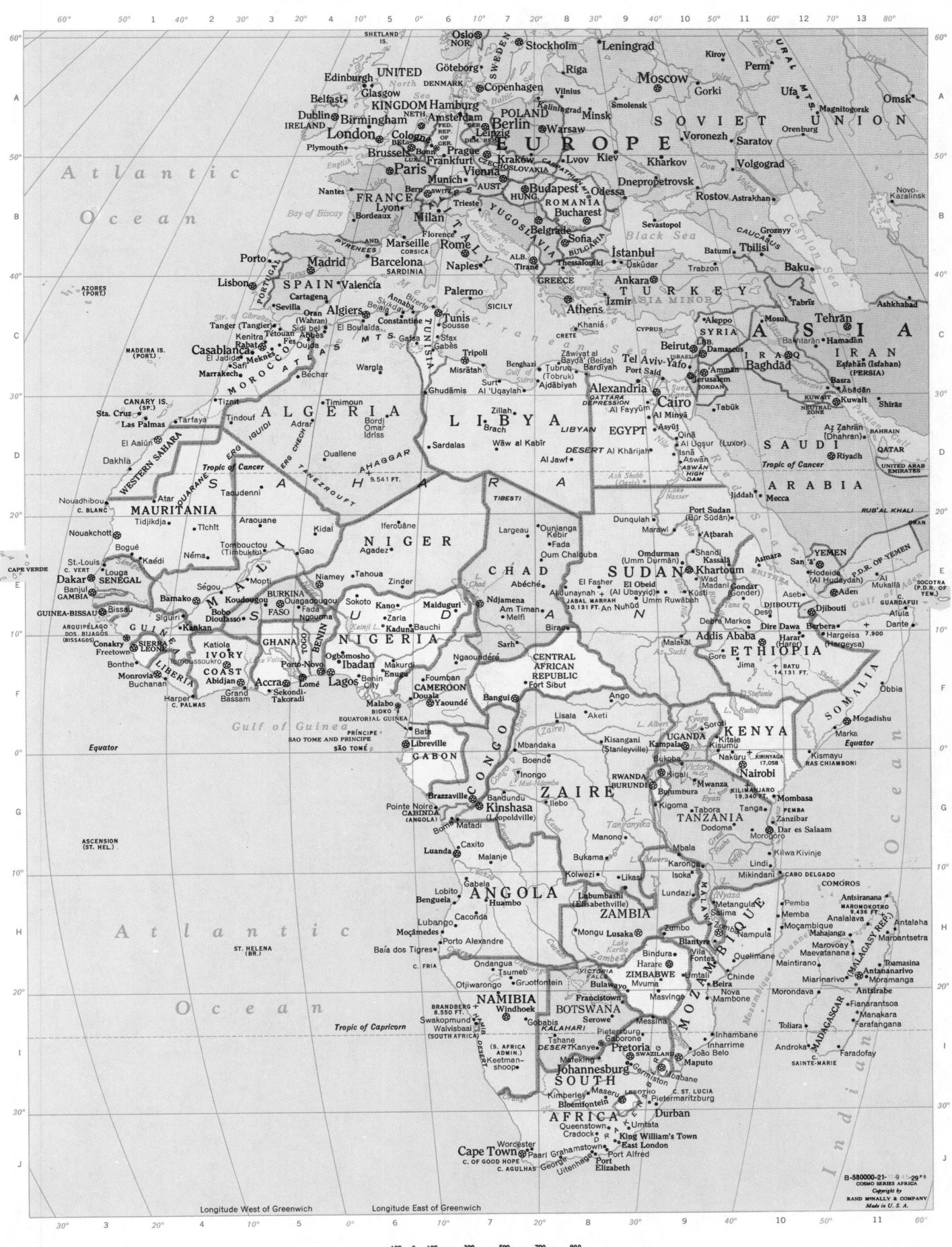

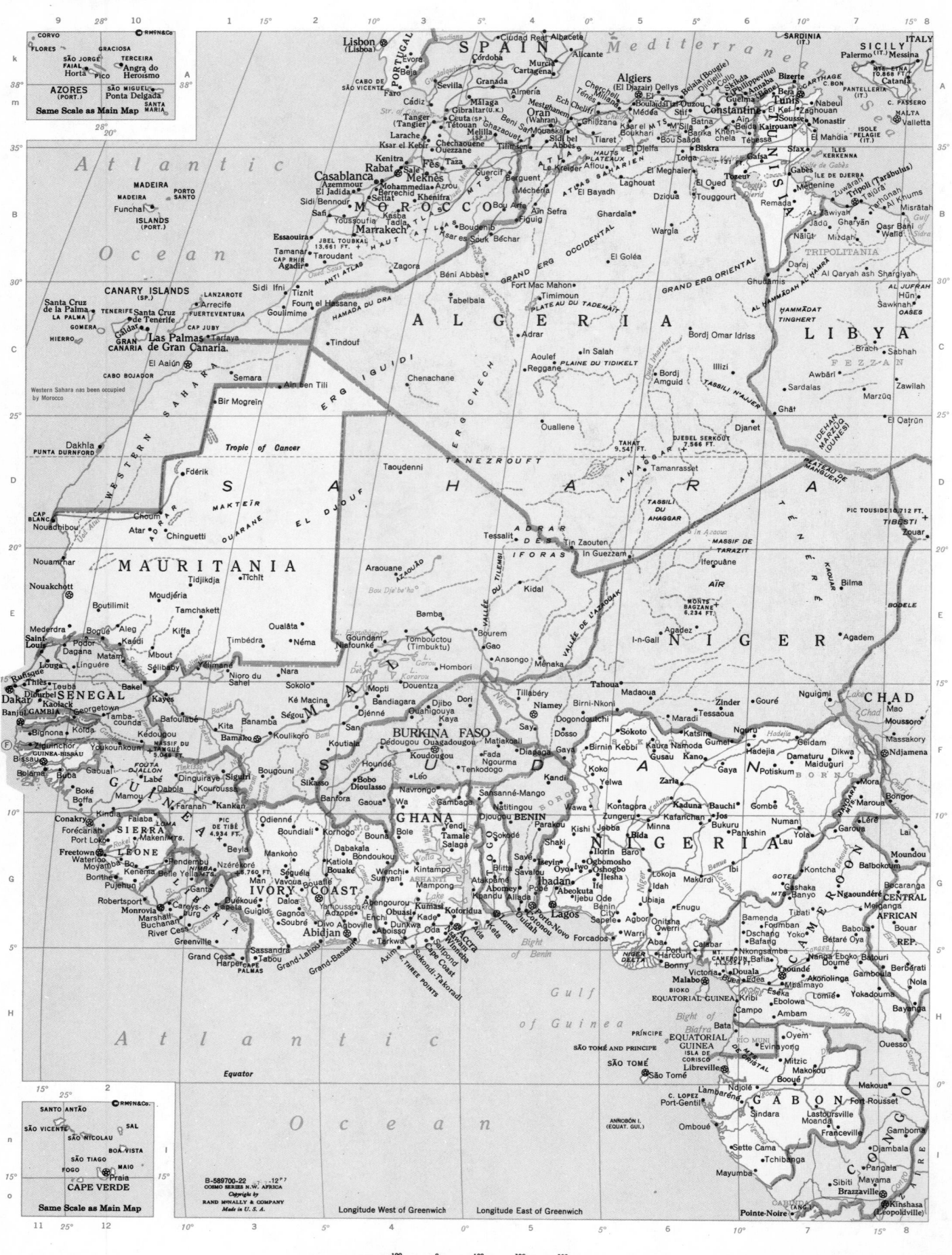

Statute Miles 100   0   100   200   300

Kilometers 100   0   100   200   300   400

Sinusoidal Projection

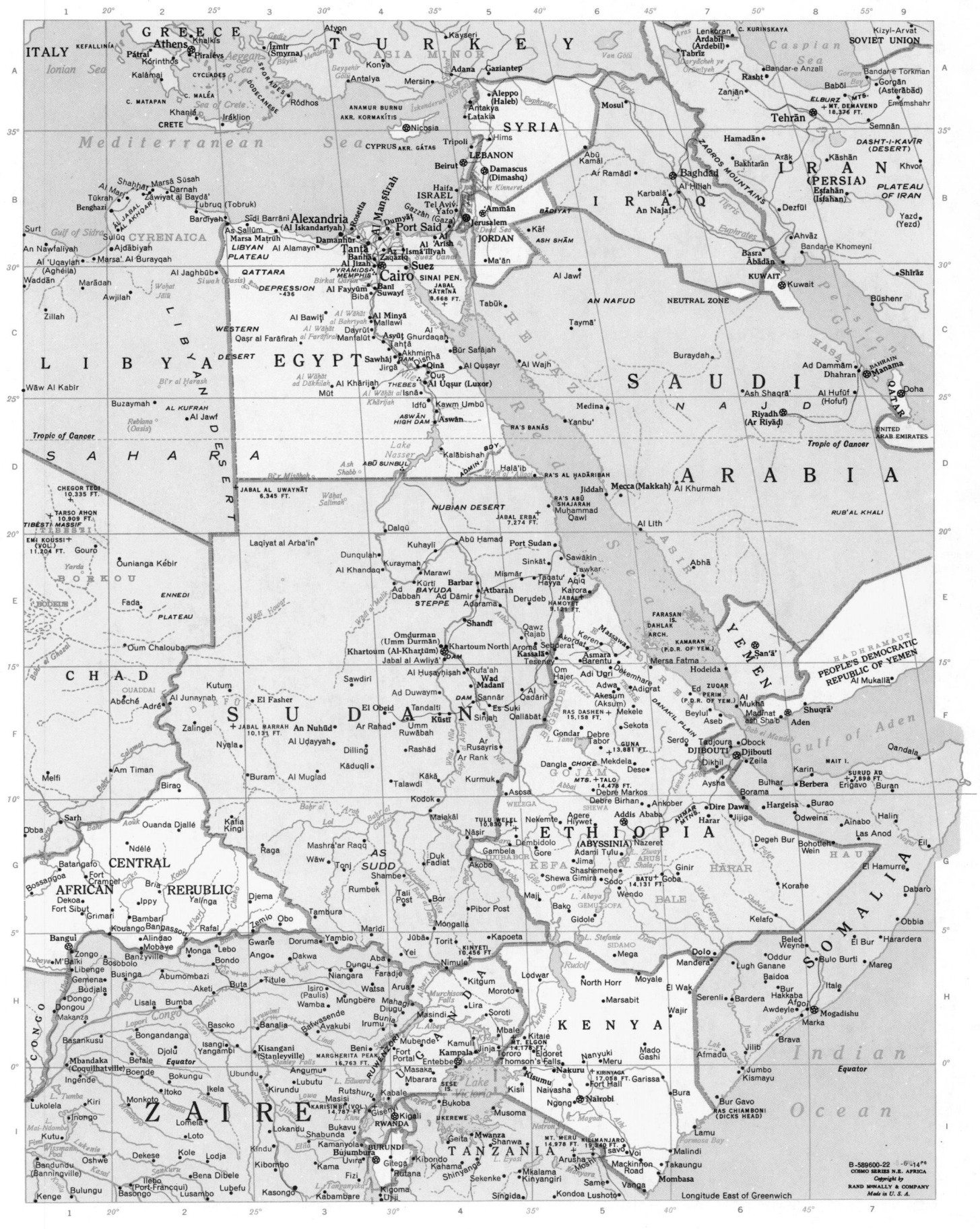

Sinusoidal Projection

Statute Miles
100   0   100   200   300

Kilometers
100 0 100 200 300 400

Longitude East of Greenwich

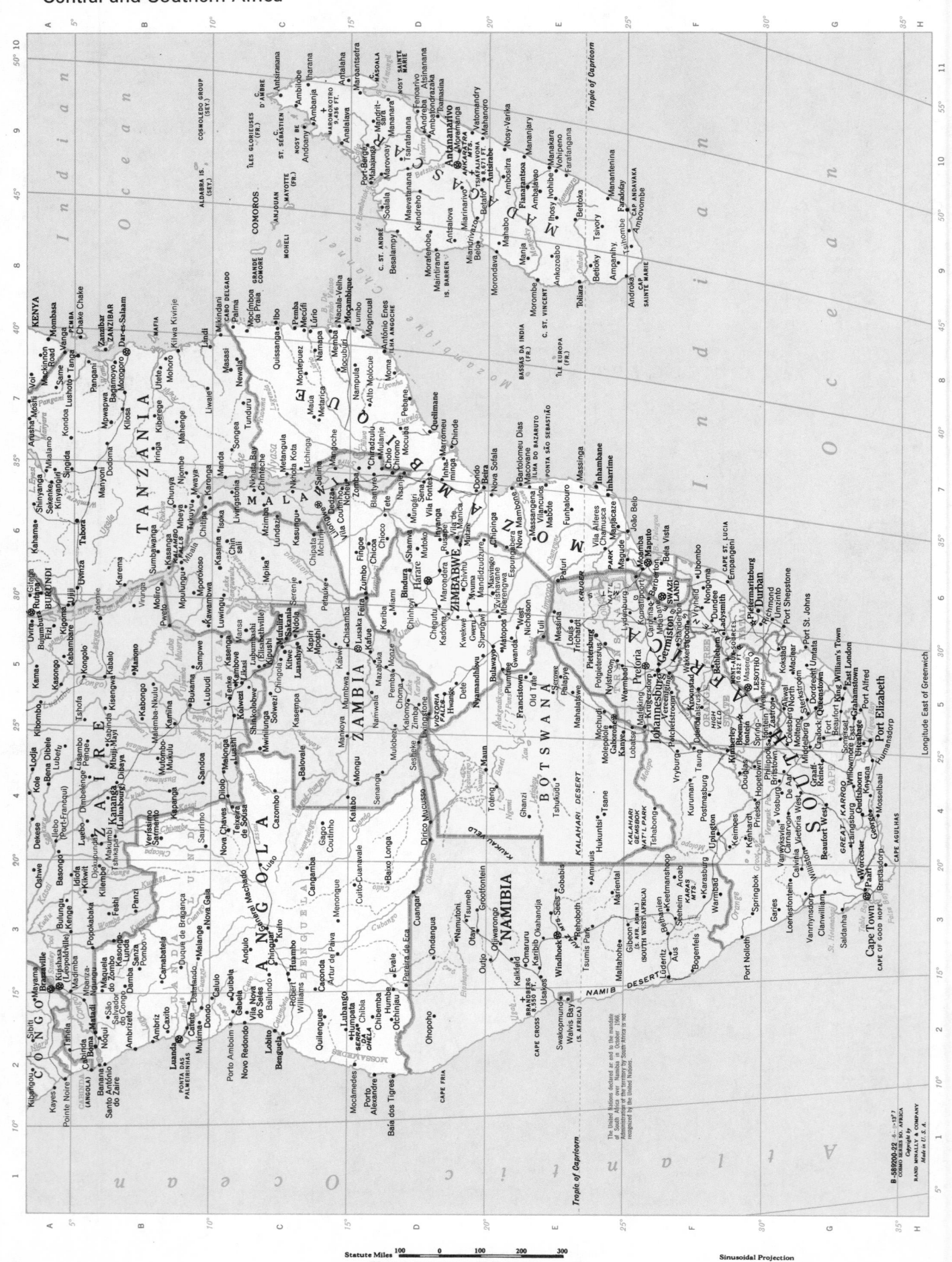

Statute Miles   100   0   100   200   300
Kilometers   100   0   100   200   300   400

Sinusoidal Projection

B-589200-22 4-13⁷
COSMO SERIES SO. AFRICA
Copyright 1966
RAND M⁈NALLY & COMPANY
Made in U.S.A.

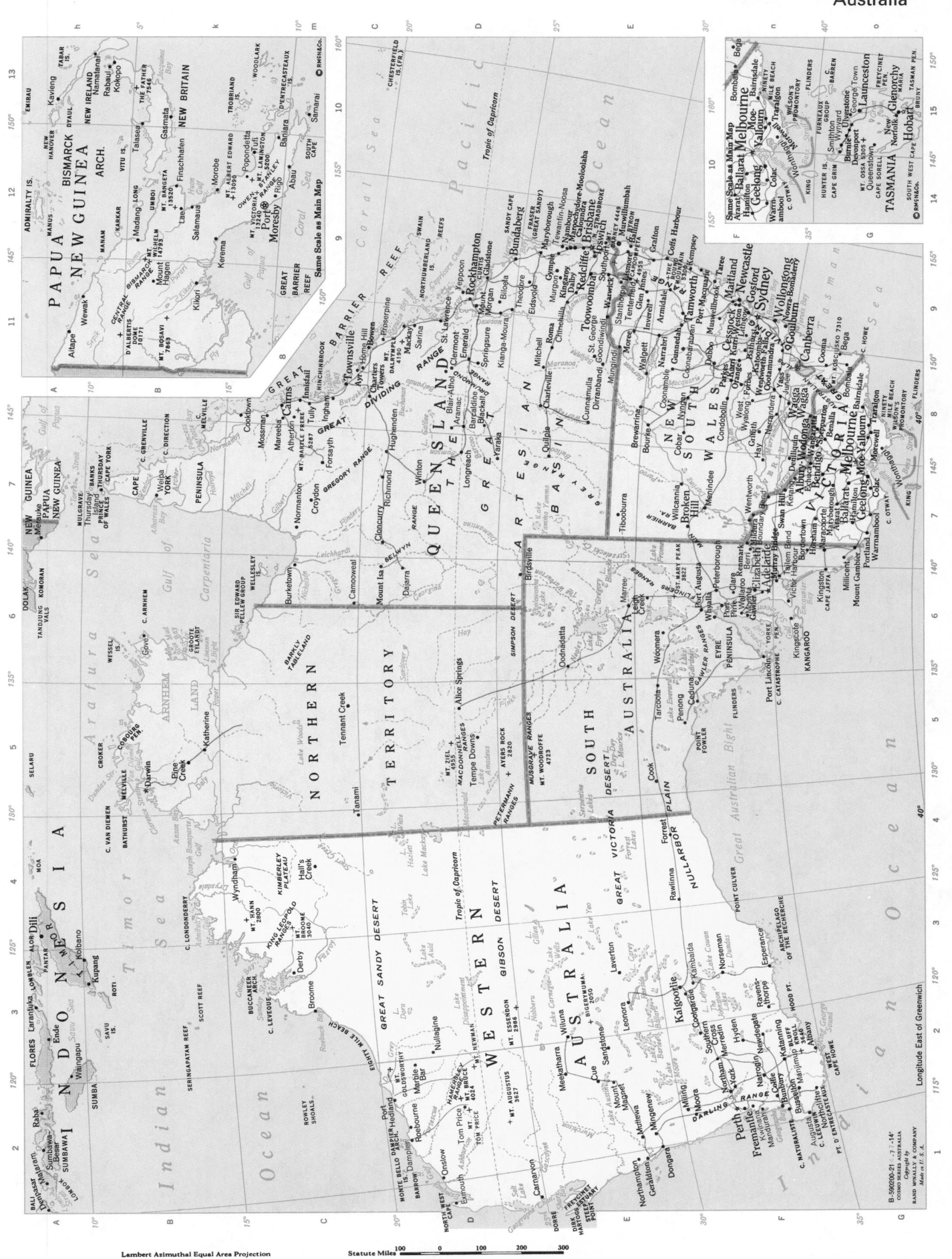

PAPUA
NEW GUINEA

BISMARCK ARCH.

NEW BRITAIN

NEW IRELAND

Port Moresby

Same Scale as Main Map

TASMANIA

Melbourne
Geelong
Launceston
Hobart

Same Scale as Main Map

INDONESIA

NEW GUINEA
PAPUA

ARNHEM LAND

NORTHERN
TERRITORY

Darwin

Tennant Creek

Alice Springs

QUEENSLAND

Cairns

Townsville

Mackay

Rockhampton

Brisbane

SOUTH
AUSTRALIA

WESTERN
AUSTRALIA

GREAT SANDY DESERT

GIBSON DESERT

GREAT VICTORIA DESERT

NULLARBOR PLAIN

Perth
Fremantle

Kalgoorlie

Adelaide

NEW SOUTH WALES

Sydney
Canberra
Wollongong
Newcastle

VICTORIA

Melbourne

Great Australian Bight

Indian Ocean

Pacific Ocean

Coral Sea

Gulf of Carpentaria

Arafura Sea

Timor Sea

Tasman Sea

Tropic of Capricorn

Lambert Azimuthal Equal Area Projection

Statute Miles
100   0   100   200   300

Kilometers
100   0   100   200   300   400

B-590200-21   -7   -14°
COSMO SERIES AUSTRALIA
Copyright by
RAND MCNALLY & COMPANY
Made in U.S.A.

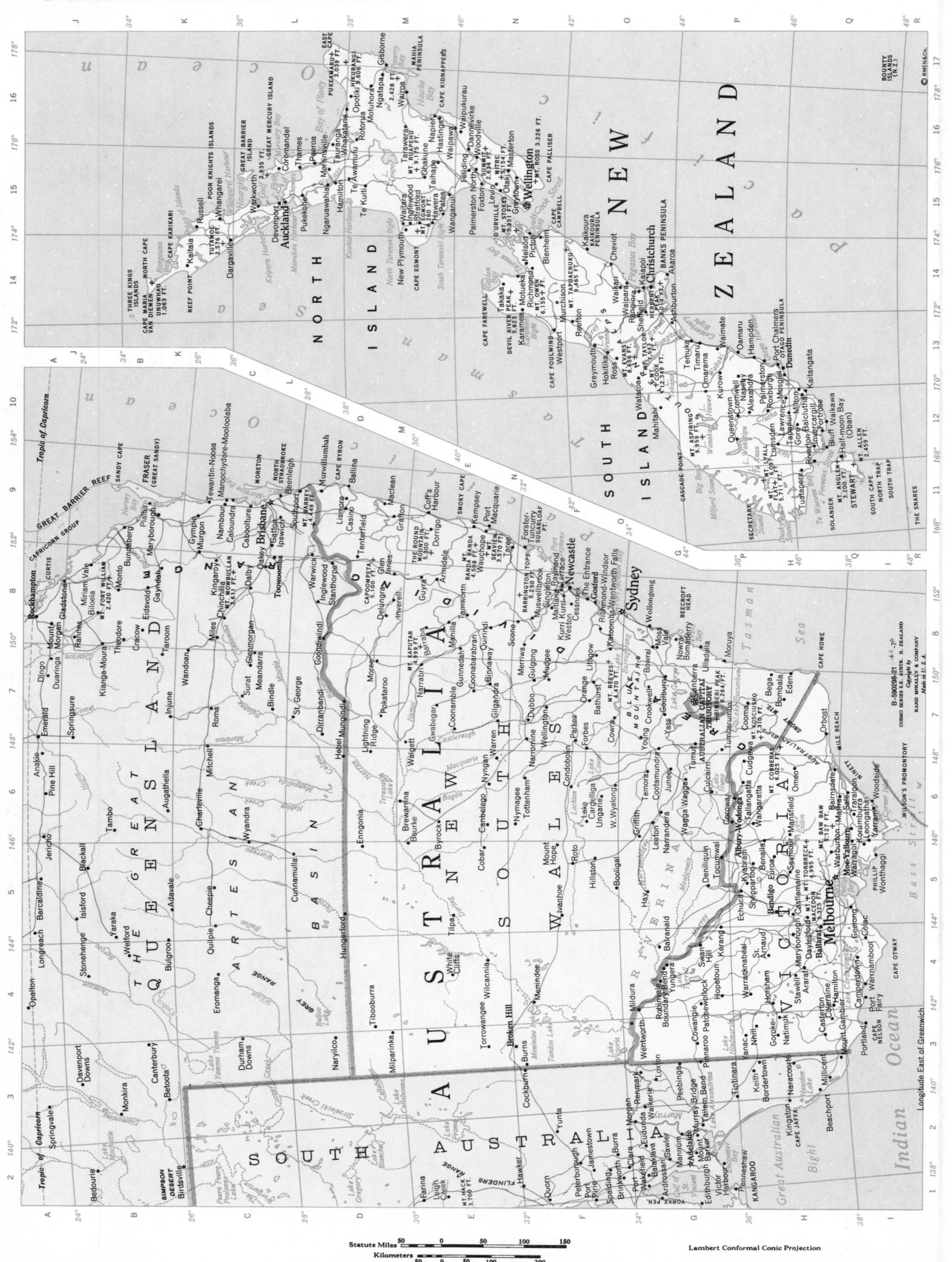

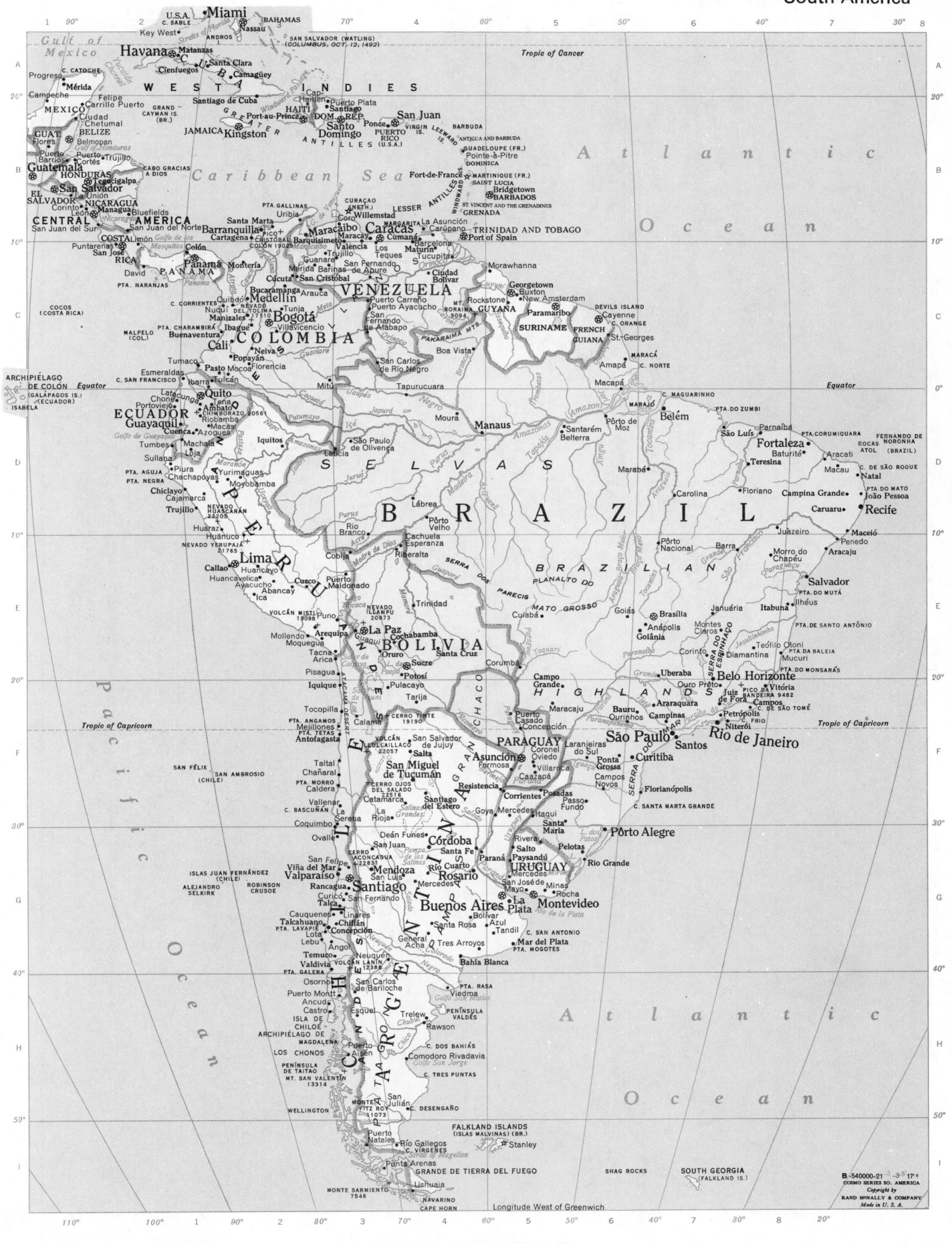

Sinusoidal Projection

Statute Miles 100 0 100 300 500 700

Kilometers 100 0 100 300 500 700 900 1100

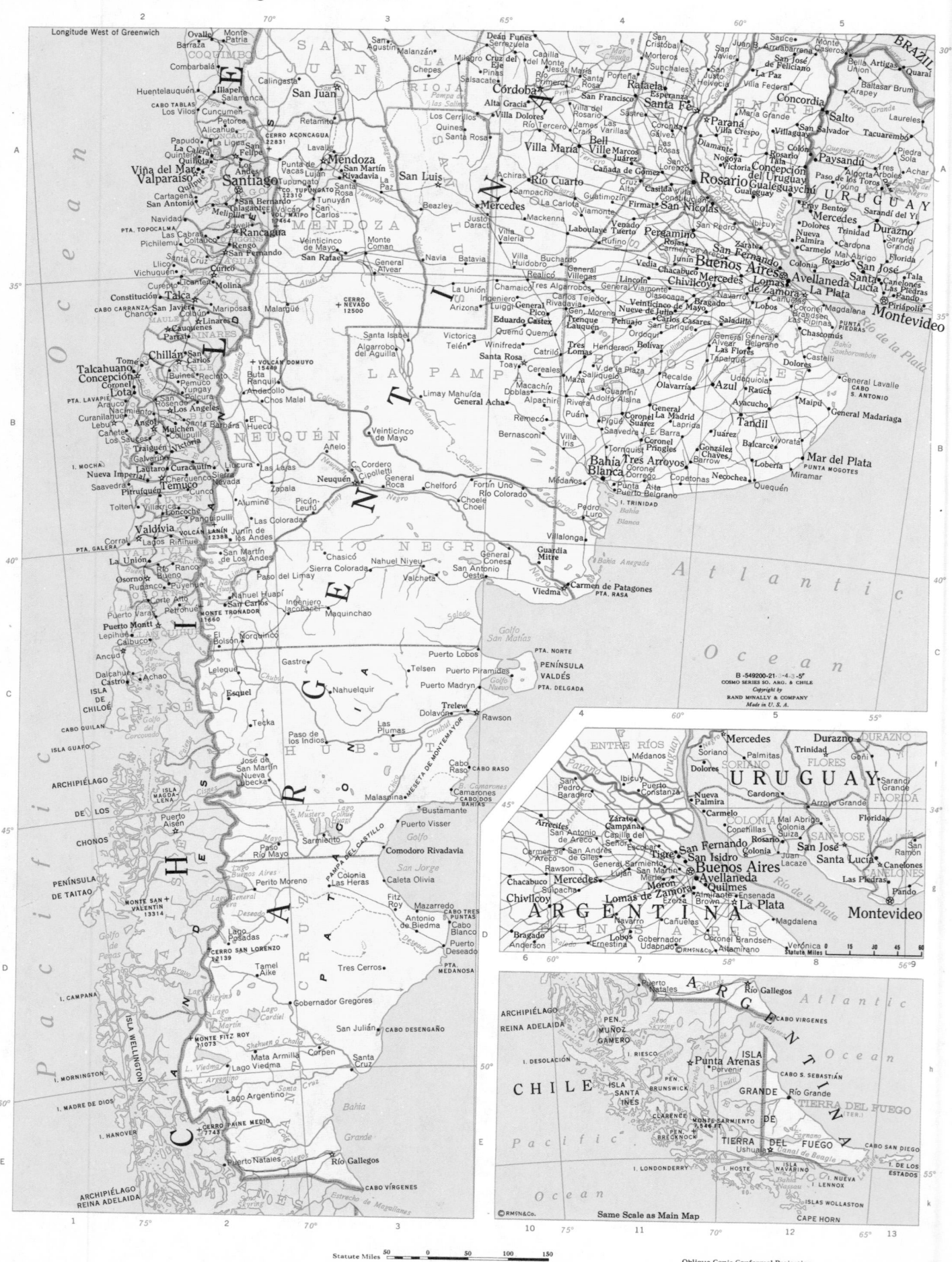

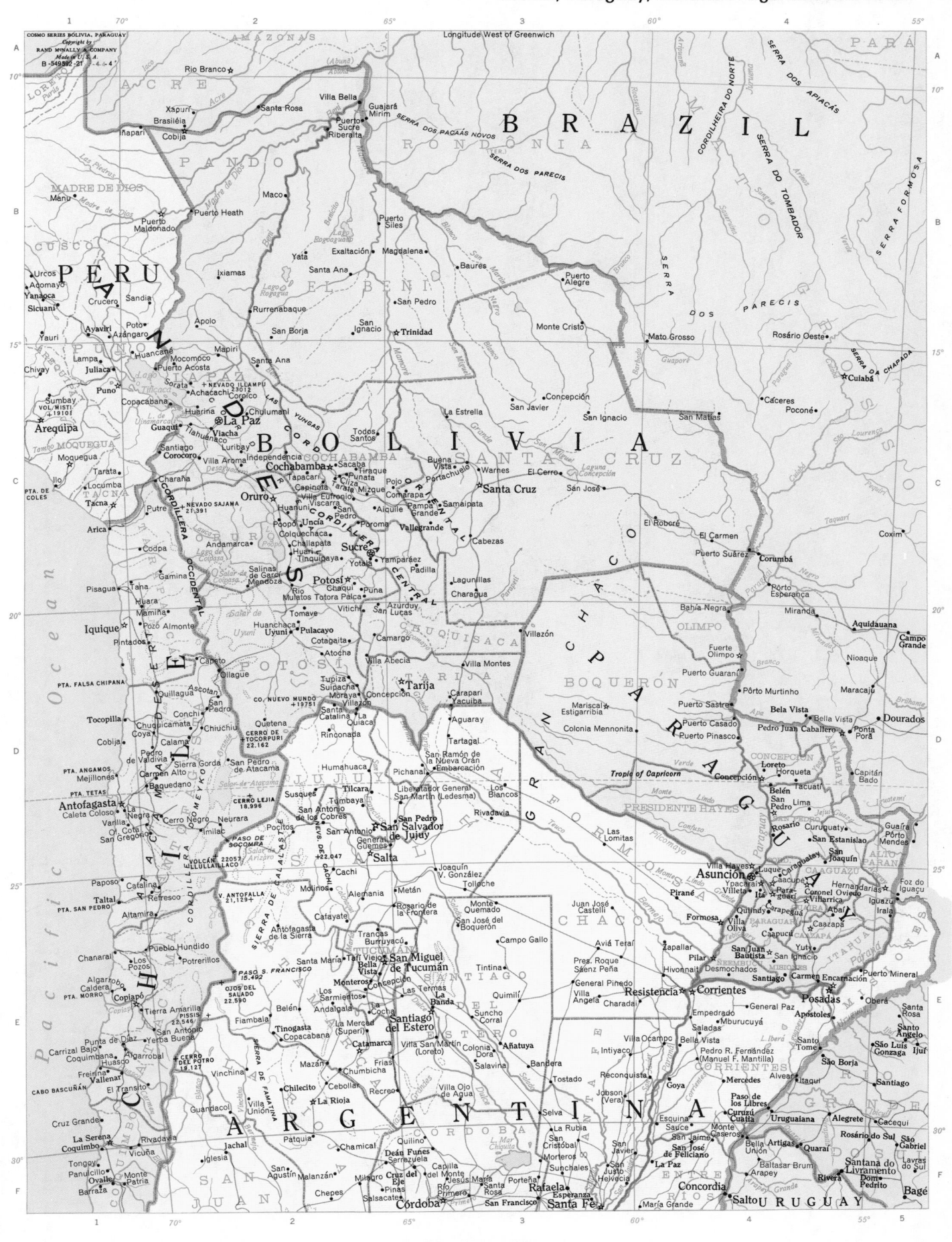

Oblique Conic Conformal Projection

Statute Miles
50 0   50   100   150

Kilometers
50 0   50 100 150 200

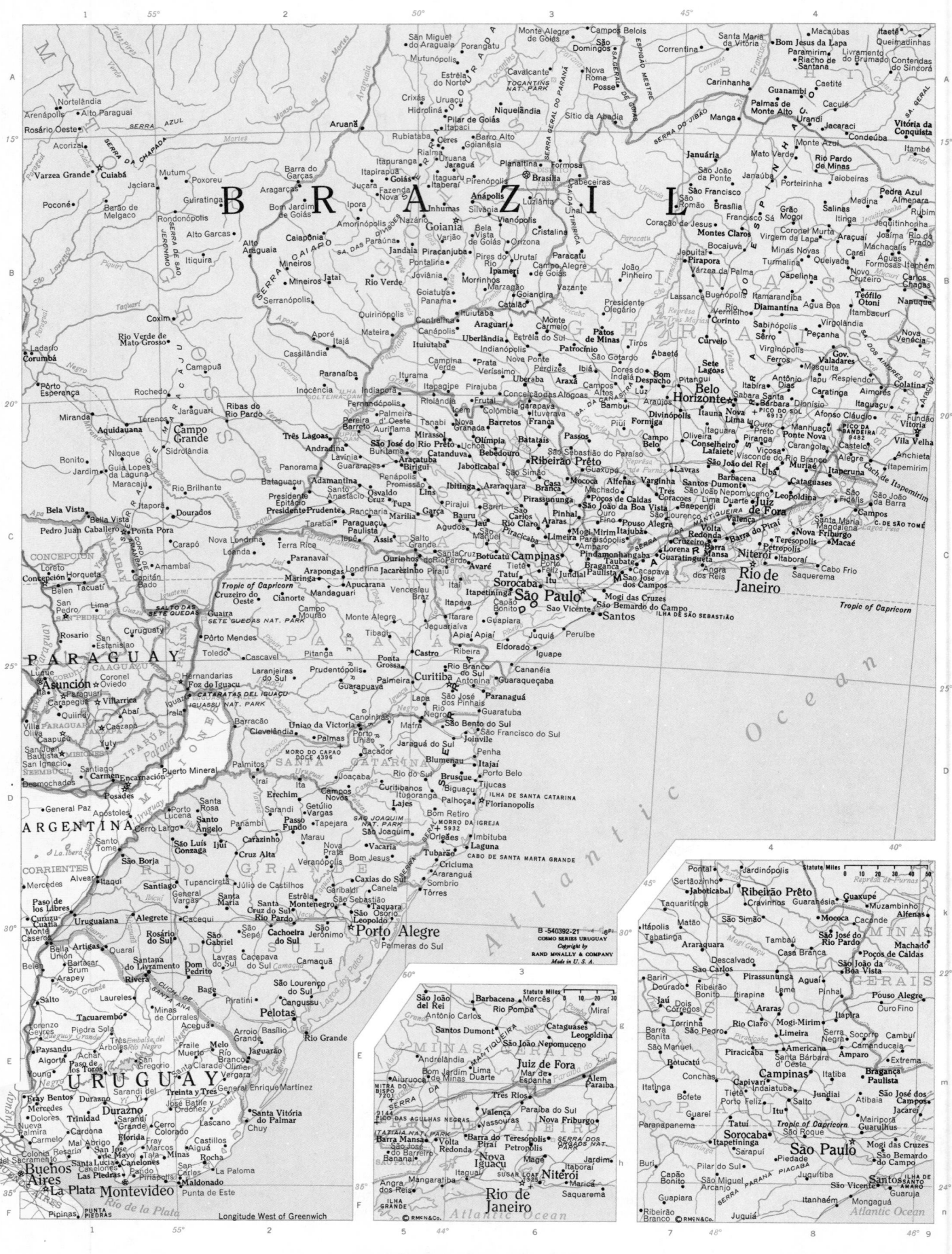

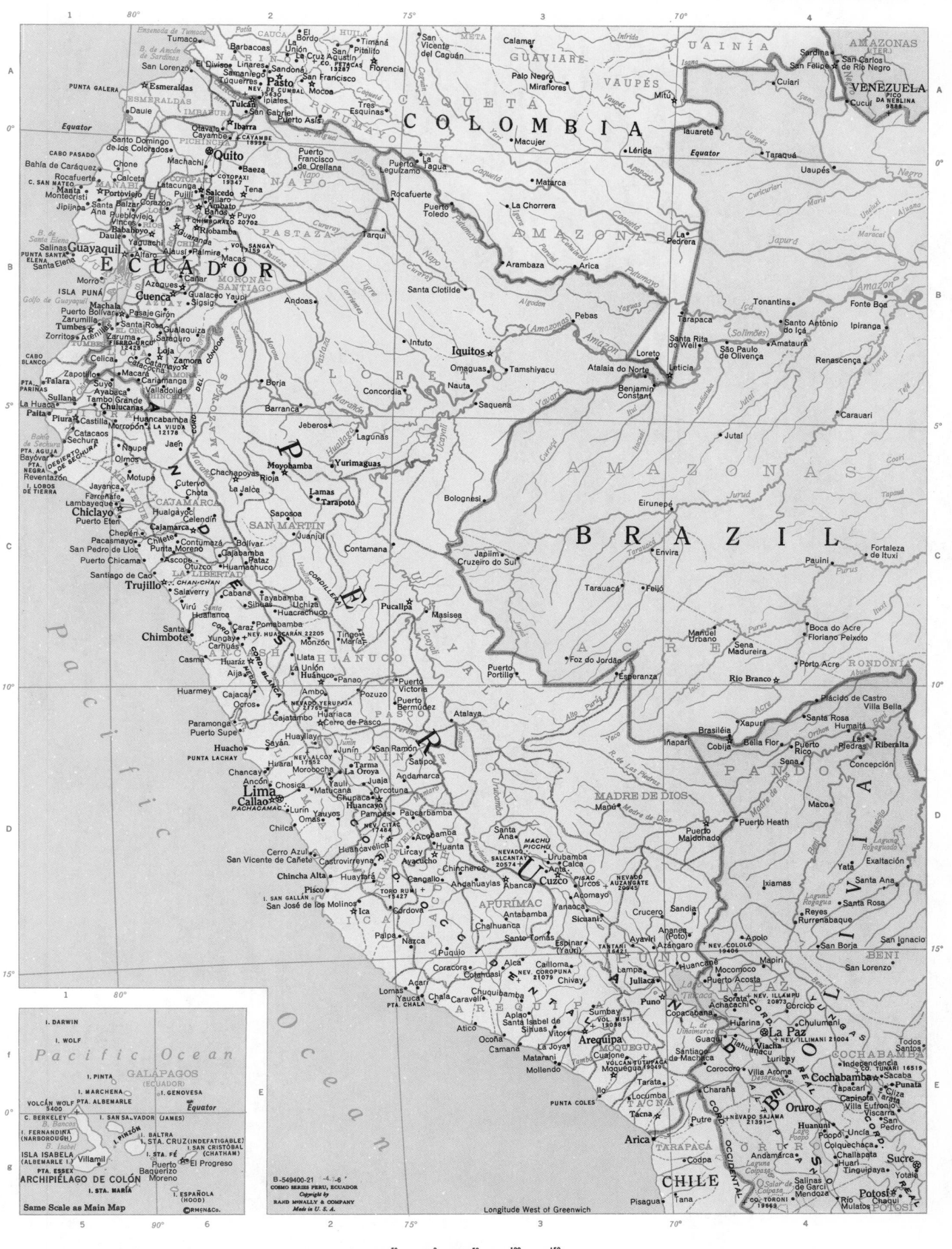

B-549400-21 4-6
COSMO SERIES PERU, ECUADOR
Copyright by
RAND McNALLY & COMPANY
Made in U.S.A.

Obliqu• Conic Conformal Projection

Longitude West of Greenwich

Statute Miles
Kilometers

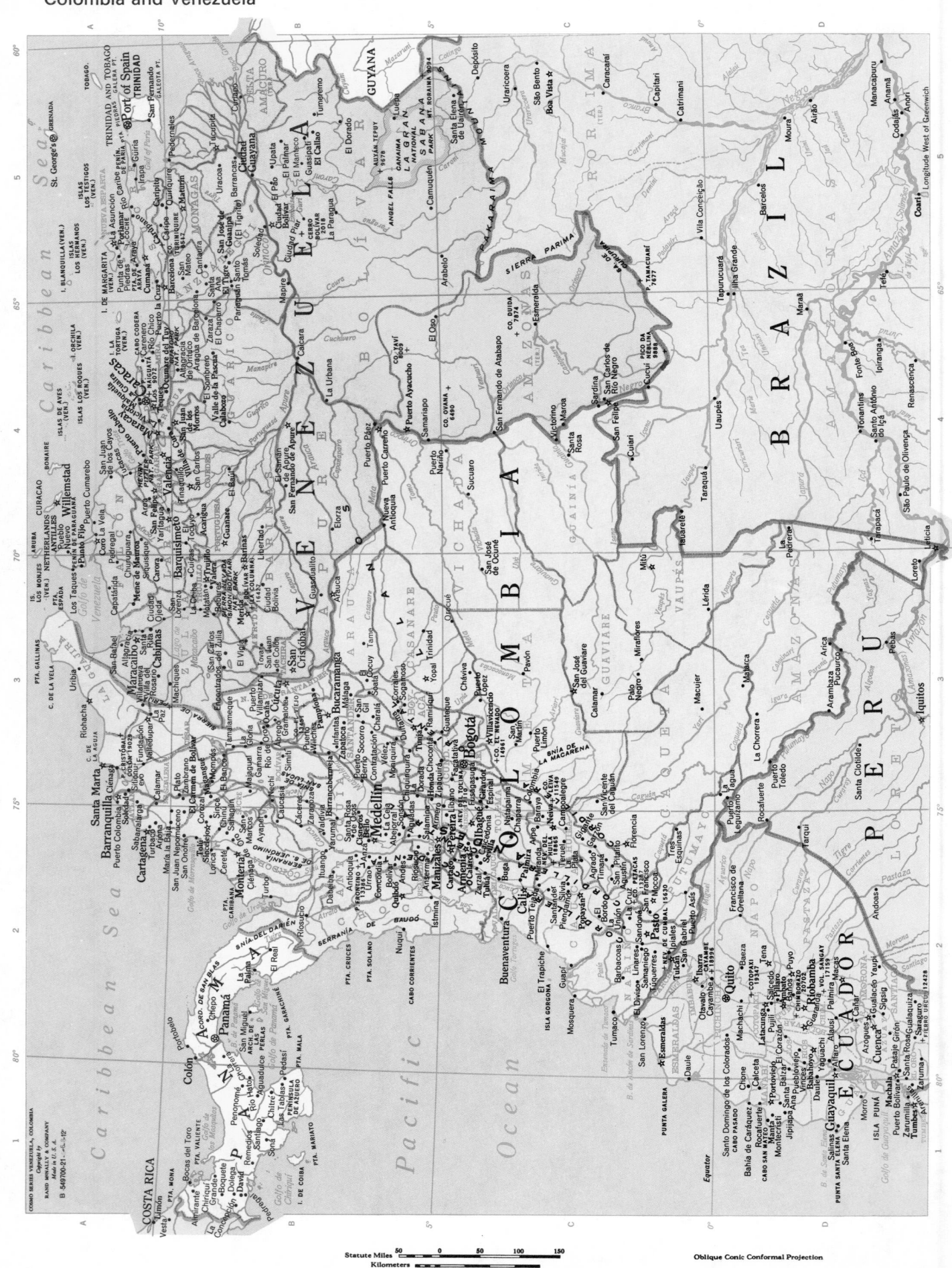

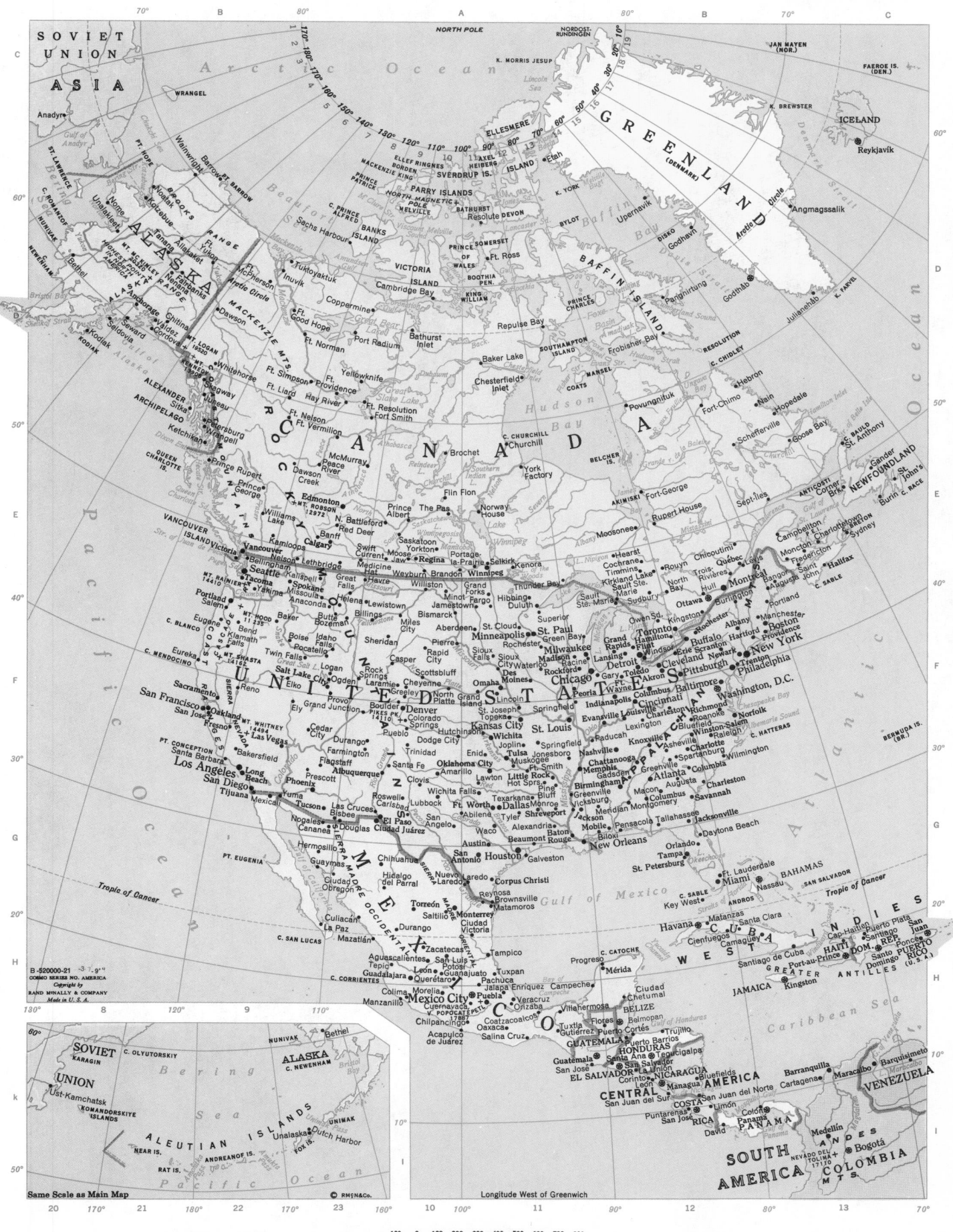

Lambert Azimuthal Equal Area Projection

Statute Miles 100 0 100 200 300 400 500 600 700 800
Kilometers 100 0 100 200 400 600 800 1000

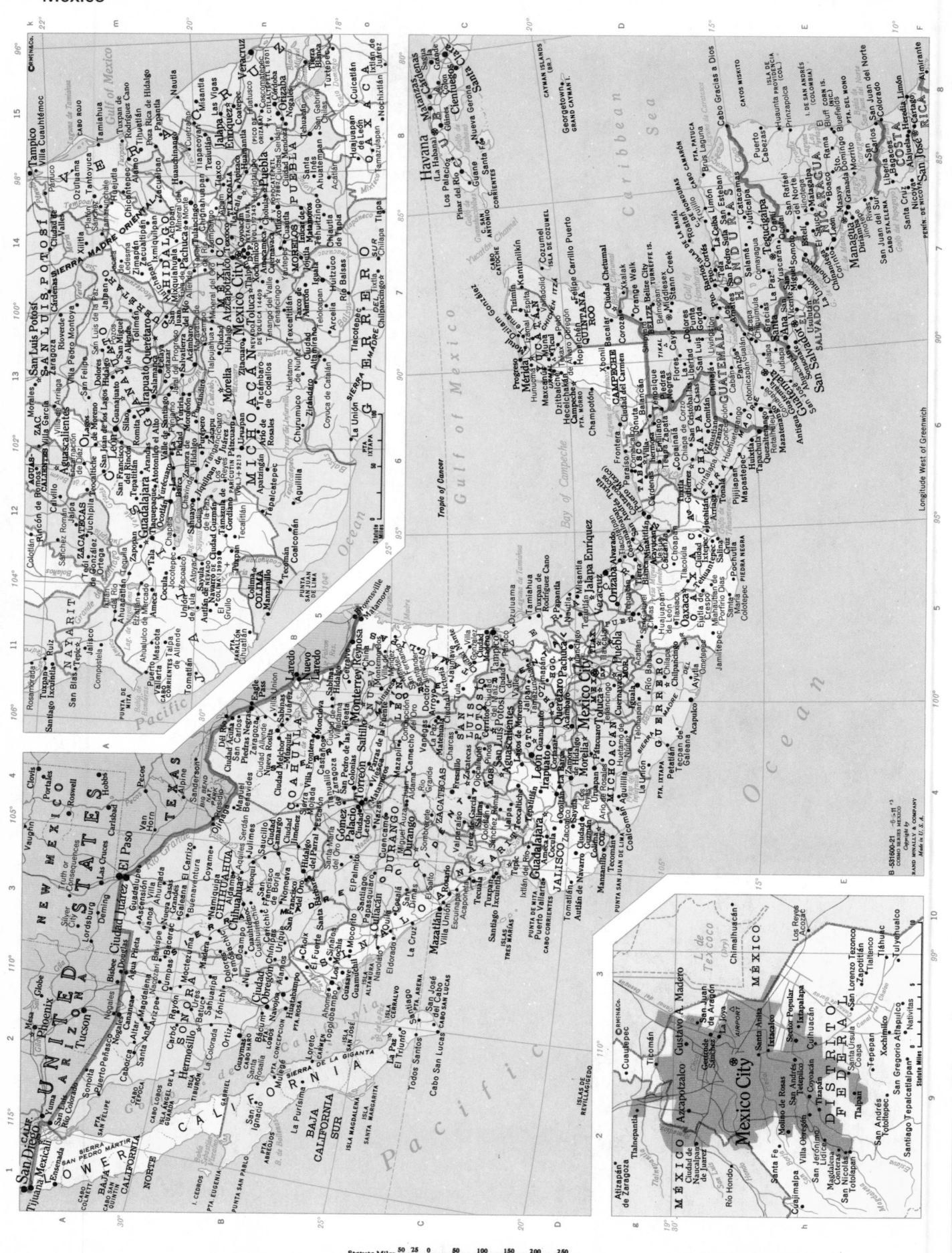

Statute Miles 50 25 0 50 100 150 200 250

Kilometers 50 0 100 200 300

Oblique Conic Conformal Projection

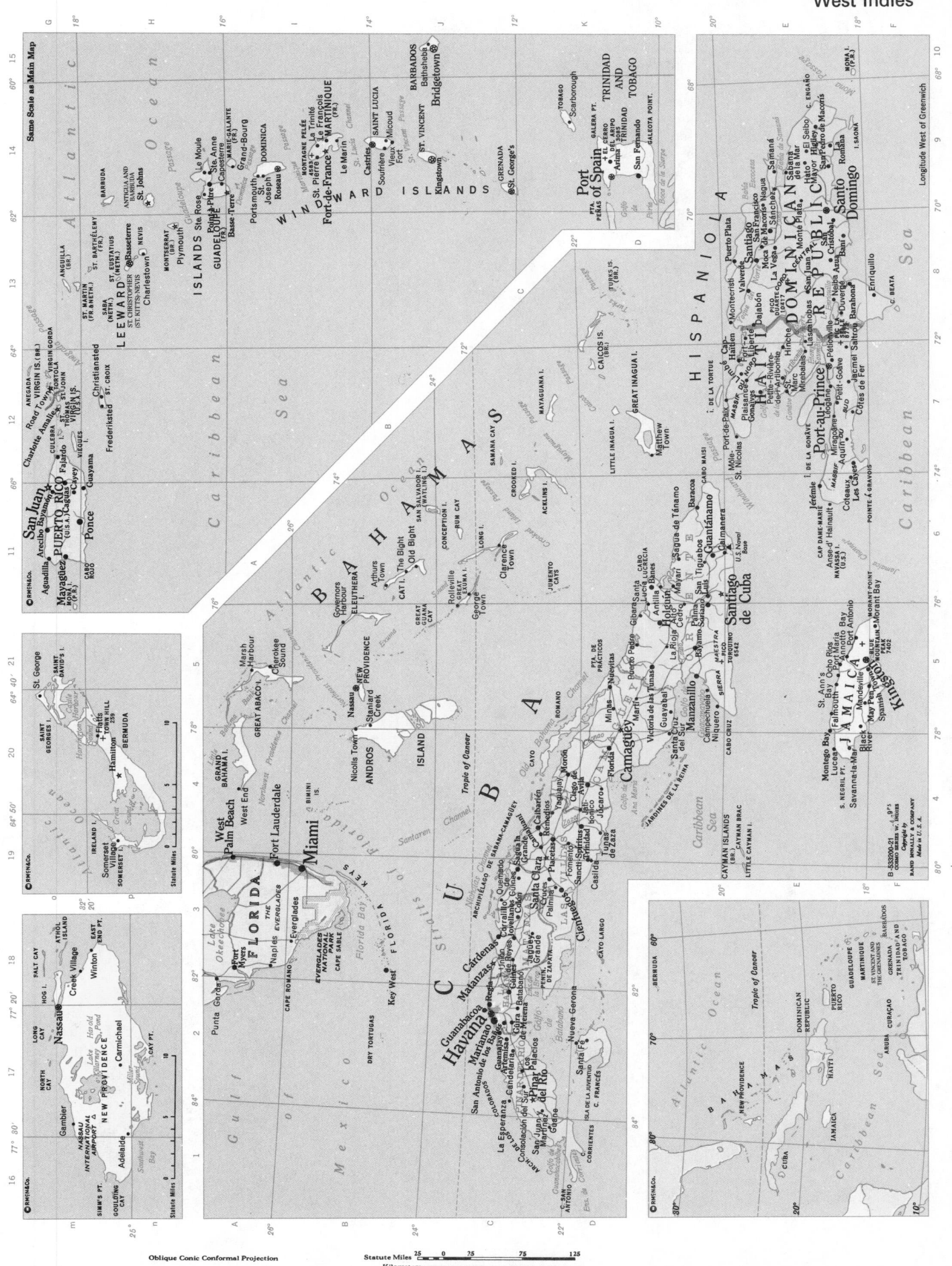

Oblique Conic Conformal Projection

Statute Miles 25 0 25 75 125

Kilometers 25 0 25 75 125 175

GREENLAND (DENMARK)

QUEEN ELIZABETH ISLANDS

ELLESMERE ISLAND

DEVON ISLAND

BAFFIN ISLAND

Same Scale as Main Map

NEWFOUNDLAND

QUEBEC

ONTARIO

MANITOBA

SASKATCHEWAN

ALBERTA

BRITISH COLUMBIA

YUKON

NORTHWEST TERRITORIES

BAFFIN ISLAND

VICTORIA ISLAND

BANKS ISLAND

PARRY ISLANDS

MELVILLE ISLAND

DISTRICT OF MACKENZIE

Hudson Bay

All islands within Hudson Bay, James Bay and Ungava Bay lie within Northwest Territories.

ALASKA

BROOKS RA.

ROCKY MTS.

COAST MTS.

FRANKLIN MTS.

RICHARDSON MTS.

SELWYN MTS.

Beaufort Sea

Mackenzie

Pacific Ocean

Atlantic Ocean

Arctic Ocean

MONTANA

NORTH DAKOTA

SOUTH DAKOTA

MINNESOTA

WISCONSIN

IOWA

WYOMING

IDAHO

NEVADA

CALIF.

OREGON

WASHINGTON

UTAH

NEW YORK

PENNSYLVANIA

OHIO

IND.

Lake Michigan

Chicago

Montreal

Toronto

Ottawa

Winnipeg

Edmonton

Calgary

Vancouver

Seattle

Philadelphia

New York

Longitude West of Greenwich

Statute Miles   100   0   100   200   300

Kilometers   100   0   100   200   300   400

Lambert Conformal Conic Projection

COSMO SERIES CANADA B
Copyright by
RAND McNALLY & COMPANY
Made in U.S.A.
B-520200-22

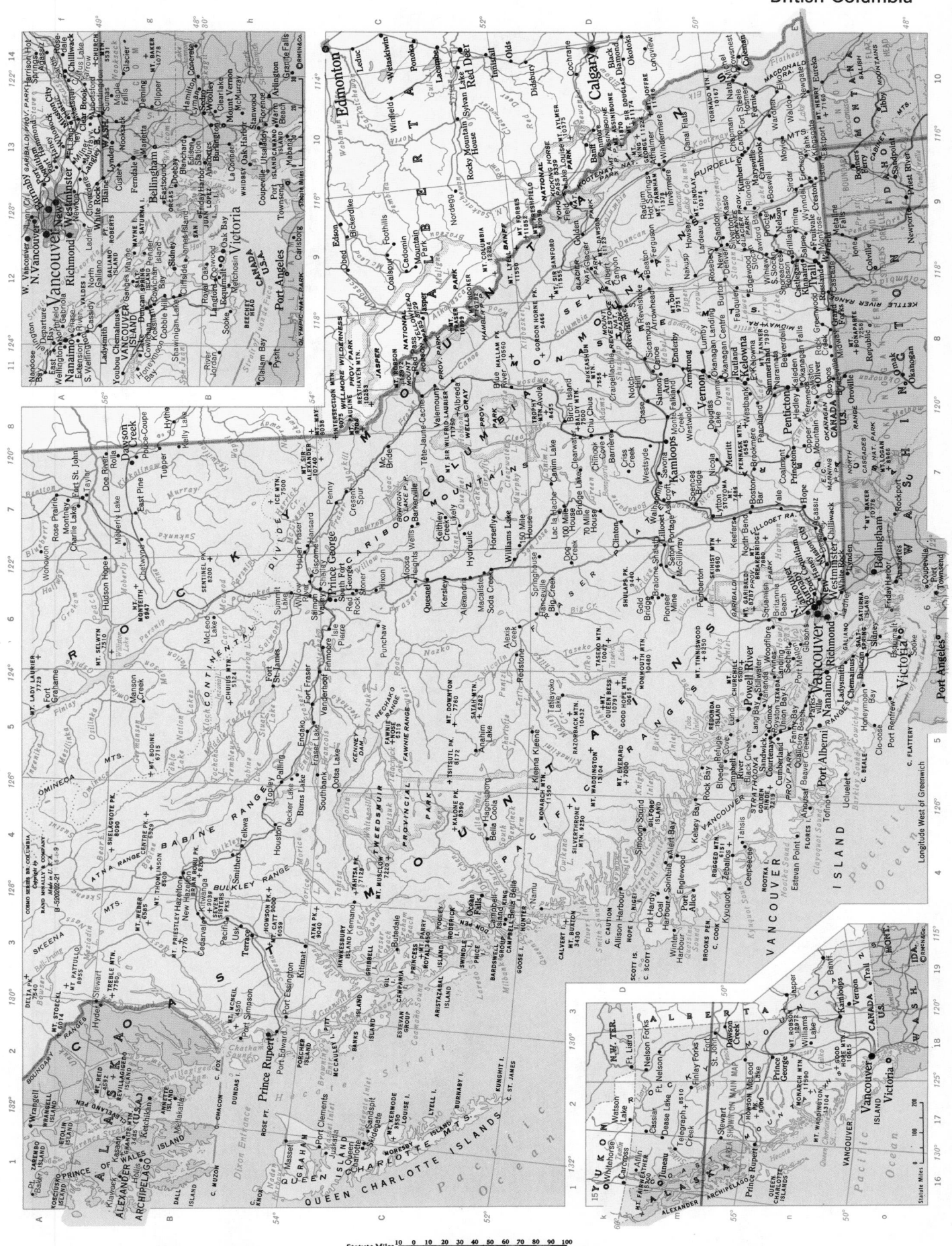

Oblique Cylindrical Projection

Statute Miles 10 0 10 20 30 40 50 60 70 80 90 100

Kilometers 0 0 10 20 40 60 80 100 120 140

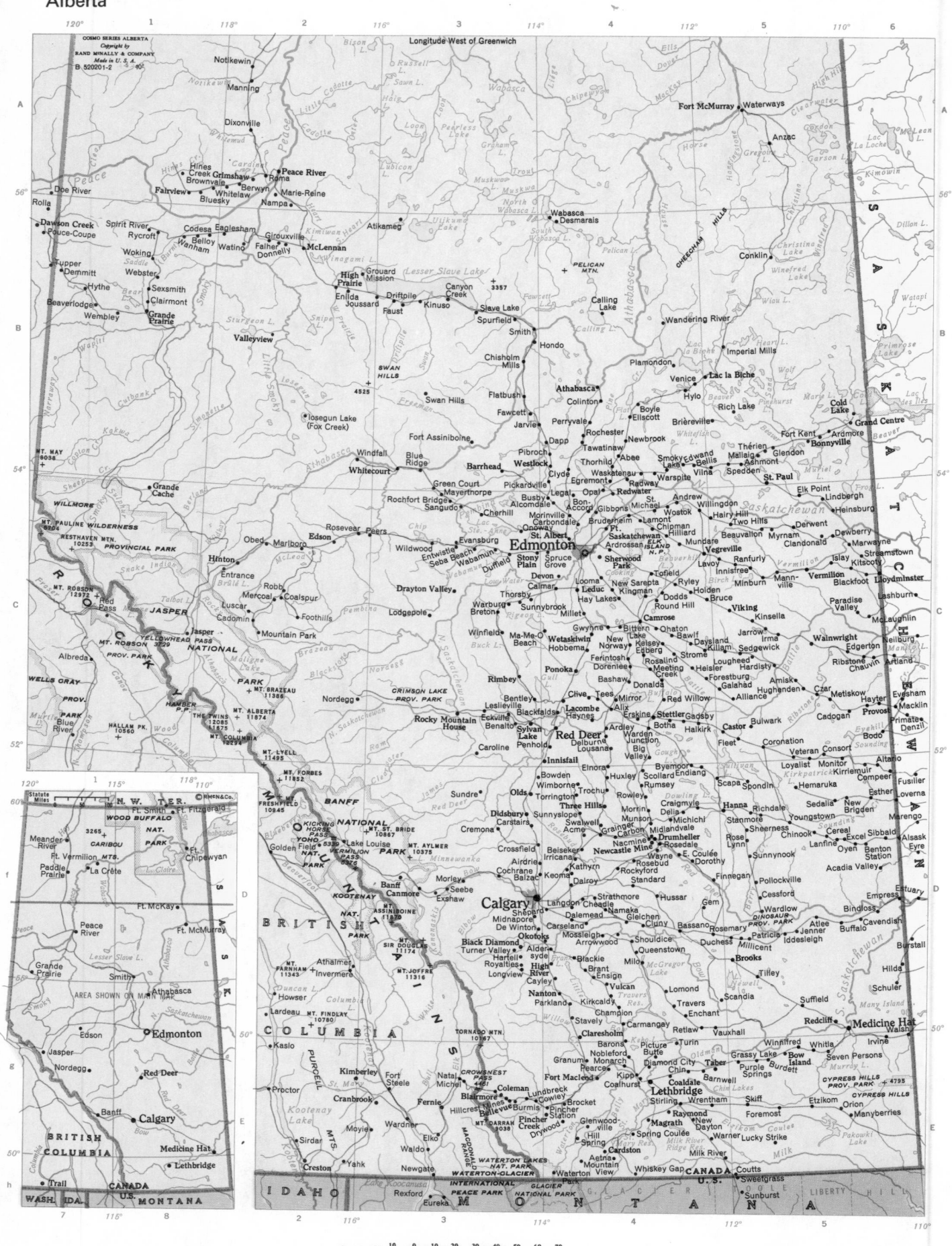

Statute Miles 10 0 10 20 30 40 50 60 70

Kilometers 10 0 10 20 40 60 80 100

Oblique Cylindrical Projection

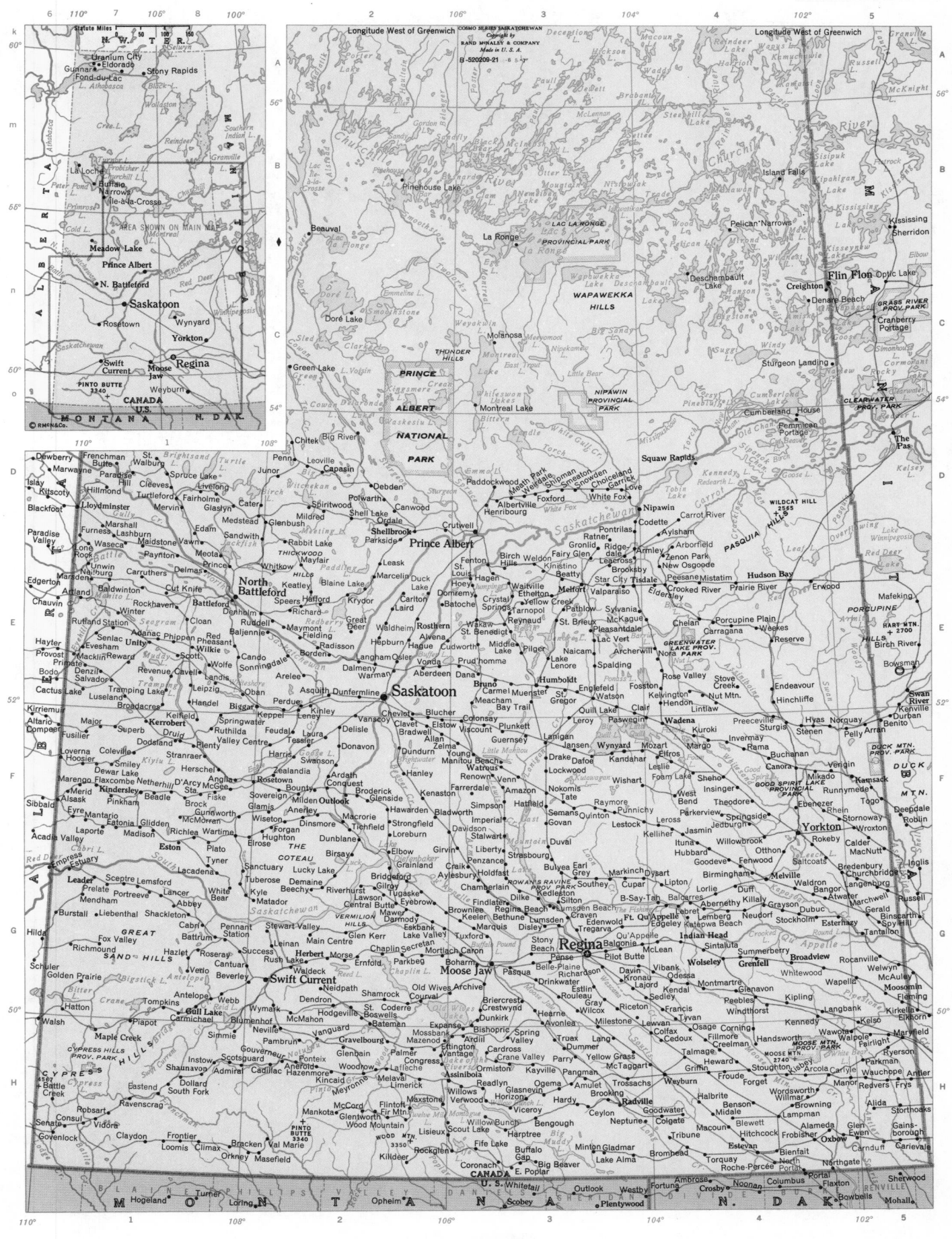

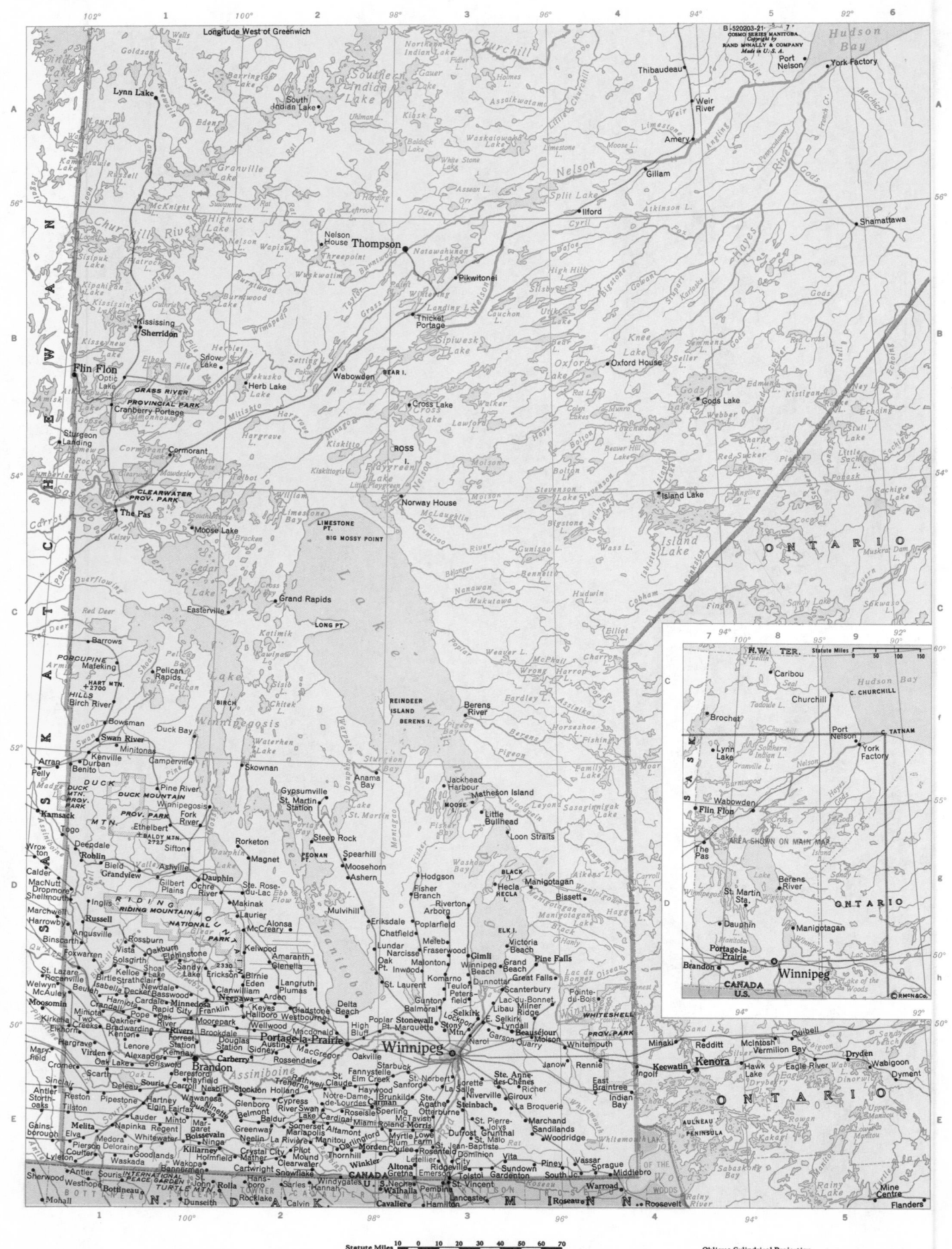

Oblique Cylindrical Projection

Statute Miles 5 0 5 10 20 30 40 50

Kilometers 5 0 5 15 25 35 45 55 65 75

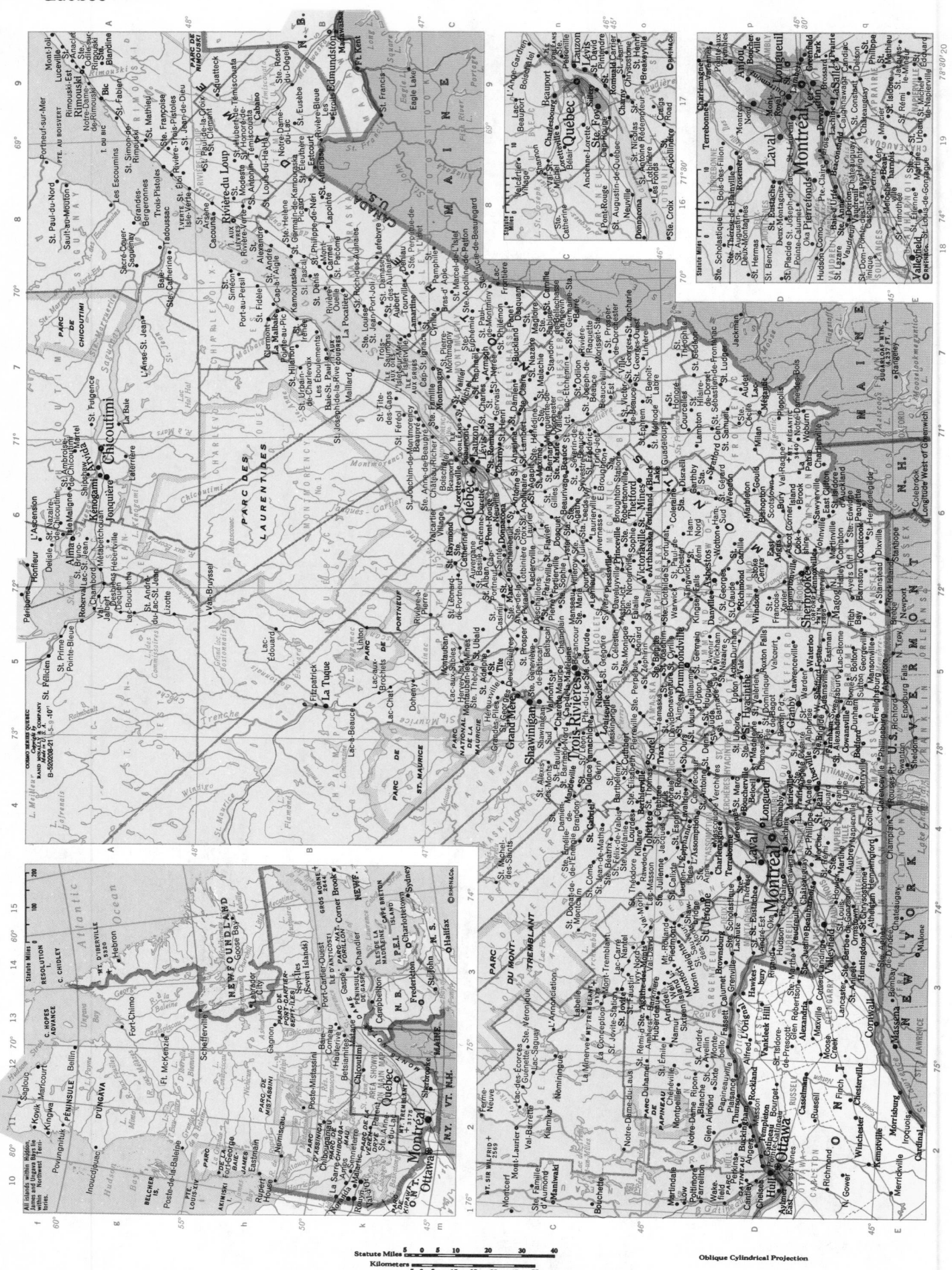

Statute Miles
Kilometers

Oblique Cylindrical Projection

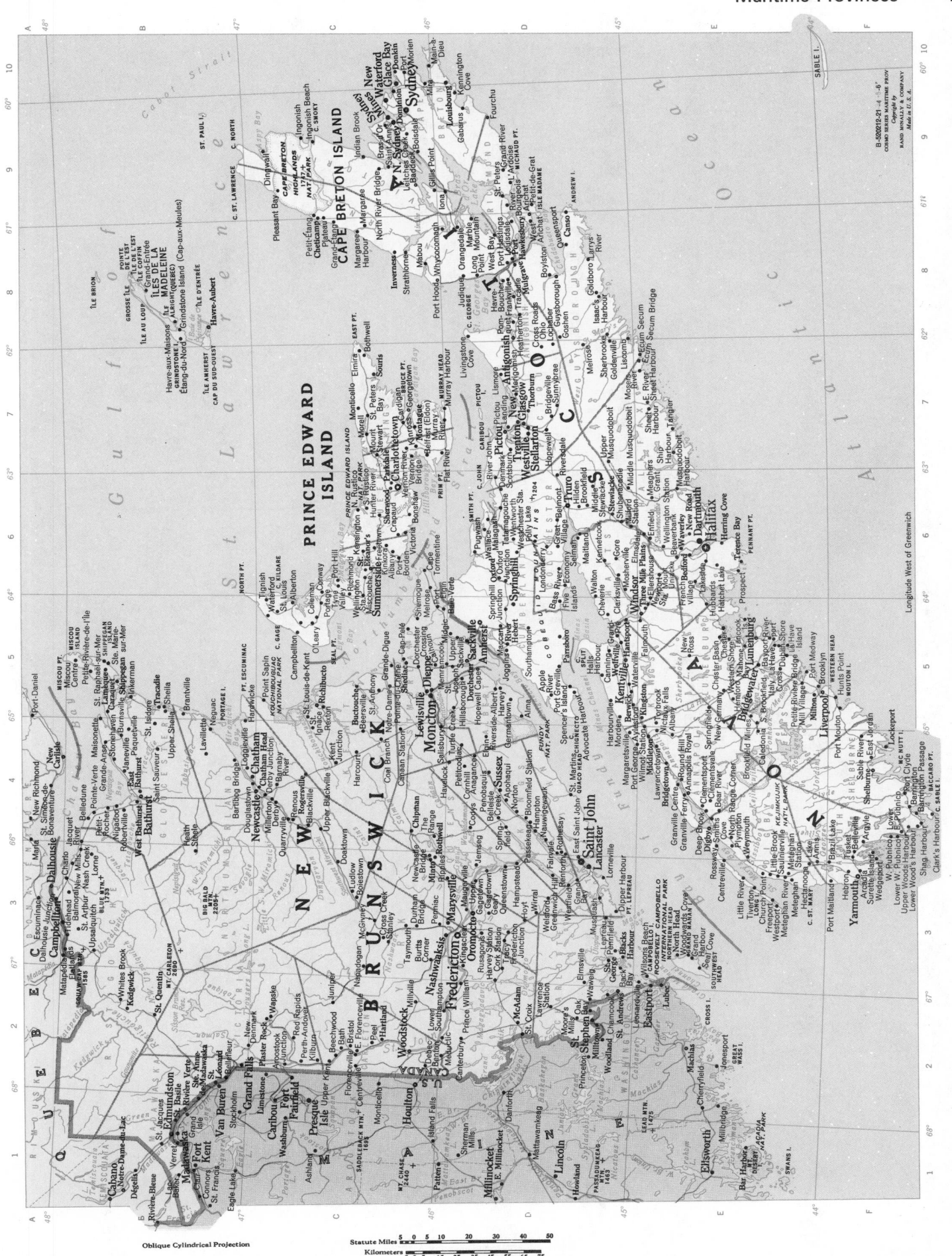

Oblique Cylindrical Projection

Statute Miles

Kilometers

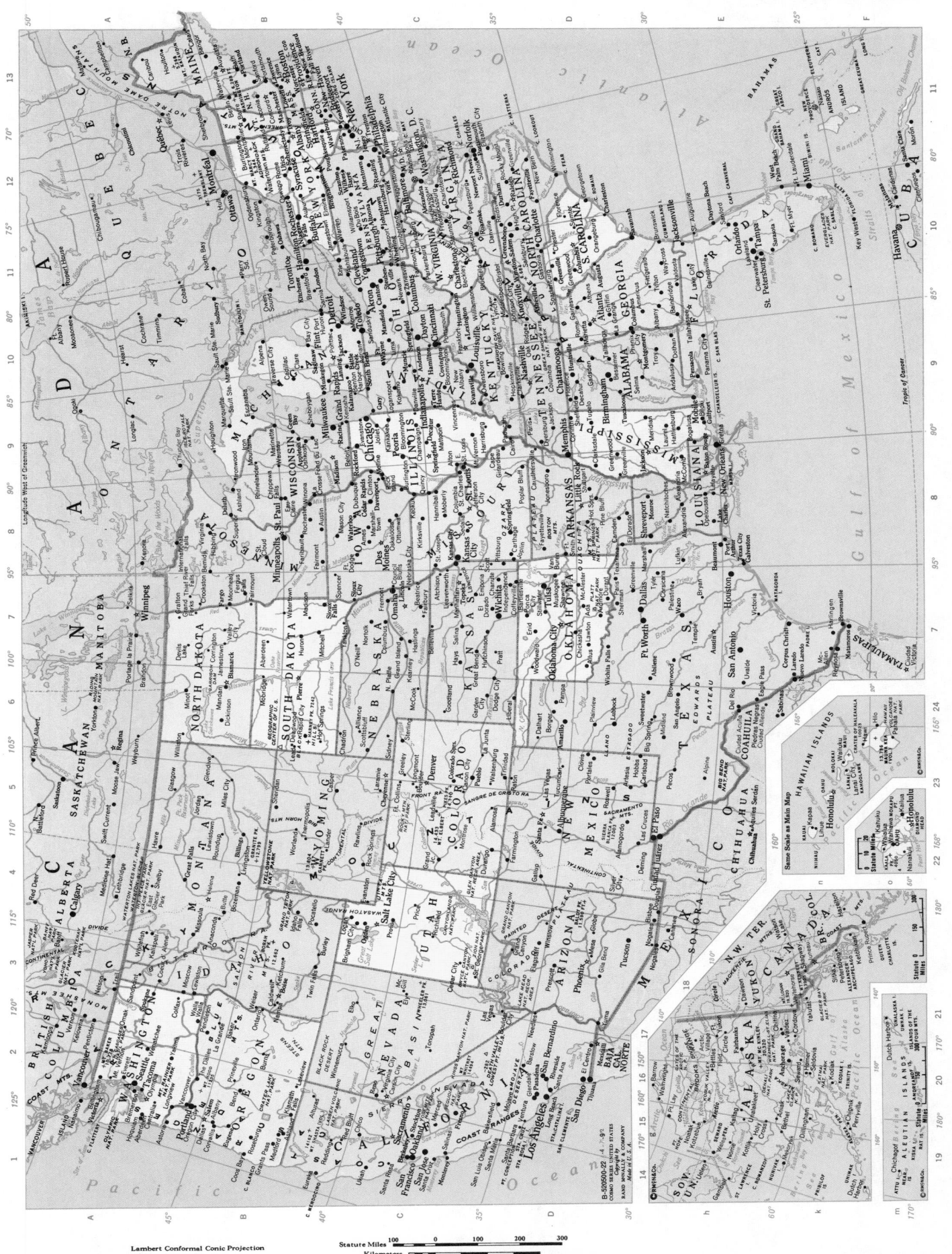

Lambert Conformal Conic Projection

Statute Miles
100   0   100   200   300

Kilometers
100   0   100   200   300   400

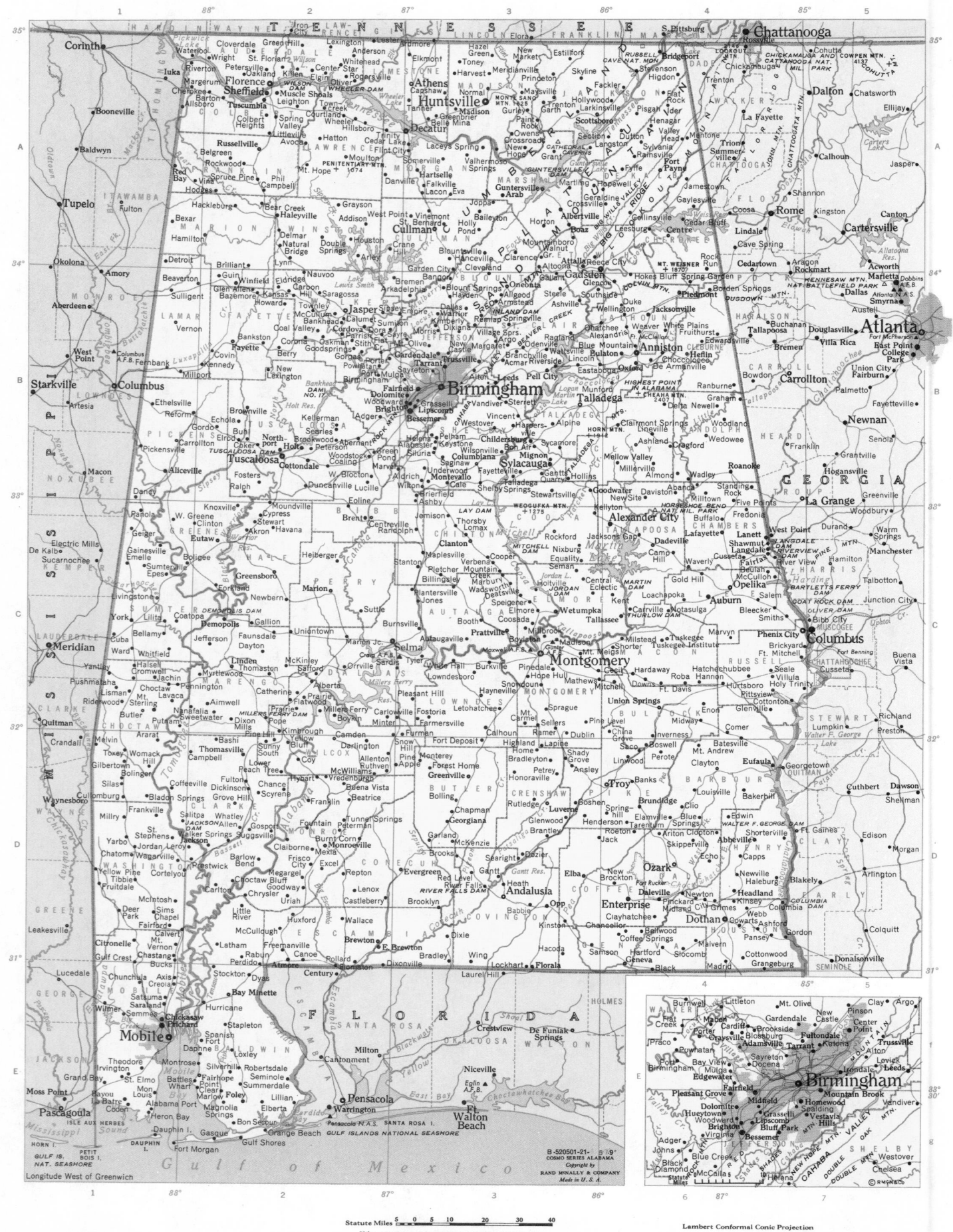

Statute Miles

Kilometers

Lambert Conformal Conic Projection

Longitude West of Greenwich

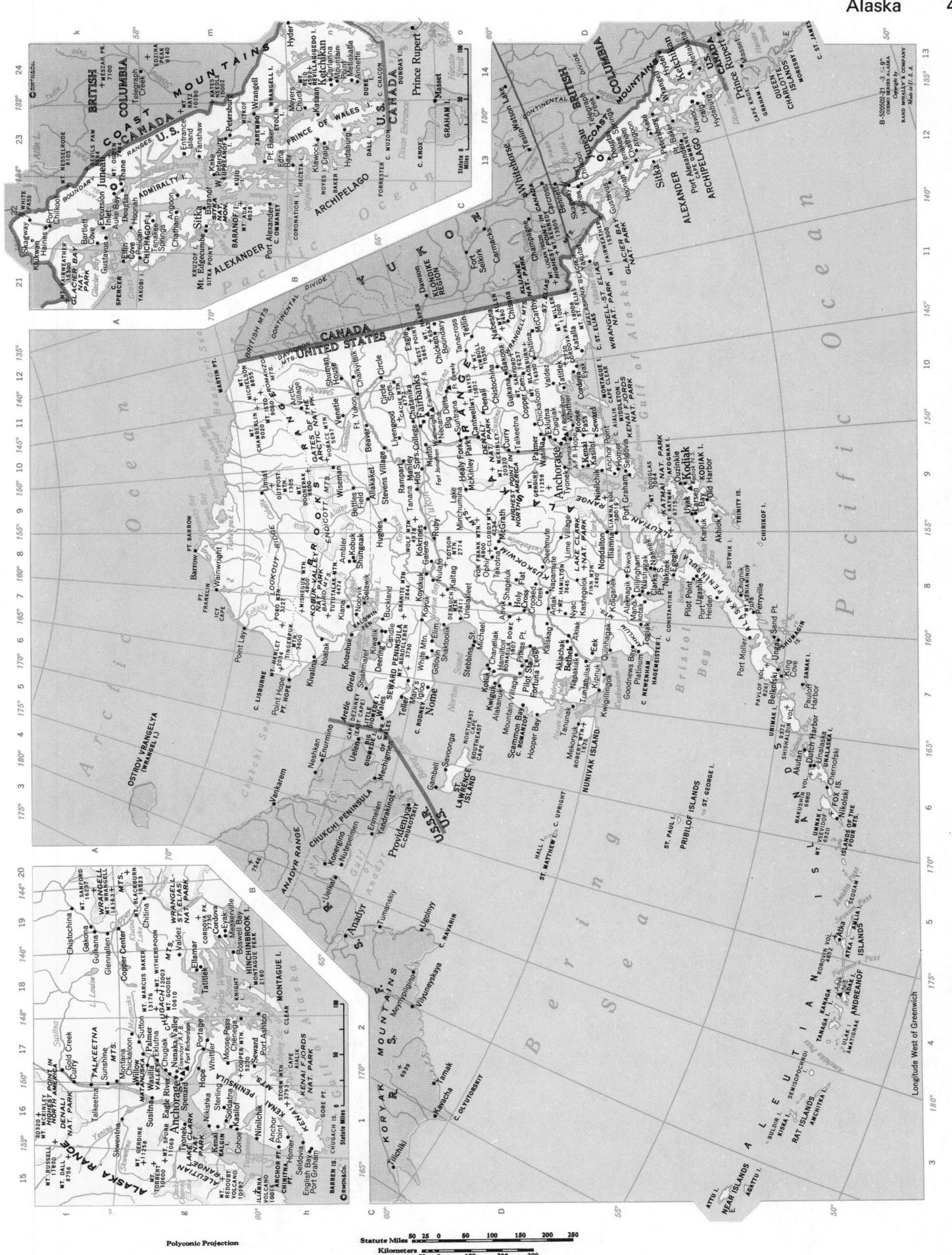

Polyconic Projection

Statute Miles 50 25 0 50 100 150 200 250

Kilometers 50 0 100 200 300

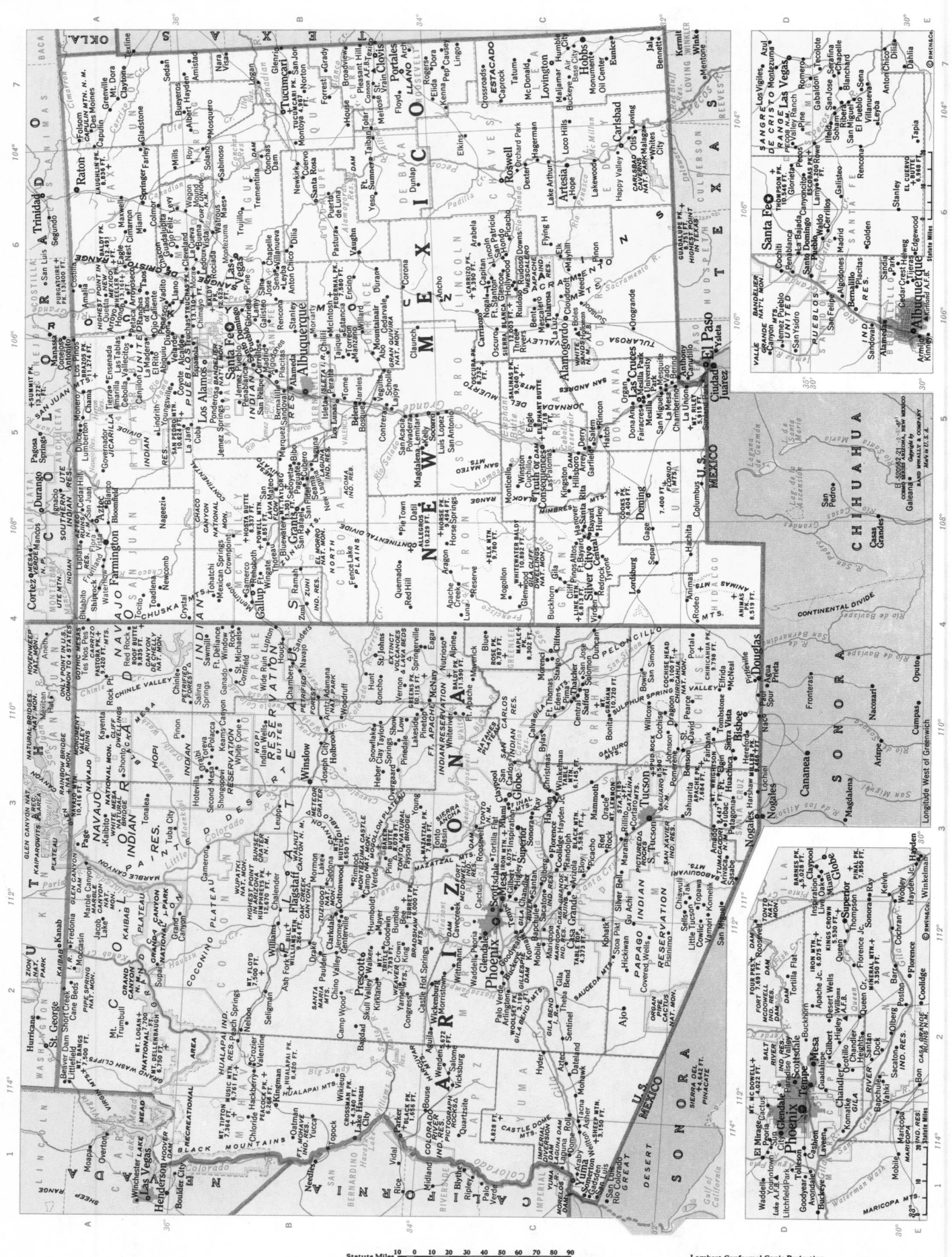

Statute Miles 10 0 10 20 30 40 50 60 70 80 90

Kilometers 10 0 10 20 40 60 80 100 120

Lambert Conformal Conic Projection

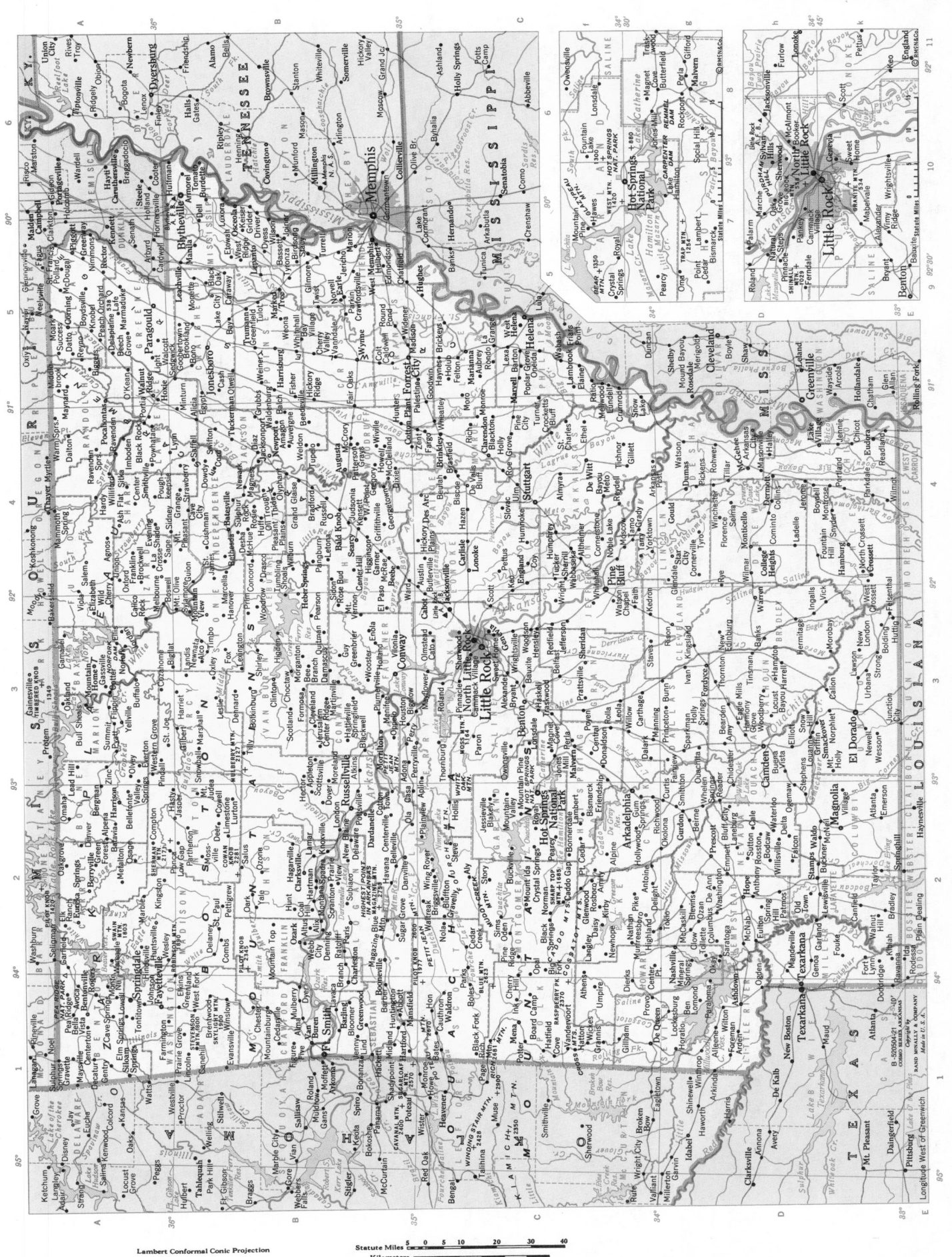

Lambert Conformal Conic Projection

Statute Miles

Kilometers

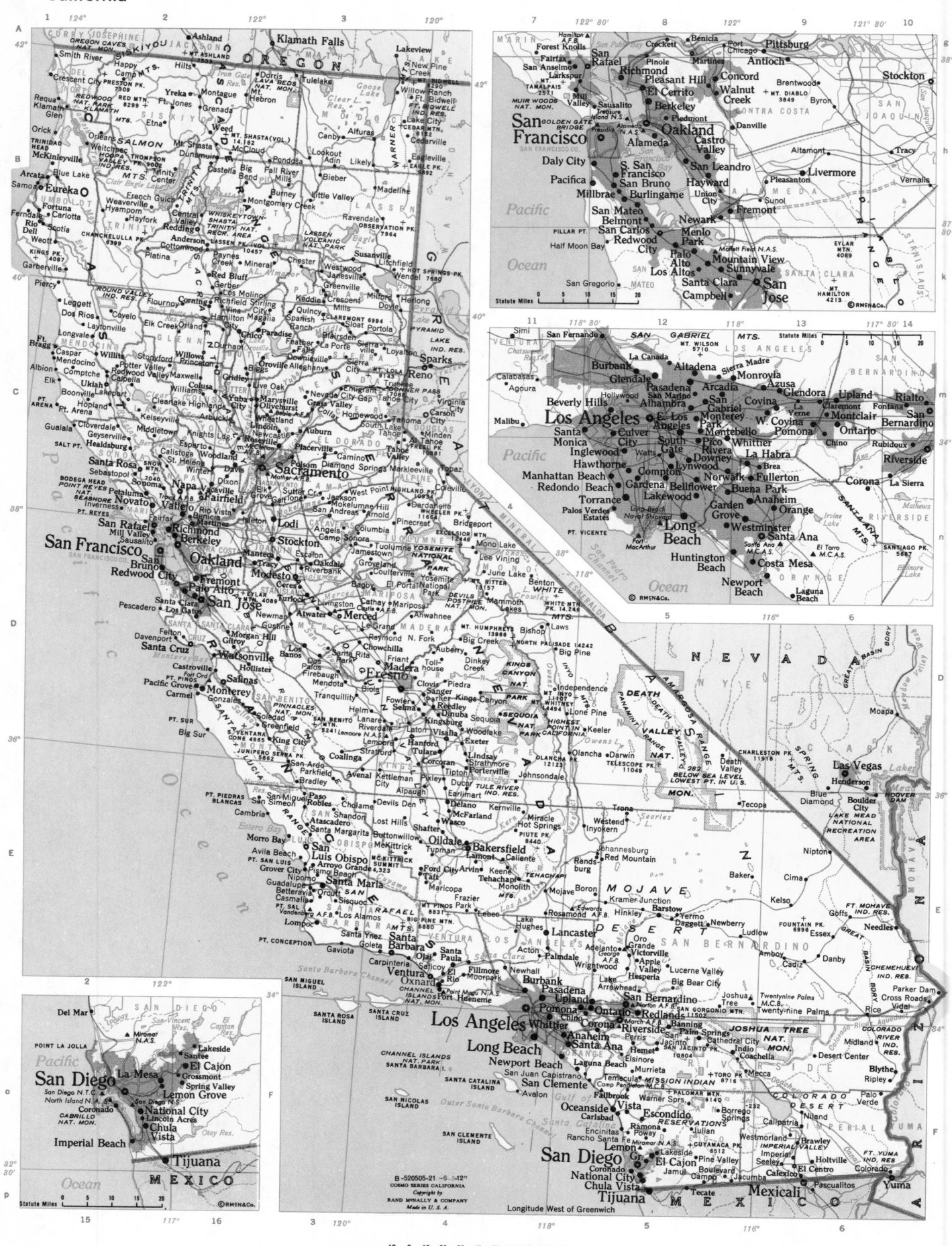

Statute Miles 10 0 10 20 30 40 50 60 70 80 90
Kilometers 10 0 10 20 40 60 80 100 120

Lambert Conformal Conic Projection

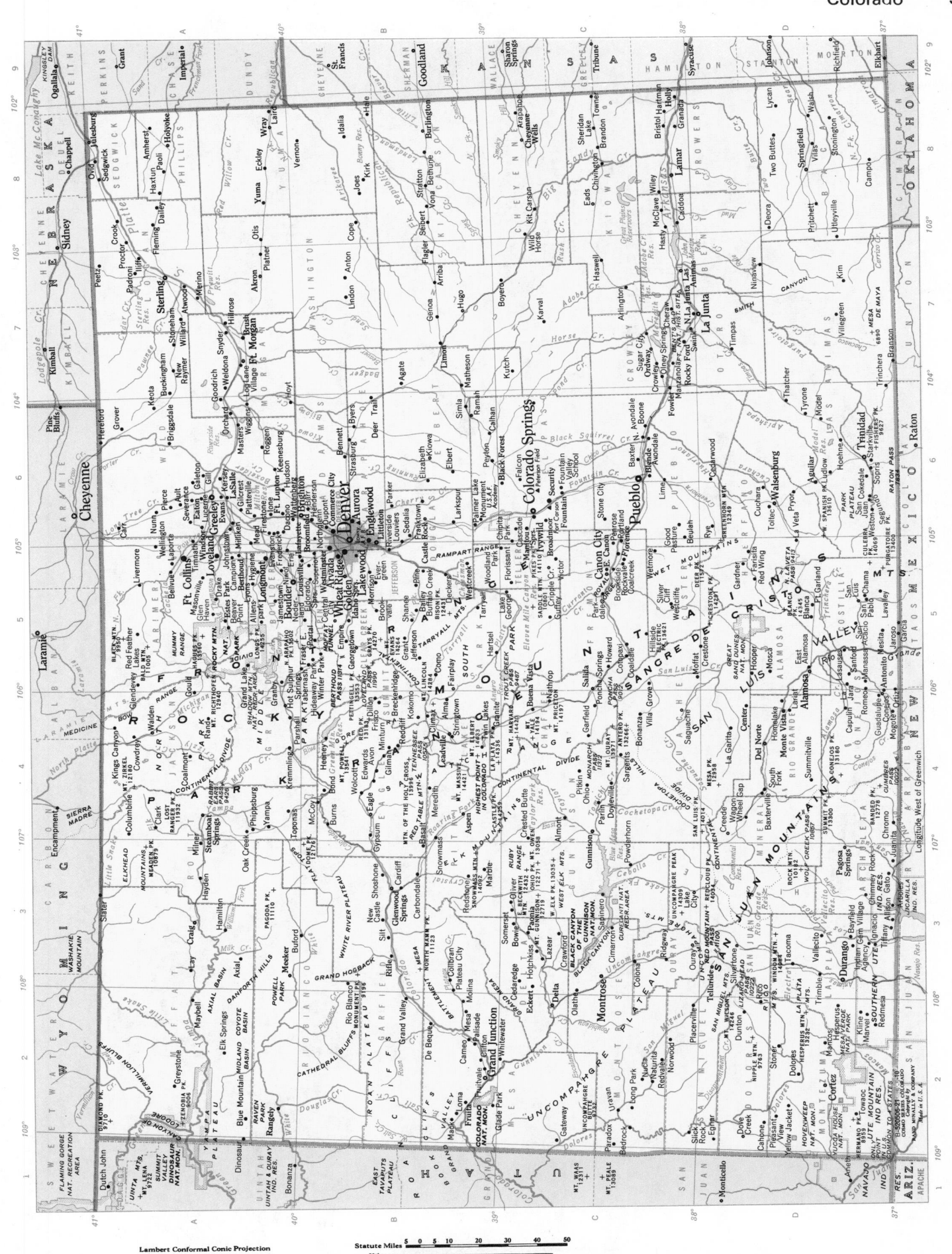

Lambert Conformal Conic Projection

Statute Miles 5 0 5 10   20   30   40   50

Kilometers 5 0 5 15   25   35   45   55   65   75

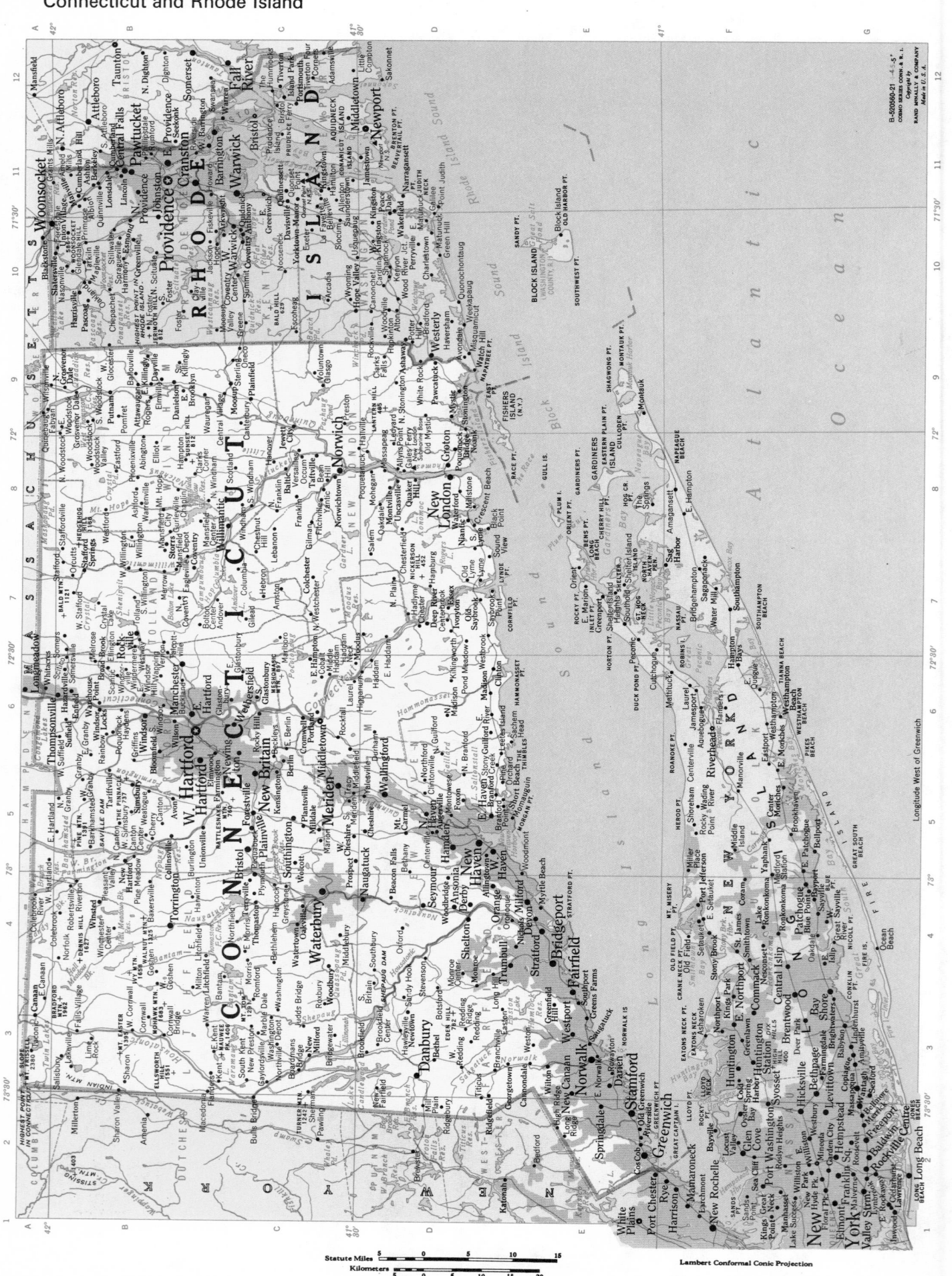

Statute Miles

Kilometers

Lambert Conformal Conic Projection

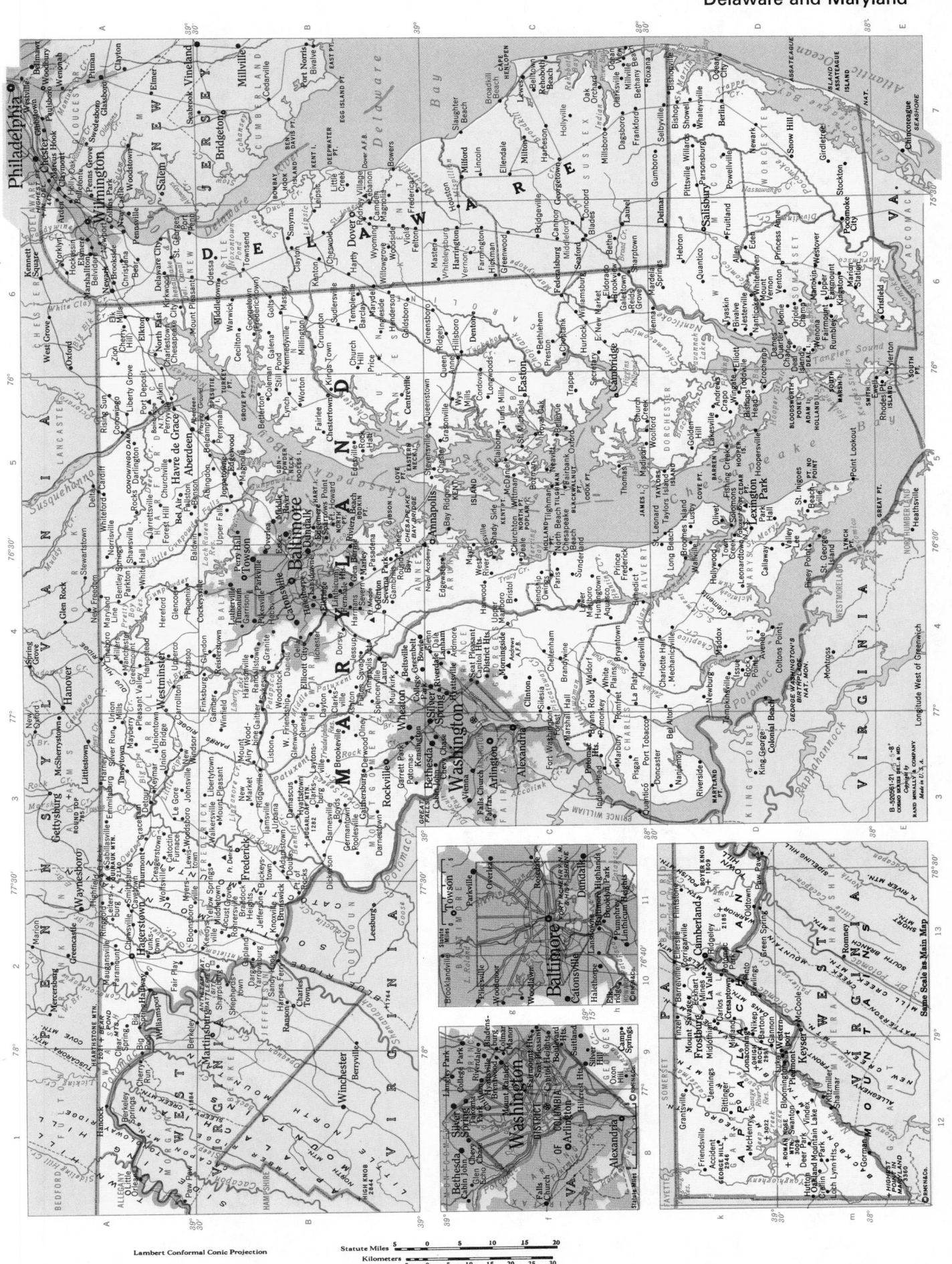

Lambert Conformal Conic Projection

Statute Miles 5   0   5   10   15   20
Kilometers 5   0   5   10   15   20   25   30

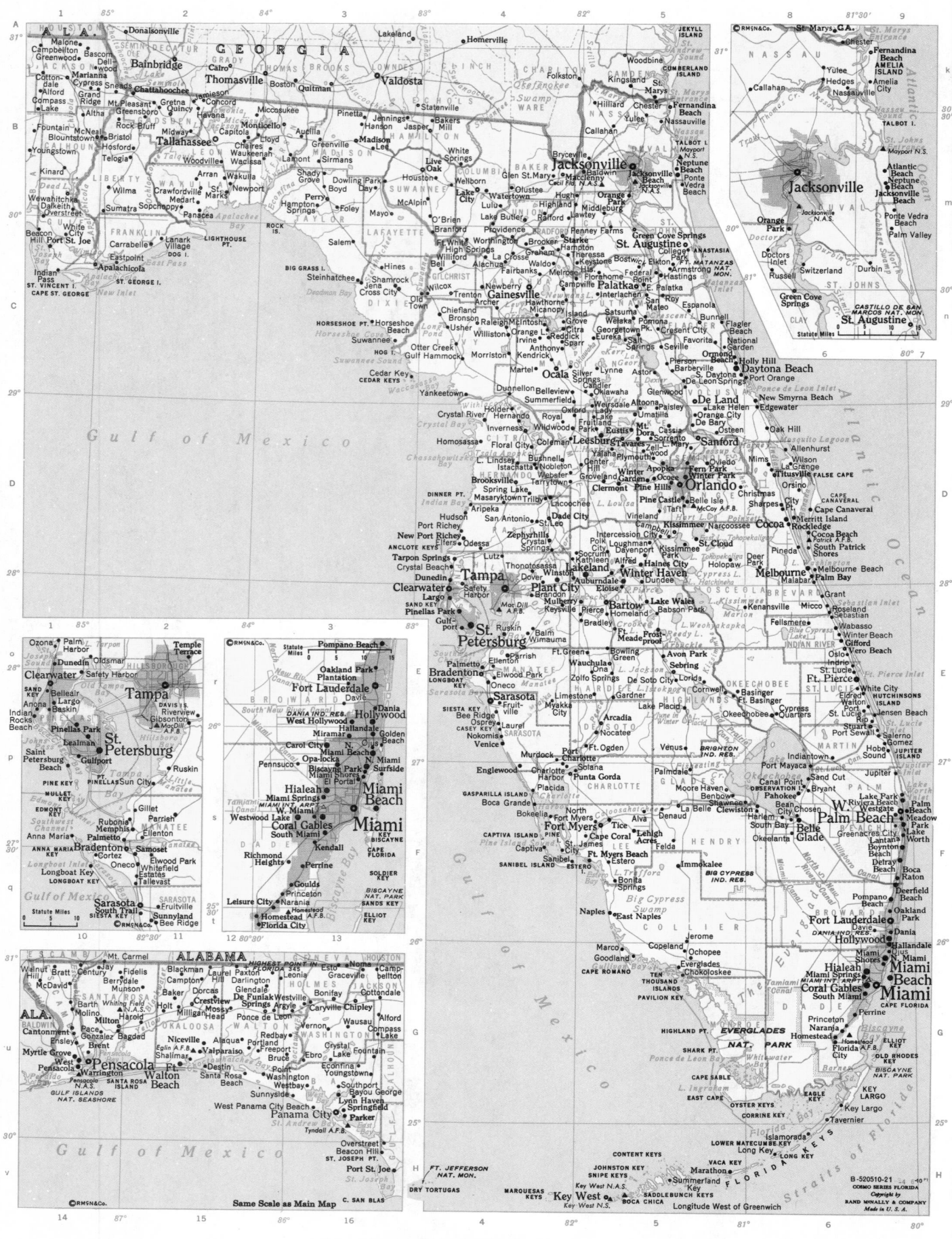

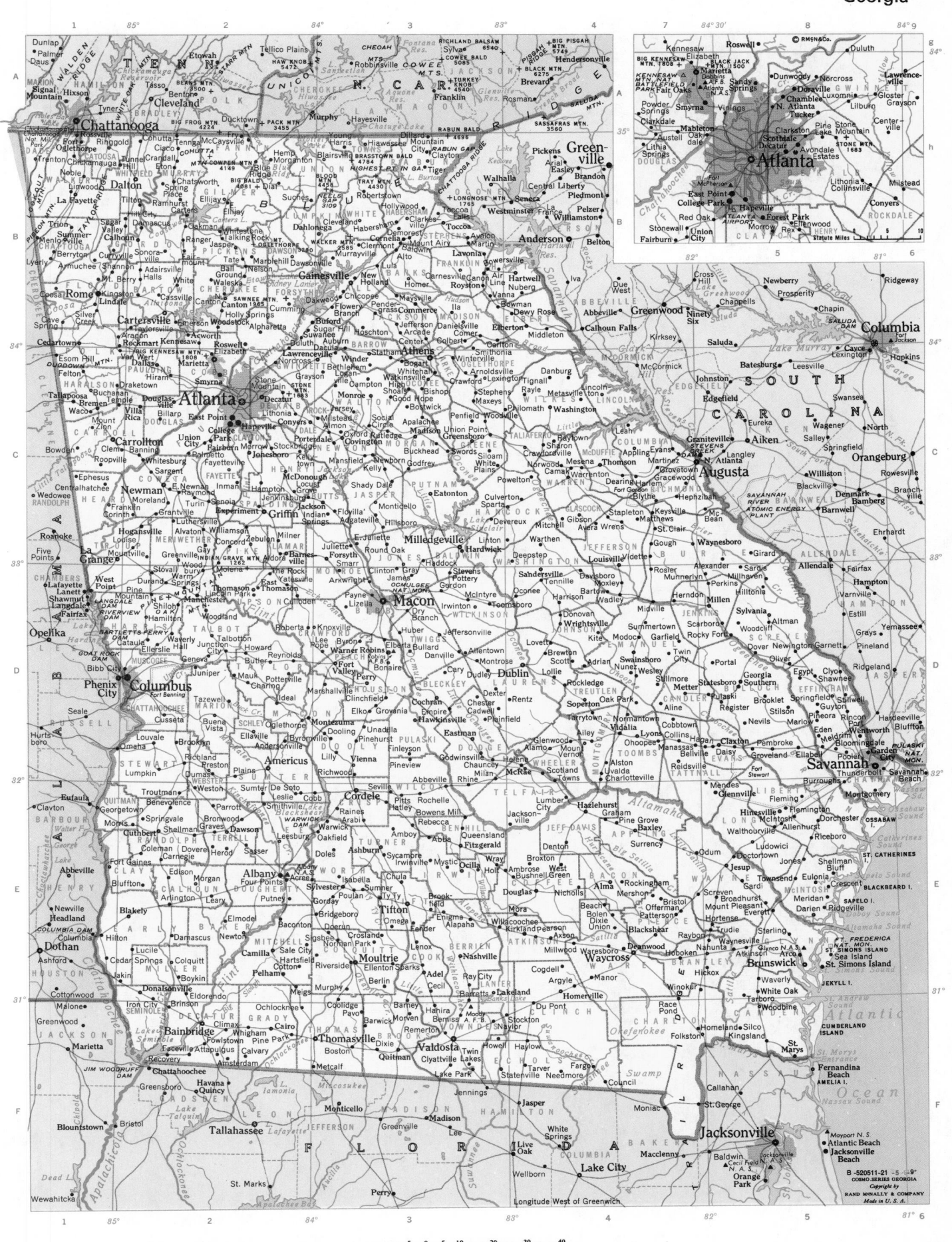

Lambert Conformal Conic Projection

Statute Miles 5 0 5 10 20 30 40

Kilometers 5 0 5 15 25 35 45 55

B-520511-21 -5 -9*
COSMO SERIES GEORGIA
Copyright by
RAND McNALLY & COMPANY
Made in U.S.A.

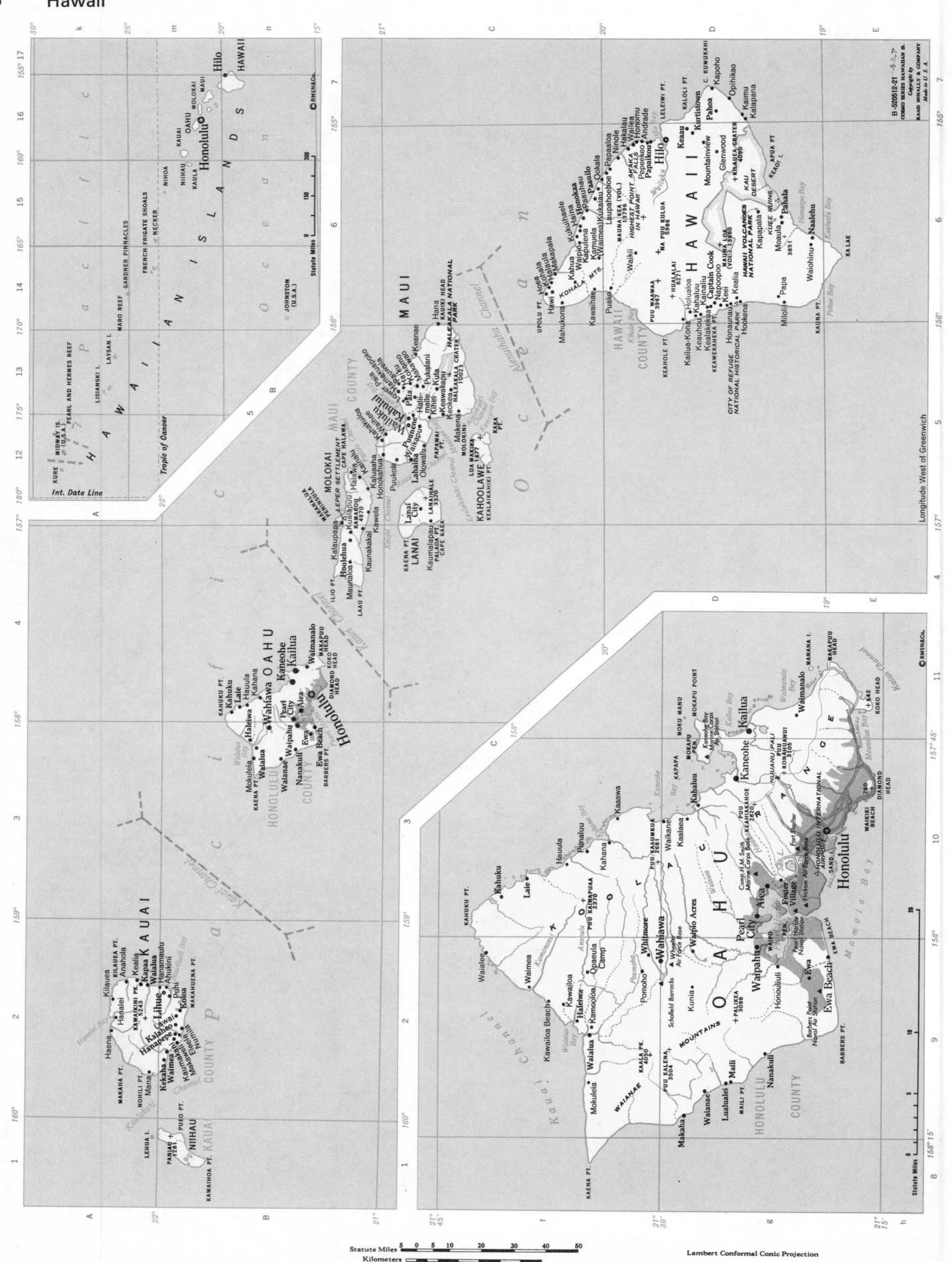

Statute Miles
Kilometers

Lambert Conformal Conic Projection

Lambert Conformal Conic Projection

Statute Miles
5 0 5 10 20 30 40 50 60

Kilometers
5 0 5 15 25 35 45 55 65 75

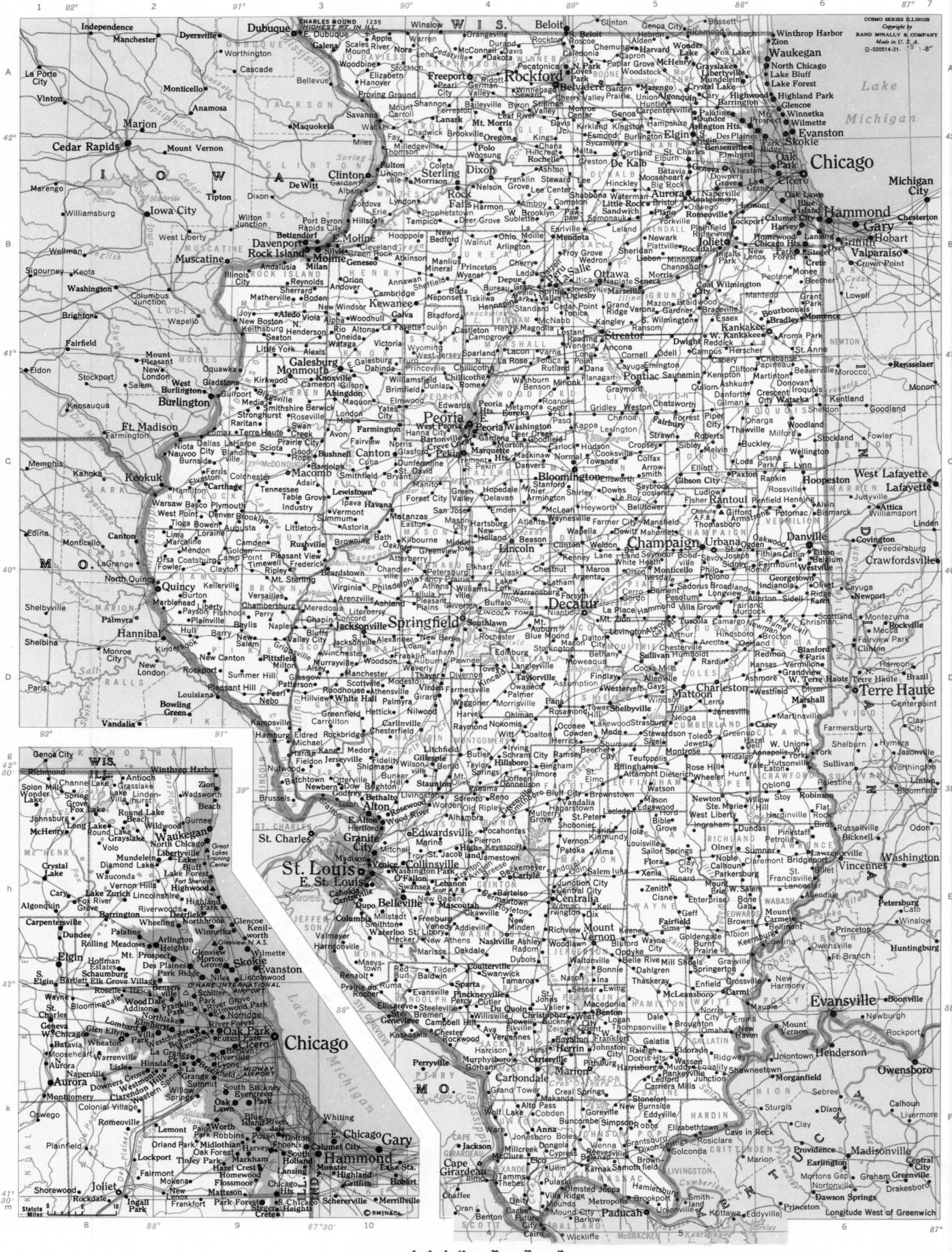

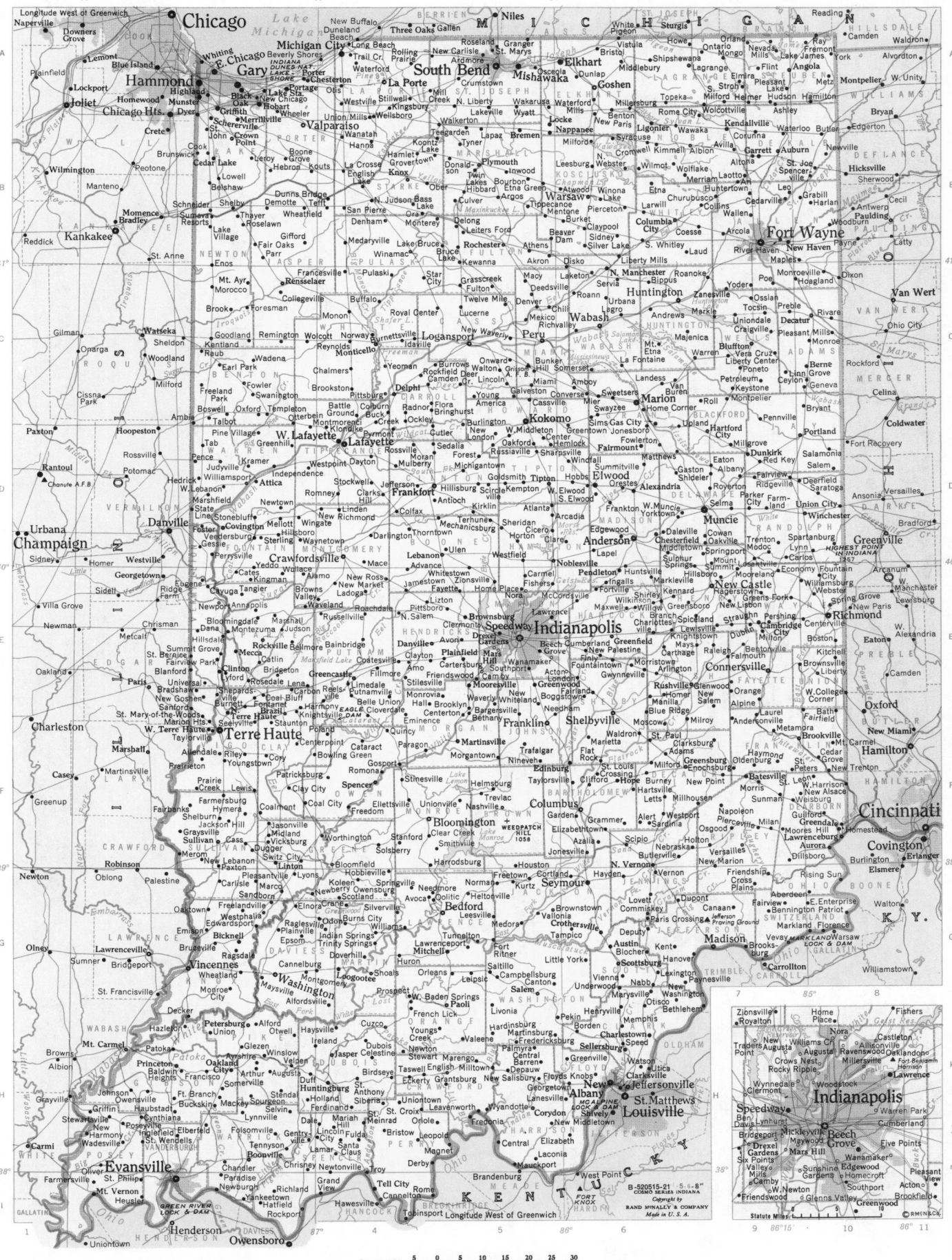

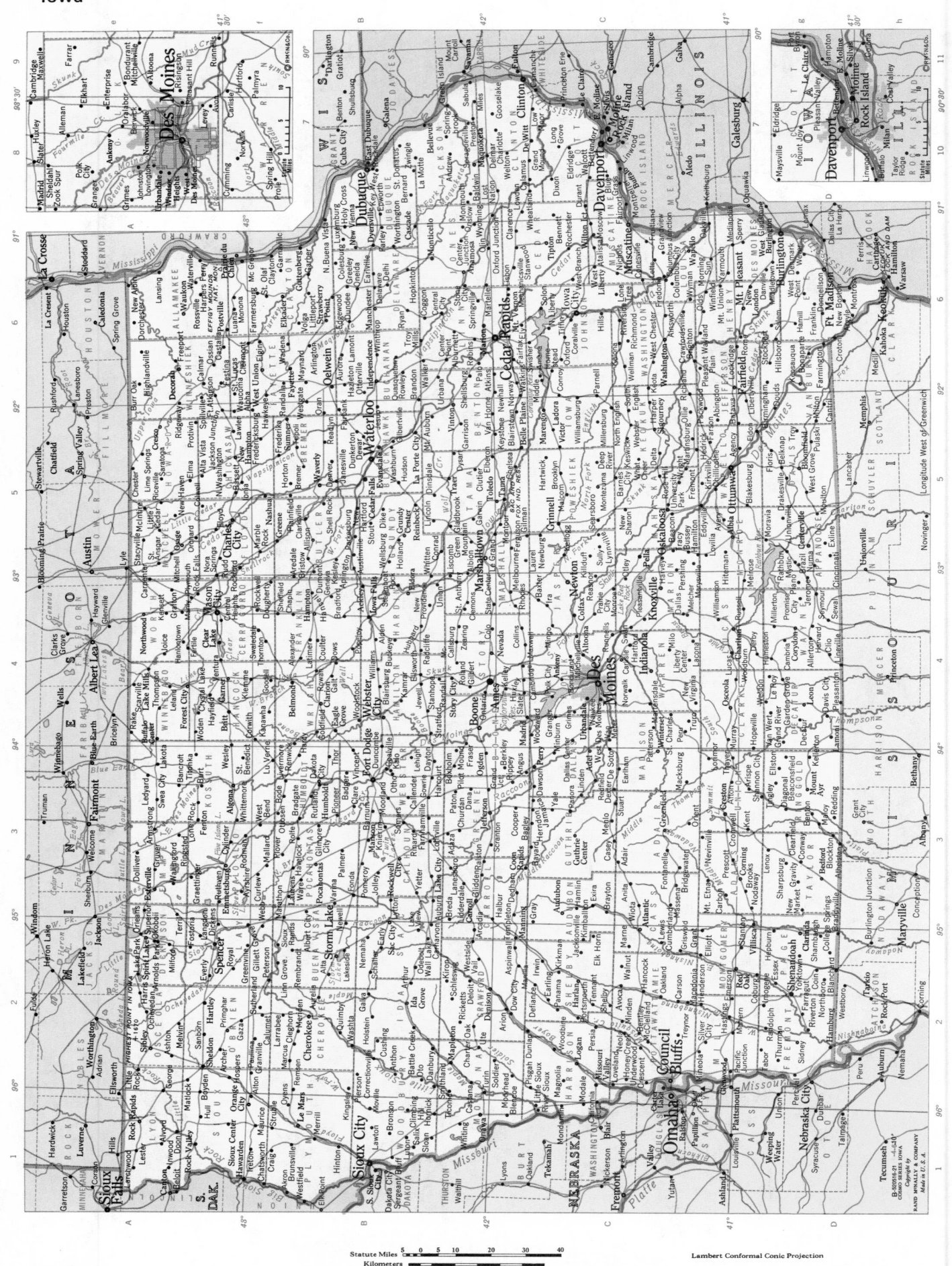

Statute Miles 5 0 5 10 20 30 40

Kilometers 5 0 5 15 25 35 45 55

Lambert Conformal Conic Projection

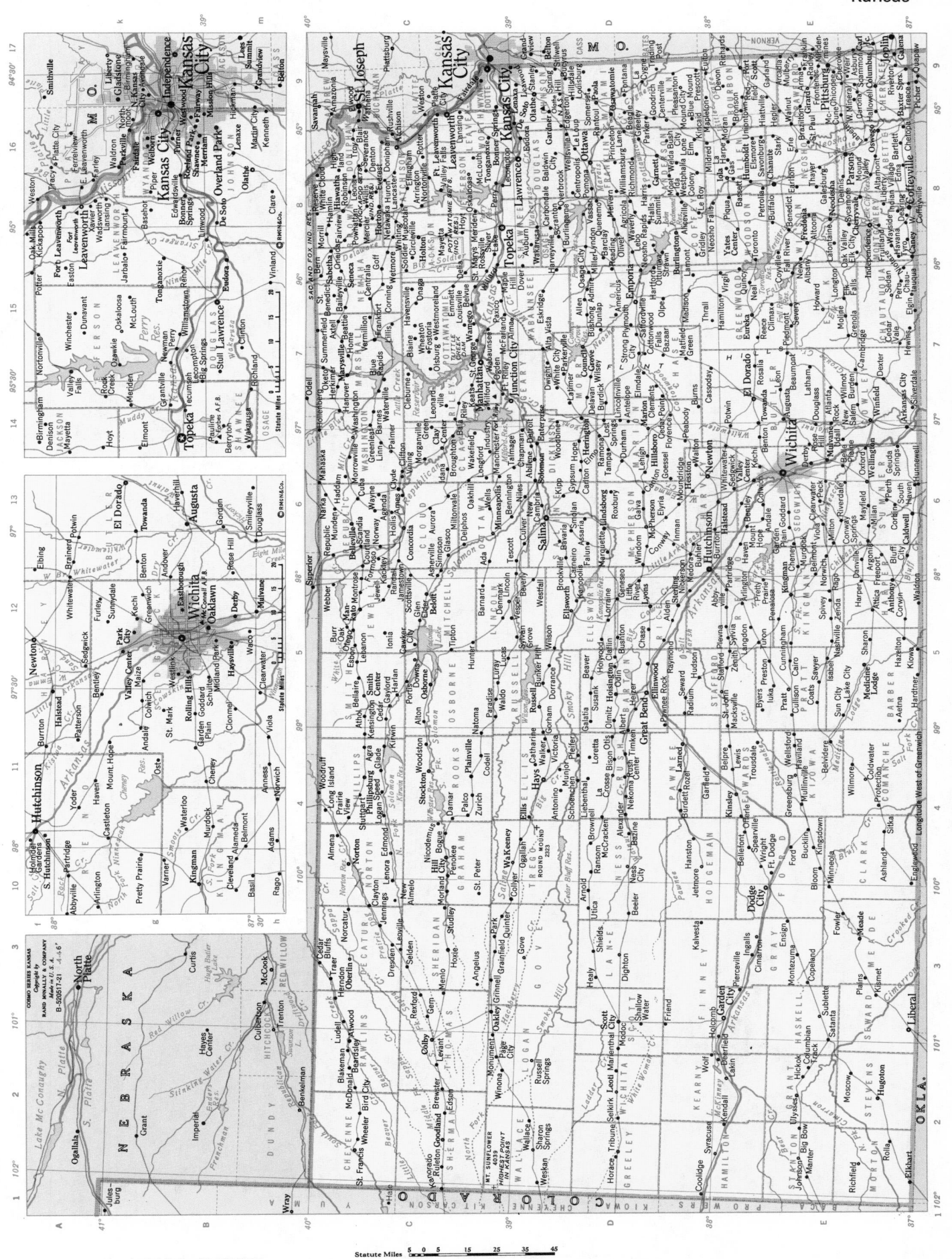

Lambert Conformal Conic Projection

Statute Miles 5 0 5 15 25 35 45
Kilometers 5 0 5 15 25 35 45 55 65

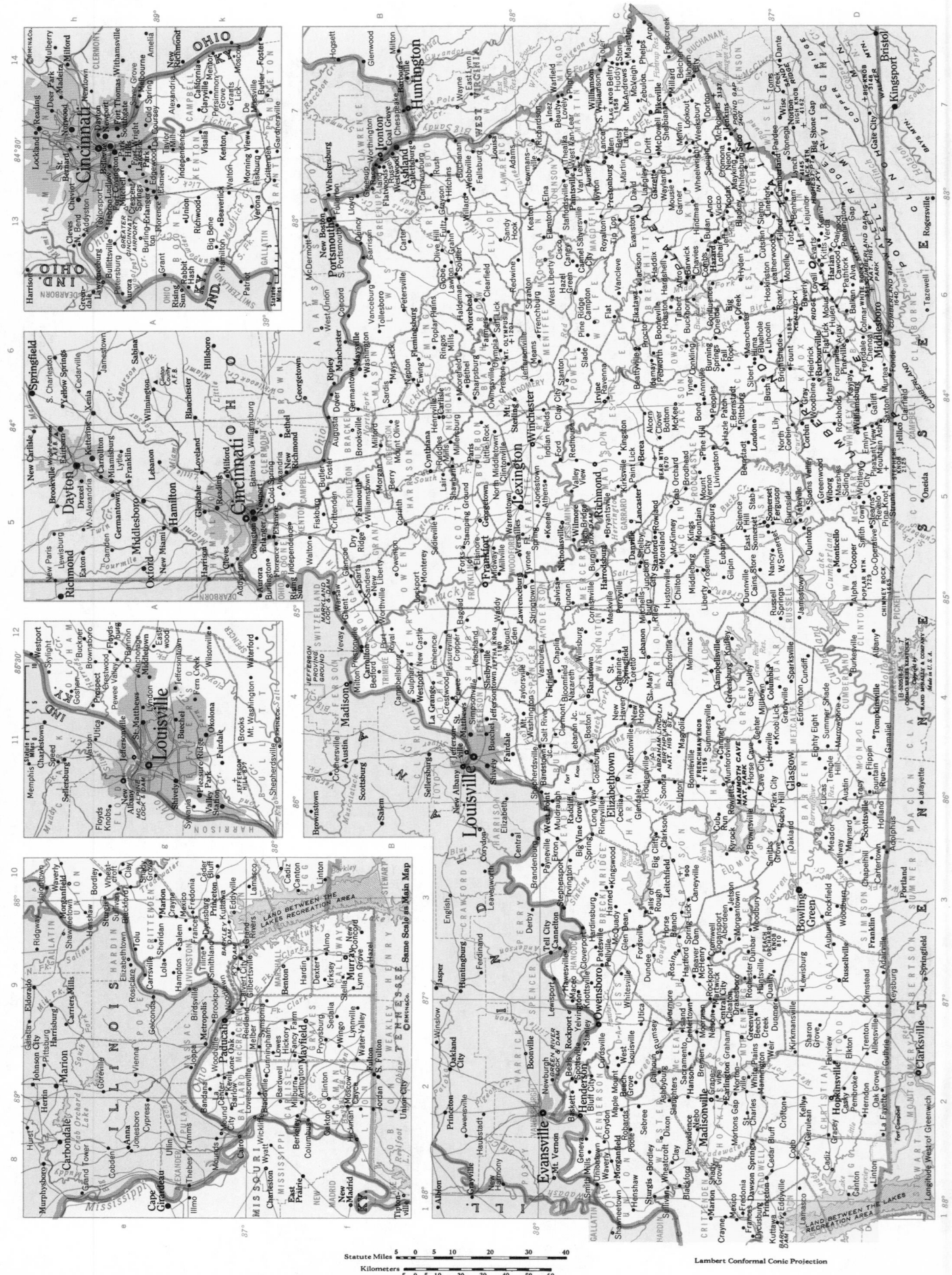

Statute Miles 5 0 5 10   20   30   40

Kilometers 5 0 5 10   20   30   40   50   60

Lambert Conformal Conic Projection

Lambert Conformal Conic Projection

Statute Miles

Kilometers

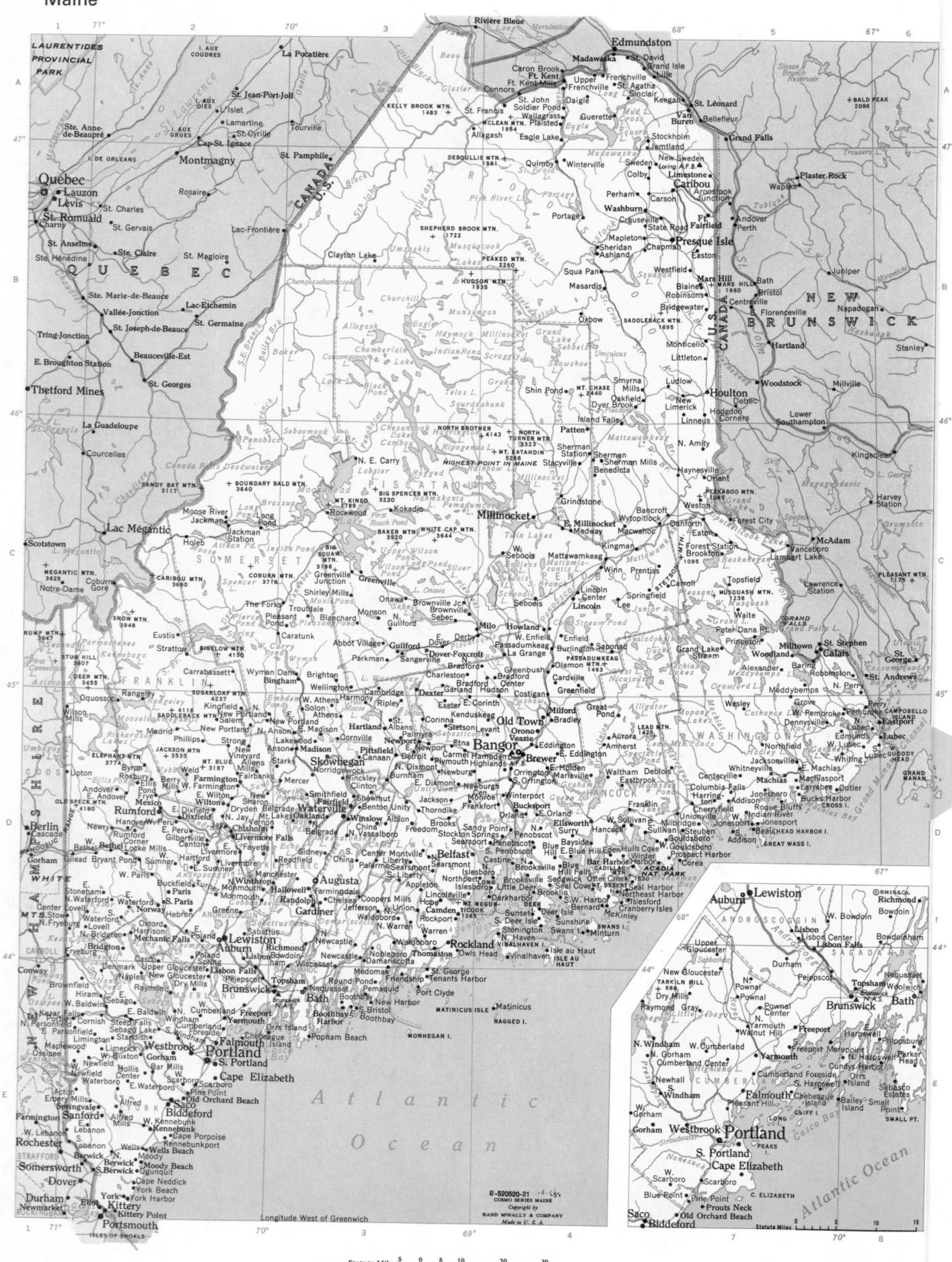

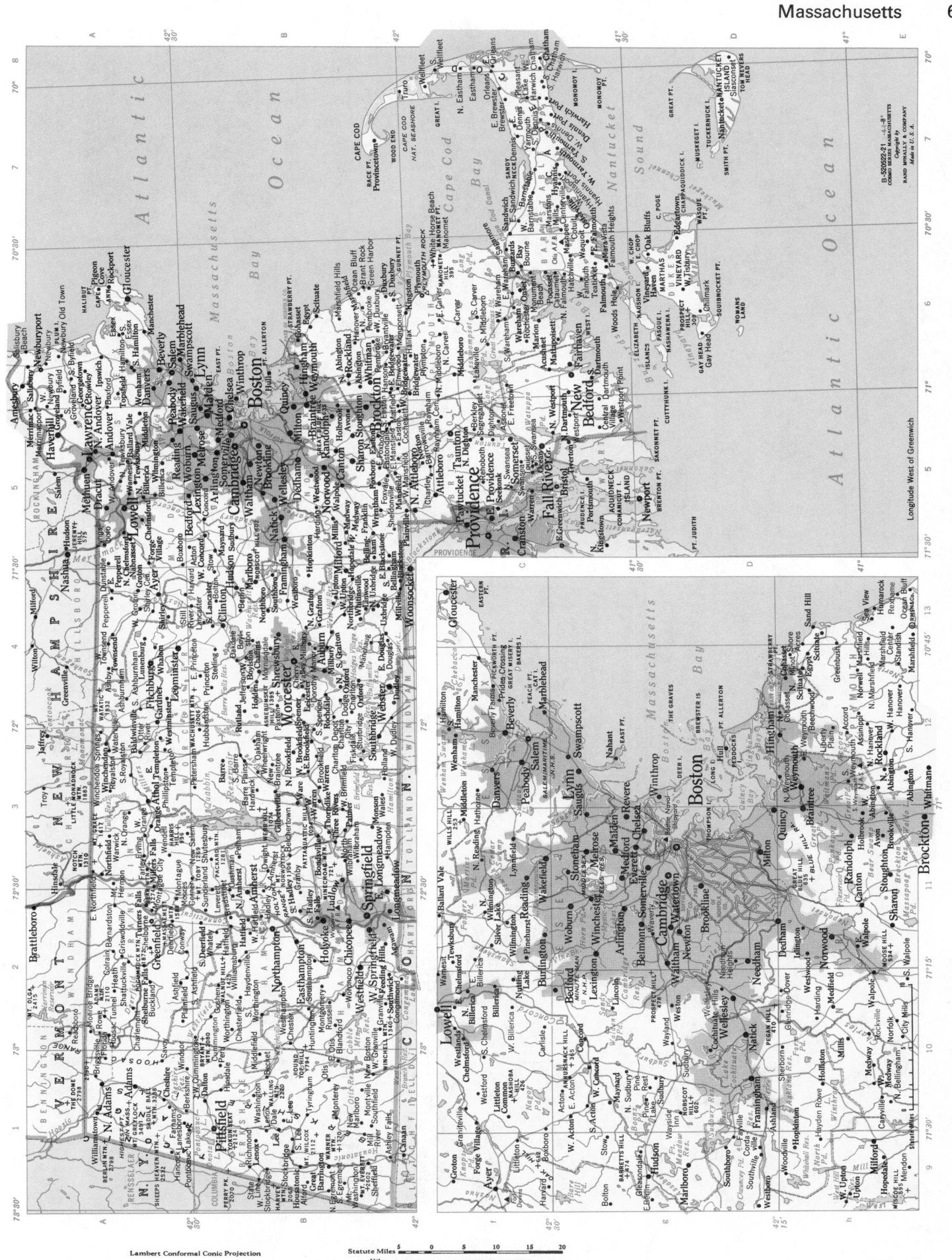

Lambert Conformal Conic Projection

Statute Miles 5 0   5   10   15   20

Kilometers 5 0 5 10 15 20 25

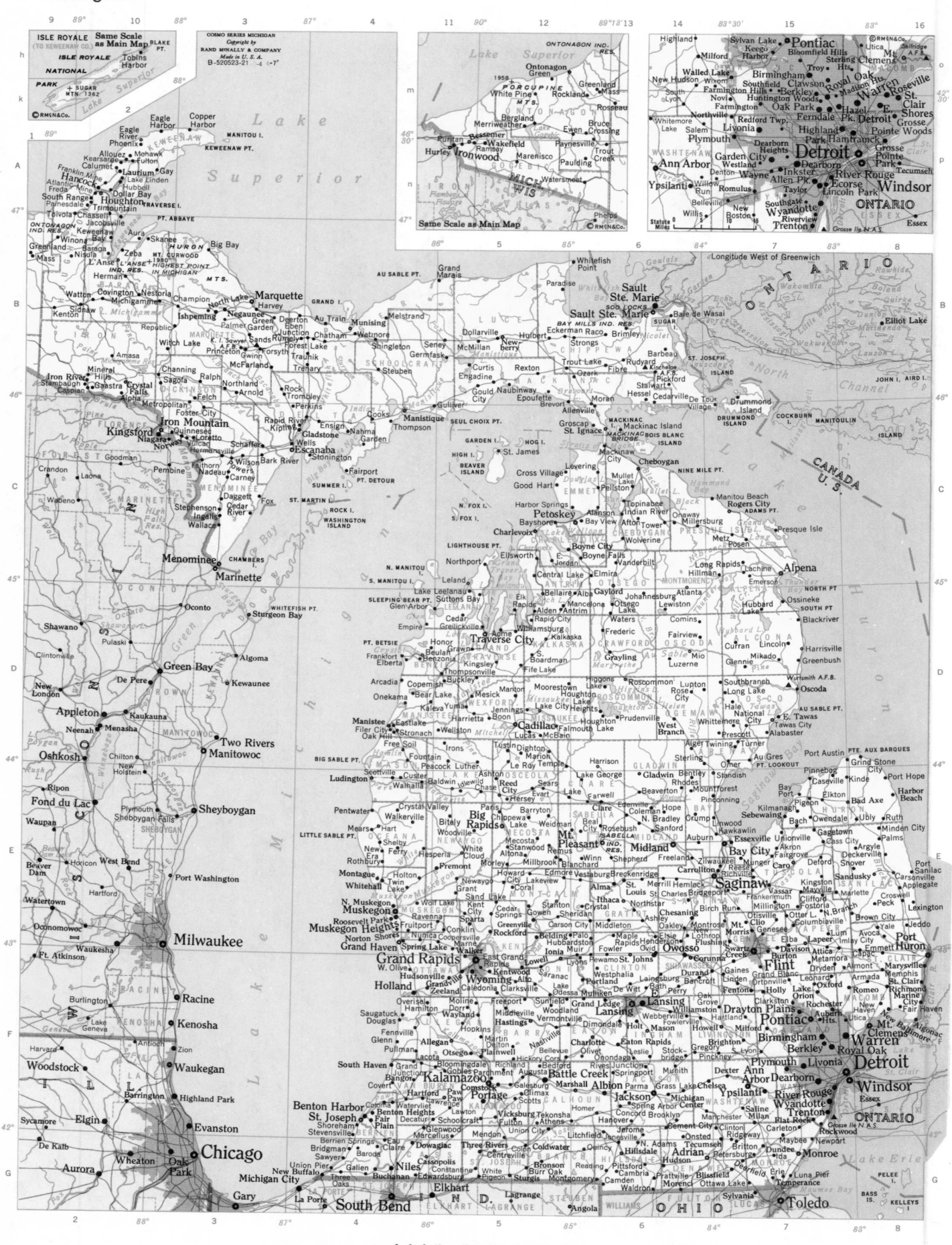

Statute Miles

Kilometers

Lambert Conformal Conic Projection

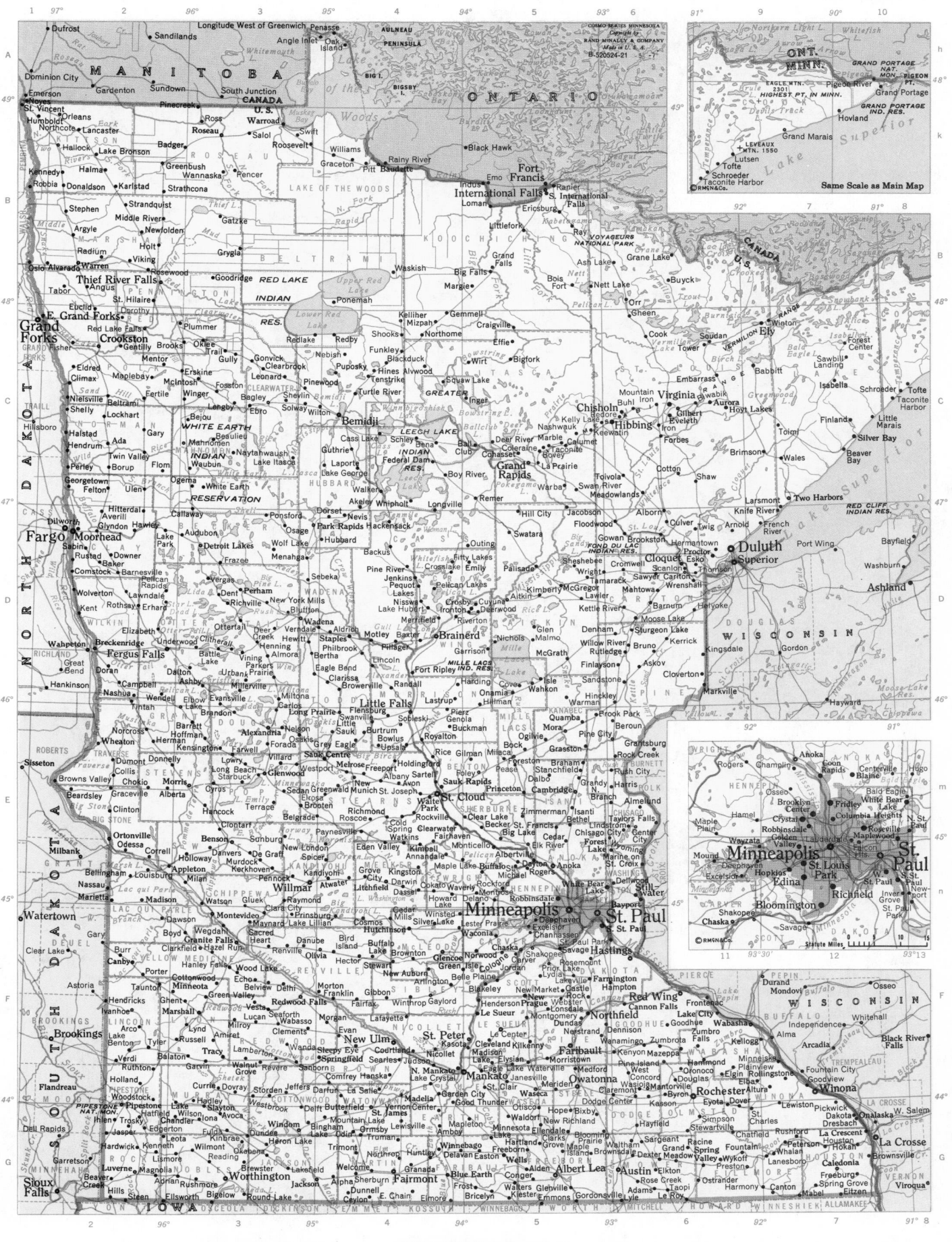

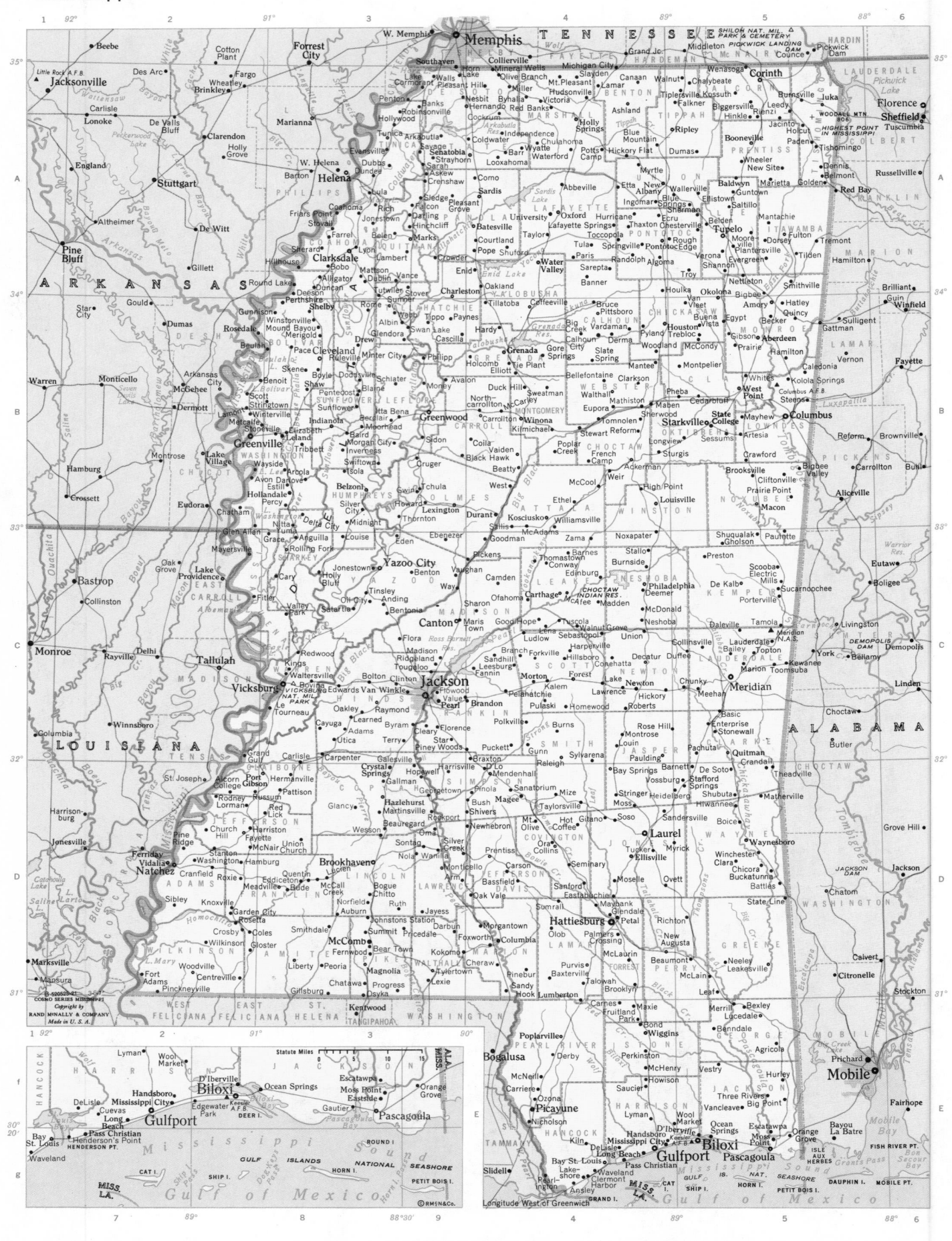

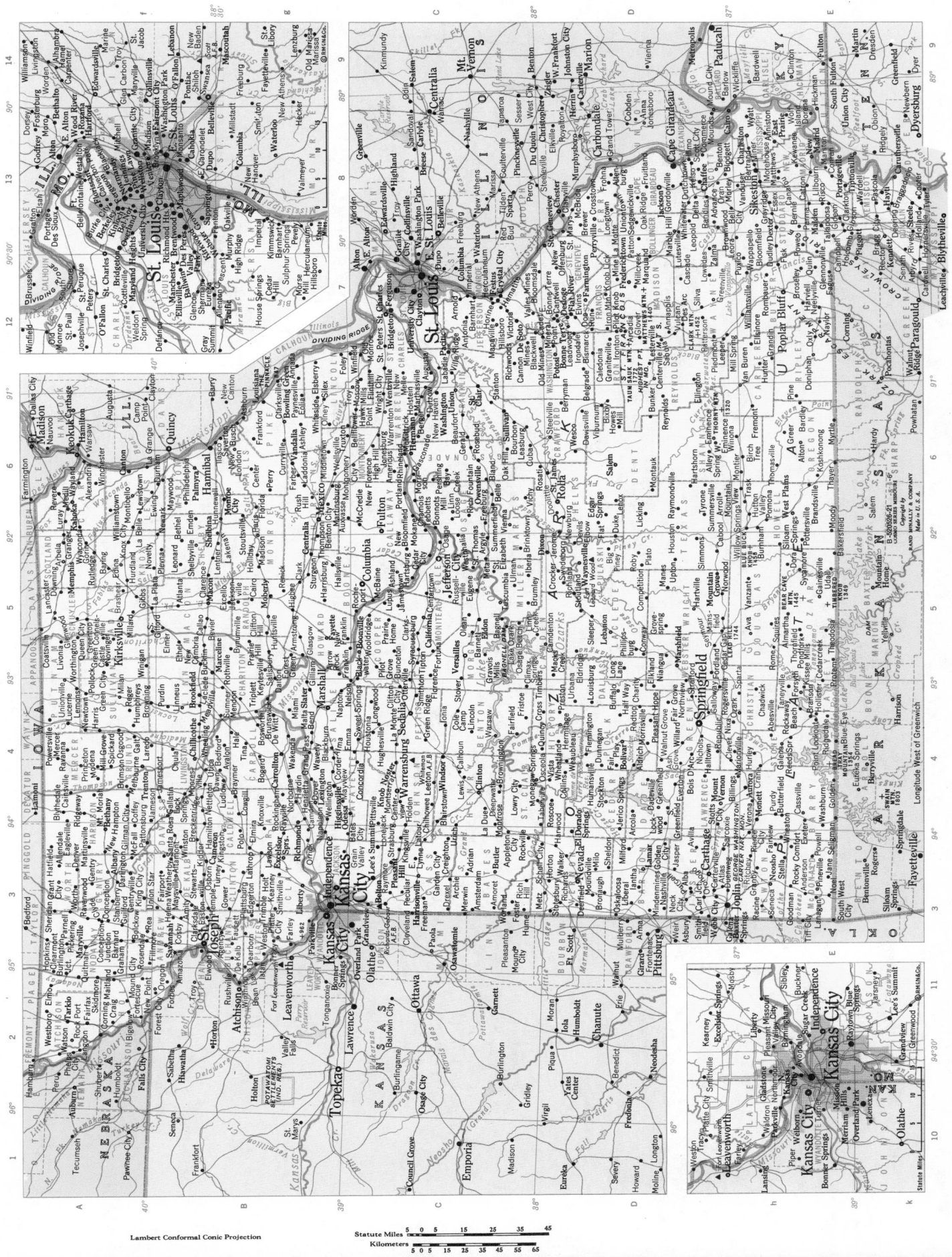

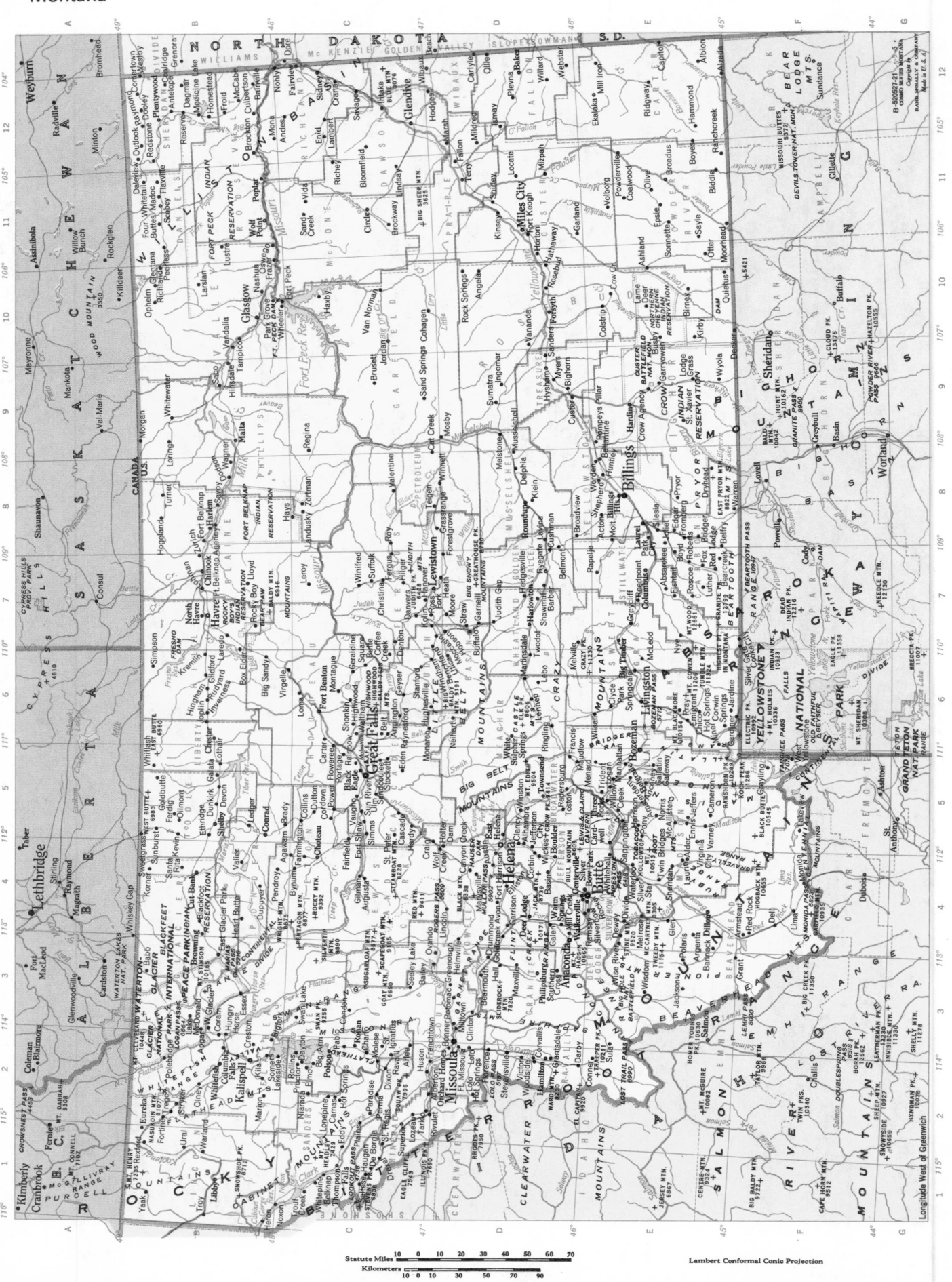

Statute Miles 10 0 10 20 30 40 50 60 70
Kilometers 10 0 10 30 50 70 90

Lambert Conformal Conic Projection

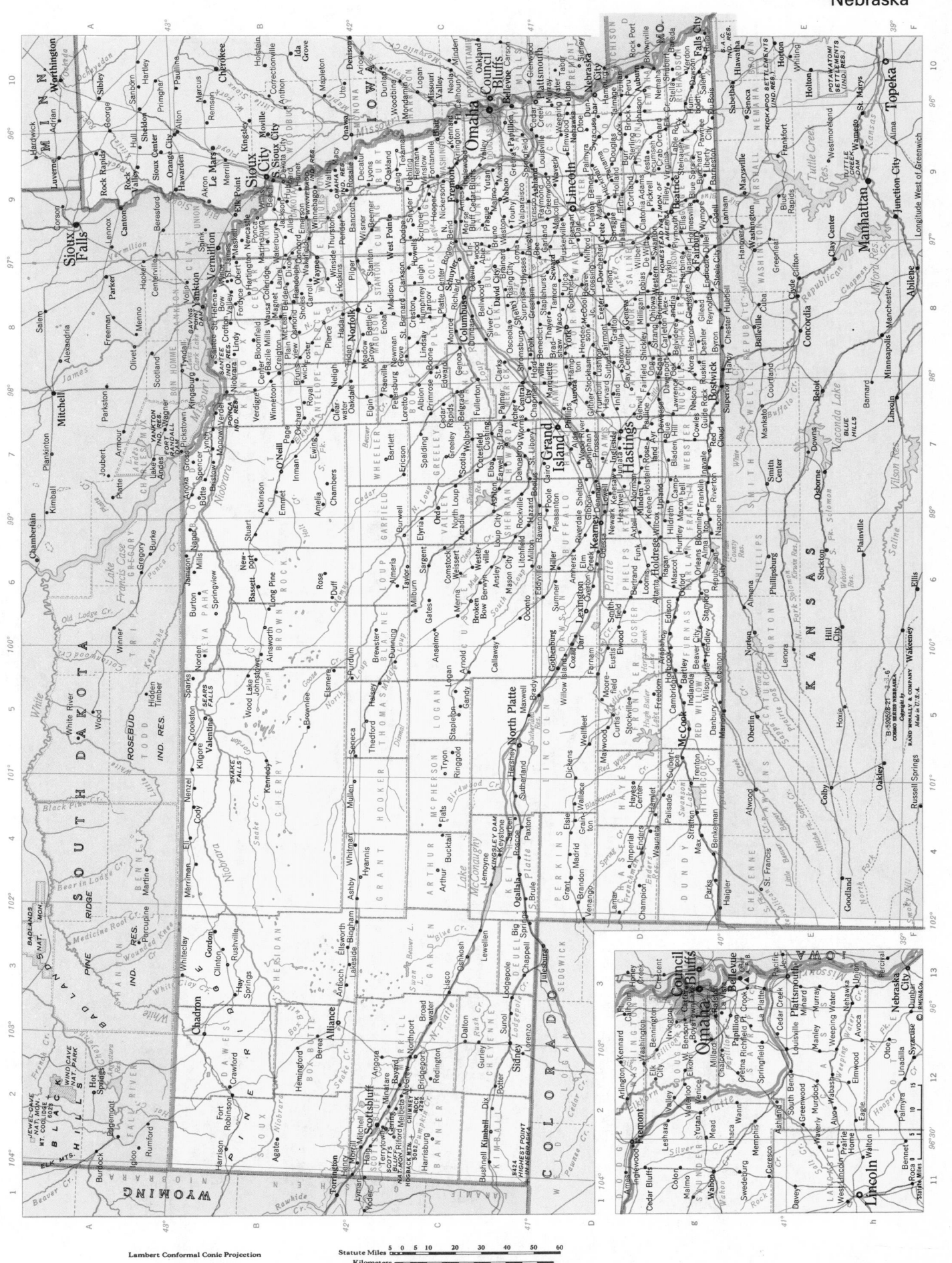

Lambert Conformal Conic Projection

Statute Miles 5 0 5 10   20   30   40   50   60

Kilometers 5 0 5 15   35   55   75   95

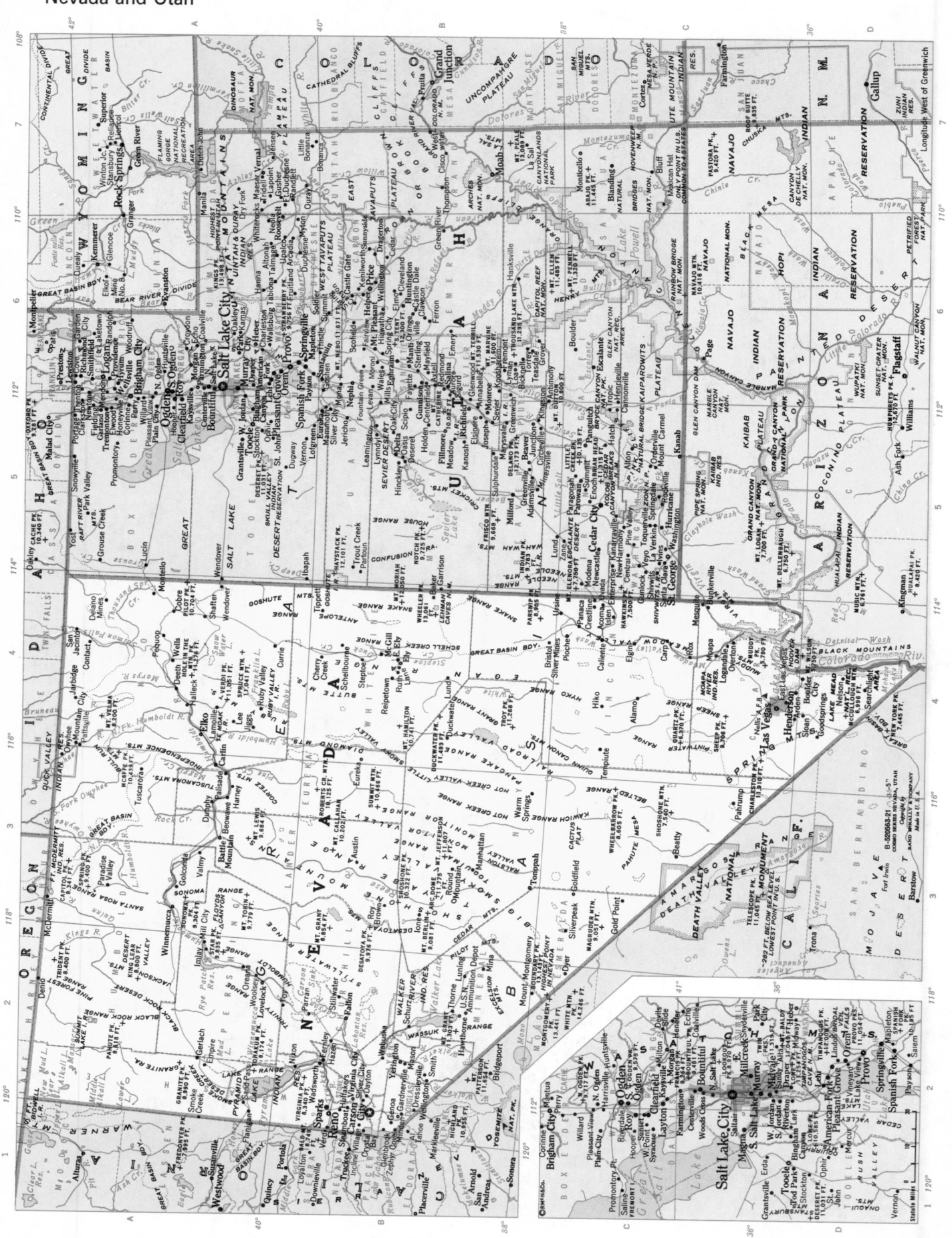

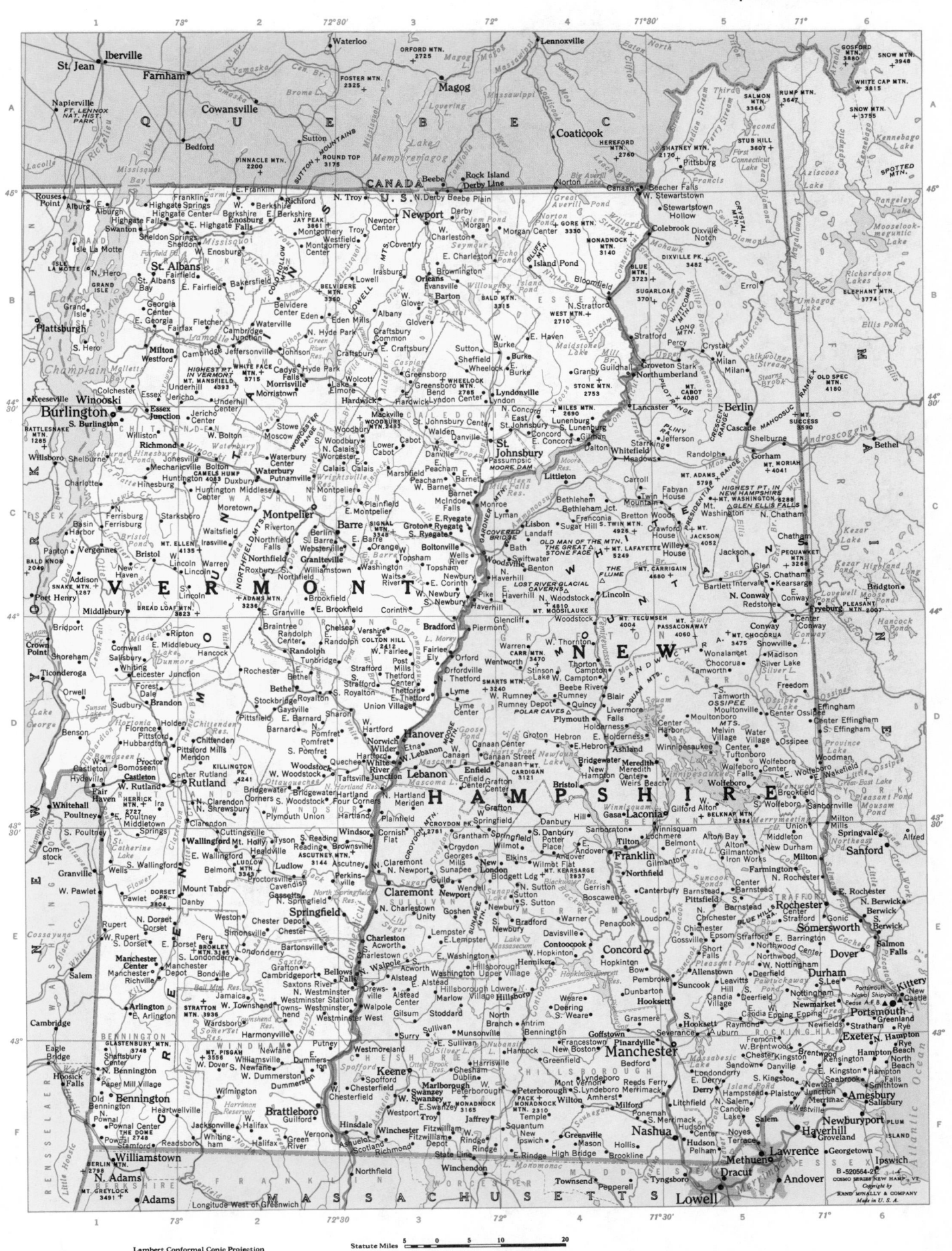

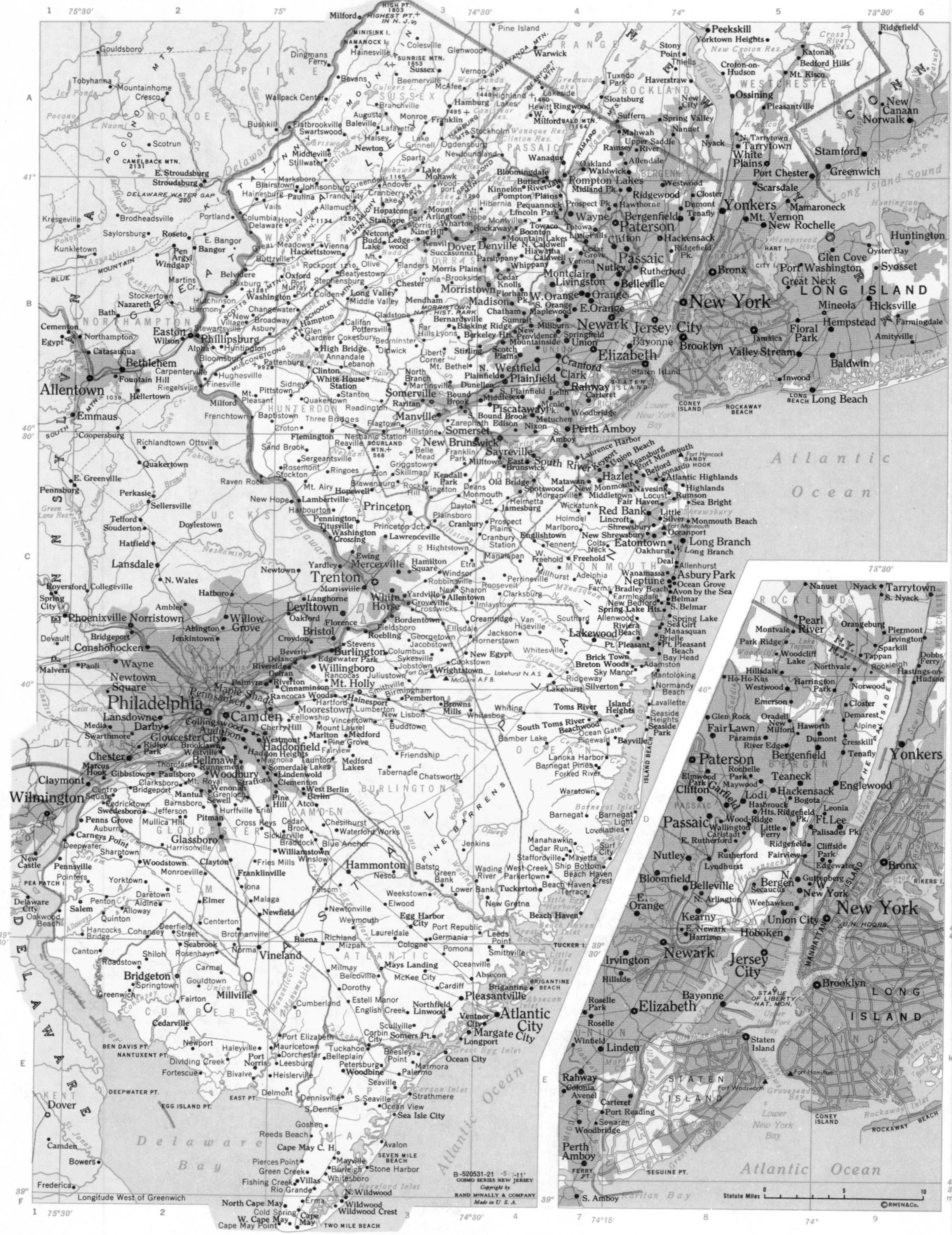

New Jersey

75°30' 1 75° 2 3 74°30' 4 74° 5 73°30' 6

Major cities and places:

Allentown, Bethlehem, Easton, Phillipsburg, Emmaus, Wilmington, Philadelphia, Camden, Trenton, Princeton, New Brunswick, Newark, New York, Jersey City, Elizabeth, Paterson, Passaic, Yonkers, Atlantic City, Vineland, Bridgeton, Millville, Toms River, Lakewood, Asbury Park, Long Branch, Red Bank, Perth Amboy, Hackensack, Bayonne, Hoboken

Counties: MONROE, PIKE, SUSSEX, PASSAIC, ROCKLAND, WESTCHESTER, NORTHAMPTON, MORRIS, BERGEN, HUNTERDON, SOMERSET, MIDDLESEX, MONMOUTH, MERCER, BUCKS, BURLINGTON, OCEAN, CAMDEN, GLOUCESTER, SALEM, CUMBERLAND, ATLANTIC, CAPE MAY, DELAWARE, KENT

Water bodies: Atlantic Ocean, Delaware Bay, Delaware River, Long Island Sound, Lower New York Bay, Raritan Bay, Barnegat Bay

Pocono, Delaware Water Gap, CAMELBACK MTN. 2131, HIGHEST PT. IN N.J., BLUE MOUNTAIN, KITTATINNY MTS., PINE BARRENS

LONG ISLAND, STATEN ISLAND, BRONX, QUEENS, KINGS

B-520531-21 -5-7-11'
COSMO SERIES NEW JERSEY
Copyright by
RAND MCNALLY & COMPANY
Made in U.S.A.

Longitude West of Greenwich

Statute Miles 5 0 5 10 15
Kilometers 5 0 5 10 15 20

Lambert Conformal Conic Projection

73°30'
Nanuet, Nyack, Tarrytown, S. Nyack, Orangeburg, Piermont, Sparkill, Dobbs Ferry, Hastings-on-Hudson, Pearl River, Montvale, Park Ridge, Woodcliff Lake, Northvale, Closter, Demarest, Alpine, Cresskill, Ho-Ho-Kus, Hillsdale, Westwood, Harrington Park, Norwood, Glen Rock, Oradell, New Milford, Haworth, Dumont, Fair Lawn, Paramus, River Edge, Bergenfield, Teaneck, Englewood, Fort Lee, Paterson, Clifton, Garfield, Lodi, Hackensack, Bogota, Leonia, Passaic, Wallington, Rutherford, Fairview, Cliffside Park, Edgewater, Nutley, Lyndhurst, Bloomfield, Belleville, North Arlington, Secaucus, Weehawken, Union City, Kearny, Harrison, East Orange, Irvington, Newark, Jersey City, Hoboken, Bayonne, Elizabeth, Linden, Rahway, Colonia, Avenel, Carteret, Port Reading, Sewaren, Woodbridge, Perth Amboy, Roselle, Roselle Park, Winfield, Hillside, New York, Brooklyn, Bronx, RIKERS I., STATEN ISLAND, Staten Island, Statue of Liberty Nat. Mon., Lower New York Bay, Coney Island, Rockaway Beach, Atlantic Ocean

Statute Miles
©R.M'N&Co.

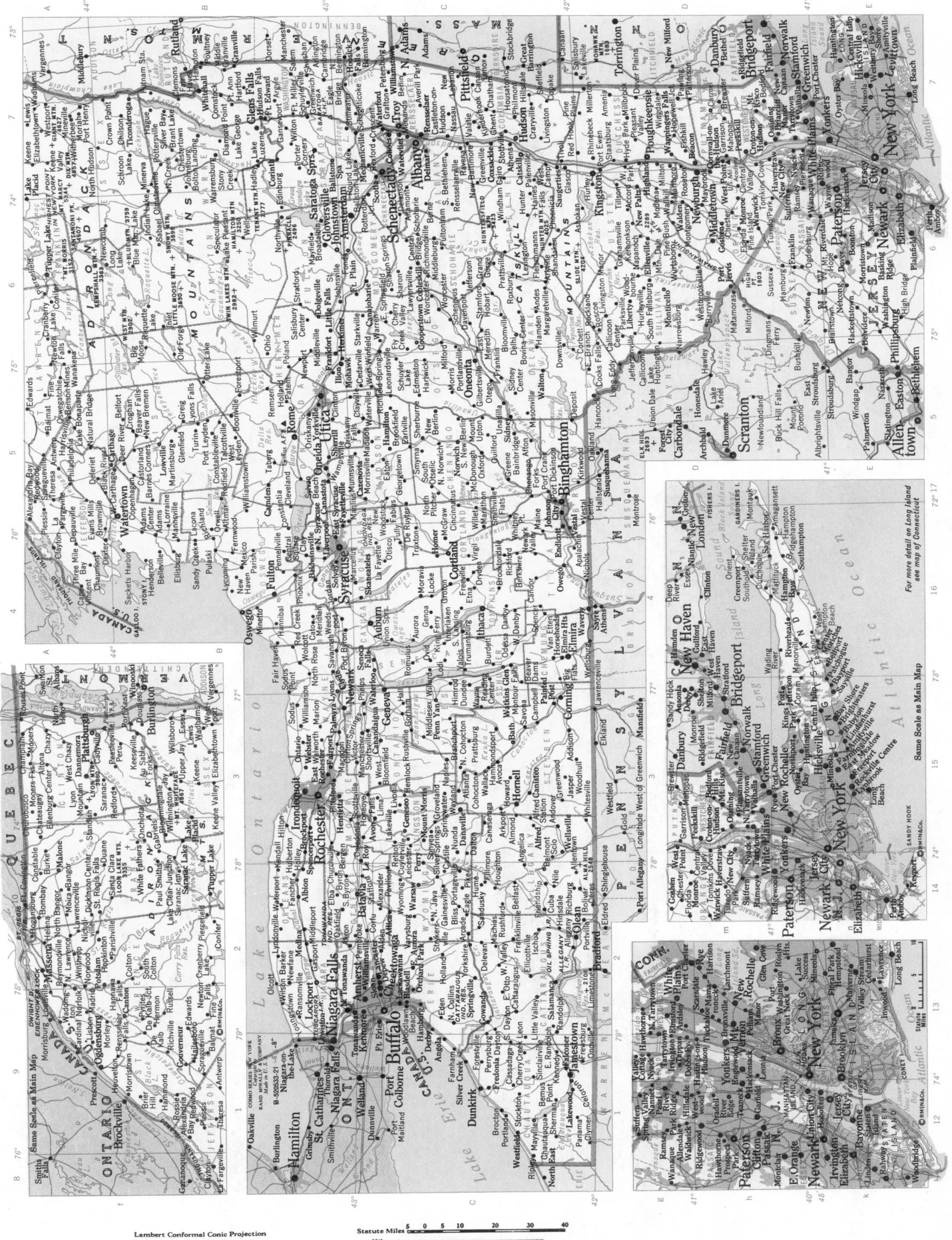

Lambert Conformal Conic Projection

Statute Miles 5 0 5 10 20 30 40

Kilometers 5 0 5 15 25 35 45 55

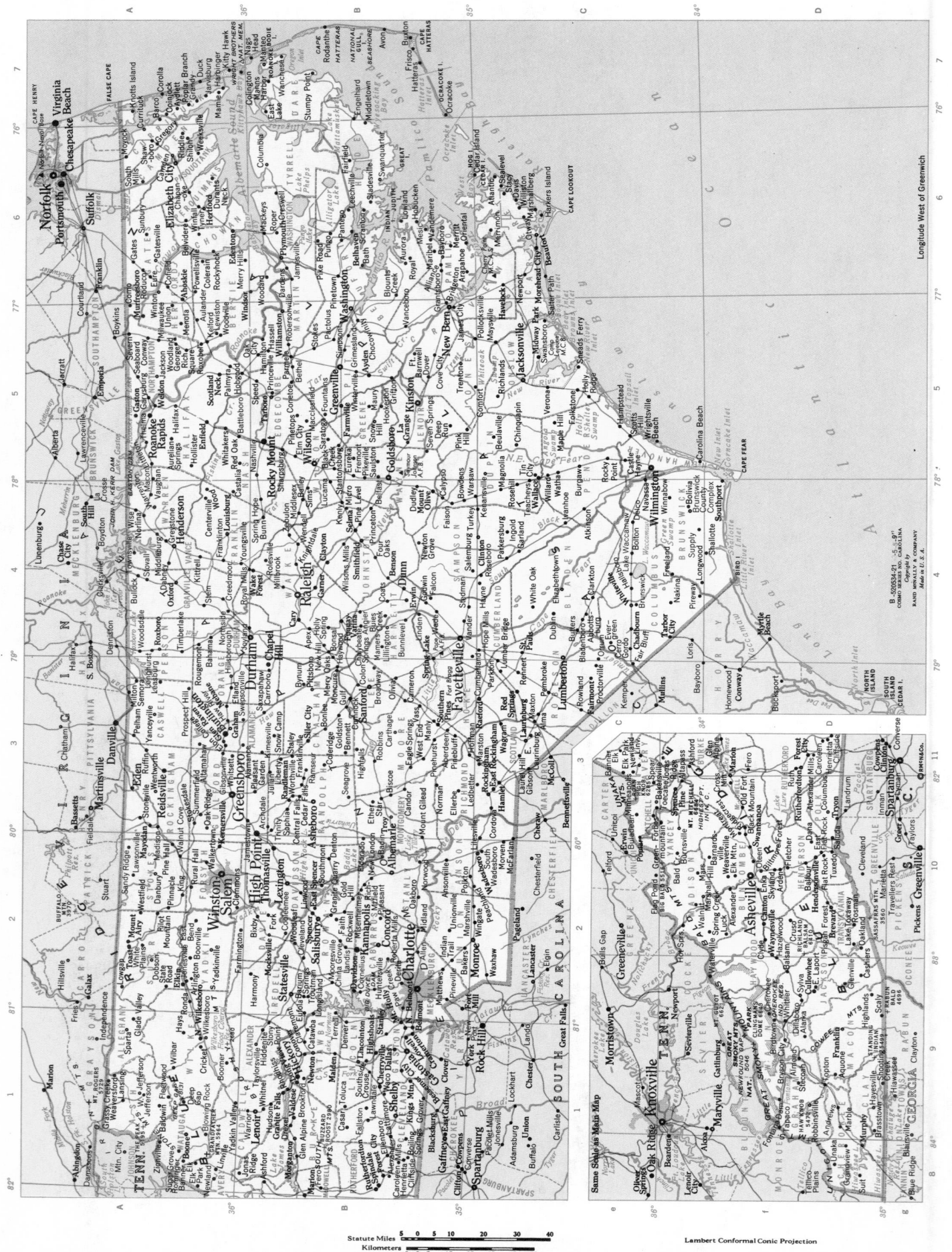

Statute Miles 5 0 5 10 20 30 40
Kilometers 5 0 5 15 25 35 45 55

Lambert Conformal Conic Projection

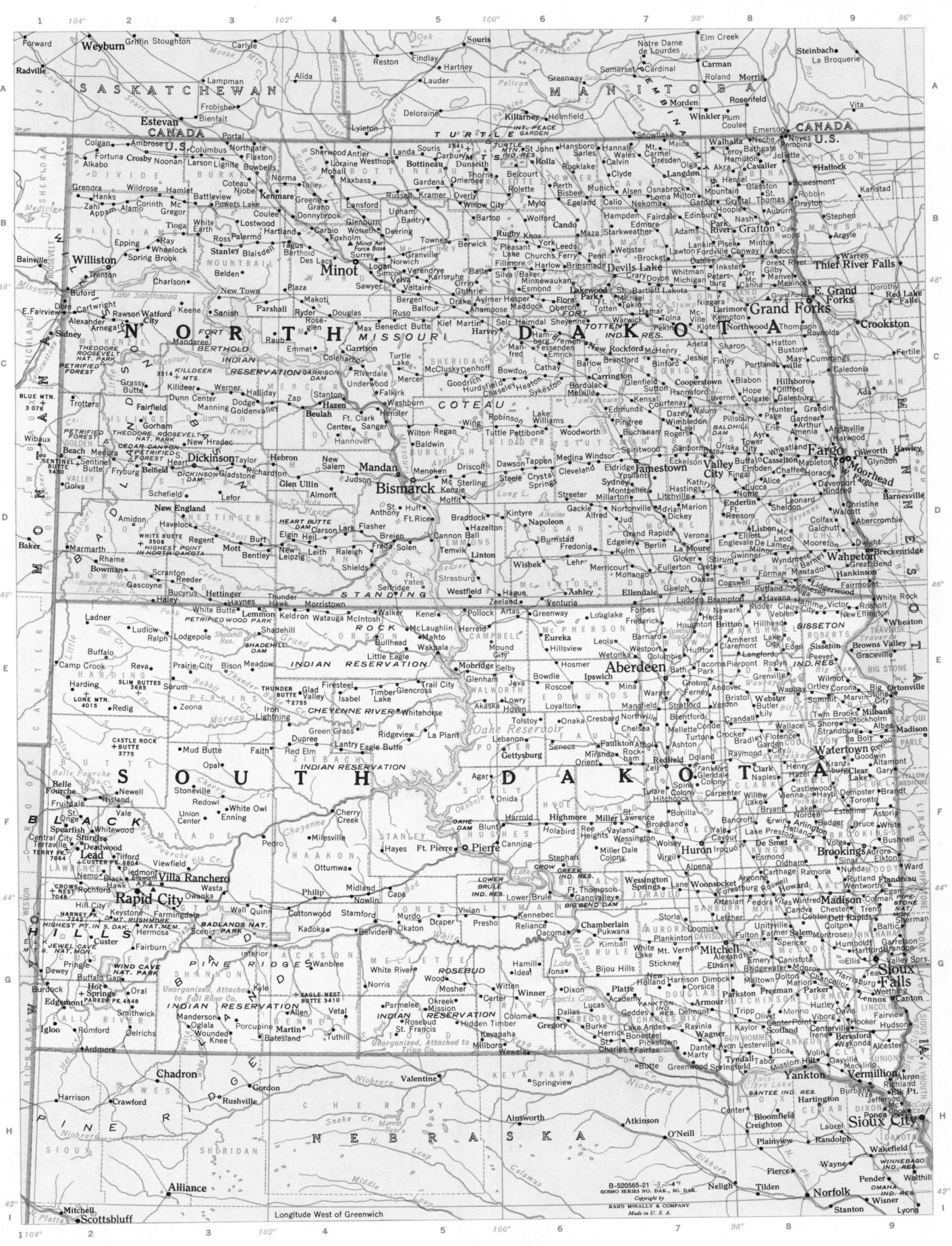

Longitude West of Greenwich

Lambert Conformal Conic Projection

Statute Miles 5 0 5 10 20 30 40 50 60

Kilometers 5 0 5 15 25 35 45 55 65 75

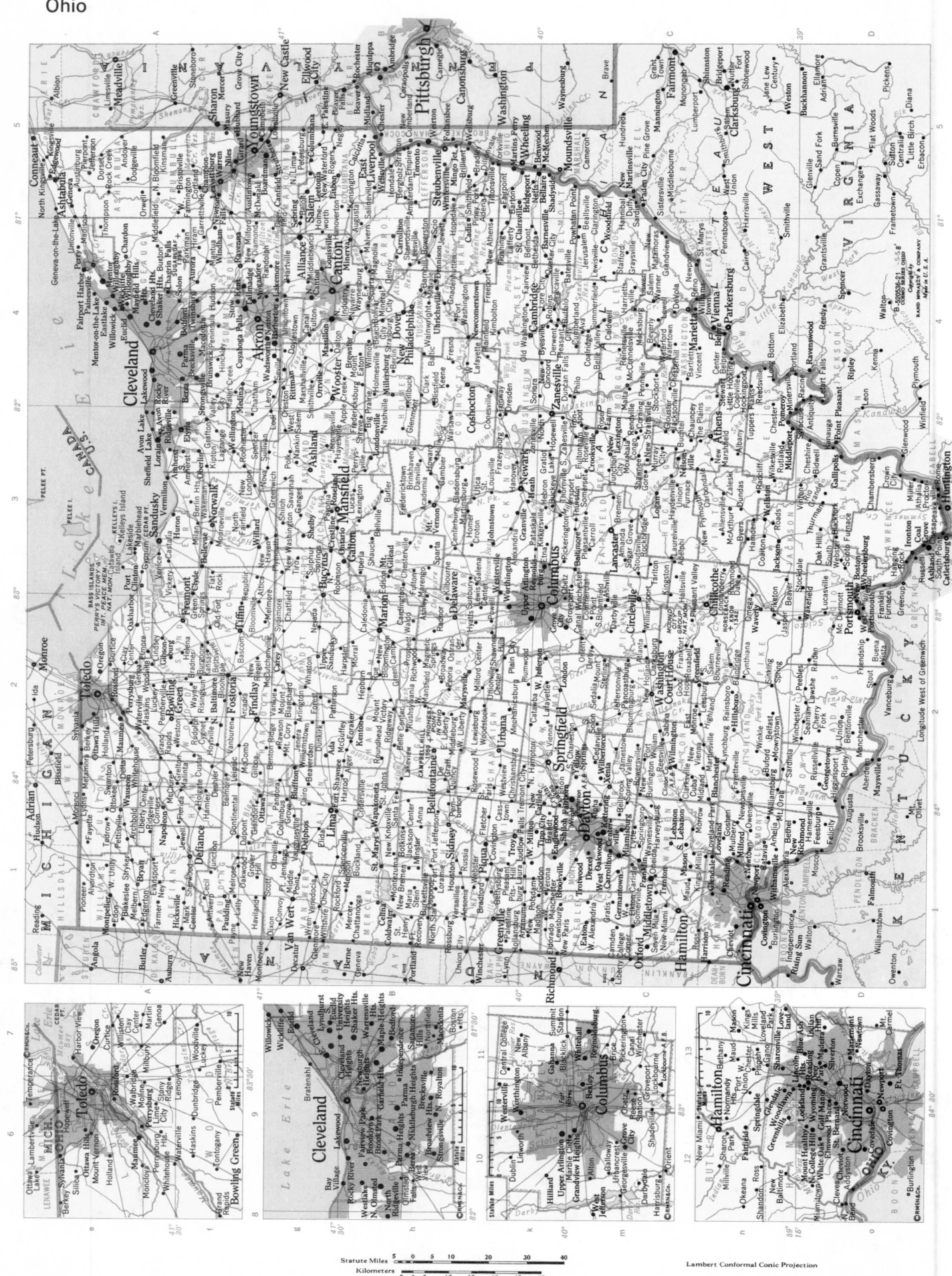

Statute Miles 5 0 5 10   20   30   40
Kilometers 5 0 5 15 25 35 45 55

Lambert Conformal Conic Projection

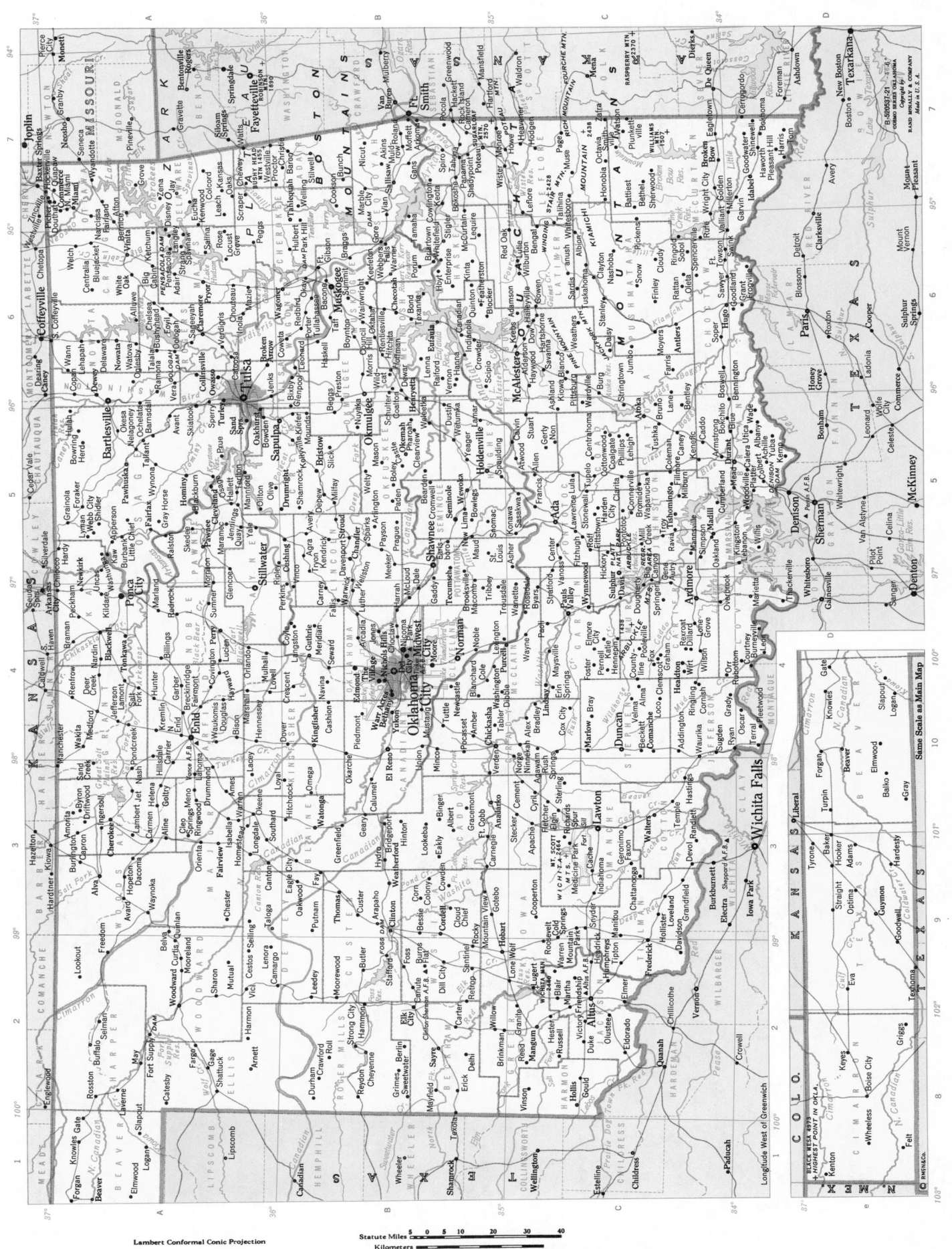

Lambert Conformal Conic Projection

Statute Miles
Kilometers

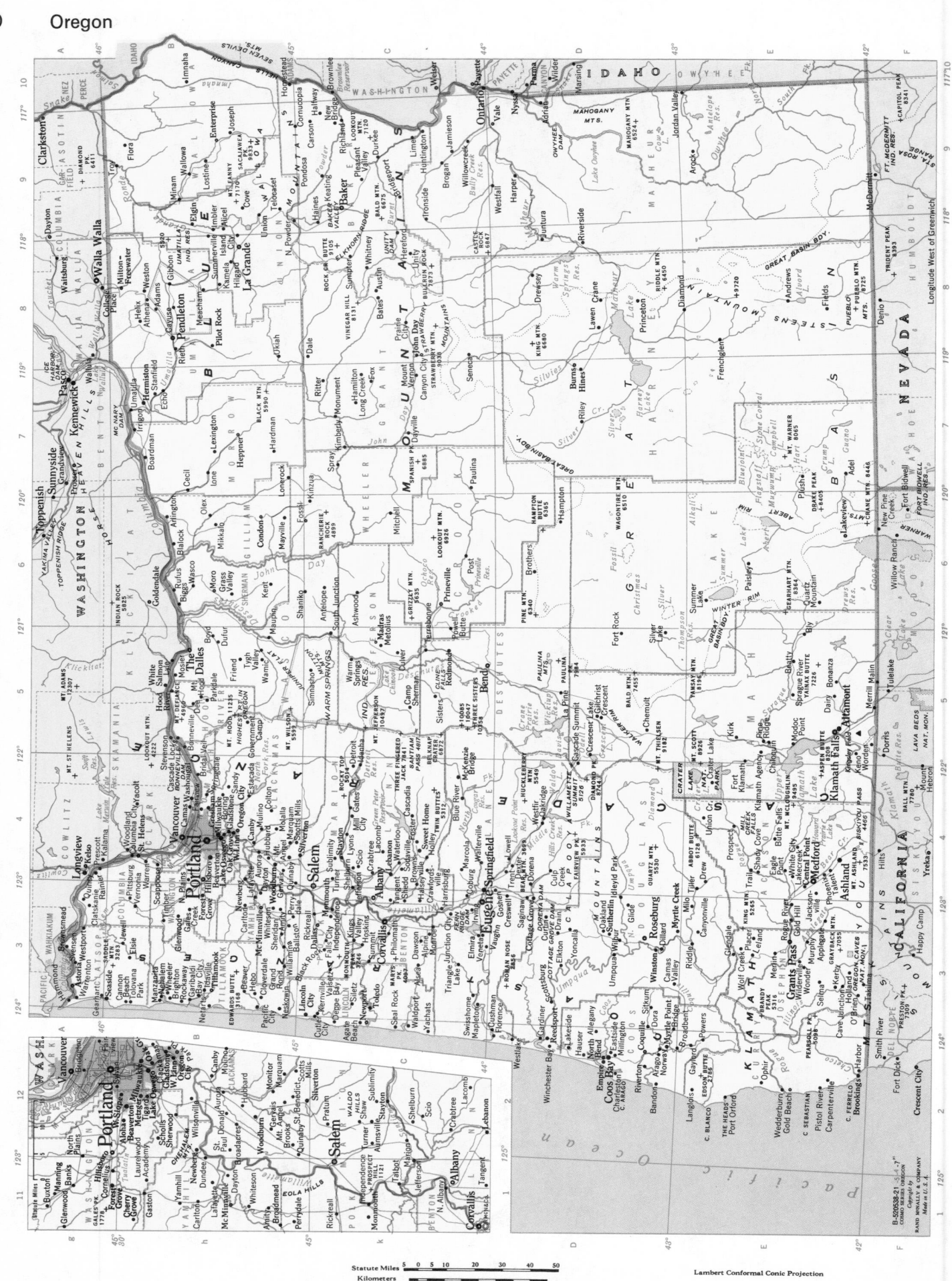

Statute Miles 5 0 5 10 20 30 40 50
Kilometers 5 0 5 15 25 35 45 55 65 75

Lambert Conformal Conic Projection

B-500538-21
COSMO SERIES OREGON
Copyright by
RAND MºNALLY & COMPANY
Made in U.S.A.

Lambert Conformal Conic Projection

Statute Miles

Kilometers

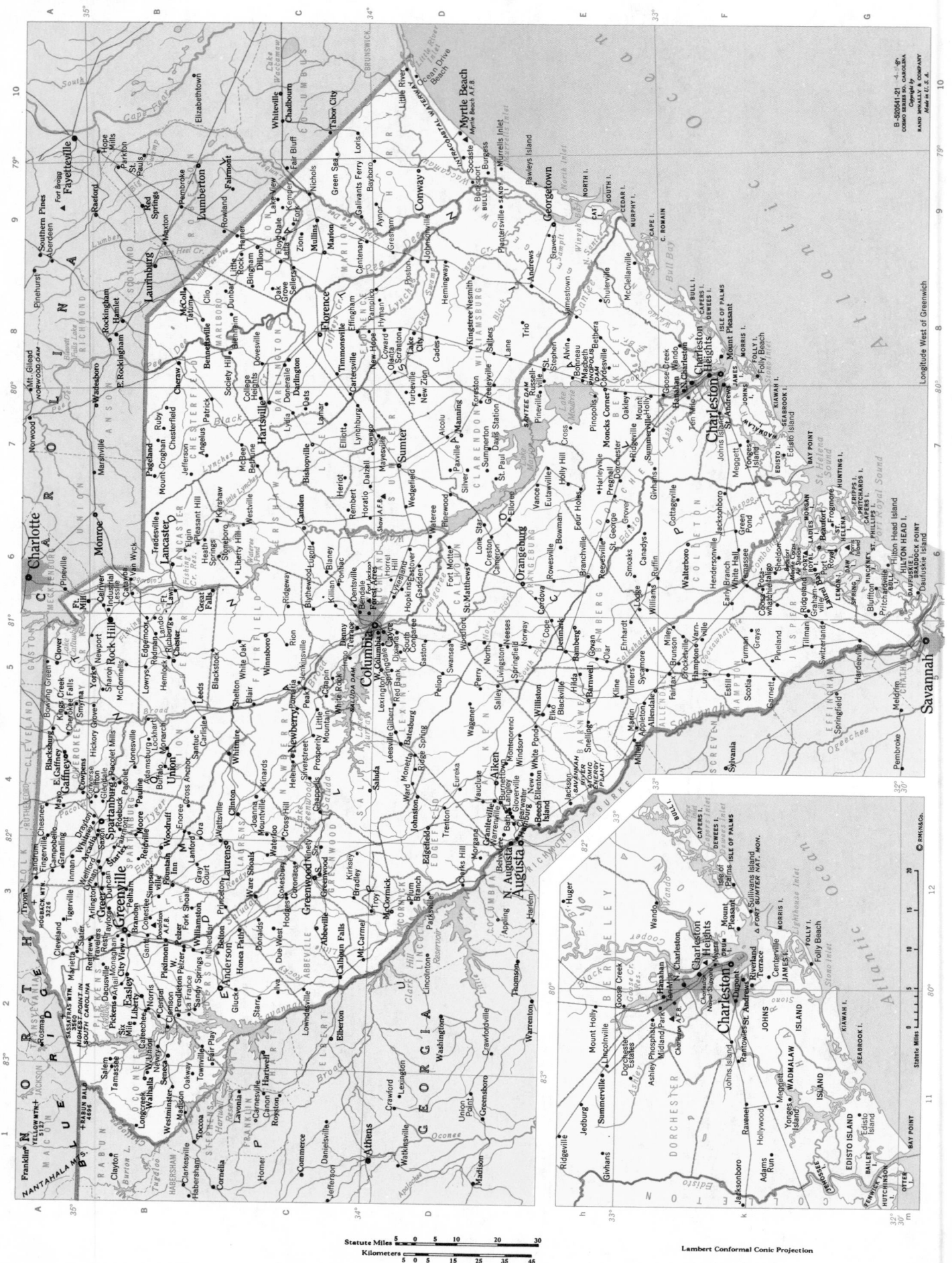

Lambert Conformal Conic Projection

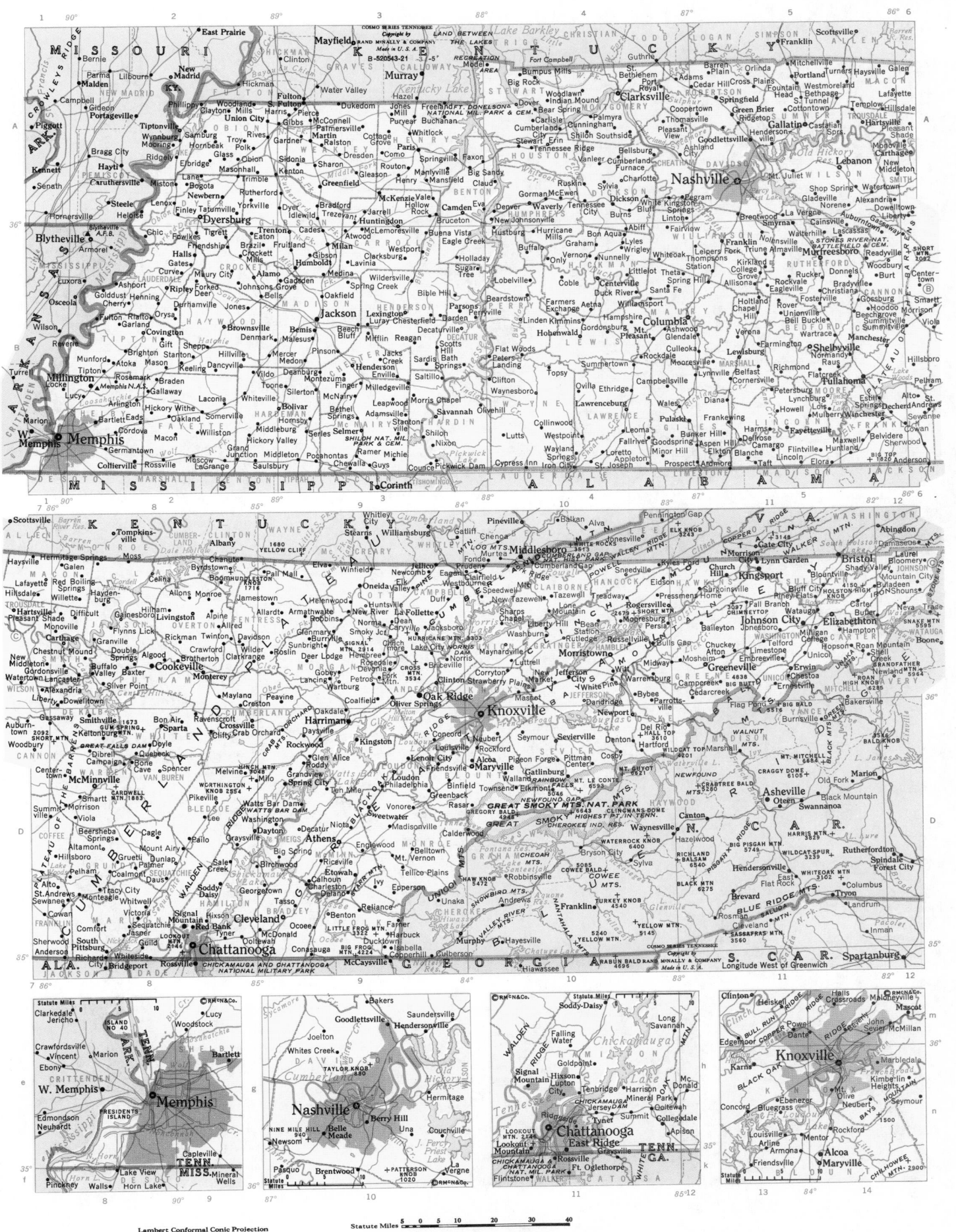

Lambert Conformal Conic Projection

Statute Miles
5 0 5 10   20   30   40

Kilometers
5 0 5 15   25   35   45   55

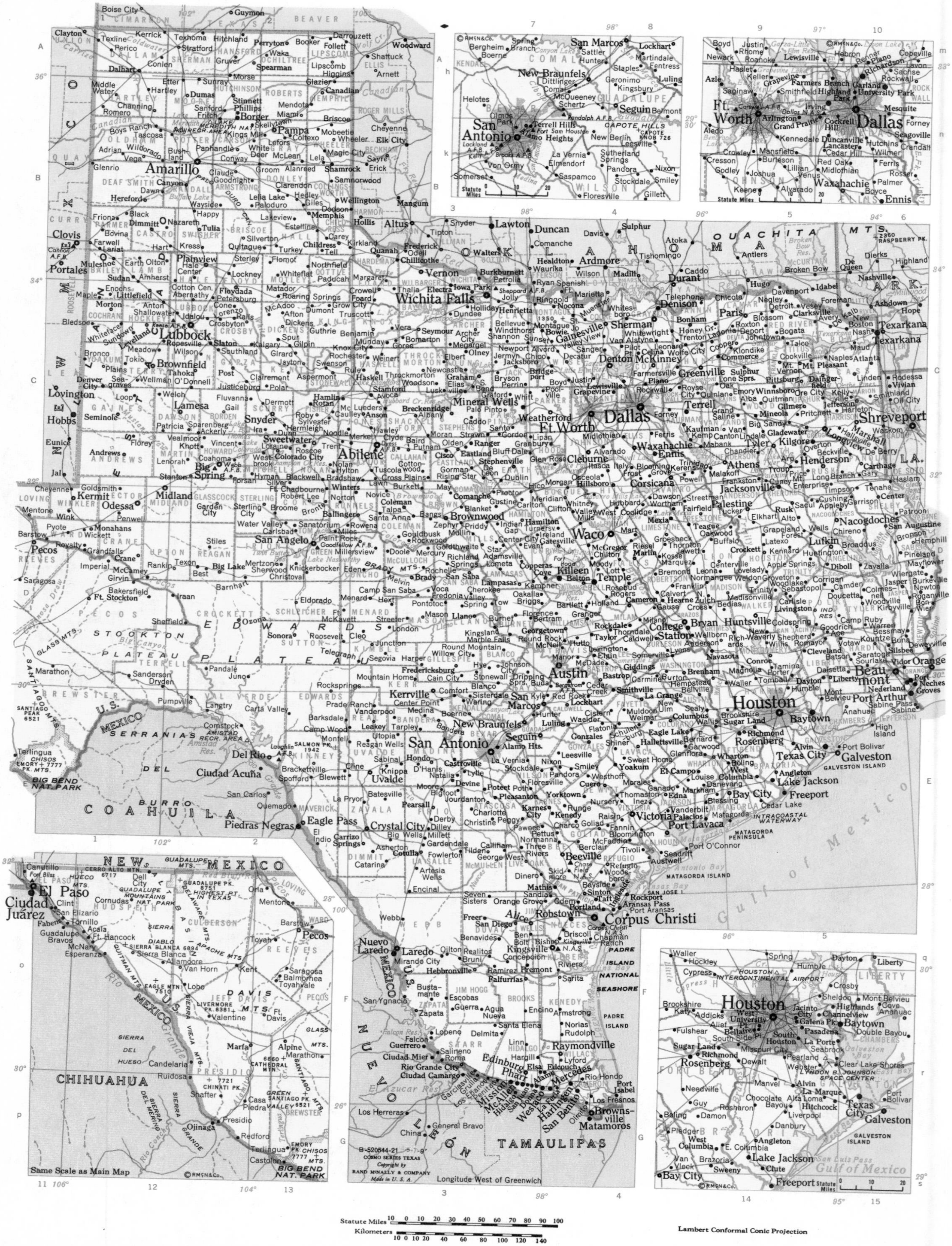
Same Scale as Main Map
B-520544-21
COSMO SERIES TEXAS
Copyright by RAND McNALLY & COMPANY
Made in U. S. A.
Longitude West of Greenwich
Gulf of Mexico
COAHUILA
CHIHUAHUA
NUEVO LEÓN
TAMAULIPAS
Statute Miles 10 0 10 20 30 40 50 60 70 80 90 100
Kilometers 10 0 10 20 40 60 80 100 120 140
Lambert Conformal Conic Projection

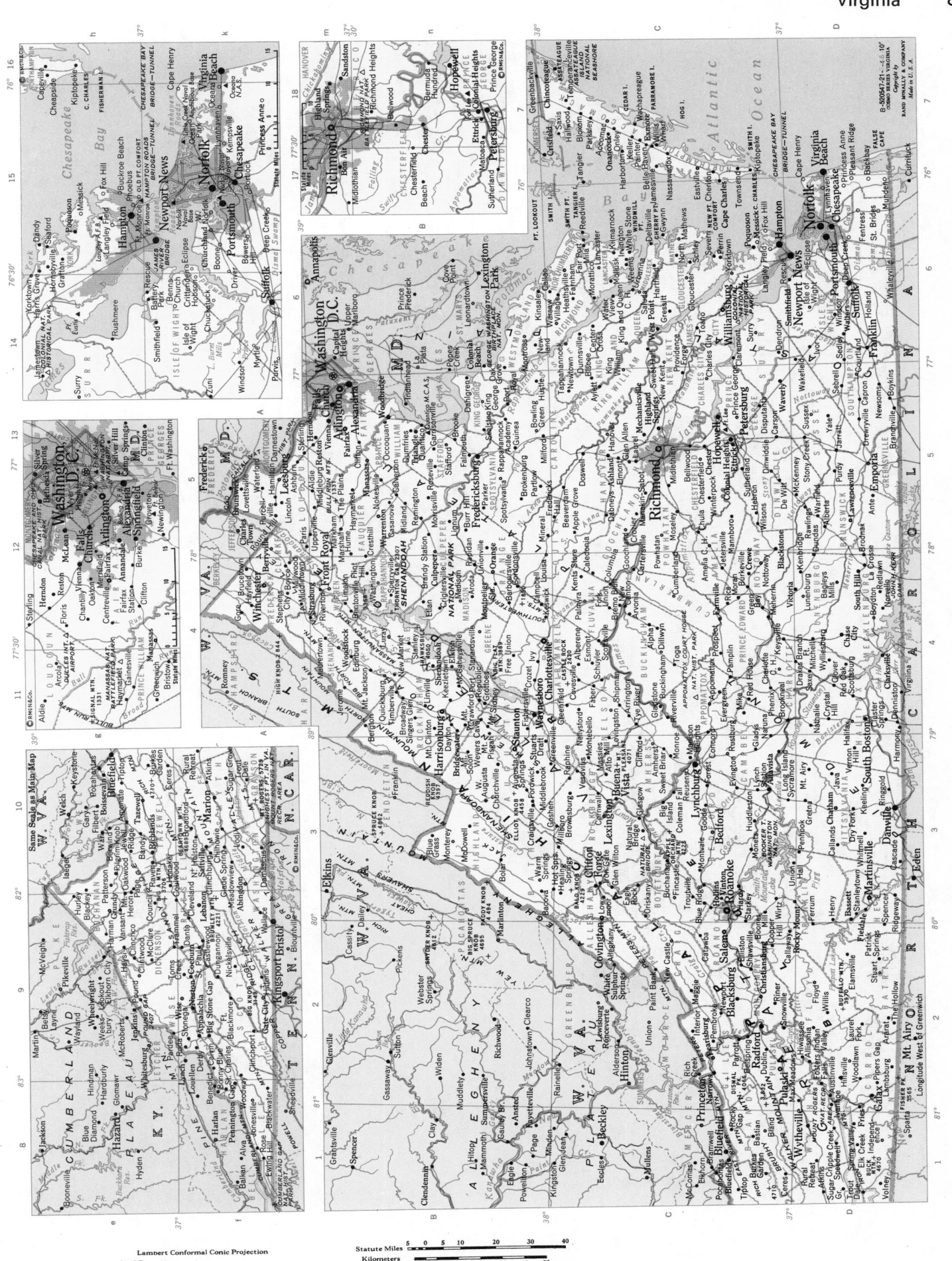

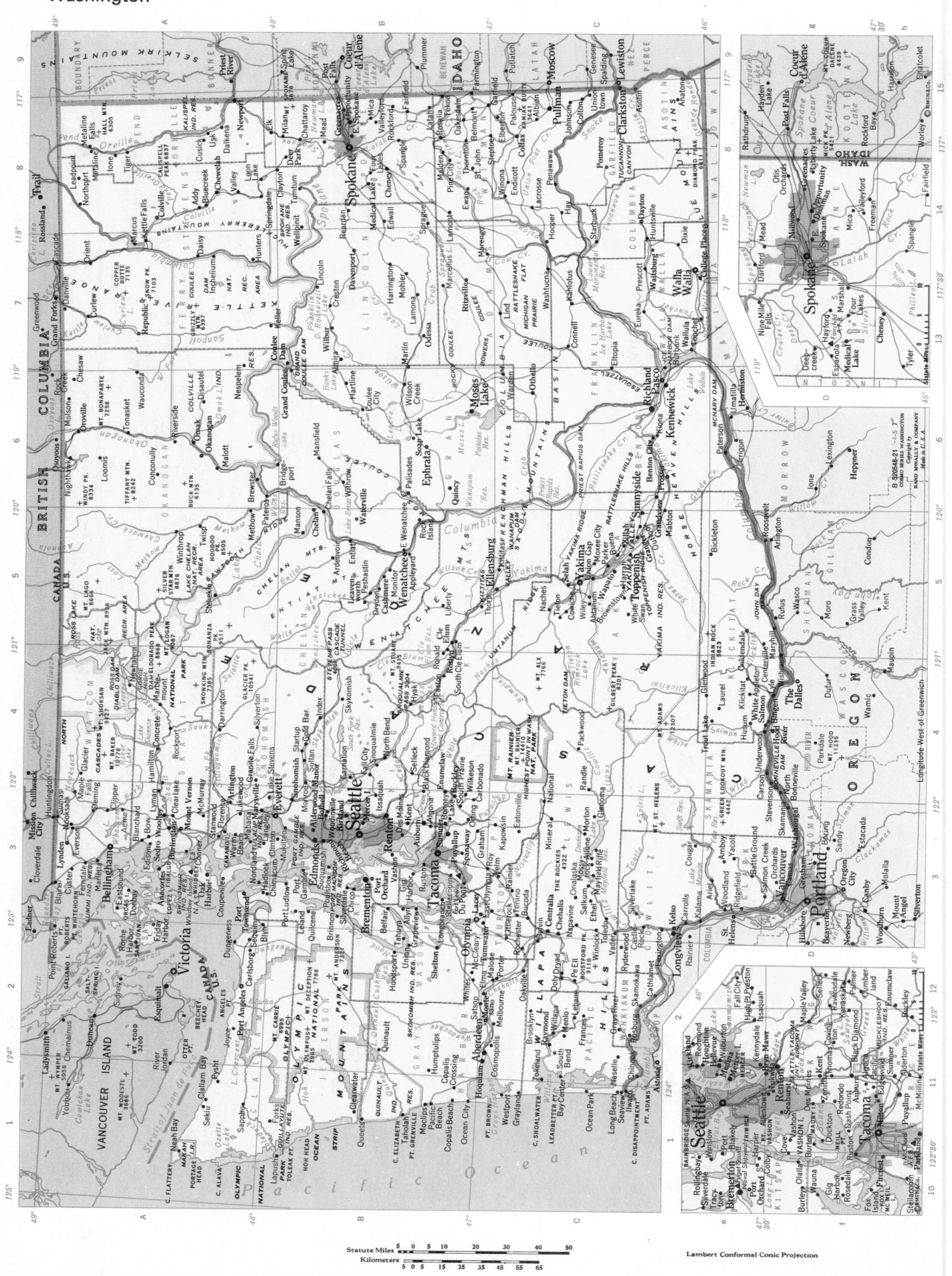

Statute Miles 5 0 5 10   20   30   40   50
Kilometers 5 0 5 15 25 35 45 55 65

Lambert Conformal Conic Projection

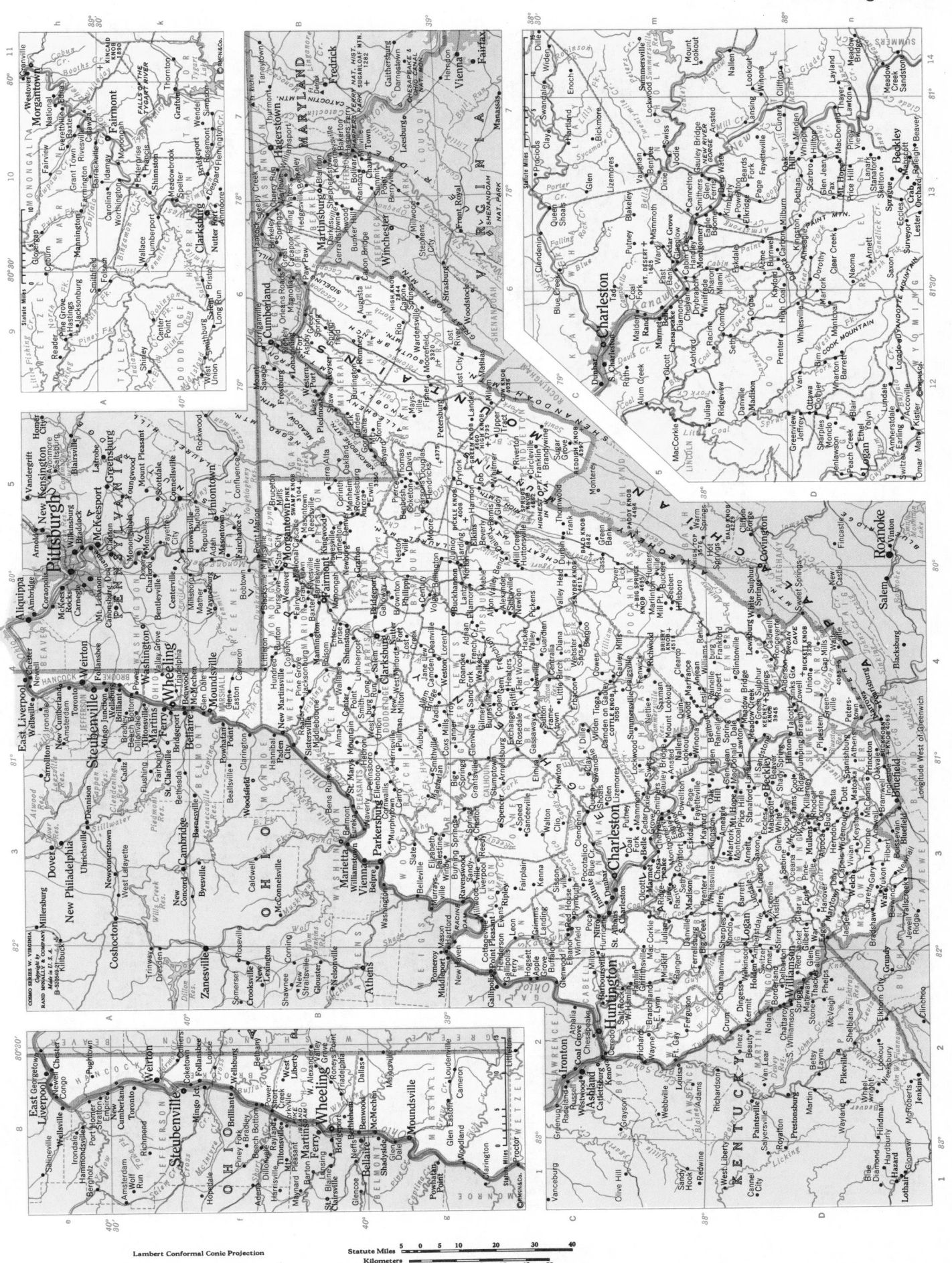

Lambert Conformal Conic Projection

Statute Miles

Kilometers

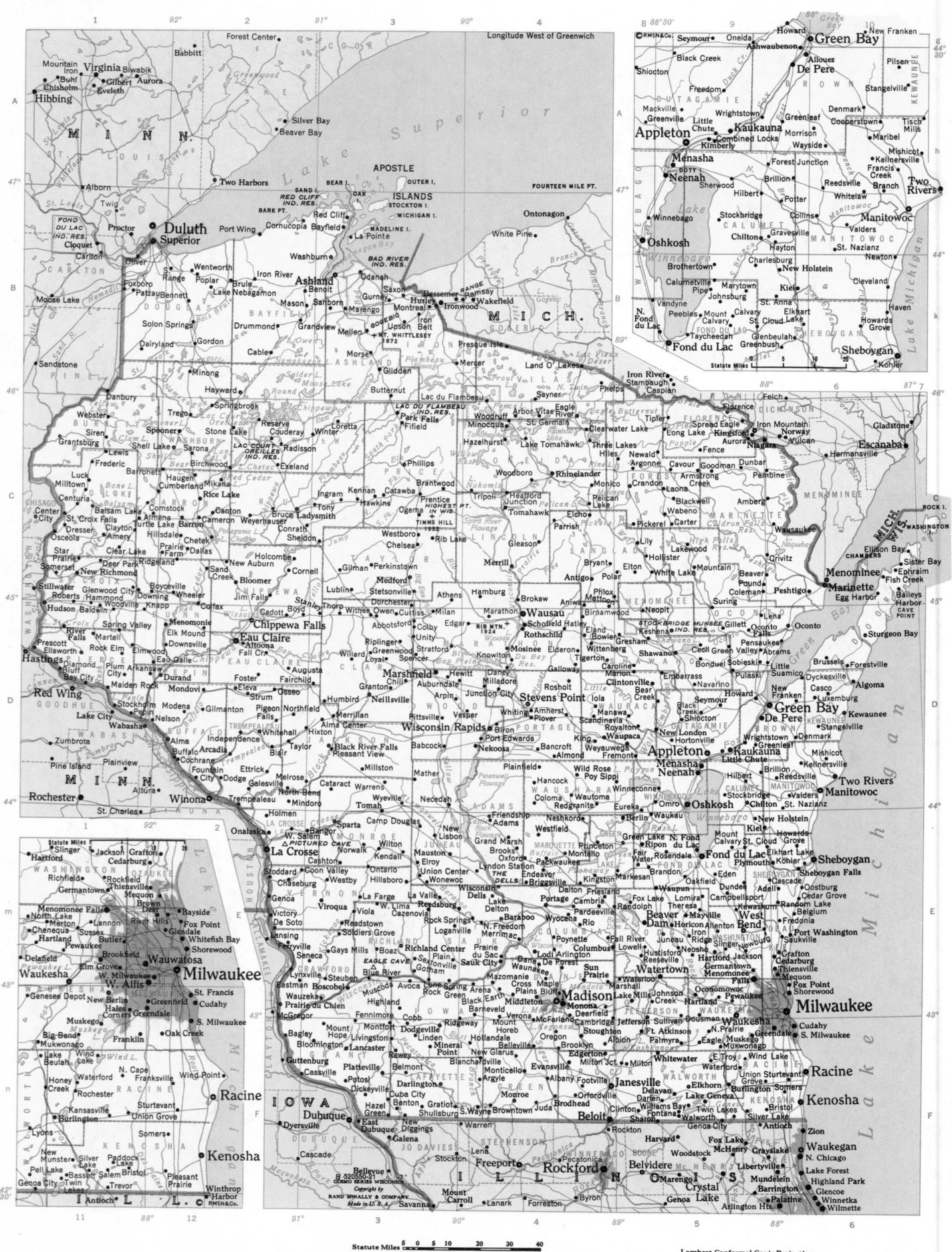

Statute Miles 5 0 5 10   20   30   40
Kilometers 5 0 5 15 25 35 45 55

Lambert Conformal Conic Projection

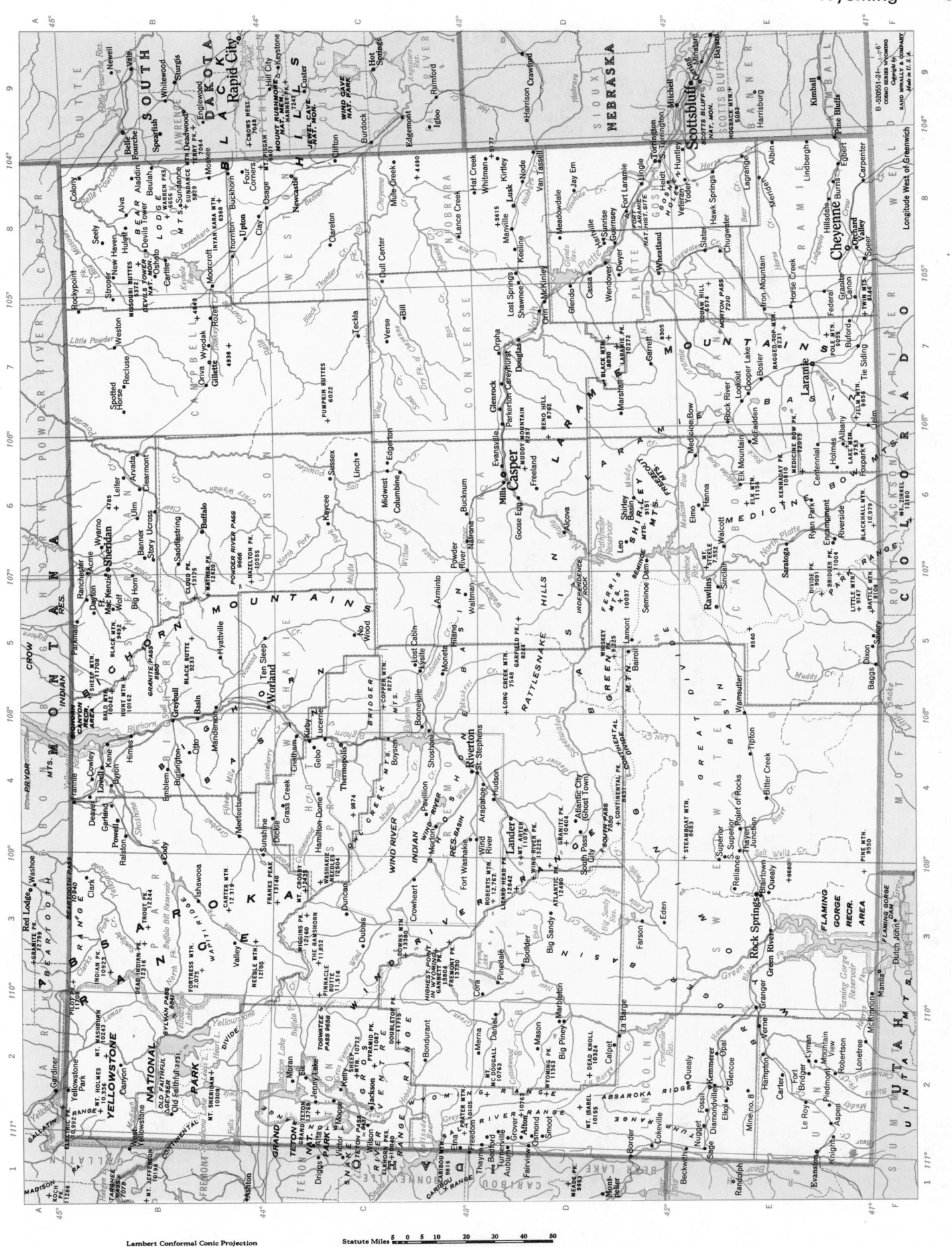

Lambert Conformal Conic Projection

Statute Miles

Kilometers

World Political Information Table

This table lists all countries and dependencies in the world, U.S. States, Canadian provinces, and other important regions and political subdivisions. Besides specifying the form of government for all political areas, the table classifies them into five groups according to their political status. Units labeled **A** are independent sovereign nations. Units labeled **B** are independent as regards internal affairs, but for purposes of foreign affairs they are under the protection of another country. Areas under military government are also labeled **B.** Units labeled **C** are colonies, overseas territories, dependencies, etc., of other countries. Together the **A, B,** and **C** areas comprise practically the entire inhabited area of the world. Units labeled **D** are States, provinces, Soviet Republics, or similar major administrative subdivisions of important countries. Units in the table with no letter designation are regions or other areas that do not constitute separate political units by themselves.

Country, Division, or Region English (Conventional)	Area* in sq. mi.	Estimated Population 1/1/84	Pop. per sq. mi.	Form of Government and Political Status	Capital: Largest City (unless same)	Predominant Language
Afars and Issas, *see* Djibouti	...	...	...	...	...	...
†**Afghanistan**	250,000	14,165,000	57	Socialist Republic A	Kābul	Dari, Pushtu
Africa	11,700,000	519,800,000	44	...	...; Cairo	...
Alabama	51,704	4,010,000	78	State (U.S.) D	Montgomery; Birmingham	English
Alaska	591,004	465,000	0.8	State (U.S.) D	Juneau; Anchorage	English, Indian, Eskimo
†**Albania**	11,100	2,600,000	234	Socialist Republic A	Tiranë	Albanian
Alberta	255,285	2,365,000	9.3	Province (Canada) D	Edmonton	English
†**Algeria**	919,595	21,290,000	23	Socialist Republic A	Algiers	Arabic, French, Berber
American Samoa	77	35,000	455	Unincorporated Territory (U.S.) C	Pago Pago	Samoan, English
Andaman and Nicobar Islands	3,202	205,000	64	Territory (India) D	Port Blair	Andaman, Nicobar Malay
Andorra	175	39,000	223	Co-Principality (Spanish and French protection) B	Andorra	Spanish, French
†**Angola**	481,353	7,735,000	16	Socialist Republic A	Luanda	Portuguese, native languages
Anguilla	35	7,000	200	Associated State (U.K.) B	The Valley; South Hill	English
Anhui	50,193	51,700,000	1,030	Province (China) D	Hefei, Huainan	Chinese
Antarctica	5,405,000	...[1]	...	...	...	...
†**Antigua and Barbuda**	170	80,000	471	Parliamentary State (Comm. of Nations) A	Saint John's	English
Arabian Peninsula	1,160,000	23,505,000	20	...	...; Riyadh	Arabic
†**Argentina**	1,068,301	28,955,000	27	Republic A	Buenos Aires	Spanish
Arizona	114,002	2,965,000	26	State (U.S.) D	Phoenix	English
Arkansas	53,191	2,315,000	44	State (U.S.) D	Little Rock	English
Armenian S.S.R.	11,506	3,200,000	278	Soviet Socialist Republic (U.S.S.R.) D	Yerevan	Armenian, Russian
Aruba	75	69,000	920	Division of Netherlands Antilles (Neth.) D	Oranjestad	Dutch, Spanish, English, Papiamento
Ascension	34	1,100	32	Dependency of St. Helena (U.K.) C	Georgetown	English
Asia	17,240,000	2,863,400,000	166	...	...; Tōkyō	...
†**Australia**	2,967,909	15,535,000	5.2	Parliamentary State (Federal) (Comm. of Nations) A	Canberra; Sydney	English
Australian Capital Territory	939	235,000	250	Territory (Australia) D	Canberra	English
†**Austria**	32,377	7,575,000	234	Federal Republic A	Vienna (Wien)	German
Azerbaidzhan S.S.R.	33,436	6,370,000	190	Soviet Socialist Republic (U.S.S.R.) D	Baku	Turkish, Russian, Armenian
Azores	868	240,000	276	Autonomous Region (Portugal) D	Ponta Delgada	Portguese
Baden-Württemberg	13,804	9,255,000	670	State (Federal Republic of Germany) D	Stuttgart	German
†**Bahamas**	5,382	225,000	42	Parliamentary State (Comm. of Nations) A	Nassau	English
†**Bahrain**	256	400,000	1,563	Constitutional Monarchy A	Manama	Arabic, English
Balearic Islands	1,936	695,000	359	Province of Spain (Baleares) D	Palma	Spanish
Baltic Republics	67,182	7,655,000	114	Part of U.S.S.R. (3 republics)	...; Rīga	Lithuanian, Latvian, Estonian, Russian
†**Bangladesh**	55,598	95,600,000	1,719	Republic (Comm. of Nations) A	Dacca	Bangla, English
†**Barbados**	166	250,000	1,506	Parliamentary State (Comm. of Nations) A	Bridgetown	English
Bavaria (Bayern)	27,238	10,920,000	401	State (Federal Republic of Germany) D	Munich (München)	German
Beijing, *see* Peking	...	...	...	...	...	...
†**Belgium**	11,781	9,870,000	838	Constitutional Monarchy A	Brussels (Bruxelles)	French, Dutch (Flemish)
†**Belize**	8,866	155,000	17	Parliamentary State (Comm. of Nations) A	Belmopan; Belize City	English, Spanish, Indian languages
Benelux	28,672	24,655,000	860	Economic Union	...; Brussels (Bruxelles)	Dutch, French, Luxumbourgish
†**Benin**	43,484	3,655,000	84	Socialist Republic A	Porto-Novo; Cotonou	French, native languages
Berlin (West)	185	1,880,000	10,162	State (Federal Republic of Germany) D	Berlin (West)	German
Bermuda	21	68,000	3,238	Colony (U.K.) C	Hamilton	English
†**Bhutan**	18,147	1,400,000	77	Monarchy (Indian protection) B	Thimbu	Dzongkha, English, Nepalese dialects
Bioko	785	77,000	98	Province of Equatorial Guinea D	Malabo	Spanish, English
†**Bolivia**	424,164	6,160,000	15	Republic A	Sucre and La Paz; La Paz	Spanish, Quechua, Aymara
Bophuthatswana[6]	15,610	1,400,000	89	Bantu Homeland (South African protection) B	Mmabatho	Sesotho, Afrikaans
Borneo, Indonesian (Kalimantan)	208,287	7,185,000	34	Part of Indonesia (4 provinces)	...; Banjarmasin	Bahasa Indonesia
†**Botswana**	231,805	1,020,000	4.4	Republic (Comm. of Nations) A	Gaborone	Setswana, English
†**Brazil**	3,265,075	133,100,000	41	Federal Republic A	Brasília; São Paulo	Portuguese
Bremen	156	690,000	4,423	State (Federal Republic of Germany) D	Bremen	German
British Columbia	366,255	2,840,000	7.8	Province (Canada) D	Victoria; Vancouver	English
British Honduras, *see* Belize	...	...	...	...	...	...
British Indian Ocean Territory	23	...[1]	...	Colony (U.K.) C	...	...
British Solomon Islands, *see* Solomon Islands	...	...	...	...	...	...
Brunei	2,226	215,000	92	Constitutional Monarchy (Comm. of Nations) A	Bandar Seri Begawan	Malay, Chinese, English
†**Bulgaria**	42,823	9,370,000	219	Socialist Republic A	Sofia (Sofiya)	Bulgarian
†**Burkina Faso (Upper Volta)**	105,869	6,525,000	62	Provisional Military Government A	Ouagadougou	French, native languages
†**Burma**	261,228	37,505,000	144	Socialist Republic A	Rangoon	Burmese, ethnic languages
†**Burundi**	10,747	4,625,000	430	Republic A	Bujumbura	Kirundi, French, Swahili
†**Byelorussian S.S.R.**	80,155	9,925,000	124	Soviet Socialist Republic (U.S.S.R.) D	Minsk	Byelorussian, Polish, Russian
California	158,704	25,300,000	159	State (U.S.) D	Sacramento; Los Angeles	English
Cambodia, *see* Kampuchea	...	...	...	...	...	...
†**Cameroon**	183,569	9,125,000	50	Republic A	Yaoundé; Douala	English, French, native languages
†**Canada**	3,831,033	25,100,000	6.6	Parliamentary State (Federal) (Comm. of Nations) A	Ottawa; Toronto	English, French
Canary Islands (Islas Canarias)	2,808	1,470,000	524	...; Part of Spain (2 provinces)	...; Las Palmas de Gran Canaria	Spanish
†**Cape Verde**	1,557	310,000	199	Republic A	Praia	Portuguese, Crioulo
Cayman Islands	100	19,000	190	Colony (U.K.) C	Georgetown	English
Celebes	73,057	11,125,000	152	Part of Indonesia (4 provinces)	...; Ujung Pandang	Bahasa Indonesia, Malay-Polynesian languages
†**Central African Republic**	240,535	2,505,000	10	Republic A	Bangui	French, Sangho
Central America	202,000	24,920,000	123	...	...; Guatemala	Spanish, Indian languages
Central Asia, Soviet	493,090	27,390,000	56	Part of U.S.S.R. (4 republics)	...; Tashkent	Uzbek, Russian, Kirghiz, Turkoman, Tadzhik
Ceylon, *see* Sri Lanka	...	...	...	...	...	...
†**Chad**	495,755	4,785,000	9.7	Provisional Military Government A	Ndjamena	French, Arabic, native languages
Channel Islands	75	133,000	1,773	...	...; St. Helier	English, French
†**Chile**	292,135	11,740,000	40	Republic A	Santiago	Spanish
†**China (excl. Taiwan)**	3,630,747	1,046,530,000	288	Socialist Republic A	Peking (Beijing); Shanghai	Chinese dialects
China (Nationalist), *see* Taiwan	...	...	...	...	...	...
Christmas Island	52	3,200	62	External Territory (Australia) C	...; Flying Fish Cove	Chinese, Malay, English
Ciskei[6]	3,205	690,000	215	Bantu Homeland (South African protection) B	Bisho; Mdantsane	Xhosa, Afrikaans
Cocos (Keeling) Islands	5.4	500	92	External Territory (Australia) C	...	Malay, English
†**Colombia**	439,737	30,285,000	69	Republic A	Bogotá	Spanish
Colorado	104,094	3,130,000	30	State (U.S.) D	Denver	English

* Areas include inland water.
† Member of the United Nations (1983).
... None, or not applicable.
[1] No permanent population.
[6] Bophuthatswana, Ciskei, Transkei, and Venda are not recognized by the United Nations.

Country, Division, or Region English (Conventional)	Area* in sq. mi.	Estimated Population 1/1/84	Pop. per sq. mi.	Form of Government and Political Status		Capital: Largest City (unless same)	Predominant Language
Cook Islands	91	18,000	198	Self-governing Territory (New Zealand protection)	B	Avarua	Malay-Polynesian languages, English
Corsica	3,352	235,000	70	Part of France (2 departments)		......; Ajaccio	French, Italian
†Costa Rica	19,730	2,395,000	121	Republic	A	San José	Spanish
†Cuba	44,218	9,850,000	223	Socialist Republic	A	Havana (La Habana)	Spanish
Curaçao	171	180,000	1,053	Division of Netherlands Antilles (Neth.)	D	Willemstad	Dutch, Spanish, English, Papiamento
†Cyprus	3,572	665,000	186	Republic (Comm. of Nations)	A	Nicosia	Greek, Turkish
†Czechoslovakia	49,378	15,415,000	312	Federal Socialist Republic	A	Prague (Praha)	Czech, Slovak, Hungarian
Dahomey, see Benin							
Delaware	2,045	615,000	301	State (U.S.)	D	Dover; Wilmington	English
†Denmark	16,633	5,110,000	307	Constitutional Monarchy	A	Copenhagen (København)	Danish
Denmark and Possessions	857,177	5,210,000	6.1			Copenhagen (København)	Danish, Faroese, Eskimo
District of Columbia	69	625,000	9,058	District (U.S.)	D	Washington	English
†Djibouti	8,880	350,000	39	Republic	A	Djibouti	Somali, French, Afar, Arabic
†Dominica	290	74,000	255	Republic (Comm. of Nations)	A	Roseau	English, French
†Dominican Republic	18,704	5,975,000	319	Republic	A	Santo Domingo	Spanish
†Ecuador	109,483	9,410,000	86	Republic	A	Quito; Guayaquil	Spanish, Quechua
†Egypt	386,643	46,465,000	120	Socialist Republic	A	Cairo (AlQāhirah)	Arabic, English, French
Ellice Islands, see Tuvalu							
†El Salvador	8,124	5,140,000	633	Republic	A	San Salvador	Spanish
England	50,362	46,465,000	923	Administrative division of U.K.	D	London	English
†Equatorial Guinea	10,831	310,000	29	Republic	A	Malabo	Spanish, English, native languages
Estonian S.S.R.	17,413	1,530,000	88	Soviet Socialist Republic (U.S.S.R.)	D	Tallinn	Estonian, Russian
†Ethiopia	472,434	31,790,000	67	Provisional Military Government	A	Addis Ababa	Amharic, Arabic, native languages
Eurasia	21,080,000	3,535,800,000	168			......; Tōkyō	
Europe	3,840,000	672,400,000	175			......; London	
Faeroe Islands	540	45,000	83	Part of Danish Realm	B	Tórshavn	Danish, Faroese
Falkland Islands (Islas Malvinas) (excl. Dependencies)	4,700	2,000	0.4	Colony (U.K.)[3]	C	Stanley	English
†Fiji	7,055	675,000	96	Parliamentary State (Comm. of Nations)	A	Suva	English, Fijian, Hindustani
†Finland	130,558	4,860,000	37	Republic	A	Helsinki	Finnish, Swedish
Florida	58,668	10,825,000	185	State (U.S.)	D	Tallahassee; Miami	English
†France (excl. Overseas Depts.)	211,208	54,730,000	259	Republic	A	Paris	French
France and Possessions	260,661	56,345,000	216			Paris	French
French Guiana	35,135	78,000	2.2	Overseas Department (France)	D	Cayenne	French
French Polynesia	1,544	160,000	104	Overseas Territory (France)	C	Papeete	Malay-Polynesian languages, French
French West Indies	1,112	615,000	553			......; Fort-de-France	French
Fujian	47,877	27,000,000	564	Province (China)	D	Fuzhou	Chinese
†Gabon	103,347	940,000	9.1	Republic	A	Libreville	French, native languages
Galapagos Islands (Archipiélago de Colón)	3,075	6,000	2.0	Province of Ecuador (Galápagos)	D	Puerto Baquerizo Moreno	Spanish
†Gambia	4,361	660,000	151	Republic (Comm. of Nations)	A	Banjul	English, native languages
Gansu	150,580	20,405,000	136	Province (China)	D	Lanzhou	Chinese, Mongolian, Tibetan dialects
Georgia	58,914	5,790,000	98	State (U.S.)	D	Atlanta	English
Georgian S.S.R.	26,911	5,195,000	193	Soviet Socialist Republic (U.S.S.R.)	D	Tbilisi	Georgic, Armenian, Russian
†German Democratic Republic	41,768	16,725,000	400	Socialist Republic	A	Berlin (East)	German
†Germany, Federal Republic of (incl. West Berlin)	96,016	61,480,000	640	Federal Republic	A	Bonn; Essen	German
Germany (Entire)	137,784	78,205,000	568			......; Essen	German
†Ghana	92,100	14,670,000	160	Provisional Military Government (Comm. of Nations)	A	Accra	English, native languages
Gibraltar	2.3	31,000	13,478	Colony (U.K.)	C	Gibraltar	Spanish, English
Gilbert Islands, see Kiribati	......	......	......	......			......
Great Britain, see United Kingdom							
†Greece	50,944	9,905,000	194	Republic	A	Athens (Athínai)	Greek
Greenland	840,004	54,000	0.06	Part of Danish Realm	B	Godthåb	Danish, Eskimo
†Grenada	133	105,000	789	Parliamentary State (Comm. of Nations)	A	Saint George's	English
Guadeloupe (incl. Dependencies)	687	310,000	451	Overseas Department (France)	D	Basse-Terre; Pointe-à-Pitre	French, Creole
Guam	209	117,000	560	Unincorporated Territory (U.S.)	D	Agana	English, Chamorro
Guangdong	84,942	61,750,000	727	Province (China)	D	Canton (Guangzhou)	Chinese, Miao-Yao
Guangxi Zhuangzu	89,190	37,990,000	426	Autonomous Region (China)	D	Nanning	Chinese, Thai, Miao-Yao
†Guatemala	42,042	7,815,000	186	Republic	A	Guatemala	Spanish, Indian languages
Guernsey (incl. Dependencies)	30	58,000	1,933	Bailiwick (U.K.)	C	St. Peter Port	English, French
†Guinea	94,926	5,500,000	58	Republic	A	Conakry	Native languages, French
†Guinea-Bissau	13,948	835,000	60	Republic	A	Bissau	Native languages, Portuguese
Guizhou	67,182	29,825,000	444	Province (China)	D	Guiyang	Chinese, Thai, Miao-Yao
†Guyana	83,000	835,000	10	Republic (Comm. of Nations)	A	Georgetown	English
†Haiti	10,714	5,185,000	484	Republic	A	Port-au-Prince	Creole, French
Hamburg	292	1,630,000	5,582	State (Federal Republic of Germany)	D	Hamburg	German
Hawaii	6,473	1,020,000	158	State (U.S.)	D	Honolulu	English, Japanese, Hawaiian
Hebei	73,359	55,150,000	752	Province (China)	D	Shijiazhuang; Tangshan	Chinese
Heilongjiang	177,607	34,000,000	191	Province (China)	D	Harbin	Chinese, Mongolian
Henan	64,093	77,440,000	1,208	Province (China)	D	Zhengzhou	Chinese
Hesse (Hessen)	8,152	5,590,000	686	State (Federal Republic of Germany)	D	Wiesbaden; Frankfurt am Main	German
Hispaniola	29,418	11,160,000	379			......; Santo Domingo	French, Spanish, Creole
Holland, see Netherlands							
†Honduras	43,277	4,155,000	96	Republic	A	Tegucigalpa	Spanish
Hong Kong	410	5,360,000	13,073	Colony (U.K.)	C	Victoria; New Kowloon	Chinese, English
Hubei	69,498	49,815,000	717	Province (China)	D	Wuhan	Chinese
Hunan	81,081	56,200,000	693	Province (China)	D	Changsha	Chinese, Miao-Yao
†Hungary	35,921	10,685,000	297	Socialist Republic	A	Budapest	Hungarian (Magyar)
†Iceland	39,769	235,000	5.9	Republic	A	Reykjavík	Icelandic
Idaho	83,566	1,000,000	12	State (U.S.)	D	Boise	English
Illinois	57,872	11,530,000	199	State (U.S.)	D	Springfield; Chicago	English
†India (incl. part of Jammu and Kashmir)	1,237,061	738,240,000	597	Federal Republic (Comm. of Nations)	A	New Delhi; Calcutta	Hindi, English, Bengali, Tegulu, Marathi, and other languages
Indiana	36,417	5,505,000	151	State (U.S.)	D	Indianapolis	English
†Indonesia	741,101	157,560,000	213	Republic	A	Jakarta	Bahasa Indonesia, Malay-Polynesian languages
Inner Mongolia (Nei Monggol)	424,772	20,200,000	48	Autonomous Region (China)	D	Hohhot; Baotou	Mongolian
Iowa	56,275	2,920,000	52	State (U.S.)	D	Des Moines	English
†Iran	636,296	43,335,000	68	Republic	A	Tehrān	Farsi, Turkish, Kurdish, Arabic
†Iraq	167,925	14,530,000	87	Republic	A	Baghdād	Arabic, Kurdish
†Ireland	27,136	3,555,000	131	Republic	A	Dublin	English, Irish Gaelic
Isle Of Man	227	67,000	295	Self-governing Territory (U.K. protection)	B	Douglas	English
†Israel	7,848	4,055,000	517	Republic	A	Jerusalem (Yerushalayim); Tel Aviv-Yafo	Hebrew, Arabic, English
Israeli Occupied Areas	2,703	1,285,000	475			......; Gaza (Ghazzah)	Hebrew, Arabic, English
†Italy	116,319	56,685,000	487	Republic	A	Rome; Milano	Italian
†Ivory Coast	123,847	8,980,000	73	Republic	A	Abidjan and Yamoussoukro; Abidjan	French, native languages
†Jamaica	4,244	2,310,000	544	Parliamentary State (Comm. of Nations)	A	Kingston	English
†Japan	145,834	119,680,000	821	Constitutional Monarchy	A	Tōkyō	Japanese
Java (incl. Madura)	51,038	97,500,000	1,910	Part of Indonesia (5 provinces)		......; Jakarta	Bahasa Indonesia, Chinese, English
Jersey	45	75,000	1,667	Bailiwick (U.K.)	C	St. Helier	English, French
Jiangsu	38,996	63,000,000	1,616	Province (China)	D	Nanjing	Chinese
Jiangxi	62,162	34,640,000	557	Province (China)	D	Nanchang	Chinese
Jilin	69,498	23,545,000	339	Province (China)	D	Changchun	Chinese, Mongolian, Korean

* Areas include inland water.
† Member of the United Nations (1983).
... None, or not applicable.
[3] Claimed by Argentina.

Country, Division, or Region English (Conventional)	Area* in sq. mi.	Estimated Population 1/1/84	Pop. per sq. mi.	Form of Government and Political Status	Capital: Largest City (unless same)	Predominant Language
†Jordan	35,135	2,420,000	69	Constitutional Monarchy .... A	'Ammān	Arabic, English
†Kampuchea	69,898	7,180,000	103	Socialist Republic .... A	Phnom Penh	Khmer (Cambodian)
Kansas	82,282	2,415,000	29	State (U.S.) .... D	Topeka; Wichita	English
Kashmir, Jammu and	86,024	9,335,000	109	In dispute (India and Pakistan) .... D	......; Srīnagar and Jammu; Srīnagar	Urdu, Kashmiri, Dogri, Balti, Ladakhi, Punjabi
Kazakh S.S.R.	1,049,155	15,445,000	15	Soviet Socialist Republic (U.S.S.R.) .... D	Alma-Ata	Turkish, Russian
Kentucky	40,414	3,740,000	93	State (U.S.) .... D	Frankfort; Louisville	English
†Kenya	224,961	18,915,000	84	Republic (Comm. of Nations) .... A	Nairobi	English, Swahili, native languages
Kerguelen Islands (Îles Kerguélen)	2,700	92	0.03	Part of French Southern and Antarctic Territory (France) C	......	French
Kirghiz S.S.R.	76,641	3,745,000	19	Soviet Socialist Republic (U.S.S.R.) .... D	Frunze	Turkish, Farsi, Russian
Kiribati	291	62,000	213	Republic (Comm. of Nations) .... A	Bairiki	Gilbertese, English
Korea, North	46,540 (4)	19,400,000	417	Socialist Republic .... A	Pyŏngyang	Korean
Korea, South	38,025 (4)	40,945,000	1,077	Republic .... A	Seoul (Sŏul)	Korean
Korea (Entire)	85,052	60,345,000	710		......; Seoul (Sŏul)	Korean
†Kuwait	6,880	1,705,000	248	Constitutional Monarchy .... A	Kuwait	Arabic, English
Labrador	112,826	30,000	0.3	Part of Newfoundland Province (Canada)	......; Labrador City	English, Eskimo
†Laos	91,429	4,035,000	44	Socialist Republic .... A	Viangchan	Lao, French
Latin America	7,916,000	392,965,000	50		......; Mexico City (Ciudad de México)	Spanish, Portuguese
Latvian S.S.R.	24,595	2,600,000	106	Soviet Socialist Republic (U.S.S.R.) .... D	Rīga	Latvian, Russian
†Lebanon	4,015	2,960,000	737	Republic .... A	Beirut (Bayrūt)	Arabic, French, English
†Lesotho	11,720	1,460,000	125	Monarchy (Comm. of Nations) .... A	Maseru	Sesotho, English
†Liaoning	57,915	37,260,000	643	Province (China) .... D	Shenyang (Mukden)	Chinese, Mongolian
†Liberia	43,000	2,260,000	53	Provisional Military Government .... A	Monrovia	Native languages, English
†Libya	679,362	3,415,000	5.0	Socialist Republic .... A	Tripoli	Arabic
Liechtenstein	62	27,000	435	Constitutional Monarchy .... A	Vaduz	German
Lithuanian S.S.R.	25,174	3,525,000	140	Soviet Socialist Republic (U.S.S.R.) .... D	Vilnius	Lithuanian, Polish, Russian
Louisiana	47,750	4,505,000	94	State (U.S.) .... D	Baton Rouge; New Orleans	English
Lower Saxony (Niedersachsen)	18,311	7,250,000	396	State (Federal Republic of Germany) .... D	Hannover	German
†Luxembourg	999	365,000	365	Constitutional Monarchy .... A	Luxembourg	Luxembourgish, French, German, English
Macao	6.0	370,000	61,667	Overseas Province (Portugal) .... D	Macao	Chinese dialects
†Madagascar	226,658	9,620,000	42	Socialist Republic .... A	Antananarivo	French, Malagasy
Madeira Islands (Arquipélago da Madeira)	307	240,000	782	Autonomous Region (Portugal) .... D	Funchal	Portuguese
Maine	33,265	1,160,000	35	State (U.S.) .... D	Augusta; Portland	English
Malagasy Republic, see Madagascar						
†Malawi	45,747	6,510,000	142	Republic (Comm. of Nations) .... A	Lilongwe; Blantyre	Chichewa, English
Malaya	50,700	12,575,000	248	Part of Malaysia (11 States)	......; Kuala Lumpur	Bahasa Malaysia, English, Chinese, Tamil
†Malaysia	128,430	15,165,000	118	Federal Constitutional Monarchy (Comm. of Nations) .... A	Kuala Lumpur	Bahasa Malaysia, English, Chinese, Tamil
†Maldives	115	160,000	1,391	Republic .... A	Male	Divehi
†Mali	478,766	7,600,000	16	Republic .... A	Bamako	French, Bambara
†Malta	122	365,000	2,992	Republic (Comm. of Nations) .... A	Valletta	English, Maltese
Manitoba	251,000	1,055,000	4.2	Province (Canada) .... D	Winnipeg	English
Maritime Provinces (excl. Newfoundland)	51,963	1,711,000	33	Part of Canada (3 provinces)	......; Halifax	English
Marshall Islands	70	33,000	471	Part of Trust Territory of the Pacific Islands (U.S. administration) .... B	Majuro (island); Jarej-Uliga-Delap	Malay-Polynesian languages, English
Martinique	425	305,000	718	Overseas Department (France) .... D	Fort-de-France	French, Creole
Maryland	10,461	4,325,000	413	State (U.S.) .... D	Annapolis; Baltimore	English
Massachusetts	8,286	5,785,000	698	State (U.S.) .... D	Boston	English
†Mauritania	397,955	1,805,000	4.5	Provisional Military Government .... A	Nouakchott	Arabic, French
†Mauritius (incl. Dependencies)	790	1,000,000	1,266	Parliamentary State (Comm. of Nations) . A	Port Louis	French, Creole, English
Mayotte	144	57,000	396	Overseas Department (France) .... D	Dzaoudzi	Swahili, French
†Mexico	761,604	75,750,000	99	Federal Republic .... A	Mexico City (Ciudad de México)	Spanish
Michigan	97,107	9,195,000	95	State (U.S.) .... D	Lansing; Detroit	English
Micronesia, Federated States of	271	78,000	288	Part of Trust Territory of the Pacific Islands (U.S. administration) .... B	Kolonia	Malay-Polynesian languages, English
Middle America	1,056,000	130,665,000	124		......; Mexico City (Ciudad de México)	Spanish, English
Midway Islands	2.0	2,300	1,150	Unincorporated Territory (U.S.) C	......	English
Minnesota	86,614	4,230,000	49	State (U.S.) .... D	St. Paul; Minneapolis	English
Mississippi	47,691	2,630,000	55	State (U.S.) .... D	Jackson	English
Missouri	69,697	5,035,000	72	State (U.S.) .... D	Jefferson City; St. Louis	English
Moldavian S.S.R.	13,012	4,075,000	313	Soviet Socialist Republic (U.S.S.R.) .... D	Kishinev	Moldavian, Russian, Ukrainian
Monaco	0.6	28,000	46,667	Constitutional Monarchy .... A	Monaco	French, Italian, English, Monegasque
†Mongolia	604,250	1,845,000	3.1	Socialist Republic .... A	Ulan Bator	Khalka Mongol
Montana	147,045	815,000	5.5	State (U.S.) .... D	Helena; Billings	English
Montserrat	40	12,000	300	Colony (U.K.) C	Plymouth	English
†Morocco (excl. Western Sahara)	172,414	23,045,000	134	Constitutional Monarchy .... A	Rabat; Casablanca	Arabic, Berber, French
†Mozambique	302,329	13,360,000	44	Socialist Republic .... A	Maputo	Portuguese, native languages
Muscat and Oman, see Oman						
Namibia (excl. Walvis Bay)	318,261	1,095,000	3.4	Under South African Administration (5) . C	Windhoek	Afrikaans, German, native languages
Nauru	8.2	8,200	1,000	Republic (Comm. of Nations) .... A	Uaboe District;	Nauruan, English
Nebraska	77,350	1,610,000	21	State (U.S.) .... D	Lincoln; Omaha	English
Nei Monggol, see Inner Mongolia						
†Nepal	56,135	15,960,000	284	Constitutional Monarchy .... A	Kathmandu	Nepali, Tibeto-Burman languages
†Netherlands	15,892	14,420,000	907	Constitutional Monarchy .... A	Amsterdam and The Hague; Amsterdam	Dutch
Netherlands Guiana, see Suriname						
Netherlands Antilles	383	275,000	718	Self-governing Territory (Netherlands protection) .... B	Willemstad	Dutch, Spanish, English, Papiamento
Nevada	110,562	955,000	8.6	State (U.S.) .... D	Carson City; Las Vegas	English
New Brunswick	28,354	715,000	25	Province (Canada) .... D	Fredericton; Saint John	English, French
New Caledonia (incl. Dependencies)	7,358	148,000	20	Overseas Territory (France) C	Nouméa	Malay-Polynesian languages, French
New England	66,674	12,580,000	189	Part of U.S. (6 states)	......; Boston	English
Newfoundland	156,185	580,000	3.7	Province (Canada) .... D	St. John's	English
Newfoundland (excl. Labrador)	43,359	550,000	13	Part of Newfoundland Province, Canada	......; St. John's	English
New Hampshire	9,278	980,000	106	State (U.S.) .... D	Concord; Manchester	English
New Hebrides, see Vanuatu						
New Jersey	7,787	7,555,000	970	State (U.S.) .... D	Trenton; Newark	English
New Mexico	121,594	1,415,000	12	State (U.S.) .... D	Santa Fe; Albuquerque	English, Spanish
New South Wales	309,433	5,435,000	• 18	State (Australia) .... D	Sydney	English
New York	52,737	17,555,000	333	State (U.S.) .... D	Albany; New York	English
†New Zealand	103,883	3,300,000	32	Parliamentary State (Comm. of Nations) .... A	Wellington; Auckland	English, Maori
†Nicaragua	50,193	3,060,000	61	Republic .... A	Managua	Spanish
†Niger	489,191	5,905,000	12	Provisional Military Government .... A	Niamey	French, Hausa, native languages
†Nigeria	356,669	84,945,000	238	Federal Republic (Comm. of Nations) ... A	Lagos	Hausa, Ibo, Yoruba, English
Ningxia Huizu	25,483	4,185,000	164	Autonomous Region (China) .... D	Yinchuan	Chinese
Niue	102	3,000	29	Self-governing Territory (New Zealand) ..... B	Alofi	Malay-Polynesian languages, English

* Areas include inland water.
† Member of the United Nations (1983).
.... None, or not applicable.
(4) The 1,262 km² or 487 sq mi of the demilitarized zone are not included in either North or South Korea.
(5) In October 1966 the United Nations terminated the South African mandate over Namibia, a decision which South Africa did not accept.

Country, Division, or Region English (Conventional)	Area* in sq. mi.	Estimated Population 1/1/84	Pop. per sq. mi.	Form of Government and Political Status		Capital: Largest City (unless same)	Predominant Language
Norfolk Island..............	14	2,300	164	External Territory (Australia)	C	Kingston	English
North America.............	9,410,000	391,100,000	42	....		......; New York	....
North Borneo, see Sabah......							
North Carolina.............	52,669	6,170,000	117	State (U.S.)	D	Raleigh; Charlotte	English
North Dakota.............	70,702	675,000	9.5	State (U.S.)	D	Bismarck; Fargo	English
Northern Ireland...........	5,452	1,560,000	286	Administrative division of United Kingdom..................	D	Belfast	English
Northern Mariana Islands......	184	19,000	103	Part of Trust Territory of the Pacific Islands (U.S. administration)	B	Saipan (island); Chalan Kanoa	Malay-Polynesian languages, English
Northern Territory, Austl.....	520,280	130,000	0.2	Territory (Australia)	D	Darwin	English, Aboriginal languages
North Rhine-Westphalia (Nordrhein-Westfalen).......	13,153	16,980,000	1,291	State (Federal Republic of Germany)......	D	Düsseldorf; Essen	German
Northwest Territories.........	1,304,903	49,000	0.04	Territory (Canada)	D	Yellowknife	English, Eskimo, Indian
†Norway (incl. Svalbard and Jan Mayen).........	149,158	4,140,000	28	Constitutional Monarchy	A	Oslo	Norwegian (Riksmal and Landsmal)
Nova Scotia..............	21,425	870,000	41	Province (Canada)	D	Halifax	English
Oceania (incl. Australia).......	3,290,000	24,000,000	7.3			......; Sydney	
Ohio...................	44,786	10,825,000	242	State (U.S.)	D	Columbus; Cleveland	English
Oklahoma...............	69,957	3,250,000	46	State (U.S.)	D	Oklahoma City	English
†Oman..................	82,030	990,000	12	Monarchy	A	Muscat; Maṭraḥ	Arabic
Ontario.................	412,582	8,875,000	22	Province (Canada)	D	Toronto	English
Oregon.................	97,076	2,715,000	28	State (U.S.)	D	Salem; Portland	English
Orkney Islands............	376	19,000	51	Part of Scotland, U.K. Orkney Island Area)	D	Kirkwall	English
Pacific Islands, Trust Territory of the	717	143,000	199	U.N. Trusteeship (Administered by U.S.)	B	Saipan (island); Jarej-Uliga-Delap	Malay-Polynesian languages, English
†Pakistan (incl. part of Jammu and Kashmir)	319,867	100,580,000	314	Federal Republic	A	Islāmābād; Karāchi	Urdu, English, Punjabi, Sindhi
Palau..................	192	13,000	68	Part of Trust Territory of the Pacific Islands (U.S. administration)	B	Koror	Malay-Polynesian languages, English
†Panama.................	29,762	2,200,000	74	Republic.....................	A	Panamá	Spanish, English
†Papua New Guinea...........	178,703	3,155,000	18	Parliamentary State (Comm. of Nations)	A	Port Moresby	Papuan and Negrito languages, English
†Paraguay	157,048	3,575,000	23	Republic.....................	A	Asunción	Spanish, Guaraní
Peking (Beijing)...........	6,487	9,735,000	1,501	Autonomous City (China)	D	Peking (Beijing)	Chinese
Pennsylvania.............	46,047	11,885,000	258	State (U.S.)	D	Harrisburg; Philadelphia	English
Persia, see Iran............							
†Peru..................	496,224	19,555,000	39	Republic.....................	A	Lima	Spanish, Quechua, Aymara
†Philippines..............	115,831	52,720,000	455	Republic.....................	A	Manila	Pilipino, English, Spanish
Pitcairn (excl. Dependencies) ...	1.8	54	30	Colony (U.K.)	C	Adamstown	English
†Poland.................	120,728	36,725,000	304	Socialist Republic	A	Warsaw (Warszawa); Katowice	Polish
†Portugal	35,516	10,230,000	288	Republic.....................	A	Lisbon (Lisboa)	Portuguese
Portuguese Guinea, see Guinea-Bissau..........							
Prairie Provinces...........	757,985	4,420,000	5.8	Part of Canada (3 provinces)		......; Winnipeg	English
Prince Edward Island.........	2,184	126,000	58	Province (Canada)	D	Charlottetown	English
Puerto Rico...............	3,515	3,365,000	957	Commonwealth (U.S. protection)........	B	San Juan	Spanish, English
†Qatar..................	4,247	270,000	64	Monarchy	A	Doha	Arabic, English
Qinghai.................	277,993	4,185,000	15	Province (China)	D	Xining	Tibetan dialects, Mongolian, Turkish, Chinese
Quebec..................	594,860	6,600,000	11	Province (Canada)	D	Québec; Montréal	French, English
Queensland..............	667,000	2,470,000	5.2	State (Australia)	D	Brisbane	English
Reunion.................	969	540,000	557	Overseas Department (France)	D	Saint-Denis	French
Rhineland-Palatinate (Rheinland-Pfalz)...............	7,663	3,625,000	473	State (Federal Republic of Germany).......	D	Mainz	German
Rhode Island.............	1,212	960,000	792	State (U.S.)	D	Providence	English
Rhodesia, see Zimbabwe.......							
Rodrigues	42	34,000	810	Part of Mauritius		......; Port Mathurin	English, French
†Romania.................	91,699	23,025,000	251	Socialist Republic	A	Bucharest (Bucureşti)	Romanian, Hungarian, German
Russian Soviet Federated Socialist Republic	6,592,846	142,705,000	22	Soviet Federated Socialist Republic (U.S.S.R.)	D	Moscow (Moskva)	Russian, Finno-Ugric languages, Farsi, Turkish, Mongolian
†Rwanda.................	10,169	5,380,000	529	Republic.....................	A	Kigali	French, English, Kinyarwanda
Saar (Saarland)............	992	1,055,000	1,064	State (Federal Republic of Germany).......	D	Saarbrücken	German
Sabah..................	29,388	1,130,000	38	State (Malaysia)	D	Kota Kinabalu	Bahasa Malaysia, Chinese, English, native languages
St. Christopher-Nevis	104	45,000	433	Parliamentary State (Comm. of Nations)	A	Basseterre	English
St. Helena (incl. Dependencies)...........	162	6,000	37	Colony (U.K.)	C	Jamestown	English
†St. Lucia................	238	120,000	504	Parliamentary State (Comm. of Nations)	A	Castries	English, French
St. Pierre and Miquelon	93	6,100	66	Overseas Department (France)		Saint-Pierre	French
†St. Vincent and the Grenadines	150	136,000	350	Parliamentary State (Comm. of Nations)	A	Kingstown	English
San Marino...............	24	22,000	917	Republic.....................	A	San Marino	Italian
†Sao Tome and Principe.......	372	89,000	239	Republic.....................	A	São Tomé	Portuguese, native languages
Sarawak.................	48,342	1,460,000	30	State (Malaysia)	D	Kuching	Bahasa Malaysia, Chinese, English, native languages
Sardinia	9,301	1,590,000	171	Part of Italy (Sardegna Autonomous Region)...................	D	Cagliari	Italian
Saskatchewan	251,700	1,000,000	4.0	Province (Canada)	D	Regina	English
†Saudi Arabia.............	830,000	10,220,000	12	Monarchy	A	Riyadh	Arabic
Scandinavia (incl. Finland and Iceland)..........	510,000	22,740,000	45		D	......; Copenhagen (København)	Swedish, Danish, Norwegian, Finnish, Icelandic
Schleswig-Holstein..........	6,070	2,605,000	429	State (Federal Republic of Germany).......	D	Kiel	German
Scotland................	30,416	5,175,000	170	Administrative division of U.K........		Edinburgh	English, Scots Gaelic
†Senegal................	75,955	6,190,000	81	Republic.....................	A	Dakar	Wolof, French, native languages
†Seychelles..............	171	65,000	380	Republic (Comm. of Nations)	A	Victoria	French, Creole, English
Shaanxi.................	76,062	30,140,000	396	Province (China)	D	Xi'an	Chinese
Shandong................	59,074	77,440,000	1,311	Province (China)	D	Jinan; Qingdao	Chinese
Shanghai................	2,239	12,455,000	5,563	Autonomous City (China)	D	Shanghai	Chinese
Shanxi..................	61,004	26,380,000	432	Province (China)	D	Taiyuan	Chinese
Shetland Islands...........	551	27,000	19	Part of Scotland, U.K. (Shetland Island Area)		Lerwick	English
Siam, see Thailand..........							
Sichuan.................	216,217	103,710,000	480	Province (China)	D	Chengdu; Chongqing	Chinese, Tibetan dialects, Miao-Yao
Sicily..................	9,926	4,880,000	492	Part of Italy (Sicilia Autonomous Region)	D	Palermo	Italian
†Sierra Leone.............	27,925	3,825,000	137	Republic (Comm. of Nations)	A	Freetown	English, Krio, native languages
†Singapore...............	224	2,540,000	11,339	Republic (Comm. of Nations)	A	Singapore	Chinese, Malay, English, Tamil
†Solomon Islands...........	11,506	260,000	23	Parliamentary State (Comm. of Nations)	A	Honiara	Malay-Polynesian languages, English
†Somalia................	246,200	7,160,000	29	Socialist Republic	A	Mogadishu (Muqdisho)	Somali, Arabic, English, Italian
†South Africa (incl. Walvis Bay).................	434,674	24,465,000	56	Republic.....................	A	Pretoria and Cape Town; Johannesburg	English, Afrikaans, native languages
South America	6,860,000	262,300,000	38			......; São Paulo	....
South Australia	380,070	1,370,000	3.6	State (Australia)	D	Adelaide	English
South Carolina	31,116	3,280,000	105	State (U.S.)	D	Columbia; Charleston	English
South Dakota	77,120	705,000	9.1	State (U.S.)	D	Pierre; Sioux Falls	English
Southern Yemen, see Yemen, People's Democratic Republic of	....	....	...	....		....	....

* Areas include inland water.
† Member of the United Nations (1983).
...None, or not applicable.

World Political Information Table (continued)

Country, Division, or Region English (Conventional)	Area° in sq. mi.	Estimated Population 1/1/84	Pop. per sq. mi.	Form of Government and Political Status		Capital: Largest City (unless same)	Predominant Language
South Georgia (incl. Dependencies)	1,580	22	0.01	Dependency of Falkland Islands (U.K.)[3]	C		English, Norwegian
South West Africa, *see* Namibia Soviet Union, *see* Union of Soviet Socialist Republics	....	....	...				....
†Spain	194,882	38,350,000	197	Constitutional Monarchy	A	Madrid	Spanish
Spanish North Africa (Sp.)[2]	12	136,000	11,333	Five Possessions (No Central Government)	C	...... ; Cueta	Spanish, Arabic, Berber
Spanish Sahara, *see* Western Sahara							
†Sri Lanka	24,962	15,510,000	621	Socialist Republic (Comm. of Nations)	A	Colombo	Sinhala, Tamil, English
†Sudan	967,500	20,500,000	21	Republic	A	Khartoum	Arabic, native languages, English
Sumatra	182,860	29,935,000	164	Part of Indonesia (7 provinces)		...... ; Medan	Bahasa Indonesia, English, Chinese
†Suriname	63,037	375,000	5.9	Republic	A	Paramaribo	Dutch, English, Sranang Tongo
Svalbard	23,958	4,200	0.2	Part of Norway		...... ; Longyearbyen	Norwegian, Russian
†Swaziland	6,704	615,000	92	Monarchy (Comm. of Nations)	A	Mbabane; Manzini	English, siSwati
†Sweden	173,780	8,350,000	48	Constitutional Monarchy	A	Stockholm	Swedish
Switzerland	15,943	6,470,000	406	Federal Republic	A	Bern; Zürich	German, French, Italian
†Syria	71,498	10,635,000	149	Socialist Republic	A	Damascus (Dimashq)	Arabic
Tadzhik S.S.R.	55,251	4,100,000	74	Soviet Socialist Republic (U.S.S.R.)	D	Dushanbe	Tadzhik, Turkish, Russian
Taiwan	13,900	18,870,000	1,358	Republic	A	Taipei	Chinese dialects
†Tanzania	364,900	20,005,000	55	Republic (Comm. of Nations)	A	Dar es Salaam	Swahili, English, native languages
Tasmania	26,383	435,000	16	State (Australia)	D	Hobart	English
Tennessee	42,143	4,765,000	113	State (U.S.)	D	Nashville; Memphis	English
Texas	266,805	15,565,000	58	State (U.S.)	D	Austin; Dallas	English, Spanish
†Thailand	198,115	51,230,000	259	Constitutional Monarchy	A	Bangkok (Krung Thep)	Thai
Tianjin	4,247	8,165,000	1,923	Autonomous City (China)	D	Tianjin (Tientsin)	Chinese, Mongolian
Tibet (Xizang)	471,044	2,095,000	4.4	Autonomous Region (China)	D	Lhasa	Tibetan dialects
†Togo	21,925	2,825,000	129	Republic	A	Lomé	Native languages, French
Tokelau	3.9	1,500	385	Island Territory (New Zealand)	C	...... ; Fakaofo	Malay-Polynesian languages, English
Tonga	270	104,000	385	Constitutional Monarchy (Comm. of Nations)	A	Nuku'alofa	Tongan, English
Transcaucasia	71,853	14,765,000	205	Part of U.S.S.R. (3 republics)		...... ; Baku	Russian, Armenian, Georgic, Turkish
Transkei[6]	15,831	2,495,000	158	Bantu Homeland (South African protection)	B	Umtata	Xhosa, Afrikaans
†Trinidad and Tobago	1,980	1,220,000	616	Republic (Comm. of Nations)	A	Port of Spain	English
Tristan da Cunha	40	300	7.5	Dependency of St. Helena (U.K.)	C	Edinburgh	English
Trucial States, *see* United Arab Emirates							
†Tunisia	63,170	6,905,000	109	Republic	A	Tunis	Arabic, French
†Turkey	300,948	47,715,000	159	Republic	A	Ankara; İstanbul	Turkish, Kurdish, Arabic
Turkey in Europe	9,175	4,495,000	490	Part of Turkey		...... ; İstanbul	Turkish
Turkmen S.S.R.	188,456	2,980,000	16	Soviet Socialist Republic (U.S.S.R.)	D	Ashkhabad	Turkish, Russian
Turks and Caicos Islands	166	8,000	48	Colony (U.K.)	C	Grand Turk	English
Tuvalu	10	7,800	780	Parliamentary State (Comm. of Nations)	A	Funafuti	English, Tuvaluan
†Uganda	91,134	14,140,000	155	Republic (Comm. of Nations)	A	Kampala	English, Swahili, Luganda, native languages
†Ukrainian S.S.R.	233,090	51,420,000	221	Soviet Socialist Republic (U.S.S.R)	D	Kiev	Ukrainian, Russian
†Union of Soviet Socialist Republics	8,600,383	273,380,000	32	Federal Socialist Republic	A	Moskow (Moskva)	Russian and other Slavic languages various Altaic and Indo-European languages
U.S.S.R. in Europe	1,920,789	177,360,000	92	Part of U.S.S.R.		...... ; Moskow (Moskva)	Russian and other Slavic languages
†United Arab Emirates	32,278	1,450,000	45	Federation of Monarchs	A	Abu Dhabi	Arabic, English, Farsi
United Arab Republic, *see* Egypt	....	....					....
†United Kingdom	94,249	56,010,000	594	Constitutional Monarchy (Comm. of Nations)	A	London	English, Gaelic
United Kingdom and Possessions	102,311	61,715,000	603			London	English
†United States	3,679,245	235,310,000	64	Federal Republic	A	Washington; New York	English
United States and Possessions	3,683,901	239,075,000	65			Washington; New York	English, Spanish
Upper Volta, *see* Burkina Faso							
†Uruguay	68,037	2,980,000	44	Republic	A	Montevideo	Spanish
Utah	84,902	1,640,000	19	State (U.S.)	D	Salt Lake City	English
Uzbek S.S.R.	172,742	16,565,000	96	Soviet Socialist Republic (U.S.S.R.)	D	Tashkent	Turkish, Sart, Russian
†Vanuatu	5,714	129,000	23	Republic (Comm. of Nations)	A	Port-Vila	Bislama, French, English
Vatican City	0.2	700	3,500	Ecclesiastical State	A	Vatican City	Italian, Latin
Venda[6]	2,774	390,000	141	Bantu Homeland (South African protection)	B	Thohoyandou; Makearela	Venda, Afrikaans
†Venezuela	352,144	15,325,000	44	Federal Republic	A	Caracas	Spanish
Vermont	9,614	530,000	55	State (U.S.)	D	Montpelier; Burlington	English
Victoria	87,884	4,100,000	47	State (Australia)	D	Melbourne	English
Vietnam	127,242	58,070,000	456	Socialist Republic	A	Hanoi; Ho Chi Minh City	Vietnamese
Virginia	40,763	5,615,000	138	State (U.S.)	D	Richmond; Norfolk	English
Virgin Islands (U.S.)	133	104,000	782	Unincorporated Territory (U.S.)	C	Charlotte Amalie	English, Spanish
Virgin Islands, British	59	13,000	220	Colony (U.K.)	C	Road Town	English
Wake Island	3.0	400	133	Unincorporated Territory (U.S.)	C		English
Wales	8,019	2,810,000	350	Administrative division of U.K.	D	Cardiff	English, Welsh
Wallis and Futuna	98	12,000	122	Overseas Territory (France)	D	Mata-Utu; Ono	French, Uvean, Futunan
Washington	68,139	4,290,000	63	State (U.S.)	D	Olympia; Seattle	English
Western Australia	975,920	1,360,000	1.4	State (Australia)	D	Perth	English
Western Sahara	102,703	150,000	1.5	Occupied by Morocco	C	El Aaiún	Arabic
†Western Samoa	1,097	160,000	146	Constitutional Monarchy (Comm. of Nations)	A	Apia	Samoan, English
West Indies	92,000	29,995,000	326			...... ; Havana	Spanish, English, French, Creole
West Virginia	24,236	1,985,000	82	State (U.S.)	D	Charleston; Huntington	English
White Russia, *see* Byelorussian S.S.R.							
Wisconsin	66,213	4,835,000	73	State (U.S.)	D	Madison; Milwaukee	English
Wyoming	97,808	535,000	5.5	State (U.S.)	D	Cheyenne	English
Xinjiang Uygur	635,910	13,710,000	22	Autonoumous Region (China)	D	Urumqi	Turkish, Mongolian, Tunguq
Xizang, *see* Tibet							
†Yemen	75,290	6,285,000	83	Republic	A	Ṣan'ā'	Arabic
†Yemen, People's Democratic Republic of	128,560	2,185,000	17	Socialist Republic	A	Aden	Arabic
†Yugoslavia	98,766	22,915,000	232	Federal Socialist Republic	A	Belgrade (Beograd)	Serbo-Croatian, Slovene, Macedonian
Yukon Territory	186,300	25,000	0.1	Territory (Canada)	D	Whitehorse	English, Eskimo, Indian
Yunnan	147,105	33,910,000	231	Province (China)	D	Kunming	Chinese, Tibetan dialects, Khmer Miao-Yao
†Zaire	905,567	31,705,000	35	Republic	A	Kinshasa (Léopoldville)	French, English, Lingala, Swahili, Kikongo, Tshiluba
†Zambia	290,586	6,435,000	22	Republic (Comm. of Nations)	A	Lusaka	English, native languages
Zanzibar	950	540,000	568	Part of Tanzania	D	Zanzibar	Swahili, English, native languages
Zhejiang	38,996	40,500,000	1,039	Province (China)	D	Hangzhou	Chinese
†Zimbabwe	150,804	8,510,000	56	Republic (Comm. of Nations)	A	Harare (Salisbury)	English, native languages
World	57,740,000	4,733,000,000	82			...... ; Tōkyō	....

° Areas include inland water.
† Member of the United Nations (1983).
.... None, or not applicable.
[2] Comprises Ceuta, Melilla, and several small islands.
[6] Bophuthatswana, Ciskei, Transkei, and Venda are not recognized by the United Nations.

World Facts and Comparisons

MOVEMENTS OF THE EARTH

The earth makes one complete revolution around the sun every 365 days, 5 hours, 48 minutes, and 46 seconds.

The earth makes one complete rotation on its axis in 23 hours and 56 minutes.

The earth revolves in its orbit around the sun at a speed of 66,700 miles per hour.

The earth rotates on its axis at an equatorial speed of more than 1,000 miles per hour.

MEASUREMENTS OF THE EARTH

Estimated age of the earth, at least 3 billion years.
Equatorial diameter of the earth, 7,926.68 miles.
Polar diameter of the earth, 7,899.99 miles.
Mean diameter of the earth, 7,918.78 miles.
Equatorial circumference of the earth, 24,902.45 miles.
Polar circumference of the earth, 24,818.60 miles.

Difference between equatorial and polar circumference of the earth, 83.85 miles.
Weight of the earth, 6,600,000,000,000,000,000,000 tons, or 6,600 billion billion tons.
Total area of the earth, 196,940,400 square miles.
Total land area of the earth (including inland water and Antarctica), 57,740,000 square miles.

THE EARTH'S INHABITANTS

Total population of the earth is estimated to be 4,733,000,000 (January 1, 1984).
Estimated population density of the earth, 82 per square mile.

THE EARTH'S SURFACE

Highest point on the earth's surface, Mount Everest, China (Tibet)–Nepal, 29,028 feet.
Lowest point on the earth's land surface, shores of the Dead Sea, Israel-Jordan, 1,299 feet below sea level.

Greatest ocean depth, the Marianas Trench, south of Guam, Pacific Ocean, 36,198 feet.

EXTREMES OF TEMPERATURE AND RAINFALL OF THE EARTH

Highest temperature ever recorded, 136.4°F. at Al 'Azīzīyah, Libya, Africa, on September 13, 1922.
Lowest temperature ever recorded, −126.9°F. at Vostok, Antarctica, on August 24, 1960.
Highest mean annual temperature, 88°F. at Lugh Ferrandi, Somalia.
Lowest mean annual temperature, −67°F. at Vostok, Antarctica.
At Cilaos, Réunion Island, in the Indian Ocean, 74 inches of rainfall was reported in a 24-hour period, March 15-16, 1952. This is believed to be the world's record for a 24-hour rainfall.
An authenticated rainfall of 366 inches in 1 month—July, 1861—was reported at Cherrapunji, India. More than 131 inches fell in a period of 7 consecutive days in June, 1931. Average annual rainfall at Cherrapunji is 450 inches.

The Continents

CONTINENT	Area (sq. mi.)	Population Estimated Jan. 1, 1984	Population per sq. mi.	Mean Elevation (feet)	Highest Elevation (Feet)	Lowest Elevation (Feet)	Highest Recorded Temperature	Lowest Recorded Temperature
North America	9,410,000	391,100,000	42	2,000	Mt. McKinley, United States (Alaska), 20,320	Death Valley, California, 282 below sea level	Death Valley, California 134°F.	Snag, Yukon, Canada, −81°F.
South America	6,860,000	262,300,000	38	1,800	Mt. Aconcagua, Argentina, 22,831	Salinas Chicas, Argentina, 138 below sea level	Rivadavia, Argentina, 120°F.	Sarmiento, Argentina, −27.4°F.
Europe	3,840,000	672,400,000	175	980	Mt. Elbrus, Soviet Union, 18,510	Caspian Sea, Soviet Union—Iran, 92 below sea level	Sevilla (Seville), Spain, 122°F.	Ust-Shchugor, Soviet Union, −67°F.
Asia	17,240,000	2,863,400,000	166	3,000	Mt. Everest, China (Tibet)-Nepal, 29,028	Dead Sea, Israel-Jordan, 1,299 below sea level	Tirat Zvi, Israel, 129.2°F.	Oymyakon, Soviet Union, −89.9°F.
Africa	11,700,000	519,800,000	44	1,900	Mt. Kilimanjaro, Tanzania, 19,340	Lac Assal, Djibouti, 509 below sea level	Al 'Azīzīyah, Libya, 139.4°F.	Ifrane, Morocco, −11.2°F.
Oceania, incl. Australia	3,290,000	24,000,000	7	. . . .	Mt. Wilhelm, Papua New Guinea, 14,793	Lake Eyre, South Australia, 52 below sea level	Cloncurry, Queensland, Australia, 127.5°F.	Charlotte Pass, New South Wales, Australia, −8°F.
Australia	2,967,909	15,535,000	5	1,000	Mt. Kosciusko, New South Wales, 7,310	Lake Eyre, South Australia, 52 below sea level	Cloncurry, Queensland, 127.5°F.	Charlotte Pass, New South Wales, −8°F.
Antarctica	5,405,000	Uninhabited	. . .	6,000	Vinson Massif, 16,864	Unknown	Esperanza (Antarctic Peninsula), 58.3°F.	Vostok, −126.9°F.
World	57,740,000	4,733,000,000	82	. . . .	Mt. Everest, China (Tibet)-Nepal, 29,028	Dead Sea, Israel-Jordan, 1,299 below sea level	Al 'Azīzīyah, Libya, 136.4°F.	Vostok, −126.9°F.

Approximate Population of the World 1650-1984*

AREA	1650	1750	1800	1850	1900	1914	1920	1939	1950	1984
North America	5,000,000	5,000,000	13,000,000	39,000,000	106,000,000	141,000,000	147,000,000	186,000,000	219,000,000	391,100,000
South America	8,000,000	7,000,000	12,000,000	20,000,000	38,000,000	55,000,000	61,000,000	90,000,000	111,000,000	262,300,000
Europe	100,000,000	140,000,000	190,000,000	265,000,000	400,000,000	470,000,000	453,000,000	526,000,000	530,000,000	672,400,000
Asia	335,000,000	476,000,000	593,000,000	754,000,000	932,000,000	1,006,000,000	1,000,000,000	1,247,000,000	1,418,000,000	2,863,400,000
Africa	100,000,000	95,000,000	90,000,000	95,000,000	118,000,000	130,000,000	140,000,000	170,000,000	199,000,000	519,800,000
Oceania, incl. Australia	2,000,000	2,000,000	2,000,000	2,000,000	6,000,000	8,000,000	9,000,000	11,000,000	13,000,000	24,000,000
Australia					4,000,000	5,000,000	6,000,000	7,000,000	8,000,000	15,535,000
World	550,000,000	725,000,000	900,000,000	1,175,000,000	1,600,000,000	1,810,000,000	1,810,000,000	2,230,000,000	2,490,000,000	4,733,000,000

*Figures prior to 1984 are rounded to the nearest million.   Figures in italics represent very rough estimates.

Largest Countries of the World in Population

	Population 1/1/84			Population 1/1/84			Population 1/1/84
1 China (excl. Taiwan)	1,046,530,000	10 Nigeria	84,945,000	17 Philippines	52,720,000
2 India (incl. part of Jammu and Kashmir)	738,240,000	11 Mexico	75,750,000	18 Thailand	51,230,000
3 Soviet Union	273,380,000	12 Federal Republic of Germany (incl. West Berlin)	61,480,000	19 Turkey	47,715,000
4 United States	235,310,000	13 Vietnam	58,070,000	20 Egypt	46,465,000
5 Indonesia	157,560,000	14 Italy	56,685,000	21 Iran	43,335,000
6 Brazil	133,100,000	15 United Kingdom	56,010,000	22 South Korea	40,945,000
7 Japan	119,680,000	16 France	54,730,000	23 Spain	38,350,000
8 Pakistan (incl. part of Jammu and Kashmir)	100,580,000			24 Burma	37,505,000
9 Bangladesh	95,600,000			25 Poland	36,725,000

Largest Countries of the World in Area

	Area (sq. mi.)		Area (sq. mi.)		Area (sq. mi.)
1 Soviet Union	8,600,383	9 Sudan	967,500	18 Mongolia	604,250
2 Canada	3,831,033	10 Algeria	919,595	19 Peru	496,224
3 United States	3,679,245	11 Zaire	905,567	20 Chad	495,755
4 China (excl. Taiwan)	3,630,747	12 Greenland	840,004	21 Niger	489,191
5 Brazil	3,265,075	13 Saudi Arabia	830,000	22 Angola	481,353
6 Australia	2,967,909	14 Mexico	761,604	23 Mali	478,766
7 India (incl. part of Jammu and Kashmir)	1,237,061	15 Indonesia	741,101	24 Ethiopia	472,434
8 Argentina	1,068,301	16 Libya	679,362	25 Colombia	439,737
		17 Iran	636,296		

Principal Mountains of the World

North America

	Height (Feet)
McKinley, △Alaska (△United States; △North America)	20,320
Logan, △Canada (△St. Elias Mts.)	19,520
Citlaltépetl (Orizaba), △Mexico	18,701
St. Elias, Alaska–Canada	18,008
Popocatépetl, Mexico	17,887
Foraker, Alaska	17,400
Ixtacihuatl, Mexico	17,343
Lucania, Yukon, Canada	17,147
Whitney, △California	14,494
Elbert, △Colorado (△Rocky Mts.)	14,433
Massive, Colorado	14,421
Harvard, Colorado	14,420
Rainier, △Washington (△Cascade Range)	14,410
Williamson, California	14,375
Blanca Pk., Colorado (△Sangre de Cristo Range)	14,345
Uncompahgre Pk., Colorado (△San Juan Mts.)	14,309
Grays Pk., Colorado (△Front Range)	14,270
Evans, Colorado	14,264
Longs Pk., Colorado	14,255
Wrangell, Alaska	14,163
Shasta, California	14,162
Pikes Peak, Colorado	14,110
Colima, Nevado de, Mexico	13,993
Tajumulco, △Guatemala (△Central America)	13,846
Gannett Pk., △Wyoming	13,804
Mauna Kea, △Hawaii (△Hawaii I.)	13,796
Grand Teton, Wyoming	13,766
Mauna Loa, Hawaii	13,680
Kings Pk., △Utah	13,528
Cloud Pk., Wyoming (△Big Horn Mts.)	13,175
Wheeler Pk., △New Mexico	13,161
Boundary Pk., △Nevada	13,143
Gunnbjörn, △Greenland	13,120
Waddington, Canada (△Coast Mts.)	13,104
Robson, Canada (△Canadian Rockies)	12,972
Granite Pk., △Montana	12,799
Borah Pk., △Idaho	12,662
Humphreys Pk., △Arizona	12,633
Chirripó Grande, △Costa Rica	12,533
Adams, Washington	12,307
San Gorgonio, California	11,502
Chiriquí, △Panama	11,411
Hood, △Oregon	11,239
Lassen Pk., California	10,457
Duarte, Pico, △Dominican Rep. (△West Indies)	10,417
Haleakala, Hawaii (△Maui)	10,023
Parícutin, Mexico	9,213
La Selle, Pic, △Haiti	8,773
Guadalupe Pk., △Texas	8,751
Olympus, Washington (△Olympic Mts.)	7,965
Monte Cristo, △El Salvador–Guatemala–Honduras	7,936
Blue Mountain Pk., △Jamaica	7,402
Harney Pk., △South Dakota (△Black Hills)	7,242
Mitchell, △North Carolina (△Appalachian Mts.)	6,684
Clingmans Dome, North Carolina–△Tennessee (△Great Smoky Mts.)	6,643
Turquino, Pico, △Cuba	6,542
Washington, △New Hampshire (△White Mts.)	6,288
Rogers, △Virginia	5,729
Marcy, △New York (△Adirondack Mts.)	5,344
Katahdin, △Maine	5,268
Kawaikini, Hawaii (△Kauai)	5,243
Spruce Knob, △West Virginia	4,862
Pelée, △Martinique	4,583
Mansfield, △Vermont (△Green Mts.)	4,393
Punta, Cerro de, △Puerto Rico	4,389
Black Mtn., △Kentucky	4,145
Kaala Pk., Hawaii (△Oahu)	4,050

South America

Aconcagua, △Argentina (△Andes Mts.; △South America)	22,831
Ojos del Salado, Argentina–△Chile	22,590
Tupungato, Argentina–Chile	22,310
Pissis, Argentina	22,241
Mercedario, Argentina	22,211
Huascarán, △Peru	22,205
Llullaillaco, Argentina–Chile	22,057
Yerupaja, Peru	21,765
Incahuasi, Argentina–Chile	21,719
Sajama, Nevado, △Bolivia	21,391
Illimani, Bolivia	21,201
Chimborazo, △Ecuador	20,561
Cotopaxi, Ecuador	19,347
Misti, Peru	19,098
Cristóbal Colón, △Colombia	19,029

Huila, Colombia (△Cordillera Central)	18,865
Bolívar (La Columna), △Venezuela	16,411
Fitz Roy, Argentina	11,073
Neblina, Pico da, △Brazil	9,888

Europe

	Height (Feet)
Elbrus, Soviet Union (△Caucasus Mts.; △Europe)	18,510
Dykh–Tau, Soviet Union	17,070
Shkhara, Soviet Union	16,594
Kazbek, Soviet Union	16,512
Blanc, Mont, △France–△Italy (△Alps)	15,771
Rosa, Monte (Dufourspitze) △Switzerland	15,200
Weisshorn, Switzerland	14,803
Matterhorn, Italy–Switzerland	14,685
Finsteraarhorn, Switzerland	14,026
Jungfrau, Switzerland	13,668
Grossglockner, △Austria	12,457
Teide, Pico de, △Spain (△Canary Is.)	12,162
Mulhacén, △Spain (continental)	11,424
Aneto, Pico de, Spain (△Pyrenees)	11,168
Etna, Italy (△Sicily)	11,122
Perdido (Perdu), Spain	11,007
Clapier, France–Italy (△Maritime Alps)	9,993
Zugspitze, Austria–△Germany, Fed. Rep. of	9,721
Coma Pedrosa, △Andorra	9,665
Musala, △Bulgaria	9,592
Corno, Italy (△Apennines)	9,560
Olympus, △Greece	9,550
Triglav, △Yugoslavia	9,393
Korab, △Albania–Yugoslavia	9,068
Cinto, France (△Corsica)	8,891
Gerlachovka, △Czechoslovakia (△Carpathian Mts.)	8,737
Moldoveanu, △Romania	8,343
Rysy, Czechoslovakia–△Poland	8,199
Glittertinden, △Norway (△Scandinavia)	8,110
Parnassós, Greece	8,061
Ídhi (Ida), Greece (△Crete)	8,058
Pico, △Portugal (△Azores Is.)	7,713
Hvannadalshnúkur, △Iceland	6,952
Kebnekaise, △Sweden	6,926
Estrela, △Portugal (continental)	6,539
Narodnaya, Soviet Union (△Ural Mts.)	6,217
Marmora, Punta la, Italy (△Sardinia)	6,017
Hekla, Iceland	4,747
Nevis, Ben, △United Kingdom (△Scotland)	4,406
Haltia, △Finland–Norway	4,357
Vesuvius, Italy	3,842
Snowdon, △Wales	3,560
Carrantuohill, △Ireland	3,414
Kékes, △Hungary	3,330
Scafell Pikes, △England	3,210

Asia

Everest, △China (△Tibet)–△Nepal (△Himalayas; △Asia; △World)	29,028
K² (Godwin Austen), China–△Pakistan (△Kashmir) (△Karakoram Range)	28,250
Känchenjunga, Nepal–△India	28,208
Makälu, China (Tibet)–Nepal	27,825
Dhaulägiri, Nepal	26,810
Nänga Parbat, Pakistan (Kashmir)	26,650
Annapurna, Nepal	26,504
Gasherbrum, Pakistan (Kashmir)	26,453
Xixabangma Mtn. (Gosainthar), China (Tibet)	26,289
Nanda Devi, India	25,645
Rakaposhi, Pakistan (Kashmir)	25,550
Kamet, India	25,447
Namcha Barwa, China (Tibet)	25,446
Guerla Mandatashan, China (Tibet)	25,354
Muztag, China (△Kunlun Mts.)	25,338
Tirich Mir, Pakistan (△Hindu Kush)	25,230
Gongga Mtn. (Minya Konka), China	24,902
Muztagata, China	24,757
Kula Kangri, △Bhutan	24,784
Communism Pk., △Soviet Union (△Pamir–Alay Mts.)	24,590
Pobedy, Peak, China–Soviet Union (△Tian Shan)	24,406
Lenin Pk., Soviet Union	23,406
Api, Nepal	23,399
Khan–Tengri, Soviet Union	22,949
Kailas, China (Tibet)	22,028
Hkakabo Razi, △Burma–China	19,296
Demavend, △Iran	18,386
Ararat, △Turkey	16,804
Jaya Pk., △Indonesia (△New Guinea)	16,503
Klyuchevskaja Sopka, Soviet Union (△Kamchatka)	15,584
Trikora Pk., Indonesia	15,584

	Height (Feet)
Belukha, Soviet Union	14,783
Tavan Bogd Uul, China–△Mongolia–Soviet Union (△Altai Mts.)	14,350
Kinabalu, △Malaysia (△Borneo)	13,432
Yu, △Taiwan (Formosa)	13,114
Türgen Mtn., Mongolia	13,051
Erciyeş, Turkey	12,848
Kerinci, Indonesia (△Sumatra)	12,467
Fuji, Japan (△Honshu)	12,388
Nabï Shu'ayb, Jabal an, △Yemen (△Arabian Peninsula)	12,336
Rinjani, Indonesia (△Lombok)	12,224
Semeru, Indonesia (△Java)	12,060
Munku–Sardyk, Mongolia–Soviet Union (△Sayan Mts.)	11,453
Rantekombola, Indonesia (△Celebes)	11,335
Sawdâ', Qurnat as, △Lebanon	10,115
Shäm, Jabal ash, △Oman	9,957
Apo, △Philippines (△Mindanao)	9,692
Pulog, Philippines (△Luzon)	9,606
Bia, △Laos	9,252
Hermon, Lebanon–△Syria	9,232
Paektu, China–△Korea	9,003
Ānai Mudi, India	8,841
Inthanon, △Thailand	8,514
Pidurutalagala, △Sri Lanka	8,281
Mayon Vol., Philippines (Luzon)	7,943
Asahi, Japan (△Hokkaido)	7,513
Tahan, Malaysia (△Malaya)	7,174
Ólimbos, △Cyprus	6,401
Kuju, Japan (△Kyushu)	5,866
Meron, △Israel	3,963
Carmel, Israel	1,791

Africa

Kilimanjaro (Kibo), △Tanzania (△Africa)	19,340
Kirinyaga (Kenya), △Kenya	17,058
Margherita Pk., △Zaire–Uganda	16,763
Ras Dashen, △Ethiopia	15,158
Meru, Tanzania	14,978
Elgon, Kenya–Uganda	14,178
Toubkal, Jbel, △Morocco (△Atlas Mts.)	13,661
Cameroun, △Cameroon	13,354
Thabana Ntlenyana, △Lesotho	11,425
Koussi, Emi, △Chad (△Tibesti Mts.)	11,204
Injasuti, △South Africa	11,182
Neiges, Piton des, △Reunion	10,069
Santa Isabel, △Equatorial Guinea (△Bioko)	9,868
Tahat, △Algeria (△Ahaggar Mts.)	9,852
Maromokotro, △Madagascar	9,436
Pico, △Cape Verde	9,281
Kâtrînâ, Jabal, △Egypt	8,668
São Tomé, Pico de, △Sao Tome	6,640

Oceania

Wilhelm, △Papua New Guinea	14,793
Giluwe, Papua New Guinea	14,330
Bangeta, Papua New Guinea	13,520
Victoria, Papua New Guinea (△Owen Stanley Range)	13,240
Cook, △New Zealand (△South Island)	12,349
Ruapehu, New Zealand (△North Island)	9,175
Balbi, △Solomon Is. (△Bougainville)	9,000
Egmont, New Zealand	8,260
Sinewit, Papua New Guinea (△Bismarck Archipelago)	8,000
Orohena, △Fr. Polynesia (△Tahiti)	7,352
Kosciusko, △Australia (△New South Wales)	7,310
Silisili, Mauga, △Western Samoa	6,095
Panié, △New Caledonia	5,341
Ossa, Australia (△Tasmania)	5,305
Bartle Frere, Australia (△Queensland)	5,287
Humboldt, New Caledonia	5,282
Woodroffe, Australia (△South Australia)	4,723
Tomaniivi (Victoria), Fiji (△Viti Levu)	4,341
Bruce, Australia (△Western Australia)	4,024

Antarctica

Vinson Massif (△Antarctica)	16,864
Kirkpatrick	14,856
Markham	14,272
Jackson	13,747
Sidley	13,717
Wade	13,396

△Highest mountain in state, country, range, or region named.

Great Oceans and Seas of the World

OCEANS AND SEAS	Area (sq. mi.)	Greatest Depth (feet)
Pacific Ocean	63,800,000	35,810
Atlantic Ocean	31,800,000	28,232
Indian Ocean	28,900,000	23,376
Arctic Ocean	5,400,000	17,881
Arabian Sea	1,492,000	19,029

OCEANS AND SEAS	Area (sq. mi.)	Greatest Depth (feet)
South China Sea	1,331,000	18,241
Caribbean Sea	1,063,000	25,197
Mediterranean Sea	967,000	16,470
Bering Sea	876,000	25,194
Bengal, Bay of	839,000	17,251

OCEANS AND SEAS	Area (sq. mi.)	Greatest Depth (feet)
Okhotsk, Sea of	610,000	11,063
Norwegian Sea	597,000	13,189
Mexico, Gulf of	596,000	14,370
Hudson Bay	475,000	850
Greenland Sea	465,000	15,899

Principal Lakes of the World

LAKES	Area (sq. mi.)
Caspian, Soviet Union–Iran (salt)	143,240
Superior, United States–Canada	31,700
Victoria, Kenya–Uganda–Tanzania	26,820
Aral, Soviet Union (salt)	24,909
Huron, United States–Canada	23,000
Michigan, United States	22,300
Tanganyika, Zaire–Tanzania–Burundi Zambia	12,350
Baikal, Soviet Union	12,160
Great Bear, Canada	12,028
Nyasa, Malawi–Tanzania–Mozambique	11,150
Great Slave, Canada	11,030
Erie, United States–Canada	9,910
Winnipeg, Canada	9,417
Ontario, United States–Canada	7,540

LAKES	Area (sq. mi.)
Balkhash, Soviet Union	△7,115
Ladoga, Soviet Union	6,835
Chad, Chad–Nigeria–Cameroon	6,300
Onega, Soviet Union	3,720
Titicaca, Peru–Bolivia	3,200
Nicaragua, Nicaragua	3,150
Mai-Ndombe, Zaire	△3,100
Athabasca, Canada	3,064
Eyre, Australia (salt)	△2,970
Reindeer, Canada	2,568
Tonle Sap, Kampuchea	△2,500
Rudolf, Kenya–Ethiopia (salt)	2,473
Issyk-Kul, Soviet Union (salt)	2,355
Torrens, Australia (salt)	△2,230
Albert, Uganda–Zaire	2,160
Vänern, Sweden	2,156

LAKES	Area (sq. mi.)
Winnipegosis, Canada	2,075
Bangweulu, Zambia	1,930
Nipigon, Canada	1,872
Nettilling, Canada	1,870
Gairdner, Australia (salt)	△1,840
Urmia, Iran (salt)	△1,815
Manitoba, Canada	1,800
Kyoga, Uganda	1,710
Khanka, China–Soviet Union	1,700
Lake of the Woods, United States–Canada	1,695
Great Salt, United States (salt)	1,680
Mweru, Zambia–Zaire	1,680
Peipus, Soviet Union	1,660
Qinghai, China (salt)	1,650
Van, Turkey (salt)	1,470

△Due to seasonal fluctuations in water level, areas of these lakes vary considerably.

Principal Rivers of the World

	Length (miles)
Nile–Kangera, Africa	4,145
Yangtze (Chang), Asia	3,915
Amazon–Ucayali, South America	3,902
Mississippi–Missouri, North America	3,740
Yellow (Huang), Asia	3,395
Ob–Irtysh, Asia	3,362
Río de la Plata–Paraná, South America	2,920
Mekong, Asia	2,796
Paraná, South America	2,796
Amur, Asia	2,744
Lena, Asia	2,734
Mackenzie, North America	2,635
Congo, Africa	2,610
Niger, Africa	2,585
Yenisey, Asia	2,543
Mississippi, North America	2,348
Missouri, North America	2,315
Ob, Asia	2,287
Volga, Europe	2,194
Murray–Darling, Australia	2,169
Madeira–Mamoré, South America	1,988
Purús, South America	1,988
Yukon, North America	1,979
Indus, Asia	1,976
Rio Grande, North America	1,885
Syrdarya, Asia	1,859
Brahmaputra, Asia	1,802
São Francisco, South America	1,802
Danube, Europe	1,777
Salween, Asia	1,770
Euphrates, Asia	1,715
Orinoco, South America	1,700
Darling, Australia	1,690
Ganges, Asia	1,678
Saskatchewan, North America	1,660
Zambezi, Africa	1,653

	Length (miles)
Tocantins, South America	1,640
Amu Darya, Asia	1,616
Murray, Australia	1,609
Kolyma, Asia	1,600
Paraguay, South America	1,584
Pilcomayo, South America	1,550
Angara, Asia	1,549
Vilyuy, Asia	1,513
Ural, Asia	1,509
Arkansas, North America	1,459
Colorado, North America (U.S.–Mexico)	1,450
Irrawaddy, Asia	1,425
Aldan, Asia	1,392
Dnepr, Europe	1,368
Araguaia, South America	1,367
Kasai, Africa	1,338
Tarim, Asia	1,328
Negro, South America	1,305
Orange, Africa	1,300
Red, North America	1,270
Kama, Europe	1,263
Juruá, South America	1,250
Columbia, North America	1,243
Xingú, South America	1,230
Ucayali, South America	1,220
Peace, North America	1,195
Tigris, Asia	1,181
Don, Europe	1,162
Songhua, Asia	1,140
Pechora, Europe	1,124
Limpopo, Africa	1,100
Tobol, Asia	1,093
Snake, North America	1,038
Uruguay, South America	1,025
Churchill, North America	1,000
Marañón, South America	1,000
Ohio, North America	981
Magdalena, South America	950
Roosevelt (River of Doubt), South America	950

	Length (miles)
Godavari, Asia	930
Xiang, Asia	930
Oka, Europe	920
Canadian, North America	906
Dnestr, Europe	876
Brazos, North America	870
Salado, South America	870
Fraser, North America	850
Parnaíba, South America	850
Colorado, North America (Texas)	840
Rhine, Europe	820
Narbada, Asia	800
Athabasca, North America	765
Donets, Europe	735
Pecos, North America	735
Green, North America	730
Elbe, Europe	720
White, North America	720
Cumberland, North America	720
James, North America	710
Ottawa, North America	696
Gambia, Africa	680
Yellowstone, North America	671
Tennessee, North America	652
Gila, North America	630
Vistula (Wisła), Europe	630
Loire, Europe	625
Tagus (Tajo) (Tejo), Europe	625
North Platte, North America	618
Albany, North America	610
Tisza (Tisa), Europe	607
Back, North America	605
Ouachita, North America	605
Cimarron, North America	600
Sava, Europe	585
Nemunas (Niemen), Europe	582
Branco, South America	580
Oder, Europe	565

Principal Islands of the World

	Area (sq. mi.)
Greenland, North America	840,004
New Guinea, Indonesia–Papua New Guinea	303,090
Borneo, Asia	258,855
Madagascar, Africa	226,658
Baffin, Canada	183,810
Sumatra, Indonesia	182,860
Great Britain, Europe	88,797
Honshū, Japan	87,805
Victoria, Canada	75,767
Ellesmere, Canada	83,896
Celebes, Indonesia	73,057
South Island, New Zealand	58,093
Java, Indonesia	51,038
North Island, New Zealand	44,297
Cuba, North America	44,218
Newfoundland, Canada	43,359
Luzon, Philippines	40,420
Iceland, Europe	39,769
Mindanao, Philippines	36,537
Ireland, Europe	32,588
Hokkaidō, Japan	30,144
Sakhalin, Soviet Union	29,498

	Area (sq. mi.)
Hispaniola, North America	29,418
Banks, Canada	27,038
Tasmania, Australia	26,383
Sri Lanka (Ceylon), Asia	24,962
Devon, Canada	21,331
Novaya Zemlya (N. part), Soviet Union	18,882
Tierra del Fuego, South America	18,600
Melville, Canada	16,274
Kyūshū, Japan	16,215
Southampton, Canada	15,913
West Spitsbergen, Norway	15,260
New Britain, Papua New Guinea	14,592
Taiwan (Formosa), Asia	13,885
Hainan, China	13,127
Timor, Indonesia	13,094
Prince of Wales, Canada	12,872
Vancouver, Canada	12,079
Sicily, Italy	9,926
Somerset, Canada	9,570
Sardinia, Italy	9,301
Shikoku, Japan	7,245
North East Land, Norway	6,350

	Area (sq. mi.)
Ceram, Indonesia	6,046
New Caledonia, Oceania	5,671
Flores, Indonesia	5,513
Samar, Philippines	5,124
Negros, Philippines	4,903
Palawan, Philippines	4,500
Panay, Philippines	4,448
Jamaica, North America	4,244
Hawaii, United States	4,021
Cape Breton, Canada	3,981
Bougainville, Papua New Guinea	3,880
Mindoro, Philippines	3,794
Kodiak, United States	3,670
Cyprus, Asia	3,572
Puerto Rico, North America	3,515
Corsica, France	3,352
Crete, Greece	3,217
New Ireland, Papua New Guinea	3,205
Leyte, Philippines	3,090
Wrangel, Soviet Union	2,819
Guadalcanal, Solomon Islands	2,500
Long Island, United States	1,401

Population of Foreign Cities and Towns, Countries and Important Political Divisions

This table includes every urban center of 50,000 or more population in the world (excluding the United States), as well as many other important or well-known cities and towns. The table also lists major political subdivisions (states, provinces, etc.) of the leading countries.

The population figures are all from recent censuses (designated C) or official estimates (designated E), except for a few cities for which only unofficial estimates are available (designated UE). The date of the census or estimate is specified for each country. Individual exceptions are dated in parentheses or with a dagger symbol (‡ or †).

For many cities, a second population figure is given accompanied by a star (★). The starred population refers to the city's entire metropolitan area, including suburbs. These metropolitan areas have been defined by Rand McNally & Company, following consistent rules to facilitate comparisons among the urban centers of various countries. Where a place is part of the metropolitan area of another city, that city's name is specified in parentheses preceded by (★). Some important places that are considered to be secondary central cities of their areas are designated by (★★) preceding the name of the metropolitan area's main city. A population marked with a triangle (▲) refers to an entire municipality, commune, or other district, which includes rural areas in addition to the urban center itself. The names of capital cities appear in CAPITALS; the largest city in each country is designated by the symbol (•).

AFGHANISTAN / Afghānestān

1973 E....18,294,000

Andkhvoy (1975 E)....46,000
Baghlān....29,000
Chārīkār....19,000
Ghaznī....24,000
Herāt (1975 E)....157,000
Jalālābād (1975 E)....58,000
•KĀBUL (1975 E)....749,000
Kandahār (Qandahār) (1975 E)....209,000
Khānābād....18,000
Kholm....22,000
Mazār-e-Sharīf (1975 E)....97,000
Meymaneh (1975 E)....29,000
Pol-e-Khomrī....25,000
Qondūz....46,000
Sheberghān....17,000

ALBANIA / Shqipëri

1976 E....2,482,000

Berat (1975 E)....30,000
Durrës....61,000
Elbasan....50,700
Fier (1975 E)....28,000
Gjirokastër (1975 E)....22,000
Kavajë (1973 E)....19,900
Korçë....50,900
Lushnje (1975 E)....21,000
Shkodër....62,500
Stalin (Kuçovë) (1971 E)....14,300
•TIRANË....192,300
Vlorë (Valona)....58,400

ALGERIA / Algérie

1974 E....16,275,000

Aïn Beïda....40,011
Aïn Benian (★Algers) (1966 C)....17,653
Aïn M'Lila (1966 C) (44,662▲)....12,632
Aïn Sefra (26,234▲)....13,100
Aïn Taya (★Algiers) (1966 C)....22,542
Aïn Témouchent....47,977
•ALGIERS (ALGER) (★1,800,000)....1,503,720
Annaba (Bône)....313,174
Arzew (1966 C)....13,080
Barika (1966 C) (40,957▲)....13,689
Batna (115,138▲)....91,500
Béchar (Colomb-Béchar)....71,081
Bejaïa (Bougie) (103,996▲)....80,000
Béni Saf (1966 C) (23,368▲)....18,507
Biskra....84,971
Blida....158,947
Bordj Bou Arreridj (85,545▲)....66,400
Bordj Ménaïel (87,736▲)....38,700
Boufarik (109,234▲)....77,700
Bouguerra (1966 C) (21,401▲)....13,373
Bouira (50,007▲)....26,800
Bou Saâda....36,433
Chelghoum el Aïd (1966 C) (27,985▲)....15,031
Cherchell (40,308▲)....17,100
Collo (40,860▲)....14,100
Constantine....350,183
Dellys (31,729▲)....13,700
Djelfa (1966 C) (30,304▲)....25,472
Djidjelli (61,545▲)....43,500
Douéra....55,993
El Affroun (67,566▲)....47,500
El Arba (1966 C) (22,857▲)....14,415
El Asnam (Orléansville) (114,327▲)....80,500
El Bayadh (33,743▲)....21,200
El Eulma (54,406▲)....41,500
El Goléa (1966 C) (16,679▲)....13,708
El Meghaier (1966 C) (23,506▲)....11,324
El Oued (1966 C) (43,547▲)....11,429
Fouka (1966 C)....10,208
Frenda (23,349▲)....16,400
Ghardaïa (85,230▲)....55,200
Ghazaouet (29,592▲)....16,600
Guelma (1966 C)....39,817
Guerrara (1966 C) (14,173▲)....12,546
Hadjout (32,334▲)....27,100
Hamma Bouziane (1966 C) (21,040▲)....11,472
Hammam Bou Hadjar (1966 C) (14,637▲)....11,219
Khemis Miliana (63,370▲)....41,400
Khenchela (49,922▲)....40,900
Koléa (48,133▲)....35,900
Ksar el Boukhari (36,986▲)....18,400
Laghouat (60,249▲)....41,900
Lakhdaria (53,780▲)....30,800
Maghnia (44,777▲)....31,000
Mascara (82,468▲)....70,600
Mecheria....23,681
Médéa (102,336▲)....70,700
Mers el Kébir (1966 C) (20,193▲)....5,624
Mila (1966 C) (33,007▲)....12,733
Miliana (46,217▲)....27,200
Mohammadia (49,730▲)....30,000
Mostaganem....101,780
M'Sila (1966 C) (36,930▲)....19,883
Oran (Ouahran)....485,139
Ouargla (69,509▲)....26,200
Oued Zenati (81,036▲)....31,900
Relizane....65,918
Rouiba (★Algiers) (87,540▲)....20,300
Saïda (59,344▲)....51,800
Sétif....157,065
Sidi bel Abbès....151,148
Sig (41,725▲)....33,900
Skikda (Philippeville)....127,968
Souk Ahras (60,551▲)....48,800
Sour el Ghozlane (67,205▲)....32,100
Tébessa....58,008
Tiaret....63,039
Tighennif (1966 C) (25,839▲)....11,834
Tizi-Ouzou (223,702▲)....108,000
Tlemcen....115,054
Touggourt (65,935▲)....34,800

AMERICAN SAMOA

1970 C....27,159

•PAGO PAGO....2,451

ANDORRA

1971 C....20,550

•ANDORRA....2,000

ANGOLA

1970 C....5,673,046

Benguela....40,996
Cabinda....21,124
Huambo (Nova Lisboa)....61,885
Lobito....59,528
•LUANDA....475,328
Lubango (Sá da Bandeira)....31,674
Malanje....31,599

ANGUILLA

1974 C....6,519

•South Hill....774
THE VALLEY....760

ANTIGUA

1970 C....65,525

•ST. JOHNS....21,814

ARGENTINA

1970 C....23,364,431

Almirante Brown (★Buenos Aires)....245,017
Avellaneda (★Buenos Aires)....337,538
Azul....36,023
Bahía Blanca (1979 E)....253,000
Balcarce....26,461
Berazategui (★Buenos Aires)....127,740
Berisso (★La Plata)....58,833
Bolívar....18,643
Bragado....23,366
•BUENOS AIRES (1979 E) (★10,300,000)....2,978,000
Campana (★Buenos Aires)....33,919
Cañada de Gómez....20,611
Caseros (Tres de Febrero) (★Buenos Aires)....313,460
Catamarca (★64,410)....57,228
Chivilcoy....37,190
Cipolletti....23,768
Comodoro Rivadavia....72,906
Concepción del Uruguay....38,967
Concordia....72,136
Córdoba (1979 E) (★1,026,000)....985,000
Corrientes (1979 E)....186,000
Cruz del Eje....23,401
Curuzú-Cuatiá....20,636
Cutral-Có....19,404
Ensenada (★La Plata)....39,154
Esquel....13,771
Esteban Echeverría (★Buenos Aires)....111,150
Florencio Varela (★Buenos Aires)....98,446
Formosa....61,071
General Pico....21,897
General Roca....29,320
General San Martín (★Buenos Aires)....360,573
General Sarmiento (★Buenos Aires)....315,457
Godoy Cruz (★Mendoza)....112,481
Goya....39,367
Gualeguay....20,401
Gualeguaychú....40,661
Guaymallén (★Mendoza)....112,081
Junín....59,020
La Banda (★Santiago del Estero)....33,032
Lanús (★Buenos Aires)....449,824
La Plata (1979 E) (★557,000)....435,000
La Rioja....46,090
Las Heras (★Mendoza)....67,789
Lomas de Zamora (★Buenos Aires)....410,806
Luján (★Buenos Aires)....38,393
Maipú....34,839
Mar del Plata (1979 E)....417,000
Mendoza (1979 E) (★677,000)....125,000
Mercedes (*San Luis Prov.*)....40,052
Mercedes (*Buenos Aires Prov.*) (★Buenos Aires)....39,760
Merlo (★Buenos Aires)....188,868
Moreno (★Buenos Aires)....114,041
Morón (★Buenos Aires)....485,983
Necochea....39,868
Neuquén....43,070
Olavarría....52,453
Paraná....127,635
Pergamino....56,078
Pilar (★Buenos Aires)....34,372
Posadas....97,514
Presidencia Roque Sáenz Peña....38,620
Punta Alta....36,805
Quilmes (★Buenos Aires)....355,265
Rafaela....43,695
Reconquista....25,333
Resistencia (1979 E)....183,000
Río Cuarto....88,852
Río Gallegos....27,833
Rosario (1979 UE) (★975,000)....810,000
Salta (1979 E)....254,000
San Carlos de Bariloche....26,799
San Fernando (★Buenos Aires)....119,565
San Francisco (★48,896)....45,023
San Isidro (★Buenos Aires)....250,008
San Juan (1979 E) (★310,000)....115,000
San Justo (★Buenos Aires)....659,193
San Lorenzo (★Rosario)....56,487
San Luis....50,771
San Martín....24,300
San Miguel de Tucumán (1979 E) (★442,000)....375,000
San Nicolás de los Arroyos....64,730
San Rafael....58,237
San Salvador de Jujuy....82,637
Santa Fe (1979 E)....282,000
Santa Rosa....33,649
Santiago del Estero (★140,000)....105,127
Tandil....65,876
Tartagal....23,696
Tigre (★Buenos Aires)....152,335
Trelew....24,214
Tres Arroyos....37,991
Ushuaia....5,373
Venado Tuerto....35,677
Vicente López (★Buenos Aires)....285,178
Villa Krause (★San Juan)....47,794
Villa María....56,087
Zárate....54,772

AUSTRALIA

1979 E....14,423,500

Adelaide (★933,300)....13,400
Albury (★54,900)....36,600
Alice Springs (1976 C)....14,149
Ashfield (★Sydney)....42,850
Auburn (★Sydney)....48,400
Ballarat (★73,200)....38,400
Bankstown (★Sydney)....159,500
Bendigo (★59,600)....33,300
Blacktown (★Sydney)....179,350
Blue Mountains (★Sydney)....51,150
Botany (★Sydney)....36,150
Box Hill (★Melbourne)....49,200
Brighton (★Melbourne)....35,000
Brisbane (★1,014,700)....702,000
Brisbane Water (★Sydney) (1976 C)....54,819
Broadmeadows (★Melbourne)....112,300
Broken Hill....28,600
Brunswick (★Melbourne)....44,800
Bundaberg (★41,900)....32,500
Burnside (★Adelaide)....37,800
Cairns (★53,000)....36,000
Camberwell (★Melbourne)....88,700
Campbelltown (★Adelaide)....42,300
Campbelltown (★Sydney)....78,000
CANBERRA (★241,500)....221,000
Canning (★Perth)....48,350
Canterbury (★Sydney)....131,900
Caulfield (★Melbourne)....74,700
Coburg (★Melbourne)....57,100
Croydon (★Melbourne)....36,400
Dandenong (★Melbourne)....54,700
Darwin (1976 C) (★46,655)....39,193
Doncaster and Templestowe (★Melbourne)....89,100
Drummoyne (★Sydney)....32,700
Dubbo....22,850
Enfield (★Adelaide)....70,200
Essendon (★Melbourne)....50,300
Fairfield (★Sydney)....120,850
Footscray (★Melbourne)....51,700
Frankston (★Melbourne)....80,300
Fremantle (★Perth)....23,500
Geelong (★141,100)....15,200
Glenorchy (★Hobart) (1980 C)....42,400
Gosnells (★Perth)....46,850
Heidelberg (★Melbourne)....67,000
Hobart (1980 E) (★170,200)....49,020
Holroyd (★Sydney)....82,600
Hurstville (★Sydney)....66,950
Ipswich (★Brisbane)....71,200
Kalgoorlie (★19,300)....9,400
Keilor (★Melbourne)....76,800
Knox (★Melbourne)....83,100
Kogarah (★Sydney)....47,850
Ku-ring-gai (★Sydney)....103,100
Lake Macquarie (★Newcastle)....140,450
Launceston (1980 E) (★86,100)....32,300
Leichhardt (★Sydney)....62,550
Lismore....31,900
Liverpool (★Sydney)....95,950
Mackay (★44,800)....21,800
Maitland (★Newcastle)....38,950
Malvern (★Melbourne)....45,900
Manly (★Sydney)....36,350
Marion (★Adelaide)....69,700
Marrickville (★Sydney)....90,150
Melbourne (★2,739,700)....65,800
Melville (★Perth)....56,900
Mitcham (★Adelaide)....59,500
Moe....16,300
Moorabbin (★Melbourne)....102,900
Mount Gambier (★20,750)....18,950
Mount Isa....26,800
Newcastle (★379,800)....139,400
Northcote (★Melbourne)....53,000
North Sydney (★Sydney)....47,900
Nunawading (★Melbourne)....95,900
Oakleigh (★Melbourne)....55,400
Orange....30,650
Parramatta (★Sydney)....134,300
Penrith (★Sydney)....94,000
Perth (★883,600)....88,850
Port Adelaide (★Adelaide)....36,400
Port Augusta (★15,650)....14,400
Port Lincoln (★11,050)....10,250
Port Pirie (★14,900)....12,150
Prahran (★Melbourne)....47,900
Preston (★Melbourne)....87,900
Queanbeyan (★Canberra)....20,100
Randwick (★Sydney)....123,750
Redcliffe (★Brisbane)....41,200
Ringwood (★Melbourne)....37,900
Rockdale (★Sydney)....86,650
Rockhampton (★54,600)....53,900
Ryde (★Sydney)....91,900
St. Kilda (★Melbourne)....52,400
Salisbury (★Adelaide)....83,800
Sandringham (★Melbourne)....32,600
Shellharbour (★Wollongong)....41,650
Shepparton (★34,100)....23,200
South Perth (★Perth)....31,400
Southport (Gold Coast) (★128,000)....102,500
South Sydney (★Sydney)....32,100
Springvale (★Melbourne)....79,000
Stirling (★Perth)....169,350
Sunshine (★Melbourne)....94,600
•Sydney (★3,193,300)....49,750
Tamworth....32,650
Tea Tree Gully (★Adelaide)....63,300
Toowoomba....72,500
Townsville (★96,100)....84,900
Unley (★Adelaide)....35,700
Wagga Wagga....38,150
Waverley (★Melbourne)....121,500
Waverley (★Sydney)....64,050
West Torrens (★Adelaide)....46,100
Whyalla (★31,150)....31,000
Willoughby (★Sydney)....52,250
Wollongong (★223,950)....172,350
Woodville (★Adelaide)....76,600
Woollahra (★Sydney)....54,500

AUSTRIA / Österreich

1971 C....7,456,745

Bruck an der Mur (★50,000)....16,359
Dornbirn....33,810
Graz (1976 E) (★275,000)....250,900
Innsbruck (1976 E) (★150,000)....120,400
Kapfenberg (★★Bruck)....26,001
Klagenfurt (1973 L)....82,512
Leoben (★48,000)....35,153
Linz (1976 E) (★290,000)....208,000
Salzburg (1976 E) (★165,000)....139,000
Sankt Pölten (1973 L)....50,144
Steyr (★54,000)....40,578
Stockerau (★Vienna) (1976 L)....12,768
Ternitz (1978 L)....16,343
Traun (★Linz)....20,843
•VIENNA (WIEN) (1979 E) (★1,925,000)....1,572,300
Villach (1973 L)....50,993
Wels (★59,000)....47,279
Wiener Neustadt (★41,000)....34,774
Wolfsberg (1974 L)....29,002

BAHAMAS

1970 C....168,812

Freeport....15,286
•NASSAU (★101,503)....3,233

BAHRAIN / Al-Bahrayn

1971 C....216,078

Al-Muḩarraq (★Manama)....37,577
•MANAMA (★145,000)....89,112

BANGLADESH

1974 C....76,398,120

Barisāl....98,127
Bhairab Bazar....43,702
Bogra....47,154
Brāhmanbāria....62,407
Chāndpur....51,668
Chittagong (★1,200,000)....497,026
Chuadanga....36,381
Comilla....86,446
•DACCA (★2,750,000)....1,563,517
Dinājpur....61,866
Doublemooring (★Chittagong)....125,453
Farīdpur....46,232
Ghorāsāl....34,321
Gopālpur....39,066
Jamālpur....60,261
Jessore (★82,817)....76,168
Jhenida....34,020
Khulna....521,543
Kishorganj....35,605
Kurigram....30,129
Kushtia....36,199
Mādārīpur....32,488
Mymensingh (★182,153)....76,036
Naogaon....34,395
Nārāyanganj (★★Dacca)....201,450
Narsingdi....39,140
Nawābganj....46,059
Noākhāli....32,490
Pābna....62,254
Pānchlāish (★Chittagong)....127,839
Pārbatipur....10,604
Rājshāhi (Rampur Boalia) (★132,909)....96,645
Rangpur....72,829
Saidpur....90,132
Sātkhira....40,507
Sherpur....35,578
Sirājganj....74,457
Sitākunda (★Chittagong)....99,929
Sylhet....59,546
Tangail....51,863
Tongi (★Dacca)....67,420

BARBADOS

1970 C....238,141

•BRIDGETOWN (★115,000)....8,789

BELGIUM / Belgique / België

1980 E....9,855,110

Provinces

Antwerpen (Anvers)....1,573,647
Brabant....2,220,699
Hainaut (Henegouwen)....1,308,931
Liège (Luik)....1,005,947
Limburg (Limbourg)....710,715
Luxembourg (Luxemburg)....222,317
Namur (Namen)....404,481
Oost-Vlaanderen; Flandre Orientale (East Flanders)....1,330,134
West-Vlaanderen; Flandre Occidentale (West Flanders)....1,078,239

Cities

Aalst (Alost) (★Brussels)....79,340
Anderlecht (★Brussels)....95,969
Antwerp (Antwerpen) (★1,105,000)....194,073
Arlon (23,218▲)....17,400
Ath (Aat) (24,171▲)....14,400
Auderghem (★Brussels)....31,174
Bastogne (11,357▲)....6,700
Berchem (★Antwerp)....46,368
Berchem-Sainte-Agathe (Sint-Agatha-Berchem) (★Brussels)....18,792
Beveren (★Antwerp) (40,510▲)....20,300
Binche....33,743
Borgerhout (★Antwerp)....44,369
Braine-l'Alleud (★Brussels)....29,116
Brasschaat (★Antwerp)....31,663
Brugge (Bruges) (★217,000)....118,243
•BRUSSELS (BRUXELLES) (BRUSSEL) (★2,400,000)....143,957
Charleroi (★495 000)....221,911
Châtelet (★Charleroi)....38,753

C Census. E Official estimate. UE Unofficial estimate.
L Population within municipal limits of year specified. • Largest city in country.

★ Population or designation of metropolitan area, including suburbs (see headnote).
▲ Population of an entire municipality, commune, or district, including rural area.
‡† Year of information specified at start of country.

Dendermonde ... 40,856
Deurne (★Antwerp) ... 78,646
Edegem (★Antwerp) ... 23,422
Eeklo ... 19,541
Ekeren (★Antwerp) ... 30,347
Etterbeek (★Brussels) ... 46,650
Eupen ... 17,072
Evere (★Brussels) ... 29,772
Forest (Vorst) (★Brussels) ... 51,314
Ganshoren (★Brussels) ... 21,593
Geel (31,450▲) ... 17,300
Genk (★★Hasselt) ... 61,512
Gent (Ghent) (★470,000) ... 241,695
Geraardsbergen (Grammont) (30,447▲) ... 14,900
Halle (Hal) (★Brussels) ... 32,124
Hamme ... 22,938
Harelbeke (★Kortrijk) ... 25,213
Hasselt (★275,000) ... 64,439
Herentals ... 23,682
Herstal (★Liège) ... 39,190
Hoboken (★Antwerp) ... 34,640
Huy ... 18,038
Ieper (Ypres) (34,446▲) ... 21,000
Ixelles (★Brussels) ... 76,545
Izegem ... 26,237
Jette (★Brussels) ... 40,361
Knokke-Heist ... 28,757
Kortrijk (Courtrai) (★200,000) ... 76,424
La Louvière (★148,000) ... 76,892
Leuven (Louvain) (★167,000) ... 85,632
Liège (Luik) (★765,000) ... 220,183
Lier (★Antwerp) ... 31,319
Lokeren ... 33,126
Maasmechelen ... 33,262
Mechelen (Malines) (★120,000) ... 77,667
Menen ... 33,972
Merksem (★Antwerp) ... 41,202
Mol (29,474▲) ... 16,600
Molenbeek St.-Jean (Sint-Jans-Molenbeek) (★Brussels) ... 70,958
Mons (Bergen) (★250,000) ... 96,784
Mortsel (★Antwerp) ... 26,834
Mouscron (Moeskroen) (★Lille, France) ... 54,553
Namur (★143,000) ... 100,712
Nivelles (21,318▲) ... 16,300
Oostende (Ostende) (★120,000) ... 70,125
Oudenaarde (Audenarde) (27,308▲) ... 13,600
Roeselare (Roulers) ... 51,752
Ronse (Renaix) ... 24,463
Saint-Gilles (Sint-Gillis) (★Brussels) ... 47,932
Schaerbeek (Schaarbeek) (★Brussels) ... 109,005
Schoten (★Antwerp) ... 31,180
Seraing (★Liège) ... 65,371
Sint-Niklaas (St.-Nicolas) ... 68,080
Sint-Truiden (St.-Trond) (36,160▲) ... 17,000
Soignies (23,344▲) ... 11,600
Spa ... 9,766
Tienen (Tirlemont) ... 32,842
Tongeren (Tongres) (29,375▲) ... 18,400
Tournai (Doornik) (69,862▲) ... 46,700
Turnhout ... 37,652
Uccle (Ukkel) (★Brussels) ... 75,861
Verviers (★103,000) ... 56,209
Veurne (Furnes) (11,212▲) ... 7,500
Vilvoorde (★Brussels) ... 33,644
Waregem ... 32,088
Waterloo (★Brussels) ... 24,536
Watermael-Boitsfort (★Brussels) ... 24,965
Wilrijk (★Antwerp) ... 43,161
Woluwe-St.-Lambert (★Brussels) ... 46,823
Woluwe-St.-Pierre (★Brussels) ... 39,166
Zottegem (25,152▲) ... 13,000

BELIZE

1972 E ... 127,200

•Belize City ... 41,500
BELMOPAN (1971 E) ... 5,000
Corozal ... 5,000
Orange Walk ... 6,100
Punta Gorda ... 2,200
San Ignacio ... 4,600
Stann Creek ... 7,400

BENIN (DAHOMEY)

1975 E ... 3,112,000

•Cotonou ... 178,000
PORTO-NOVO ... 104,000

BERMUDA

1970 C ... 52,330

•HAMILTON (★13,757) ... 2,060
St. George ... 1,604

BHUTAN / Druk-Yul

1977 E ... 1,232,000

THIMBU ... 8,982

BOLIVIA

1976 C ... 4,647,816

Cobija ... 3,636
Cochabamba ... 205,002
•LA PAZ ... 654,713
Oruro ... 124,121
Potosí ... 77,334
Santa Cruz ... 256,946
SUCRE ... 62,207
Tarija ... 39,087
Trinidad ... 27,583

BOTSWANA

1971 C ... 574,094

Francistown ... 18,613
•GABORONE (GABERONES) ... 18,799
Kanye ... 10,664
Lobatse ... 11,936
Mahalapye ... 12,056
Mochudi ... 6,945
Molepolole ... 9,448
Serowe ... 15,723

BRAZIL / Brasil

1975 E ... 107,145,200

States

Acre ... 249,100
Alagoas ... 1,786,200
Amapá (Ter.) ... 142,100
Amazonas ... 1,089,700
Bahia ... 8,438,900
Ceará ... 5,111,600
Distrito Federal (Brasília) ... 763,000
Espírito Santo ... 1,725,100
Fernando de Noronha (Ter.) (1970 C) ... 1,239
Goiás ... 3,558,100
Maranhão ... 3,330,000
Mato Grosso (1978 L) ... 753,700
Mato Grosso do Sul (1978 L) ... 1,253,200
Minas Gerais ... 12,550,600
Pará ... 2,544,300
Paraíba ... 2,675,100
Paraná ... 8,449,200
Pernambuco ... ‡5,853,400
Piauí ... 1,988,200
Rio de Janeiro ... 10,400,200
Rio Grande do Norte ... 1,855,700
Rio Grande do Sul ... 7,457,600
Rondônia (Ter.) ... 141,300
Roraima (Ter.) ... 48,200
Santa Catarina ... 3,351,400
São Paulo ... 20,636,900
Sergipe ... 992,400

‡Includes 1975 estimated population for Fernando de Noronha

Cities (1970 C or †1975 E)

Alagoinhas ... 53,891
Alegrete ... 45,522
Alvorada ... 39,485
Americana ... 62,387
Anápolis ... 89,405
Andradina ... 43,465
Anil ... 37,719
Apucarana ... 41,800
Aracaju ... 179,512
Araçatuba ... 85,660
Araguari ... 48,702
Arapiraca ... 43,875
Arapongas ... 36,628
Araraquara ... 82,607
Araras ... 40,945
Araxá ... 31,498
Arcoverde ... 33,308
Assis ... 45,531
Bagé ... 57,036
Barbacena ... 57,766
Barra do Piraí ... 42,713
Barra Mansa (★★Volta Redonda) ... 75,006
Barretos ... 53,050
Bauru ... 120,178
Bayeux (★João Pessoa) ... 34,681
Belém (★660,000) ... 565,097
Belford Roxo (★Rio de Janeiro) ... 173,427
Belo Horizonte (★1,945,000) ... †1,557,464
Blumenau ... 85,942
Boa Vista (*Roraima Ter.*) ... 16,720
Boa Vista (*Santa Catarina State*) ... 33,503
Botucatu ... 42,252
Bragança Paulista ... 39,573
BRASÍLIA (1975 UE) (★750,000) ... 350,000
Brusque ... 32,427
Cabedelo (★João Pessoa) ... 12,811
Cachoeira do Sul ... 50,001
Cachoeiro de Itapemirim ... 58,968
Camarajibe (★Recife) ... 41,216
Campina Grande ... 163,206
Campinas ... 328,629
Campo Grande ... 130,792
Campos ... 153,310
Campos Elyseos (★Rio de Janeiro) ... 104,636
Canoas (★Porto Alegre) ... 148,798
Carapicuíba (★São Paulo) ... 54,907
Caruaru ... 101,006
Cascavel ... 33,809
Cataguases ... 32,515
Catanduva ... 48,446
Cavaleiro (★Recife) ... 58,811
Caxias ... 31,089
Caxias do Sul ... 107,487
Coelho da Rocha (★Rio de Janeiro) ... 100,781
Colatina ... 46,012
Conselheiro Lafaiete ... 44,894
Corumbá ... 48,607
Crato ... 36,836
Criciúma ... 50,430
Cruz Alta ... 43,568
Cruzeiro ... 42,366
Cubatão (★Santos) ... 37,255
Cuiabá ... 83,621
Curitiba (★680,000) ... 483,038
Curvelo ... 30,225
Diadema (★São Paulo) ... 68,552
Divinópolis ... 69,872
Duque de Caxias (★Rio de Janeiro) ... 256,582
Erechim ... 32,426
Feira de Santana ... 127,105
Florianópolis ... 115,665
Fortaleza (★1,175,000) ... †1,109,837
Franca ... 86,852
Garanhuns ... 49,579
Goiânia ... 362,152
Governador Valadares ... 125,174
Guaratinguetá ... 55,069
Guarujá (★Santos) ... 30,741
Guarulhos (★São Paulo) ... 221,639
Ijuí ... 31,879
Ilhéus ... 58,529
Imperatriz ... 34,709
Inhomirim (★Rio de Janeiro) ... 40,322
Ipatinga ... 35,808
Ipiíba (★Rio de Janeiro) ... 55,486
Itabira ... 40,143
Itabuna ... 89,928
Itajaí ... 54,135
Itajubá ... 42,485
Itapetinga ... 30,578
Itapetininga ... 42,331
Itaquari (★Vitória) ... 64,559
Itaúna ... 32,731
Itu ... 35,907
Ituiutaba ... 46,784
Jaboatão (★Recife) ... 52,537
Jacareí ... 48,684
Jaú ... 40,989
Jequié ... 62,341
João Monlevade ... 38,689
João Pessoa (★310,000) ... 197,398
Joinvile ... 77,760
Juàzeiro ... 36,273
Juàzeiro do Norte ... 79,796
Juiz de Fora ... 218,832
Jundiaí ... 145,785
Lajes ... 82,325
Lavras ... 35,489
Limeira ... 77,243
Limoeiro ... 30,726
Lins ... 38,080
Londrina ... 156,675
Lorena ... 39,653
Macapá ... 51,567
Maceió ... 242,860
Manaus ... 284,118
Marília ... 73,165
Maringá ... 51,620
Mauá (★São Paulo) ... 101,569
Mesquita (★Rio de Janeiro) ... 93,926
Mogi das Cruzes (★São Paulo) ... 90,330
Monjolo (★Rio de Janeiro) ... 46,793
Montes Claros ... 81,572
Mossoró ... 77,251
Muriaé ... 34,118
Muribeca dos Guararapes (★Recife) ... 74,963
Nanuque ... 34,714
Natal ... 250,787
Neves (★Rio de Janeiro) ... 112,912
Nilópolis (★Rio de Janeiro) ... 86,720
Niterói (★Rio de Janeiro) ... †376,033
Nova Friburgo ... 65,732
Nova Iguaçu (★Rio de Janeiro) ... 331,457
Nôvo Hamburgo (★Porto Alegre) ... 81,248
Olinda (★Recife) ... 187,553
Olinda (★Rio de Janeiro) ... 41,378
Osasco (★São Paulo) ... 283,303
Ourinhos ... 40,733
Paranaguá ... 51,510
Parnaíba ... 57,031
Parque Industrial (★Belo Horizonte) ... 80,572
Passo Fundo ... 69,135
Passos ... 39,184
Patos ... 39,850
Patos de Minas ... 42,215
Paulo Afonso ... 38,494
Pelotas ... 150,278
Petrolina ... 37,801
Petrópolis (★Rio de Janeiro) ... 116,080
Pinheirinho (★Curitiba) ... 50,302
Piracicaba ... 125,490
Poços de Caldas ... 51,844
Ponta Grossa ... 92,344
Porto Alegre (★1,760,000) ... †1,043,964
Porto Velho ... 41,146
Presidente Prudente ... 91,188
Queimados (★Rio de Janeiro) ... 62,560
Recife (★2,100,000) ... †1,249,821
Ribeirão Prêto ... 190,897
Rio Branco ... 34,531
Rio Claro ... 69,240
Rio de Janeiro (★8,235,000) ... †4,857,716
Rio Grande ... 98,863
Salvador (★1,270,000) ... †1,237,373
Santa Maria ... 120,667
Santana do Livramento ... 48,448
Santarém ... 51,123
Santo André (★São Paulo) ... 415,025
Santo Ângelo ... 36,020
Santos (★610,000) ... 341,317
São Bernardo do Campo (★São Paulo) ... 187,368
São Caetano do Sul (★São Paulo) ... 150,171
São Carlos ... 74,835
São Gonçalo (★Rio de Janeiro) ... 161,392
São João del Rei ... 45,019
São João de Meriti (★Rio de Janeiro) ... 163,934
São José do Rio Prêto ... 108,319
São José dos Campos ... 130,118
São Leopoldo (★Porto Alegre) ... 62,861
São Luís ... 167,529
São Mateus (★Rio de Janeiro) ... 38,393
•São Paulo (★9,900,000) ... †7,198,608
São Vicente (★Santos) ... 116,075
Sapucaia do Sul (★Porto Alegre) ... 41,154
Sete Lagoas ... 61,063
Sete Pontes (★Rio de Janeiro) ... 53,766
Sobral ... 51,864
Sorocaba ... 165,990
Taboão da Serra (★São Paulo) ... 40,959
Taubaté ... 98,933
Teófilo Otoni ... 64,568
Teresina ... 181,071
Teresópolis ... 53,462
Três Lagoas ... 40,157
Tubarão ... 51,121
Uberaba ... 108,576
Uberlândia ... 110,463
Uruguaiana ... 60,667
Varginha ... 36,447
Vicente de Carvalho (★Santos) ... 59,767
Vila Velha (Espírito Santo) (★Vitória) ... 43,177
Vitória (★345,000) ... 121,978
Vitória da Conquista ... 82,477
Vitória de Santo Antão ... 41,130
Volta Redonda (★205,000) ... 120,645

BRITISH VIRGIN ISLANDS

See Virgin Islands, British

BRUNEI

1971 C ... 136,256

•BANDAR SERI BEGAWAN (BRUNEI) (★37,000) ... 17,410
Seria ... 20,824

BULGARIA / Bâlgarija

1979 E ... 8,846,417

Asenovgrad (1969 E) ... 38,500
Blagoevgrad (Gorna Dzhumaya) ... 57,457
Burgas ... 165,994
Dimitrovgrad (1969 E) ... 44,200
Gabrovo ... 78,092
Gorna Oryakhovitsa (1969 E) ... 28,300
Karlovo (Levskigrad) (1969 E) ... 22,900
Karnobat (Polyanovgrad) (1969 E) ... 20,500
Kazanlŭk ... 56,483
Khaskovo ... 82,636
Kŭrdzhali ... 52,487
Kyustendil ... 52,118
Lom (1969 E) ... 29,100
Lovech (1969 E) ... 40,000
Mikhaylovgrad (1969 E) ... 34,200
Nova Zagora (1969 E) ... 21,000
Panagyurishte (1969 E) ... 21,800
Pazardzhik ... 71,933
Pernik (Dimitrovo) ... 91,428
Petrich (1969 E) ... 21,900
Pleven ... 122,916
Plovdiv ... 342,000
Razgrad (1969 E) ... 35,600
Ruse ... 170,594
Samokov (1969 E) ... 23,800
Sevlievo (1969 E) ... 21,900
Shumen (Kolarovgrad) ... 92,157
Silistra ... 53,085
Sliven ... 96,090
Smolyan (1969 E) ... 20,300
•SOFIA (SOFIYA) (★1,133,733) ... 1,047,920
Stanke Dimitrov (1969 E) ... 37,800
Stara Zagora ... 133,201
Svishtov (1969 E) ... 22,900
Tolbukhin (Dobrich) ... 94,132
Tŭrgovishte (Eski Dzhumaya) (1969 E) ... 31,100
Varna ... 286,382
Veliko Tŭrnovo (Tŭrnovo) ... 62,565
Vidin ... 58,213
Vratsa ... 64,697
Yambol ... 81,477

BURKINA FASO see Upper Volta

BURMA / Myanma

1977 E ... 31,512,000

Bassein ... 138,000
Henzada (1970 E) ... 85,000
Insein (★Rangoon) (1973 C) ... 143,625
Kanbe (★Rangoon) (1973 C) ... 253,600
Mandalay ... 458,000
Meiktila (1953 C) ... 25,180
Mergui (1953 C) ... 33,697
Monywa (1953 C) ... 26,172
Moulmein ... 188,000
Myaungmya (1953 C) ... 24,532
Myingyan (1970 E) ... 65,000
Pakokku (1953 C) ... 30,943
Pegu ... 135,000
Prome (Pyè) (1970 E) ... 65,000
•RANGOON (★3,000,000) ... 2,276,000
Sittwe (Akyab) (1970 E) ... 82,000
Tavoy (1970 E) ... 53,000
Thaton (1953 C) ... 38,047
Thingangyun (★Rangoon) (1973 C) ... 141,210
Toungoo (1953 C) ... 31,589

BURUNDI

1976 E ... 3,864,000

•BUJUMBURA ... 157,000
Gitega (1970 E) ... 15,000
Muyinga (1970 E) ... 19,000

CAMBODIA

See Kampuchea

CAMEROON / Cameroun

1976 C ... 7,663,246

Bafoussam ... 62,239
Bamenda ... 48,111
•Douala ... 458,246
Foumban ... 33,944
Garoua ... 63,900
Kumba ... 44,175
Maroua ... 67,187
Ngaoundere ... 38,992
Nkongsamba ... 71,298
Victoria ... 27,016
YAOUNDÉ ... 313,706

CANADA

1976 C ... 22,992,604

CANADA/ALBERTA ... 1,838,037

Banff ... 3,410
Blairmore (★7,292) ... 2,321
Brooks ... 6,339
Calgary ... 469,917
Camrose ... 10,104
Cardston ... 3,043
Claresholm ... 3,276
Coaldale ... 3,654
Drayton Valley ... 4,303
Drumheller ... 6,154
Edmonton (★554,228) ... 461,361
Edson ... 4,038
Fort MacLeod ... 3,067
Fort McMurray ... 15,424
Fort Saskatchewan (★Edmonton) ... 8,304
Grand Cache ... 4,116
Grande Prairie ... 17,626
High River ... 3,598
Hinton ... 6,731
Jasper ... 3,404
Lacombe ... 3,888
Leduc ... 8,576
Lethbridge ... 46,752
Lloydminster (*Alta. and Sask.*) ... 10,311
Medicine Hat (★36,326) ... 32,811
Olds ... 3,658
Peace River ... 4,840
Pincher Creek ... 3,448
Ponoka ... 4,636
Redcliff (★Medicine Hat) ... 3,006
Red Deer ... 32,184
Rocky Mountain House ... 3,432
St. Albert (★Edmonton) ... 24,129
St. Paul ... 4,337
Sherwood Park (★Edmonton) ... 26,534
Slave Lake ... 3,561
Spruce Grove ... 6,907
Stettler ... 4,182
Taber ... 5,296
Vegreville ... 4,158
Wainwright ... 3,890
Westlock ... 3,721
Wetaskiwin ... 6,754
Whitecourt ... 3,878

CANADA/BRITISH COLUMBIA ... 2,466,608

Burnaby (★Vancouver) ... 131,599
Campbell River ... 11,781
Castlegar ... 6,255
Chemainus ... 2,129
Chilliwack (★37,525) ... 8,634
Clear Brook ... 4,849
Comox (★Courtenay) ... 5,359
Courtenay (★19,012) ... 7,733
Cranbrook ... 13,510
Creston ... 3,552
Dawson Creek ... 10,528
Duncan (★20,410) ... 4,106
Esquimalt (★Victoria) ... 15,053
Fernie ... 4,608
Fort Nelson ... 2,916
Fort St. John ... 8,947
Kamloops ... 58,311
Kelowna ... 51,955
Kimberley ... 7,111
Kitimat ... 11,791
Ladysmith ... 4,004
Langley (★Vancouver) ... 10,123
MacKenzie ... 5,266
Merritt ... 5,680
Mission City ... 8,278
Nanaimo ... 40,336
Nelson ... 9,235
New Westminster (★Vancouver) ... 38,393
North Vancouver (★Vancouver) ... 31,934
Oak Bay (★Victoria) ... 17,658
Penticton ... 21,344
Port Alberni (★26,254) ... 19,585
Port Coquitlam (★Vancouver) ... 23,926
Port Moody (★Vancouver) ... 11,649
Powell River ... 13,694
Prince George ... 59,929
Prince Rupert ... 14,754
Quesnel ... 7,637
Richmond (★Vancouver) ... 80,034
Sidney (★Victoria) ... 6,732
Smithers ... 3,783
Summerland ... 6,724
Terrace (★15,000) ... 10,251
Trail (★15,649) ... 9,976
Vancouver (★1,166,348) ... 410,188
Vernon (★22,541) ... 17,546
Victoria (★218,250) ... 62,551
West Vancouver (★Vancouver) ... 37,144
White Rock (★Vancouver) ... 12,497
Williams Lake (★15,966) ... 6,199

CANADA/MANITOBA ... 1,021,506

Brandon ... 34,901
Churchill ... 1,699
Dauphin ... 9,109
Flin Flon (*Man. and Sask.*) (★10,306) ... 8,560
Morden ... 3,886
Neepawa ... 3,508
Portage-la-Prairie ... 12,555
Selkirk ... 9,862
Steinbach ... 5,979
Swan River ... 3,742
The Pas ... 6,602
Thompson ... 17,291
Winkler ... 3,749
Winnipeg (★578,217) ... 560,874

C Census. E Official estimate. UE Unofficial estimate.
L Population within municipal limits of year specified. • Largest city in country.

★ Population or designation of metropolitan area, including suburbs (see headnote).
▲ Population of an entire municipality, commune, or district, including rural area.
‡† Year of information specified at start of country.

CANADA/ NEW BRUNSWICK ... 677,250

Bathurst (★19,500) ... 16,301
Beresford (★Bathurst) ... 3,199
Campbellton (★11,144) ... 9,282
Caraquet (★5,678) ... 3,950
Chatham (★★Newcastle) ... 7,601
Dalhousie ... 5,640
Dieppe (★Moncton) ... 7,460
Edmundston (★15,851) ... 12,710
Fairvale (★Saint John) ... 3,258
Fredericton ... 45,248
Grand Falls ... 6,223
Minto ... 3,714
Moncton (★77,571) ... 55,934
Newcastle (★18,419) ... 6,423
Oromocto ... 10,276
Quispamsis (★Saint John) ... 4,968
Riverview (★Moncton) ... 14,177
Sackville ... 5,755
St. Basile (★Edmundston) ... 3,072
Saint John (★112,974) ... 85,956
St. Stephen ... 5,264
Shediac ... 4,216
Sussex ... 3,938
Woodstock ... 4,869

CANADA/ NEWFOUNDLAND ... 557,725

Bay Roberts (★5,640) ... 4,072
Bishop's Falls ... 4,504
Bonavista ... 4,299
Botwood ... 4,554
Carbonear (★11,326) ... 5,026
Channel-Port-aux-Basques ... 6,187
Conception Bay South (St. John's) ... 9,743
Corner Brook ... 25,198
Deer Lake ... 4,546
Gander ... 9,301
Grand Bank ... 3,802
Grand Falls (★15,078) ... 8,729
Happy Valley ... 8,075
Labrador City (★15,781) ... 12,012
Lewisporte ... 3,782
Marystown ... 5,915
Mount Pearl (★St. John's) ... 10,193
St. John's (★143,390) ... 86,576
Springdale ... 3,513
Stephenville ... 10,284
Wabana ... 4,824
Wabush (★Labrador City) ... 3,769
Windsor (★Grand Falls) ... 6,349

CANADA/ NORTHWEST TERRITORIES ... 42,609

Fort Smith ... 2,288
Frobisher Bay ... 2,320
Hay River ... 3,268
Inuvik ... 3,116
Pine Point ... 1,915
Yellowknife ... 8,256

CANADA/NOVA SCOTIA ... 828,571

Amherst ... 10,263
Antigonish ... 5,442
Bible Hill (★Truro) ... 4,266
Bridgewater ... 6,010
Dartmouth (★Halifax) ... 65,341
Glace Bay (★★Sydney) ... 21,836
Halifax (★267,991) ... 117,882
Kentville (★12,973) ... 5,056
Liverpool ... 3,336
Louisbourg ... 1,519
New Glasgow (★23,513) ... 10,672
New Waterford (★Sydney) ... 9,223
North Sydney (★★Sydney Mines) ... 8,319
Pictou ... 4,588
Port Hawkesbury ... 4,008
Sackville ... 14,590
Springhill ... 5,220
Stellarton (★New Glasgow) ... 5,366
Sydney (★88,614) ... 30,645
Sydney Mines (★35,455) ... 8,965
Truro (★27,551) ... 12,840
Westville (★New Glasgow) ... 4,251
Windsor ... 3,702
Yarmouth ... 7,801

CANADA/ONTARIO ... 8,264,465

Ajax (★Toronto) ... 20,774
Amherstburg ... 5,566
Amherstview ... 5,295
Ancaster (★Hamilton) ... 14,255
Arnprior (★10,662) ... 6,111
Atikokan ... 5,668
Aurora (★Toronto) ... 14,249
Aylmer West ... 5,125
Barrie (★49,228) ... 34,389
Belleville ... 35,311
Blackburn Hamlet (★Ottawa) ... 8,290
Bracebridge ... 8,428
Bradford ... 5,080
Brampton (★Toronto) ... 103,459
Brantford (★82,800) ... 66,950
Brockville (★26,883) ... 19,903
Burlington (★Hamilton) ... 104,314
Caledon (★Toronto) ... 22,434
Cambridge (Galt) (★★Kitchener) ... 72,383
Capreol ... 4,089
Carleton Place ... 5,256
Chatham ... 38,685
Cobourg (★20,256) ... 11,421
Cochrane ... 4,974
Collingwood ... 11,114
Collins Bay (★Kingston) ... 6,897
Cornwall ... 46,121
Deep River ... 5,565
Delhi ... 3,929
Dryden ... 6,799
Dundas (★Hamilton) ... 19,179
Dunnville ... 11,642
East York (★Toronto) ... 106,950
Elliot Lake ... 8,849
Elmira ... 7,034
Espanola ... 5,926
Essex (★Windsor) ... 5,577
Etobicoke (★Toronto) ... 297,109
Exeter ... 3,494
Fergus (★11,727) ... 6,001
Fort Erie ... 24,031
Fort Frances ... 9,325
Gananoque ... 5,103
Goderich ... 7,385
Gravenhurst ... 7,986
Grimsby (★Hamilton) ... 15,567
Guelph (★70,388) ... 67,538
Haileybury (★12,596) ... 4,939
Haldimand ... 16,375
Halton Hills ... 34,477
Hamilton (★529,371) ... 312,003
Hanover ... 5,691
Hawkesbury (★11,306) ... 9,789
Hearst ... 5,195
Huntsville ... 11,123
Ingersoll ... 8,198
Iroquois Falls ... 6,887
Kanata (★Ottawa) ... 6,304
Kapuskasing ... 12,676
Kenora (★12,519) ... 10,565
Kincardine ... 4,182
Kingston (★90,741) ... 56,032
Kingsville (★11,836) ... 4,692
Kirkland Lake ... 13,567
Kitchener (★272,158) ... 131,870
Lambeth (★London) ... 2,876
Leamington ... 11,169
Lincoln ... 14,460
Lindsay ... 13,062
Listowel ... 5,126
London (★270,383) ... 240,392
Manitouwadge Lake ... 3,507
Marathon ... 2,258
Markham (★Toronto) ... 56,206
Meaford ... 4,319
Midland (★26,239) ... 11,568
Milton ... 20,756
Mississauga (★Toronto) ... 250,017
Mount Forest ... 3,376
Nanticoke ... 19,489
Napanee ... 4,844
Newcastle ... 31,928
New Hamburg ... 3,628
New Liskeard (★Haileybury) ... 5,601
Newmarket (★Toronto) ... 24,795
Niagara Falls (★★St. Catharines) ... 69,423
Niagara-on-the-Lake (★St. Catharines) ... 12,485
Nickel Centre (★Sudbury) ... 13,157
North Bay (★53,961) ... 51,639
North York (★Toronto) ... 558,398
Oakville (★Toronto) ... 68,950
Onaping Falls ... 6,776
Orangeville ... 12,021
Orillia ... 24,412
Oshawa (★135,196) ... 107,023
OTTAWA (★693,288) ... 304,462
Owen Sound ... 19,525
Paris (★Brantford) ... 6,713
Parry Sound ... 5,501
Pelham (★St. Catharines) ... 10,071
Pembroke (★18,468) ... 14,927
Penetanguishene (★Midland) ... 5,460
Perth ... 5,675
Petawawa (★14,326) ... 5,815
Peterborough (★65,293) ... 59,683
Petrolia ... 4,393
Pickering (★Toronto) ... 27,879
Picton ... 4,629
Port Colborne (★St. Catharines) ... 20,536
Port Elgin (★9,481) ... 5,069
Port Hope ... 9,788
Prescott ... 4,975
Rayside-Balfour (★Sudbury) ... 16,035
Renfrew ... 8,617
Richmond Hill (★Toronto) ... 34,716
St. Catharines (★301,921) ... 123,351
St. Marys ... 4,843
St. Thomas ... 27,206
Sarnia (★81,342) ... 55,576
Sault Ste. Marie (★81,992) ... 81,048
Scarborough (★Toronto) ... 387,149
Simcoe ... 14,189
Smiths Falls (★13,327) ... 9,279
Stoney Creek (★Hamilton) ... 30,294
Stratford ... 25,657
Strathroy ... 7,769
Sturgeon Falls ... 6,400
Sudbury (★157,030) ... 97,604
Tecumseh (★Windsor) ... 5,326
Thorold (★St. Catharines) ... 14,944
Thunder Bay (★119,253) ... 111,476
Tilbury ... 4,248
Tillsonburg ... 9,404
Timmins ... 44,747
•Toronto (★2,803,101) ... 633,318
Trenton (★32,634) ... 15,465
Valley East (★Sudbury) ... 19,591
Vanier (Eastview) (★Ottawa) ... 19,812
Vaughan (Woodbridge) (★Toronto) ... 17,782
Walden (★Sudbury) ... 10,453
Walkerton ... 4,626
Wallaceburg ... 11,132
Waterloo (★Kitchener) ... 46,623
Wawa (Jamestown) ... 4,272
Welland (★★St. Catharines) ... 45,047
Whitchurch Stouffville (★Toronto) ... 12,884
Whitby (★Oshawa) ... 28,173
Windsor (★247,582) ... 196,526
Woodstock ... 26,779
York (★Toronto) ... 141,367

CANADA/PRINCE EDWARD ISLAND ... 118,229

Charlottetown (★24,837) ... 17,063
Kensington ... 1,150
Montague ... 1,827
Parkdale (★Charlottetown) ... 2,172
St. Eleanors (★Summerside) ... 2,495
Sherwood (★Charlottetown) ... 5,602
Souris ... 1,447
Summerside (★14,145) ... 8,592

CANADA/QUEBEC ... 6,234,445

Acton Vale ... 4,326
Alma ... 25,638
Amos ... 9,213
Amqui ... 3,949
Ancienne-Lorette (Notre-Dame-de-Lorette) (★Québec) ... 11,694
Anjou (★Montréal) ... 36,596
Arthabaska (★Victoriaville) ... 5,907
Asbestos (★14,395) ... 9,075
Aylmer East (★Ottawa) ... 25,714
Baie-Comeau (★26,635) ... 11,911
Baie-d'Urfé (★Montréal) ... 3,955
Baie-St. Paul ... 4,062
Beaconsfield (★Montréal) ... 20,417
Beauceville ... 4,276
Beauharnois (★Montréal) ... 7,665
Beauport (★Québec) ... 55,339
Beaupré (★7,490) ... 2,821
Bécancour ... 9,043
Beloeil (★Montréal) ... 15,913
Berthierville ... 4,249
Black Lake (★Thetford Mines) ... 4,051
Blainville (★Montréal) ... 12,517
Boisbriand (★Montréal) ... 10,132
Bois-des-Filion (★Montréal) ... 4,346
Boucherville (★Montréal) ... 25,530
Bromptonville ... 2,992
Brossard (★Montréal) ... 37,641
Brownsburg (★Lachute) ... 3,114
Buckingham ... 14,328
Cabano ... 3,193
Candiac (★Montréal) ... 7,166
Cap-aux-Meules (★6,847) ... 1,305
Cap-Chat ... 3,617
Cap-de-la-Madeleine (★Trois-Rivières) ... 32,126
Carignan (★Montréal) ... 3,585
Chambly (★Montréal) ... 11,815
Chandler ... 4,011
Chapais ... 3,147
Charlemagne (★Montréal) ... 4,025
Charlesbourg (★Québec) ... 63,147
Charny (★Québec) ... 6,461
Châteauguay (★Montréal) ... 36,329
Château-Richer (★Québec) ... 3,075
Chibougamau ... 10,536
Chicoutimi (★128,643) ... 57,737
Clermont ... 3,518
Coaticook ... 6,392
Côte-St.-Luc (★Montréal) ... 25,721
Cowansville ... 11,902
Deux-Montagnes (★Montréal) ... 8,957
Dolbeau (★13,924) ... 8,451
Dollard-des-Ormeaux (★Montréal) ... 36,837
Donnacona (★7,876) ... 5,800
Dorion-Vaudreuil (Dorion) (★Montréal) ... 5,843
Dorval (★Montréal) ... 19,131
Drummondville (★45,018) ... 29,286
Drummondville-Sud (★Drummondville) ... 9,420
East Angus ... 4,417
East Broughton Station (★2,562) ... 1,191
Farnham ... 6,476
Forestville (★4,358) ... 1,819
Gaspé ... 16,842
Gatineau (★Ottawa) ... 73,479
Granby (★41,462) ... 37,132
Grande-Rivière ... 4,390
Grand'Mere (★Shawinigan) ... 15,999
Greenfield Park (★Montréal) ... 18,430
Hampstead (★Montréal) ... 7,562
Hauterive (★Baie-Comeau) ... 14,724
Havre-St.-Pierre ... 3,208
Hébertville-Station (★3,621) ... 1,362
Hudson (★Montréal) ... 4,480
Hull (★Ottawa) ... 61,039
Iberville (★St.-Jean) ... 8,897
Île-Perrot (★Montréal) ... 5,272
Joliette (★30,116) ... 18,118
Jonquière (★★Chicoutimi) ... 60,691
Kirkland (★Montréal) ... 7,476
La Baie ... 20,116
Lac-Brome ... 4,117
Lachenaie (★Montréal) ... 7,118
Lachine (★Montréal) ... 41,503
Lachute (★15,042) ... 11,928
Lac-Mégantic ... 6,457
La Malbaie (★5,135) ... 4,069
La Pocatière ... 4,319
Laprairie (★Montréal) ... 9,173
La Salle (★Montréal) ... 76,713
La Sarre ... 4,978
L'Assomption (★Montréal) ... 4,832
La Tuque ... 12,067
Lauzon (★Québec) ... 12,663
Laval (Ville de Laval) (★Montréal) ... 246,243
LeMoyne (★Montréal) ... 7,202
Lévis (★Québec) ... 17,819
Longueuil (★Montréal) ... 122,429
Loretteville (★Québec) ... 14,767
Louiseville ... 3,993
Magog (★14,598) ... 13,290
Malartic ... 5,092
Maniwaki ... 5,969
Marieville (★Montréal) ... 4,853
Mascouche (★Montréal) ... 14,266
Matane ... 12,726
Mercier (Ste.-Philomène) (★Montréal) ... 4,957
Métabetchouan ... 3,016
Mirabel ... 13,486
Mistassini (★Dolbeau) ... 5,473
Mont-Joli ... 6,508
Mont-Laurier ... 8,565
Montmagny ... 12,326
Montréal (★2,802,485) ... 1,080,546
Montréal-Est (★Montréal) ... 4,372
Montréal-Nord (★Montréal) ... 97,250
Montréal-Ouest (★Montréal) ... 5,980
Mont-Royal (★Montréal) ... 20,514
Mont-St.-Hilaire (★Montréal) ... 7,688
Murdochville ... 3,704
Napierville ... 2,166
New Richmond ... 4,295
Nicolet ... 4,818
Noranda (★★Rouyn) ... 9,809
Notre-Dame-des-Prairies ... 5,714
Otterburn Park (★Montréal) ... 4,159
Outremont (★Montréal) ... 27,089
Percé ... 5,198
Pierrefonds (★Montréal) ... 35,402
Pierreville (★2,510) ... 1,311
Pincourt (★Montréal) ... 7,892
Plessisville ... 7,238
Pohénégamook ... 3,627
Pointe-aux-Trembles (★Montréal) ... 35,618
Pointe-Claire (★Montréal) ... 25,917
Pontiac ... 3,365
Pont-Rouge ... 3,342
Port-Cartier ... 8,139
Portneuf (★3,225) ... 1,320
Price ... 2,461
Princeville ... 3,852
Québec (★542,158) ... 177,082
Rawdon ... 2,808
Repentigny (★Montréal) ... 26,698
Richmond ... 4,021
Rimouski (★30,225) ... 27,897
Rivière-du-Loup ... 13,103
Roberval ... 8,543
Rock Island (★3,548) ... 1,230
Rosemère (★Montréal) ... 7,112
Rouyn (★27,487) ... 17,678
Roxboro (★Montréal) ... 7,106
Ste.-Adèle (★6,273) ... 4,186
Ste.-Agathe-des-Monts ... 5,435
St.-Ambroise-de-Chicoutimi ... 3,169
Ste.-Anne-de-Bellevue (★Montréal) ... 3,738
Ste.-Anne-des-Monts (★7,606) ... 5,945
St.-Antoine (★St.-Jérôme) ... 6,872
St.-Basile-le-Grand (★Montréal) ... 5,843
St.-Boniface-de-Shawinigan ... 2,680
St.-Bruno (★Montréal) ... 21,272
Ste.-Catherine (★Montréal) ... 5,036
St.-Césaire ... 2,701
St.-Constant (★Montréal) ... 7,659
St.-David-de-l'Auberivière (★Québec) ... 4,386
St.-Eustache (★Montréal) ... 21,248
St.-Félicien ... 4,985
St.-Ferdinand (Bernierville) ... 2,182
Ste.-Foy (★Québec) ... 71,237
Ste.-Geneviève (★Montréal) ... 2,869
St.-Georges-Ouest (★Ville-St.-Georges) ... 6,478
St.-Hubert (★Montréal) ... 49,706
St.-Hyacinthe (★40,202) ... 37,500
St.-Jacques ... 2,095
St.-Jean (★50,363) ... 34,363
St.-Jérôme (★36,489) ... 25,175
St.-Joseph-de-Beauce ... 3,213
St.-Joseph-de-Sorel (★Sorel) ... 2,811
St.-Jovite ... 3,595
Ste.-Julie (★Montréal) ... 8,666
St.-Lambert (★Montréal) ... 20,318
St.-Laurent (★Montréal) ... 64,404
St.-Léonard (★Montréal) ... 78,452
St.-Luc (★St.-Jean) ... 7,103
St.-Marc-des-Carrières ... 2,625
Ste.-Marie-de-Beauce ... 4,462
St.-Pamphile ... 3,450
St.-Paul-l'Ermite (★Montréal) ... 6,107
St.-Pierre (★Montréal) ... 6,039
St.-Raymond ... 3,742
St. Rémi ... 4,866
St.-Romuald-d'Etchemin (★Québec) ... 9,160
Ste.-Thérèse-de Blainville (★Montréal) ... 17,479
St.-Tite ... 3,128
Sayabec ... 1,818
Schefferville ... 3,429
Senneterre ... 4,289
Sept-Îles (Seven Islands) ... 30,617
Shawinigan (★55,414) ... 24,921
Shawinigan-Sud (★Shawinigan) ... 11,155
Sherbrooke (★104,505) ... 76,804
Sillery (★Québec) ... 13,580
Sorel (★37,029) ... 19,666
Témiscaming ... 2,165
Terrebonne (★Montréal) ... 11,204
Thetford Mines (★28,826) ... 20,784
Thurso ... 3,066
Tracy (★Sorel) ... 12,284
Trois-Pistoles ... 4,554
Trois-Rivières (★98,583) ... 52,518
Trois-Rivières-Ouest (★Trois-Rivières) ... 10,564
Val-Bélair (★Québec) ... 10,716
Val-d'Or (★21,378) ... 19,915
Valleyfield (Salaberry-de) (★35,920) ... 29,716
Vanier (Québec-Ouest) (★Québec) ... 10,683
Varennes (★Montréal) ... 6,469
Vaudreuil (★Montréal) ... 5,630
Verdun (★Montréal) ... 68,013
Victoriaville (★27,732) ... 21,825
Ville-St.-Georges (★15,083) ... 8,605
Warwick ... 2,865
Waterloo ... 4,746
Westmount (★Montréal) ... 22,153
Windsor ... 5,637

CANADA/ SASKATCHEWAN ... 921,323

Assiniboia ... 2,738
Battleford (★North Battleford) ... 2,569
Biggar ... 2,491
Canora ... 2,689
Esterhazy ... 2,894
Estevan ... 8,847
Hudson Bay ... 2,280
Humboldt ... 4,265
Kamsack ... 2,726
Kindersley ... 3,523
Lloydminster (*Sask. and Alta.*) ... 10,311
Maple Creek ... 2,330
Meadow Lake ... 3,662
Melfort ... 5,141
Melville ... 5,149
Moose Jaw (★34,829) ... 32,581
Nipawin ... 4,317
North Battleford (★16,124) ... 13,158
Prince Albert ... 28,631
Regina (★151,191) ... 149,593
Rosetown ... 2,551
Saskatoon ... 133,750
Shaunavon ... 2,183
Swift Current ... 14,264
Tisdale ... 3,026
Unity ... 2,244
Uranium City ... 1,765
Weyburn ... 8,892
Wynyard ... 2,045
Yorkton ... 14,119

CANADA/YUKON ... 21,836

Dawson ... 838
Elsa ... 456
Faro ... 1,544
Watson Lake ... 808
Whitehorse ... 13,311

CAPE VERDE / Cabo Verde

1970 C ... 272,071

•Mindelo ... 28,797
PRAIA ... 21,494

CAYMAN IS.

1970 C ... 10,652

•GEORGETOWN ... 3,975

CENTRAL AFRICAN REPUBLIC
République centrafricaine

1971 E ... 1,637,000

Bambari (1968 E) ... 35,300
•BANGUI ... 187,000
Bouar (1968 E) ... 24,600

CHAD / Tchad

1975 E ... 4,030,000

Abéché ... 32,000
Kélo ... 18,500
Koumra ... 18,800
Moundou ... 45,000
•NDJAMENA (FORT-LAMY) ... 224,000
Sarh (Fort-Archambault) ... 50,000

CHILE

1970 C ... 8,880,889

Angol ... 22,123
Antofagasta ... 138,821
Apoquindo (★Santiago) ... 90,722
Arica ... 87,726
Calama ... 45,863
Chillán ... 87,555
Concepción (★395,000) ... 175,853
Conchalí (★Santiago) ... 246,046
Copiapó ... 45,194
Coquimbo ... 50,405
Coronel ... 37,312
Curicó ... 41,262
Iquique ... 65,040
La Cisterna (★Santiago) ... 246,537
La Granja (★Santiago) ... 163,882
La Serena ... 61,897
Las Rejas (★Santiago) ... 44,681
Linares ... 37,913
Lo Prado Arriba (★Santiago) ... 112,548
Los Ángeles ... 49,175
Lota ... 48,166
Ñuñoa (★Santiago) ... 280,733
Osorno ... 68,815
Ovalle ... 31,756
Providencia (★Santiago) ... 85,678
Puente Alto (★Santiago) ... 61,077
Puerto Montt ... 62,726
Punta Arenas ... 61,813
Quillota ... 35,488
Quilpué (★Valparaíso) ... 40,163
Quinta Normal (★Santiago) ... 138,007
Rancagua ... 86,404
Renca (★Santiago) ... 68,440
San Antonio ... 46,744
San Bernardo (★Santiago) ... 100,225
San Fernando ... 27,997
San Miguel (★Santiago) ... 320,883
•SANTIAGO (★2,925,000) ... 517,473
Talca ... 94,449
Talcahuano (★★Concepción) ... 152,755
Temuco ... 110,335
Tocopilla ... 22,241
Tomé ... 29,597
Valdivia ... 82,362
Vallenar ... 26,800
Valparaíso (★530,000) ... 250,358
Victoria ... 16,509
Villa Alemana ... 29,605
Viña del Mar (★Valparaíso) ... 188,811

C Census. E Official estimate. UE Unofficial estimate.
L Population within municipal limits of specified year. • Largest city in country.

★ Population or designation of metropolitan area, including suburbs (see headnote).
▲ Population of an entire municipality, commune, or district, including rural area.
‡† Year of information specified at start of country.

CHINA / Zhongguo

1982 C ... 1,008,175,288

Provinces

Anhui ... 49,665,724
Beijing (Auton. City) ... 9,230,687
Fujian ... 25,873,259
Gansu ... 19,569,261
Guangdong ... 59,299,220
Guangxi Zhuang (Auton. Region) ... 36,420,960
Guizhou ... 28,552,997
Hebei ... 53,005,875
Heilongjiang ... 32,665,546
Henan ... 74,422,739
Hubei ... 47,804,150
Hunan ... 54,008,851
Jiangsu ... 60,521,114
Jiangxi ... 33,184,827
Jilin ... 22,560,053
Liaoning ... 35,721,693
Nei Monggol (Auton. Region) ... 19,274,279
Ningxia Huizu (Auton. Region) ... 3,895,578
Qinghai ... 3,895,706
Shaanxi ... 28,904,423
Shandong ... 74,419,054
Shanghai (Auton. City) ... 11,859,748
Shanxi ... 25,291,389
Sichuan ... 99,713,310
Tianjin (Auton. City) ... 7,764,141
Xinjiang Uygur (Auton. Region) ... 13,081,681
Xizang (Auton. Region) ... 1,892,393
Yunnan ... 32,553,817
Zhejiang ... 38,884,603

Cities (1982C, † 1981E or ‡ 1975UE)

Acheng ... ‡60,000
Anda ... ‡60,000
Anqing ... ‡135,000
Anshan (1,215,000▲) ... 1,028,000
Anshun ... ‡50,000
Anyang ... ‡175,000
Baicheng ... ‡125,000
Baiyin ... ‡50,000
Baoding (Paoting) ... ‡350,000
Baoji (Paoki) ... ‡250,000
Baotou (1,026,000▲) ... †846,000
Baoying ... ‡50,000
Bei'an ... ‡80,000
Beihai ... ‡95,000
Beipiao ... ‡100,000
Bengbu (Pengpu) ... ‡400,000
Benxi (778,000▲) ... †643,000
Boshan ... ‡100,000
Boxian ... ‡90,000
Butha Qi ... ‡55,000
Cangzhou ... ‡100,000
Canton (Guangzhou) (1,296,000▲) ... 827,000
Changchun (Hsinking) (1,696,000▲) ... †1,309,000
Changde ... ‡125,000
Changsha (1,047,000▲) ... †835,000
Changshu ... ‡95,000
Changzhi ... ‡100,000
Changzhou (Changchow) ... ‡300,000
Chao'an ... ‡95,000
Chaoyang (*Liaoning prov.*) ... ‡120,000
Chaoyang (*Guangdong prov.*) ... ‡60,000
Chengde ... ‡90,000
Chengdu (2,428,000▲) ... †1,376,000
Chenghai ... ‡50,000
Chengxian ... ‡60,000
Chifeng ... ‡75,000
Chongqing (Chungking) (2,597,000▲) ... †1,900,000
Dachangzhen ... ‡50,000
Dandong (Antung) ... ‡300,000
Datong (872,000▲) ... †590,000
Deyang ... ‡50,000
Dezhou ... ‡70,000
Didao ... ‡50,000
Dongguan ... ‡55,000
Dongtai ... ‡50,000
Dukou ... ‡120,000
Dunhua ... ‡60,000
Duyun ... ‡75,000
Erenhot ... ‡60,000
Foshan ... ‡125,000
Fushun (Foochow) (1,193,000▲) ... 1,038,000
Fuxian ... ‡85,000
Fuxin (619,000▲) ... †516,000
Fuyang ... ‡70,000
Fuzhou (1,130,000▲) ... 710,000
Fuzhou ... ‡55,000
Ganzhou ... ‡140,000
Gejiu ... ‡100,000
Guilin (Kweilin) ... ‡250,000
Guiyang (1,296,000▲) ... †827,000
Haicheng ... ‡90,000
Haikou (Hoihow) ... ‡275,000
Hailar ... ‡85,000
Hami ... ‡50,000
Handan (895,000▲) ... †656,000
Hangu ... ‡100,000
Hangzhou (1,192,000▲) ... 933,000
Hanzhong ... ‡90,000
Harbin (2,460,000▲) ... †2,094,000
Hebi ... ‡100,000
Hechuan ... ‡60,000
Hefei (795,000▲) ... †539,000
Hegang (Hokang) ... ‡250,000
Hengyang ... ‡350,000
Hepu ... ‡50,000
Hohhot (Kweisui) ... ‡450,000
Horqin Youyi Qianqi (Ulan Hot) ... ‡80,000
Huadian ... ‡55,000
Huaian ... ‡50,000
Huaide ... ‡75,000
Huaibei ... ‡75,000
Huainan (1,015,000▲) ... †539,000
Huangshi ... ‡140,000
Huizhou ... ‡80,000
Hulan ... ‡75,000
Hunjiang ... ‡50,000
Jiamusi (Kiamusze) ... ‡300,000
Ji'an ... ‡110,000
Jiangmen ... ‡120,000
Jiaozuo (Tsiaotso) ... ‡275,000
Jiawang ... ‡50,000
Jiaxing ... ‡150,000
Jieyang ... ‡65,000
Jilin (Kirin) (1,049,000▲) ... †815,000
Jinan (Tsinan) (1,338,000▲) ... 1,048,000
Jingdezhen (Kingtechen) ... ‡300,000
Jinhua ... ‡55,000
Jining ... ‡100,000
Jining (Tsining) ... ‡130,000
Jinshi ... ‡65,000
Jinxi ... ‡50,000
Jinxian ... ‡75,000
Jinzhou (Chinchow) ... ‡450,000
Jiujiang ... ‡100,000
Jixi (Chihsi) (773,000▲) ... †606,000
Kaifeng ... ‡350,000
Kaiyuan ... ‡50,000
Karamay ... ‡60,000
Kashi ... ‡100,000
Kunming (1,399,000▲) ... †997,000
Lanzhou (1,381,000▲) ... †1,075,000
Leshan ... ‡70,000
Lhasa ... ‡80,000
Lianyungang ... ‡250,000
Liaoyang ... ‡250,000
Liaoyuan (Shwangliao) ... ‡250,000
Linfen ... ‡50,000
Linqing ... ‡65,000
Linxia ... ‡65,000
Liuzhou ... ‡300,000
Liyujiang ... ‡50,000
Lu'an ... ‡55,000
Lüda (Dairen) (1,425,000▲) ... 1,185,000
Luohe ... ‡60,000
Luoyang (951,000▲) ... †563,000
Lüshun (Port Arthur) ... ‡40,000
Luzhou ... ‡175,000
Ma'anshan ... ‡60,000
Manzhouli ... ‡65,000
Maoming ... ‡100,000
Meixian ... ‡50,000
Mianyang ... ‡50,000
Minhang ... ‡60,000
Mudanjiang (Mutankiang) ... ‡350,000
Nancha ... ‡50,000
Nanchang (1,033,000▲) ... †815,000
Nanchong ... ‡225,000
Nanjing (Nanking) (2,134,000▲) ... 1,740,000
Nanning (657,000▲) ... †505,000
Nanping ... ‡50,000
Nantong ... ‡275,000
Nanyang ... ‡60,000
Neijiang ... ‡225,000
Ningbo ... ‡300,000
PEKING (BEIJING) (★6,100,000) (9,230,687▲) ... 5,597,972
Pingdingshan ... ‡85,000
Pingliang ... ‡80,000
Pingxiang ... ‡120,000
Qingdao (1,174,000▲) ... 1,031,000
Qingjiang ... ‡100,000
Qinhuangdao (Chinwangtao) ... ‡275,000
Qiqihar (1,193,000▲) ... †899,000
Quanzhou ... ‡130,000
Quxian ... ‡50,000
Sanmenxia ... ‡60,000
Shache ... ‡50,000
•Shanghai (★9,000,000) (11,859,748▲) ... 6,320,872
Shangqiu ... ‡100,000
Shangrao ... ‡60,000
Shantou (Swatow) ... ‡325,000
Shaoguan ... ‡100,000
Shaoxing ... ‡150,000
Shaoyang ... ‡215,000
Shashi ... ‡120,000
Shenyang (Mukden) (4,003,000▲) ... 3,700,000
Shijiazhuang (1,066,000▲) ... 837,000
Shiquaigou ... ‡50,000
Shuangyashan ... ‡150,000
Siping ... ‡165,000
Songjiang ... ‡60,000
Suihua ... ‡70,000
Suining ... ‡60,000
Suxian ... ‡50,000
Suzhou (Soochow) (658,000▲) ... †556,000
Tai'an ... ‡50,000
Taiyuan (1,775,000▲) ... 1,292,000
Taizhou ... ‡175,000
Tangshan (1,338,000▲) ... 895,000
Tao'an ... ‡75,000
Tianjin (Tientsin) (7,764,141▲) ... 4,300,000
Tianshui ... ‡85,000
Tieling ... ‡75,000
Tongchuan ... ‡75,000
Tonghua ... ‡175,000
Tongliao ... ‡60,000
Tongling ... ‡65,000
Tongxian ... ‡80,000
Tunxi ... ‡65,000
Ürümqi (942,000▲) ... †880,000
Wanxian ... ‡120,000
Weifang ... ‡240,000
Wenzhou ... ‡260,000
Wuhan (Hankow) (3,157,000▲) ... †2,662,000
Wuhu ... ‡325,000
Wuxi (Wusih) (781,000▲) ... †618,000
Wuzhou ... ‡160,000
Xaimen (Amoy) ... ‡300,000
Xi'an (Sian) (2,197,000▲) ... 1,618,000
Xiangfan ... ‡110,000
Xiangtan (Siangtan) ... ‡325,000
Xianyang ... ‡85,000
Xinghua ... ‡85,000
Xingtai ... ‡115,000
Xinhui ... ‡50,000
Xining (Sining) ... ‡300,000
Xinwen ... ‡50,000
Xinxiang (Sinsiang) ... ‡250,000
Xinyang ... ‡100,000
Xuanhua ... ‡140,000
Xuchang ... ‡100,000
Xuguit Qi ... ‡50,000
Xuzhou (Süchow) (750,000▲) ... †648,000
Ya'an ... ‡50,000
Yancheng ... ‡60,000
Yangjiang ... ‡60,000
Yangquan (Yangchüan) ... ‡275,000
Yangzhou ... ‡175,000
Yanji ... ‡90,000
Yantai ... ‡150,000
Yibin (Ipin) ... ‡250,000
Yichang ... ‡120,000
Yichun (Ichun) (788,000▲) ... †736,000
Yidu ... ‡50,000
Yinchuan ... ‡125,000
Yingcheng ... ‡50,000
Yingkou ... ‡50,000
Yingkou (Yingkow) ... ‡175,000
Yining ... ‡90,000
Yiyang ... ‡110,000
Yuci ... ‡90,000
Yueyang ... ‡60,000
Yumen ... ‡90,000
Zaozhuang (1,238,000▲) ... 80,000
Zhangjiakou (Kalgan) ... ‡300,000
Zhangzhou ... ‡110,000
Zhanjiang ... ‡200,000
Zhaodong ... ‡65,000
Zhaoqing ... ‡75,000
Zhengzhou (1,381,000▲) ... †859,000
Zhenjiang ... ‡225,000
Zhongshan ... ‡90,000
Zhoucun ... ‡50,000
Zhoukouzhen ... ‡90,000
Zhuzhou (Chuchow) ... ‡250,000
Zibo (Tzupo) (2,192,000▲) ... †623,000
Zigong (Tzekung) ... ‡325,000
Zunyi (Tsunyi) ... ‡250,000

COLOMBIA

1973 C ... 22,551,811

Armenia (1979 E) (★205,000) ... 164,000
Barrancabermeja (1979 E) ... 115,000
Barranquilla (1979 E) (★950,000) ... 859,000
Bello (★Medellín) ... 121,204
•BOGOTÁ (1979 E) (★4,150,000) ... 4,067,000
Bucaramanga (1979 E) (★470,000) ... 402,000
Buenaventura (1979 E) ... 144,000
Buga (84,057▲) ... 71,016
Caicedonia ... 23,567
Calarcá (★Armenia) (49,936▲) ... 29,349
Caldas ... 27,394
Cali (1979 E) (★1,340,000) ... 1,293,000
Cartagena (1979 E) ... 388,000
Cartago (77,890▲) ... 69,154
Ciénaga (89,723▲) ... 42,546
Cúcuta (1979 UE) ... 355,000
Dos Quebradas (★Pereira) ... 37,837
Duitama (48,459▲) ... 36,551
Envigado (★Medellín) ... 69,921
Espinal ... 32,475
Facatativá ... 27,892
Florencia ... 31,817
Floridablanca (★Bucaramanga) ... 38,446
Fusagasugá ... 25,456
Girardot (★78,000) ... 61,829
Ibaqué (1979 E) ... 257,000
Ipiales ... 30,871
Itagüí (★Medellín) ... 96,972
La Dorada ... 30,962
Líbano (42,832▲) ... 19,132
Lorica (59,757▲) ... 18,251
Magangué (62,746▲) ... 34,396
Manizales (1979 UE) ... 252,000
Medellín (1979 E) (★2,025,000) ... 1,477,000
Montería (1979 E) ... 123,000
Neiva (1979 E) ... 145,000
Ocaña ... 38,352
Palmira (1979 E) ... 168,000
Pamplona ... 31,817
Pasto (1979 E) ... 171,000
Pereira (1979 UE)](★325,000) ... 260,000
Popayán (1977 E) ... 88,768
Pradera ... 15,732
Puerto Berrío ... 19,579
Quibdó (1977 E) ... 33,588
Ríohacha (1977 E) ... 35,000
Santa Marta (1979 UE) ... 155,000
Santa Rosa de Cabal (★Pereira) (42,717▲) ... 28,368
Sevilla ... 31,143
Sincelejo (1977 E) ... 86,569
Sogamoso (67,738▲) ... 48,891
Soledad (★Barranquilla) ... 64,469
Sonsón ... 15,990
Tuluá (1979 E) ... 113,000
Tumaco (87,448▲) ... 38,742
Tunja (1977 E) ... 64,551
Valledupar (1979 E) ... 164,000
Villavicencio (1979 E) ... 133,000

COMOROS / Comores

1974 E ... 292,000

•MORONI ... 12,000
Mutsamudu (1966 C) ... 7,652

CONGO (PEOPLE'S REPUBLIC OF THE CONGO)

1970 C ... 1,089,300

•BRAZZAVILLE ... 175,000
Jacob (1969 E) ... 18.000
Loubomo (1969 E) ... 15,000
Pointe-Noire ... 135,000

COOK IS.

1971 C ... 21,227

•AVARUA (1961 E) ... 4,000

COSTA RICA

1976 E ... 1,993,800

Alajuela ... 35,000
Cartago ... 23,100
Desamparados (★San José) ... 32,700
Guadalupe (★San José) ... 29,100
Heredia ... 24,200
Liberia (18,000▲) ... 11,600
Limón (43,800▲) ... 31,900
Puntarenas ... 29,000
•SAN JOSÉ (1978 E) (★519,400) ... 239,800
San Juan (★San José) ... 19,600
San Pedro (★San José) ... 25,100
San Vicente (★San José) ... 16,400

CUBA

1970 C ... 8,553,400

Amancio Rodríguez (37,900▲) ... 12,300
Artemisa ... 31,200
Banes (39,300▲) ... 27,100
Baracoa (35,600▲) ... 20,900
Bauta (★Havana) (25,400▲) ... 21,100
Bayamo (1976 E) (88,994▲) ... 68,900
Camagüey (1976 E) ... 230,891
Camajuaní (32,300▲) ... 15,900
Cárdenas ... 55,700
Chaparra (51,000▲) ... 8,400
Ciego de Avila (1976 E) (66,542▲) ... 57,700
Cienfuegos (1976 E) (92,210▲) ... 86,600
Colón (40,800▲) ... 26,000
Consolación del Sur (42,000▲) ... 15,100
Contramaestre (43,900▲) ... 22,900
Cruces (32,100▲) ... 19,100
Florida (37,500▲) ... 32,700
Fomento (33,600▲) ... 12,900
Guanabacoa (★Havana) ... 69,700
Guantánamo (1976 E) ... 155,217
Güines (45,300▲) ... 41,400
Guisa (44,100▲) ... 9,000
•HAVANA (LA HABANA) (1976 E) (★2,000,000) ... 1,961,674
Holguín (1976 E) (160,965▲) ... 129,800
Manzanillo (88,900▲) ... 77,900
Matanzas (1976 E) ... 99,003
Mayarí (34,000▲) ... 17,600
Mayarí Arriba (31,400▲) ... 2,300
Morón (31,100▲) ... 29,000
Niquero (36,500▲) ... 11,300
Nueva Gerona (1976 E) (28,342▲) ... 24,300
Nuevitas (21,500▲) ... 20,700
Palma Soriano (59,600▲) ... 41,200
Pinar del Rio (1976 E) ... 89,978
Placetas (48,400▲) ... 32,300
Sagua la Grande (41,900▲) ... 35,800
San Antonio de los Baños (30,000▲) ... 25,300
Sancti-Spíritus (1976 E) (67,569▲) ... 58,600
San Germán (30,200▲) ... 12,400
San José de las Lajas (33,600▲) ... 24,900
San Juan y Martínez (45,700▲) ... 11,100
San Luis (35,000▲) ... 17,400
Santa Clara (1976 E) ... 152,361
Santiago de Cuba (1976 E) ... 326,066
Santiago de las Vegas (★Havana) ... 29,300
Trinidad (37,000▲) ... 31,500
Vertientes (32,600▲) ... 14,000
Victoria de las Tunas (1976 E) (65,767▲) ... 54,400

CYPRUS / Kípros / Kıbrıs

1974 E ... 639,000

Ammókhostos (Famagusta) ... 39,400
Kirínia ... 3,900
Lárnax (Larnaca) ... 19,800
Lemesós (Limassol) (★80,600) ... 55,000
•NICOSIA (LEVKOSÍA) (★117,100) ... 51,000
Páfos ... 9,100

CZECHOSLOVAKIA / Československo

1979 E ... 15,280,148

Banská Bystrica ... 66,279
Beroun (★26,000) ... 18,149
Bratislava ... 374,860
Břeclav ... 24,258
Brno ... 372,793
České Budějovice (Budweis) ... 89,399
Cheb ... 31,030
Chomutov ... 49,960
Děčín ... 48,424
Frýdek-Místek (★Ostrava) ... 54,112
Gottwaldov (Zlín) ... 82,926
Havířov (★Ostrava) ... 93,832
Havlíčkův Brod ... 24,859
Hlohovec (★26,000) ... 16,815
Hodonín ... 25,504
Hradec Králové ... 93,165
Humenné ... 26,885
Jablonec [nad Nisou] ... 39,692
Jihlava ... 50,995
Karlovy Vary (Karlsbad) ... 61,212
Karviná (★★Ostrava) ... 80,017
Kladno (★86,000) ... 66,370
Kolín ... 31,169
Komárno ... 30,886
Košice ... 200,943
Krnov ... 26,393
Kroměříž ... 26,166
Levice ... 25,610
Liberec (★96,000) ... 85,119
Liptovský Mikuláš ... 23,795
Litvínov ... 23,572
Lučenec ... 26,300
Martin ... 56,294
Michalovce ... 28,012
Mladá Boleslav ... 43,876
Most ... 61,411
Náchod ... 19,812
Nitra ... 72,140
Nové Zámky ... 32,694
Nový Jičín ... 31,101
Olomouc ... 102,501
Opava ... 59,481
Orlová (★Ostrava) ... 30,938
Ostrava (★745,000) ... 325,473
Pardubice ... 93,042
Piešt'any ... 30,070
Pisek ... 28,067
Plzeň (Pilsen) ... 169,466
Poprad ... 36,428
Považská Bystrica ... 24,747
•PRAGUE (PRAHA) (★1,275,000) ... 1,193,345
Přerov ... 47,933
Prešov ... 69,453
Příbram ... 36,441
Prievidza ... 38,948
Prostějov ... 48,516
Ružomberok ... 26,803
Sokolov ... 27,338
Spišská Nová Ves ... 31,537
Šumperk ... 29,872
Tábor ... 31,005
Teplice ... 53,822
Třebíč ... 27,708
Trenčín ... 47,832
Třinec ... 34,226
Trnava ... 61,617
Trutnov ... 27,402
Uherské Hradiště ... 35,909
Ústí nad Labem (★103,000) ... 80,309
Valašské Meziříčí ... 24,485
Vsetín ... 29,023
Žilina ... 67,204
Znojmo ... 35,711
Zvolen ... 35,754

DENMARK / Danmark

1980 E ... 5,122,065

Åbenrå (21,172▲) ... 18,200
Albertslund (★Copenhagen) ... 30,425
Ålborg ... 153,948
Århus ... 244,839
Ballerup-Måløv (★Copenhagen) ... 48,938
Brøndby (★Copenhagen) ... 38,034
•COPENHAGEN (KØBENHAVN) (★1,470,000) ... 498,850
Esbjerg ... 79,310
Fredericia ... 45,820
Frederiksberg (★Copenhagen) ... 88,287
Frederikshavn ... 35,038
Gentofte (★Copenhagen) ... 67,300
Gladsakse (★Copenhagen) ... 64,954
Glostrup (★Copenhagen) ... 19,573
Haderslev (29,973▲) ... 23,100
Helsingør (Elsinore) ... 56,566
Herlev (★Copenhagen) ... 28,530
Herning (56,033▲) ... 47,900
Hillerød ... 33,686
Hjørring (34,456▲) ... 24,900
Høje Tåstrup (★Copenhagen) ... 43,292
Holbæk (29,578▲) ... 23,300
Holstebro (36,777▲) ... 29,900
Horsens ... 54,533
Hvidovre (★Copenhagen) ... 50,608
Køge (34,511▲) ... 30,300
Kolding ... 55,769
Lyngby (Kongens Lyngby)-Tårbæk (★Copenhagen) ... 52,013
Middelfart ... 17,996
Næstved (45,237▲) ... 39,800
Odense ... 168,528
Randers ... 62,486
Rødovre (★Copenhagen) ... 38,020
Roskilde ... 48,746
Silkeborg (46,774▲) ... 40,300
Søllerød (★Copenhagen) ... 31,920
Sønderborg ... 27,790
Svendborg (37,996▲) ... 33,200
Tårnby (★Copenhagen) ... 42,075
Vejle ... 49,471
Viborg (38,757▲) ... 32,600

DJIBOUTI

1971 E ... 125,000

•DJIBOUTI ... 40,000

DOMINICA

1970 C ... 70,302

•ROSEAU ... 10,157

DOMINICAN REPUBLIC / República Dominicana

1976 E ... 4,835,207

Baní ... 31,763
Barahona ... 53,912
Bonao ... 32,132
La Romana ... 49,498
La Vega ... 41,658
Mao (Valverde) ... 32,723
Moca ... 32,621
Puerto Plata ... 44,113
San Cristóbal ... 36,504
San Francisco de Macorís ... 60,821
San Juan [de la Maguana] ... 43,417
San Pedro de Macorís ... 66,022
Santiago [de los Caballeros] ... 219,846
•SANTO DOMINGO ... 979,608

C Census. E Official estimate. UE Unofficial estimate.
L Population within municipal limits of year specified. • Largest city in country.
★ Population or designation of metropolitan area, including suburbs (see headnote).
▲ Population of an entire municipality, commune, or district, including rural area.
‡† Year of information specified at start of country.

ECUADOR

1974 C ... 6,521,710

Ambato (1976 E) ... 80,000
Azogues ... 10,939
Babahoyo ... 28,345
Chone ... 23,647
Cuenca (1978 E) ... 128,788
Esmeraldas ... 60,132
Guaranda ... 11,387
•Guayaquil (1978 E) ... 1,022,010
Ibarra ... 41,057
Jipijapa ... 19,719
Latacunga ... 22,106
Loja ... 47,268
Machala ... 68,379
Manta ... 63,514
Milagro ... 53,058
Pasaje ... 20,822
Portoviejo ... 59,404
Quevedo ... 43,123
QUITO (1978 E) ... 742,858
Riobamba ... 58,029
Santo Domingo ... 30,487
Tulcán ... 24,443

EGYPT / Mişr

1966 C ... 30,083,419

Abnūb ... 31,195
Abū Kabīr ... 41,789
Abū Tīj ... 28,161
Akhmīm ... 44,829
Al-'Arīsh ... ††40,338
Al-Badārī ... 26,531
Alexandria (Al-Iskandarīyah) (1978 E) (*2,850,000) ... 2,409,000
Al-Fashn ... 27,746
Al-Fayyūm (1976 C) ... 167,081
Al-Ḥawāmidīyah (*Cairo) ... 36,227
Al-Ismā'īlīyah (Ismailia) (1976 C) (*185,000) ... 145,478
Al-Jīzah (Giza) (*Cairo) (1976 C) ... 1,246,713
Al Madīnah al Fikrīyah ... 21,504
Al-Maḥallah al Kubrā (1976 C) ... 292,853
Al-Manshāh ... 25,027
Al-Manṣūrah (El Mansura) (1976 C) (*290,000) ... 257,866
Al-Manzilah ... 33,298
Al-Maṭarīyah ... 41,105
Al-Minyā (1976 C) ... 146,423
Al Qanāṭir al Khayrīyah ... 22,477
Al-Quṣayr ... 5,525
Al-Qūṣīyah ... 25,991
Al-Uqṣur (Luxor) ... 77,578
Armant ... 38,308
Ashmūn ... 32,168
Ash Shuhadā' ... 21,947
As-Sallūm ... 2,483
As-Sinbillāwayn ... 40,686
Aswān (1976 C) ... 144,377
Asyūṭ (1976 C) ... 213,983
Aṭ Ṭalibīyah ... 20,438
Az-Zaqāzīq (1976 C) ... 202,637
Bahtīm (*Cairo) ... 32,510
Banhā ... 63,849
Banī Mazār ... 34,053
Banī Suwayf (1976 C) ... 118,148
Bibā ... 22,871
Bilbays ... 58,070
Bilqās Qism Awwal ... 41,067
Biyalā ... 33,008
Būsh ... 21,174
•CAIRO (AL QĀHIRAH) (1978 E) (*8,500,000) ... 5,278,000
Damanhūr (1976 C) ... 188,927
Dayrūṭ ... 27,646
Dishnā ... 21,857
Disūq ... 45,580
Dumyāṭ (Damietta) (1975 E) ... 113,200
Fāqūs ... 40,561
Fuwah ... 30,654
Giheina al Gharbiya ... 24,203
Ḥawsh 'Īsá ... 30,006
Idfū ... 27,346
Idkū ... 42,239
Isnā ... 27,383
Jirjā ... 44,150
Kafr ad-Dawwār (*Alexandria) (1976 C) ... 160,554
Kafr ash-Shaykh ... 51,544
Kafr az-Zayyāt ... 34,084
Kafr Salīm (*Alexandria) ... 40,381
Kawm Umbū ... 27,227
Maghāghah ... 33,211
Mallawī ... 59,938
Manfalūṭ ... 34,132
Minūf ... 48,256
Minyā al-Qamḥ ... 31,533
Mīt Ghamr (*82,000) ... 43,665
Nafīshah (*Al-Ismā'īlīyah) ... 29,483
Port Said (Bur Sa'īd) (1978 E) ... 271,000
Qalyūb ... 49,303
Qinā ... 68,536
Qūṣ ... 27,462
Rashīd (Rosetta) ... 36,711
Samālūṭ ... 37,861
Samannūd ... 29,749
Sāqiyat Makkī ... 22,967
Sawhāj (1976 C) ... 101,758
Shibīn al-Kawm (1976 C) ... 102,844
Shirbīn ... 25,089
Shubrā al-Khaymah (*Cairo) (1976 C) ... 393,700
Sīdī Sālim ... 21,096
Sinnūris ... 34,855
Suez (As Suways) (1978 E) ... 204,000
Ṭahṭā ... 38,915
Ṭalā ... 25,448
Ṭanṭā (1976 C) ... 284,636
Ṭimā ... 29,293
Warrāq al-'Arab (*Cairo) ... 31,263
Ziftá (**Mīt Ghamr) ... 37,883

††31,733 per 1967 census taken by Israeli occupation authorities.

EL SALVADOR

1977 E ... 4,255,000

Ahuachapán (63,600▲) ... 18,100
Chalchuapa (51,200▲) ... 22,000
Delgado (*San Salvador) (77,100▲) ... 53,600
Mejicanos (*San Salvador) (85,000▲) ... 70,500
Nueva San Salvador (63,500▲) ... 44,000
San Miguel (144,900▲) ... 72,900
•SAN SALVADOR (*720,000) ... 397,100
Santa Ana (189,000▲) ... 112,800
San Vicente (56,900▲) ... 21,500
Sonsonate (61,000▲) ... 40,100
Soyapango (*San Salvador) (56,900▲) ... 32,700
Usulután (57,600▲) ... 25,100
Zacatecoluca (71,500▲) ... 20,200

EQUATORIAL GUINEA / Guinea Ecuatorial

1965 C ... 254,684

Bata (1960 C) (27,024▲) ... 4,000
•MALABO (SANTA ISABEL) (37,152▲) ... 17,500

ETHIOPIA / Yaltopya

1978 E ... 29,408,200

•ADDIS ABABA ... 1,125,340
Asmera ... 373,827
Bahir Dar ... 45,955
Dabra-Mārk'os ... 35,818
Debre Zeyt ... 43,654
Desē ... 65,571
Dirē Dawa ... 72,202
Gonder ... 67,790
Hārer ... 55,401
Jimā ... 56,278
Keren ... 33,368
Mak'alē ... 41,235
Mitsiwa ... 29,064
Nazreth (Adāmā) ... 61,468

FAEROE IS. / Føroyar

1977 E ... 41,575

•TÓRSHAVN ... 11,586

FALKLAND ISLANDS

1972 C ... 1,957

•STANLEY ... 1,081

FIJI

1976 C ... 588,068

Lautoka (*28,847) ... 22,672
•SUVA (*117,827) ... 63,628

FINLAND / Suomi

1978 E ... 4,758,088

Espoo (Esbo) (*Helsinki) ... 129,758
Hämeenlinna ... 41,303
•HELSINKI (HELSINGFORS) (*885,000) ... 484,879
Hyvinkää ... 37,104
Iisalmi ... 22,131
Imatra ... 36,593
Joensuu ... 43,940
Jyväskylä (*86,000) ... 62,937
Kajaani ... 33,662
Kotka ... 61,320
Kouvola (*53,000) ... 30,524
Kuopio ... 73,567
Kuusankoski (**Kouvola) ... 22,649
Lahti (*109,000) ... 94,980
Lappeenranta ... 53,393
Mikkeli ... 27,919
Nokia (*Tampere) ... 23,612
Oulu (*112,000) ... 93,497
Pori ... 79,815
Rauma ... 30,429
Tampere (*241,000) ... 165,519
Turku (Åbo) (*221,000) ... 164,586
Vaasa (Vasa) ... 53,774
Vantaa (Vanda) (*Helsinki) ... 127,403
Varkaus ... 24,536

FRANCE

1980 E ... 53,589,000

Regions and Departments

ALSACE ... 1,560,000
Bas-Rhin ... 904,300
Haut-Rinh ... 655,700
AQUITAINE ... 2,576,700
Dordogne ... 365,800
Gironde ... 1,089,000
Landes ... 292,000
Lot-et-Garonne ... 287,800
Pyrénées-Atlantiques (Basses-Pyrénées) ... 542,100
AUVERGNE ... 1,319,500
Allier ... 365,400
Cantal ... 160,500
Haute-Loire ... 199,300
Puy-de-Dôme ... 594,300
BASSE-NORMANDIE ... 1,314,000
Calvados ... 579,100
Manche ... 444,600
Orne ... 290,300
BOURGOGNE ... 1,589,600
Côte-d'Or ... 474,100
Nièvre ... 239,500
Saône-et-Loire ... 569,000
Yonne ... 307,000
BRETAGNE ... 2,652,800
Côtes-du-Nord ... 531,700
Finistère ... 817,800
Ille-et-Vilaine ... 731,600
Morbihan ... 571,700
CENTRE ... 2,224,000
Cher ... 319,100
Eure-et-Loir ... 352,700
Indre ... 243,000
Indre-et-Loire ... 498,700
Loiret ... 521,900
Loir-et-Cher ... 288,600
CHAMPAGNE-ARDENNE ... 1,346,600
Ardennes ... 300,700
Aube ... 286,900
Haute-Marne ... 205,700
Marne ... 553,300
CORSE (CORSICA) ... 229,400
Corse-du-Sud ... 102,400
Haute-Corse ... 127,000
FRANCHE-COMTÉ ... 1,085,800
Belfort, Territoire de ... 132,000
Doubs ... 492,500
Haute-Saône ... 223,500
Jura ... 237,800
HAUTE-NORMANDIE ... 1,638,500
Eure ... 443,800
Seine-Maritime ... 1,194,700
ÎLE-DE-FRANCE ... 10,064,700
Essonne ... 1,087,600
Hauts-de-Seine ... 1,350,000
Paris ... 2,050,500
Seine-et-Marne ... 889,400
Seine-Saint-Denis ... 1,292,400
Val-de-Marne ... 1,226,000
Val-d'Oise ... 921,000
Yvelines ... 1,247,800
LANGUEDOC-ROUSSILLON ... 1,832,100
Aude ... 265,200
Gard ... 500,000
Hérault ... 685,500
Lozère ... 72,300
Pyrénées-Orientales ... 309,100
LIMOUSIN ... 733,500
Corrèze ... 238,600
Creuse ... 138,100
Haute-Vienne ... 356,800
LORRAINE ... 2,312,900
Meurthe-et-Moselle ... 716,500
Meuse ... 191,400
Moselle ... 1,007,200
Vosges ... 397,800
MIDI-PYRÉNÉES ... 2,272,100
Ariège ... 135,500
Aveyron ... 268,300
Gers ... 167,200
Haute-Garonne ... 816,600
Hautes-Pyrénées ... 222,200
Lot ... 148,300
Tarn ... 334,900
Tarn-et-Garonne ... 179,100
NORD-PAS-DE-CALAIS ... 3,920,300
Nord ... 2,521,300
Pas-de-Calais ... 1,399,000
PAYS DE LA LOIRE ... 2,860,800
Loire-Atlantique ... 977,700
Maine-et-Loire ... 652,700
Mayenne ... 264,700
Sarthe ... 499,500
Vendée ... 466,200
PICARDIE ... 1,714,600
Aisne ... 527,200
Oise ... 642,100
Somme ... 545,300
POITOU-CHARENTES ... 1,537,200
Charente ... 334,200
Charente-Maritime ... 499,800
Deux-Sèvres ... 338,000
Vienne ... 365,200
PROVENCE-ALPES-CÔTE D'AZUR ... 3,873,100
Alpes-de-Haute-Provence (Basses-Alpes) ... 115,800
Alpes-Maritimes ... 862,600
Bouches-du-Rhône ... 1,715,400
Hautes-Alpes ... 99,800
Var ... 667,300
Vaucluse ... 412,200
RHÔNE-ALPES ... 4,930,800
Ain ... 398,000
Ardèche ... 252,000
Drôme ... 366,700
Haute-Savoie ... 483,400
Isère ... 903,900
Loire ... 735,500
Rhône ... 1,478,900
Savoie ... 312,400

Cities (1975 C)

Aix-en-Provence ... 110,659
Aix-les-Bains ... 22,210
Ajaccio ... 50,726
Albi ... 46,162
Alençon ... 33,680
Alès (*67,513) ... 44,245
Alfortville (*Paris) ... 38,057
Amiens (*152,997) ... 131,476
Angers (*188,695) ... 137,587
Angoulême (*100,528) ... 47,221
Annecy (*103,543) ... 53,262
Antibes (**Cannes) ... 55,960
Antony (*Paris) ... 57,540
Arcachon (*38,000) ... 13,892
Argenteuil (*Paris) ... 102,530
Arles (50,059▲) ... 37,340
Armentières (*58,000) ... 26,346
Arras (*79,783) ... 46,446
Asnières [-sur-Seine] (*Paris) ... 75,431
Athis-Mons (*Paris) ... 30,737
Aubervilliers (*Paris) ... 72,976
Aulnay-sous-Bois (*Paris) ... 78,137
Aurillac ... 30,863
Autun ... 21,556
Auxerre ... 38,342
Avignon (*162,562) ... 90,786
Avranches ... 10,136
Bagneux (*Paris) ... 40,674
Bagnolet (*Paris) ... 35,906
Barentin (*12,000) ... 10,773
Bar-le-Duc ... 19,288
Bastia (*56,984) ... 50,718
Bayeux ... 13,457
Bayonne (*121,474) ... 42,938
Beauvais ... 54,089
Belfort (*75,795) ... 54,615
Besançon (*126,349) ... 120,315
Béthune (*145,155) ... 26,982
Béziers (*88,619) ... 84,029
Biarritz (**Bayonne) ... 27,595
Blois ... 49,778
Bobigny (*Paris) ... 43,125
Bois-Colombes (*Paris) ... 26,657
Bondy (*Paris) ... 48,333
Bordeaux (*612,456) ... 223,131
Boulogne-Billancourt (*Paris) ... 103,578
Boulogne-sur-Mer (*100,581) ... 48,440
Bourg-en-Bresse ... 42,181
Bourges (*86,041) ... 77,300
Brest (*190,812) ... 166,826
Briançon ... 9,489
Brive-la-Gaillarde ... 51,864
Bron (*Lyon) ... 44,563
Bruay-en-Artois (*116,340) ... 25,714
Caen (*181,390) ... 119,474
Cagnes [-sur-Mer] (*Nice) (29,538▲) ... 23,353
Cahors ... 20,311
Calais (*100,327) ... 78,820
Caluire-et-Cuire (*Lyon) ... 43,041
Cambrai (*51,357) ... 39,049
Cannes (*210,000) ... 70,527
Carcassonne ... 42,154
Carmaux (*23,000) ... 13,208
Castres ... 45,978
Châlons-sur-Marne (*63,407) ... 52,275
Chalon-sur-Saône (*72,407) ... 58,187
Chambéry (*88,081) ... 54,415
Chamonix-Mont-Blanc ... 6,285
Champigny-sur-Marne (*Paris) ... 80,291
Chantilly ... 10,552
Charleville-Mézières (*69,124) ... 60,176
Chartres (*72,246) ... 38,928
Châteauroux (*66,836) ... 53,429
Châtellerault (*66,836) ... 37,080
Châtenay-Malabry (*Paris) ... 30,497
Châtillon (*Paris) ... 26,574
Chatou (*Paris) ... 26,550
Chaumont ... 27,226
Chauny (*21,000) ... 14,405
Chelles (*Paris) ... 36,516
Cherbourg (*82,539) ... 32,536
Chinon ... 5,391
Choisy-le-Roi (*Paris) ... 38,705
Cholet ... 52,976
Clamart (*Paris) ... 52,952
Clermont-Ferrand (*253,244) ... 156,900
Clichy (*Paris) ... 47,764
Cognac ... 22,237
Colmar (*83,435) ... 64,771
Colombes (*Paris) ... 83,390
Compiègne (*57,210) ... 37,699
Concarneau (18,759▲) ... 15,096
Corbeil-Essonnes (*Paris) ... 38,859
Courbevoie (*Paris) ... 54,488
Coutances ... 8,349
Creil (*77,225) ... 32,509
Créteil (*Paris) ... 59,023
Dax (*27,000) ... 19,137
Deauville ... 5,664
Decazeville (*26,000) ... 10,231
Denain (**Valenciennes) ... 26,204
Dieppe (*40,000) ... 25,822
Dijon (*208,432) ... 151,705
Dinard ... 9,234
Dives-sur-Mer (*11,500) ... 5,872
Dole ... 29,295
Douai (*210,508) ... 45,239
Douarnenez ... 19,096
Drancy (*Paris) ... 64,430
Dreux ... 33,101
Dunkerque (*186,314) ... 83,163
Elbeuf (*48,000) ... 19,116
Épernay ... 29,677
Épinal (*53,522) ... 39,525
Épinay-sur-Seine (*Paris) ... 46,578
Étaples (*22,000) ... 10,559
Eu (*21,000) ... 8,626
Évreux ... 47,412
Fécamp ... 21,910
Foix ... 9,599
Fontaine (*Grenoble) ... 25,036
Fontainebleau (*36,000) ... 16,778
Fontenay-sous-Bois (*Paris) ... 46,475
Forbach (*62,000) ... 25,244
Fougères ... 26,610
Fréjus (*50,000) ... 28,851
Gagny (*Paris) ... 36,772
Gap (28,233▲) ... 25,052
Garges-lès-Gonesse (*Paris) ... 37,927
Gennevilliers (*Paris) ... 50,290
Givors (*35,000) ... 21,968
Granville ... 13,330
Grasse (34,579▲) ... 24,442
Grenoble (*389,088) ... 166,037
Guebwiller (*25,566) ... 11,072
Guéret ... 14,855
Haguenau ... 25,147
Hayange (*75,000) ... 20,426
Hendaye ... 9,470
Hénin-Beaumont (Hénin-Liétard) (**Lens) ... 26,359
Houilles (*Paris) ... 30,345
Hyères (**Toulon) (36,123▲) ... 29,611
Issy-les-Moulineaux (*Paris) ... 47,561
Ivry-sur-Seine (*Paris) ... 62,856
Jœuf (*30,000) ... 10,649
La Baule-Escoublac (*St.-Nazaire) ... 15,006
La Ciotat (32,721▲) ... 29,319
La Courneuve (*Paris) ... 37,958
La Garenne-Colombes (*Paris) ... 24,038
La Grand' Combe (*17,500) ... 10,452
Lambersart (*Lille) ... 29,642
Laon ... 27,914
La Rochelle (*100,649) ... 75,367
La Roche-sur-Yon ... 44,713
La Seyne-sur-Mer (*Toulon) ... 51,155
Laval ... 51,544
Le Blanc-Mesnil (*Paris) ... 49,107
Le Creusot ... 33,366
Le Grand-Quevilly (*Rouen) ... 31,963
Le Havre (*264,422) ... 217,881
Le Mans (*192,057) ... 152,285
Lens (*328,741) ... 40,199
Le Perreux-sur-Marne (*Paris) ... 28,333
Le Puy-en-Velay (*41,000) ... 26,594
Les Sables-d'Olonne (*29,000) ... 17,463
Levallois-Perret (*Paris) ... 52,523
Le Vésinet (*Paris) ... 17,986
L'Hay-les-Roses (*Paris) ... 31,412
Libourne ... 21,651
Liévin (*Lens) ... 33,070
Lille (*1,015,000) ... 172,280
Limoges (*167,664) ... 143,689
Lisieux ... 25,521
Livry-Gargan (*Paris) ... 32,917
Loches ... 6,738
Lomme (*Lille) ... 29,255
Longwy (*83,000) ... 20,131
Lons-le-Saunier ... 20,942
Lorient (*105,797) ... 69,769
Lourdes ... 17,870
Lunéville ... 22,709
Lyon (*1,170,660) ... 456,716
Mâcon ... 39,344
Maisons-Alfort (*Paris) ... 54,146
Maisons-Laffitte (*Paris) ... 23,504
Malakoff (*Paris) ... 34,121
Mantes-la-Jolie ... 42,465
Marcq-en-Baroeul (*Lille) ... 36,126
Marignane (*Marseille) ... 26,477
Marseille (*1,070,912) ... 908,600
Martigues (38,373▲) ... 26,897
Massy (*Paris) ... 41,344
Maubeuge (*105,000) ... 35,399
Mazamet (*28,000) ... 14,440
Meaux ... 42,243
Melun (*77,272) ... 37,705
Mende ... 10,451
Menton (*34,000) ... 25,129
Mérignac (*Bordeaux) ... 50,652
Metz (*181,191) ... 111,869
Meudon (*Paris) ... 52,806
Millau ... 21,907
Montargis (*50,200) ... 18,380
Montauban (48,053▲) ... 35,940
Montbéliard (*132,343) ... 30,425
Montceau-les-Mines (*51,385) ... 28,177
Mont-de-Marsan ... 26,166
Montélimar ... 28,058
Montereau-faut-Yonne ... 21,568
Montigny-lès-Metz (*Metz) ... 24,519
Montluçon (*71,988) ... 56,468
Montmorency (*Paris) ... 20,860
Montpellier (*211,430) ... 191,354
Montreuil-sous-Bois (*Paris) ... 96,587
Montrouge (*Paris) ... 40,304
Morlaix (19,237▲) ... 17,256
Moulins (*42,000) ... 26,067
Moyeuvre-Grande (*77,000) ... 12,523
Mulhouse (*218,743) ... 117,013
Nancy (*280,569) ... 107,902
Nanterre (*Paris) ... 95,032
Nantes (*453,500) ... 256,693
Narbonne ... 39,342
Neuilly-sur-Seine (*Paris) ... 65,983
Nevers (*59,424) ... 45,480
Nice (*437,566) ... 344,481
Nîmes (*131,638) ... 127,933
Niort (*64,128) ... 62,267
Nogent-sur-Marne (*Paris) ... 25,634
Noisy-le-Grande (*Paris) ... 26,662
Noisy-le-Sec (*Paris) ... 37,734
Noyon ... 13,889
Orange (25,371▲) ... 20,779
Orléans (*209,234) ... 106,246
Orly (*Paris) ... 26,109
Oullins (*Lyon) ... 27,772
Oyonnax ... 23,007
Palaiseau (*Paris) ... 28,716
Pantin (*Paris) ... 42,739
Paray-le-Monial ... 11,545
•PARIS (1980 E) (*9,450,000) ... 2,050,500
Pau (*126,859) ... 83,498
Périgueux (*57,830) ... 35,120
Perpignan (*117,689) ... 106,426
Pessac (*Bordeaux) ... 51,360
Poissy (*Paris) ... 37,431
Poitiers (*98,554) ... 81,313
Pont-à-Mousson (*23,000) ... 14,830
Pontoise (*Paris) ... 27,240
Port-de-Bouc ... 21,424
Privas ... 10,808
Puteaux (*Paris) ... 35,514
Quimper ... 55,977
Reims (*197,021) ... 178,381
Rennes (*229,310) ... 198,305
Rezé (*Nantes) ... 35,730
Rive-de-Gier (*38,000) ... 17,706
Roanne (*83,561) ... 55,195
Rochefort ... 28,155
Rodez (*35,000) ... 25,550
Romainville (*Paris) ... 26,260
Romans-sur-Isère (*46,000) ... 33,030
Rosny-sous-Bois (*Paris) ... 35,784
Roubaix (**Lille) ... 109,553
Rouen (*388,711) ... 114,927
Royan (*29,000) ... 18,062
Rueil-Malmaison (*Paris) ... 62,727
St.-Avold (*28,000) ... 17,955
St. Brieuc (*82,148) ... 52,559
St.-Chamond ... 40,250
St.-Cloud (*Paris) ... 28,139
St. Cyr-l'École (*Paris) ... 16,537
St.-Denis (*Paris) ... 96,132
St.-Dié ... 25,423
St.-Dizier ... 37,266
Saintes ... 26,891
St.-Étienne (*334,846) ... 220,070

C Census. E Official estimate. UE Unofficial estimate.
L Population within municipal limits of year specified. • Largest city in country.

* Population or designation of metropolitan area, including suburbs (see headnote).
▲ Population of an entire municipality, commune, or district, including rural area.
‡† Year of information specified at start of country.

St.-Étienne-du-Rouvray (★Rouen)....37,242
St.-Germain-en-Laye (★Paris)....37,509
St.-Jean-de-Luz (★23,000)....11,854
St.-Lô....23,221
St.-Malo....45,030
St.-Martin-d'Hères (★Grenoble)....38,052
St.-Maur-des-Fossés (★Paris)....80,920
St.-Nazaire (★119,418)....69,251
St.-Omer (★27,000)....16,932
St.-Ouen (★Paris)....43,588
St.-Quentin (★75,056)....67,243
St.-Tropez....4,523
Salon-de-Provence....34,576
Sarcelles (★Paris)....55,007
Sarreguemines....25,729
Sartrouville (★Paris)....42,253
Saumur....32,515
Savigny-sur-Orge (★Paris)....34,607
Schiltigheim (★Strasbourg)....30,144
Sedan....23,995
Senlis....13,639
Sens....26,463
Sète....39,258
Sèvres (★Paris)....21,149
Soissons (★49,000)....30,009
Sotteville (★Rouen)....31,659
Stains (★Paris)....35,545
Strasbourg (★390,000)....253,384
Suresnes (★Paris)....37,537
Talence (★Bordeaux)....34,127
Tarbes (★78,645)....54,897
Thann (★28,187)....8,519
Thionville (★141,881)....43,020
Thonon-les-Bains....26,354
Toul (★23,000)....16,454
Toulon (★378,430)....181,801
Toulouse (★509,939)....373,796
Tourcoing (★★Lille)....102,239
Tours (★245,631)....140,686
Trouville-sur-Mer (★16,000)....6,618
Troyes (★126,611)....72,167
Tulle....20,100
Valence (★104,330)....68,460
Valenciennes (★350,599)....42,473
Vannes....40,359
Vanves (★Paris)....22,528
Vénissieux (★Lyon)....74,347
Verdun....23,621
Versailles (★Paris)....94,145
Vesoul....18,173
Vichy (★59,062)....32,117
Vienne....27,830
Vierzon....35,699
Villefranche (★Nice)....7,200
Villefranche-sur-Saône (★42,000)....30,341
Villejuif (★Paris)....55,606
Villemomble (★Paris)....28,727
Villeneuve-d'Ascq (★Lille)....36,769
Villeneuve-St.-Georges (★Paris)....31,664
Villeurbanne (★Lyon)....116,535
Vincennes (★Paris)....44,261
Viry-Châtillon (★Paris)....32,411
Vitry-le-François....19,372
Vitry-sur-Seine (★Paris)....87,316
Voiron (★31,000)....19,420
Wattrelos (★Lille)....45,440

FRENCH GUIANA / Guyane française

1974 C....55,125

•CAYENNE....30,461
St.-Laurent-du-Maroni....3,182

FRENCH POLYNESIA / Polynésie française

1977 C....137,382

•PAPEETE (★42,000)....23,453

GABON

1976 E....530,000

Lambaréné....24,000
•LIBREVILLE....251,000
Port-Gentil....85,000

GAMBIA

1978 E....569,000

•BANJUL (BATHURST) (★88,000)....45,600

GAZA STRIP

1967 C....356,261

•GAZA (GHAZZAH)....118,272
Jabālyah....43,604
Khān Yūnis....52,997
Rafaḩ....49,812

GERMAN DEMOCRATIC REPUBLIC (EAST GERMANY) / Deutsche Demokratische Republik

1978 E....16,751,375

Altenburg....54,281
Annaberg-Buchholz....25,584
Apolda....28,961
Arnstadt....29,820
Aschersleben....35,259
Aue....30,053
Bautzen....47,450
•BERLIN, EAST (OST-BERLIN) (★★Berlin)....1,128,983
Bernburg....43,221
Bitterfeld (★105,000)....24,644
Blankenburg....18,143
Borna....23,326
Brandenburg....94,505
Burg [bei Magdeburg]....28,805
Coswig (★Dresden)....26,250
Cottbus....107,623
Crimmitschau....27,208
Delitzsch....24,124
Dessau (★135,000)....101,322
Döbeln....27,549
Dresden (★640,000)....514,508
Eberswalde....50,994
Eilenburg....21,969
Eisenach....49,850
Eisenhüttenstadt....48,677
Eisleben....27,785
Erfurt....208,800
Falkensee (★Berlin)....24,442
Finsterwalde....23,335
Forst [Lausitz]....27,030
Frankfurt an der Oder....77,175
Freiberg....50,808
Freital (★Dresden)....46,626
Fürstenwalde [Spree]....33,570
Gera....121,251
Glauchau....29,690
Görlitz....81,963
Gotha....58,369
Greifswald....60,636
Greiz....36,606
Güstrow....36,794
Halberstadt....47,919
Halle (★485,000)....232,543
Halle-Neustadt (★Halle)....91,860
Heidenau (★Dresden)....20,644
Hennigsdorf bei Berlin (★Berlin)....26,899
Hettstedt....19,646
Hoyerswerda....70,133
Ilmenau....24,026
Jena....102,025
Karl-Marx-Stadt (Chemnitz) (★460,000)....313,850
Köthen [Anhalt]....34,651
Lauchhammer....25,710
Leipzig (★710,000)....563,980
Leuna (★Halle) (1977 E)....10,132
Limbach-Oberfrohna (★Karl-Marx-Stadt)....24,272
Lübbenau [Spreewald]....22,365
Luckenwalde....27,677
Ludwigsfelde....20,081
Magdeburg (★395,000)....283,109
Meissen....40,858
Merseburg (★★Halle)....51,684
Mühlhausen (Thomas-Müntzer-Stadt)....43,678
Naumburg [an der Saale]....34,675
Neubrandenburg....73,258
Neuruppin....25,258
Neustrelitz....27,342
Nordhausen....46,317
Oranienburg (★Berlin)....24,258
Parchim....22,998
Pirna....48,233
Plauen....79,190
Potsdam (★Berlin)....126,262
Prenzlau....22,283
Quedlinburg....29,179
Radebeul (★Dresden)....35,497
Rathenow....32,341
Reichenbach [Vogtland]....25,909
Riesa....51,411
Rostock....224,834
Rudolstadt....31,435
Saalfeld [Saale]....33,876
Salzwedel....22,732
Sangerhausen....33,494
Schneeberg....21,842
Schönebeck....44,485
Schwedt [Oder]....52,228
Schwerin....115,950
Senftenberg....31,447
Sömmerda....21,933
Sondershausen....23,148
Sonneberg....28,663
Spremberg....22,582
Stassfurt....26,404
Stendal....42,942
Stralsund....73,889
Strausberg (★Berlin)....22,930
Suhl....42,324
Torgau....21,627
Waren....23,322
Weimar....62,803
Weissenfels....40,958
Weisswasser....29,632
Werdau....21,028
Wernigerode....35,435
Wilhelm-Pieck-Stadt Guben....36,826
Wismar....57,055
Wittenberg [Lutherstadt]....53,211
Wittenberge....32,893
Wolfen (★★Bitterfeld)....34,284
Zeitz....44,135
Zittau....41,822
Zwickau (★170,000)....123,446

GERMANY, FEDERAL REPUBLIC OF (WEST GERMANY) / Bundesrepublik Deutschland

1979 E....61,439,342

States

BADEN-WÜRTTEMBERG....9,190,052
BAYERN (BAVARIA)....10,870,968
BERLIN (WEST)....1,902,250
BREMEN....695,115
HAMBURG....1,653,043
HESSEN (HESSE)....5,576,085
NIEDERSACHSEN (LOWER SAXONY)....7,234,000
NORDRHEIN-WESTFALEN (NORTH RHINE-WESTPHALIA)....17,017,075
RHEINLAND-PFALZ (RHINE-LAND-PALATINATE)....3,633,195
SAARLAND....1,068,555
SCHLESWIG-HOLSTEIN....2,599,004

Cities

Aachen (★540,000)....242,971
Aalen (★80,000)....62,854
Achern....20,442
Achim (★Bremen)....27,442
Ahaus....27,824
Ahlen....53,681
Ahrensburg (★Hamburg)....25,416
Albstadt....48,192
Alfeld (Leine)....23,447
Alsdorf (★Aachen)....46,328
Altena....24,729
Amberg....44,541
Andernach (★★Neuwied)....26,897
Ansbach....38,338
Arnsberg....78,282
Aschaffenburg (★145,000)....59,054
Augsburg (★390,000)....245,940
Aurich....34,344
Backnang....29,104
Baden-Baden....49,399
Bad Harzburg (★Goslar)....25,095
Bad Hersfeld....28,240
Bad Homburg (★Frankfurt)....50,909
Bad Honnef am Rhein (★Bonn)....20,877
Bad Kissingen....22,331
Bad Kreuznach....41,255
Bad Nauheim (★Frankfurt)....26,852
Bad Neuenahr-Ahrweiler....26,027
Bad Oeynhausen....44,126
Bad Oldesloe....20,009
Bad Reichenhall....17,919
Bad Salzuflen (★★Herford)....51,181
Bad Vilbel (★Frankfurt)....25,875
Baesweiler (★Aachen)....23,471
Balingen....29,638
Bamberg (★120,000)....71,993
Barsinghausen (★Hannover)....32,699
Bayreuth (★89,000)....70,210
Beckum....37,952
Bensheim....32,874
Berchtesgaden....8,276
Bergheim (Erft) (★Cologne)....53,205
Bergisch Gladbach (★Cologne)....101,007
Bergkamen (★Essen)....47,533
Berlin, West- (★3,775,000)....1,902,250
Biberach....28,122
Bielefeld (★525,000)....312,357
Bietigheim-Bissingen (★Stuttgart)....33,982
Bingen....23,837
Böblingen (★Stuttgart)....41,065
Bocholt....65,346
Bochum (★★Essen)....402,988
BONN (★555,000)....286,184
Borken....31,939
Bornheim (★Bonn)....33,819
Bottrop (★Essen)....114,510
Brake....17,511
Bramsche....23,762
Braunschweig (Brunswick) (★335,000)....261,669
Bremen (★800,000)....556,128
Bremerhaven (★190,000)....138,987
Bretten....22,615
Brilon....24,439
Bruchsal....37,232
Brühl (★Cologne)....43,012
Buchholz in der Nordheide (★Hamburg)....27,999
Bückeburg....20,626
Bünde....39,871
Burgdorf (★Hannover)....27,949
Butzbach....21,096
Buxtehude (★Hamburg)....31,162
Calw....22,881
Castrop-Rauxel (★Essen)....79,264
Celle....72,804
Cloppenburg....20,681
Coburg....45,906
Coesfeld....31,093
Cologne (Köln) (★1,815,000)....976,136
Crailsheim....24,636
Cuxhaven....58,891
Dachau (★Munich)....34,162
Darmstadt (★305,000)....138,661
Datteln (★Essen)....37,004
Deggendorf....30,455
Delmenhorst (★★Bremen)....72,140
Detmold....67,116
Dillingen (★Saarlouis)....20,722
Dinslaken (★Essen)....58,334
Dormagen (★Cologne)....55,826
Dorsten (★Essen)....68,862
Dortmund (★★Essen)....609,954
Duderstadt....22,886
Duisburg (★★Essen)....559,066
Dülmen....38,074
Düren (★110,000)....86,308
Düsseldorf (★1,225,000)....594,770
Einbeck....28,923
Elmshorn....41,628
Emden....51,607
Emmendingen....24,448
Emmerich....29,378
Emsdetten....30,900
Ennepetal (★Essen)....35,965
Erftstadt (★Cologne)....42,905
Erkelenz....35,579
Erkrath (★Düsseldorf)....42,637
Erlangen (★★Nürnberg)....100,760
Eschwege....24,097
Eschweiler (★★Aachen)....53,065
Espelkamp....23,124
•Essen (★5,125,000)....652,501
Esslingen (★Stuttgart)....91,733
Ettlingen (★Karlsruhe)....36,259
Euskirchen....44,593
Fellbach (★Stuttgart)....41,653
Filderstadt (★Stuttgart)....36,757
Flensburg (★103,000)....88,810
Forchheim....28,932
Frankenthal (★Mannheim)....43,511
Frankfurt am Main (★1,880,000)....628,203
Frechen (★Cologne)....43,161
Freiburg (★220,000)....174,121
Freising....34,252
Friedrichshafen....51,541
Fulda (★79,000)....57,114
Fürstenfeldbruck (★Munich)....31,354
Fürth (★★Nürnberg)....98,266
Gaggenau....28,611
Garbsen (★Hannover)....57,406
Garmisch-Partenkirchen....27,765
Geldern....25,730
Gelsenkirchen (★★Essen)....306,323
Georgsmarienhütte (★Osnabrück)....30,857
Gevelsberg (★Essen)....31,138
Giessen (★160,000)....76,485
Gifhorn....33,006
Gladbeck (★Essen)....80,434
Goch....28,634
Göppingen (★155,000)....53,034
Goslar (★84,000)....52,815
Göttingen....128,118
Greven....28,414
Grevenbroich (★Düsseldorf)....58,644
Gronau (★Enschede, Netherlands)....41,042
Gummersbach....48,344
Gütersloh (★★Bielefeld)....77,792
Hagen (★★Essen)....220,676
Haltern (★Essen)....30,783
Hamburg (★2,260,000)....1,653,043
Hameln (★72,000)....59,005
Hamm....171,595
Hanau [am Main] (★★Frankfurt)....86,144
Hannover (★1,005,000)....535,854
Hattingen (★Essen)....57,255
Heidelberg (★★Mannheim)....128,773
Heidenheim (★89,000)....48,470
Heilbronn (★230,000)....111,426
Heinsberg....36,343
Helmstedt....26,816
Hemer....32,891
Hennef (★Siegburg)....28,835
Heppenheim (★Mannheim)....23,908
Herford (★120,000)....62,977
Herne (★Essen)....183,065
Herten (★Essen)....69,400
Herzogenrath (★Aachen)....42,425
Hilden (★Düsseldorf)....52,708
Hildesheim (★139,000)....102,512
Hof....53,398
Hofheim am Taunus (★Frankfurt)....33,262
Homburg (★★Zweibrücken)....41,581
Höxter....32,457
Hückelhoven....34,919
Hürth (★Cologne)....50,654
Ibbenbüren....42,149
Idar-Oberstein....35,811
Ingolstadt (★135,000)....89,467
Iserlohn....94,478
Itzehoe....33,707
Jülich....30,495
Kaarst (★Düsseldorf)....37,595
Kaiserslautern (★138,000)....99,197
Kamen (★Essen)....43,278
Kamp-Lintfort (★Essen)....37,859
Karlsruhe (★485,000)....271,417
Kassel (★370,000)....196,224
Kaufbeuren....42,204
Kempen (★Essen)....30,101
Kempten....57,390
Kerpen (★Cologne)....53,932
Kiel (★335,000)....250,750
Kirchheim (★Stuttgart)....31,756
Kleve (Cleves)....44,036
Koblenz (★180,000)....113,795
Königswinter (★Bonn)....34,935
Konstanz....67,948
Krefeld (★★Essen)....222,750
Kreuztal (★Siegen)....30,295
Kulmbach....28,324
Laatzen (★Hannover)....33,919
Lage....32,044
Lahr....35,516
Lampertheim (★Mannheim)....31,307
Landau....36,502
Landshut....55,538
Langen (★Frankfurt)....29,198
Langenfeld (★Düsseldorf)....46,590
Langenhagen (★Hannover)....46,825
Leer....31,316
Lehrte (★Hannover)....38,271
Leichlingen (★Cologne)....24,616
Leinfelden-Echterdingen (★Stuttgart)....35,044
Lemgo....39,512
Leonberg (★Stuttgart)....37,848
Leverkusen (★Cologne)....161,453
Lingen....43,864
Lippstadt....61,692
Löhne....37,111
Lörrach (★Basel, Switzerland)....41,522
Lübeck (★265,000)....222,120
Lüdenscheid....74,561
Ludwigsburg (★Stuttgart)....81,049
Ludwigshafen (★★Mannheim)....160,479
Lüneburg....62,198
Lünen (★Essen)....85,685
Mainz (★★Wiesbaden)....186,200
Mannheim (★1,395,000)....303,247
Marburg an der Lahn....74,724
Marl (★Essen)....89,441
Meerbusch (★Düsseldorf)....49,794
Melle....40,757
Memmingen....37,885
Menden [Sauerland]....53,101
Meppen....28,062
Merzig....30,008
Meschede....31,352
Mettmann (★Düsseldorf)....36,724
Minden (★125,000)....77,989
Moers (★Essen)....100,110
Mönchengladbach (★410,000)....258,001
Monheim (★Düsseldorf)....39,932
Mülheim an der Ruhr (★Essen)....182,465
Münden....26,047
Munich (München) (★1,940,000)....1,299,693
Münster....267,478
Nettetal....37,366
Neuburg an der Donau....23,945
Neu Isenburg (★Frankfurt)....35,899
Neumarkt in der Oberpfalz....30,226
Neumünster....80,331
Neunkirchen (★135,000)....52,216
Neuss (★Düsseldorf)....149,333
Neustadt am Rübenberge (★Hannover)....37,941
Neustadt an der Weinstrasse....50,405
Neu-Ulm (★Ulm)....47,263
Neuwied (★150,000)....60,461
Niederkassel (★Cologne)....25,460
Nienburg....30,207
Nordenham (★★Bremerhaven)....30,320
Norderstedt (★Hamburg)....64,302
Nordhorn....48,580
Northeim....32,307
Nürnberg (★1,025,000)....484,184
Nürtingen (★Stuttgart)....35,046
Oberammergau....4,800
Oberhausen (★★Essen)....229,613
Oberursel (★Frankfurt)....39,477
Oelde....27,335
Oer-Erkenschwick (★Essen)....26,702
Offenbach (★Frankfurt)....111,310
Offenburg....50,471
Oldenburg....136,155
Osnabrück (★270,000)....158,150
Paderborn....109,218
Papenburg....27,420
Passau....50,323
Peine....47,559
Pforzheim (★220,000)....106,677
Pinneberg (★Hamburg)....36,823
Pirmasens....50,250
Pulheim (★Cologne)....43,501
Rastatt....36,942
Ratingen (★Düsseldorf)....89,039
Ravensburg (★74,000)....42,081
Recklinghausen (★Essen)....119,472
Regensburg (★200,000)....132,399
Remagen (★Bonn)....14,342
Remscheid (★★Wuppertal)....129,507
Rendsburg....32,860
Reutlingen (★155,000)....94,737
Rheda-Wiedenbrück (★Bielefeld)....37,723
Rheinbach (★Bonn)....21,609
Rheinberg (★Essen)....26,205
Rheine....71,525
Rodgau (★Frankfurt)....34,854
Rosenheim....51,485
Rottenburg am Neckar....31,468
Rottweil....23,732
Rüsselsheim (★★Wiesbaden)....62,606
Saarbrücken (★390,000)....194,452
Saarlouis (★115,000)....39,028
Salzgitter....113,427
Sankt Augustin (★Bonn)....47,288
Sankt Ingbert....41,896
Sankt Wendel....26,880
Schleswig....30,118
Schmallenberg....24,929
Schorndorf (★Stuttgart)....33,527
Schwabach (★Nürnberg)....34,693
Schwäbisch Gmünd....56,621
Schwäbisch Hall....31,548
Schweinfurt (★110,000)....53,035
Schwelm (★Wuppertal)....31,207
Schwerte (★Essen)....47,333
Seelze (★Hannover)....30,293
Seevetal (★Hamburg)....35,409
Selb....21,428
Siegburg (★160,000)....34,475
Siegen (★205,000)....112,740
Sindelfingen (★Stuttgart)....54,153
Singen....43,653
Soest....40,373
Solingen (★★Wuppertal)....166,654
Speyer....43,663
Springe....30,528
Stade....42,519
Steinfurt....32,090
Stolberg (★★Aachen)....57,552
Straubing....42,718
Stuttgart (★1,935,000)....581,989
Sundern (Sauerland)....25,400
Trier (★125,000)....95,736
Troisdorf (★★Siegburg)....57,733
Tübingen....72,167
Tuttlingen....31,555
Uelzen....36,536
Ulm (★210,000)....99,560
Unna (★Essen)....56,903
Velbert (★Essen)....93,302
Verden....24,275
Viernheim (★Mannheim)....29,645
Viersen (★★Mönchengladbach)....81,419
Villingen-Schwenningen....78,465
Voerde (★Essen)....31,442
Völklingen (★★Saarbrücken)....44,901
Waiblingen (★Stuttgart)....44,968
Warendorf....32,909
Warstein....28,413
Wedel (★Hamburg)....30,075
Weiden....44,319
Weinheim (★Mannheim)....41,498
Wermelskirchen (★Wuppertal)....34,730
Wesel....56,760
Wetzlar (★105,000)....52,138
Wiesbaden (★795,000)....273,267
Wilhelmshaven (★135,000)....99,426
Willich (★Essen)....38,916
Witten (★Essen)....106,185
Wolfenbüttel (★★Braunschweig)....50,218
Wolfsburg....126,942
Worms (★★Mannheim)....73,505
Wunstorf (★Hannover)....37,318
Wuppertal (★870,000)....394,605
Würselen (★Aachen)....34,802
Würzburg (★205,000)....127,370
Zweibrücken (★105,000)....35,074

C Census. E Official estimate. UE Unofficial estimate.
L Population within municipal limits of year specified. • Largest city in country.

★ Population or designation of metropolitan area, including suburbs (see headnote).
▲ Population of an entire municipality, commune, or district, including rural area.
‡† Year of information specified at start of country.

GHANA

1970 C 8,559,313

•ACCRA (★738,498) 633,880
Bawku 20,567
Bolgatanga 18,896
Cape Coast 71,594
Ho 24,199
Keta 14,446
Koforidua 46,235
Kumasi 345,117
Nkawkaw 23,219
Nsawam 25,518
Obuasi 31,005
Oda 20,957
Sekondi-Takoradi 160,868
Tamale 83,653
Tarkwa 14,702
Tema 60,767
Wa 21,374
Winneba 30,778
Yendi 22,072

GIBRALTAR

1979 E 29,760

•GIBRALTAR 29,760

GREECE / Ellás

1971 C 8,768,641

Agrínion (★41,794) 30,973
Aiyáleo (★Athens) 79,961
Aíyion (★23,756) 18,829
Akharnaí (Acharnae) 24,621
Alexandroúpolis 22,995
Amaliás 14,177
Amaroúsion (★Athens) 27,112
Ambelókipoi (★Thessaloníki) 24,892
Árgos 18,890
Árta 19,498
•ATHENS (ATHÍNAI) (★2,540,241) 867,023
Ayía Varvára (★Athens) 26,409
Áyioi Anáryiroi (★Athens) 26,094
Áyios Dhimítrios (★Athens) 40,968
Dháfni (★Athens) 26,608
Dráma 29,692
Édhessa 13,967
Elevsís (Eleusis) 18,535
Ermoúpolis (Síros) (★16,082) 13,502
Flórina (Phlorina) 11,164
Galátsion (★Athens) 27,240
Glifádha (★Athens) 23,449
Grevená 8,016
Ilioúpolis (★Athens) 49,215
Ioánnina (Yanina) 40,130
Iráklion (Candia) (★84,710) 77,506
Iráklion (★Athens) 24,302
Kaisarianí (★Athens) 26,833
Kalámai (★40,402) 39,133
Kalamákion (★Athens) 26,957
Kalamariá 36,978
Kallithéa (★Athens) 82,438
Kardhítsa 25,685
Kastoría 15,407
Kateríni (★30,512) 28,808
Kavála 46,234
Keratsínion (★Athens) 67,672
Kérkira (Corfu) 28,630
Khaïdhárion (★Athens) 34,673
Khálandrion (★Athens) 35,944
Khalkís (Chalcis) 36,300
Khaniá (Canea) (★53,026) 40,564
Khíos (Chios) (★30,021) 24,084
Kifisiá (★Athens) 20,082
Komotiní 28,896
Koridhallós (★Athens) 47,335
Kórinthos (Corinth) 20,773
Kozáni 23,240
Lamía 37,872
Lárisa 72,336
Levádhia (Lebadea) 15,445
Mégara 17,294
Néa Ionía (★Athens) 54,906
Néa Liósia (★Athens) 56,217
Néa Smírni (★Athens) 42,512
Níkaia (★Athens) 86,269
Palaión Fáliron (★Athens) 35,066
Pátrai (Patras) (★120,847) 111,607
Peristérion (★Athens) 118,413
Piraiévs (Piraeus) (★★Athens) 187,362
Pírgos (Pyrgos) 20,599
Ródhos (Rhodes) 32,092
Salamís 18,256
Sérrai 39,897
Spárti (Sparta) (★13,432) 10,549
Thessaloníki (Salonika) (★557,360) 345,799
Thívai (Thebes) 15,971
Tríkkala 34,794
Trípolis (Tripolitza) 20,209
Véroia 29,528
Víron (★Athens) 44,021
Vólos (★88,096) 51,290
Xánthi 24,867
Zákinthos 9,339
Zografós (★Athens) 56,722

GREENLAND / Grønland

1977 E 49,719

Angmagssalik 1,023
Egedesminde 3,347
•GODTHÅB 8,545
Holsteinsborg 3,741
Julianehåb 2,670
Sukkertoppen 2,937
Thule 357

GRENADA

1976 E 109,609

•ST. GEORGE'S (★26,000) 10,000

GUADELOUPE

1974 C 324,530

BASSE-TERRE (★25,202) 15,457
Capesterre (18,143▲) 6,861
Les Abymes (★Pointe-à-Pitre) (53,605▲) 10,573
•Pointe-à-Pitre (★59,000) 23,889

GUAM

1980 C 105,816

•AGANA (★25,000) 881
Dededo 23,659

GUATEMALA

1973 C 5,211,929

Amatitlán 15,372
Antigua Guatemala 17,692
Chiquimula 16,181
Coatepeque 15,949
Escuintla 37,180
•GUATEMALA (★945,000) 717,322
Mazatenango 24,156
Puerto Barrios 19,696
Quezaltenango 45,977
Retalhuleu 20,222

GUERNSEY

1971 C 53,734

•ST. PETER PORT (★36,000) 16,303

GUINEA / Guinée

1967 E 3,702,000

•CONAKRY (1967 C) 197,267
Kankan 50,000
Kindia 45,000
Labé 26,000
Mamou 18,000
Nzérékoré 26,000
Siguiri 15,000

GUINEA-BISSAU

1970 C 487,448

•BISSAU 71,169

GUYANA

1976 E 783,000

•GEORGETOWN (★187,056) 72,049
New Amsterdam (1970 C) 17,782

HAITI / Haïti

1975 E 4,583,785

Cap-Haïtien 52,220
Gonaïves 33,837
Jérémie 19,227
Les Cayes 24,931
Pétionville (★Port-au-Prince) (1971 C) 35,257
•PORT-AU-PRINCE (1978 E) (★800,000) 745,700
Port-de-Paix 16,151
St.-Marc 19,354

HONDURAS

1977 E 2,998,700

Choluteca 29,300
Comayagua (1974 C) 15,941
El Progreso 32,800
La Ceiba 44,900
La Lima (1974 C) 14,631
Puerto Cortés 30,200
San Pedro Sula 172,900
•TEGUCIGALPA 316,800
Tela 22,700

HONG KONG

1976 C 4,402,990

Kowloon (★★Victoria) 749,600
New Kowloon (★Victoria) 1,628,880
Tai Wan Tsun (Ngau Tau Kok) (★Victoria) (1961 C) 53,836
Tsun Wan (★Victoria) 455,270
•VICTORIA (HONG KONG) (★3,975,000) 1,026,870

HUNGARY / Magyarország

1980 C 10,710,000

Ajka 30,000
Baja 39,000
Békés (22,000▲) 17,900
Békéscsaba (66,000▲) 57,400
•BUDAPEST (★2,600,000) 2,060,000
Cegléd (40,000▲) 32,500
Csongrád (22,000▲) 19,100
Debrecen 195,000
Dunaújváros 60,000
Eger 60,000
Érd (★Budapest) 40,000
Esztergom 31,000
Gödöllö (★Budapest) 26,000
Gyöngyös 38,000
Györ 125,000
Gyula (34,000▲) 29,300
Hajdúböszörmény (32,000▲) 28,600
Hajdúszoboszló 24,000
Hatvan 24,000
Hódmezövásárhely (54,000▲) 45,100
Jászberény (31,000▲) 24,900
Kaposvár 73,000
Karcag 24,000
Kazincbarcika 37,000
Kecskemét (93,000▲) 74,200
Kiskunfélegyháza (36,000▲) 27,300
Kiskunhalas (31,000▲) 22,700
Komló 30,000
Makó 30,000
Miskolc 210,000
Mohács (21,000▲) 17,700
Mosonmagyaróvár 30,000
Nagykanizsa 48,000
Nagykörös (27,000▲) 21,600
Nyíregyháza (107,000▲) 84,600
Orosháza (36,000▲) 31,500
Ózd 47,000
Pápa 32,000
Pécs 170,000
Salgótarján 49,000
Sopron 56,000
Szeged 175,000
Székesfehérvár 102,000
Szekszárd 34,000
Szentes (35,000▲) 30,600
Szolnok 77,000
Szombathely 82,000
Tata 24,000
Tatabánya 75,000
Törökszentmiklós (26,000▲) 22,500
Vác 34,000
Várpalota 28,000
Veszprém 55,000
Zalaegerszeg 55,000

ICELAND / Ísland

1979 E 226,724

Akureyri 13,137
Hafnarfjördur (★Reykjavík) 12,158
Keflavík 6,539
Kópavogur (★Reykjavík) 13,533
•REYKJAVIK (★120,085) 83,536

INDIA / Bhārat

1976 E 609,264,000

(total excludes Sikkim, annexed in 1975)

States

Andaman and Nicobar Islands (Ter.) 128,000
Andhra Pradesh 47,944,000
Arunachal Pradesh (Ter.) 520,000
Assam 17,354,000
Bihār 61,790,000
Chandīgarh (Ter.) 285,000
Dādra and Nagar Haveli (Ter.) 83,000
Delhi (Ter.) 5,116,000
Goa, Damān and Diu (Ter.) 954,000
Gujarāt 30,269,000
Haryana 11,221,000
Himāchal Pradesh 3,657,000
Jammu and Kashmīr 5,120,000
Karnataka (Mysore) 32,448,000
Kerala 23,955,000
Lakshadweep (Ter.) 36,000
Madhya Pradesh 47,167,000
Mahārāshtra 56,341,000
Manipur (Ter.) 1,195,000
Meghalaya 1,125,000
Mizoram (pop. included with Assam)
Nāgāland 557,000
Orissa 24,391,000
Pondicherry (Ter.) 524,000
Punjab 14,954,000
Rājasthān 29,005,000
Sikkim (1971 E) 196,852
Tamil Nadu (Madras) 45,434,000
Tripura (Ter.) 1,731,000
Uttar Pradesh 96,172,000
West Bengal 49,788,000

Cities (1971 C)

Abohar 58,925
Achalpur (Ellichpur) (★66,451) 42,326
Ādilābād 30,368
Ādoni 85,311
Agartala (★100,264) 59,625
Āgra (★634,622) 591,917
Āgra Cantonment (★Āgra) 37,074
Ahmadābād (★1,950,000) 1,585,544
Ahmadnagar (★148,405) 118,236
Aijal 31,740
Ajmer (★264,291) 262,851
Akola 168,438
Akot 41,534
Alandur (★Madras) 65,039
Alīgarh 252,314
Alīpur Duār (★54,454) 36,667
Allahābād (★513,036) 490,622
Alleppey 160,166
Almora (★20,881) 19,671
Alwar 100,378
Amalāpuram 30,518
Amalner 55,544
Ambāla (★186,126) 83,633
Ambāla Cantonment (★Ambāla) 102,493
Ambarnāth (★Bombay) 56,276
Ambāsamudram (★49,255) 27,709
Ambattur (★Madras) 45,586
Āmbūr 54,011
Amrāvati (Amraoti) (★221,277) 193,800
Amreli (★43,794) 39,520
Amritsar (★458,029) 407,628
Amroha 82,702
Anakapalle 57,273
Ānand 59,155
Anantapur 80,069
Arcot (★75,911) 30,230
Arkonam 43,347
Arni 38,664
Arrah 92,919
Aruppukkottai 62,223
Asansol (★925,000) 155,968
Ashoknagar-Kalyangarh (★Hābra) 41,916
Āttūr 41,569
Aurangābād (★165,253) 150,483
Avadi (★Madras) 77,413
Azamgarh 40,963
Badagara 53,938
Bāgalkot 51,746
Bahraich 73,931
Baidyabāti (★Calcutta) 54,130
Balasore 46,239
Ballarpur 34,268
Ballia 47,101
Balrāmpur 36,191
Bālurghāt 67,088
Bānda 50,575
Bangalore (★1,750,000) 1,540,741
Bangaon 50,538
Bānkura 79,129
Bansbāria (★Calcutta) 61,748
Bāpatla 41,947
Baranagar (★Calcutta) 136,842
Bārāsat (★Calcutta) 42,642
Baraut 31,264
Bareilly (★326,106) 296,248
Barmer 38,630
Barnāla 31,388
Baroda (Vadodara) (★467,487) 466,696
Barrackpore (★Calcutta) 96,889
Bārsi 62,374
Basīrhāt 63,816
Basti 49,635
Batāla (★76,488) 58,200
Beāwar 66,114
Begusarai (★44,084) 35,736
Behāla (South Suburban) (★Calcutta) 272,600
Belgaum (★213,872) 192,427
Bellampalle 30,290
Bellary 125,183
Berhampore (*West Bengal state*) (★78,909) 72,605
Berhampur (*Orissa state*) 117,662
Bettiah 51,018
Betūl 30,862
Bhadrakh 40,487
Bhadrāvati (★101,358) 40,203
Bhadreswar (★Calcutta) 45,586
Bhāgalpur 172,202
Bhandāra 39,423
Bharatpur (★69,902) 68,036
Bhatinda (★65,318) 53,684
Bhātpāra (★Calcutta) 204,750
Bhaunagar (★225,974) 225,358
Bhavāni (★56,696) 23,114
Bhilai (Bhilainagar) (★245,124) 157,173
Bhīlwāra 82,155
Bhīmavaram 63,762
Bhind (★45,794) 42,371
Bhiwandi (★Bombay) 79,576
Bhiwāni 73,086
Bhopāl (★384,859) 298,022
Bhubaneswar 105,491
Bhuj (★52,861) 52,177
Bhusāwal (★104,708) 96,800
Bīdar 50,670
Bihar 100,046
Bijāpur 103,931
Bijnor 43,290
Bīkaner (★208,894) 188,518
Bilāspur (★130,740) 98,410
Bīr (Bhir) 49,965
Bishnupur 38,135
Bodhan 37,589
Bodināyakkanūr 54,176
Bokāro Steel City (★107,159) 94,007
Bolāngir 35,748
Bombay (★6,750,000) 5,970,575
Botād 32,179
Broach (Bharuch) (★92,251) 91,589
Budaun 72,204
Budge Budge (★Calcutta) 51,039
Bulandshahr 59,505
Bulsār (Valsad) (★54,966) 43,254
Būndi 34,279
Burdwān 143,318
Burhānpur (★105,335) 105,246
Buxar 31,691
•Calcutta (★9,100,000) 3,148,746
Calicut (Kozhikode) 333,979
Cambay 62,097
Cannanore (★59,912) 55,162
Chaibāsā 35,386
Chākdaha 46,345
Chakradharpur (★34,967) 22,709
Chālakudi 37,562
Chālisgaon 41,720
Champdāni (★Calcutta) 58,596
Chandannagar (Chandernagore) (★Calcutta) 75,238
Chandausi 53,393
Chandīgarh (★232,940) 218,743
Chandrapur 75,134
Changanācheri 48,545
Chāpra (★98,401) 83,101
Chhatarpur 32,271
Chhindwāra (★53,508) 53,492
Chidambaram (★57,658) 48,811
Chikmagalūr 41,639
Chilakalūrupet 41,543
Chingleput 38,419
Chīrāla 54,487
Chitradurga 50,254
Chittaranjan 40,736
Chittoor 63,035
Chopda 32,656
Churu (★53,185) 52,502
Cochin 439,066
Coimbatore (★750,000) 356,368
Cooch Behār (★62,664) 53,684
Coonoor (★70,813) 38,007
Cuddalore 101,335
Cuddapah 66,195
Cumbum 40,796
Cuttack (★205,759) 194,068
Dabhoi 37,892
Dabra (★21,430) 18,623
Dalhousie (★5,123) 4,296
Daltonganj 32,367
Damān 17,317
Damoh (★59,983) 59,489
Dānāpur (★Patna) 42,694
Darbhanga 132,059
Darjeeling 42,873
Datia 36,439
Dāvangere 121,110
Dehra Dūn (★203,464) 166,073
Dehri 46,037
Delhi (★4,500,000) 3,706,558
Delhi Cantonment (★Delhi) 57,339
Deoband 38,194
Deoghar (★45,060) 40,356
Deolāli (★★Nāsik) 55,436
Deoria 38,161
Dewās (★51,866) 51,545
Dhānbād (★600,000) 79,838
Dhār 36,172
Dhārāpuram 34,500
Dharmapuri 40,086
Dholka 35,520
Dholpur 31,865
Dhorāji (★60,080) 59,773
Dhrāngadhra 40,791
Dhubri (★45,589) 36,503
Dhule 137,129
Dibrugarh 80,348
Digboi (★32,388) 16,538
Dindigul 128,429
Dohad (★51,406) 44,506
Dombivli (★Bombay) 51,108
Dum-Dum (★Calcutta) 31,363
Durg (★★Bhilai) 67,892
Durgapur 206,638
Dwarka 17,801
Elūru (Ellore) 127,023
English Bāzār (★68,026) 61,335
Erode (★169,613) 105,111
Etah 33,514
Etāwah 85,894
Faizābād (★109,806) 102,835
Farīdābād New Township (★Delhi) 85,762
Farrukhābād (★110,835) 102,768
Fatehābād 22,630
Fatehpur 54,665
Fatehpur Sīkri 13,561
Fāzilka 36,281
Fīrozābād 133,863
Fīrozpur (Ferozepore) (★97,709) 49,545
Gadag 95,426
Garden Reach (★Calcutta) 154,913
Garulia (★Calcutta) 44,271
Gauhāti (★200,377) 123,783
Gaya 179,884
Ghāziābād (★Delhi) 118,836
Ghāzīpur 45,635
Giridih 40,308
Godhra (★66,853) 66,403
Gonda 52,662
Gondal (★55,329) 54,928
Gondia 77,992
Gopichettipālaiyam 36,356
Gorakhpur 230,911
Govindpura (★Bhopāl) 53,922
Gūdalūr 32,843
Gudivāda 61,068
Gudiyāttam (★67,966) 63,007
Gūdūr 33,778
Gulbarga 145,588
Guna 40,006
Guntakal 66,320
Guntūr 269,991
Gurdāspur 32,064
Gurgaon 57,151
Gwalior (★406,140) 384,772
Hābra (★93,351) 51,435
Hājīpur 41,890
Haldwāni 52,205
Hālisahar (★Calcutta) 68,906
Hānsi 41,108
Hāpur 71,266
Hardoi 46,639
Hardwār (★79,277) 77,864
Harihar 33,888
Haripād 31,145
Hassan 51,325
Hāthras 74,349
Hazārībāgh 54,818
Hindupur 42,959
Hinganghāt 44,349
Hingoli 31,948
Hisār 89,437
Hooghly-Chinsura (★Calcutta) 105,241
Hoshiārpur 57,691
Hospet 65,196
Howrah (★Calcutta) 737,877
Hubli-Dhārwār 379,166
Hyderābād (★2,000,000) 1,607,396
Ichalkaranji 87,731
Imphāl 100,366
Indore (★560,936) 543,381
Itārsi (★46,866) 44,191
Jabalpur (★534,845) 426,224
Jabalpur Cantonment (★Jabalpur) 50,195
Jagādhri (★115,020) 35,094
Jagannāthnagar (★Rānchī) 55,663
Jagraon 32,999
Jagtiāl 30,900
Jaipur (★636,768) 615,258
Jālgaon 106,711
Jālna 91,099
Jalpaiguri 55,159
Jamālpur (★★Monghyr) 61,731
Jammu (★164,207) 155,338
Jāmnagar (★227,640) 199,709
Jamshedpur (★456,146) 341,576
Jaora 37,235
Jaridih Bazar (★69,321) 33,084
Jaunpur 80,737
Jetpur (★41,943) 41,926

C Census. E Official estimate. UE Unofficial estimate.
L Population within municipal limits of year specified. • Largest city in country.

★ Population or designation of metropolitan area, including suburbs (see headnote).
▲ Population of an entire municipality, commune, or district, including rural area.
‡† Year of information specified at start of country.

Jeypore 34,319
Jhānsi (★198,135) 173,292
Jharia (★★Dhānbād) 45,236
Jīnd 38,161
Jodhpur 317,612
Jorhāt (★70,674) 30,247
Jullundur (★329,830) 296,106
Junāgadh (★95,900) 95,485
Kadaiyanallūr 50,295
Kadiri 33,810
Kairāna 32,353
Kaithal 45,199
Kākināda 164,200
Kālol (★Ahmadābād) 50,321
Kalyān (★Bombay) 99,547
Kamarhati (★Calcutta) 169,404
Kāmthi (★Nāgpur) 53,412
Kānchipuram (Conjeeveram) (★119,693) 110,657
Kānchrāpāra (★Calcutta) 78,768
Kānpur (★1,320,000) 1,154,388
Kānpur Cantonment (★Kānpur) 69,452
Kapadvanj 30,748
Kapūrthala 35,482
Karād 42,329
Kāraikkudi (★88,371) 55,449
Kāranja 31,150
Karimganj 31,618
Karīmnagar 48,918
Karnāl 92,784
Karūr 65,706
Kāsaragod 34,984
Kāsganj 46,467
Kāshīpur 33,457
Katihār (★80,121) 67,014
Kayankulam (Kayamkulam) 54,102
Kerkend (★Dhānbād) 51,314
Khadki (Kirkee) (★Pune) 65,497
Khāmgaon 53,692
Khammam 56,919
Khandwa (★85,403) 84,517
Khanna 34,182
Kharagpur (★161,257) 61,783
Khargone 41,316
Khurja 50,245
Kilikollūr 41,871
Kishanganj 36,893
Kishangarh 37,405
Kohima 21,545
Kolār 43,418
Kolār Gold Fields (★118,861) 76,112
Kolhāpur (★267,513) 259,050
Konnagar (★Calcutta) 34,424
Kota 212,991
Kot Kapūra (★34,116) 33,907
Kottagūdem 75,542
Kottayam 59,714
Kovilpatti 48,509
Krishnanagar 85,923
Kulti (★★Asansol) 29,665
Kumbakonam (★119,655) 113,130
Kundla 37,957
Kurichi (★Coimbatore) 40,537
Kurnool 136,710
Lakhīmpur 43,752
Lalitpur 34,462
Lātūr 70,156
Leh 5,519
Lucknow (★840,000) 749,239
Lucknow Cantonment (★Lucknow) 39,338
Ludhiāna (★401,176) 397,850
Machilīpatnam (Bandar) 112,612
Madras (★3,200,000) 2,469,449
Madakulam (★Madurai) 46,317
Madanapalle 36,458
Madgaon (Margao) (★48,593) 41,655
Madhubani 32,919
Madurai (★725,000) 549,114
Mahbūbnagar 51,756
Mahuva 39,497
Mainpurī 43,849
Mālegaon 191,847
Māler Kotla (★48,859) 48,536
Malkāpur 35,476
Manappārai 32,092
Mandasor (★56,988) 52,347
Mandya 72,132
Mangalagiri 32,850
Mangalore (★215,122) 165,174
Mannārgudi 42,783
Mānsa 31,351
Mathura (★140,150) 132,028
Maunath Bhanjan 64,058
Māyūram 60,195
Meerut (★367,754) 270,993
Meerut Cantonment (★Meerut) 85,415
Mehsāna (Mahesāna) (★51,713) 51,598
Melappālaiyam (★Tirunelveli) 47,731
Mettupālaiyam 48,365
Mettūr 38,380
Mhow (★63,739) 59,037
Midnapore 71,326
Mira (★★Sāngli) 77,606
Mirzāpur 105,939
Modinagar 43,470
Moga (★61,625) 55,270
Mokameh 38,164
Monghyr (★164,205) 102,474
Morādābād (★272,652) 258,590
Morena 44,901
Mormugão 44,065
Morvi 60,976
Motihāri (★40,352) 37,032
Muktsar 36,750
Murtazāpur 23,141
Murwāra (Katni) (★86,535) 54,864
Mussoorie 18,038
Muzaffarnagar 114,783
Muzaffarpur 126,379
Mysore 355,685
Nabadwip 94,204
Nābha 34,761
Nadiād 108,269
Nāgappattinam (★74,019) 68,026
Nāgaur 36,448
Nāgda 32,569
Nāgercoil 141,288
Nagīna 37,066
Nāgpur (★950,000) 866,076
Naihāti (★Calcutta) 82,080
Naini Tāl (★25,167) 23,986
Najībābād 42,586
Nalgonda 33,126
Nānded 126,538
Nandurbār 54,070
Nandyāl 63,193
Nangi (★Calcutta) 47,555
Narasapur 36,147
Narasaraopet 43,467
Nārnaul 31,875
Nāsik (★271,681) 176,091
Navsāri (★80,101) 72,979
Nawābganj 35,395
Neemuch (★49,748) 47,113
Nellikkuppam 37,638
Nellore 133,590
NEW DELHI (★★Delhi) 301,801
Neyveli 58,285
Nipāni 35,116
Nizāmābād 115,640
North Barrackpore (★Calcutta) 76,335
North Dum-Dum (★Calcutta) 63,873
Nowgong 56,537
Ongole 53,330
Ootacamund 63,310
Orai 42,513
Outer Burnpur (★Asansol) 56,900
Pālakollu 36,196
Pālanpur 42,114
Pālayankottai (★★Tirunelveli) 70,070
Pālghāt 95,788
Pāli 49,834
Pallavaram (★Madras) 51,374
Palni (★51,664) 49,575
Palwal 36,207
Panaji (Panjim) (Nova Goa) (★59,258) 34,953
Pānchur (★Calcutta) 59,021
Pandharpur 53,638
Pandu (★Gauhati) 38,876
Pānihāti (★Calcutta) 148,046
Pānīpat 87,981
Panruti 34,065
Paramagudi 48,880
Parbhani 61,570
Parli 31,078
Pātan 64,519
Pattukkottai 37,682
Pathānkot (★78,192) 76,355
Patiāla (★151,041) 148,686
Patna (★625,000) 473,001
Periyakulam 41,561
Petlād 39,535
Phagwāra (★55,012) 50,863
Pīlibhīt 68,273
Pimpri-Chinchwad (★Pune) 83,542
Pithāpuram 31,391
Pollāchi (★93,838) 68,655
Pondicherry (★153,325) 90,637
Ponnāni 35,723
Porbandar (★106,727) 96,881
Port Blair 26,218
Proddatūr 70,822
Pudukkottai 66,384
Pulgaon 33,382
Puliyangudi 38,742
Pune (Poona) (★1,175,000) 856,105
Pune Cantonment (★Pune) 77,774
Puri 72,674
Purnea (★71,311) 56,484
Purūlia 57,708
Quilon 124,208
Rabkavi Banhatti 37,509
Rāe-Bareli 38,765
Rāichūr 79,831
Raiganj 43,191
Raigarh (★48,049) 46,745
Raipur (★205,986) 174,518
Rājahmundry (★188,805) 165,912
Rājapālaiyam 86,952
Rājkot 300,612
Rāj-Nāndgaon (★55,827) 41,183
Rājpur (★Calcutta) 34,393
Rāmanāthapuram 36,122
Rāmpur 161,417
Rānāghāt 47,815
Rānchī (★255,551) 175,934
Rānībennur 40,749
Rānīganj (★★Asansol) 40,104
Ratangarh 31,506
Ratlām (★119,247) 106,666
Ratnāgiri 37,551
Raurkela (★172,502) 125,426
Rewa 69,182
Rewāri 43,885
Rishīkesh 17,646
Rishra (★Calcutta) 63,486
Rohtak 124,755
Roorkee (★62,456) 47,561
Sāgar (★154,785) 118,574
Sahāranpur 225,396
Sāhibganj 35,640
Salem (★416,440) 308,716
Sāmalkot 34,607
Sambalpur (★105,085) 64,675
Sambhal 86,323
Sāngli (★201,597) 115,138
Sāntipur 61,166
Sardārshahr 37,703
Sāsarām 48,282
Sātāra 66,433
Satna (★62,162) 57,531
Secunderābād Cantonment (★Hyderābād) 94,416
Sehore 35,657
Seoni 38,396
Serampore (★Calcutta) 102,023
Shāhābād 33,408
Shāhjahānpur (★144,065) 135,604
Shāmli 36,959
Shikohābād 31,442
Shillong (★122,752) 87,659
Shimoga 102,709
Shivpuri (★50,858) 42,120
Sholāpur 398,361
Sidhpur (★41,334) 40,521
Sīkar 70,987
Silchar 52,596
Silīguri (★136,343) 97,484
Simla 55,368
Sindri (★★Dhānbād) 46,385
Singānallūr (★Coimbatore) 112,206
Sirsa 48,808
Sītāpur 66,715
Sivakāsi (★60,753) 44,883
Siwān 33,162
Sonīpat 62,393
South Dum-Dum (★Calcutta) 174,342
Sri Gangānagar (Gangānagar) 90,042
Srīkākulam 45,179
Srīnagar (★423,253) 403,413
Srīrangam (★Tiruchchirāppalli) 51,069
Srīvilliputtūr 53,855
Sūjāngarh 39,073
Sultānpur 32,330
Surat (★493,001) 471,656
Surendranagar (★97,251) 66,667
Sūri 30,110
Tādepallegūdem 43,610
Tādpatri 31,618
Tāmbaram (★Madras) 58,805
Tandā 41,611
Tanuku 34,197
Tellicherry 68,759
Tenāli 102,937
Tenkāsi 42,627
Tezpur 39,870
Thāna (★Bombay) 170,675
Thanjāvūr (Tanjore) 140,547
Theni-Allinagaram 34,854
Tindivanam 45,058
Tinsukia 54,911
Tiruchchirāppalli (Trichinopoly) (★475,000) 307,400
Tiruchendūr (★55,636) 18,126
Tiruchengodu 36,990
Tirunelveli (★266,688) 108,498
Tirupati (★71,984) 65,843
Tiruppattūr 40,357
Tiruppur (★151,127) 113,302
Tiruvannāmalai 61,370
Tiruvottiyūr (★Madras) 82,853
Titāgarh (★Calcutta) 88,218
Tonk 55,866
Trichūr 76,241
Trivandrum 409,627
Tumkūr 70,476
Tuticorin (★181,913) 155,310
Udaipur 161,278
Udamalpet 39,311
Udgīr 30,647
Ujjain (★208,561) 203,278
Ulhāsnagar (★Bombay) 168,462
Upleta 35,326
Uttarpara-Kotrung (★Calcutta) 67,568
Valparai 95,175
Vāniyambādi (★57,686) 51,810
Vārānasi (Benares) (★606,271) 583,856
Vellore (★178,554) 139,082
Verāval (★75,520) 58,771
Vidisha 43,212
Vijayawāda (★344,607) 317,258
Vikramasingapuram 40,274
Villupuram 60,242
Viramgām 43,790
Virudunagar 61,902
Vishākhapatnam (★363,467) 352,504
Visnagar 34,863
Vizianagaram 86,608
Warangal 207,520
Wardha 69,037
Yādgīr 32,756
Yamunānagar (★★Jagādhri) 72,594
Yavatmāl 64,836

INDONESIA

1979 E ....†144,911,000

Island Groups

BORNEO, INDONESIAN (KALIMANTAN) 6,406,000
CELEBES 10,605,000
JAVA AND MADURA 90,780,000
LESSER SUNDA ISLANDS †8,153,000
MOLUCCAS 2,481,000
SUMATRA 26,486,000

†Total excludes Timor Timur, annexed in 1976

Cities (‡1971 C or 1961 C)

Amahai 18,256
Ambon (Amboina) (1976 E) 91,000
Amuntai 27,383
Balikpapan ‡137,340
Banda Aceh (Kutaradja) ‡53,668
Bandung (★1,250,000) ‡1,201,730
Bangil 28,275
Bangkalan 28,300
Banjarmasin ‡281,673
Bantul 30,572
Banyuwangi ‡89,303
Baubau 21,060
Bekasi ‡45,694
Bengkulu ‡31,866
Binjai ‡59,882
Blitar ‡67,856
Blora ‡53,504
Bogor ‡195,882
Bojonegoro ‡52,597
Bondowoso 35,760
Brebes ‡44,456
Bukittinggi ‡63,132
Ciamis 35,189
Cianjur (Tjiandjur) 62,546
Cilacap (Tjilatjap) ‡82,043
Cimahi (Tjimahi) ‡72,367
Cirebon (Tjirebon) ‡178,529
Denpasar ‡88,142
Dili (1970 C) (65,451▲) 6,730
Ende 26,843
Garut ‡81,234
Gorontalo ‡82,328
Gresik ‡48,561
Indramayu 25,710
●JAKARTA (DJAKARTA) (1979 UE) (★6,500,000) 6,400,000
Jambi (Telanaipura) ‡158,559
Jayapura (Sukarnapura) (1976 E) 61,054
Jember ‡122,712
Jepara 18,921
Jombang ‡45,450
Kediri ‡178,865
Klaten 33,400
Kotabumi 37,496
Krawang ‡61,361
Kualakapuas 18,573
Kudus ‡87,767
Kuningan 21,542
Kupang ‡52,698
Lahat ‡41,030
Langsa ‡55,016
Lawang 35,852
Lhokseumawe 28,386
Lumajang ‡48,995
Madiun ‡136,147
Magelang ‡110,308
Magetan 26,818
Majalengka 14,361
Majene 24,259
Makale 32,578
Malang ‡422,428
Manado ‡169,684
Martapura ‡69,729
Medan ‡635,562
Mojokerto ‡60,013
Nganjuk 23,499
Ngawi 29,220
Padang ‡196,339
Padangpanjang ‡30,711
Padangsidempuan ‡49,090
Pakanbaru ‡145,030
Palangkaraya ‡27,132
Palembang ‡582,961
Palopo 29,724
Palu 16,977
Pamekasan ‡41,416
Pangkalpinang ‡74,733
Parepare ‡72,538
Pasuruan ‡75,266
Pati ‡46,037
Payakumbuh ‡63,388
Pekalongan ‡111,537
Pemalang ‡77,672
Pematangsiantar ‡129,232
Perabumulih 41,951
Pinrang 23,818
Ponorogo ‡67,711
Pontianak ‡217,555
Praya 26,729
Probolinggo ‡82,008
Purbolinggo 22,698
Purwakarta ‡49,703
Purwokerto ‡94,023
Purworejo ‡52,956
Raba 29,881
Rangkasbitung 30,822
Salatiga ‡69,831
Samarinda ‡137,521
Semarang ‡646,590
Serang ‡56,263
Sibolga ‡42,223
Sidoarjo ‡41,254
Singaraja ‡42,289
Singkawang 35,169
Situbondo ‡55,348
Solok ‡24,771
Sragen 25,685
Subang ‡42,437
Sukabumi ‡96,242
Sungaipenuh 36,766
Surabaya (★1,400,000) ‡1,332,249
Surakarta ‡414,285
Tangerang ‡50,893
Tanjungbalai ‡33,604
Tanjungkarang-Telukbetung ‡198,986
Tanjungpandan 29,412
Tanjungpinang 37,638
Tarutung 24,998
Tasikmalaya ‡136,004
Tebingtinggi ‡30,314
Tegal ‡105,752
Ternate 24,287
Tidore 26,160
Tual 38,403
Tuban 38,575
Tulungagung ‡68,899
Ujung Pandang (Makasar) ‡434,766
Watampone ‡54,720
Yogyakarta (Jogjakarta) ‡342,267

IRAN / Īrān

1976 C 33,591,875

Ābādān 296,081
Ahvāz 329,006
Āmol 68,782
Arāk 114,507
Ardabīl 147,404
Bābol 67,790
Bakhtarān 290,861
Bandar 'Abbās 89,103
Bandar-e Anzalī (Bandar-e Pahlavī) 55,978
Behbehān (1966 C) 39,874
Behshahr (1966 C) 26,032
Bīrjand (1966 C) 25,854
Bojnūrd (1966 C) 31,248
Borūjerd 100,103
Dezfūl 110,287
Emāmshahr (Shahrūd) (1966 C) 30,767
Eşfahān (Isfahan) 671,825
Gonbad-e Qābūs 59,868
Gorgān 88,348
Hamadān 155,846
Homāyunshahr (1966 C) 46,836
Jahrom (1966 C) 38,236
Karaj 138,774
Kāshān 84,545
Kāzerūn 51,309
Kermān 140,309
Khorramābād 104,928
Khorramshahr 146,709
Khvoy 70,040
Lāhījān (1966 C) 25,725
Lār (1966 C) 21,576
Mahābād (1966 C) 28,610
Malāyer (1966 C) 28,434
Marāgheh 60,820
Marand (1966 C) 23,818
Marv Dasht (1966 C) 25,498
Mashhad (Meshed) 670,180
Masjed Soleymān 77,161
Mīāneh (1966 C) 28,447
Najafābād 76,236
Neyshābūr 59,101
Ōrūmīyeh (Reẓā'īyeh) 163,991
Qā'emshahr (Shāhī) 63,289
Qazvīn 138,527
Qom 246,831
Qūchān (1966 C) 29,133
Rasht 187,203
Sabzevār 69,174
Sanandaj 95,834
Sārī 70,936
Semnān (1966 C) 31,058
Shīrāz 416,408
Tabrīz 598,576
●TEHRĀN (★4,700,000) 4,496,159
Torbat-e Ḩeydarīyeh (1966 C) 30,106
Yazd 135,978
Zāhedān 92,628
Zanjān 99,967

IRAQ / Al-'Irāq

1970 E 9,465,800

Ad-Dīwānīyah 62,300
Al-'Amārah 80,100
Al-Başrah (Basra) 370,900
Al-Fallūjah (1965 C) 38,072
Al-Ḩillah (Hilla) 128,800
Al-Kūfah (1965 C) 30,862
Al-Mawşil (Mosul) 293,100
An-Najaf 179,200
An-Nāşirīyah 62,400
Ar-Ramādī (1965 C) 28,723
As-Samāwah (1965 C) 33,473
As-Sulaymānīyah 98,100
Az-Zubayr (1965 C) 41,408
●BAGHDĀD (★2,183,800) 1,300,000
Ba'qūbah (1965 C) 34,575
Irbīl 107,400
Karbalā' 107,500
Kirkūk 207,900
Kūt al-Imāra (Al-Kūt) (1965 C) 42,116
Sāmarrā (1965 C) 24,746
Tall 'Afar (1965 C) 36,837

IRELAND / Eire

1979 C 3,368,217

An Uaimh (Navan) (★7,000) 4,277
Arklow (Inbhear Mór) 8,446
Athlone (Áth Luain) (★12,500) 9,760
Ballina (Béal Átha an Fheadha) 6,941
Ballinasloe (Béal Átha na Sluagh) 6,461
Bray (Brí Chualann) (★Dublin) 21,672
Carlow (Ceatharlach) 11,404
Carrick-on-Suir (Carraig na Siúire) 5,510
Castlebar (Caisleán an Bharraigh) 6,482
Clonmel (Cluain Meala) 12,411
Cobh 6,670
Cork (Corcaigh) (★175,000) 138,267
Drogheda (Droichead Átha) 22,555
Droichead Nua (1971 C) 5,053
●DUBLIN (BAILE ÁTHA CLIATH) (★1,110,000) 544,586
Dundalk (Dún Dealgan) 25,281
Dungarvan (Dún Garbháin) 6,578
Dún Laoghaire (★Dublin) 54,244
Ennis (Inis) (★12,000) 6,277
Enniscorthy (Inis Coirthe) 5,253
Galway (Gaillimh) 36,824
Kilkenny (Cill Choinnigh) (★14,800) 10,075
Killarney (Cill Áirne) 7,724
Limerick (Luimneach) (★80,000) 60,665
Mallow (Mala) 6,609
Monaghan (Muineachán) 6,173
Mullingar (Muileann Cearr) (1971 C) (★9,245) 6,790
Naas (Nás na Ríogh) (★Dublin) 7,740
Nenagh (Aonach Urmhumhan) 5,647
New Ross (Ros Mhic Treoin) 5,230
Portlaoise (1971 C) (★6,470) 3,902
Sligo (Sligeach) 16,836
Thurles (Durlas Éile) 7,436
Tipperary (Tiobrad Árann) 4,929
Tralee (Tráighlí) 15,011
Tuam (Tuaim) (1971 C) (★4,952) 3,808
Tullamore (Tulach Mhór) 7,720
Waterford (Port Láirge) (★42,000) 32,617
Wexford (Loch Garman) 11,848
Youghal (Eochaill) 5,739

ISLE OF MAN

1976 C 61,723

●DOUGLAS (★28,500) 20,262
Peel 3,338
Ramsey 5,458

C Census. E Official estimate. UE Unofficial estimate.
L Population within municipal limits of specified year. ● Largest city in country.

★ Population or designation of metropolitan area, including suburbs (see headnote).
▲ Population of an entire municipality, commune, or district, including rural area.
‡† Year of information specified at start of country.

ISRAEL / Yisra'el

1979 E ... †3,836,200

'Afula ... 19,700
'Akko (Acre) (★Haifa) ... 37,900
Ashdod ... 62,300
Ashqelon ... 52,000
Bat Yam (★Tel Aviv-Yafo) ... 130,100
Be'er Sheva' (Beersheba) ... 107,000
Bene Beraq (★Tel Aviv-Yafo) ... 89,600
Dimona ... 27,800
Elat (Elath) ... 18,900
Giv'atayim (★Tel Aviv-Yafo) ... 49,300
Hadera ... 37,800
Haifa (Hefa) (★415,000) ... 229,300
Herzliyya (★Tel Aviv-Yafo) ... 56,400
Holon (★Tel Aviv-Yafo) ... 128,400
JERUSALEM (YERUSHALAYIM) (AL-QUDS) *(includes Old City area occupied in 1967)* (★420,000) ... 398,200
Kefar Ata (★Haifa) ... 31,400
Kefar Sava (★Tel Aviv-Yafo) ... 38,100
Lod (Lydda) ... 39,400
Nahariyya ... 28,200
Nazerat (Nazareth) (★63,000) ... 40,400
Nazerat 'Illit (★Nazerat) ... 21,400
Nes Ziyyona ... 13,700
Netanya ... 95,900
Or Yehuda (★Tel Aviv-Yafo) ... 19,400
Petah Tiqwa (★Tel Aviv-Yafo) ... 117,000
Qiryat Bialik (★Haifa) ... 27,500
Qiryat Gat ... 24,300
Qiryat Motzkin (★Haifa) ... 23,200
Qiryat Ono (★Tel Aviv-Yafo) ... 22,500
Qiryat Shemona ... 15,800
Qiryat Yam (★Haifa) ... 28,400
Ra'anana (★Tel Aviv-Yafo) ... 29,700
Ramat Gan (★Tel Aviv-Yafo) ... 120,400
Ramat HaSharon (★Tel Aviv-Yafo) ... 30,100
Ramla ... 40,600
Rehovot ... 63,700
Rishon le Ziyyon (★Tel Aviv-Yafo) ... 87,800
•Tel Aviv-Yafo (Tel Aviv-Jaffa) (★1,350,000) ... 336,300
Teverya (Tiberias) ... 28,300
Tirat Karmel (★Haifa) ... 15,500
Umm el Fahm ... 18,600
Zefat ... 15,500

ITALY / Italia

1979 E ... 56,999,047

Regions and Provinces

ABRUZZI ... 1,239,738
Chieti ... 372,791
L'Aquila ... 302,480
Pescara ... 291,592
Teramo ... 272,875
APULIA, see PUGLIA
BASILICATA (LUCANIA) ... 618,703
Matera ... 204,273
Potenza ... 414,430
CALABRIA ... 2,078,264
Catanzaro ... 748,166
Cosenza ... 735,673
Reggio di Calabria ... 594,425
CAMPANIA ... 5,457,838
Avellino ... 440,712
Benevento ... 294,438
Caserta ... 753,207
Napoli (Naples) ... 2,945,181
Salerno ... 1,024,300
EMILIA-ROMAGNA ... 3,964,538
Bologna ... 937,136
Ferrara ... 385,503
Forlì ... 598,672
Modena ... 590,547
Parma ... 399,560
Piacenza ... 280,981
Ravenna ... 361,634
Reggio nell'Emilia ... 410,505
FRIULI-VENEZIA GIULIA ... 1,245,130
Gorizia ... 146,600
Pordenone ... 274,550
Trieste ... 291,581
Udine ... 532,399
LAZIO (LATIUM) ... 5,059,174
Frosinone ... 464,439
Latina ... 434,787
Rieti ... 143,983
Roma (Rome) ... 3,747,003
Viterbo ... 268,962
LIGURIA ... 1,844,779
Genova ... 1,065,846
Imperia ... 229,936
La Spezia ... 244,558
Savona ... 304,439
LOMBARDIA (LOMBARDY) ... 8,941,704
Bergamo ... 890,540
Brescia ... 1,015,350
Como ... 772,532
Cremona ... 333,403
Mantova ... 380,413
Milano ... 4,065,584
Pavia ... 519,369
Sondrio ... 175,188
Varese ... 789,325
MARCHE (MARCHES) ... 1,415,563
Ancona ... 434,091
Ascoli Piceno ... 354,667
Macerata ... 292,728
Pesaro e Urbino ... 334,077
MOLISE ... 334,091
Campobasso ... 238,564
Isernia ... 95,527
PIEMONTE (PIEDMONT) ... 4,531,141
Alessandria ... 472,865
Asti ... 217,982
Cuneo ... 548,236
Novara ... 509,830
Torino (Turin) ... 2,380,674
Vercelli ... 401,554
PUGLIA (APULIA) ... 3,917,029
Bari ... 1,471,563
Brindisi ... 400,092
Foggia ... 692,245
Lecce ... 778,830
Taranto ... 574,299
SARDEGNA (SARDINIA) ... 1,601,586
Cagliari ... 730,333
Nuoro ... 278,267
Oristano ... 157,151
Sassari ... 435,835
SICILIA (SICILY) ... 4,999,032
Agrigento ... 489,020
Caltanissetta ... 295,817
Catania ... 1,014,493
Enna ... 204,114
Messina ... 686,764
Palermo ... 1,206,291
Ragusa ... 276,312
Siracusa ... 397,818
Trapani ... 428,403
TOSCANA (TUSCANY) ... 3,600,233
Arezzo ... 313,801
Firenze ... 1,209,407
Grosseto ... 223,661
Livorno ... 346,395
Lucca ... 388,576
Massa-Carrara ... 205,535
Pisa ... 388,560
Pistoia ... 266,526
Siena ... 257,772
TRENTINO-ALTO ADIGE ... 876,249
Bolzano ... 432,073
Trento ... 444,176
UMBRIA ... 808,351
Perugia ... 579,311
Terni ... 229,040
VALLE D'AOSTA ... 114,591
VENETO (VENETIA) ... 4,351,313
Belluno ... 224,829
Padova ... 813,289
Rovigo ... 254,466
Treviso ... 716,250
Venezia (Venice) ... 844,391
Verona ... 774,347
Vicenza ... 723,741

Cities

Abano Terme ... 16,115
Acerra (★Naples) (37,629▲) ... 33,100
Acireale (49,813▲) ... 30,600
Adrano ... 34,190
Afragola (★Naples) ... 58,927
Agrigento ... 51,725
Alassio ... 13,943
Alba ... 31,309
Albano Laziale (★Rome) (27,889▲) ... 22,000
Alberobello ... 9,983
Alcamo ... 43,593
Alessandria ... 101,684
Alghero (37,892▲) ... 31,700
Altamura ... 49,878
Amalfi ... 6,446
Ancona ... 108,371
Andria ... 83,734
Anzio ... 27,223
Aosta ... 39,072
Arezzo ... 92,245
Ascoli Piceno ... 56,200
Assisi (24,910▲) ... 19,400
Asti ... 79,407
Augusta ... 38,181
Avellino ... 59,324
Aversa (★Naples) ... 51,837
Avezzano (34,353▲) ... 29,800
Avola ... 30,565
Bagheria ... 41,373
Barcellona Pozzo di Gotto (37,737▲) ... 26,000
Bari (★460,000) ... 387,266
Barletta ... 81,414
Bassano del Grappa ... 37,801
Battipaglia (40,604▲) ... 32,200
Belluno ... 37,003
Benevento (62,524▲) ... 52,800
Bergamo (★340,000) ... 125,544
Biella ... 55,857
Bisceglie ... 46,962
Bitonto ... 48,052
Bollate (★Milan) ... 43,115
Bologna (★550,000) ... 471,554
Bolzano (Bozen) ... 106,199
Bordighera (12,014▲) ... 9,600
Brescia ... 212,265
Bresso (★Milan) ... 34,245
Brindisi ... 89,241
Busto Arsizio (★Milan) ... 81,139
Cagliari (★305,000) ... 241,472
Caltagirone ... 38,525
Caltanissetta (61,461▲) ... 54,700
Camaiore (31,110▲) ... 22,700
Camerino (8,085▲) ... 3,400
Campobasso ... 47,316
Canicattì ... 32,603
Canosa di Puglia ... 30,781
Cantù ... 36,664
Capannori (43,972▲) ... 36,900
Capua ... 18,435
Carbonia ... 33,162
Carpi (59,824▲) ... 51,800
Carrara (★★Massa) ... 70,227
Casale Monferrato ... 42,711
Cascina ... 35,073
Caserta ... 67,257
Casoria (★Naples) ... 67,242
Cassino (32,181▲) ... 27,200
Castel Gandolfo (★Rome) (5,953▲) ... 3,400
Castellammare di Stabia (★Naples) ... 74,452
Castelvetrano ... 31,382
Catania (★515,000) ... 398,426
Catanzaro ... 93,845
Cattolica ... 15,811
Cava de' Tirreni (★Salerno) (51,611▲) ... 45,500
Cefalù (13,624▲) ... 11,600
Cerignola (51,349▲) ... 45,300
Cesano Maderno (★Milan) ... 32,637
Cesena (90,269▲) ... 68,100
Cesenatico (20,222▲) ... 15,900
Chiavari ... 30,508
Chieri (31,012▲) ... 26,400
Chieti ... 57,140
Chioggia (53,611▲) ... 38,200
Chivasso ... 27,064
Ciampino (★Rome) ... 30,561
Cinisello Balsamo (★Milan) ... 80,387
Cittadella (17,182▲) ... 7,000
Città di Castello (37,497▲) ... 28,600
Civitanova Marche (36,002▲) ... 31,500
Civitavecchia ... 48,342
Collegno (★Turin) ... 46,326
Cologno Monzese (★Milan) ... 51,855
Como (★160,000) ... 96,665
Conegliano (36,000▲) ... 29,500
Corato ... 41,623
Corsico (★Milan) ... 43,769
Cortina d'Ampezzo ... 8,326
Cosenza (★130,000) ... 102,338
Crema ... 34,742
Cremona ... 82,056
Crotone ... 57,009
Cuneo ... 55,784
Desio (★Milan) ... 33,051
Domodossola ... 20,704
Eboli ... 29,044
Empoli ... 45,725
Enna ... 29,370
Ercolano (Resina) (★Naples) ... 57,114
Erice ... 26,282
Este ... 18,283
Faenza (55,538▲) ... 40,100
Fano (53,273▲) ... 44,000
Fasano (36,420▲) ... 23,300
Favara ... 33,046
Fermo (35,186▲) ... 27,000
Ferrara (152,752▲) ... 125,200
Fiesole (★Florence) ... 14,760
Florence (Firenze) (★660,000) ... 462,690
Foggia ... 157,727
Foligno (52,580▲) ... 46,300
Forlì (110,523▲) ... 92,500
Francavilla Fontana ... 34,565
Frascati (★Rome) ... 19,587
Frattamaggiore (★Naples) ... 38,134
Frosinone ... 45,725
Gaeta ... 24,437
Gallarate (★Milan) ... 47,741
Gela ... 75,201
Genoa (Genova) (★855,000) ... 782,476
Giugliano in Campania (★Naples) ... 42,347
Gorizia ... 42,580
Gravina in Puglia ... 36,628
Grosseto (69,699▲) ... 61,600
Grottaglie ... 28,477
Grugliasco (★Turin) ... 34,202
Gubbio (32,164▲) ... 9,900
Guidonia Montecelio (★Rome) ... 48,821
Iesi (Jesi) (41,974▲) ... 35,600
Iglesias ... 29,561
Imola (60,234▲) ... 48,000
Imperia ... 42,159
Isernia (19,121▲) ... 14,500
Ivrea ... 28,650
L'Aquila ... 66,644
La Spezia (★192,000) ... 117,761
Latina (94,910▲) ... 83,200
Lecce ... 90,121
Lecco ... 52,806
Legnago ... 27,044
Legnano (★Milan) ... 49,600
Lentini ... 34,350
Licata ... 42,250
Limbiate (★Milan) ... 32,815
Lissone (★Milan) ... 30,482
Livorno (Leghorn) ... 176,757
Lodi ... 43,927
Loreto (10,851▲) ... 6,000
Lucca ... 91,256
Lucera (33,307▲) ... 28,500
Lugo (34,518▲) ... 20,300
Macerata (44,492▲) ... 37,700
Maddaloni (33,228▲) ... 26,100
Magenta ... 23,627
Manduria ... 30,488
Manfredonia (53,052▲) ... 45,800
Mantova ... 64,008
Marino (★Rome) ... 30,464
Marsala (86,051▲) ... 50,400
Martina Franca (44,340▲) ... 32,600
Massa (★145,000) ... 66,060
Matera ... 50,424
Mazara del Vallo ... 43,825
Merano (Meran) ... 34,460
Messina ... 271,660
•Milan (Milano) (★3,800,000) ... 1,677,109
Milazzo (30,710▲) ... 20,500
Modena ... 180,428
Modica (47,742▲) ... 31,400
Molfetta ... 66,699
Moncalieri (★Turin) ... 65,066
Monfalcone ... 31,053
Monopoli (44,017▲) ... 29,800
Monreale ... 25,416
Montecatini Terme ... 21,843
Montepulciano (14,255▲) ... 9,500
Monte Sant'Angelo ... 17,421
Monza (★Milan) ... 123,834
Naples (Napoli) (★2,740,000) ... 1,223,228
Nardò (30,916▲) ... 24,200
Nettuno (29,321▲) ... 25,300
Nicastro (Lamezia Terme) (62,069▲) ... 29,800
Nichelino (★Turin) ... 45,092
Nocera Inferiore (51,533▲) ... 43,300
Nola (29,282▲) ... 22,400
Novara ... 101,947
Novi Ligure ... 31,783
Nuoro ... 36,503
Oristano ... 29,769
Orvieto (23,414▲) ... 17,500
Otranto ... 4,748
Paderno Dugnano (★Milan) ... 38,885
Padova (★280,000) ... 242,216
Pagani ... 32,713
Palermo ... 693,949
Parma ... 176,945
Partinico ... 28,162
Paternò ... 48,992
Pavia ... 87,005
Perugia ... 139,871
Pesaro ... 90,705
Pescara ... 137,059
Piacenza ... 108,888
Pinerolo ... 36,589
Piombino ... 39,659
Pisa ... 103,772
Pistoia (94,344▲) ... 84,300
Poggibonsi ... 26,743
Pompei (★Naples) (22,526▲) ... 13,300
Pontedera ... 28,254
Pordenone ... 52,106
Portici (★Naples) ... 83,372
Portoferraio ... 11,212
Portofino ... 773
Potenza ... 64,513
Pozzuoli (★Naples) (70,429▲) ... 61,400
Prato (★201,000) ... 158,229
Ragusa (66,545▲) ... 55,200
Rapallo ... 29,809
Ravello (2,387▲) ... 1,400
Ravenna (139,392▲) ... 102,300
Reggio di Calabria ... 181,293
Reggio nell'Emilia ... 130,005
Rho (★Milan) ... 49,657
Riccione ... 31,688
Rieti (43,277▲) ... 38,700
Rimini ... 127,714
Riva [del Garda] ... 13,240
Rivoli (★Turin) ... 50,992
ROME (ROMA) (★3,195,000) ... 2,911,671
Rosignano Marittimo ... 29,402
Rovereto ... 33,082
Rovigo ... 52,588
Salerno (★240,000) ... 161,997
Salsomaggiore Terme ... 17,982
San Benedetto del Tronto ... 46,256
San Donà di Piave (32,058▲) ... 22,500
San Gimignano (7,521▲) ... 2,800
San Giorgio a Cremano (★Naples) ... 65,245
San Remo (63,423▲) ... 52,400
San Severo ... 54,914
Santa Maria Capua Vetere ... 32,529
Saronno ... 36,683
Sassari ... 119,597
Sassuolo ... 39,471
Savona (★120,000) ... 78,216
Scandicci (★Florence) ... 54,102
Schio ... 36,388
Sciacca (36,148▲) ... 32,300
Senigallia (40,567▲) ... 34,500
Seregno (★Milan) ... 37,717
Sesto Fiorentino (★Florence) ... 44,862
Sesto San Giovanni (★Milan) ... 98,151
Settimo Torinese (★Turin) ... 44,895
Siena ... 63,961
Siracusa ... 116,755
Sorrento (★42,900) ... 16,868
Spoleto (37,593▲) ... 32,200
Taranto ... 247,681
Teramo (51,768▲) ... 41,000
Termini Imerese ... 26,815
Terni ... 113,241
Tivoli (★Rome) ... 46,201
Todi (17,244▲) ... 3,900
Torre Annunziata (★Naples) ... 57,659
Torre del Greco (★Naples) ... 101,905
Trani ... 43,243
Trapani (72,036▲) ... 62,400
Trento ... 99,052
Treviso ... 89,121
Trieste ... 260,291
Turin (Torino) (★1,670,000) ... 1,160,686
Udine (★128,000) ... 102,973
Urbino (16,211▲) ... 13,000
Varese ... 91,100
Venice (Venezia) (★445,000) ... 355,865
Verbania ... 33,384
Vercelli ... 54,063
Verona ... 269,763
Viareggio ... 59,600
Vicenza ... 117,571
Vigevano ... 67,034
Villa San Giovanni (12,106▲) ... 9,000
Viterbo (58,529▲) ... 50,000
Vittoria ... 50,739
Vittorio Veneto ... 30,897
Voghera ... 42,781

IVORY COAST / Côte d'Ivoire

1978 E ... 7,613,000

Abengourou (1975 C) ... 31,239
•ABIDJAN ... 1,100,000
Agboville (1975 C) ... 27,192
Bouaké ... 230,000
Daloa ... 70,000
Danane (1975 C) ... 19,872
Dimbokro (1975 C) ... 30,986
Divo (1975 C) ... 37,896
Gagnoa (1975 C) ... 42,362
Grand-Bassam (1975 C) ... 25,808
Korhogo (1975 C) ... 47,657
Man ... 55,000
Séguéla (1975 C) ... 12,587

JAMAICA

1978 E ... 2,137,300

•KINGSTON ... 665,050
Mandeville (1970 C) ... 14,421
May Pen (1970 C) ... 26,074
Montego Bay (1970 C) ... 43,754
Ocho Rios (1970 C) ... 6,900
Port Antonio (1970 C) ... 10,538
Savanna-la-Mar (1970 C) ... 11,759
Spanish Town (1970 C) ... 40,731

JAPAN

1979 E ... 116,133,000

Districts and Prefectures

CHUBU ... 19,844,000
Aichi ... 6,176,000
Fukui ... 792,000
Gifu ... 1,945,000
Ishikawa ... 1,110,000
Nagano ... 2,071,000
Niigata ... 2,437,000
Shizuoka ... 3,420,000
Toyama ... 1,098,000
Yamanashi ... 795,000
CHUGOKU ... 7,557,000
Hiroshima ... 2,723,000
Okayama ... 1,865,000
Shimane ... 782,000
Tottori ... 599,000
Yamaguchi ... 1,588,000
HOKKAIDŌ ... 5,532,000
Hokkaidō ... 5,532,000
KANTŌ (KWANTŌ) ... 34,428,000
Chiba ... 4,617,000
Gumma ... 1,826,000
Ibaraki ... 2,503,000
Kanagawa ... 6,809,000
Saitama ... 5,309,000
Tochigi ... 1,768,000
Tōkyō ... 11,596,000
KINKI ... 21,158,000
Hyōgo ... 5,139,000
Kyōto ... 2,515,000
Mie ... 1,674,000
Nara ... 1,190,000
Ōsaka ... 8,487,000
Shiga ... 1,063,000
Wakayama ... 1,090,000
KYŪSHŪ ... 13,985,000
Fukuoka ... 4,527,000
Kagoshima ... 1,770,000
Kumamoto ... 1,776,000
Miyazaki ... 1,141,000
Nagasaki ... 1,592,000
Ōita ... 1,224,000
Okinawa ... 1,096,000
Saga ... 859,000
SHIKOKU ... 4,143,000
Ehime ... 1,499,000
Kagawa ... 995,000
Kōchi ... 828,000
Tokushima ... 821,000
TŌHOKU ... 9,486,000
Akita ... 1,251,000
Aomori ... 1,514,000
Fukushima ... 2,015,000
Iwate ... 1,411,000
Miyagi ... 2,054,000
Yamagata ... 1,241,000

Cities (1975 C or †1979 E)

Abashiri (43,825▲) ... 34,900
Abiko (★Tōkyō) ... 76,218
Ageo (★Tōkyō) ... †163,985
Aioi ... 42,008
Aizu-wakamatsu ... †113,175
Akashi (★Ōsaka) (1980 C) ... 254,873
Akishima (★Tōkyō) ... 83,864
Akita (1980 C) ... 284,830
Akō ... 49,583
Amagasaki (★Ōsaka) (1980 C) ... 523,657
Amagi (42,725▲) ... 25,700
Anan (60,439▲) ... 37,200
Anjō ... †121,178
Aomori (1980 C) ... 287,609
Arao (★Ōmuta) (58,296▲) ... 47,300
Arida ... 34,865
Asahikawa (1980 C) ... 352,620
Asaka (★Tōkyō) ... 81,755
Ashibetsu (36,520▲) ... 29,100
Ashikaga ... †165,024
Ashiya (★Ōsaka) ... 76,211
Atami ... 51,437
Atsugi (★Tōkyō) ... †136,652
Ayabe (43,490▲) ... 29,000
Ayase (★Tōkyō) ... 50,365
Beppu ... †137,477
Bibai (38,416▲) ... 29,200
Bisai ... 54,247
Chiba (★Tōkyō) (1980 C) ... 746,428
Chichibu ... 61,798
Chigasaki (★Tōkyō) ... †168,849
Chikugo ... 39,520
Chikushino (★Fukuoka) ... 47,741
Chiryū (★Nagoya) ... 47,209
Chita (★Nagoya) ... 56,560
Chitose ... 61,031
Chōfu (★Tōkyō) ... †179,631
Chōshi ... 90,374
Daitō (★Ōsaka) ... †115,678
Ebetsu ... 77,624
Ebina (★Tōkyō) ... 59,783
Fuchū *(Hiroshima pref.)* ... 50,217
Fūchū (★Hiroshima) *(Hiroshima pref.)* ... 47,538
Fuchū (★Tōkyō) ... †190,048
Fuji (1980 C) (★325,000) ... 205,752
Fujieda (101,216▲) ... †72,000
Fujiidera (★Ōsaka) ... 59,515
Fujimi (★Tōkyō) ... 70,391
Fujinomiya (★★Fuji) (106,524▲) ... †82,800
Fujioka (49,169▲) ... 30,000
Fujisawa (★Tōkyō) (1980 C) ... 300,181
Fuji-yoshida ... 51,976
Fukaya (75,748▲) ... 53,100
Fukuchiyama (60,003▲) ... 43,000
Fukui (1980 C) ... 240,264
Fukuoka (1980 C) (★1,575,000) ... 1,088,617
Fukuroi (42,581▲) ... 25,700
Fukushima (1980 C) ... 262,847
Fukuyama (1980 C) ... 346,031
Funabashi (★Tōkyō) (1980 C) ... 479,437
Furukawa (54,356▲) ... 31,100
Fussa (★Tōkyō) ... 46,457
Futtsu ... 56,653

C Census. E Official estimate. UE Unofficial estimate.
L Population within municipal limits of year specified. • Largest city in country.

★ Population or designation of metropolitan area, including suburbs (see headnote).
▲ Population of an entire municipality, commune, or district, including rural area.
‡† Year of information specified at start of country.

Gamagōri	85,282
Gifu (1980 C)	410,368
Ginowan	53,835
Gose (★Ōsaka)	37,554
Gotemba (62,722▲)	49,300
Gushikawa	42,133
Gyōda	66,069
Habikino (★Ōsaka)	†102,217
Hachinohe (1980 C)	238,208
Hachiōji (★Tōkyō) (1980 C)	387,162
Hadano (★Tōkyō)	†118,528
Hagi (52,724▲)	42,100
Hakodate (1980 C)	320,152
Hamada	50,316
Hamakita (67,180▲)	49,600
Hamamatsu (1980 C)	490,827
Hanamaki (65,826▲)	38,200
Handa	85,824
Hannō (★Tōkyō)	55,926
Haranomachi (43,483▲)	26,800
Hashima (52,570▲)	40,500
Hatogaya (★Tōkyō)	56,693
Hekinan	60,680
Higashihiroshima (★Hiroshima)	66,231
Higashikurume (★Tōkyō)	†106,566
Higashimatsuyama	57,684
Higashimurayama (★Tōkyō)	†119,684
Higashiōsaka (★Ōsaka) (1980 C)	521,635
Higashiyamato (★Tōkyō)	58,464
Hikari (★Tokuyama)	48,794
Hikone	85,066
Himeji (1980 C)	446,255
Himi (61,789▲)	38,600
Hino (★Tōkyō)	†142,982
Hirakata (★Ōsaka) (1980 C)	353,360
Hiratsuka (★Tōkyō) (1980 C)	214,299
Hirosaki (173,550▲)	†112,300
Hiroshima (1980 C) (★1,525,000)	899,394
Hisai	36,587
Hita (63,969▲)	47,300
Hitachi (1980 C)	204,612
Hōfu (109,762▲)	†86,100
Honjō	51,090
Hōya (★Tōkyō)	91,546
Hyūga (53,448▲)	40,600
Ibaraki (★Ōsaka) (1980 C)	234,059
Ichihara (★Tōkyō) (1980 C)	216,395
Ichikawa (★Tōkyō) (1980 C)	364,244
Ichinomiya (1980 C)	253,138
Ichinoseki (59,122▲)	36,000
Iida (77,112▲)	51,900
Iizuka (★103,000)	75,417
Ikeda (★Ōsaka)	†101,872
Ikoma (★Ōsaka)	48,848
Imabari	†123,928
Imaichi (46,760▲)	29,800
Imari (60,913▲)	36,600
Ina (54,468▲)	32,500
Inagi (★Tōkyō)	43,924
Inazawa (★Nagoya)	88,606
Innoshima	41,683
Inuyama (★Nagoya)	58,731
Iruma (★Tōkyō)	83,997
Isahaya (73,341▲)	49,400
Ise (Uji-yamada)	†105,624
Isehara (★Tōkyō)	61,616
Isesaki	†104,300
Ishinomaki	†119,758
Ishioka (43,679▲)	30,400
Itami (★Ōsaka)	†177,745
Itō	68,072
Itsukaichi (★Hiroshima)	64,885
Iwai	38,304
Iwaki (Taira) (1980 C) (342,076▲)	271,800
Iwakuni	†112,200
Iwakura (★Nagoya)	41,935
Iwamizawa (72,305▲)	56,800
Iwata	67,665
Iwatsuki (★Tōkyō) (83,825▲)	60,900
Iyo-mishima	38,409
Izumi (★Ōsaka)	†122,464
Izumi *(Kagoshima pref.)*	37,483
Izumi (★Sendai)	70,087
Izumi-ōtsu (★Ōsaka)	66,250
Izumi-sano (★Ōsaka)	86,139
Izumo (71,568▲)	47,700
Joetsu	†126,474
Jōyō (★Ōsaka)	58,923
Kadoma (★Ōsaka)	†142,167
Kaga (61,599▲)	47,400
Kagoshima (1980 C)	505,077
Kainan	53,250
Kaizuka (★Ōsaka)	79,506
Kakamigahara	†112,802
Kakegawa (61,731▲)	38,600
Kakogawa (★Ōsaka) (1980 C)	212,232
Kamagaya (★Tōkyō)	63,288
Kamaishi	68,981
Kamakura (★Tōkyō)	†173,331
Kameoka (58,184▲)	36,400
Kamifukuoka (★Tōkyō)	58,332
Kanazawa (1980 C)	417,681
Kanonji (44,131▲)	31,700
Kanoya (67,951▲)	38,500
Kanuma (81,799▲)	55,800
Karatsu	75,224
Kariya (★Nagoya)	†103,643
Karuizawa	13,951
Kasai (50,161▲)	30,600
Kasaoka (63,413▲)	42,700
Kashihara (★Ōsaka)	†105,691
Kashiwa (★Tōkyō) (1980 C)	239,199
Kashiwara (★Ōsaka)	63,586
Kashiwazaki (80,351▲)	53,500
Kasuga (★Fukuoka)	55,160
Kasugai (★Nagoya) (1980 C)	244,114
Kasukabe (★Tōkyō)	†151,083
Katano (★Ōsaka)	52,732
Katsuta	79,996
Kawachi-nagano (★Ōsaka)	66,936
Kawagoe (★Tōkyō)	259,317
Kawaguchi (★Tōkyō) (1980 C)	379,357
Kawanishi (★Ōsaka)	†128,861
Kawanoe	35,961
Kawasaki (★Tōkyō) (1980 C)	1,040,698
Kazo (45,183▲)	27,900
Kesennuma	66,616
Kimitsu	76,016
Kiryū	†132,950
Kisarazu	†108,065
Kishiwada (★Ōsaka)	†179,038
Kitaibaraki (44,332▲)	33,500
Kitakami (48,759▲)	28,200
Kitakyūshū (1980 C) (★1,515,000)	1,065,084
Kitami (91,519▲)	73,000
Kitamoto (★Tōkyō)	46,632
Kiyose (★Tōkyō)	60,574
Kobayashi	38,325
Kōbe (★★Ōsaka) (1980 C)	1,367,392
Kōchi (1980 C)	300,830
Kodaira (★Tōkyō)	†156,758
Kōfu	†197,803
Koga (★Tōkyō)	55,973
Koganei (★Tōkyō)	†103,487
Kokubunji (★Tōkyō)	88,159
Komae (★Tōkyō)	70,043
Komaki (★Nagoya)	†101,299
Komatsu	†103,606
Komatsushima (42,203▲)	32,300
Kōnan	90,426
Kōnosu (★Tōkyō)	51,632
Kōriyama (1980 C) (286,497▲)	195,700
Koshigaya (★Tōkyō) (1980 C)	223,243
Kudamatsu (★★Tokuyama)	55,825
Kuki (★Tōkyō)	45,797
Kumagaya	†134,347
Kumamoto (1980 C)	525,613
Kunitachi (★Tōkyō)	64,495
Kurashiki (1980 C)	403,785
Kurayoshi (50,785▲)	34,800
Kure (★★Hiroshima) (1980 C)	234,550
Kurume (1980 C)	216,974
Kusatsu (★Ōsaka)	64,873
Kushiro (1980 C)	214,694
Kuwana	83,440
Kyōto (★★Ōsaka) (1980 C)	1,472,993
Machida (★Tōkyō) (1980 C)	295,354
Maebashi (1980 C)	265,171
Maizuru (97,780▲)	82,600
Marugame	65,662
Masuda (50,734▲)	34,400
Matsubara (★Ōsaka)	†135,741
Matsudo (★Tōkyō) (1980 C)	400,870
Matsue	†134,190
Matsumoto	†190,780
Matsuyama (1980 C)	401,682
Matsuzaka (112,870▲)	†81,800
Mihara	83,679
Miki (★Ōsaka) (55,731▲)	41,200
Minamiashigara	36,928
Minō (★Ōsaka)	79,621
Mino-kamo	37,524
Misato (★Tōkyō)	79,355
Misawa (37,437▲)	28,600
Mishima (★★Numazu)	89,248
Mitaka (★Tōkyō)	†166,514
Mito (1980 C)	215,563
Mitsuke (40,954▲)	30,900
Miura	47,888
Miyako	61,912
Miyakonojō (127,528▲)	†82,200
Miyazaki (1980 C)	264,858
Mizusawa (52,266▲)	34,700
Mobara	64,942
Mōka (47,345▲)	20,700
Mombetsu (32,825▲)	28,000
Moriguchi (★Ōsaka)	†164,716
Morioka (1980 C)	229,123
Moriyama	41,439
Mukō (★Ōsaka)	45,886
Muroran (★220,000)	†162,731
Musashi-murayama (★Tōkyō)	50,842
Musashino (★Tōkyō)	†138,874
Mutsu	44,646
Nagahama	54,064
Nagano (1980 C) (324,360▲)	244,300
Nagaoka	†178,201
Nagaokakyo (★Ōsaka)	65,557
Nagareyama (★Tōkyō)	†103,864
Nagasaki (1980 C)	447,091
Nagoya (1980 C) (★3,700,000)	2,087,884
Naha (1980 C)	295,801
Nakama (★Kitakyūshū)	43,145
Nakatsu (59,111▲)	44,200
Nakatsugawa (51,183▲)	36,800
Nanao (49,493▲)	38,800
Nankoku (42,832▲)	25,500
Nara (★Ōsaka) (1980 C)	297,893
Narashino (★Tōkyō)	†120,257
Narita (50,915▲)	30,500
Naruto (61,959▲)	50,600
Natori (46,730▲)	29,700
Naze	46,335
Nemuro	45,817
Neyagawa (★Ōsaka) (1980 C)	255,864
Nichinan (52,171▲)	38,200
Niigata (1980 C)	457,783
Niihama	†133,178
Niitsu (58,970▲)	42,900
Niiza (★Tōkyō)	†119,991
Nikkō	26,279
Nishinomiya (★Ōsaka) (1980 C)	410,329
Nishio (82,524▲)	62,600
Nishiwaki	38,108
Nobeoka	†136,572
Noboribetsu (★Muroran)	50,885
Noda (★Tōkyō)	78,193
Nōgata	58,551
Noshiro (59,215▲)	43,600
Numata (45,255▲)	32,000
Numazu (1980 C) (★435,000)	203,699
Obihiro	†150,337
Ōbu (★Nagoya)	56,211
Ōda	37,449
Ōdate (71,828▲)	50,200
Odawara	†177,047
Ōfunato (39,632▲)	32,700
Ōgaki	†141,877
Ōita (1980 C)	360,484
Ojiya (44,375▲)	26,900
Ōkawa	50,395
Okaya	61,776
Okayama (1980 C)	545,737
Okazaki (1980 C)	262,370
Okegawa (★Tōkyō)	48,034
Okinawa	91,347
Ōme (★Tōkyō)	86,152
Ōmi-hachiman (★Ōsaka) (51,537▲)	34,100
Ōmiya (★Tōkyō) (1980 C)	354,082
Ōmura (60,919▲)	44,200
Ōmuta (★225,000)	†163,436
Ōno *(Fukui pref.)* (41,918▲)	25,800
Ōno *(Hyōgo pref.)*	40,576
Onojo (★Fukuoka)	52,169
Onoda (★Ube)	43,804
Onomichi	†102,190
Ōsaka (1980 C) (★15,200,000)	2,648,158
Ōta	†120,472
Ōtake	38,457
Otaru	†185,737
Ōtawara (42,332▲)	22,900
Ōtsu (★Ōsaka) (1980 C)	215,318
Ōtsuki	36,766
Oyama (125,565▲)	†81,000
Rumoi	36,882
Ryūgasaki (40,565▲)	25,000
Sabae (57,252▲)	45,700
Saga	†162,038
Sagamihara (★Tōkyō) (1980 C)	439,257
Saijō (52,615▲)	39,100
Saiki (52,863▲)	42,200
Sakado (★Tōkyō)	51,230
Sakai (★Ōsaka) (1980 C)	810,120
Sakaide	67,624
Sakaiminato	35,821
Sakata (101,454▲)	†73,900
Saku (56,143▲)	32,500
Sakura (★Tōkyō) (80,804▲)	61,500
Sakurai (54,314▲)	42,800
Sanda (★Ōsaka)	35,261
Sanjō	81,806
Sano	75,844
Sapporo (1980 C) (★1,450,000)	1,401,758
Sasebo (1980 C)	251,188
Sawara (48,670▲)	26,000
Sayama (★Tōkyō)	†121,433
Seki	53,881
Sendai *(Kagoshima pref.)* (61,788▲)	34,700
Sendai *(Miyagi pref.)* (1980 C) (★925,000)	664,799
Sennan (★Ōsaka)	46,741
Seto	†119,473
Settsu (★Ōsaka)	76,704
Shibata (74,025▲)	48,700
Shibukawa	47,071
Shijōnawate (★Ōsaka)	52,368
Shimabara (45,179▲)	34,000
Shimada	68,820
Shimizu (★★Shizuoka) (1980 C)	241,578
Shimminato (★Takaoka)	44,700
Shimodate (57,778▲)	36,500
Shimonoseki (★★Kitakyūshū) (1980 C)	268,964
Shingū	39,023
Shinjō (42,227▲)	28,100
Shiogama (★Sendai)	59,235
Shiojiri (47,421▲)	29,200
Shirakawa (42,685▲)	32,300
Shizuoka (1980 C) (★735,000)	458,342
Sōja	47,027
Sōka (★Tōkyō)	†186,759
Suita (★Ōsaka) (1980 C)	332,413
Sukagawa (54,922▲)	33,700
Sumoto (44,137▲)	35,700
Suwa	49,594
Suzaka	49,513
Suzuka (152,431▲)	†106,900
Tachikawa (★Tōkyō)	†142,793
Tagajō (★Sendai)	44,862
Tajimi	68,901
Takaishi (★Ōsaka)	66,824
Takamatsu (1980 C)	316,662
Takaoka (★220,000)	†174,334
Takarazuka (★Ōsaka)	†179,394
Takasago (★Ōsaka)	77,080
Takasaki (1980 C)	221,432
Takatsuki (★Ōsaka) (1980 C)	340,722
Takawa	61,464
Takayama	60,504
Takefu (65,012▲)	48,700
Takehara	36,273
Takikawa	50,090
Tama (★Tōkyō)	65,466
Tamana (42,837▲)	28,100
Tamano	78,516
Tanabe (66,999▲)	51,800
Tanashi (★Tōkyō)	67,433
Tatebayashi	66,410
Tateyama (56,139▲)	40,700
Tatsuno	39,646
Tendō (48,082▲)	27,900
Tenri (62,909▲)	45,200
Toba	29,346
Tochigi	83,189
Toda (★Tōkyō)	77,137
Tokai (★Nagoya)	95,457
Tōkamachi (50,211▲)	33,400
Toki	63,324
Tokoname	54,865
Tokorozawa (★Tōkyō) (1980 C)	236,477
Tokushima (1980 C)	249,343
Tokuyama (★255,000)	†111,347
•TŌKYŌ (1980 C) (★25,800,000)	8,349,209
Tomakomai	†146,088
Tomioka (46,821▲)	29,200
Tondabayashi (★Ōsaka)	91,393
Toride (★Tōkyō)	52,816
Tosu	50,733
Tottori	†128,789
Towada (54,365▲)	27,900
Toyama (1980 C)	305,054
Toyoake (★Nagoya)	45,837
Toyohashi (1980 C)	304,274
Toyokawa	†102,484
Toyonaka (★Ōsaka) (1980 C)	403,185
Toyooka (46,210▲)	33,000
Toyota (1980 C)	281,609
Tsu	†144,587
Tsubame	43,265
Tsuchiura	†110,912
Tsuruga	60,205
Tsuruoka (95,932▲)	74,600
Tsushima	58,241
Tsuyama (79,907▲)	56,500
Ube (★222,000)	†167,732
Ueda	†110,340
Ueno (59,716▲)	42,500
Uji (★Ōsaka)	†150,869
Uozu	48,419
Urawa (★Tōkyō) (1980 C)	358,180
Usa (50,677▲)	25,400
Usuki (39,163▲)	28,200
Utsunomiya (1980 C)	377,748
Uwajima	70,428
Wakayama (1980 C)	401,462
Wakkanai	55,464
Warabi (★Tōkyō)	76,311
Yachiyo (★Tōkyō)	†132,989
Yaizu	†103,544
Yamagata (1980 C)	236,984
Yamaguchi (111,725▲)	†80,800
Yamato (★Tōkyō)	†165,858
Yamato-kōriyama (★Ōsaka)	71,001
Yamato-takada (★Ōsaka)	58,637
Yame	38,843
Yao (★Ōsaka) (1980 C)	272,706
Yashio (★Tōkyō)	56,127
Yatsushiro (107,200▲)	†80,000
Yawata (★Ōsaka)	50,131
Yawatahama (45,259▲)	34,700
Yokkaichi (1980 C)	255,442
Yokohama (★★Tōkyō) (1980 C)	2,773,322
Yokosuka (★Tōkyō) (1980 C)	421,112
Yonago	†125,291
Yonezawa (91,974▲)	71,400
Yono (★Tōkyō)	71,044
Yūbari	50,131
Yukuhashi (53,750▲)	39,300
Zama (★Tōkyō)	80,562
Zushi (★Tōkyō)	56,298

JERSEY

1976 C	**74,470**
•ST. HELIER (★45,000)	26,343

JORDAN / Al-Urdunn

1979 E	**2,152,273**
Al-'Aqabah ('Aqaba)	26,986
Al-Karak	11,805
Al-Khalīl (Hebron) (††1971 E)	43,000
Al-Mafraq (1973 E)	15,500
•AMMĀN	648,587
Arīḥā (Jericho) (††1967 C)	6,829
Ar-Ramthā (1973 E)	19,000
As-Salt	32,866
Az-Zarqā'	215,687
Bayt Laḥm (Bethlehem) (††1971 E)	25,000
Irbid	112,864
Janīn (††1971 E)	20,000
Jerusalem (★Jerusalem, Israel) (††1976 E)	90,000
Ma'ān	11,308
Nābulus (††1971 E)	64,000

††*Located in area occupied by Israel in 1967. See note under Israel.*

KAMPUCHEA / Kâmpŭchéa Prâchéathĭpâtéyy

1962 C	**5,728,711**
Battambang	38,780
Kompong Cham	28,532
•PHNUM PÉNH	393,995

KENYA

1979 C	**15,322,000**
Eldoret	50,000
Kisumu	150,000
Mombasa	342,000
•NAIROBI	835,000
Nakuru	93,000
Nyeri	36,000
Thika	41,000

KOREA, NORTH / Chosŏn Minjujuŭi In'min Konghwaguk

1967 E	**12,700,000**
Aoji (1944 C)	39,616
Ch'ŏngjin	265,000
Haeju	115,000
Hamhŭng (1944 C)	112,184
Hŭngnam (1944 C)	143,600
Kaesŏng	140,000
Kilchu (1944 C)	30,026
Kimch'aek (Sŏngjin)	265,000
Najin (1944 C)	34,338
Namp'o (Chinnamp'o)	130,000
Ongjin (1949 C)	32,965
Pukch'ŏng (1944 C)	30,709
•P'YONGYANG	840,000
Sariwŏn (1944 C)	42,957
Sinŭiju	165,000
Songnim (1944 C)	53,035
Tanch'ŏn (1944 C)	32,761
Wŏnsan	215,000

KOREA, SOUTH / Taehan-Min'guk

1978 E	**37,019,000**
Andong (101,494▲)	85,000
Anyang (★Seoul)	187,887
Bucheon (★Seoul)	163,341
Ch'angwŏn	70,707
Chech'ŏn (80,124▲)	55,400
Cheju (152,486▲)	83,100
Chinhae	108,730
Chinju	174,918
Ch'ŏnan (109,324▲)	76,800
Ch'ŏngju	223,016
Chŏngŭp (1975 C) (54,864▲)	37,600
Chŏnju	348,053
Ch'unch'ŏn	152,606
Ch'ungju (110,091▲)	76,500
Chungmu	71,511
Inch'ŏn (★★Seoul)	936,497
Iri (132,272▲)	109,800
Kangnŭng (102,153▲)	67,100
Kimch'ŏn (70,348▲)	53,200
Kumi	89,612
Kunsan	167,422
Kwangju	694,646
Kyŏngju (113,921▲)	68,100
Masan	391,874
Mokp'o	210,922
Namwŏn (55,043▲)	37,900
P'ohang (1975 C) (134,404▲)	110,000
Pusan	2,879,570
Pyŏngtaek	56,324
Samch'ŏnp'o (61,701▲)	37,100
Sangju (55,242▲)	29,500
Seongnam (★Seoul)	324,064
•SEOUL (SŎUL) (1979 E) (★10,775,000)	8,114,000
Sŏkch'o	71,737
Songjŏng (47,070▲)	29,900
Sunch'ŏn (114,588▲)	76,900
Suwŏn (★Seoul)	266,135
Taegu	1,487,098
Taejŏn	508,574
Ŭijŏngbu (★Seoul)	117,849
Ulsan (364,456▲)	247,000
Wŏnju	131,047
Yŏngju (1975 C) (70,793▲)	50,800
Yŏsu	151,337

KUWAIT / Al-Kuwayt

1975 C	**994,837**
Abraq Khīṭān (★Kuwait)	59,443
Al-Farwānīyah (★Kuwait)	44,875
Al-Jahrah (★Kuwait)	52,302
As-Sālimīyah (★Kuwait)	113,943
Ḩawallī (★Kuwait)	130,565
•KUWAIT (Al-Kuwayt) (★780,000)	78,116

LAOS / Lao

1973 E	**3,181,000**
Louangphrabang	43,000
Pakxé	44,860
Savannakhet	50,691
Sayaboury	13,760
•VIANGCHAN (VIENTIANE)	174,229

LEBANON / Al-Lubnān

1970 E	**2,126,355**
Ba'labakk (Baalbek)	16,000
•BEIRUT (BAYRŪT) (★1,010,000)	474,870
Şaydā (Sidon)	34,000
Şūr (Tyre)	12,500
Ţarābulus (Tripoli)	157,320
Zaḩlah	29,500

LESOTHO

1972 E	**972,000**
•MASERU	17,000

LIBERIA

1974 C	**1,503,368**
Buchanan	23,994
•MONROVIA	204,210

LIBYA / Lībiyā

1970 E	**1,938,000**
Ajdābiyah (1964 C)	15,400
Beida (1964 C)	12,800
Benghāzī (Bengasi)	170,000
Darnah (Derna) (1964 C)	21,400
Misrātah	44,000
•TRIPOLI (ŢARĀBULUS)	264,000
Ţubruq (Tobruk) (1964 C)	15,900

LIECHTENSTEIN

1977 E	**24,715**
•VADUZ	4,704

LUXEMBOURG

1976 E	**358,000**
Bettembourg	7,100
Clervaux (1970 C)	1,428
Diekirch	5,500
Differdange (★Esch-sur-Alzette)	18,000
Dudelange	14,600
Echternach (1970 C)	3,792
Esch-sur-Alzette (★98,000)	27,600
Ettelbruck	6,100
•LUXEMBOURG (★110,000)	79,300
Pétange (★★Longwy, France)	12,100
Sanem (★Esch-sur-Alzette)	10,900
Wtilz (1970 C)	3,920

C Census. E Official estimate. UE Unofficial estimate.
L Population within municipal limits of year specified. • Largest city in country.

★ Population or designation of metropolitan area, including suburbs (see headnote).
▲ Population of an entire municipality, commune, or district, including rural area.
‡† Year of information specified at start of country.

MACAO

1970 C..........248,636

•MACAO (*248,636)..........241,413

MADAGASCAR / Madagasikara

1977 E..........8,520,000

•ANTANANARIVO (TANANARIVE)..........484,000
Antsirabe (85,000▲)..........45,000
Diégo-Suarez (Antsirane)..........43,000
Fianarantsoa..........73,000
Majunga..........71,000
Manakara (1972 E) (25,070▲)..........23,225
Marovoay (1972 E)..........20,780
Tamatave..........83,000
Tuléar..........49,000

MALAWI

1977 C..........5,561,821

•Blantyre..........229,000
LILONGWE..........102,924
Mzuzu..........16,000
Zomba..........16,000

MALAYSIA

1970 C..........10,319,324

Alor Setar (*85,748).......... 66,179
Ayer Itam (*Pinang).......... 25,640
Batu Pahat..........53,291
Bentong..........22,683
Bukit Mertajam..........26,631
Butterworth (**Pinang)..........61,187
Chukai..........12,514
George Town (Pinang) (*450,000)..........270,019
Ipoh (*257,309)..........247,689
Johor Baharu (*Singapore)..........136,229
Kajang..........21,950
Kampar..........26,591
Kangar..........8,758
Kelang..........113,607
Keluang..........43,272
Kota Baharu (*69,756)..........55,052
Kota Kinabalu (Jesselton)..........40,939
•KUALA LUMPUR (*750,000)..........451,728
Kuala Terengganu (*59,494)..........53,353
Kuantan..........43,358
Kuching..........63,535
Kulim..........18,505
Melaka (Malacca) (*99,782)..........86,357
Miri..........35,702
Muar (Bandar Maharani)..........61,218
Petaling Jaya (*Kuala Lumpur)..........93,447
Sandakan..........42,413
Segamat..........17,796
Seremban (*90,062)..........79,915
Sibu..........50,635
Sungai Petani..........35,959
Sungai Siput..........21,383
Taiping..........54,645
Tawau..........24,247
Telok Anson..........44,524

MALDIVES

1978 C..........143,046

•MALE..........29,555

MALI

1972 E..........5,257,000

•BAMAKO (1976 C)..........404,022
Gao..........17,000
Kati (1971 E)..........13,800
Kayes..........37,000
Kita (1971 E)..........11,700
Koulikoro..........15,000
Koutiala..........16,000
Mopti..........43,000
Nioro du Sahel (1971 E)..........13,200
San..........18,000
Ségou..........40,000
Sikasso..........29,000
Tombouctou (Timbuktu) (1971 E)..........11,900

MALTA

1979 E..........346,970

Birkirkara (*Valletta)..........16,832
Cospicua (*Valletta)..........9,440
Gzira (*Valletta)..........10,046
Hamrun (*Valletta)..........13,875
Msida (*Valletta)..........12,448
Paola (*Valletta)..........11,974
Qormi (*Valletta)..........15,784
Rabat..........11,823
Sliema (*Valletta)..........20,095
•VALLETTA (*215,000)..........14,042
Victoria (*Gozo I.*)..........5,249
Zabbar (*Valletta)..........10,366
Zejtun..........10,252

MARTINIQUE

1974 C..........324,832

•FORT-DE-FRANCE (*113,556)..........98,807
Le Lamentin (23,145▲)..........7,558
Saint-Pierre..........5,358
Schœlcher (*Fort-de-France) (14,749▲)..........13,792

MAURITANIA / Mauritanie

1971 E..........1,190,000

Atar (1967 E)..........8,500
Kaédi (1967 E)..........10,000
Nouadhibou (1966 E)..........11,000
•NOUAKCHOTT..........35,000

MAURITIUS

1978 E..........924,663

Beau Bassin (*Port Louis)..........83,714
Curepipe (*Port Louis)..........54,356
•PORT LOUIS (*405,000)..........142,853
Quatre Bornes (*Port Louis)..........53,835
Vacoas-Phoenix (*Port Louis)..........51,793

MEXICO / México

1976 E..........62,329,000

States

Aguascalientes..........430,000
Baja California Norte..........1,253,000
Baja California Sur..........181,000
Campeche..........337,000
Chiapas..........1,933,000
Chihuahua..........2,000,000
Coahuila..........1,334,000
Colima..........317,000
Distrito Federal (Federal District)..........8,906,000
Durango..........1,122,000
Guanajuato..........2,811,000
Guerrero..........2,013,000
Hidalgo..........1,409,000
Jalisco..........4,157,000
México..........6,245,000
Michoacán..........2,805,000
Morelos..........866,000
Nayarit..........699,000
Nuevo León..........2,344,000
Oaxaca..........2,337,000
Puebla..........3,055,000
Querétaro..........618,000
Quintana Roo..........131,000
San Luis Potosí..........1,527,000
Sinaloa..........1,714,000
Sonora..........1,414,000
Tabasco..........1,054,000
Tamaulipas..........1,901,000
Tlaxcala..........498,000
Veracruz..........4,917,000
Yucatán..........904,000
Zacatecas..........1,097,000

Cities (1970 C)

Acámbaro..........32,257
Acaponeta..........11,844
Acapulco [de Juárez] (1978 E)..........421,100
Acayucan..........21,173
Actopan..........11,037
Agua Dulce..........21,060
Agua Prieta..........20,754
Aguascalientes (1978 E)..........247,800
Alvarado..........15,792
Ameca..........21,018
Amecameca [de Juárez]..........16,276
Apatzingán..........44,849
Apizaco..........21,189
Arandas..........18 934
Arriaga..........13,193
Atlixco..........41,967
Atotonilco el Alto..........16,271
Autlán de Navarro..........20,398
Caborca..........20,771
Campeche (1978 E)..........103,600
Cananea..........17,518
Cárdenas..........15,643
Celaya (1978 E)..........114,400
Cerro Azul..........20,259
Chihuahua (1978 E)..........369,500
Chilpancingo [de los Bravos]..........36,193
Cholula [de Rivadabia]..........15,399
Ciudad Acuña..........30,276
Ciudad Camargo..........24,030
Ciudad Chetumal..........23,685
Ciudad del Carmen..........34,656
Ciudad de Valles..........47,587
Ciudad Guzmán..........48,166
Ciudad Hidalgo..........24,692
Ciudad Ixtepec..........14,025
Ciudad Jiménez..........18,095
Ciudad Juárez (**El Paso, Tex.) (1978 E)..........597,100
Ciudad Lerdo (*Torreón)..........19,803
Ciudad Madero (*Tampico) (1978 E)..........135,100
Ciudad Mante..........51,247
Ciudad Melchor Múzquiz..........18,868
Ciudad Mendoza (*Orizaba)..........18,696
Ciudad Obregón (1978 E)..........173,000
Ciudad Serdán..........9,581
Ciudad Victoria (1978 E)..........121,400
Coatepec..........21,542
Coatzacoalcos (1978 E)..........120,100
Colima..........58,450
Comalcalco..........14,963
Comitán [de Domínguez]..........21,249
Córdoba (1978 E)..........116,100
Cortazar..........25,794
Cosamaloapan..........19,766
Cumauhtéoc..........26,598
Cuautla..........13,946
Cuernavaca (1978 E)..........226,600
Culiacán (1978 E)..........302,200
Delicias..........52,446
Dolores Hidalgo..........16,849
Durango (1978 E)..........218,600
Ecatepec de Morelos (*Mexico City)..........11,899
El Grullo..........10,538
Empalme..........24,927
Encarnación de Díaz..........10,474
Ensenada..........77,687
Escuinapa de Hidalgo..........16,442
Fresnillo [de González Echeverría]..........44,475
Garza García (*Monterrey)..........20,934
Gómez Palacio (**Torreón) (1978 E)..........100,200
Guadalajara (1978 E) (*2,350,000)..........1,813,100
Guadalupe (*Monterrey)..........51,899
Guamúchil..........17,151
Guanajuato..........36,809
Guasave..........26,080
Guaymas..........57,492
Hermosillo (1978 E)..........299,700
Hidalgo del Parral..........57,619
Huajuapan de León..........13,822
Huamantla..........15,565
Huatabampo..........18,506
Huauchinango..........16,826
Huixtla..........15,737
Iguala..........45,355
Irapuato (1978 E)..........155,600
Izúcar de Matamoros..........21,164
Jacona de Plancarte..........22,724
Jalapa Enríquez (1978 E)..........191,100
Jalostotitlán..........11,719
Jerez de García Salinas..........20,325
Juchitán [de Zaragoza]..........30,218
La Barca..........18,055
Lagos de Moreno..........33,782
La Paz..........46,011
La Piedad [Cavadas]..........34,963
Las Choapas..........20,166
Léon [de los Aldamas] (1978 E)..........590,000
Linares..........24,456
Loma Bonita..........15,804
Los Mochis (1978 E)..........111,800
Los Reyes..........19,452
Magdalena..........10,281
Manzanillo..........20,777
Martínez de la Torre..........17,203
Matamoros (**Brownsville, Tex.) (1978 E)..........186,500
Matamoros de la Laguna..........15,125
Matehuala..........28,799
Matías Romero..........13,200
Mazatlán (1978 E)..........177,700
Meoqui..........12,308
Mérida (1978 E)..........263,200
Mesa de Tijuana (*San Diego, Calif.)..........50,094
Mexicali (1978 E)(*355,000)..........338,400
•MEXICO CITY (CIUDAD DE MÉXICO) (1978 E) (*14,400,000)..........8,988,200
Minatitlán (1978 E)..........112,600
Mineral del Monte..........8,887
Monclova (1978 E)..........130,900
Montemorelos..........18,642
Monterrey (1978 E) (*1,925,000)..........1,054,000
Morelia (1978 E)..........239,400
Moroleón..........25,620
Motul de Felipe Carrillo Puerto..........12,949
Navojoa..........43,817
Netzahualcóyotl (*Mexico City)..........580,438
Nogales (*Sonora*)..........52,108
Nogales (*Veracruz*) (*Orizaba)..........14,254
Nueva Rosita..........34,706
Nuevo Casas Grandes..........20,023
Nuevo Laredo (**Laredo, Tex.) (1978 E)..........214,200
Oaxaca [de Juárez] (1978 E)..........131,200
Ocotlán..........35,367
Ojinaga..........12,757
Orizaba (1978 E) (*265,000)..........118,400
Pachuca [de Soto] (1978 E)..........105,200
Pánuco..........14,277
Papantla [de Olarte]..........26,773
Parras de la Fuente..........18,707
Pátzcuaro..........17,299
Pénjamo..........9,245
Piedras Negras..........41,033
Poza Rica de Hidalgo (1978 E)..........188,900
Progreso..........17,518
Puebla [de Zaragoza] (1978 E)..........678,000
Puerto Vallarta..........24,155
Puruándiro..........9,956
Querétaro (1978 E)..........176,200
Reynosa (1978 E)..........218,700
Río Bravo..........39,018
Ríoverde..........16,804
Romita..........11,947
Rosario..........10,276
Sabinas..........20,538
Sabinas Hidalgo..........17,439
Sahuayo..........28,727
Salamanca..........61,039
Salina Cruz..........22,004
Saltillo (1978 E)..........245,700
Salvatierra..........18,975
San Andrés Tuxtla..........24,267
San Cristóbal de las Casas..........25,700
San Francisco del Oro..........12,116
San Francisco del Rincón..........27,079
San Juan de los Lagos..........19,570
San Juan del Río..........15,422
San Juan Teotihuacán (*Mexico City)..........2,238
San Luis de la Paz..........12,654
San Luis Potosí (1978 E)..........315,200
San Luis Río Colorado..........49,990
San Martín Texmelucan..........23,355
San Miguel de Allende..........24,286
San Miguel el Alto..........7,909
San Nicolás de los Garzas (*Monterrey)..........28,803
San Pedro de las Colonias..........26,882
Santa Ana Chiautempan..........12,327
Santa Bárbara..........16,978
Santa Cruz de Juventino Rosas..........15,859
Santa Inés Zacatelco..........14,117
Santa Rosalía..........7,356
Santiago Ixcuintla..........17,321
Sayula..........14,339
Silao..........31,825
Sombrerete..........11,077
Tala..........15,744
Tamazula de Gordiano..........13,521
Tamazunchale..........12,302
Tampico (1978 E) (*420,000)..........240,000
Tangancícuaro [de Arista]..........12,650
Tapachula..........60,620
Taxco de Alarcón..........27,089
Tecomán..........31,625
Tecuala..........12,461
Tehuacán..........47,497
Tehuantepec..........16,179
Teocaltiche..........13,745
Tepatitlán [de Morelos]..........29,292
Tepic (1978 E)..........133,400
Tequila..........11,839
Texcoco [de Mora] (*Mexico City)..........18,044
Teziutlán..........23,948
Ticul..........14,341
Tierra Blanca..........22,727
Tijuana (**San Diego, Calif.) (1978 E)..........535,000
Tizimín..........18,343
Tlalnepantla (*Mexico City)..........45,575
Tlapacoyan..........13,172
Tlaquepaque (*Guadalajara)..........59,760
Tlaxcala [de Xicohténcatl]..........9,972
Toluca [de Lerdo] (1978 E)..........222,900
Tonalá..........15,611
Torreón (1978 E) (*450,000)..........268,700
Tulancingo..........35,799
Tuxpan (*Jalisco*)..........14,693
Tuxpan (*Nayarit*)..........20,322
Tuxpan de Rodríguez Cano (*Veracruz*)..........33,901
Tuxtepec..........17,700
Tuxtla Gutiérrez (1978 E)..........101,700
Umán..........8,371
Unión de Tula..........6,399
Uriangato..........14,626
Uruapan [del Progreso] (1978 E)..........138,300
Valladolid..........14,663
Valle de Santiago..........16,517
Valle Hermoso..........19,278
Venustiano Carranza..........23,624
Veracruz [Llave] (1978 E) (*365,000)..........295,300
Vicente Guerrero (*Tlaxcala*)..........18,280
Vicente Guerrero (*Veracruz*) (*Orizaba)..........11,688
Villa Frontera..........25,761
Villahermosa (1978 E)..........165,500
Xicotepec de Juárez..........12,656
Yautepec..........13,952
Yurécuaro..........13,611
Yuriria..........10,085
Zaachila..........7,270
Zacapu..........31,989
Zacatecas..........50,251
Zacatepec..........16,839
Zacoalco de Torres..........11,343
Zamora de Hidalgo..........57,775
Zapopan (*Guadalajara)..........18,512
Zapotiltic..........11,733
Zihuatanejo..........4,879
Zitácuaro..........36,911
Zumpango..........12,923

MONACO

1975 E..........25,000

•MONACO (*50,000)..........25,000

MONGOLIA / Mongol Ard Uls

1969 C..........1,197,600

Cecerleg (Tsetserleg)..........12,400
Choibalsan..........20,500
Darchan..........22,800
Jirgalanta (Chovd)..........12,400
Süchbaatar..........10,000
•ULAN BATOR (URGA) (1970 E)..........287,000

MONTSERRAT

1970 C..........11,458

•PLYMOUTH..........1,267

MOROCCO / Al-Magreb

1971 C..........15,379,259

Agadir..........61,192
Beni-Mellal..........53,826
Berkane..........39,015
Berrechid..........20,113
•Casablanca (Dar-el-Beida) (*1,575,000)..........1,506,373
El-Jadida (Mazagan)..........55,501
Essaouira (Mogador)..........30,061
Fès (Fez)..........325,327
Fkih Ben Salah..........26,918
Jerada..........30,633
Kenitra..........139,206
Khemisset..........21,811
Khenifra..........25,526
Khouribga..........73,667
Ksar-el-Kebir..........48,262
Ksar-es-Souk..........16,775
Larache..........45,710
Marrakech..........332,741
Meknès..........248,369
Mohammedia (Fedala)..........70,392
Nador..........32,490
Ouarzazate..........11,142
Oued-Zem..........33,323
Ouezzane..........33,267
Oujda..........175,532
RABAT (*540,000)..........367,620
Safi..........129,113
Salé (**Rabat)..........155,557
Sefrou..........28,607
Settat..........42,325
Sidi Ifni..........13,650
Sidi Kacem..........26,831
Sidi Slimane..........20,398
Tanger (Tangier)..........187,894
Taroudant..........22,272
Taza..........55,157
Tétouan..........139,105
Villa Alhucemas (Al Hoceima)..........18,686
Youssoufia..........22,435

MOZAMBIQUE / Moçambique

1970 C..........8,168,933

Beira..........110,752
Inhambane..........24,090
João Belo..........63,494
•MAPUTO (LOURENÇO MARQUES)..........341,922
Nampula..........120,188
Quelimane..........71,289
Tete..........51,453
Villa Cabral..........41,251

NAMIBIA

1970 C..........722,867

Gobabis..........4,428
Keetmanshoop..........10,297
Lüderitz..........6,642
Mariental..........4,629
Otjiwarongo..........8,018
Rehoboth..........5,363
Swakopmund..........5,681
Tsumeb..........12,338
•WINDHOEK..........61,260

NEPAL / Nepāl

1971 C..........11,555,983

Bhaktapur..........40,112
Birātnagar..........45,100
•KATHMANDU (*215,000)..........150,402
Lalitpur (*Katmandu)..........59,049
Nepālganj..........23,523

NETHERLANDS / Nederland

1980 E..........14,091,014

(includes 1,546 persons with no fixed residence in any province)

Provinces

Drenthe..........418,479
Dronten..........19,658
Friesland..........583,989
Gelderland..........1,694,416
Groningen..........553,709
Lelystad..........38,971
Limburg..........1,069,038
North Brabant (Noord-Brabant)..........2,051,195
North Holland (Noord-Holland)..........2,307,646
Overijssel..........1,018,208
Southern IJsselmeer Polders (Zuidelijke IJsselmeerpolders) (not part of any province)..........6,872
South Holland (Zuid-Holland)..........3,083,555
Utrecht..........895,464
Zeeland..........348,268

Cities

Aalsmeer..........20,486
Alkmaar (*107,000)..........71,245
Almelo..........63,381
Alphen aan den Rijn..........51,780
Amersfoort (*128,678)..........88,097
Amstelveen (*Amsterdam)..........69,488
•AMSTERDAM (*1,810,000)..........716,919
Apeldoorn..........138,164
Arnhem (*287,305)..........127,846
Assen..........45,036
Bergen op Zoom..........43,715
Beverwijk (*Amsterdam)..........35,980
Breda (*151,236)..........117,259
Brunssum (*Heerlen)..........26,281
Bussum (*Amsterdam)..........35,316
Castricum (*Amsterdam)..........22,783
De Bilt (*Utrecht)..........32,397
Delft (*The Hague)..........83,939
Delfzijl..........25,433
Den Helder..........61,761
Deventer..........64,561
Doetinchem (36,995▲)..........27,800
Dordrecht (*195,792)..........107,453
Edam-Volendam (*Amsterdam)..........23,091
Ede (82,829▲)..........43,500
Eindhoven (*369,352)..........194,451
Emmen (89,763▲)..........35,500
Enschede (*285,000)..........143,042
Geldrop (*Eindhoven)..........26,474
Geleen (*181,250)..........35,371
Goes..........30,193
Gorinchem..........28,957
Gouda..........58,784
Groningen (*200,467)..........161,322
Haarlem (*Amsterdam)..........158,291
Haarlemmermeer (77,657▲)..........10,600
Harderwijk..........30,174
Harlingen..........15,427
Heemstede (*Amsterdam)..........26,729
Heerenveen (36,729▲)..........20,400
Heerlen (*267,003)..........71,102
Helmond..........58,490
Hengelo (**Enschede)..........75,216
Hilversum (*Amsterdam)..........92,964
Hoensbroek (*Heerlen)..........22,748
Hoogeveen (43,645▲)..........33,000
Hoorn..........39,300
IJmuiden (Velsen) (*Amsterdam)..........61,202
Kampen..........30,353
Katwijk aan Zee..........38,163
Kerkrade (*Heerlen)..........47,001
Leeuwarden..........84,518
Leiden (*173,386)..........103,046
Lelystad (38,971▲)..........9,900
Maassluis (*Rotterdam)..........32,937
Maastricht (*145,346)..........109,285
Meppel..........22,377
Middelburg..........38,077
Nijmegen (*217,951)..........147,614
Oldenzaal..........28,134
Oss..........43,462

C Census. E Official estimate. UE Unofficial estimate.
L Population within municipal limits of year specified. • Largest city in country.

* Population or designation of metropolitan area, including suburbs (see headnote).
▲ Population of an entire municipality, commune, or district, including rural area.
‡† Year of information specified at start of country.

Papendrecht (★Dordrecht) ... 24,995
Purmerend (★Amsterdam) ... 32,565
Renkum (★Arnhem) (34,168▲) ... 12,600
Rheden (★Arnhem) (48,637▲) ... 10,100
Ridderkerk (★Rotterdam) ... 45,908
Rijswijk (★The Hague) ... 52,605
Roermond ... 37,539
Roosendaal ... 54,838
Rotterdam (★1,085,000) ... 579,194
Schiedam (★Rotterdam) ... 74,895
's-Hertogenbosch (★183,583) ... 87,897
Sittard (★★Geleen) ... 33,702
Sliedrecht ... 22,504
Sneek ... 28,457
Soest (★Amersfoort) ... 40,581
Spijkenisse (★Rotterdam) ... 36,863
Tegelen (★Venlo) ... 18,079
Terneuzen (35,393▲) ... 22,200
THE HAGUE ('s-GRAVENHAGE) (★775,000) ... 456,886
Tiel ... 28,919
Tilburg (★216,873) ... 151,799
Utrecht (★481,875) ... 237,037
Valkenswaard (★Eindhoven) ... 27,441
Veendam ... 28,169
Veenendaal ... 39,210
Veldhoven (★Eindhoven) ... 33,382
Venlo (★86,000) ... 62,595
Vlaardingen (★Rotterdam) ... 79,531
Vlissingen (Flushing) (45,726▲) ... 26,200
Voorburg (★The Hague) ... 44,227
Vught (★'s-Hertogenbosch) ... 23,582
Waalwijk ... 28,514
Wageningen ... 30,447
Wassenaar (★The Hague) ... 26,989
Weert (38,311▲) ... 27,800
Winschoten ... 21,101
Woerden ... 23,715
Zaanstad (Zaandam) (★Amsterdam) ... 128,809
Zeist (★Utrecht) ... 61,532
Zoetermeer (★The Hague) ... 63,832
Zutphen ... 31,767
Zwijndrecht (★★Dordrecht) ... 39,641
Zwolle ... 82,190

NETHERLANDS ANTILLES / Nederlandse Antillen

1960 C ... 188,914

Kralendijk (*Bonaire*) (1953 E) ... 600
Oranjestad (*Aruba*) (1965 E) ... 14,700
•WILLEMSTAD (*Curaçao*) (★94,133) ... 43,547

NEW CALEDONIA / Nouvelle-Calédonie

1976 C ... 133,233

•NOUMEA (★70,600) ... 56,100

NEW HEBRIDES
see Vanuatu

NEW ZEALAND

1979 E ... 3,144,700

•Auckland (★775,000) ... 147,600
Birkenhead (★Auckland) ... 20,600
Blenheim ... 17,450
Christchurch (★309,000) ... 171,300
Dunedin (★113,000) ... 81,600
East Coast Bays (★Auckland) ... 24,500
Gisborne (★32,000) ... 30,000
Hamilton (★97,400) ... 90,900
Hastings (★★Napier) ... 35,500
Invercargill (★53,800) ... 49,900
Lower Hutt (★Wellington) ... 65,100
Manukau (★Auckland) ... 143,500
Masterton (★21,200) ... 19,650
Mount Albert (★Auckland) ... 28,300
Mount Eden (★Auckland) ... 19,500
Mount Roskill (★Auckland) ... 34,800
Mount Wellington (★Auckland) ... 20,500
Napier (★110,600) ... 47,900
Nelson (★42,800) ... 33,100
New Plymouth (★44,700) ... 38,300
Palmerston North (★64,900) ... 58,800
Papakura (★Auckland) ... 22,200
Papatoetoe (★Auckland) ... 23,100
Porirua (★Wellington) ... 42,500
Rotorua (★47,400) ... 37,700
Takapuna (★Auckland) ... 63,700
Tauranga (★49,000) ... 34,300
Timaru (★30,100) ... 29,500
Tokoroa ... 19,150
Upper Hutt (★Wellington) ... 31,300
Wainuiomata (★Wellington) (1978 E) ... 19,650
Waitemata (★Auckland) ... 81,900
Wanganui (★39,800) ... 37,500
WELLINGTON (★349,900) ... 137,600
Whangarei (★39,600) ... 35,900

NICARAGUA

1978 E ... 2,451,418

Bluefields ... 18,252
Chinandega ... 44,435
Granada ... 56,232
León ... 81,647
•MANAGUA ... 552,900
Masaya ... 47,276
Matagalpa ... 26,986
Rivas ... 16,222

NIGER

1977 E ... 5,098,000

Maradi ... 45,900
•NIAMEY ... 225,300
Tahoua ... 31,300
Zinder ... 58,400

NIGERIA

1963 C ... 55,670,052

Aba (1975 E) ... 177,000
Abeokuta (1975 E) ... 253,000
Ado-Ekiti (1975 E) ... 213,000
Afikpo ... 36,096
Agege ... 45,986
Akure ... 71,106
Awka ... 48,725
Bauchi ... 37,778
Benin City (1975 E) ... 136,000
Bida ... 55,007
Calabar (1975 E) ... 103,000
Deba ... 60,679
Ede (1975 E) ... 182,000
Effon-Alaiye ... 67,090
Ejigbo ... 46,410
Enugu (1975 E) ... 187,000
Epe ... 44,268
Gombe ... 47,265
Gusau ... 69,231
Ibadan (1975 E) ... 847,000
Ife (1975 E) ... 176,000
Igboho ... 46,776
Ihiala ... 40,198
Ijebu-Igbo ... 43,180
Ijebu-Ode ... 68,543
Ijero Ekiti ... 41,935
Ikare ... 61,696
Ikerre (1975 E) ... 145,000
Ikire ... 54,022
Ikirun ... 79,516
Ikorodu ... 81 024
Ikot Ekpene ... 38,107
Ila (1975 E) ... 155,000
Ilawe ... 80,833
Ilegboro ... 44,543
Ilesha (1975 E) ... 224,000
Ilobu ... 87,223
Ilorin (1975 E) ... 282,000
Inisa ... 52,482
Ise Ekiti ... 45,323
Iseyin (1971 E) ... 115,000
Iwo (1975 E) ... 214,000
Jos ... 90,402
Kaduna (1975 E) ... 202,000
Kano (1975 E) ... 399,000
Katsina (1971 E) ... 109,000
Kishi ... 42,374
Kumo ... 64,878
Lafia ... 53,667
•LAGOS (1975 E) (★1,450,000) ... 1,060,800
Maiduguri (1975 E) ... 189,000
Makurdi ... 53,967
Minna ... 59,988
Mushin (★Lagos) (1975 E) ... 197,000
Nguru ... 43,234
Offa ... 86,425
Ogbomosho (1975 E) ... 432,000
Oka ... 62,761
Ondo ... 74,343
Onitsha (1975 E) ... 220,000
Oshogbo (1975 E) ... 282,000
Owo ... 89,693
Oyo (1975 E) ... 152,000
Port Harcourt (1975 E) ... 242,000
Sapele ... 61,007
Shagamu ... 51,371
Shaki ... 76,290
Shomolu (★Lagos) ... 64,731
Sokoto ... 89,817
Ugep ... 44,945
Warri ... 55,254
Zaria (1975 E) ... 224,000

NORWAY / Norge

1979 E ... 4,073,000

Ålesund ... 34,744
Arendal (1980 E) (★20,000) ... 11,400
Bergen (1980 E) (★238,000) ... 209,000
Bodø ... 32,163
Drammen (1980 E) (★71,000) ... 49,700
Eigersund ... 11,694
Fredrikstad (1980 E) (★48,000) ... 28,000
Gjøvik ... 26,150
Grimstad ... 13,588
Halden ... 26,810
Hamar ... 16,053
Hammerfest ... 7,457
Harstad ... 21,579
Haugesund ... 27,081
Horten ... 13,476
Kongsberg ... 20,385
Kongsvinger ... 17,018
Kristiansand ... 60,722
Kristiansund ... 18,412
Larvik (1980 E) (★16,500) ... 8,300
Lillehammer ... 21,762
Mandal ... 11,847
Mo (1970 C) ... 21,033
Molde ... 20,886
Moss ... 25,407
Namsos ... 11,640
Narvik ... 19,202
Notodden ... 12,973
•OSLO (1980 E) (★725,000) ... 454,819
Porsgrunn (★★Skien) (1980 E) ... 31,365
Ringerike ... 26,839
Sandefjord ... 34,405
Sandnes (★Stavanger) (1980 E) ... 36,200
Sarpsborg (1980 E) (★37,500) ... 12,100
Skien (1980 E) (★78,815) ... 47,450
Stavanger (1980 E) (★128,000) ... 90,000
Steinkjer ... 20,526
Tønsberg (1980 E) (★35,000) ... 9,200
Tromsø ... 45,360
Trondheim ... 134,683
Vadsø ... 6,054

OMAN / 'Umān

1962 E ... 565,000

•Maṭraḥ ... 14,000
MUSCAT (MASQAṬ) ... 6,000

PACIFIC ISLANDS TRUST TERRITORY

1973 C ... 114,773

Island Groups
Caroline Islands ... 75,394
Mariana Islands (excl. Guam) ... 14,335
Marshall Islands ... 25,044

PAKISTAN / Pākistān

1972 C ... 64,979,732

(excl. population in section of Jammu and Kashmir occupied by Pakistan)

Abbottābād (★47,122) ... 27,963
Ahmadpur East ... 43,312
Bahāwalnagar ... 50,991
Bahāwalpur (★133,782) ... 115,660
Baldia (★Karāchi) ... 79,529
Bannu (★43,795) ... 33,000
Bhakkar ... 34,638
Burewala ... 57,741
Campbellpore (★29,172) ... 21,633
Chakwāl ... 29,143
Chārsadda ... 45,555
Chiniot ... 70,108
Dādu ... 30,184
Dera Ghāzi Khān ... 72,343
Dera Ismāil Khān (★58,778) ... 57,296
Faisalabad (Lyallpur) ... 823,343
Gujrānwāla (★360,478) ... 323,880
Gujrāt ... 100,333
Gwādar ... 15,758
Hāfizābād ... 61,597
Hyderābād (★660,000) ... 600,796
ISLĀMĀBĀD (★★Rāwalpindi) ... 77,000
Jacobābād ... 57,596
Jhang Maghiāna ... 131,843
Jhelum (★70,157) ... 63,676
Kamālia ... 50,934
Kāmoke ... 50,257
•Karāchi (1975 E) (★4,500,000) ... 2,800,000
Karāchi Cantonment (★Karāchi) ... 133,176
Kasūr ... 102,531
Khānewāl ... 67,746
Khānpur ... 49,235
Kohāt (★65,202) ... 48,096
Lahore (★2,200,000) ... 2,022,577
Lahore Cantonment (★Lahore) ... 147,165
Landhi Korangi (★Karāchi) ... 551,236
Lārkāna ... 71,893
Leiah ... 33,549
Mardān (★115,194) ... 105,157
Miānwāli ... 48,304
Mīrpur-Khās ... 81,965
Multān (★538,949) ... 504,365
Nawābshāh ... 81,045
New Karāchi No. 1 (★Karāchi) ... 85,398
New Karāchi No. 2 (★Karāchi) ... 67,682
Nowshera (★55,916) ... 31,101
Okāra (★101,052) ... 84,334
Orangi (★Karāchi) ... 109,979
Peshāwar (★284,833) ... 219,562
Quetta (★158,026) ... 137,659
Rahīmyār Khān (★85,699) ... 74,262
Rāwalpindi (★725,000) ... 372,919
Rāwalpindi Cantonment (★Rāwalpindi) ... 241,890
Sāhiwāl (Montgomery) ... 106,648
Sargodha (★200,460) ... 166,391
Shekhūpura ... 80,560
Shikārpur ... 70,924
Shujāābād ... 24,422
Siālkot (★203,650) ... 183,685
Sibi ... 19,989
Sukkur ... 158,781
Turbat ... 27,671
Wah Cantonment ... 107,510

PANAMA / Panamá

1970 C ... †1,472,280

†Includes former Canal Zone

Balboa (★Panamá) ... 2,569
Balboa Heights (★Panamá) ... 232
Colón (1976 E) (★82,000) ... 73,600
David ... 35,677
Gamboa ... 2,102
La Chorrera ... 25,873
•PANAMÁ (1978 E) (★645,000) ... 439,800
Puerto Armuelles ... 12,015
San Miguelito (★Panamá) (1977 E) ... 135,100
Santiago ... 14,595

PAPUA NEW GUINEA

1977 E ... 2,905,000

Lae ... 45,100
Madang ... 20,100
•PORT MORESBY ... 106,600
Rabaul ... 13,400
Wewak ... 18,100

PARAGUAY

1972 C ... 2,357,955

•ASUNCIÓN (1978 E) (★655,000) ... 463,700
Caacupé ... 7,278
Concepción ... 19,392
Coronel Oviedo ... 13,786
Encarnación ... 23,343
Fernando de la Mora (★Asunción) ... 36,834
Lambaré (★Asunción) ... 31,656
Luque (★Asunción) ... 13,921
Paraguarí ... 5,036
Pedro Juan Caballero ... 21,033
Pilar ... 12,506
Villa Hayes ... 4,749
Villarrica ... 17,687

PERU / Perú

1972 C ... 13,572,052

Arequipa (★304,653) ... 98,605
Ayacucho (★43,304) ... 34,593
Barranco (★Lima) ... 46,449
Barrio Obrero Industrial (★Lima) ... 238,402
Breña (★Lima) ... 123,345
Cajamarca ... 37,608
Callao (★★Lima) ... 196,919
Cerro de Pasco (★47,178) ... 35,975
Chiclayo (★189,685) ... 148,932
Chimbote ... 159,045
Chorrillos (★Lima) ... 87,021
Cuzco (★120,881) ... 67,658
Huacho ... 36,697
Huancayo (★115,693) ... 64,777
Huánuco ... 41,123
Ica ... 73,883
Iquitos ... 111,327
Jesús María (★Lima) ... 82,988
Juliaca ... 38,475
La Victoria (★Lima) ... 265,157
•LIMA (★3,250,000) ... 340,339
Lince (★Lima) ... 82,749
Magdalena del Mar (★Lima) ... 54,855
Miraflores (★Lima) ... 93,926
Pisco ... 41,429
Piura (★126,702) ... 81,683
Pucallpa ... 57,525
Pueblo Libre (★Lima) ... 76,279
Puno ... 41,166
Rímac (★Lima) ... 165,340
San Isidro (★Lima) ... 61,682
Sullana ... 60,112
Surco (★Lima) ... 70,949
Surquillo (★Lima) ... 89,201
Tacna ... 55,752
Trujillo (★241,882) ... 127,535
Tumbes ... 32,972
Vitarte (★Lima) ... 54,417

PHILIPPINES / Pilipinas

1975 C ... 42,070,660

Angeles ... 151,164
Antipolo (40,944▲) ... 35,672
Bacolod ... 223,392
Bacoor (★Manila) ... 62,225
Baguio ... 97,449
Baliuag ... 61,624
Batangas (125,363▲) ... 18,592
Biñan (★Manila) ... 67,444
Bocaue ... 40,577
Butuan (132,682▲) ... 53,578
Cabanatuan (115,258▲) ... 32,003
Cadiz (127,653▲) ... 26,581
Cagayan de Oro (165,220▲) ... 37,272
Calamba (97,432▲) ... 33,321
Calapan (55,608▲) ... 13,982
Caloocan (★Manila) ... 397,201
Cavite (★160,000) ... 82,456
Cebu (★500,000) ... 413,025
Cotabato (67,097▲) ... 49,134
Dagupan ... 90,092
Davao (484,678▲) ... 214,849
General Santos (Dadiangas) (91,154▲) ... 37,527
Gingoog (66,577▲) ... 16,590
Ilagan (70,075▲) ... 12,234
Iligan (118,778▲) ... 10,367
Iloilo ... 227,027
Iriga (75,885▲) ... 13,938
Isabela (Basilan) (27,261▲) ... 7,204
Jolo ... 37,623
Koronadal (62,764▲) ... 15,066
La Carlota (40,984▲) ... 20,251
Laoag (66,259▲) ... 31,336
Lapu-Lapu ... 79,484
Las Piñas (★Manila) ... 81,610
Legazpi (88,378▲) ... 37,724
Lingayen (59,034▲) ... 16,096
Lipa (106,094▲) ... 18,330
Lucena ... 92,336
Maasin (54,737▲) ... 12,348
Makati (★Manila) ... 334,448
Malabon (★Manila) ... 174,878
Malaybalay (65,198▲) ... 10,207
Malolos ... 83,491
Mandaluyong (★Manila) ... 182 267
Mandaue (★Cebu) ... 75,904
•MANILA (★5,500,000) ... 1,479,116
Marawi ... 63,332
Marikina (★Manila) ... 168,453
Mati (73,125▲) ... 18,188
Mecauayan (★Manila) ... 60,225
Muntinglupa (★Manila) ... 94,563
Naga ... 83,337
Navotas (★Manila) ... 97,098
Olongapo ... 147,109
Ormoc (89,466▲) ... 13,075
Ozamiz (71,559▲) ... 17,372
Pagadian (66,062▲) ... 28,645
Parañaque (★Manila) ... 158,974
Pasay (★Manila) ... 254,999
Pasig (★Manila) ... 209,915
Puerto Princesa (45,709▲) ... 18,480
Quezon City (★Manila) ... 956,864
Roxas (Capiz) (71,305▲) ... 18,869
Sagay (95,421▲) ... 32,417
San Carlos (*Negros Occidental Prov.*) (90,982▲) ... 23,950
San Carlos (*Pangasinan Prov.*) (90,882▲) ... 12,003
San Fernando (*La Union Prov.*) (61,166▲) ... 14,133
San Fernando (*Pampanga Prov.*) ... 98,382
San Juan del Monte (★Manila) ... 122,492
San Pablo (116,607▲) ... 42,489
San Pedro ... 43,439
Santa Cruz ... 52,672
Santa Rosa (★Manila) ... 47,639
Tacloban (80,707▲) ... 63,693
Tagbilaran ... 37,335
Tagig (★Manila) ... 73,702
Valenzuela (★Manila) ... 150,605
Zamboanga (265,023▲) ... 53,678

POLAND / Polska

1979 E ... 35,414,000

Będzin (★Katowice) ... 75,000
Biała Podlaska ... 38,100
Białystok ... 218,700
Bielawa (Langenbielau) (★★Dzierżoniów) ... 32,100
Bielsko-Biała ... 160,300
Bolesławiec (Bunzlau) ... 39,200
Brzeg (Brieg) ... 35,300
Bydgoszcz ... 343,800
Bytom (Beuthen) (★★Katowice) ... 231,600
Chełm ... 51,200
Chojnice ... 31,100
Chorzów (★★Katowice) ... 149,900
Częstochowa ... 232,400
Dąbrowa Górnicza (★Katowice) ... 137,300
Dzierżoniów (Reichenbach) (★85,000) ... 35,800
Elbląg (Elbing) ... 108,100
Ełk (Lyck) ... 37,300
Gdańsk (Danzig) (★820,000) ... 449,200
Gdynia (★★Gdańsk) ... 232,500
Gliwice (Gleiwitz) (★★Katowice) ... 195,300
Głogów (Glogau) ... 49,200
Gniezno ... 61,100
Gorzów Wielkopolski (Landsberg) ... 102,500
Grudziądz ... 88,700
Inowrocław ... 65,100
Jarosław ... 34,900
Jastrzębie Zdrój ... 97,800
Jaworzno (★Katowice) ... 88,200
Jelenia Góra (Hirschberg) ... 86,000
Kalisz ... 97,700
•Katowice (★2,590,000) ... 351,300
Kędzierzyn-Koźle (Heydebreck) ... 68,700
Kielce ... 181,000
Knurów (★Katowice) ... 40,200
Kołobrzeg (Kolberg) ... 37,500
Konin ... 65,300
Koszalin (Köslin) ... 90,000
Kraków (★780,000) ... 706,100
Krosno ... 38,000
Kutno ... 40,500
Legionowo (★Warsaw) ... 37,200
Legnica (Liegnitz) ... 88,400
Leszno ... 47,500
Łódź (★1,025,000) ... 830,800
Łomża ... 38,100
Lubin (Lüben) ... 63,000
Lublin (★345,000) ... 297,600
Mielec ... 41,300
Mysłowice (★Katowice) ... 78,100
Nowa Sól (Neusalz) ... 38,000
Nowy Sącz ... 62,600
Nysa (Neisse) ... 40,700
Olsztyn (Allenstein) ... 130,400
Opole (Oppeln) ... 114,000
Ostrowiec Świętokrzyski ... 62,300
Ostrów Wielkopolski ... 61,400
Oświęcim ... 44,200
Otwock (★Warsaw) ... 47,400
Pabianice (★Łódź) ... 69,800
Piekary Śląskie (★Katowice) ... 63,500
Piła (Schneidemühl) ... 57,200
Piotrków Trybunalski ... 70,900
Płock ... 99,800
Poznań (★610,000) ... 545,600
Pruszków (★Warsaw) ... 49,000
Przemyśl ... 60,100
Pszczyna ... 34,800
Puławy ... 44,800
Racibórz (Ratibor) ... 52,900
Radom ... 187,600
Radomsko ... 39,900
Ruda Śląska (★Katowice) ... 156,800
Rybnik ... 118,200
Rzeszów ... 116,900
Siedlce ... 52,500
Siemianowice Śląskie (★Katowice) ... 77,200
Skarżysko-Kamienna ... 43,100
Słupsk (Stolp) ... 84,200
Sopot (Zoppot) (★Gdańsk) ... 51,800
Sosnowiec (★★Katowice) ... 241,700
Stalowa Wola ... 52,200
Starachowice ... 48,400
Stargard Szczeciński ... 57,200
Starogard Gdański ... 43,300
Suwałki ... 38,500
Świdnica (Schweidnitz) ... 55,700
Świętochłowice (★Katowice) ... 57,700
Świnoujście (Swinemünde) ... 46,000
Szczecin (Stettin) (★425,000) ... 388,000
Szczecinek (Neustettin) ... 35,200
Tarnobrzeg ... 35,200
Tarnów ... 102,800
Tarnowskie Góry (★Katowice) ... 65,900
Tczew ... 52,300
Tomaszów Mazowiecki ... 62,800
Toruń ... 170,100
Tychy (★Katowice) ... 160,700
Wałbrzych (Waldenburg) (★195,000) ... 132,900
Wałcz (Deutsch Krone) ... 22,000
WARSAW (WARSZAWA) (★2,080,000) ... 1,576,600
Wejherowo ... 41,600
Włocławek ... 104,400
Wodzisław Śląski ... 104,500
Wołomin (★Warsaw) ... 30,600
Wrocław (Breslau) ... 609,100
Zabrze (Hindenburg) (★★Katowice) ... 195,000
Zamość ... 45,700
Żary (Sorau) ... 34,700
Zawiercie ... 61,600
Zduńska Wola ... 38,200
Zgierz (★Łódź) ... 52,100
Zgorzelec ... 32,800
Zielona Góra (Grünberg) ... 98,000
Żyrardów (★Warsaw) ... 36,700

C Census. E Official estimate. UE Unofficial estimate.
L Population within municipal limits of specified year. • Largest city in country.
★ Population or designation of metropolitan area, including suburbs (see headnote).
▲ Population of an entire municipality, commune, or district, including rural area.
‡† Year of information specified at start of country.

PORTUGAL

1970 C ... 8,568,703

Almada (★Lisbon) 38,714
Amadora (★Lisbon) 66,189
Angra do Heroísmo (*Azores Is.*) 14,328
Aveiro 20,651
Barreiro (★Lisbon) 53,200
Beja 15,909
Braga 49,693
Bragança 10,001
Coimbra 56,568
Covilhã 27,018
Évora 24,003
Faro 20,687
Funchal (*Madeira Is.*) 40,057
Guimarães 25,113
Horta (*Azores Is.*) 6,025
•LISBON (LISBOA) (1975 E) (★1,950,000) 829,900
Matosinhos (★Porto) 22,475
Montijo (★Lisbon) 25,949
Moscavide (★Lisbon) 21,647
Odivelas (★Lisbon) 25,978
Piedade (★Lisbon) 21,004
Ponta Delgada (*Azores Is.*) 21,262
Portimão 10,389
Porto (Oporto) (1975 E) (★1,150,000) 335,700
Póvoa de Varzim 17,555
Queluz (★Lisbon) 25,913
Santarem 18,069
Setúbal 50,730
Sintra (★Lisbon) (1960 C) 7,705
Vila do Conde 16,390
Vila Nova de Gaia (★Porto) 50,219
Viseu 16,636

PUERTO RICO

1980 C ... 3,187,570

Adjuntas (18,617▲) 5,184
Aguadilla (52,627▲) 20,879
Aibonito (22,230▲) 9,369
Arecibo (86,660▲) 48,586
Bayamón (★San Juan) 184,854
Cabo Rojo (33,909▲) 10,254
Caguas (★San Juan) (118,020▲) 87,218
Carolina (★San Juan) 147,100
Cataño (★San Juan) 26,318
Cayey (40,927▲) 23,315
Cidra (28,135▲) 6,065
Coamo (30,752▲) 12,834
Corozal (28,218▲) 5,891
Fajardo (32,011▲) 26,845
Guánica (18,784▲) 9,627
Guayama (40,137▲) 21,044
Guayanilla (21,012▲) 6,191
Guaynabo (★San Juan) 65,091
Humacao (45,916▲) 19,135
Isabela (37,451▲) 12,097
Juncos (25,433▲) 7,898
Manatí (36,480▲) 17,254
Mayagüez (★132,814) 82,703
Ponce (★252,420) 161,260
San Germán (32,941▲) 13,093
•SAN JUAN (★1,535,000) 422,701
San Lorenzo (32,333▲) 8,886
San Sebastian (35,877▲) 10,792
Trujillo Alto (★San Juan) (51,389▲) 41,097
Utuado (34,384▲) 11,049
Vega Alta (★San Juan) (28,225▲) 10,584
Vega Baja (★San Juan) (46,841▲) 18,020
Yabucoa (30,559▲) 6,782
Yauco (37,682▲) 14,598

QATAR / Qaṭar

1971 E ... 160,000

•DOHA (AD-DAWḤAH) 95,000

REUNION / Réunion

1974 C ... 476,675

Le Port (25,068▲) 21,621
•ST. DENIS (103,512▲) 80,802
St. Pierre (46,060▲) 22,022

RHODESIA see Zimbabwe

ROMANIA / România

1978 E ... 21,854,622

Aiud 25,929
Alba-Iulia 44,870
Alexandria 39,531
Arad 174,411
Bacău 135,841
Baia-Mare 107,945
Bîrlad 57,954
Bistriţa 48,959
Blaj 21,465
Bocşa 21,317
Borşa 25,427
Botoşani 68,325
Brăila 200,435
Braşov 268,226
•BUCHAREST (BUCUREŞTI) (★2,050,000) 1,858,418
Buzău 102,868
Călăraşi 50,601
Caracal 31,433
Caransebeş 28,437
Carei 24,473
Cîmpia Turzii 23,750
Cîmpina 33,554
Cîmpulung 33,329
Cluj 273,199
Codlea 23,691
Constanţa (★301,758) 267,612
Craiova 230,721
Cugir 27,892
Curtea de Argeş 26,081
Dej 33,350
Deva 65,009
Dorohoi 22,332
Drobeta-Turnu-Severin 80,200
Făgăraş 35,831
Feteşti 28,257
Focşani 60,038
Galaţi 252,592
Gheorghe Gheorghiu-Dej 43,282
Giurgiu 53,072
Hunedoara 81,963
Huşi 23,652
Iaşi 278,545
Lugoj 45,957
Lupeni 27,857
Mangalia 30,404
Medgidia 41,792
Mediaş 66,795
Miercurea Ciuc 33,884
Odorheiu Secuiesc 30,756
Olteniţa 25,185
Oradea 179,780
Petroşani (★74,000) 41,720
Piatra-Neamţ 83,168
Piteşti 133,081
Ploieşti (★270,000) 206,138
Rădăuţi 22,750
Reghin 31,035
Reşiţa 90,664
Rîmnicu-Sărat 29,246
Rîmnicu-Vîlcea 72,915
Roman 53,797
Roşiori de Vede 29,462
Săcele 31,615
Satu-Mare 107,852
Sebeş 26,881
Sfîntu Gheorghe 45,739
Sibiu 157,519
Sighetul Marmaţiei 39,095
Sighişoara 33,359
Slatina 50,683
Slobozia 33,701
Suceava 66,527
Tecuci 37,423
Timişoara 277,779
Tîrgovişte 67,024
Tîrgu-Jiu 67,694
Tîrgu-Mureş 136,679
Tîrnăveni 26,877
Tulcea 66,054
Turda 56,350
Turnu-Măgurele 33,404
Vaslui 42,718
Vulcan 29,216
Zalău 35,734
Zărneşti 24,317

RWANDA

1978 C ... 4,819,000

Butare 21,700
•KIGALI 117,700
Ruhengeri 16,000

ST. HELENA
(*excl. Dependencies*)

1976 C ... 5,147

•JAMESTOWN 1,516

ST. KITTS-NEVIS

1970 C ... 47,457

•BASSETERRE (*St. Kitts*) 13,055
Charlestown (*Nevis*) 1,880

SAINT LUCIA

1978 E ... 117,500

•CASTRIES 47,600

ST. PIERRE & MIQUELON / Saint-Pierre-et-Miquelon

1974 C ... 5,840

•ST.-PIERRE 5,232

ST. VINCENT

1970 C ... 89,129

•KINGSTOWN (★23,782) 17,258

SAN MARINO

1977 E ... 20,000

•SAN MARINO 4,628

SAO TOME & PRINCIPE / São Tomé e Príncipe

1970 C ... 73,631

•SÃO TOMÉ 17,380

SAUDI ARABIA / Al-'Arabīyah as-Sa'ūdīyah

1974 C ... 7,012,642

Abhā 30,150
Ad-Dammām 127,844
Al-Hufūf (Hofuf) 101,271
Al-Jawf (1961 UE) 20,000
Al-Khubar 48,817
Al-Madīnah (Medina) 198,186
Al-Mubarraz 54,325
Al-Qaṭīf (1961 UE) 30,000
At-Ṭā'if 204,857
Aẓ-Ẓahrān (Dhahran) (1974 UE) 25,000
Buraydah 69,940
Ḥā'il 40,502
Juddah (Jidda) 561,104
Khamīs Mushayṭ 49,581
Mecca (Makkah) 366,801
Najran 47,501
Qal'at Bīshah (1961 UE) 20,000
Qīzān 32,812
•RIYADH (AR-RIYĀḌ) 666,840
Tabūk 74,825
Yanbu' (1961 UE) 20,000

SENEGAL / Sénégal

1976 C ... 5,085,388

•DAKAR 798,792
Diourbel 51,000
Kaolack 106,899
Rufisque (★Dakar) (1973 E) 54,000
Saint-Louis 88,000
Thiès 117,333
Ziguinchor 73,000

SEYCHELLES

1971 C ... 52,437

•VICTORIA 13,622

SIERRA LEONE

1974 C ... 2,730,000

Bo 30,000
Bonthe (1963 C) 6,230
•FREETOWN (★335,000) 274,000
Kenema 15,000
Kissy (★Freetown) (1963 C) 13,143
Koidu (1963 C) 11,706
Lunsar (1963 C) 12,132
Makeni 12,000
Port Loko (1963 C) 5,809

SINGAPORE

1980 E ... 2,390,800

•SINGAPORE (★2,600,000) 2,390,800

SOLOMON ISLANDS

1976 C ... 196,823

•HONIARA 14,942

SOMALIA / Somaliya

1972 E ... 2,941,000

Afgoi (1964 C) 16,575
Berbera (1966 E) 14,000
Hargeisa (1966 E) 42,000
Kismayu (1968 C) 17,872
Marka (Merca) (1967 E) 17,700
•MOGADISHU (MOGADISCIO) 230,000

SOUTH AFRICA / Suid-Afrika

1970 C ... 21,794,328

Provinces

Cape (Kaap) 6,827,756
Natal 4,315,847
Orange Free State (Oranje-Vrystaat) 1,749,671
Transvaal 8,901,054

Cities

Alberton (★Johannesburg) 23,988
Alexandra (★Johannesburg) 57,040
Aliwal North 12,311
Beaufort West 17,862
Bellville (★Cape Town) 49,026
Benoni (★Johannesburg) 151,294
Bethal 17,337
Bethlehem 29,918
Bishop Levis (★Cape Town) 26,386
Bloemfontein (★182,329) 149,836
Boksburg (★Johannesburg) 106,126
Brakpan (★Johannesburg) 73,210
CAPE TOWN (KAAPSTAD) (★1,125,000) 697,514
Carletonville 93,096
Clermont (★Durban) 26,125
Cradock 20,822
De Aar 18,057
Dundee 17,162
Durban (★1,040,000) 736,852
East London (Oos-Londen) (★190,000) 119,727
Edendale (★Pietermaritzburg) 41,194
Edenvale (★Johannesburg) 25,126
Elsies River (★Cape Town) 64,539
Ermelo 19,036
Ga-Rankuwa 45,631
George 24,625
Germiston (★★Johannesburg) 221,972
Goodwood (★Cape Town) 31,592
Graaff-Reinet 22,392
Grahamstown 41,302
Grassy Park (★Cape Town) 32,709
Hammarsdale 21,657
Harrismith 16,082
•Johannesburg (★2,550,000) 654,232
Kempton Park (★Johannesburg) 37,205
Kimberley 105,258
Klerksdorp (★175,000) 63,558
Kroonstad 51,988
Krugersdorp (★Johannesburg) 92,725
Ladysmith 28,920
Mabopane 22,559
Madadeni 32,398
Mafeking 6,515
Mariannhill (★Durban) 22,484
Mdantsane (★East London) 67,501
Middelburg 26,942
Mosselbaai 17,574
Nelspruit 25,092
Newcastle 14,407
Nigel 41,179
Odendaalsrus (★29,026) 15,603
Orkney (★★Klerksdorp) 22,117
Oudtshoorn 26,907
Paarl 49,244
Parow (★Cape Town) 60,768
Parys 17,447
Pietermaritzburg (★160,855) 114,822
Pietersburg 27,174
Port Elizabeth (★475,869) 392,231
Potchefstroom 57,443
Potgietersrus 6,667
PRETORIA (★575,000) 545,450
Queenstown 39,304
Randburg (★Johannesburg) 46,011
Randfontein (★Johannesburg) 50,481
Roodepoort-Maraisburg (★Johannesburg) 115,366
Rustenburg 22,303
Sandton (★Johannesburg) 49,022
Sasolburg (★Vereeniging) 29,056
Soweto (★Johannesburg) 602,043
Springs (★Johannesburg) 142,812
Standerton 21,038
Stellenbosch 29,955
Stilfontein (★Klerksdorp) 70,661
Strand (★Cape Town) 24,503
Tembisa (★Johannesburg) 83,637
Uitenhage (★★Port Elizabeth) 70,517
Umlazi (★Durban) 123,495
Umtata 25,216
Upington 28,632
Vanderbijlpark (★★Vereeniging) 80,375
Vereeniging (★310,188) 172,549
Virginia 46,138
Welkom (★132,880) 67,472
Westonaria (★Johannesburg) 36,253
Witbank 37,456
Worcester 41,198
Zwelitsha 22,131

SOVIET UNION
See Union of Soviet Socialist Republics

SPAIN / España

1978 E ... 38,141,157

Regions and Provinces

ANDALUSIA (ANDALUCÍA) 6,560,445
Almería 418,471
Cádiz 1,016,340
Córdoba 751,833
Granada 780,848
Huelva 427,991
Jaén 677,756
Málaga 1,013,346
Sevilla 1,473,860
ARAGON (ARAGÓN) 1,204,244
Huesca 218,364
Teruel 157,454
Zaragoza 828,426
ASTURIAS 1,172,301
Oviedo 1,172,301
BALEARIC IS. (BALEARES) 642,702
Baleares 642,702
BASQUE PROVINCES (VASCONGADAS) 2,192,755
Álava 256,883
Guipúzcoa 714,690
Vizcaya 1,221,182
CANARY IS. (CANARIAS) 1,410,665
Las Palmas 704,389
Santa Cruz de Tenerife 706,276
CATALONIA (CATALUÑA) 6,071,953
Barcelona 4,724,063
Gerona 467,749
Lérida 358,430
Tarragona 521,711
ESTREMADURA (EXTREMADURA) 1,110,457
Badajoz 666,389
Cáceres 444,068
GALICIA 2,895,467
La Coruña 1,126,202
Lugo 418,770
Orense 447,980
Pontevedra 902,515
LEON (LEÓN) 1,156,113
León 549,709
Salamanca 368,833
Zamora 237,571
MURCIA 1,300,878
Albacete 343,868
Murcia 957,010
NAVARRE (NAVARRA) 511,699
Navarra 511,699
NEW CASTILE (CASTILLA LA NUEVA) 6,010,575
Ciudad Real 498,205
Cuenca 226,496
Guadalajara 143,520
Madrid 4,659,478
Toledo 482,876
OLD CASTILE (CASTILLA LA VIEJA) 2,261,956
Ávila 194,913
Burgos 368,302
Logroño 252,110
Palencia 192,102
Santander 515,109
Segovia 153,771
Soria 104,595
Valladolid 481,054
VALENCIA 3,638,947
Alicante 1,142,323
Castellón 430,845
Valencia 2,065,779

Cities (1975 C or ‡1978 E)

Aguilas (18,900▲) 16,900
Albacete ‡107,725
Alcalá [de Guadaira] (39,593▲) 33,500
Alcalá de Henares (★Madrid) ‡114,788
Alcalá la Real (20,184▲) 9,300
Alcantarilla 21,891
Alcázar de San Juan 26,930
Alcira 35,428
Alcobendas (★Madrid) ‡57,951
Alcorcón (★Madrid) ‡124,348
Alcoy ‡65,078
Algeciras ‡92,933
Algemesí 23,623
Algorta (66,306▲) ‡29,500
Alicante ‡235,868
Almadén 10,312
Almendralejo 22,074
Almería ‡136,720
Andújar (34,459▲) 28,400
Antequera (40,113▲) 27,500
Aranjuez 31,275
Arcos de la Frontera (24,867▲) 15,500
Arizgoiti (Basauri) (★Bilbao) (55,303▲) ‡46,800
Arrecife (*Canary Is.*) 25,201
Ávila ‡38,105
Avilés (★129,000) ‡90,458
Badajoz (112,573▲) ‡89,500
Badalona (★Barcelona) ‡216,041
Baracaldo (★Bilbao) ‡123,178
Barcelona (★3,975,000) ‡1,902,713
Baza (20,113▲) 14,400
Bilbao (★995,000) ‡452,921
Burgos ‡148,487
Burjasot (★Valencia) 30,739
Burriana 23,846
Cabra (20,140▲) 15,900
Cáceres ‡64,539
Cádiz (★230,000) ‡156,328
Camas (★Sevilla) 23,840
Carmona 21,548
Cartagena (165,557▲) ‡135,200
Castellón de la Plana ‡118,648
Chiclana [de la Frontera] 31,711
Cieza 28,228
Ciudad Real ‡48,871
Córdoba ‡276,255
Cornellá (★Barcelona) ‡95,933
Cuenca ‡39,064
Daimiel 16,986
Don Benito 26,117
Dos Hermanas 47,800
Écija (33,505▲) 25,400
Éibar 37,838
Elche (165,203▲) ‡136,400
Elda ‡53,558
El Ferrol del Caudillo (★126,000) ‡90,317
El Puerto de Santa María ‡52,350
Esplugas Llobregat (★Barcelona) 38,110
Figueras 28,102
Gandía (41,565▲) 32,600
Gavá (★Barcelona) 30,586
Gerona ‡85,522
Getafe (★Madrid) ‡128,523
Gijón ‡256,904
Granada ‡229,108
Granollers (★Barcelona) 36,366
Guadalajara ‡49,130
Guadix (19,234▲) 14,900
Guernica y Luno (17,271▲) 11,704
Hellín (22,327▲) 16,109
Hospitalet (★Barcelona) ‡294,280
Huelva ‡125,810
Huesca ‡38,986
Ibiza 20,552
Igualada 30,024
Irún ‡54,781
Jaén ‡91,198
Játiva 22,613
Jerez de la Frontera (183,534▲) ‡137,700
La Coruña ‡228,637
La Línea ‡57,940
Langreo (Sama de Langreo) (63,128▲) ‡10,600
La Orotava (*Canary Is.*) (30,190▲) 9,300
Las Palmas de Gran Canaria (*Canary Is.*) ‡357,158
Leganés (★Madrid) ‡151,353
Léon (★144,000) ‡122,827
Lérida (108,212▲) ‡86,100
Linares (56,356▲) ‡50,520
Logroño ‡104,928
Loja (22,001▲) 11,700
Lorca (65,806▲) 27,400
Lucena 29,373
Lugo (72,686▲) ‡60,900
•MADRID (★4,415,000) ‡3,367,438
Mahón 21,619
Málaga ‡467,637
Manacor 24,275
Manresa ‡68,213
Marbella (59,445▲) ‡35,200
Martos (21,375▲) 16,300
Mataró ‡98,589
Mérida 38,319
Mieres (62,826▲) ‡22,200
Miranda de Ebro 35,354
Mislata (★Valencia) 26,100
Morón de la Frontera (26,047▲) 22,700
Móstoles (★Madrid) ‡108,290
Motril (35,471▲) 28,100
Murcia (290,414▲) ‡190,600
Onteniente 26,297
Orense (89,485▲) ‡77,600
Orihuela (51,163▲) ‡20,000
Oviedo ‡181,556
Palencia ‡67,755
Palma [de Mallorca] ‡287,389
Pamplona ‡175,833

C Census. E Official estimate. UE Unofficial estimate.
L Population within municipal limits of year specified. • Largest city in country.
★ Population or designation of metropolitan area, including suburbs (see headnote).
▲ Population of an entire municipality, commune, or district, including rural area.
‡† Year of information specified at start of country.

Peñarroya-Pueblonuevo 13,579
Plasencia 28,574
Ponferrada ....‡53,400
Pontevedra (64,722▲) ....‡33,500
Portugalete (★Bilbao) ....‡57,053
Prat de Llobregat (★Barcelona) ....‡57,330
Priego [de Córdoba] (20,560▲) 12,300
Puente-Genil (25,277▲) 21,900
Puerto de la Cruz (*Canary Is.*) (50,173▲) 37,100
Puertollano ....‡52,722
Rentería (★San Sebastián) 46,329
Reus ....‡84,986
Ronda (30,099▲) 22,100
Rota 25,702
Rubí (★Barcelona) 35,855
Sabadell (★Barcelona) ....‡188,344
Sagunto ....‡57,840
Salamanca ....‡144,446
San Adrián de Besós (★Barcelona) 37,286
San Baudilio de Llobregat (★Barcelona) ....‡67,321
San Cristóbal de la Laguna (Canary Is.) (114,183▲) ....‡24,900
San Fernando (★★Cádiz) ....‡69,123
Sanlúcar (43,867▲) 31,500
San Sebastián (★290,000) ....‡176,023
Santa Coloma de Gramanet (★Barcelona) ....‡143,568
Santa Cruz de Tenerife (*Canary Is.*) ....‡186,949
Santander ....‡176,363
Santiago de Compostela (83,841▲) ....‡61,100
Santurce-Antiguo (★Bilboa) ....‡55,159
Segovia ....‡49,583
Sestao (★Bilbao) 41,399
Sevilla (Seville) (★740,000) ....‡630,329
Soria ....‡29,315
Sueca 22,522
Talavera de la Reina ....‡60,964
Tarragona ....‡109,969
Tarrasa (★Barcelona) ....‡160,403
Telde (*Canary Is.*) (58,503▲) ....‡17,300
Teruel ....‡24,856
Toledo ....‡56,414
Tomelloso 26,089
Torrejón de Ardoz (★Madrid) ....‡63,500
Torrelavega (55,695▲) ....‡25,900
Torrente (★Valencia) 46,686
Tortosa (47,246▲) 20,400
Ubeda 30,223
Valencia (★1,140,000) ....‡750,994
Valladolid ....‡315,486
Vall de Uxó 25,087
Vélez-Málaga (38,249▲) 18,700
Vich 27,615
Vigo ....‡260,059
Villanueva y Geltrú 41,229
Vitoria ....‡185,271
Zamora ....‡55,822
Zaragoza (Saragossa) ....‡563,375

SPANISH NORTH AFRICA / Plazas de Soberanía en el Norte de África

1978 E 120,719

•Ceuta 64,567
Melilla 56,152

SRI LANKA

1977 E 13,940,000

Anuradhapura 38,000
Badulla 38,000
Battaramulla (★Colombo) (1971 C) 43,057
Batticaloa 40,000
•COLOMBO (★1,540,000) 616,000
Dalugama (★Colombo) (1971 C) ..41,200
Dehiwala-Mount Lavinia (★Colombo) 169,000
Galle 79,000
Jaffna 118,000
Kalutara 32,000
Kandy 103,000
Kegalla 14,000
Kotikawatta (★Colombo) (1971 C) 43,764
Kotte (★Colombo) 102,000
Kurunegala 28,000
Maharagama (★Colombo) (1971 C) 40,378
Matale 34,000
Matara 40,000
Moratuwa (★Colombo) 104,000
Negombo 63,000
Ratnapura 32,000
Trincomalee 46,000

SUDAN / As-Sūdān

1973 C 12,427,795

Al-Fāshir 51,932
Al-Junaynah 35,424
Al-Khurṭūm Baḥrī (Khartoum North (★Khartoum) 150,991
Al-Qaḍārif 66,465
Al-Ubayyiḍ (El Obeid) 90,060
'Aṭbarah 66,116
Būr-Sūdān (Port Sudan) 132,631
Jūbā 56,737
Kassalā 98,751
•KHARTOUM (AL-KHARṬŪM) (★790,000) 333,921
Kūstī 65,257
Malakāl 34,898
Nyala 59,852
Umm Durmān (Omdurman) (★★Khartoum) 299,401
Wad Madanī 106,776
Wāw 52,752

SURINAME

1971 C 384,900

•PARAMARIBO (★175,000) 102,300

SWAZILAND

1976 C 494,534

•Manzini (★26,000) 10,019
MBABANE 23,109

SWEDEN / Sverige

1979 E 8,303,010

Counties

Älvsborg 424,240
Blekinge 154,135
Gävleborg 293,959
Göteborg och Bohus 713,242
Gotland 55,261
Halland 229,211
Jämtland 134,653
Jönköping 302,475
Kalmar 241,448
Kopparberg 285,545
Kristianstad 278,917
Kronoberg 172,401
Malmöhus 743,133
Norrbotten 266,983
Örebro 274,223
Östergötland 392,390
Skaraborg 268,702
Södermanland 252,026
Stockholm 1,524,266
Uppsala 241,722
Värmland 284,615
Västerbotten 241,898
Västernorrland 267,895
Västmanland 259,670

Cities

Alingsås (29,109▲) 19,800
Angelholm (29,397▲) 16,700
Arvika (26,962▲) 13,600
Avesta (26,471▲) 18,600
Boden (28,770▲) 20,200
Bollnäs (27,683▲) 11,100
Borås 102,914
Borlänge 46,318
Enköping (32,286▲) 18,800
Eskilstuna 90,414
Eslöv (26,939▲) 14,000
Falkenberg (34,610▲) 14,800
Falun (50,079▲) 31,600
Gällivare (24,661▲) 8,500
Gävle 87,364
Göteborg (Gothenburg) (★665,000) 434,699
Halmstad (75,663▲) 50,400
Härnösand (27,616▲) 19,400
Hässleholm (48,751▲) 17,000
Helsingborg 101,370
Huddinge (★Stockholm) 66,038
Hudiksvall (37,336▲) 15,200
Järfälla (★Stockholm) 52,442
Jönköping 107,652
Kalmar (52,657▲) 32,200
Karlshamn (31,907▲) 17,400
Karlskoga 37,070
Karlskrona (60,270▲) 33,400
Karlstad 73,904
Katrineholm (32,308▲) 22,700
Kiruna 30,177
Koping (27,291▲) 19,700
Kristianstad (68,675▲) 31,300
Kristinehamn (27,166▲) 20,700
Kungsbacka (42,905▲) 13,400
Landskrona 37,027
Lidingö (★Stockholm) 37,390
Linköping 111,866
Ljungby (27,097▲) 13,400
Ludvika 31,976
Luleå 67,190
Lund 78,003
Malmö (★305,000) 235,111
Mariestad (24,377▲) 16,200
Mjölby (25,885▲) 12,700
Mölndal (★Göteborg) 47,692
Motala (41,945▲) 25,100
Nacka (★Stockholm) 56,825
Nässjö (31,891▲) 18,200
Norrköping 119,993
Norrtälje (40,400▲) 31,200
Nyköping (63,918▲) 31,000
Örebro 116,877
Örnsköldsvik (60,665▲) 29,600
Oskarshamn (28,021▲) 19,000
Östersund (55,440▲) 41,000
Piteå (38,146▲) 17,400
Ronneby (30,270▲) 12,000
Sandviken 43,139
Skellefteå (73,647▲) 29,800
Skövde (45,847▲) 30,200
Söderhamn (31,264▲) 14,200
Södertälje (★Stockholm) 79,396
Sollefteå (26,133▲) 8,900
Sollentuna (★Stockholm) 45,864
Solna (★Stockholm) 51,324
•STOCKHOLM (★1,384,310) 649,384
Sundbyberg (★Stockholm) 25,676
Sundsvall (94,358▲) 52,500
Täby (★Stockholm) 46,142
Trelleborg (34,473▲) 22,300
Trollhättan 49,846
Uddevalla (46,139▲) 32,300
Umeå (79,930▲) 52,800
Uppsala 145,032
Vänersborg (34,613▲) 20,600
Varberg (43,829▲) 19,800
Värnamo (30,156▲) 15,700
Västerås 117,257
Västervik (41,303▲) 21,000
Växjö (63,763▲) 41,500
Vetlanda (28,714▲) 12,400
Visby (Gotland) (55,261▲) 20,200

SWITZERLAND / Schweiz / Suisse / Svizzera

1980 E 6,314,200

Aarau (★51,100) 15,900
Adliswil (★Zürich) 16,100
Allschwil (★Basel) 18,000
Altdorf 8,200
Appenzell 5,300
Arbon (★15,100) 11,500
Arosa (1970 C) 2,717
Baar (★Zug) 15,300
Baden (★67,300) 13,900
Basel (Bâle) (★575,000) 180,900
Bellinzona (★33,700) 17,200
BERN (BERNE) (★282,400) 141,300
Biel (Bienne) (★87,000) 56,800
Bolligen (★Bern) 32,500
Bülach 12,200
Burgdorf (★17,900) 14,900
Château d'Oex (1970 C) 3,203
Chiasso 8,900
Chur (Coire) 32,500
Davos 11,200
Delémont 11,600
Einsiedeln 9,700
Emmen (★Luzern) 22,800
Frauenfeld 18,600
Fribourg (Freiburg) (★51,800) 37,700
Genève (Geneva) (★425,000) 151,100
Glarus 5,800
Grenchen (★25,300) 16,800
Herisau 13,900
Illnau (★Zürich) 14,600
Interlaken (1970 C) 4,735
Köniz (★Bern) 34,400
Kreuzlingen 16,100
Kriens (★Luzern) 21,200
La Chaux-de-Fonds 38,100
Langenthal (★21,900) 13,400
Lausanne (★225,200) 128,800
Lauterbrunnen (1970 C) 3,431
Le Locle 12,600
Liestal (★Basel) 11,700
Locarno (★41,600) 15,100
Lugano (★69,100) 28,000
Luzern (Lucerne) (★156,400) 62,400
Martigny 11,100
Meiringen (1970 C) 3,759
Monthey 11,400
Montreux (★★Vevey) 20,200
Morges (★19,100) 13,300
Neuchâtel (Neuenburg) (★59,000) 34,900
Nyon 12,500
Olten (★47,200) 19,200
Opfikon (★Zürich) 11,200
Riehen (★Basel) 20,600
Rorschach (★23,000) 9,800
Sankt Gallen (St.-Gall) (★112,000) 73,800
Schaffhausen (Schaffhouse) (★51,300) 31,900
Schwyz 12,100
Sierre 14,200
Sion (Sitten) 23,400
Solothurn (Soleure) (★34,500) 15,600
Thun (Thoune) (★65,400) 37,000
Uster 23,000
Vernier (★Genève) 28,000
Vevey (★60,400) 15,700
Wädenswil 18,300
Wettingen (★Baden) 18,200
Wil (★21,500) 15,100
Winterthur (★106,800) 86,100
Wohlen (★15,700) 11,600
Yverdon (Iferten) 20,800
Zug (Zoug) (★52,200) 21,900
•Zürich (★780,000) 374,200

SYRIA / As-Sūrīyah

1978 E 8,401,100

Aleppo (Ḥalab) 878,000
Al-Ḥasakah 29,900
Al-Lādhiqīyah (Latakia) 204,000
Al-Qāmishlī (1970 C) 47,714
Ar-Raqqah 48,500
As-Suwaydā' 30,400
•DAMASCUS (DIMASHQ) (1979 E) (★1,550,000) 1,156,000
Dayr az-Zawr 99,100
Dūmā (★Damascus) (1970 C) 30,980
Ḥamāh 180,000
Ḥimṣ (Homs) 306,000
Idlib 52,600
Mukhayyam al-Yarmūk (★Damascus) (1970 C) 64,273

TAIWAN / T'aiwan

1977 E 16,813,127

Changhua (166,612▲) 129,000
Chiai 252,972
Chilung (Keelung) 345,392
Chungho (★T'aipei) 175,778
Chungli (Chunli) (180,689▲) 151,000
Chutung 52,000
Fengshan (Kaohsiunghsien) (★Kaohsiung) 177,982
Fengyüan (T'aichunghsien) (121,491▲) 94,000
Hsichih 51,000
Hsinchu 233,459
Hsinchuang (★T'aipei) 124,609
Hsintien (★T'aipei) 145,809
Hsinying (T'ainanhsien) 45,000
Hualien 101,010
Ilan (78,983▲) 66,000
Kangshan 58,000
Kaohsiung (★1,480,000) 1,172,977
Lotung 49,000
Lukang (Luchiang) 32,000
Makung (Penghuhsien) 23,000
Miaoli 66,000
Nant'ou 60,000
Panch'iao (T'aipeihsien) (★T'aipei) 314,848
Peikang 31,000
P'ingtung 182,114
Sanch'ung (★T'aipei) 292,909
Shulin (★T'aipei) 54,000
T'aichung 585,205
T'ainan 572,590
•T'AIPEI (★3,825,000) 2,196,237
T'aitung (111,647▲) 78,000
T'aoyüan 163,404
Touliu (Yünlin) 31,000
Yungho (★T'aipei) 162,731

TANZANIA

1978 C 17,557,000

Arusha 48,000
•DAR-ES-SALAAM 870,000
Dodoma (1970 E) 28,000
Iringa (1967 C) 21,746
Morogoro (1970 E) 30,000
Moshi 52,000
Mwanza 171,000
Tabora (1970 E) 23,000
Tanga 144,000
Ujiji (1967 C) 21,369
Zanzibar (1975 E) 80,000

THAILAND / Prathet Thai

1972 E 36,286,000

Ayutthaya 46,664
•BANGKOK (KRUNG THEP) (★3,375,000) 3,133,834
Ban Pong 22,036
Chachoengsao 27,071
Chiang Mai 93,353
Chon Buri 46,368
Hat Yai 57,255
Hua Hin 24,041
Khon Kaen 35,055
Lampang 42,007
Lop Buri 33,302
Nakhon Phanom 21,019
Nakhon Pathom 37,807
Nakhon Ratchasima 77,397
Nakhon Sawan 51,378
Nakhon Si Thammarat 50,761
Narathiwat 24,069
Nong Khai 24,680
Nonthaburi (★Bangkok) 25,654
Pattani 26,243
Phayao 22,217
Phet Buri 32,928
Phitsanulok 70,649
Phuket 38,493
Rat Buri 34,966
Samut Prakan (★Bangkok) 44,916
Samut Sakhon 39,982
Sara Buri 23,300
Songkhla 50,687
Suphan Buri 20,128
Surat Thani (Ban Don) 35,560
Surin 27,995
Trang 35,859
Ubon Ratchathani 52,171
Udon Thani 70,110
Warin Chamrap 25,850
Yala 39,983

TOGO

1977 E 2,348,000

•LOMÉ 229,400
Palimé 25,500
Sokodé 33,500

TONGA

1976 C 90,085

•NUKUALOFA 18,312

TRINIDAD & TOBAGO

1977 E 1,118,500

Arima (1970 C) 11,792
Débé (★Port of Spain) (1970 UE) 13,200
Point Fortin (1970 C) 7,738
•PORT OF SPAIN (★395,000) 42,950
Princess Town (1970 C) 7,784
San Fernando (★73,000) 36,650
San Juan (★Port of Spain) (1970 C) 30,802
Scarborough (*Tobago*) (1970 C) ...1,724
Tunapuna (★Port of Spain) (1970 C) 11,984

TUNISIA / Tunisie

1975 C 5,588,209

Ariana (★Tunis) 47,833
Béja 39,226
Bizerte (Binzert) 62,856
Gabès 40,585
Gafsa 42,225
Hammam Lif (★Tunis) 35,634
Kairouan 54,546
Kasserine 22,594
La Goulette (★Tunis) 41,912
Le Bardo (★Tunis) 49,367
Menzel Bourguiba 42,111
Moknine 26,035
Monastir 26,759
Msaken 33,559
Nabeul 30,476
Sfax (★260,000) 171,297
Sousse 69,530
•TUNIS (★915,000) 550,404

TURKEY / Türkiye

1980 C 45,217,556

(Cities designated (E) are in Turkey in Europe)

Adana 568,513
Adapazarı 131,400
Adıyaman 55,030
Afyonkarahisar 73,832
Akhisar 60,061
Aksaray 65,306
Akşehir 40,418
Alaşehir 25,605
Alibeyköy (★İstanbul) (1975 C) ...33,387
Amasya 48,010
ANKARA (★2,290,000) 2,203,729
Antakya (Antioch) 91,551
Antalya 176,446
Aydın 71,576
Bafra 50,167
Balıkesir 124,122
Bandırma 53,187
Batman 86,034
Bayburt 22,540
Bayrampaşa (E) (★İstanbul) (1975 C) 157,367
Bergama 34,386
Bolu 38,400
Bolvadin 30,733
Bornova (★İzmir) 54,965
Buca (★İzmir) (1975 C) 70,715
Burdur 44,750
Bursa 466,178
Çamdibi (★İzmir) (1975 C) 42,376
Çanakkale 39,943
Çankiri 35,040
Çarşamba 28,524
Ceyhan 57,097
Çorlu (E) 45,675
Çorum 76,020
Denizli 134,673
Diyarbakır 233,289
Düzce 37,659
Edirne (E) 71,570
Elâzığ 142,787
Ereğli (*Konya prov.*) 61,100
Ereğli (*Zonguldak prov.*) 50,096
Erzincan 73,335
Erzurum 190,121
Esenler (E) (★İstanbul) (1975 C) ..49,379
Eskişehir 309,335
Gaziantep 371,000
Gebze (★Izmit) 58,212
Gelibolu (Gallipoli) (E) 14,554
Giresun 46,068
Gölcük 45,006
İnegöl 45,314
İskenderun (Alexandretta) 120,985
Isparta 91,544
•İstanbul (E) (★4,765,000) 2,853,539
İzmir (Smyrna) (★1,190,000) 753,749
İzmit (Kocaeli) 191,340
Kadirli 38,125
Kâğıthane (E) (★İstanbul) (1975 C) 164,448
Karabük 84,975
Karaköse (Ağrı) 41,103
Karaman 51,868
Kars 58,651
Kartal (★İstanbul) 67,627
Kastamonu 35,636
Kayseri 273,362
Keşan (E) 28,428
Kilis 58,686
Kırıkhan 47,688
Kırıkkale 175,235
Kırklareli (E) 36,183
Kırşehir 50,063
Konya 325,850
Kozan 42,410
Küçükçekmece (★İstanbul) (1975 C) 58,709
Kütahya 101,087
Lüleburgaz (E) 35,643
Malatya 184,390
Manisa 93,970
Maraş 177,919
Mardin 37,750
Mersin 215,300
Merzifon 32,031
Muğla 27,162
Muş 40,297
Mustafakemalpaşa 30,099
Nazilli 64,015
Nevşehir 37,106
Niğde 39,972
Nizip 39,267
Ödemiş 40,652
Ordu 52,080
Osmaniye 84,338
Polatlı 43,514
Reyhanlı 30,843
Rize 41,740
Salihli 51,638
Samsun 198,266
Siirt 42,692
Silvan 44,412
Sinop 18,381
Sivas 173,831
Siverek 30,000
Söke 37,362
Tarsus 120,270
Tatvan 40,324
Tekirdağ (E) 51,327
Tire 32,242
Tokat 60,369
Trabzon 107,412
Turgutlu 55,575
Turhal 47,364
Urfa 148,434
Uşak 70,822
Uzunköprü (E) 27,706
Van 93,823
Viranşehir 41,934
Yozgat 36,220
Zile 30,066
Zonguldak (★195,000) 108,661

C Census. E Official estimate. UE Unofficial estimate.
L Population within municipal limits of year specified. • Largest city in country.

★ Population or designation of metropolitan area, including suburbs (see headnote).
▲ Population of an entire municipality, commune, or district, including rural area.
‡† Year of information specified at start of country.

TURKS & CAICOS IS.

1970 C...5,607
•GRAND TURK...2,287

UGANDA

1969 C...9,548,847
Arua...10,837
Bugembe...46,884
Entebbe...21,096
Fort Portal...7,949
Gulu...18,170
Jinja...52,509
Kabale...8,234
•KAMPALA...330,700
Lugazi...12,000
Masaka...12,987
Mbale...23,544
Soroti...12,398
Tororo...15,977

UNION OF SOVIET SOCIALIST REPUBLICS / Sojuz Sovetskich Socialističeskich Respublik

1980 E...264,486,000
UNION OF SOVIET SOCIALIST REPUBLICS IN EUROPE...172,022,000

Soviet Socialist Republics

Byelorussia (White Russia)...9,611,000
Estonia...1,474,000
Latvia...2,529,000
Lithuania...3,420,000
Moldavia...3,968,000
Russian Soviet Federated Socialist Republic (part)...101,067,000
Ukraine...49,953,000

Cities (1974 E, ‡1980 E)

Abdulino...25,000
Akhtubinsk...44,000
Akhtyrka...43,000
Alatyr...46,000
Aleksandriya...‡84,000
Aleksandrov...‡61,000
Aleksin...‡68,000
Almetyevsk...‡111,000
Alytus...‡57,000
Anapa...30,000
Antratsit (**Krasnyy Luch)...‡62,000
Apatity...‡64,000
Apsheronsk...33,000
Arkhangelsk...‡387,000
Armavir...‡163,000
Artemovsk...‡88,000
Arzamas...‡95,000
Astrakhan...‡465,000
Atkarsk...30,000
Avdeyevka (*Donetsk)...33,000
Azov...‡76,000
Bakhchisaray...20,000
Balakhna (*Gorkiy)...37,000
Balakleya...31,000
Balakovo...‡156,000
Balashikha (*Moscow)...‡119,000
Balashov...‡94,000
Baranovichi...‡135,000
Bataysk (*Rostov-na-Donu)...‡91,000
Belaya Kalitva...35,000
Belaya Tserkov...‡157,000
Belebey...39,000
Belgorod...‡248,000
Belgorod-Dnestrovskiy...37,000
Belorechensk...38,000
Beloretsk...‡72,000
Beltsy...‡128,000
Bendery...‡104,000
Berdichev...‡81,000
Berdyansk...‡124,000
Berezniki...‡186,000
Bezhetsk...30,000
Bobruysk...‡197,000
Bogoroditsk...32,000
Bogorodsk (*Gorkiy)...37,000
Bologoye...34,000
Bor (*Gorkiy)...‡63,000
Borislav...36,000
Borisoglebsk...‡67,000
Borispol'...36,000
Borisov...‡115,000
Borovichi...‡60,000
Boyarka (*Kiev)...31,000
Brest...‡186,000
Brezhnev...‡319,000
Brovary (*Kiev)...‡60,000
Bryanka (*Stakhanov)...‡63,000
Bryansk...‡401,000
Bugulma...‡81,000
Buguruslan...‡54,000
Buy...28,000
Buynaksk...42,000
Buzuluk...‡77,000
Chapayevsk...‡85,000
Chaykovskij...‡71,000
Cheboksary...‡323,000
Chekhov...‡53,000
Cherepovets...‡274,000
Cherkassy...‡234,000
Cherkessk...‡92,000
Chernigov...‡245,000
Chernovtsy...‡221,000
Chernyakhovsk (Insterburg)...34,000
Chervonograd...‡56,000
Chistopol...‡65,000
Chusovoy...‡57,000
Daugavpils...‡117,000
Debaltsevo...37,000
Derbent...‡71,000
Dimitrov (**Krasnoarmeysk)...‡59,000
Dimitrovgrad (Melekess)...‡108,000
Dmitrov...‡59,000
Dneprodzerzhinsk (**Dnepropetrovsk)...‡253,000
Dnepropetrovsk (*1,460,000)...‡1,083,000
Dobropolye...31,000
Dolgoprudnyy (*Moscow)...‡66,000
Domodedovo (*Moscow)...39,000
Donetsk (*Donetsk obl.*) (*2,075,000)...‡1,032,000
Donetsk (*Rostov obl.*)...42,000
Donskoy (*Novomoskovsk)...34,000
Drogobych...‡68,000
Druzhkovka (*Kramatorsk)...‡66,000
Dubna...‡56,000
Dzerzhinsk (*Gorkiy)...‡260,000
Dzerzhinsk (*Gorlovka)...46,000
Dzhankoy...46,000
Elektrostal...‡141,000
Elista...‡72,000
Engels (**Saratov)...‡165,000
Fastov...‡52,000
Feodosiya...‡78,000
Frolovo...38,000
Fryazino (*Moscow)...39,000
Furmanov...41,000
Galich...21,000
Gatchina (*Leningrad)...‡76,000
Gelendzhik...31,000
Georgiu-Dezh (Liski)...‡52,000
Georgiyevsk...‡55,000
Glazov...‡83,000
Glukhov...30,000
Gomel...‡393,000
Gorkiy (Gorki) (*1,900,000)...‡1,358,000
Gorlovka (*700,000)...‡337,000
Gorodets...35,000
Gremyachinsk...27,000
Grodno...‡202,000
Groznyy...‡377,000
Gryazi...42,000
Gubakha...32,000
Gubkin...‡65,000
Gudermes...34,000
Gukovo...‡69,000
Gusev...23,000
Gus-Khrustalnyy...‡72,000
Ilichevsk...43,000
Ingulets...35,000
Inta...‡51,000
Ishimbay...‡58,000
Ivano-Frankovsk...‡159,000
Ivanovo...‡466,000
Ivanteyevka (*Moscow)...41,000
Izberbash...20,000
Izmail...‡84,000
Izyum...‡61,000
Jelgava...‡69,000
Jurmala (*Rīga)...‡62,000
Kagul...31,000
Kakhovka...35,000
Kalinin...‡416,000
Kaliningrad (*Moscow)...‡135,000
Kaliningrad (Königsberg)...‡361,000
Kaluga...‡270,000
Kalush...‡61,000
Kamenets-Podolskiy...‡86,000
Kamenka...32,000
Kamensk-Shakhtinskiy...‡72,000
Kamyshin...‡112,000
Kanash...46,000
Kandalaksha...43,000
Kapsukas...33,000
Kashira...42,000
Kasimov...34,000
Kaspiysk...42,000
Kaunas...‡377,000
Kazan (*1,050,000)...‡1,002,000
Kerch...‡158,000
Kharkov (*1,750,000)...‡1,464,000
Khartsyzsk (*Donetsk)...‡59,000
Khasavyurt...‡67,000
Kherson...‡324,000
Khimki (*Moscow)...‡120,000
Khmelnitskiy...‡179,000
Kiev (Kiyev) (*2,430,000)...‡2,192,000
Kimovsk...44,000
Kimry...‡58,000
Kinel'...40,000
Kineshma...‡102,000
Kirishi...34,000
Kirov (*Kirov obl.*)...‡392,000
Kirov (*Kaluga obl.*)...30,000
Kirovo-Chepetsk...‡74,000
Kirovograd...‡242,000
Kirovsk (*Murmansk obl.*)...40,000
Kirovsk (*Voroshilovgrad obl.*) (*Stakhanov)...40,000
Kishinev...‡519,000
Kislovodsk...‡102,000
Kizel...42,000
Klaipėda (Memel)...‡178,000
Klimovsk (*Moscow)...‡55,000
Klin...‡92,000
Klintsy...‡69,000
Kobrin...28,000
Kohtla-Järve...‡73,000
Kolchugino...43,000
Kolomna...‡149,000
Kolomyya...‡53,000
Kolpino (*Leningrad)...‡118,000
Kommunarsk (*Stakhanov)...‡120,000
Komrat...24,000
Konakovo...33,000
Kondopoga...32,000
Konotop...‡84,000
Konstantinovka...‡113,000
Korosten...‡66,000
Kostroma...‡255,000
Kotel'nich...31,000
Kotlas...‡63,000
Kotovsk (*Odessa obl.*)...39,000
Kotovsk (*Tambov obl.*)...36,000
Kovel...40,000
Kovrov...‡144,000
Kramatorsk (*445,000)...‡180,000
Krasnoarmeysk (*155,000)...‡61,000
Krasnodar...‡572,000
Krasnodon...46,000
Krasnogorsk (*Moscow)...‡80,000
Krasnokamsk...‡56,000
Krasnyy Luch (*230,000)...‡107,000
Krasnyy Sulin...43,000
Kremenchug...‡212,000
Krichev...28,000
Krivoy Rog...‡657,000
Kronshtadt (*Leningrad) (1970 C)...39,477
Kropotkin...‡71,000
Krymsk (Krymskaya)...43,000
Kstovo (*Gorkiy)...‡60,000
Kudymkar (1975 E)...27,000
Kulebaki...46,000
Kumertau...‡54,000
Kungur...‡80,000
Kupyansk...34,000
Kurganinsk...38,000
Kursk...‡383,000
Kuybyshev (*1,440,000)...‡1,226,000
Kuznetsk...‡94,000
Labinsk...‡55,000
Leningrad (*5,360,000)...‡4,119,000
Leninogorsk...‡68,000
Lida...‡67,000
Liepāja...‡108,000
Lipetsk...‡405,000
Lisichansk (*365,000)...‡120,000
Livny...42,000
Lobnya (*Moscow)...‡53,000
Lomonosov (*Leningrad)...43,000
Lozovaya...‡55,000
Lubny...‡55,000
Luga...35,000
Lutsk...‡146,000
Lvov...‡676,000
Lysva...‡75,000
Lytkarino (*Moscow)...42,000
Lyubertsy (*Moscow)...‡162,000
Lyubotin...33,000
Lyudinovo...36,000
Makeyevka (**Donetsk)...‡439,000
Makhachkala...‡261,000
Marganets...‡51,000
Marks...22,000
Maykop...‡130,000
Mednogorsk...36,000
Melitopol...‡163,000
Michurinsk...‡102,000
Mikhaylovka...‡59,000
Millerovo...37,000
Mineralnyye Vody...‡68,000
Minsk (*1,330,000)...‡1,295,000
Mogilev...‡300,000
Molodechno...‡74,000
Monchegorsk...‡53,000
Morshansk (1977 E)...50,000
•MOSCOW (MOSKVA) (*11,950,000)...‡7,915,000
Mozdok...33,000
Mozhga...41,000
Mozyr...‡75,000
Mtsensk...34,000
Mukachevo...‡74,000
Murmansk...‡388,000
Murom...‡116,000
Mytishchi (*Moscow)...‡143,000
Nalchik...‡211,000
Naro-Fominsk...‡57,000
Narva...‡74,000
Neftekamsk...‡72,000
Nevinnomyssk...‡106,000
Nezhin...‡71,000
Nikolayev...‡449,000
Nikopol...‡149,000
Nizhnekamsk...‡139,000
Noginsk...‡120,000
Novaya Kakhovka...‡54,000
Novgorod...‡192,000
Novocheboksarsk...‡89,000
Novocherkassk...‡185,000
Novo-Ekonomicheskoye (**Krasnoarmeysk) (1970 C)...31,214
Novograd-Volynskiy...44,000
Novokuybyshevsk (*Kuybyshev)...‡110,000
Novomoskovsk (*Dnepropetrovsk obl.*)...‡70,000
Novomoskovsk (*Tula obl.*) (*370,000)...‡147,000
Novopolotsk...‡70,000
Novorossiysk...‡162,000
Novoshakhtinsk...‡105,000
Novo-Troitsk...‡97,000
Novovolynsk...44,000
Novozybkov...39,000
Nyandoma...23,000
Obninsk...‡76,000
Odessa (*1,120,000)...‡1,057,000
Odintsovo (*Moscow)...‡104,000
Oktyabr'sk...33,000
Oktyabr'skiy...‡91,000
Onega...25,000
Ordzhonikidze (*Severo-Osetinsk obl.*)...‡283,000
Ordzhonikidze (*Dnepropetrovsk obl.*)...39,000
Orekhovo-Zuyevo (*200,000)...‡133,000
Orel...‡309,000
Orenburg...‡471,000
Orsha...‡113,000
Orsk...‡252,000
Otradnyy...46,000
Panevėžys...‡104,000
Pärnu...‡51,000
Pavlograd...‡111,000
Pavlovo...‡69,000
Pavlovskiy Posad...‡71,000
Pechora...‡57,000
Penza...‡490,000
Pereslavl-Zalesskiy...33,000
Pereval'sk (*Stakhanov)...32,000
Perm (*1,075,000)...‡1,008,000
Pervomaysk (*Stakhanov) (*Voroshilovgrad obl.*)...46,000
Pervomaysk (*Nikolayev obl.*)...‡73,000
Petrodvorets (*Leningrad)...‡74,000
Petrovsk...34,000
Petrozavodsk...‡238,000
Pinsk...‡93,000
Podolsk (*Moscow)...‡203,000
Polotsk...‡72,000
Poltava...‡282,000
Priluki...‡66,000
Prokhladnyy...44,000
Pskov...‡177,000
Pugachev...35,000
Pushkin (*Leningrad)...‡89,000
Pushkino...‡71,000
Pyatigorsk...‡112,000
Ramenskoye (*Moscow)...‡79,000
Rasskazovo...40,000
Rechitsa...‡62,000
Reutov (*Moscow)...‡62,000
Rēzekne...34,000
Rīga (*920,000)...‡843,000
Rodniki...30,000
Romny...‡53,000
Roslavl...‡56,000
Rossosh'...38,000
Rostov...31,000
Rostov-na-Donu (*1,075,000)...‡946,000
Rovenki...‡62,000
Rovno...‡185,000
Rtishchevo...41,000
Rubezhnoye (**Lisichansk)...‡66,000
Ruzayevka...44,000
Ryazan...‡462,000
Rybinsk...‡241,000
Rybnitsa...39,000
Rzhev...‡69,000
Safonovo...‡53,000
Salavat...‡140,000
Salsk...‡58,000
Saransk...‡271,000
Sarapul...‡107,000
Saratov (*1,090,000)...‡864,000
Serdobsk...37,000
Serpukhov...‡141,000
Sevastopol...‡308,000
Severodonetsk (**Lisichansk)...‡115,000
Severodvinsk (Molotovsk)...‡203,000
Severomorsk...‡51,000
Shakhtersk (**Torez)...‡70,000
Shakhty...‡212,000
Shchekino...‡71,000
Shchelkovo (*Moscow)...‡101,000
Shebekino...36,000
Shepetovka...42,000
Shostka...‡82,000
Shumerlya...35,000
Shuya...‡72,000
Šiauliai...‡121,000
Sibay...40,000
Simferopol...‡307,000
Slantsy...42,000
Slavyansk (**Kramatorsk)...‡141,000
Slavyansk-na-Kubani...‡55,000
Slobodskoy...36,000
Slutsk...39,000
Smela...‡63,000
Smolensk...‡305,000
Snezhnoye (*Torez)...‡67,000
Sochi...‡291,000
Sokol...48,000
Soligorsk...‡68,000
Solikamsk...‡102,000
Solnechnogorsk (*Moscow)...37,000
Solntsevo (*Moscow)...‡62,000
Sovetsk...40,000
Stakhanov (Kadiyevka) (*590,000)...‡108,000
Staraya Russa...37,000
Staryy Oskol...‡123,000
Stavropol...‡265,000
Sterlitamak...‡224,000
Stryy...‡56,000
Stupino...‡71,000
Sumy...‡233,000
Suzdal (1959 C)...9,000
Sverdlovsk...‡75,000
Svetlogorsk...‡56,000
Svetlovodsk (Kremges)...41,000
Syktyvkar...‡175,000
Syzran...‡168,000
Taganrog...‡278,000
Tallinn...‡436,000
Tambov...‡270,000
Tartu...‡106,000
Ternopol...‡149,000
Teykovo...42,000
Tikhoretsk...‡64,000
Tikhvin...‡61,000
Timashevsk...31,000
Tiraspol...142,000
Tokmak...39,000
Tolyatti (Stavropol)...‡517,000
Torez (Chistyakovo) (*295,000)...‡87,000
Torzhok (1977 E)...50,000
Tuapse...‡61,000
Tula (*615,000)...‡518,000
Tuymazy...42,000
Ufa (*1,000,000)...‡986,000
Uglich...37,000
Ukhta...‡89,000
Ulyanovsk...‡473,000
Uman...‡80,000
Uryupinsk...39,000
Ustinov...‡562,000
Ust'-Labinsk...38,000
Uzhgorod...‡93,000
Uzlovaya (**Novomoskovsk)...‡65,000
Valuyki...30,000
Velikiye Luki...‡103,000
Velikiy Ustyug...38,000
Ventspils...44,000
Vichuga...‡52,000
Vidnoye...40,000
Vilnius...‡492,000
Vinnitsa...‡323,000
Vitebsk...‡303,000
Vladimir...‡301,000
Vogodonsk...‡109,000
Volgograd (Stalingrad) (*1,230,000)...‡939,000
Volkhov...48,000
Vologda...‡241,000
Volsk...‡65,000
Volzhsk...‡53,000
Volzhskiy (*Volgograd)...‡214,000
Vorkuta...‡101,000
Voronezh...‡796,000
Voroshilovgrad (Lugansk)...‡469,000
Voskresensk...‡77,000
Votkinsk...‡92,000
Voznesensk...39,000
Vyatskiye Polyany...35,000
Vyazma...‡52,000
Vyazniki...44,000
Vyborg...‡77,000
Vyksa...‡54,000
Vyshniy Volochek...‡71,000
Yalta...‡81,000
Yaroslavl...‡603,000
Yartsevo...39,000
Yasinovataya...39,000
Yefremov...‡53,000
Yegoryevsk...‡73,000
Yelabuga...35,000
Yelets...‡112,000
Yenakiyevo (**Gorlovka)...‡115,000
Yessentuki...‡79,000
Yevpatoriya...‡95,000
Yeysk...‡72,000
Yoshkar-Ola...‡207,000
Yuryev-Polskiy...23,000
Zagorsk...‡108,000
Zaporozhye...‡799,000
Zavolzh'ye...38,000
Zelenodolsk...‡85,000
Zelenograd (*Moscow)...‡132,000
Zelenokumsk...30,000
Zhdanov...‡507,000
Zheleznodorozhnyy (*Moscow)...‡78,000
Zheleznogorsk...‡67,000
Zheltyye Vody...‡53,000
Zhigulevsk (1977 E)...50,000
Zhitomir...‡250,000
Zhlobin...29,000
Zhmerinka...38,000
Zhukovskiy...‡92,000

UNION OF SOVIET SOCIALIST REPUBLICS IN ASIA...92,464,000

Soviet Socialist Republics

Armenia...3,074,000
Azerbaidzhan...6,112,000
Georgia...5,041,000
Kazakh S.S.R....14,858,000
Kirghiz S.S.R....3,588,000
Russian Soviet Federated Socialist Republic (part)...37,298,000
Tadzhik S.S.R....3,901,000
Turkmen S.S.R....2,827,000
Uzbek S.S.R....15,765,000

Cities (1974 E, ‡1980 E)

Abakan...‡133,000
Abay...41,000
Abovyan (*Yerevan)...32,000
Achinsk...‡117,000
Akhaltsikhe...19,000
Aktyubinsk...‡197,000
Alapayevsk (1977 E)...52,000
Aldan...20,000
Aleysk...37,000
Ali-Bayramly...38,000
Alma-Ata (*970,000)...‡928,000
Almalyk...‡102,000
Andizhan...‡233,000
Angarsk...‡241,000
Angren...‡108,000
Anzhero-Sudzhensk...‡107,000
Aral'sk...39,000
Arkalyk (1975 E)...35,000
Arsenyev...‡61,000
Artem...‡69,000
Artemovskiy...38,000
Arys...28,000
Asbest...‡80,000
Asha...38,000
Ashkhabad...‡318,000
Asino...31,000
Atbasar...39,000
Ayaguz...40,000
Baku (*1,800,000)...‡1,030,000
Balkhash...‡78,000
Barabinsk...37,000
Barnaul (*600,000)...‡542,000
Batumi...‡124,000
Bayram-Ali...36,000
Bekabad (Begovat)...‡69,000
Belogorsk...‡64,000
Belovo...‡112,000
Berdsk (*Novosibirsk)...‡68,000
Berezovskiy (*Sverdlovsk)...39,000
Berezovskiy (*Kemerovo obl.*)...37,000
Birobidzhan...‡70,000
Biysk...‡213,000
Blagoveshchensk...‡175,000
Bratsk...‡219,000
Bukhara...‡188,000
Chardzhou...‡143,000
Chebarkul'...42,000
Chelkar...20,000
Chelyabinsk (*1,215,000)...‡1,042,000
Cheremkhovo...‡75,000
Chernogorsk...‡73,000
Chimkent...‡327,000
Chirchik (*Tashkent)...‡134,000
Chita...‡308,000
Chu...35,000
Chust...31,000
Dudinka (1975 E)...23,000
Dushanbe...‡501,000
Dzhalal-Abad...‡55,000
Dzhambul...‡270,000
Dzhetygara...39,000
Dzhezkazgan...‡92,000
Dzhizak...‡71,000
Echmiadzin (*Yerevan)...37,000
Ekibastuz...‡74,000

C Census. E Official estimate. UE Unofficial estimate.
L Population within municipal limits of year specified. • Largest city in country.
* Population or designation of metropolitan area, including suburbs (see headnote).
▲ Population of an entire municipality, commune, or district, including rural area.
‡† Year of information specified at start of country.

Fergana ‡177,000
Frunze ‡543,000
Gagra 22,000
Geokchay 30,000
Gori ‡57,000
Gorno-Altaysk (1975 E) 39,000
Gulistan (1975 E) 39,000
Guryev ‡134,000
Igarka 16,000
Irbit ‡52,000
Irkutsk ‡561,000
Ishim ‡62,000
Iskitim ‡60,000
Kachkanar 38,000
Kafan 31,000
Kagan 38,000
Kamen-na-Obi 40,000
Kamensk-Uralskiy ‡189,000
Kamyshlov 31,000
Kansk ‡100,000
Karaganda ‡577,000
Karpinsk 37,000
Karshi ‡113,000
Kartaly 44,000
Katta-Kurgan ‡54,000
Kemerovo ‡478,000
Kentau ‡52,000
Kerki (1967E) 18,000
Khabarovsk ‡538,000
Khanty-Mansiysk (1975 E) 26,000
Khiva 26,000
Khodzheyli 40,000
Kholmsk 43,000
Khorog (1975 E) 15,000
Kirovabad ‡237,000
Kirovakan ‡149,000
Kiselevsk (★★Prokopyevsk) ‡122,000
Kokand ‡154,000
Kokchetav ‡106,000
Komsomolsk-na-Amure ‡269,000
Kopeysk (★Chelyabinsk) ‡146,000
Korkino ‡63,000
Korsakov 40,000
Krasnokamensk 54,000
Krasnotur'insk ‡61,000
Krasnoufimsk 40,000
Krasnouralsk 40,000
Krasnovodsk ‡53,000
Krasnoyarsk ‡807,000
Kuba 19,000
Kulyab ‡57,000
Kurgan ‡316,000
Kurgan-Tyube 39,000
Kushva 43,000
Kustanay ‡169,000
Kutaisi ‡197,000
Kuybyshev 44,000
Kyakhta 16,000
Kyshtym 39,000
Kyzyl ‡67,000
Kyzyl-Kiya 33,000
Kzyl-Orda ‡159,000
Leninabad ‡132,000
Leninakan ‡210,000
Leninogorsk ‡54,000
Leninsk 31,000
Leninsk-Kuznetskiy ‡133,000
Lenkoran 38,000
Lesozavodsk 38,000
Magadan ‡124,000
Magnitogorsk ‡410,000
Margelan ‡112,000
Mariinsk 40,000
Mary ‡76,000
Mezhdurechensk ‡93,000
Miass ‡152,000
Mingechaur ‡63,000
Minusinsk ‡61,000
Myski 38,000
Nakhichevan-na-Arakse (1975 E) 37,000
Nakhodka ‡136,000
Namangan ‡234,000
Naryn (1975 E) 26,000
Navoy ‡86,000
Nazarovo ‡55,000
Nazyvayevsk 15,000
Nebit-Dag ‡73,000
Nefteyugansk 51,000
Nev'yansk 31,000
Nikolayevsk-na-Amure 33,000
Nizhneudinsk 42,000
Nizhnevartovsk ‡122,000
Nizhniy Tagil ‡400,000
Norilsk ‡182,000
Novoaltaysk (★Barnaul) ‡50,000
Novokazalinsk (1970 C) 34,815
Novokuznetsk ‡545,000
Novosibirsk (★1,460,000) ‡1,328,000
Nukus ‡113,000
Omsk (★1,040,000) ‡1,028,000
Osh ‡173,000
Osinniki ‡60,000
Partizansk (Suchan) 49,000
Pavlodar ‡281,000
Pervouralsk ‡130,000
Petropavlovsk ‡209,000
Petropavlovsk-Kamchatskiy ‡219,000
Polevskoy ‡64,000
Poti (1977 E) 54,000
Prokopyevsk (★395,000) ‡266,000
Przhevalsk ‡52,000
Razdan 33,000
Revda ‡63,000
Rezh 34,000
Rubtsovsk ‡158,000
Rudnyy ‡111,000
Rustavi (★Tbilisi) ‡132,000
Rybachye 33,000
Samarkand ‡481,000
Saran ‡56,000
Satka 44,000
Semipalatinsk ‡286,000
Serov ‡101,000
Shadrinsk ‡82,000
Shakhtinsk ‡51,000
Shchuchinsk 46,000
Sheki (Nukha) 44,000
Shevchenko ‡116,000
Spassk-Dalniy ‡53,000
Sukhumi ‡116,000
Sumgait ★Baku) ‡196,000
Surgut ‡121,000
Sverdlovsk (★1,450,000) ‡1,225,000
Svobodnyy ‡75,000
Taldy-Kurgan ‡91,000
Tashauz ‡87,000
Tashkent (★2,015,000) ‡1,816,000
Tavda 47,000
Tayshet 35,000
Tbilisi (★1,240,000) ‡1,080,000
Temirtau ‡215,000
Termez ‡58,000
Tobolsk ‡64,000
Tokmak ‡60,000
Tomsk ‡431,000
Troitsk ‡83,000
Tselinograd (Akmolinsk) ‡237,000
Tskhinvali (1975 E) 34,000
Tulun ‡52,000
Turkestan ‡69,000
Tyumen ‡369,000
Ulan-Ude ‡305,000
Uralsk ‡170,000
Ura-Tyube 36,000
Urgench ‡103,000
Usolye-Sibirskoye ‡104,000
Ussuriysk ‡148,000
Ust-Ilimsk ‡76,000
Ust-Kamenogorsk ‡280,000
Ust-Kut ‡51,000
Verkhniy Ufaley 38,000
Verkhnyaya Pyshma (★Sverdlovsk) 40,000
Verkhnyaya Salda ‡55,000
Vladivostok ‡558,000
Yakutsk ‡155,000
Yangi-Yul ‡64,000
Yerevan (★1,155,000) ‡1,036,000
Yermak 40,000
Yurga ‡80,000
Yuzhno-Sakhalinsk ‡143,000
Zima (1977 E) 51,000
Zlatoust ‡199,000
Zugdidi 41,000
Zyryanovsk ‡52,000

UNITED ARAB EMIRATES / Ittiḥād al-Imārāt al-'Arabīyah

1968 C 180,200

ABU DHABI (ABŪ ẒABY) (1973 E) 50,000
'Ajmān 3,725
Al Fujayrah 760
Ash Shāriqah 19,200
•Dubai (Dubayy) (1970 E) 60,000
Ra's al Khaymah 5,300
Umm al Qaywayn 2,900

UNITED KINGDOM

1979 E 55,880,000

Political Divisions

ENGLAND 46,396,100
WALES 2,774,700
SCOTLAND 5,167,000
NORTHERN IRELAND 1,542,200

ENGLAND

Metropolitan Counties

Greater London 6,877,100
Greater Manchester 2,648,300
South York 1,301,300
Tyne & Wear 1,155,900
West Midlands 2,696,000
West York 2,064,100

Non-metropolitan Counties

Avon 924,200
Bedford 498,800
Berks 682,000
Buckingham 535,800
Cambridge 579,300
Cheshire 926,500
Cleveland 568,600
Cornwall & Isles of Scilly 419,300
Cumbria 469,900
Derby 898,300
Devon 952,100
Dorset 591,100
Durham 603,200
East Sussex 654,600
Essex 1,446,700
Gloucester 497,100
Hampshire 1,459,500
Hereford & Worcester 617,900
Hertford 952,000
Humberside 849,600
Isle of Wight 115,300
Kent 1,456,100
Lancashire 1,369,700
Leicester 836,300
Lincoln 533,800
Merseyside 1,531,600
Norfolk 686,300
Northampton 523,300
Northumberland 289,800
North York 663,200
Nottingham 974,100
Oxford 542,100
Shropshire 369,500
Somerset 415,500
Stafford 999,900
Suffolk 597,600
Surrey 993,700
Warwick 468,900
West Sussex 643,800
Wilts 516,400

Cities ★(1979 E or ‡1973 E)

Abingdon (★Oxford) ‡20,130
Accrington (Hyndburn) (★★Blackburn) 79,400
Adur (★Brighton) 57,700
Aldershot (Rushmoor) (★London) 81,000
Aldridge-Brownhills (Walsall) ‡89,370
Andover ‡27,620
Ashford ‡36,380
Ashton-under-Lyne (Tameside) (★★Manchester) 218,500
Aycliffe (1971 C) 20,190
Aylesbury ‡41,420
Banbury ‡31,060
Barnsley 221,800
Barnstaple ‡17,820
Barrow-in-Furness 71,100
Basildon (★London) 148,200
Basingstoke ‡60,910
Bath 83,900
Batley (★Leeds) ‡41,630
Battle (1971 C) 4,987
Bebington (Wirral) ‡62,500
Bedford ‡74,390
Bedworth (Nuneaton) ‡41,600
Beeston & Stapleford (★Nottingham) ‡65,360
Benfleet (Castle Point) (★London) 84,400
Berkhamsted (★London) ‡15,920
Berwick-upon-Tweed ‡11,610
Bexhill-on-Sea ‡34,680
Birkenhead (Wirral) (★Liverpool) 342,300
Birmingham (★2,660,000) 1,033,900
Bishop Auckland ‡32,940
Bishop's Stortford (★London) ‡21,720
Blackburn (★221,900) 142,500
Blackpool (★275,000) 145,400
Bletchley ‡33,450
Blyth (Blyth Valley) 75,700
Blyth Valley see Blyth
Bodmin ‡10,430
Bognor Regis ‡34,620
Bolton (★★Manchester) 260,100
Bootle (★Liverpool) ‡71,160
Boston ‡26,700
Bournemouth (★315,000) 144,200
Bracknell (★London) (1971 C) 33,953
Bradford (★★Leeds) 461,600
Bradford-on-Avon ‡8,310
Braintree ‡26,300
Brentwood (★London) ‡58,690
Bridgwater ‡26,600
Bridlington ‡26,920
Brighouse (★Halifax) ‡35,320
Brighton (★425,000) 152,700
Bristol (★635,000) 408,000
Broadstairs and St. Peters ‡21,670
Bromsgrove (★Birmingham) ‡41,430
Broxbourne see Cheshunt
Burgess Hill (★London) ‡20,030
Burnham-on-Sea ‡12,690
Burnley (★160,000) 92,300
Burton-upon-Trent ‡49,480
Bury (★★Manchester) 178,600
Bury St. Edmunds ‡26,800
Buxton ‡20,050
Camborne-Redruth ‡43,970
Cambridge 101,600
Cannock (Cannock Chase) (★Birmingham) 83,600
Cannock Chase see Cannock
Canterbury ‡34,510
Carlisle ‡70,930
Carlton (Gedling) (★Nottingham) 102,800
Castleford (★Leeds) ‡37,650
Castle Point see Benfleet
Caterham & Warlingham (★London) ‡35,840
Chatham (Medway) (★London) 147,400
Cheadle and Gatley (Stockport) ‡62,460
Chelmsford (★London) ‡58,320
Cheltenham 85,000
Chertsey (Runnymede) (★London) 72,800
Chesham (★London) ‡20,830
Cheshunt (Broxbourne) (★London) 79,200
Chester ‡61,370
Chesterfield (★127,000) 96,300
Chester-le-Street (★Newcastle) ‡20,720
Chichester ‡20,940
Chigwell (★London) ‡54,220
Chippenham ‡18,550
Chorley (★★Preston) ‡31,800
Christchurch (★Bournemouth) 38,600
Cirencester ‡14,500
Clacton-on-Sea ‡39,380
Cleethorpes (★Grimsby) ‡37,200
Clevedon ‡15,140
Coalville ‡28,740
Colchester ‡79,600
Consett (★Newcastle) ‡35,080
Corby 53,000
Coventry (★655,000) 339,300
Cowes ‡19,190
Crawley (★London) 71,800
Crewe ‡50,450
Crosby (★Liverpool) ‡56,750
Cuckfield (★London) ‡26,500
Darlington ‡85,120
Dartford (★London) ‡44,130
Dartmouth ‡6,720
Dawley ‡30,720
Deal ‡26,840
Derby (★270,000) 215,900
Dewsbury (★★Leeds) ‡50,560
Doncaster (★160,000) ‡81,530
Dorchester ‡13,880
Dorking (★London) ‡22,410
Dover ‡34,160
Dronfield (★Sheffield) ‡20,000
Dudley (★★Birmingham) 296,000
Dunstable (★Luton) ‡32,090
Durham ‡29,490
Eastbourne 73,100
East Grinstead (★London) ‡19,420
Eastleigh (★Southampton) ‡46,340
East Retford ‡18,260
Ellesmere Port (★Liverpool) ‡63,870
Elmbridge see Walton and Weybridge
Ely ‡10,630
Epsom and Ewell (★London) 70,500
Esher (Elmbridge) ‡63,970
Eton (★London) ‡4,950
Evesham ‡14,090
Exeter 95,600
Exmouth ‡26,840
Falmouth ‡17,530
Fareham (★Portsmouth) 85,000
Farnham (★London) ‡33,140
Faversham ‡15,010
Felixstowe ‡19,460
Fleet (★London) ‡22,930
Fleetwood (★★Blackpool) ‡30,070
Folkestone ‡45,610
Formby (★Liverpool) ‡24,850
Frimley & Camberley (★London) ‡47,390
Frome ‡13,780
Gainsborough ‡17,440
Gateshead (★Newcastle) 212,200
Gedling see Carlton
Gillingham (★London) 92,800
Glastonbury ‡6,580
Glossop (★Manchester) ‡24,820
Gloucester (★115,000) 91,300
Goole ‡17,920
Gosport (★Portsmouth) 79,400
Grantham ‡27,830
Gravesend (Gravesham) (★London) 95,900
Gravesham see Gravesend
Great Yarmouth ‡49,410
Grimsby (★145,000) 91,900
Guildford (★London) ‡58,470
Halesowen (Dudley) ‡54,120
Halifax (★173,000) ‡88,580
Haltemprice (★Hull) ‡54,850
Halton see Widnes
Harlow (★London) 79,100
Harrogate ‡64,620
Hartlepool (★★Middlesbrough) 95,100
Harwich ‡15,280
Hastings 74,200
Havant (★Portsmouth) 116,100
Haverhill ‡14,550
Heanor ‡24,590
Hemel Hempstead (★London) ‡71,150
Hemsworth ‡14,680
Henley-on-Thames ‡11,860
Hereford 46,800
Herne Bay ‡26,510
Hertford (★London) ‡20,760
Hertsmere (★London) 87,800
Hexham ‡9,820
High Wycombe ‡61,190
Hinckley (★★Coventry) ‡49,310
Hitchin ‡29,190
Horsham (★London) ‡26,770
Hove (★Brighton) 87,800
Hucknall (★Nottingham) ‡27,110
Huddersfield (★209,000) ‡130,060
Huntingdon & Godmanchester ‡17,200
Huyton-with-Roby (Knowsley) (★Liverpool) 179,700
Hyndburn see Accrington
Hythe ‡12,210
Ilkeston (★Nottingham) ‡33,690
Ipswich 118,900
Keighley (Bradford) ‡56,040
Kendal ‡22,440
Kenilworth (★Coventry) ‡19,730
Keswick ‡4,790
Kettering ‡44,480
Kidderminster ‡49,960
King's Lynn ‡29,990
Kingston-upon-Hull (Hull) (★350,000) 274,500
Kingswood (★Bristol) 82,100
Kirkby (Knowsley) ‡59,100
Knowsley see Huyton-with-Roby
Lancaster (★100,000) ‡50,570
Leamington Spa (★★Coventry) ‡44,950
Leatherhead (★London) ‡40,830
Leeds (★1,540,000) 724,300
Leek ‡19,460
Leicester (★480,000) 276,600
Leighton-Linslade ‡22,590
Letchworth ‡31,520
Lewes ‡14,170
Leyland (South Ribble) (★Preston) 96,100
Lichfield ‡23,690
Lincoln 71,900
Littlehampton ‡20,320
Liverpool (★1,535,000) 520,200
•LONDON (★11,050,000) 6,877,100
Longbenton (North Tyneside) ‡50,120
Long Eaton (★Nottingham) ‡33,560
Loughborough ‡49,010
Lowestoft ‡53,260
Ludlow (1971 C) 7,466
Luton (★215,000) 160,300
Lymington ‡36,760
Lytham St. Annes (★Blackpool) ‡42,120
Macclesfield ‡45,420
Maidenhead (★London) ‡48,210
Maidstone ‡72,110
Malvern ‡30,420
Manchester (★2,800,000) 479,100
Mansfield (★198,000) ‡58,450
Margate ‡50,290
Market Harborough ‡15,230
Marlborough ‡6,370
Matlock ‡20,300
Medway see Chatham
Melton Mowbray ‡20,680
Middlesbrough (★580,000) 153,000
Middleton (Rochdale) ‡53,340
Morecambe [& Heysham] (★★Lancaster) ‡42,010
Morley (Leeds) ‡44,790
Nelson (★★Burnley) ‡31,220
Newark-upon-Trent ‡24,760
Newbury ‡24,850
Newcastle-under-Lyme (★★Stoke-on-Trent) ‡75,940
Newcastle-upon-Tyne (★1,295,000) 287,300
Newmarket ‡13,370
Newport ‡22,430
Newton Abbot ‡19,940
Northampton 154,900
North Tyneside see Tynemouth
Northwich ‡17,710
Norwich (★220,000) 119,300
Nottingham (★645,000) 278,600
Nuneaton (★★Coventry) 110,300
Oadby and Wigston (★Leicester) 52,300
Oakengates ‡17,340
Oakham ‡7,280
Oldham (★★Manchester) 223,500
Ormskirk (★Liverpool) ‡28,860
Oxford (★240,000) 122,400
Penrith ‡11,400
Penzance ‡19,360
Peterborough ‡72,270
Peterlee (1971 C) 21,836
Plymouth (★295,000) 255,500
Poole (★★Bournemouth) 115,500
Portsmouth (★490,000) 191,000
Preston (★245,000) 126,200
Queenborough-in-Sheppey ‡31,550
Ramsgate ‡40,090
Rawtenstall ‡20,950
Rayleigh (★London) ‡26,740
Reading (★200,000) 138,400
Redditch (★Birmingham) 64,300
Reigate and Banstead (★London) 114,000
Rickmansworth (★London) ‡29,030
Ripon ‡12,580
Rochdale (★★Manchester) 209,000
Rochester (Medway) (★London) ‡56,030
Rotherham (★★Sheffield) 248,800
Rugby ‡60,380
Runnymede see Chertsey
Rushden ‡21,840
Rushmoor see Aldershot
Ryde ‡23,170
Rye ‡4,530
Saint Albans (★London) 124,300
St. Austell [with Fowey] ‡32,710
St. Helens 188,700
Sale (Trafford) ‡59,060
Salford (★Manchester) 252,600
Salisbury ‡35,460
Sandwell see Smethwick
Sandwich ‡4,420
Scarborough ‡43,300
Scunthorpe 67,200
Seaford ‡18,020
Seaham (★Newcastle) ‡22,470
Selby ‡11,590
Sevenoaks (★London) ‡18,160
Sheffield (★705,000) 544,200
Shrewsbury ‡56,120
Sittingbourne & Milton ‡32,830
Skelmersdale [& Holland] (★Manchester) ‡35,850
Slough (★London) 98,400
Smethwick (Sandwell) (★Birmingham) 306,900
Solihull (★Birmingham) 198,300
Southampton (★410,000) 207,800
Southend-on-Sea (★London) 154,700
Southport (★★Liverpool) ‡86,030
South Ribble see Leyland
South Shields (South Tyneside) (★★Newcastle) 162,600
South Tyneside see South Shields
Spenborough (★Leeds) ‡41,460
Spennymoor ‡19,050
Stafford ‡54,860
Staines (Spelthorne) (★London) 93,500
Stamford ‡14,980
Stanley (★Newcastle) ‡42,280
Stevenage 73,100
Stockport (★Manchester) 291,700
Stockton-on-Tees (★★Middlesbrough) 171,800
Stoke-on-Trent (★445,000) 257,200
Stourbridge (Dudley) ‡56,530
Stratford-on-Avon ‡20,080
Stretford (Trafford) (★Manchester) 224,000
Stroud ‡19,600
Sudbury ‡8,860
Sunderland (★★Newcastle) 300,800
Sutton Coldfield (Birmingham) ‡83,630
Sutton-in-Ashfield (★★Mansfield) ‡40,330
Swadlincote ‡21,060
Swindon (Thamesdown) 143,800
Tameside see Ashton-under-Lyne
Tamworth 60,300
Taunton ‡37,570
Tewkesbury ‡9,210
Thamesdown see Swindon
Thetford ‡15,690
Thornton Cleveleys (★Blackpool) ‡27,090
Thurrock (★London) 127,100
Tiverton ‡16,190
Todmorden ‡14,540
Tonbridge (★London) ‡31,410
Torquay (Torbay) 108,700
Trafford see Stretford

(England continued)

C Census. E Official estimate. UE Unofficial estimate.
L Population within municipal limits of year specified. • Largest city in country.
★ Population or designation of metropolitan area, including suburbs (see headnote).
▲ Population of an entire municipality, commune, or district, including rural area.
‡† Year of information specified at start of country.
* Italicized place names are now a part of the city shown in parentheses following the place name. These changes are part of the April 1974 reorganization of local administrative areas.

(England continued)

Trowbridge ... ‡20,120
Truro ... ‡15,690
Tunbridge Wells ... ‡44,800
Tynemouth (North Tyneside) (*Newcastle) ... 193,000
Ulverston ... ‡12,370
Wakefield (**Leeds) ... ‡58,490
Wallasey (Wirral) ... *‡94,520*
Walsall (**Birmingham) ... 263,400
Walton and Weybridge (Elmbridge) (*London) ... 110,000
Wansbeck ... 61,000
Warrington ... 168,200
Warwick (**Coventry) ... ‡17,870
Watford (*London) ... 76,500
Wellingborough ... ‡39,570
Wells ... ‡8,960
Welwyn Garden City (*London) ... ‡39,900
West Bridgford (*Nottingham) ... ‡28,340
West Bromwich (Sandwell) ... *‡162,740*
Weston-super-Mare ... ‡51,960
Weymouth and Portland ... 57,700
Whitby ... ‡12,710
Whitehaven ... ‡26,260
Whitstable ... ‡26,980
Widnes (Halton) ... 120,700
Wigan (**Manchester) ... 311,200
Wilmslow (*Manchester) ... ‡31,250
Winchester ... ‡31,070
Windermere ... ‡7,860
Windsor (New Windsor) (*London) ... ‡29,660
Winsford ... ‡26,920
Wirral see Birkenhead
Woking (*London) ... 80,500
Wokingham ... ‡22,390
Wolverhampton (**Birmingham) ... 258,200
Worcester ... 75,000
Workington ... ‡28,260
Worksop ... ‡36,590
Worthing (**Brighton) ... 90,600
Yeovil ... ‡26,180
York (*140,000) ... 100,900

WALES

Counties

Clwyd ... 385,100
Dyfed ... 325,600
Gwent ... 435,900
Gwynedd ... 226,300
Mid Glamorgan ... 537,500
Powys ... 107,100
South Glamorgan ... 390,600
West Glamorgan ... 366,600

Cities (1973 E)

Aberdare ... 38,030
Abertillery (*Newport) ... 20,550
Aberystwyth ... 10,900
Bangor ... 16,030
Barry (*Cardiff) ... 42,780
Brecon ... 6,460
Bridgend ... 14,690
Caernarfon ... 8,840
Caerphilly (*Cardiff) ... 42,190
•CARDIFF (1979 E) (*625,000) ... 282,000
Carmarthen ... 12,860
Colwyn Bay ... 25,370
Ebbw Vale ... 25,670
Flint ... 15,070
Islwyn (*Newport) (1979 E) ... 63,400
Llandudno ... 17,700
Llanelli ... 25,870
Merthyr Tydfil ... 53,680
Milford Haven ... 13,960
Monmouth ... 7,000
Neath (**Swansea) ... 27,280
Newport (1979 E) (*310,000) ... 132,800
Pembroke ... 14,570
Pontypool (Torfaen) (**Newport) (1979 E) ... 90,400
Pontypridd (*Cardiff) ... 34,180
Port Talbot (*132,000) ... 50,200
Prestatyn ... 15,480
Rhondda (**Cardiff) (1979 E) ... 81,800
Rhyl ... 22,150
Swansea (1979 E) (*270,000) ... 186,900
Torfaen see Pontypool
Wrexham ... 39,530

SCOTLAND

Regions (1979 E)

Borders ... 99,938
Central ... 271,177
Dumfries and Galloway ... 142,547
Fife ... 340,170
Grampian ... 469,168
Highland ... 190,507
Lothian ... 750,728
Orkney (Island Area) ... 18,134
Shetland (Island Area) ... 22,111
Strathclyde ... 2,431,101
Tayside ... 401,661
Western Isles (Island Area) ... 29,758

Cities (‡1979 E or 1974 E)

Aberdeen ... ‡209,189
*Airdrie (Monklands) (*Glasgow)* ... *38,833*
Alloa ... 13,498
Arbroath ... 23,207
Ardrossan (**Irvine) ... 11,166
Ayr (*97,000) ... 47,991
Bearsden and Milngavie (*Glasgow) ... ‡38,812
Clydebank (*Glasgow) ... ‡52,835
Cumbernauld (*Glasgow) ... ‡49,300
Dumbarton (*Glasgow) ... 25,440
Dumfries ... 29,431
Dundee ... ‡190,793
Dunfermline (*124,893) ... 53,418
East Kilbride (*Glasgow) ... ‡76,000
EDINBURGH (*635,000) ... ‡455,126
Elgin ... 17,589
Falkirk (*142,058) ... 36,589
Forfar ... 11,395
•Glasgow (*1,830,000) ... ‡794,316
Glenrothes (**Kirkcaldy) ... ‡36,500
Grangemouth (**Falkirk) ... 24,347
Hamilton (*Glasgow) ... ‡107,490
Hawick ... 16,378
Helensburgh (*Glasgow) ... 13,956
Inverclyde (Greenock) ... ‡102,598
Inverness ... 36,595
Irvine (*97,000) ... ‡57,900
Johnstone (*Glasgow) ... 23,603
Kilmarnock (*82,000) ... 50,318
Kirkcaldy (*148,028) ... 50,063
Kirkintilloch (*Glasgow) ... 26,845
Kirkwall ... 4,814
Lerwick ... 6,307
Livingston ... ‡35,900
Monklands (Coatbridge) ... ‡109,645
Montrose ... 10,112
Motherwell (*Glasgow) ... ‡150,857
Oban ... 6,410
*Paisley (Renfrew) (*Glasgow)* ... *94,025*
Perth ... 44,066
Peterhead ... 14,994
Port Glasgow (Inverclyde) ... *22,278*
Prestwick (*Ayr) ... 13,138
Renfrew (**Glasgow) ... ‡214,534
St. Andrews ... 13,137
Stirling (*58,000) ... 29,818
Stranraer ... 10,170
Thurso ... 9,107
Wick ... 7,842

NORTHERN IRELAND

Cities (1971 C)

Armagh ... 13,606
•BELFAST (1978 E) (*710,000) ... 354,400
Castlereagh (*Belfast) (1978 E) ... 63,900
Enniskillen ... 9,679
Larne ... 18,482
Lisburn (*Belfast) ... 31,836
Londonderry (1973 E) (*87,000) ... 51,200
Lurgan (*59,000) ... 25,431
Newry ... 20,279
Newtownabbey (*Belfast) (1978 E) ... 75,000
North Down (Bangor) (*Belfast) (1978 E) ... 61,500
Omagh ... 14,594
Portadown (**Lurgan) ... 22,207

UPPER VOLTA (BURKINA FASO)

1977 E ... 6,390,000

Bobo Dioulasso ... 120,000
Koudougou ... 38,000
•OUAGADOUGOU ... 180,000
Quahigouya ... 27,000

URUGUAY

1975 C ... 2,763,964

Artigas ... 29,256
Canelones (1963 C) ... 14,180
Colonia del Sacramento (1963 C) ... 12,839
Dolores (1963 C) ... 12,483
Durazno ... 25,811
Florida ... 25,030
Fray Bentos (1963 C) ... 20,755
La Paz (*Montevideo) (1963 C) ... 13,204
Las Piedras (*Montevideo) ... 53,983
Maldonado (1963 C) ... 15,361
Melo ... 38,260
Mercedes ... 34,667
Minas ... 35,433
•MONTEVIDEO (*1,350,000) ... 1,229 748
Paysandú ... 62,412
Rivera ... 49 013
Rocha (1963 C) ... 19,063
Salto ... 71,881
San Carlos (1963 C) ... 13,663
San José de Mayo ... 28,427
Santa Lucía (1963 C) ... 12,630
Tacuarembo ... 34,157
Treinta y Tres ... 25,757
Trinidad (1963 C) ... 15,460

VANUATU

1979 C ... 112,596

•VILA (*14,801) ... 10,158

VATICAN CITY / Città del Vaticano

1977 E ... 723

VENEZUELA

1971 C ... 10,721,522

Acarigua ... 56,743
Altagracia de Orituco ... 18,717
Anaco ... 29,003
Araure ... 22,466
Bachaquero ... 17,896
Barcelona ... 78,201
Barinas ... 56,329
Barquisimeto ... 330,815
Baruta (*Caracas) ... 121,066
Boconó ... 15,915
Cabimas ... 118,037
Cagua ... 29,601
Calabozo ... 38,360
Caraballeda (*Caracas) ... 20,725
•CARACAS (*2,475,000) ... 1,658,500
Caripito ... 19,053
Carora ... 36,115
Carúpano ... 50,935
Catia La Mar (*Caracas) ... 62,200
Chacao (*Caracas) ... 78,528
Chivacoa ... 19,210
Ciudad Bolívar ... 103,728
Ciudad Guayana (Santo Tomé de Guayana) ... 143,540
Ciudad Ojeda (Lagunillas) ... 83,083
Coro ... 68,701
Cumaná ... 119,751
El Tigre ... 49,801
El Tocuyo ... 19,351
El Vigía ... 20,970
Guacara ... 38,793
Guanare ... 34,148
Guarenas (*Caracas) ... 33,374
Guatire (*Caracas) ... 18,604
Güigüe ... 18,067
La Guaira (*Caracas) ... 20,344
La Victoria ... 40,731
Los Dos Caminos (*Caracas) ... 59,211
Los Teques (*Caracas) ... 63,106
Machiques ... 18,898
Maiquetía (*Caracas) ... 59,238
Maracaibo ... 651,574
Maracay ... 255,134
Mariara ... 24,284
Maturín ... 98,188
Mérida ... 74,214
Morón ... 19,451
Ocumare del Tuy ... 24,229
Palo Negro ... 19,173
Petare (*Caracas) ... 227,727
Porlamar ... 31,985
Pozuelos ... 44,011
Puerto Cabello ... 72,103
Puerto la Cruz ... 63,276
Punta Cardón ... 18,182
Punto Fijo ... 55,483
San Antonio del Táchira ... 20,342
San Carlos ... 21,029
San Carlos del Zulia ... 26,762
San Cristobal ... 151,717
San Felipe ... 42,905
San Fernando de Apure ... 38,960
San José de Guanipa ... 22,530
San Juan de Colón ... 16,615
San Juan de los Morros ... 38,265
San Mateo ... 17,389
Táriba ... 15,683
Trujillo ... 25,921
Tucupita ... 21,417
Turmero ... 43,832
Upata ... 22,793
Valencia ... 367,171
Valera ... 76,740
Valle de la Pascua ... 36,809
Villa de Cura ... 27,832
Villa del Rosario ... 17,491
Yaritagua ... 21,363
Zaraza ... 15,480

VIETNAM / Viet-nam Dan-chu Cong-hoa

1967 E ... 37,073,000

Bac-ninh (1960 C) ... 22,520
Ban-me-thuot ... 37,500
Bien-hoa ... 52,200
Cam-pha (1971 E) ... 90,000
Cam-ranh ... 46,600
Can-tho ... 61,100
Chau-phu (1971 E) ... 40,400
Da-lat (1971 E) ... 86,600
Da-nang (1971 E) ... 437,700
Gia-dinh (*Saigon) (1968 E) ... 151,100
Ha-dong (1960 C) ... 25,001
Hai-duong (1960 C) ... 24,752
Hai-phong (1971 E) (650,000▲) ... 400,000
HANOI (1971 E) ... 1,600,000
•Ho Chi Minh City (Than-pho Ho Chi Minh) (Saigon) (1971 E) (*2,750,000) ... 1,804,900
Hon-gai (1960 C) ... 35,412
Hue (1971 E) ... 199,900
Khanh-hung ... 40,300
Long-xuyen ... 45,800
My-tho ... 62,700
Nam-dinh (1960 C) ... 86,132
Nha-trang ... 59,600
Phan-rang ... 21,900
Phan-thiet ... 58,300
Phu-cuong (1971 E) ... 34,400
Phu-vinh (1971 E) ... 51,500
Pleiku ... 23,700
Quang-tri (1971 E) ... 16,900
Quan-long ... 33,500
Qui-nhon ... 50,000
Rach-gia ... 56,000
Sa-dec ... 34,800
Truc-giang ... 45,200
Vinh (1960 C) ... 43,954
Vinh-loi ... 41,700
Vinh-long (1971 E) ... 35,300
Vung-tau ... 54,200

VIRGIN ISLANDS, BRITISH

1970 C ... 10,484

•ROAD TOWN ... 2,183

VIRGIN ISLANDS OF THE U.S.

1970 C ... 62,468

•CHARLOTTE AMALIE ... 12,220
Christiansted ... 3,020

WALLIS AND FUTUNA
Wallis et Futuna

1976 C ... 9,192

MATA-UTU ... 558
•Ono ... 624

WESTERN SAHARA

1974 E ... 108,000

•EL AAIÚN (AIÚN) ... 20,000

WESTERN SAMOA

1976 C ... 151,983

•APIA ... 32,099

YEMEN / Al-Yaman

1979 E ... 5,785,000

Hodeida (Al Ḩudaydah) (1978 E) ... 106,080
Mocha (Al-Mukhā) (1975 C) ... 1,110
•ṢAN'Ā' ... 192,045
Ta'izz (1975 C) ... 81,000

YEMEN, PEOPLE'S DEMOCRATIC REPUBLIC OF / Al-Yaman ash-Sha'bīyah

1973 E ... 1,555,000

•ADEN (1977 E) ... 271,600
Al Mukallā (1970 E) ... 65,000
Madīnat ash Sha'b (Al-Ittiḩad) (1966 UE) ... 10,000

YUGOSLAVIA / Jugoslavija

1976 E ... 21,560,000

People's Republics

Bosnia-Hercegovina (Bosna i Hercegovina) ... 4,029,000
Croatia (Hrvatska) ... 4,530,000
Macedonia (Makedonija) ... 1,784,000
Montenegro (Crna Gora) ... 565,000
Serbia (Srbija) ... 8,860,000
Slovenia (Slovenija) ... 1,792,000

Cities (1971 C)

Banja Luka ... 89 866
Bečej ... 26,470
•BELGRADE (BEOGRAD) (*1,150,000) ... 770,140
Bihać ... 24,026
Bijeljina ... 24,722
Bitola ... 65,851
Bor ... 29,039
Brčko ... 25,422
Čačak ... 38,170
Celje ... 31,788
Cetinje ... 11,892
Djakovica ... 29,638
Dubrovnik ... 31,106
Karlovac ... 47,532
Kikinda ... 37,487
Kosovska Mitrovica ... 42,241
Kragujevac ... 71,180
Kraljevo ... 27,817
Kranj ... 27,209
Kruševac ... 29,469
Kumanovo ... 46,406
Leskovac ... 44,255
Ljubljana ... 173,662
Maribor ... 97,167
Mostar ... 47,606
Nikšić ... 28,547
Niš ... 127,178
Novi Pazar ... 29,072
Novi Sad ... 141,712
Ohrid ... 26,370
Osijek ... 93,912
Pančevo (*Belgrade) ... 54,269
Peč ... 42,113
Pirot ... 29,228
Požarevac ... 33,121
Prilep ... 48,242
Priština ... 69,524
Prizren ... 41,661
Pula ... 47,414
Rijeka ... 132,933
Šabac ... 42,307
Sarajevo ... 244,045
Šibenik ... 30,090
Sisak ... 38,421
Skopje ... 312,092
Slavonski Brod ... 38,762
Smederevo ... 40,289
Sombor ... 43,971
Split ... 151,875
Sremska Mitrovica ... 31,921
Štip ... 27,289
Subotica ... 88,787
Svetozarevo ... 27,542
Tetovo ... 35,792
Titograd ... 54,509
Titovo Užice ... 34,312
Titov Veles ... 36,026
Tuzla ... 53,825
Valjevo ... 26,367
Varaždin ... 34,270
Vinkovci ... 29,072
Vranje ... 25,685
Vršac ... 34,231
Vukovar ... 30,149
Zadar ... 43,187
Zagreb ... 566,084
Zaječar ... 27,677
Zenica ... 51,279
Zrenjanin ... 59 580

ZAIRE / Zaïre

1974 E ... 24,222,000

Bandundu (1970 C) ... 74,467
Boma (1970 E) ... 61,100
Bukavu ... 182 000
Gandajika (1970 E) ... 60,100
Goma (1970 E) ... 48,600
Isiro (1970 E) ... 49,300
Kabinda (1970 E) ... 60,500
Kalemie (Albertville) (1970 E) ... 62,300
Kamina (1970 E) ... 56,300
Kananga (Luluabourg) ... 601,000
Kikwit ... 150,000
•KINSHASA (LÉOPOLDVILLE) (1975 E) ... 2,202,000
Kisangani (Stanleyville) ... 311,000
Kolwezi (1970 E) ... 81,600
Likasi (Jadotville) (1970 C) ... 146,394
Lubumbashi (Élisabethville) ... 404,000
Matadi ... 144,000
Mbandaka (Coquilhatville) ... 134,000
Mbanza Ngungu (1970 E) ... 55,800
Mbuji-Mayi (Bakwanga) ... 337,000
Mwene-Ditu (1970 E) ... 71,100

ZAMBIA

1980 E ... 5,834,000

Chililabombwe (Bancroft) ... 77,000
Chingola ... 192,000
Kabwe (Broken Hill) ... 147,000
Kalulushi ... 60,000
Kitwe ... 341,000
Livingstone ... 80,000
Luanshya ... 164,000
•LUSAKA ... 641,000
Mufulira ... 187,000
Ndola ... 323,000

ZIMBABWE (RHODESIA)

1979 E ... 7,130,000

Bulawayo (*363,000) ... 85,700
Fort Victoria (*24,000) ... 11,300
Gatooma (*33,000) ... 4,700
Gwelo (*70,000) ... 22,500
•HARARE (SALISBURY) (*633,000) ... 118,500
Harari (*Salisbury) (1969 C) ... 58,007
Highfield (*Salisbury) (1969 C) ... 52,560
Que Que (*51,000) ... 17,700
Sinoia (*27,000) ... 7,200
Umtali (*64,000) ... 20,800
Wankie (*33,000) ... 14,700

C Census. E Official estimate. UE Unofficial estimate.
L Population within municipal limits of year specified. • Largest city in country.
* Population or designation of metropolitan area, including suburbs (see headnote).
▲ Population of an entire municipality, commune, or district, including rural area.
‡† Year of information specified at start of country.
* Italicized place names are now a part of the city shown in parentheses following the place name. These changes are part of the April 1974 reorganization of local administrative areas.

United States City and County Populations and ZIP Codes

The following alphabetical list shows populations for nearly 18,000 cities and counties and ZIP codes for cities. The state abbreviation following each name is that used by the United States Postal Service.

ZIP codes are listed for cities and towns after the state abbreviations. For each city with more than one ZIP code, the range of numbers assigned to the city is shown. For example, the ZIP code range for Chicago is 60601-99, and this indicates that the numbers between 60601 and 60699 are valid Chicago ZIP codes. ZIP code ranges are not listed for counties.

Populations for cities and towns appear as *italics* after the ZIP codes, and populations for counties appear after the state abbreviations. These populations are either 1980 census figures or, where census data are not available, estimates created by Rand McNally & Company. City populations are for central cities, not metropolitan areas. For New England, 1980 census populations are given for incorporated cities. Estimates are used for unincorporated places that are not treated separately by the census. "Town" (or "township") populations are not included unless the town is considered to be primarily urban and contains only one commonly used place-name.

Counties are identified by a square symbol (□).

Abbreviations for State Names

AK	Alaska
AL	Alaska
AR	Arkansas
AZ	Arizona
CA	California
CO	Colorado
CT	Connecticut
DC	District of Columbia
DE	Delaware
FL	Florida
GA	Georgia
HI	Hawaii
IA	Iowa
ID	Idaho
IL	Illinois
IN	Indiana
KS	Kansas
KY	Kentucky
LA	Louisiana
MA	Massachusetts
MD	Maryland
ME	Maine
MI	Michigan
MN	Minnesota
MO	Missouri
MS	Mississippi
MT	Montana
NC	North Carolina
ND	North Dakota
NE	Nebraska
NH	New Hampshire
NJ	New Jersey
NM	New Mexico
NV	Nevada
NY	New York
OH	Ohio
OK	Oklahoma
OR	Oregon
PA	Pennsylvania
RI	Rhode Island
SC	South Carolina
SD	South Dakota
TN	Tennessee
TX	Texas
UT	Utah
VA	Virginia
VT	Vermont
WA	Washington
WI	Wisconsin
WV	West Virginia
WY	Wyoming

A

Abbeville, AL 36310 • 3,155
Abbeville, GA 31001 • 985
Abbeville, LA 70510 • 12,391
Abbeville, SC 29620 • 5,833
Abbeville □, SC • 22,627
Abbotsford, WI 54405 • 1,901
Abbott Run Valley, RI 02864 • 1,300
Abbottstown, PA 17301 • 689
Aberdeen, ID 83210 • 1,528
Aberdeen, MD 21001 • 11,533
Aberdeen, MS 39730 • 7,184
Aberdeen, NC 28315 • 1,945
Aberdeen, OH 45101 • 1,566
Aberdeen, SD 57401 • 25,851
Aberdeen, WA 98520 • 18,739
Abernathy, TX 79311 • 2,904
Abilene, KS 67410 • 6,572
Abilene, TX 79601-99 • 98,315
Abingdon, IL 61410 • 4,210
Abingdon, VA 24210 • 4,318
Abington, MA 02351 • 13,517
Abington, PA 19001 • 7,900
Abita Springs, LA 70420 • 1,072
Absarokee, MT 59001 • 750
Absecon, NJ 08201 • 6,859
Academia, OH 43050 • 1,447
Acadia □, LA • 56,427
Accomack □, VA • 31,268
Ackerman, MS 39735 • 1,598
Ackley, IA 50601 • 1,900
Acton, CA 93510 • 900
Acton, MA 01720 • 2,500
Acushnet, MA 02743 • 6,400
Acworth, GA 30101 • 3,648
Ada, MN 56510 • 1,971
Ada, OH 45810 • 5,669
Ada, OK 74820 • 15,902
Ada □, ID • 173,036
Adair, IA 50002 • 883
Adair □, IA • 9,509
Adair □, KY • 15,233
Adair □, MO • 24,870
Adair □, OK • 18,575
Adairsville, GA 30103 • 1,739
Adairville, KY 42202 • 1,105
Adams, MA 01220 • 10,381
Adams, MN 55909 • 797
Adams, NY 13605 • 1,701
Adams, WI 53910 • 1,744
Adams □, CO • 245,944
Adams □, ID • 3,347
Adams □, IL • 71,622
Adams □, IN • 29,619
Adams □, IA • 5,731
Adams □, MS • 38,035
Adams □, NE • 30,656
Adams □, ND • 3,584
Adams □, OH • 24,328
Adams □, PA • 68,292
Adams □, WA • 13,267
Adams □, WI • 13,457
Adams Center, NY 13606 • 800
Adams City, CO 80022 • 2,200
Adamston, NJ 08723 • 1,300
Adamstown, PA 19501 • 1,119
Adamsville, AL 35005 • 2,498
Adamsville, TN 38310 • 1,453
Addis, LA 70710 • 1,320
Addison, AL 35540 • 746
Addison, CT 06033 • 1,100
Addison, IL 60101 • 29,826
Addison, NY 14801 • 2,028
Addison, TX 75001 • 5,553
Addison □, VT • 29,406
Addyston, OH 45001 • 1,195
Adel, GA 31620 • 5,592
Adel, IA 50003 • 2,846
Adelanto, CA 92301 • 2,164
Adena, OH 43901 • 1,062
Adobe Acres, NM 87105 • 3,400
Adrian, GA 31002 • 756
Adrian, MI 49221 • 21,186
Adrian, MN 56110 • 1,336
Adrian, MO 64720 • 1,484
Advance, MO 63730 • 1,054
Affton, MO 63123 • 23,181
Afton, IA 50830 • 985
Afton, MN 55001 • 2,550
Afton, NY 13730 • 982
Afton, OK 74331 • 1,174
Afton, WY 83110 • 1,481
Agate Beach, OR 97365 • 700
Agawam, MA 01001 • 10,300
Agency, IA 52530 • 657
Agua Fria, NM 87501 • 850
Aguilar, CO 81020 • 624
Ahoskie, NC 27910 • 4,887
Ahwahnee, CA 93601 • 900
Aiea, HI 96701 • 15,200
Aiken, SC 29801 • 14,978
Aiken □, SC • 105,625
Ainsworth, NE 69210 • 2,256
Air Park West, NE 68524 • 3,100
Aitkin, MN 56431 • 1,770
Aitkin □, MN • 13,404
Ajo, AZ 85321 • 5,189
Akron, AL 35441 • 604
Akron, CO 80720 • 1,716
Akron, IN 46910 • 1,045
Akron, IA 51001 • 1,517
Akron, NY 14001 • 2,971
Akron, OH 44301-99 • 237,177
Akron, PA 17501 • 3,471
Alabaster, AL 35007 • 7,079
Alachua, FL 32615 • 3,561
Alachua □, FL • 151,348
Alamance □, NC • 99,319
Alameda, CA 94501 • 63,852
Alameda, NM 87114 • 7,800
Alameda □, CA • 1,105,379
Alamo, GA 30411 • 993
Alamo, TN 38001 • 2,615
Alamo, TX 78516 • 5,831
Alamogordo, NM 88310 • 24,024
Alamo Heights, TX 78209 • 6,252
Alamosa, CO 81101 • 6,830
Alamosa □, CO • 11,799
Alamosa East, CO 81101 • 1,175
Alapaha, GA 31622 • 771
Albany, CA 94706 • 15,130
Albany, GA 31701-08 • 74,550
Albany, IL 61230 • 1,014
Albany, IN 47320 • 2,625
Albany, KY 42602 • 2,083
Albany, LA 70711 • 857
Albany, MN 56307 • 1,569
Albany, MO 64402 • 2,152
Albany, NY 12201-99 • 101,727
Albany, OH 45710 • 905
Albany, OR 97321 • 26,678
Albany, TX 76430 • 2,450
Albany, WI 53502 • 1,051
Albany □, NY • 285,909
Albany □, WY • 29,062
Albemarle, NC 28001 • 15,110
Albemarle □, VA • 55,783
Albert City, IA 50510 • 818
Albert Lea, MN 56007 • 19,200
Albertson, NY 11507 • 11,200
Albertville, AL 35950 • 12,039
Albia, IA 52531 • 4,184
Albion, IL 62806 • 2,285
Albion, IN 46701 • 1,637
Albion, IA 50005 • 739
Albion, MI 49224 • 11,059
Albion, NE 68620 • 1,997
Albion, NY 14411 • 4,897
Albion, PA 16401 • 1,818
Albion, RI 02802 • 1,200
Albion, WA 99102 • 631
Albuquerque, NM 87101-99 • 331,767
Alburtis, PA 18011 • 1,428
Alcalde, NM 87511 • 800
Alcester, SD 57001 • 885
Alcoa, TN 37701 • 6,870
Alcona □, MI • 9,740
Alcorn □, MS • 33,036
Alda, NE 68810 • 601
Alden, IA 50006 • 953
Alden, MN 56009 • 687
Alden, NY 14004 • 2,488
Alden, PA 18634 • 800
Alderson, WV 24910 • 1,375
Aledo, IL 61231 • 3,881
Aledo, TX 76008 • 1,027
Alex, OK 73002 • 769
Alexander □, IL • 12,264
Alexander □, NC • 24,999
Alexander City, AL 35010 • 13,807
Alexander Mills, NC 28043 • 643
Alexandria, IN 46001 • 6,028
Alexandria, KY 41001 • 4,735
Alexandria, LA 71301-03 • 51,565
Alexandria, MN 56308 • 7,608
Alexandria, TN 37012 • 689
Alexandria, VA 22301-99 • 103,217
Alexandria Bay, NY 13607 • 1,265
Alexis, IL 61412 • 1,076
Alfalfa □, OK • 7,077
Alfred, NY 14802 • 4,967
Alger, OH 45812 • 992
Alger □, MI • 9,225
Algoma, WI 54201 • 3,656
Algona, IA 50511 • 6,289
Algona, WA 98002 • 1,467
Algonac, MI 48001 • 4,412
Algonquin, IL 60102 • 5,834
Algood, TN 38501 • 2,406
Alhambra, CA 91801-99 • 64,615
Alhambra, IL 62001 • 643
Alice, TX 78332 • 20,961
Aliceville, AL 35442 • 3,207
Aliquippa, PA 15001 • 17,094
Allamakee □, IA • 15,108
Allardt, TN 38504 • 654
Allegan, MI 49010 • 4,576
Allegan □, MI • 81,555
Allegany, NY 14706 • 2,078
Allegany □, MD • 80,548
Allegany □, NY • 51,742
Alleghany □, NC • 9,587
Alleghany □, VA • 14,333
Allegheny □, PA • 1,450,085
Allen, OK 74825 • 998
Allen, TX 75002 • 8,314
Allen □, IN • 294,335
Allen □, KS • 1,564
Allen □, KY • 14,128
Allen □, LA • 21,390
Allen □, OH • 112,241
Allendale, IL 62410 • 613
Allendale, NJ 07401 • 5,901
Allendale, SC 29810 • 4,400
Allendale □, SC • 10,700
Allenhurst, GA 31301 • 606
Allenhurst, NJ 07711 • 912
Allen Park, MI 48101 • 34,196
Allentown, NJ 08501 • 1,962
Allentown, PA 18101-99 • 103,758
Allerton, IA 50008 • 670
Alliance, NE 69301 • 9,920
Alliance, NC 28509 • 616
Alliance, OH 44601 • 24,315
Allison, IA 50602 • 1,132
Allison, PA 15413 • 1,040
Allison Park, PA 15101 • 5,600
Allouez, WI 54301 • 13,753
Alloway, NJ 08001 • 1,370
Allyn, WA 98524 • 900
Alma, AR 72921 • 2,755
Alma, GA 31510 • 3,819
Alma, KS 66401 • 925
Alma, MI 48801 • 9,652
Alma, NE 68920 • 1,369
Alma, WI 54610 • 876
Almont, MI 48003 • 1,857
Aloha, OR 97007 • 10,000
Alondra, CA 90249 • 12,096
Alpaugh, CA 93201 • 900
Alpena, MI 49707 • 12,214
Alpena □, MI • 32,315
Alpha, IL 61413 • 815
Alpha, NJ 08865 • 2,644
Alpharetta, GA 30201 • 3,128
Alpine, NJ 07620 • 1,549
Alpine, TX 79830 • 5,465
Alpine, UT 84003 • 2,649
Alpine □, CA • 1,097
Alsip, IL 60658 • 17,134
Alta, IA 51002 • 1,720
Altadena, CA 91001 • 40,983
Altamont, IL 62411 • 2,389
Altamont, KS 67330 • 1,054
Altamont, NY 12009 • 1,292
Altamont, OR 97601 • 19,805
Altamont, TN 37301 • 679
Altamonte Springs, FL 32701 • 22,028
Altavista, VA 24517 • 3,849
Altheimer, AR 72004 • 1,231
Alto, GA 30510 • 618
Alto, TX 75925 • 1,203
Alton, IL 62002 • 34,171
Alton, IA 51003 • 986
Alton, MO 65606 • 721
Alton, NH 03809 • 900
Altona, IL 61414 • 610
Alton Bay, NH 03810 • 900
Altoona, AL 35952 • 928
Altoona, FL 32702 • 1,300
Altoona, IA 50009 • 5,764
Altoona, PA 16601-03 • 57,078
Altoona, WI 54720 • 4,393
Alturas, CA 96101 • 3,025
Altus, OK 73521 • 23,101
Alum Rock, CA 95127 • 17,471
Alva, FL 33920 • 1,200
Alva, OK 73717 • 6,416
Alvarado, TX 76009 • 2,701
Alvin, TX 77511 • 16,515
Alvord, TX 76225 • 874
Ama, LA 70031 • 875
Amador □, CA • 19,314
Amagansett, NY 11930 • 1,800
Amanda, OH 43102 • 720
Amarillo, TX 79101-99 • 149,230
Ambler, PA 19002 • 6,628
Amboy, IL 61310 • 2,377
Amboy, MN 56010 • 606
Ambridge, PA 15003 • 9,575
Amelia, LA 70340 • 3,612
Amelia, OH 45102 • 1,108
Amelia □, VA • 8,405
Amelia Court House, VA 23002 • 700
Amenia, NY 12501 • 1,157
American Falls, ID 83211 • 3,626
American Fork, UT 84003 • 12,693
Americus, GA 31709 • 16,120
Americus, KS 66835 • 915
Amery, WI 54001 • 2,404
Ames, IA 50010 • 45,775
Amesbury, MA 01913 • 13,971
Amherst, MA 01002 • 26,300
Amherst, NH 03031 • 750
Amherst, NY 14226 • 66,100
Amherst, OH 44001 • 10,638
Amherst, TX 79312 • 971
Amherst, VA 24521 • 1,135
Amherst, WI 54406 • 701
Amherst □, VA • 29,122
Amherstdale, WV 25607 • 800
Amite, LA 70422 • 4,301
Amite □, MS • 13,369
Amity, AR 71921 • 859
Amity, OR 97101 • 1,092
Amityville, NY 11701 • 9,076
Ammon, ID 83401 • 4,669
Amory, MS 38821 • 7,307
Amsterdam, NY 12010 • 21,872
Amsterdam, OH 43903 • 783
Anacoco, LA 71403 • 820
Anaconda, MT 59711 • 12,518
Anacortes, WA 98221 • 9,013
Anadarko, OK 73005 • 6,378
Anaheim, CA 92801-99 • 219,494
Anahola, HI 96703 • 915
Anahuac, TX 77514 • 1,840
Anamosa, IA 52205 • 4,958
Anandale, LA 71301 • 2,000
Anawalt, WV 24808 • 652
Anchorage, AK 99501-40 • 174,431
Anchorage, KY 40223 • 1,726
Andalusia, AL 36420 • 10,415
Andalusia, IL 61232 • 1,238
Anderson, CA 96007 • 7,381
Anderson, IN 46011-18 • 64,695
Anderson, MO 64831 • 1,237
Anderson, SC 29621-24 • 27,965
Anderson □, KS • 8,749
Anderson □, KY • 12,567
Anderson □, SC • 133,235
Anderson □, TN • 67,346
Anderson □, TX • 38,381
Andover, IL 61233 • 612
Andover, KS 67002 • 2,801
Andover, MA 01810 • 8,445
Andover, MN 55303 • 9,387
Andover, NY 14806 • 1,120
Andover, OH 44003 • 1,205
Andrew □, MO • 13,980
Andrews, IN 46702 • 1,243
Andrews, NC 28901 • 1,621
Andrews, SC 29510 • 3,129
Andrews, TX 79714 • 11,061
Andrews □, TX • 13,323
Androscoggin □, ME • 99,657
Angelica, NY 14709 • 982
Angelina □, TX • 64,172
Angels Camp, CA 95222 • 2,302
Angier, NC 27501 • 1,709
Angleton, TX 77515 • 13,929
Angola, IN 46703 • 5,486
Angola, NY 14006 • 2,292
Anguilla, MS 38721 • 950
Anita, IA 50020 • 1,153
Ankeny, IA 50021 • 15,429
Anna, IL 62906 • 5,408
Anna, OH 45302 • 1,038
Annalee Heights, VA 22042 • 1,750
Anna Maria, FL 33501 • 1,537
Annandale, MN 55302 • 1,568
Annandale, NJ 08801 • 1,040
Annandale, VA 22003 • 35,300
Annapolis, MD 21401-99 • 31,740
Ann Arbor, MI 48103-09 • 107,966
Annawan, IL 61234 • 908
Anne Arundel □, MD • 370,775
Anniston, AL 36201-05 • 29,523
Annville, PA 17003 • 4,493
Anoka, MN 55303 • 15,634
Anoka □, MN • 195,998
Ansley, NE 68814 • 644
Anson, ME 04911 • 900
Anson, TX 79501 • 2,831
Anson □, NC • 25,649
Ansonia, CT 06401 • 19,039
Ansonia, OH 45303 • 1,267
Ansonville, NC 28007 • 794
Ansted, WV 25812 • 1,952
Antelope □, NE • 8,675
Anthon, IA 51004 • 687
Anthony, FL 32617 • 1,200
Anthony, KS 67003 • 2,661
Anthony, NM 88021 • 3,285
Anthony, RI 02816 • 4,500
Antigo, WI 54409 • 8,653
Antioch, CA 94509 • 42,683
Antioch, IL 60002 • 4,419
Antlers, OK 74523 • 2,989
Anton, TX 79313 • 1,180
Antonito, CO 81120 • 1,103
Antrim, NH 03440 • 1,142
Antrim □, MI • 16,194
Antwerp, NY 13608 • 749
Antwerp, OH 45813 • 1,765
Apache, OK 73006 • 1,560
Apache □, AZ • 52,108
Apache Junction, AZ 85220 • 9,935
Apalachicola, FL 32320 • 2,565
Apalachin, NY 13732 • 1,233
Apex, NC 27502 • 2,847
Aplington, IA 50604 • 1,027
Apollo, PA 15613 • 2,212
Apopka, FL 32703 • 6,019
Appalachia, VA 24216 • 2,418
Appanoose □, IA • 15,511

Apple Creek, OH 44606 • 741
Applegate, OR 97530 • 800
Appleton, MN 56208 • 1,842
Appleton, WI 54911-19 • 58,913
Appleton City, MO 64724 • 1,257
Apple Valley, CA 92307 • 14,305
Apple Valley, MN 55124 • 21,818
Applewood, CO 80401 • 7,200
Appleyard, WA 98801 • 1,500
Appling □, GA • 15,565
Appomattox, VA 24522 • 1,345
Appomattox □, VA • 11,971
Aptos, CA 95003 • 7,039
Aquebogue, NY 11931 • 1,300
Arab, AL 35016 • 5,967
Arabi, LA 70032 • 10,248
Aragon, GA 30104 • 855
Aransas □, TX • 14,260
Aransas Pass, TX 78336 • 7,173
Arapaho, OK 73620 • 851
Arapahoe, NE 68922 • 1,107
Arapahoe □, CO • 293,621
Arbuckle, CA 95912 • 1,306
Arbyrd, MO 63821 • 704
Arcade, CA 95821 • 37,600
Arcade, NY 14009 • 2,052
Arcadia, CA 91006 • 45,994
Arcadia, FL 33821 • 6,002
Arcadia, IN 46030 • 1,801
Arcadia, LA 71001 • 3,403
Arcadia, MO 63621 • 683
Arcadia, SC 29320 • 2,088
Arcadia, WI 54612 • 2,109
Arcanum, OH 45304 • 2,002
Arcata, CA 95521 • 12,850
Archbald, PA 18403 • 6,295
Archbold, OH 43502 • 3,318
Archdale, NC 27263 • 5,326
Archer, FL 32618 • 1,230
Archer □, TX • 7,266
Archer City, TX 76351 • 1,862
Archie, MO 64725 • 753
Archuleta □, CO • 3,664
Arco, ID 83213 • 1,241
Arcola, IL 61910 • 2,714
Arden. CA 95825 • 49,130
Arden Hills, MN 55112 • 8,012
Ardmore, AL 35739 • 1,096
Ardmore, IN 46628 • 3,400
Ardmore, MD 20706 • 900
Ardmore, OK 73401 • 23,689
Ardmore, PA 19003 • 13,600
Ardmore, TN 38449 • 835
Ardsley, NY 10502 • 4,183
Arenac □, MI • 14,706
Argenta, IL 62501 • 994
Argos, IN 46501 • 1,547
Argyle, MN 56713 • 741
Argyle, WI 53504 • 720
Ariton, AL 36311 • 844
Arizona Sunsites, AZ 85625 • 900
Arjay, KY 40902 • 650
Arkadelphia, AR 71923 • 10,005
Arkansas □, AR • 24,175
Arkansas City, AR 71630 • 668
Arkansas City, KS 67005 • 13,201
Arkoma, OK 74901 • 2,175
Arkport, NY 14807 • 811
Arkwright, RI 02816 • 1,500
Arlington, GA 31713 • 1,572
Arlington, KS 67514 • 631
Arlington, LA 70808 • 850
Arlington, MA 02174 • 48,219
Arlington, MN 55307 • 1,779
Arlington, NE 68002 • 1,117
Arlington, NC 28642 • 872
Arlington, NY 12603 • 11,203
Arlington, OH 45814 • 1,187
Arlington, SD 57212 • 991
Arlington, TN 38002 • 1,778
Arlington, TX 76010-19 • 160,113
Arlington, VT 05250 • 800
Arlington, VA 22201-99 • 152,700
Arlington, WA 98223 • 3,282
Arlington □, VA • 152,599
Arlington Heights, IL 60004-08 • 66,116
Arma, KS 66712 • 1,676
Armada, MI 48005 • 1,392
Armijo, NM 87105 • 18,900
Armonk, NY 10504 • 5,900
Armour, SD 57313 • 819
Armstrong, IA 50514 • 1,153
Armstrong □, PA • 77,768
Armstrong □, TX • 1,994
Arnaudville, LA 70512 • 1,679
Arnett, OK 73832 • 714
Arnold, CA 95223 • 2,385
Arnold, MN 55803 • 1,350
Arnold, MO 63010 • 19,141
Arnold, NE 69120 • 813
Arnold, PA 15068 • 6,853
Arnolds Park, IA 51331 • 1,051
Aroma Park, IL 60910 • 673
Aroostook □, ME • 91,331
Arp, TX 75750 • 939
Arrowhead Village, NJ 08723 • 3,100
Arroyo Grande, CA 93420 • 11,290
Artesia, CA 90701 • 14,301
Artesia, NM 88210 • 10,385
Arthur, IL 61911 • 2,122
Arthur □, NE • 513
Arundel Village, MD 21225 • 5,300
Arvada, CO 80001-05 • 84,576
Arvin, CA 93203 • 6,863
Arvonia, VA 23004 • 700
Asbury Park, NJ 07712 • 17,015
Ascension □, LA • 50,068
Ashaway, RI 02804 • 1,747
Ashburn, GA 31714 • 4,766
Ashburnham, MA 01430 • 1,150
Ashdown, AR 71822 • 4,218
Ashe □, NC • 22,325
Asheboro, NC 27203 • 15,252
Asher, OK 74826 • 659
Asherton, TX 78827 • 1,574
Asheville, NC 28801-99 • 53,583
Ashford, AL 36312 • 2,165
Ash Grove, MO 65604 • 1,157
Ashkum, IL 60911 • 735
Ashland, AL 36251 • 2,052
Ashland, CA 94541 • 13,893
Ashland, IL 62612 • 1,351
Ashland, KS 67831 • 1,096
Ashland, KY 41101 • 27,064
Ashland, ME 04732 • 800
Ashland, MA 01721 • 9,165
Ashland, MO 65010 • 1,021
Ashland, NE 68003 • 2,274
Ashland, NH 03217 • 1,479
Ashland, OH 44805 • 20,326
Ashland, OR 97520 • 14,943
Ashland, PA 17921 • 4,235
Ashland, VA 23005 • 4,640
Ashland, WI 54806 • 9,115
Ashland □, OH • 46,178
Ashland □, WI • 16,783
Ashland City, TN 37015 • 2,329
Ashley, IL 62808 • 658
Ashley, IN 46705 • 841
Ashley, ND 58413 • 1,192
Ashley, OH 43003 • 1,057
Ashley, PA 18706 • 3,512
Ashley □, AR • 26,538
Ashmore, IL 61912 • 883
Ashtabula, OH 44004 • 23,449
Ashtabula □, OH • 104,215
Ashton, ID 83420 • 1,219
Ashton, IL 61006 • 1,140
Ashton, MD 20861 • 1,010
Ashton, RI 02864 • 875
Ashville, AL 35953 • 1,489
Ashville, OH 43103 • 2,046
Ashwaubenon, WI 54304 • 14,486
Asotin, WA 99402 • 943
Asotin □, WA • 16,823
Aspen, CO 81611 • 3,678
Aspen Hill, MD 20906 • 9,800
Aspermont, TX 79502 • 1,357
Aspinwall, PA 15215 • 3,284
Assinippi, MA 02339 • 1,400
Assonet, MA 02702 • 900
Assumption, IL 62510 • 1,283
Assumption □, LA • 22,084
Aston, PA 19014 • 6,900
Astor, FL 32002 • 950
Astoria, IL 61501 • 1,370
Astoria, OR 97103 • 9,998
Atascadero, CA 93422 • 16,232
Atascosa □, TX • 25,055
Atchison, KS 66002 • 11,407
Atchison □, KS • 18,397
Atchison □, MO • 8,605
Atco, NJ 08004 • 2,100
Athena, OR 97813 • 965
Athens, AL 35611 • 14,558
Athens, GA 30601-13 • 42,549
Athens, IL 62613 • 1,371
Athens, MI 49011 • 960
Athens, NY 12015 • 1,738
Athens, OH 45701 • 19,743
Athens, PA 18810 • 3,622
Athens, TN 37303 • 12,080
Athens, TX 75751 • 10,197
Athens, WV 24712 • 1,147
Athens, WI 54411 • 988
Athens □, OH • 56,399
Atherton, CA 94025 • 7,797
Athol, MA 01331 • 10,634
Atkins, AR 72823 • 3,002
Atkinson, IL 61235 • 1,138
Atkinson, NE 68713 • 1,521
Atkinson, NH 03811 • 900
Atkinson □, GA • 6,141
Atlanta, GA 30301-99 • 425,022
Atlanta, IL 61723 • 1,807
Atlanta, IN 46031 • 657
Atlanta, MI 49709 • 650
Atlanta, NY 14808 • 750
Atlanta, TX 75551 • 6,272
Atlantic, IA 50022 • 7,789
Atlantic, NC 28511 • 900
Atlantic □, NJ • 194,119
Atlantic Beach, FL 32233 • 7,847
Atlantic City, NJ 08401-99 • 40,199
Atlantic Highlands, NJ 07716 • 4,950
Atmore, AL 36502 • 8,789
Atoka, OK 74525 • 3,409
Atoka, TN 38004 • 691
Atoka □, OK • 12,748
Attala □, MS • 19,865
Attalla, AL 35954 • 7,737
Attapulgus, GA 31715 • 623
Attica, IN 47918 • 3,841
Attica, KS 67009 • 730
Attica, NY 14011 • 2,659
Attica, OH 44807 • 865
Attleboro, MA 02703 • 34,196
Atwater, CA 95301 • 17,530
Atwater, MN 56209 • 1,128
Atwood, IL 61913 • 1,464
Atwood, KS 67730 • 1,665
Atwood, TN 38220 • 1,143
Auberry, CA 93602 • 1,100
Auburn, AL 36830 • 28,471
Auburn, CA 95603 • 7,540
Auburn, GA 30203 • 692
Auburn, IL 62615 • 3,616
Auburn, IN 46706 • 8,122
Auburn, KS 66402 • 890
Auburn, KY 42206 • 1,467
Auburn, ME 04210 • 23,128
Auburn, MA 01501 • 14,845
Auburn, MI 48611 • 1,921
Auburn, NE 68305 • 3,482
Auburn, NY 13021 • 32,548
Auburn, PA 17922 • 999
Auburn, WA 98002-03 • 26,417
Auburndale, FL 33823 • 6,501
Auburndale, WI 54412 • 641
Auburn Heights, MI 48057 • 4,000
Audrain □, MO • 26,458
Audubon, IA 50025 • 2,841
Audubon, NJ 08106 • 9,533
Audubon □, IA • 8,559
Auglaize □, OH • 42,554
Au Gres, MI 48703 • 768
Augusta, AR 72006 • 3,496
Augusta, GA 30901-99 • 47,532
Augusta, IL 62311 • 764
Augusta, KS 67010 • 6,968
Augusta, KY 41002 • 1,455
Augusta, ME 04330 • 21,819
Augusta, MI 49012 • 913
Augusta, WI 54722 • 1,560
Augusta □, VA • 53,732
Aulander, NC 27805 • 1,214
Ault, CO 80610 • 1,056
Aumsville, OR 97325 • 1,432
Aurelia, IA 51005 • 1,143
Aurora, CO 80010-17 • 158,588
Aurora, IL 60504-07 • 81,293
Aurora, IN 47001 • 3,816
Aurora, MN 55705 • 2,670
Aurora, MO 65605 • 6,437
Aurora, NE 68818 • 3,717
Aurora, NC 27806 • 698
Aurora, NY 13026 • 926
Aurora, OH 44202 • 8,177
Aurora, UT 84620 • 874
Aurora □, SD • 3,628
Au Sable, MI 48750 • 1,240
Au Sable Forks, NY 12912 • 2,100
Austell, GA 30001 • 3,939
Austin, IN 47102 • 4,857
Austin, MN 55912 • 23,020
Austin, PA 16720 • 740
Austin, TX 78701-99 • 345,496
Austin □, TX • 17,726
Austintown, OH 44512 • 33,636
Austinville, VA 24312 • 800
Autauga □, AL • 32,259
Autaugaville, AL 36003 • 843
Auxier, KY 41602 • 900
Auxvasse, MO 65231 • 858
Ava, IL 62907 • 811
Ava, MO 65608 • 2,761
Avalon, CA 90704 • 2,022
Avalon, NJ 08202 • 2,162
Avalon, PA 15202 • 6,240
Avella, PA 15312 • 1,100
Avenal, CA 93204 • 4,137
Avenel, MD 20783 • 5,600
Avenel, NJ 07001 • 11,500
Averill Park, NY 12018 • 1,500
Avery □, NC • 14,409
Avilla, IN 46710 • 1,272
Avis, PA 17721 • 1,718
Aviston, IL 62216 • 846
Avoca, IA 51521 • 1,650
Avoca, NY 14809 • 1,144
Avoca, PA 18641 • 3,536
Avocado Heights, CA 91746 • 11,721
Avon, CT 06001 • 1,434
Avon, IL 61415 • 1,019
Avon, MA 02322 • 5,026
Avon, MN 56310 • 804
Avon, NY 14414 • 3,006
Avon, OH 44011 • 7,241
Avon by the Sea, NJ 07717 • 2,337
Avondale, AZ 85323 • 8,168
Avondale, CO 81022 • 800
Avondale, LA 70094 • 6,699
Avondale, MO 64117 • 612
Avondale, OH 45404 • 5,000
Avondale, PA 19311 • 891
Avondale Estates, GA 30002 • 1,313
Avon Lake, OH 44012 • 13,222
Avonmore, PA 15618 • 1,234
Avon Park, FL 33825 • 8,026
Avoyelles □, LA • 41,393
Axtell, NE 68924 • 602
Ayden, NC 28513 • 4,361
Ayer, MA 01432-33 • 6,993
Aynor, SC 29511 • 643
Azalea Park, FL 32807 • 8,304
Azle, TX 76020 • 5,822
Aztec, NM 87410 • 5,512
Azusa, CA 91702 • 29,380

B

Babbitt, MN 55706 • 2,435
Babbitt, NV 89416 • 1,800
Babson Park, FL 33827 • 950
Babylon, NY 11702-04 • 12,388
Baca □, CO • 5,419
Bacon □, GA • 9,379
Baconton, GA 31716 • 763
Bad Axe, MI 48413 • 3,184
Baden, PA 15005 • 5,318
Badger, IA 50516 • 653
Badin, NC 28009 • 1,514
Bagdad, AZ 86321 • 2,331
Bagdad, FL 32530 • 1,479
Bagley, MN 56621 • 1,321
Bailey, NC 27807 • 685
Bailey □, TX • 8,168
Bailey Island, ME 04003 • 650
Baileys Crossroads, VA 22041 • 4,600
Bainbridge, GA 31717 • 10,553
Bainbridge, IN 46105 • 644
Bainbridge, NY 13733 • 1,603
Bainbridge, OH 45612 • 1,042
Baird, TX 79504 • 1,696
Bairdford, PA 15006 • 950
Baker, CA 92309 • 650
Baker, LA 70714 • 12,865
Baker, MT 59313 • 2,354
Baker, OR 97814 • 9,471
Baker □, FL • 15,289
Baker □, GA • 3,808
Baker □, OR • 16,134
Bakersfield, CA 93301-99 • 105,735
Bakerstown, PA 15007 • 1,000
Bala-Cynwyd, PA 19004 • 8,600
Balaton, MN 56115 • 752
Balch Springs, TX 75180 • 13,746
Bald Knob, AR 72010 • 2,756
Baldwin, FL 32234 • 1,526
Baldwin, GA 30511 • 1,080
Baldwin, LA 70514 • 2,644
Baldwin, MI 49304 • 674
Baldwin, NY 11510 • 35,100
Baldwin, PA 15234 • 24,712
Baldwin, SC 29706 • 700
Baldwin, WI 54002 • 1,620
Baldwin □, AL • 78,556
Baldwin □, GA • 34,686
Baldwin City, KS 66006 • 2,829
Baldwin Park, CA 91706 • 50,554
Baldwinsville, NY 13027 • 6,446
Baldwinville, MA 01436 • 1,709
Baldwyn, MS 38824 • 3,427
Balfour, NC 28706 • 1,772
Ball, LA 71405 • 3,405
Ballard □, KY • 8,798
Ballardvale, MA 01810 • 1,300
Ball Ground, GA 30107 • 640
Ballinger, TX 76821 • 4,207
Ballston Spa, NY 12020 • 4,711
Ballwin, MO 63011 • 12,656
Bally, PA 19503 • 1,051
Balmville, NY 12550 • 3,214
Balsam Lake, WI 54810 • 749
Baltic, CT 06330 • 1,500
Baltic, SD 57003 • 679
Baltimore, MD 21201-99 • 786,775
Baltimore, OH 43105 • 2,689
Baltimore □, MD • 655,615
Baltimore Highlands, MD 21227 • 6,750
Bamberg, SC 29003 • 3,672
Bamberg □, SC • 18,118
Bancroft, IA 50517 • 1,082
Bancroft, MI 48414 • 618
Bandera, TX 78003 • 947
Bandera □, TX • 7,084
Bandon, OR 97411 • 2,311
Bangor, ME 04401 • 31,643
Bangor, MI 49013 • 2,001
Bangor, PA 18013 • 5,006
Bangor, WI 54614 • 1,012
Bangor Township, MI 48706 • 17,494
Bangs, TX 76823 • 1,716
Banks □, GA • 8,702
Banner □, NE • 918
Banner Elk, NC 28604 • 1,087
Banning, CA 92220 • 14,020
Bannock □, ID • 65,421
Bantam, CT 06750 • 860
Baraboo, WI 53913 • 8,081
Baraga, MI 49908 • 1,055
Baraga □, MI • 8,484
Barataria, LA 70036 • 1,123
Barber □, KS • 6,548
Barberton, OH 44203 • 29,751
Barbour □, AL • 24,756
Barbour □, WV • 16,639
Barboursville, WV 25504 • 2,871
Barbourville, KY 40906 • 3,333
Bardstown, KY 40004 • 6,155
Bardwell, KY 42023 • 988
Bargersville, IN 46106 • 1,647
Bar Harbor, ME 04609 • 2,685
Barker Heights, NC 28739 • 1,267
Barling, AR 72923 • 3,761
Barlow, KY 42024 • 746
Bar Mills, ME 04004 • 825
Barnegat, NJ 08005 • 1,012
Barnegat Light, NJ 08006 • 619
Barnes □, ND • 13,960
Barnesboro, PA 15714 • 2,741
Barnesville, GA 30204 • 4,887
Barnesville, MN 56514 • 2,207
Barnesville, OH 43713 • 4,633
Barnhart, MO 63012 • 800
Barnsdall, OK 74002 • 1,501
Barnstable, MA 02630 • 2,033
Barnstable □, MA • 147,925
Barnwell, SC 29812 • 5,572
Barnwell □, SC • 19,868
Baroda, MI 49101 • 627
Barrackville, WV 26559 • 1,815
Barre, MA 01005 • 1,136
Barre, VT 05641 • 9,824
Barren □, KY • 34,009
Barrett, WV 25013 • 800
Barrington, IL 60010 • 9,029
Barrington, NJ 08007 • 7,418
Barrington, RI 02806 • 16,174
Barron, WI 54812 • 2,595
Barron □, WI • 38,730
Barron Lake, MI 49120 • 1,600
Barrow, AK 99723 • 2,207
Barrow □, GA • 21,354
Barry, IL 62312 • 1,487
Barry □, MI • 45,781
Barry □, MO • 24,408
Barstow, CA 92311 • 17,690
Barstow, TX 79719 • 637
Bartholomew □, IN • 65,088
Bartlesville, OK 74003-06 • 34,568
Bartlett, IL 60103 • 13,254
Bartlett, NH 03812 • 700
Bartlett, TN 38134 • 17,170
Bartlett, TX 76511 • 1,567
Barton, MD 21521 • 617
Barton, OH 43905 • 1,039
Barton, VT 05822 • 1,062
Barton □, KS • 31,343
Barton □, MO • 11,292
Bartonville, IL 61607 • 6,137
Bartow, FL 33830 • 14,780
Bartow □, GA • 40,760
Barview, OR 97420 • 1,462
Basehor, KS 66007 • 1,483
Basile, LA 70515 • 2,635
Basin, WY 82410 • 1,349
Baskin, FL 33540 • 800
Basking Ridge, NJ 07920 • 4,800
Bassett, NE 68714 • 1,009
Bassett, VA 24055 • 2,950
Bass Lake, IN 46534 • 1,500
Bastrop, LA 71220 • 15,527
Bastrop, TX 78602 • 3,789
Bastrop □, TX • 24,726
Batavia, IL 60510 • 12,574
Batavia, NY 14020 • 16,703
Batavia, OH 45103 • 1,896
Bates □, MO • 15,873
Batesburg, SC 29006 • 4,023
Batesville, AR 72501 • 8,263
Batesville, IN 47006 • 4,152
Batesville, MS 38606 • 4,692
Batesville, TX 78829 • 800
Bath, ME 04530 • 10,246
Bath, NY 14810 • 6,042
Bath, PA 18014 • 1,953
Bath, SC 29816 • 2,242
Bath □, KY • 10,025
Bath □, VA • 5,860
Baton Rouge, LA 70801-99 • 219,419
Batson, TX 77519 • 650
Battleboro, NC 27809 • 632
Battle Creek, IA 51006 • 919
Battle Creek, MI 49014-17 • 56,339
Battle Creek, NE 68715 • 948
Battle Ground, IN 47920 • 812
Battle Ground, WA 98604 • 2,774
Battle Lake, MN 56515 • 708
Battle Mountain, NV 89820 • 2,755
Baudette, MN 56623 • 1,170
Bawcomville, LA 71291 • 2,500
Baxley, GA 31513 • 3,586
Baxter, IA 50028 • 951
Baxter, MN 56401 • 2,625
Baxter, TN 38544 • 1,411
Baxter □, AR • 27,409
Baxter Springs, KS 66713 • 4,730
Bay, AR 72411 • 1,605
Bay □, FL • 97,740
Bay □, MI • 119,881
Bayard, IA 50029 • 637
Bayard, NE 69334 • 1,435
Bayard, NM 88023 • 3,036
Bayberry, NY 13088 • 5,900
Bayboro, NC 28515 • 759
Bay City, MI 48706-08 • 41,593
Bay City, OR 97107 • 986
Bay City, TX 77414 • 17,837
Bayfield, CO 81122 • 724
Bayfield, WI 54814 • 778
Bayfield □, WI • 13,822
Bay Head, NJ 08742 • 1,340
Baylor □, TX • 4,919
Bay Minette, AL 36507 • 7,455
Bayonne, NJ 07002 • 65,047
Bayou George, FL 32401 • 1,500
Bayou Goula, LA 70716 • 800
Bayou La Batre, AL 36509 • 2,005
Bay Port, MI 48720 • 800
Bayport, MN 55003 • 2,932
Bayport, NY 11705 • 8,900
Bay Ridge, MD 21403 • 1,989
Bay Saint Louis, MS 39520 • 7,891
Bay Shore, NY 11706 • 31,200
Bayshore Gardens, FL 33507 • 14,945
Bayside, WI 53217 • 4,724
Bay Springs, MS 39422 • 1,884
Baytown, TX 77520-22 • 56,923
Bayview, AL 35005 • 830
Bay View, MI 49770 • 1,000
Bay Village, OH 44140 • 17,846
Bayville, NJ 08721 • 900

Bayville, NY 11709 • 7,034
Beach, IL 60085 • 4,650
Beach, ND 58621 • 1,381
Beach City, OH 44608 • 1,083
Beach Haven, NJ 08008 • 1,714
Beachwood, NJ 08722 • 7,687
Beachwood, OH 44122 • 9,983
Beacon, NY 12508 • 12,937
Beacon Falls, CT 06403 • 1,500
Beadle □, SD • 19,195
Beallsville, OH 43716 • 601
Bear, DE 19701 • 950
Bearden, AR 71720 • 1,191
Beardstown, IL 62618 • 6,338
Bear Lake □, ID • 6,931
Bear Town, MS 39648 • 1,277
Beatrice, NE 68310 • 12,891
Beatty, NV 89003 • 900
Beattyville, KY 41311 • 1,068
Beaufort, NC 28516 • 3,826
Beaufort, SC 29902 • 8,634
Beaufort □, NC • 40,355
Beaufort □, SC • 65,364
Beaumont, CA 92223 • 6,818
Beaumont, MS 39423 • 1,112
Beaumont, TX 77701–99 • 118,102
Beauregard □, LA • 29,692
Beaver, OK 73932 • 1,939
Beaver, PA 15009 • 5,441
Beaver, UT 84713 • 1,792
Beaver, WV 25813 • 1,400
Beaver □, OK • 6,806
Beaver □, PA • 204,441
Beaver □, UT • 4,378
Beaver City, NE 68926 • 775
Beavercreek, OH 45385 • 31,589
Beaverdale, PA 15921 • 1,579
Beaver Dam, KY 42320 • 3,185
Beaver Dam, WI 53916 • 14,149
Beaver Falls, PA 15010 • 12,525
Beaverhead □, MT • 8,186
Beaver Meadows, PA 18216 • 1,078
Beaver Springs, PA 17812 • 725
Beaverton, MI 48612 • 1,025
Beaverton, OR 97005–07 • 30,582
Beavertown, PA 17813 • 853
Beckemeyer, IL 62219 • 1,119
Becker, MN 55308 • 601
Becker □, MN • 29,336
Beckham □, OK • 19,243
Beckley, WV 25801 • 20,492
Beckville, TX 75631 • 945
Bedford, IN 47421 • 14,410
Bedford, IA 50833 • 1,692
Bedford, KY 40006 • 835
Bedford, MA 01730 • 13,067
Bedford, NH 03102 • 1,300
Bedford, OH 44146 • 15,056
Bedford, PA 15522 • 3,326
Bedford, TX 76021–22 • 20,821
Bedford, VA 24523 • 5,991
Bedford □, PA • 46,784
Bedford □, TN • 27,916
Bedford □, VA • 34,927
Bedford Heights, OH 44146 • 13,214
Bedford Hills, NY 10507 • 3,200
Bee □, TX • 26,030
Beebe, AR 72012 • 3,599
Beech Creek, PA 16822 • 760
Beecher, IL 60401 • 2,024
Beecher, MI 48505 • 17,178
Beech Grove, IN 46107 • 13,196
Beech Island, SC 29841 • 1,300
Beemer, NE 68716 • 853
Bee Ridge, FL 33578 • 3,313
Beersheba Springs, TN 37305 • 643
Beeville, TX 78102 • 14,574
Beggs, OK 74421 • 1,428
Bel Air, MD 21014 • 7,814
Bel Aire, KS 67220 • 2,650
Bel Aire Estates, CT 06355 • 900
Belcamp, MD 21017 • 650
Belchertown, MA 01007 • 2,531
Belcourt, ND 58316 • 1,803
Belding, MI 48809 • 5,634
Belen, NM 87002 • 5,617
Belfast, ME 04915 • 6,243
Belfast, NC 27530 • 950
Belfast, NY 14711 • 900
Belfield, ND 58622 • 1,274
Belford, NJ 07718 • 6,000
Belfry, KY 41514 • 900
Belgium, WI 53004 • 892
Belgrade, MN 56312 • 805
Belgrade, MT 59714 • 2,336
Belhaven, NC 27810 • 2,430
Belington, WV 26250 • 2,038
Belknap □, NH • 42,884
Bell, CA 90201 • 25,450
Bell □, KY • 34,330
Bell □, TX • 157,820
Bellair, FL 32073 • 5,200
Bellaire, MI 49615 • 1,063
Bellaire, OH 43906 • 8,241
Bellaire, TX 77401 • 14,950
Bellamy, AL 36901 • 750
Bella Vista, AR 72712 • 2,589
Bellbrook, OH 45305 • 5,174
Belle, MO 65013 • 1,233
Belle, WV 25015 • 1,621
Belleair, FL 33516 • 5,200
Belle Center, OH 43310 • 930
Belle Chasse, LA 70037 • 5,412
Bellefontaine, OH 43311 • 11,888
Bellefontaine Neighbors, MO 63137 • 12,082
Bellefonte, DE 19809 • 1,279
Bellefonte, PA 16823 • 6,300
Belle Fourche, SD 57717 • 4,692
Belle Glade, FL 33430 • 16,535
Belle Isle, FL 32809 • 2,848
Belle Meade, TN 37205 • 3,182
Belle Plaine, IA 52208 • 2,903
Belle Plaine, KS 67013 • 1,706
Belle Plaine, MN 56011 • 2,754
Belle Rose, LA 70341 • 700
Belle Vernon, PA 15012 • 1,489
Belleview, FL 32620 • 1,913
Belle View, VA 22307 • 3,500
Belleville, IL 62220–25 • 41,580
Belleville, KS 66935 • 2,805
Belleville, MI 48111 • 3,366
Belleville, NJ 07109 • 35,367
Belleville, PA 17004 • 1,817
Belleville, WI 53508 • 1,302
Bellevue, ID 83313 • 1,016
Bellevue, IA 52031 • 2,450
Bellevue, KY 41073 • 7,678
Bellevue, MI 49021 • 1,289
Bellevue, NE 68005 • 21,813
Bellevue, OH 44811 • 8,187
Bellevue, PA 15202 • 10,128
Bellevue, WA 98004–09 • 73,903
Bellflower, CA 90706 • 53,441
Bell Gardens, CA 90201 • 34,117
Bellingham, MA 02019 • 14,300
Bellingham, WA 98225–27 • 45,794
Bellmawr, NJ 08031 • 13,721
Bellmead, TX 76705 • 7,569
Bellmore, NY 11710 • 18,431
Bellows Falls, VT 05101 • 3,456
Bellport, NY 11713 • 2,809
Bells, TN 38006 • 1,571
Bellville, OH 44813 • 1,714
Bellville, TX 77418 • 2,860
Bellwood, IL 60104 • 19,811
Bellwood, PA 16617 • 2,114
Belmar, NJ 07719 • 6,771
Belmond, IA 50421 • 2,505
Belmont, CA 94002 • 24,505
Belmont, MA 02178 • 26,100
Belmont, MS 38827 • 1,420
Belmont, NH 03220 • 900
Belmont, NC 28012 • 4,607
Belmont, NY 14813 • 1,024
Belmont, OH 43718 • 714
Belmont, WV 26134 • 887
Belmont, WI 53510 • 826
Belmont □, OH • 82,569
Bel-Nor, MO 63133 • 2,047
Beloit, KS 67420 • 4,367
Beloit, OH 44609 • 1,093
Beloit, WI 53511 • 35,207
Beloit North, WI 53511 • 5,912
Belpre, OH 45714 • 7,193
Belt, MT 59412 • 825
Belton, MO 64012 • 12,708
Belton, SC 29627 • 5,312
Belton, TX 76513 • 10,660
Beltrami □, MN • 30,982
Beltsville, MD 20705 • 12,760
Belvedere, SC 29841 • 6,859
Belvedere Park, GA 30032 • 17,766
Belvidere, DE 19804 • 1,100
Belvidere, IL 61008 • 15,176
Belvidere, NJ 07823 • 2,475
Belzoni, MS 39038 • 2,982
Bement, IL 61813 • 1,770
Bemidji, MN 56601 • 10,949
Bemis, TN 38314 • 1,883
Benavides, TX 78341 • 1,978
Benbrook, TX 76126 • 13,579
Bend, OR 97701–09 • 17,263
Benedict, MD 20612 • 700
Benewah □, ID • 8,292
Benham, KY 40807 • 936
Ben Hill □, GA • 16,000
Benicia, CA 94510 • 15,376
Benkelman, NE 69021 • 1,235
Benld, IL 62009 • 1,638
Bennett, CO 80102 • 942
Bennett □, SD • 3,044
Bennettsville, SC 29512 • 8,774
Bennington, NE 68007 • 631
Bennington, VT 05201 • 9,349
Bennington □, VT • 33,345
Bennion, UT 84107 • 950
Bensenville, IL 60106 • 16,124
Bensley, VA 23234 • 3,300
Benson, AZ 85602 • 4,190
Benson, MN 56215 • 3,656
Benson, NC 27504 • 2,792
Benson □, ND • 7,944
Bent □, CO • 5,945
Bentleyville, PA 15314 • 2,525
Benton, AR 72015 • 17,717
Benton, IL 62812 • 7,778
Benton, KS 67017 • 609
Benton, KY 42025 • 3,700
Benton, LA 71006 • 1,864
Benton, MO 63736 • 674
Benton, PA 17814 • 981
Benton, TN 37307 • 1,115
Benton, WI 53803 • 983
Benton □, AR • 78,115
Benton □, IN • 10,218
Benton □, IA • 23,649
Benton □, MN • 25,187
Benton □, MS • 8,153
Benton □, MO • 12,183
Benton □, OR • 68,211
Benton □, TN • 14,901
Benton □, WA • 109,444
Benton City, WA 99320 • 1,980
Benton Harbor, MI 49022 • 14,707
Benton Heights, MI 49022 • 6,787
Bentonville, AR 72712 • 8,756
Benwood, WV 26031 • 1,994
Benzie □, MI • 11,205
Berea, KY 40403 • 8,226
Berea, OH 44017 • 19,567
Berea, SC 29611 • 7,500
Beresford, SD 57004 • 1,865
Bergen, NY 14416 • 976
Bergen □, NJ • 845,385
Bergenfield, NJ 07621 • 25,568
Bergholz, OH 43908 • 914
Bergland, MI 49910 • 700
Berkeley, CA 94701–99 • 103,328
Berkeley, IL 60162 • 5,467
Berkeley, MO 63134 • 15,922
Berkeley, RI 02864 • 930
Berkeley □, SC • 94,727
Berkeley □, WV • 46,775
Berkeley Heights, NJ 07922 • 12,549
Berkeley Springs, WV 25411 • 789
Berkley, MI 48072 • 18,637
Berks □, PA • 312,509
Berkshire □, MA • 145,110
Berlin, CT 06037 • 2,000
Berlin, MD 21811 • 2,162
Berlin, NH 03570 • 13,084
Berlin, NJ 08009 • 5,786
Berlin, NY 12022 • 850
Berlin, OH 44610 • 800
Berlin, PA 15530 • 1,999
Berlin, WI 54923 • 5,478
Berlin Heights, OH 44814 • 756
Bernalillo, NM 87004 • 3,012
Bernalillo □, NM • 419,700
Bernardston, MA 01337 • 700
Bernardsville, NJ 07924 • 6,715
Berne, IN 46711 • 3,300
Bernice, LA 71222 • 1,956
Bernie, MO 63822 • 1,975
Bernville, PA 19506 • 798
Berrien □, GA • 13,525
Berrien □, MI • 171,276
Berrien Springs, MI 49103 • 2,042
Berry, AL 35546 • 916
Berry Hill, TN 37204 • 1,113
Berryville, AR 72616 • 2,966
Berryville, VA 22611 • 1,752
Berthoud, CO 80513 • 2,362
Bertie □, NC • 21,024
Bertram, TX 78605 • 824
Bertrand, MI 49120 • 5,000
Bertrand, MO 63823 • 688
Bertrand, NE 68927 • 775
Berwick, LA 70342 • 4,466
Berwick, ME 03901 • 2,378
Berwick, PA 18603 • 11,850
Berwyn, IL 60402 • 46,849
Berwyn, PA 19312 • 9,300
Bessemer, AL 35020–23 • 31,729
Bessemer, MI 49911 • 2,553
Bessemer, PA 16112 • 1,293
Bessemer City, NC 28016 • 4,787
Bethalto, IL 62010 • 8,630
Bethany, CT 06525 • 890
Bethany, IL 61914 • 1,550
Bethany, MO 64424 • 3,095
Bethany, OK 73008 • 22,130
Bethany, WV 26032 • 1,336
Bethel, AK 99559 • 3,576
Bethel, CT 06801 • 8,755
Bethel, ME 04217 • 1,225
Bethel, NC 27812 • 1,825
Bethel, OH 45106 • 2,231
Bethel, VT 05032 • 1,016
Bethel Acres, OK 74801 • 747
Bethel Park, PA 15102 • 34,755
Bethel Springs, TN 38315 • 873
Bethesda, MD 20814–17 • 63,022
Bethesda, OH 43719 • 1,429
Bethlehem, CT 06751 • 1,762
Bethlehem, NH 03574 • 700
Bethlehem, PA 18015–18 • 70,419
Bethpage, NY 11714 • 29,900
Betsy Layne, KY 41605 • 900
Bettendorf, IA 52722 • 27,381
Bettsville, OH 44815 • 752
Beulah, ND 58523 • 2,908
Beulaville, NC 28518 • 1,060
Beverly, MA 01915 • 37,655
Beverly, NJ 08010 • 2,919
Beverly, OH 45715 • 1,471
Beverly Hills, CA 90210–13 • 32,367
Beverly Hills, MI 48009 • 11,598
Beverly Shores, IN 46301 • 864
Bexar □, TX • 988,798
Bexley, OH 43209 • 13,405
Bibb □, AL • 15,723
Bibb □, GA • 150,256
Bibb City, GA 31904 • 667
Bicknell, IN 47512 • 4,713
Biddeford, ME 04005 • 19,638
Bienville □, LA • 16,387
Big Bear City, CA 92314 • 3,500
Big Bend, WI 53103 • 1,345
Big Creek, CA 93605 • 700
Big Flats, NY 14814 • 2,500
Bigfork, MT 59911 • 1,080
Biggs, CA 95917 • 1,413
Big Horn □, MT • 11,096
Big Horn □, WY • 11,896
Big Lake, MN 55309 • 2,210
Big Lake, TX 76932 • 3,404
Biglerville, PA 17307 • 991
Big Pine, CA 93513 • 1,510
Bigpoint, MS 39567 • 900
Big Rapids, MI 49307 • 14,361
Big Run, PA 15715 • 822
Big Sandy, MT 59520 • 835
Big Sandy, TN 38221 • 650
Big Sandy, TX 75755 • 1,258
Big Spring, TX 79720 • 24,804
Big Stone □, MN • 7,716
Big Stone City, SD 57216 • 672
Big Stone Gap, VA 24219 • 4,748
Big Timber, MT 59011 • 1,690
Big Wells, TX 78830 • 939
Billerica, MA 01821 • 6,400
Billings, MO 65610 • 911
Billings, MT 59101–99 • 66,842
Billings, OK 74630 • 632
Billings □, ND • 1,138
Billings Heights, MT 59105 • 8,480
Biloxi, MS 39530–34 • 49,311
Biltmore Forest, NC 28803 • 1,499
Bingen, WA 98605 • 644
Binger, OK 73009 • 791
Bingham, ME 04920 • 1,074
Bingham □, ID • 36,489
Binghamton, NY 13901–99 • 55,860
Biola, CA 93606 • 800
Birch Run, MI 48415 • 1,196
Birch Tree, MO 65438 • 622
Birchwood City, MD 20745 • 8,000
Birchwood Park, DE 19711 • 1,500
Bird Island, MN 55310 • 1,372
Birdsboro, PA 19508 • 3,481
Birmingham, AL 35201–99 • 286,799
Birmingham, MI 48008–12 • 21,689
Birnamwood, WI 54414 • 688
Biron, WI 54494 • 698
Bisbee, AZ 85603 • 7,154
Biscayne Gardens, FL 33168 • 13,000
Biscayne Park, FL 33161 • 3,088
Biscoe, NC 27209 • 1,334
Bishop, CA 93514 • 3,333
Bishop, TX 78343 • 3,706
Bishopville, SC 29010 • 3,429
Bismarck, IL 61814 • 750
Bismarck, MO 63624 • 1,625
Bismarck, ND 58501 • 44,485
Biwabik, MN 55708 • 1,428
Bixby, OK 74008 • 6,969
Black Creek, WI 54106 • 1,097
Black Diamond, WA 98010 • 1,170
Blackduck, MN 56630 • 653
Black Eagle, MT 59414 • 1,100
Black Earth, WI 53515 • 1,145
Blackfoot, ID 83221 • 10,065
Blackford □, IN • 15,570
Black Forest, CO 80908 • 3,372
Black Hawk, SD 57718 • 1,608
Black Hawk □, IA • 137,961
Black Jack, MO 63031 • 5,293
Black Lick, PA 15716 • 1,074
Blacklick Estates, OH 43227 • 11,223
Black Mountain, NC 28711 • 4,083
Black Oak, IN 46406 • 10,000
Black River, NY 13612 • 1,384
Black River Falls, WI 54615 • 3,434
Black Rock, AR 72415 • 848
Blacksburg, SC 29702 • 1,873
Blacksburg, VA 24060 • 30,638
Blackshear, GA 31516 • 3,222
Blackstone, MA 01504 • 5,100
Blackstone, VA 23824 • 3,624
Blackville, SC 29817 • 2,840
Blackwell, OK 74631 • 8,400
Blackwood, NJ 08012 • 5,219
Bladen □, NC • 30,491
Bladenboro, NC 28320 • 1,428
Bladensburg, MD 20710 • 7,691
Blades, DE 19973 • 664
Blaine, ME 04734 • 620
Blaine, MN 55433 • 28,558
Blaine, TN 37709 • 1,147
Blaine, WA 98230 • 2,363
Blaine □, ID • 9,841
Blaine □, MT • 6,999
Blaine □, NE • 867
Blaine □, OK • 13,443
Blair, NE 68008 • 6,418
Blair, OK 73526 • 1,092
Blair, WI 54616 • 1,142
Blair □, PA • 136,621
Blairstown, IA 52209 • 695
Blairsville, PA 15717 • 4,166
Blakely, GA 31723 • 5,880
Blakely, PA 18447 • 7,438
Blanchard, LA 71009 • 1,128
Blanchard, OK 73010 • 1,688
Blanchard, PA 16826 • 750
Blanchardville, WI 53516 • 803
Blanchester, OH 45107 • 3,202
Blanco, TX 78606 • 1,179
Blanco □, TX • 4,681
Bland, MO 65014 • 662
Bland □, VA • 6,349
Blandburg, PA 16619 • 775
Blandford, MA 01008 • 800
Blanding, UT 84511 • 3,118
Blandinsville, IL 61420 • 886
Blanford, IN 47831 • 700
Blasdell, NY 14219 • 3,288
Blauvelt, NY 10913 • 5,426
Blawnox, PA 15238 • 1,653
Bleckley □, GA • 10,767
Bledsoe □, TN • 9,478
Blende, CO 81006 • 1,500
Blennerhassett, WV 26101 • 2,200
Blessing, TX 77419 • 950
Blissfield, MI 49228 • 3,107
Block Island, RI 02807 • 620
Bloomdale, OH 44817 • 744
Bloomer, WI 54724 • 3,342
Bloomfield, CT 06002 • 7,400
Bloomfield, IN 47424 • 2,705
Bloomfield, IA 52537 • 2,849
Bloomfield, KY 40008 • 954
Bloomfield, MO 63825 • 1,795
Bloomfield, NE 68718 • 1,393
Bloomfield, NJ 07003 • 47,792
Bloomfield, NM 87413 • 4,881
Bloomfield Hills, MI 48013 • 3,985
Bloomingburg, OH 43106 • 869
Bloomingdale, GA 31302 • 1,855
Bloomingdale, IL 60108 • 12,659
Bloomingdale, NJ 07403 • 7,867
Bloomingdale, NY 12913 • 608
Bloomingdale, TN 37660 • 9,000
Blooming Grove, TX 76626 • 823
Blooming Prairie, MN 55917 • 1,969
Bloomington, CA 92316 • 6,674
Bloomington, IL 61701 • 44,189
Bloomington, IN 47401 • 52,044
Bloomington, MN 55420 • 81,831
Bloomington, TX 77951 • 1,750
Bloomington, WI 53804 • 743
Bloomsburg, PA 17815 • 11,717
Bloomsbury, NJ 08804 • 864
Bloomville, OH 44818 • 1,019
Blossburg, PA 16912 • 1,757
Blossom, TX 75416 • 1,487
Blount □, AL • 36,459
Blount □, TN • 77,770
Blountstown, FL 32424 • 2,632
Blountsville, AL 35031 • 1,509
Blountville, TN 37617 • 2,554
Blowing Rock, NC 28605 • 1,337
Blue Ash, OH 45242 • 9,506
Blue Earth, MN 56013 • 4,132
Blue Earth □, MN • 52,314
Bluefield, VA 24605 • 5,946
Bluefield, WV 24701 • 16,060
Blue Grass, IA 52726 • 1,377
Blue Hill, ME 04614 • 700
Blue Hill, NE 68930 • 883
Blue Hills, CT 06002 • 6,600
Blue Island, IL 60406 • 21,855
Blue Lake, CA 95525 • 1,201
Blue Mound, IL 62513 • 1,338
Blue Mountain, MS 38610 • 867
Blue Rapids, KS 66411 • 1,280
Blue Ridge, GA 30513 • 1,376
Blue Ridge, VA 24064 • 1,200
Blue Ridge Summit, PA 17214 • 800
Blue Springs, MO 64015 • 25,927
Bluewell, WV 24701 • 1,000
Bluff City, TN 37618 • 1,121
Bluffdale, UT 84065 • 1,300
Bluff Park, AL 35226 • 12,000
Bluffs, IL 62621 • 821
Bluffton, IN 46714 • 8,705
Bluffton, OH 45817 • 3,310
Bluford, IL 62814 • 728
Bly, OR 97622 • 750
Blythe, CA 92225 • 6,805
Blytheville, AR 72315 • 23,844
Boalsburg, PA 16827 • 950
Boardman, OH 44512 • 39,161
Boardman, OR 97818 • 1,261
Boaz, AL 35957 • 7,151
Bobtown, PA 15315 • 1,055
Boca Grande, FL 33921 • 1,200
Boca Raton, FL 33431–34 • 49,505
Boerne, TX 78006 • 3,229
Bogalusa, LA 70427 • 16,976
Bogart, GA 30622 • 819
Bogata, TX 75417 • 1,508
Boger City, NC 28092 • 2,252
Bogota, NJ 07603 • 8,344
Bohemia, NY 11716 • 9,800
Boiling Springs, NC 28017 • 2,381
Boiling Springs, PA 17007 • 1,521
Boise, ID 83701–99 • 102,160
Boise □, ID • 2,999
Boise City, OK 73933 • 1,761
Boissevain, VA 24606 • 900
Bokchito, OK 74726 • 628
Bokeelia, FL 33922 • 900
Boling, TX 77420 • 1,000
Bolingbrook, IL 60439 • 37,261
Bolivar, MO 65613 • 5,919
Bolivar, NY 14715 • 1,345
Bolivar, OH 44612 • 989
Bolivar, PA 15923 • 706
Bolivar, TN 38008 • 6,597
Bolivar, WV 25425 • 672
Bolivar □, MS • 45,965
Bollinger □, MO • 10,301
Bolton, MS 39041 • 664
Bolton Landing, NY 12814 • 1,500
Bon Air, VA 23235 • 13,000
Bonaire, GA 31005 • 800
Bond □, IL • 16,224
Bondsville, MA 01009 • 1,906
Bonduel, WI 54107 • 1,160
Bondurant, IA 50035 • 1,283
Bonham, TX 75418 • 7,338
Bon Homme □, SD • 8,059
Bonifay, FL 32425 • 2,534
Bonita Springs, FL 33923 • 3,400
Bonneauville, PA 17325 • 920

Bonner □, ID • 24,163
Bonners Ferry, ID 83805 • 1,906
Bonner Springs, KS 66012 • 6,266
Bonne Terre, MO 63628 • 3,797
Bonneville □, ID • 65,980
Bonney Lake, WA 98390 • 5,328
Bonnie Doone, NC 28303 • 5,950
Bono, AR 72416 • 967
Booker, TX 79005 • 1,219
Boomer, WV 25031 • 1,100
Boone, IA 50036 • 12,602
Boone, NC 28607 • 10,191
Boone □, AR • 26,067
Boone □, IL • 28,630
Boone □, IN • 36,446
Boone □, IA • 26,184
Boone □, KY • 45,842
Boone □, MO • 100,376
Boone □, NE • 7,391
Boone □, WV • 30,447
Booneville, AR 72927 • 3,718
Booneville, MS 38829 • 6,199
Boonsboro, MD 21713 • 1,908
Boonton, NJ 07005 • 8,620
Boonville, CA 95415 • 1,000
Boonville, IN 47601 • 6,300
Boonville, MO 65233 • 6,959
Boonville, NC 27011 • 1,028
Boonville, NY 13309 • 2,344
Boothbay Harbor, ME 04538 • 2,207
Boothwyn, PA 19061 • 7,100
Borden □, TX • 859
Bordentown, NJ 08505 • 4,441
Borger, TX 79007 • 15,837
Boron, CA 93516 • 2,040
Borrego Springs, CA 92004 • 1,405
Boscobel, WI 53805 • 2,662
Bosque □, TX • 13,401
Bossert Estates, NJ 08505 • 2,800
Bossier □, LA • 80,721
Bossier City, LA 71111–13 • 50,817
Boston, GA 31626 • 1,424
Boston, MA 02101–99 • 562,994
Boston Heights, OH 44236 • 781
Boswell, IN 47921 • 810
Boswell, OK 74727 • 702
Boswell, PA 15531 • 1,480
Botetourt □, VA • 23,270
Bothell, WA 98011–12 • 7,943
Botkins, OH 45306 • 1,372
Bottineau, ND 58318 • 2,829
Bottineau □, ND • 9,239
Boulder, CO 80301–99 • 76,685
Boulder, MT 59632 • 1,441
Boulder □, CO • 189,625
Boulder City, NV 89005 • 9,590
Boulder Hill, IL 60538 • 9,333
Boulevard Heights, MD 20743 • 1,700
Boundary □, ID • 7,289
Bound Brook, NJ 08805 • 9,710
Bountiful, UT 84010 • 32,877
Bourbon, IN 46504 • 1,522
Bourbon, MO 65441 • 1,259
Bourbon □, KS • 15,969
Bourbon □, KY • 19,405
Bourbonnais, IL 60914 • 13,280
Bourg, LA 70343 • 2,073
Bourne, MA 02532 • 800
Boutte, LA 70039 • 1,200
Bovey, MN 55709 • 813
Bovina, TX 79009 • 1,499
Bowdle, SD 57428 • 644
Bowdon, GA 30108 • 1,743
Bowie, MD 20715–16 • 33,695
Bowie, TX 76230 • 5,610
Bowie □, TX • 75,301
Bowling Green, FL 33834 • 2,310
Bowling Green, KY 42101 • 40,450
Bowling Green, MO 63334 • 3,022
Bowling Green, OH 43402 • 25,728
Bowling Green, SC 29703 • 850
Bowling Green, VA 22427 • 665
Bowman, GA 30624 • 890
Bowman, ND 58623 • 2,071
Bowman, SC 29018 • 1,137
Bowman □, ND • 4,229
Bowmanstown, PA 18030 • 1,078
Bow Mar, CO 80120 • 930
Box Butte □, NE • 13,696
Box Elder, SD 57719 • 3,186
Box Elder □, UT • 33,222
Boxford, MA 01921 • 1,841
Boyce, LA 71409 • 1,198
Boyceville, WI 54725 • 862
Boyd, TX 76023 • 889
Boyd, WI 54726 • 660
Boyd □, KY • 55,513
Boyd □, NE • 3,331
Boyden, IA 51234 • 708
Boyertown, PA 19512 • 3,979
Boykins, VA 23827 • 791
Boyle, MS 38730 • 888
Boyle □, KY • 25,066
Boylston, MA 01505 • 950
Boyne City, MI 49712 • 3,348
Boynton Beach, FL 33435–37 • 35,624
Boys Ranch, TX 79010 • 650
Boys Town, NE 68010 • 622
Bozeman, MT 59715 • 21,645
Braceville, IL 60407 • 721
Bracken □, KY • 7,738
Brackenridge, PA 15014 • 4,297
Brackettville, TX 78832 • 1,676
Braddock, PA 15104 • 5,634
Braddock Heights, MD 21714 • 4,223
Bradenton, FL 33505–08 • 30,170
Bradenville, PA 15620 • 1,200
Bradford, AR 72020 • 950
Bradford, IL 61421 • 924
Bradford, OH 45308 • 2,166
Bradford, PA 16701 • 11,211
Bradford, RI 02808 • 1,354
Bradford, TN 38316 • 1,146
Bradford, VT 05033 • 831
Bradford □, FL • 20,023
Bradford □, PA • 62,919
Bradfordwoods, PA 15015 • 1,264
Bradley, AR 71826 • 790
Bradley, FL 33835 • 1,108
Bradley, IL 60915 • 11,008
Bradley, ME 04411 • 625
Bradley, WV 25818 • 1,200
Bradley □, AR • 13,803
Bradley □, TN • 67,547
Bradley Beach, NJ 07720 • 4,772
Bradner, OH 43406 • 1,175
Bradshaw, MD 21021 • 800
Bradshaw, WV 24817 • 628
Brady, TX 76825 • 5,969
Braham, MN 55006 • 1,015
Braidwood, IL 60408 • 3,429
Brainerd, MN 56401 • 11,489
Braintree, MA 02184 • 36,337
Bramwell, WV 24715 • 989
Branch □, MI • 40,188
Branchville, SC 29432 • 1,769
Brandenburg, KY 40108 • 1,831
Brandon, FL 33511 • 29,100
Brandon, MS 39042 • 9,626
Brandon, SC 29611 • 2,170
Brandon, SD 57005 • 2,589
Brandon, VT 05733 • 1,925
Brandon, WI 53919 • 862
Brandywine, MD 20613 • 1,319
Branford, CT 06405 • 5,438
Branford, FL 32008 • 622
Branford Hills, CT 06405 • 2,200
Branford Point, CT 06405 • 700
Branson, MO 65616 • 2,550
Brant Lake, NY 12815 • 700
Brantley, AL 36009 • 1,151
Brantley □, GA • 8,701
Brant Rock, MA 02020 • 1,500
Bratenahl, OH 44108 • 1,485
Brattleboro, VT 05301 • 8,596
Brawley, CA 92227 • 14,946
Braxton □, WV • 13,894
Braymer, MO 64624 • 986
Brazil, IN 47834 • 7,852
Brazoria, TX 77422 • 3,025
Brazoria □, TX • 169,587
Brazos □, TX • 93,588
Brea, CA 92621 • 27,913
Breathitt □, KY • 17,004
Breaux Bridge, LA 70517 • 5,922
Breckenridge, CO 80424 • 818
Breckenridge, MI 48615 • 1,495
Breckenridge, MN 56520 • 3,909
Breckenridge, TX 76024 • 6,921
Breckenridge Hills, MO 63114 • 5,666
Breckinridge □, KY • 16,861
Brecksville, OH 44141 • 10,132
Breese, IL 62230 • 3,516
Bremen, GA 30110 • 3,966
Bremen, IN 46506 • 3,565
Bremen, OH 43107 • 1,432
Bremer □, IA • 24,820
Bremerton, WA 98310–15 • 36,208
Bremond, TX 76629 • 1,025
Brenham, TX 77833 • 10,966
Brent, AL 35034 • 2,862
Brent, FL 32503 • 4,100
Brenton, WV 24818 • 800
Brentwood, CA 94513 • 4,434
Brentwood, MD 20722 • 2,988
Brentwood, MO 63144 • 8,209
Brentwood, NY 11717 • 48,800
Brentwood, OH 45231 • 5,508
Brentwood, PA 15227 • 11,861
Brentwood, SC 29405 • 2,000
Brentwood, TN 37027 • 9,431
Breton Woods, NJ 08723 • 1,300
Brevard, NC 28712 • 5,323
Brevard □, FL • 272,959
Brewer, ME 04412 • 9,017
Brewster, MA 02631 • 1,744
Brewster, NY 10509 • 1,650
Brewster, OH 44613 • 2,321
Brewster, WA 98812 • 1,337
Brewster □, TX • 7,573
Brewton, AL 36426 • 6,680
Briarcliff, PA 19036 • 9,300
Briarcliff Manor, NY 10510 • 7,115
Briceville, TN 37710 • 800
Brick, NJ 08723–24 • 3,200
Bridge City, LA 70094 • 2,500
Bridgehampton, NY 11932 • 950
Bridgeport, AL 35740 • 2,974
Bridgeport, CA 93517 • 900
Bridgeport, CT 06601–99 • 142,546
Bridgeport, IL 62417 • 2,281
Bridgeport, MI 48722 • 3,500
Bridgeport, NE 69336 • 1,668
Bridgeport, NJ 08014 • 900
Bridgeport, OH 43912 • 2,642
Bridgeport, PA 19405 • 4,843
Bridgeport, TX 76026 • 3,737
Bridgeport, WA 98813 • 1,174
Bridgeport, WV 26330 • 6,604
Bridger, MT 59014 • 724
Bridgeton, MO 63044 • 18,445
Bridgeton, NJ 08302 • 18,795
Bridgetown, OH 45211 • 11,460
Bridgeview, IL 60455 • 14,155
Bridgeville, DE 19933 • 1,238
Bridgeville, PA 15017 • 6,154
Bridgewater, MA 02324 • 6,781
Bridgewater, NJ 08807 • 5,800
Bridgewater, SD 57319 • 653
Bridgewater, VA 22812 • 3,289
Bridgman, MI 49106 • 2,235
Bridgton, ME 04009 • 1,639
Brielle, NJ 08730 • 4,068
Brigantine, NJ 08203 • 8,318
Brigham City, UT 84302 • 15,596
Brighton, AL 35020 • 5,308
Brighton, CO 80601 • 12,773
Brighton, IL 62012 • 2,364
Brighton, IA 52540 • 804
Brighton, MI 48116 • 4,268
Brighton, NY 14610 • 35,776
Brighton, TN 38011 • 976
Brilliant, AL 35548 • 871
Brilliant, OH 43913 • 1,751
Brillion, WI 54110 • 2,907
Brimfield, IL 61517 • 890
Brinkley, AR 72021 • 4,909
Briscoe □, TX • 2,579
Bristol, CT 06010 • 57,370
Bristol, FL 32321 • 1,044
Bristol, IN 46507 • 1,203
Bristol, NH 03222 • 1,258
Bristol, PA 19007 • 10,867
Bristol, RI 02809 • 20,128
Bristol, TN 37620 • 23,986
Bristol, VT 05443 • 1,793
Bristol, VA 24201 • 19,042
Bristol □, MA • 474,641
Bristol □, RI • 46,942
Bristow, OK 74010 • 4,702
Britt, IA 50423 • 2,185
Britton, MI 49229 • 693
Britton, SD 57430 • 1,590
Broadalbin, NY 12025 • 1,415
Broad Brook, CT 06016 • 1,548
Broadmoor, CO 80906 • 1,900
Broadus, MT 59317 • 712
Broadview, IL 60153 • 8,618
Broadview Heights, OH 44141 • 10,920
Broadview Park, FL 33314 • 6,022
Broadwater □, MT • 3,267
Broadway, NC 27505 • 908
Broadway, VA 22815 • 1,234
Brockport, NY 14420 • 9,776
Brockton, MA 02401–99 • 95,172
Brockway, PA 15824 • 2,376
Brocton, NY 14716 • 1,416
Broderick, CA 95605 • 9,900
Brodhead, KY 40409 • 686
Brodhead, WI 53520 • 3,153
Broken Arrow, OK 74012–14 • 35,761
Broken Bow, NE 68822 • 3,979
Broken Bow, OK 74728 • 3,965
Bronson, FL 32621 • 853
Bronson, MI 49028 • 2,271
Bronte, TX 76933 • 983
Bronx □, NY • 1,168,972
Bronxville, NY 10708 • 6,267
Brook, IN 47922 • 926
Brooke □, WV • 31,117
Brookfield, CT 06804 • 1,000
Brookfield, IL 60513 • 19,395
Brookfield, MA 01506 • 1,037
Brookfield, MO 64628 • 5,555
Brookfield, VA 22021 • 2,500
Brookfield, WI 53005 • 34,035
Brookfield Center, CT 06805 • 900
Brookhaven, MS 39601 • 10,800
Brookhaven, PA 19015 • 7,912
Brookhaven, WV 26505 • 1,200
Brookings, OR 97415 • 3,384
Brookings, SD 57006 • 14,951
Brookings □, SD • 24,332
Brookland, AR 72417 • 840
Brooklawn, NJ 08030 • 2,133
Brooklet, GA 30415 • 1,035
Brookline, MA 02146 • 55,062
Brooklyn, CT 06234 • 900
Brooklyn, IN 46111 • 889
Brooklyn, IA 52211 • 1,509
Brooklyn, MI 49230 • 1,110
Brooklyn, MS 39425 • 800
Brooklyn, OH 44144 • 12,342
Brooklyn, SC 29720 • 1,800
Brooklyn, WI 53521 • 627
Brooklyn Center, MN 55429 • 31,230
Brooklyn Park, MD 21225 • 11,508
Brooklyn Park, MN 55443 • 43,332
Brookneal, VA 24528 • 1,454
Brook Park, OH 44142 • 26,195
Brookport, IL 62910 • 1,128
Brookridge, CO 80120 • 1,200
Brooks, KY 40109 • 1,344
Brooks □, GA • 15,255
Brooks □, TX • 8,428
Brookshire, TX 77423 • 2,175
Brookside, AL 35036 • 1,409
Brookside, DE 19713 • 15,255
Brookston, IN 47923 • 1,701
Brooksville, FL 33512 • 5,582
Brooksville, KY 41004 • 680
Brooksville, MS 39739 • 1,038
Brookville, IN 47012 • 2,874
Brookville, MA 02343 • 950
Brookville, NY 11545 • 3,290
Brookville, OH 45309 • 4,322
Brookville, PA 15825 • 4,568
Brookwood, NJ 08527 • 4,000
Broomall, PA 19008 • 23,642
Broome □, NY • 213,648
Broomfield, CO 80020 • 20,730
Brooten, MN 56316 • 647
Broussard, LA 70518 • 2,923
Broward □, FL • 1,018,200
Browardale, FL 33311 • 7,571
Browerville, MN 56438 • 693
Brown □, IL • 5,411
Brown □, IN • 12,377
Brown □, KS • 11,955
Brown □, MN • 28,645
Brown □, NE • 4,377
Brown □, OH • 31,920
Brown □, SD • 36,962
Brown □, TX • 33,057
Brown □, WI • 175,280
Brown City, MI 48416 • 1,163
Brown Deer, WI 53209 • 12,921
Brownfield, TX 79316 • 10,387
Brownfields, LA 70811 • 1,800
Browning, MT 59417 • 1,226
Brownsburg, IN 46112 • 6,242
Brownsdale, MN 55918 • 691
Browns Mills, NJ 08015 • 10,568
Brownstown, IL 62418 • 708
Brownstown, IN 47220 • 2,704
Brownstown, PA 15906 • 800
Browns Valley, MN 56219 • 887
Brownsville, FL 33142 • 18,058
Brownsville, KY 42210 • 674
Brownsville, LA 71291 • 3,000
Brownsville, OR 97327 • 1,261
Brownsville, PA 15417 • 4,043
Brownsville, TN 38012 • 9,307
Brownsville, TX 78520–26 • 84,997
Brownton, MN 55312 • 697
Brownville, NY 13615 • 1,099
Brownville Junction, ME 04415 • 775
Brownwood, TX 76801 • 19,396
Broxton, GA 31519 • 1,117
Broyhill Park, VA 22042 • 3,600
Bruce, MS 38915 • 2,208
Bruce, WI 54819 • 905
Bruceton, TN 38317 • 1,579
Bruceville, IN 47516 • 646
Brule □, SD • 5,245
Brundidge, AL 36010 • 3,213
Brunswick, GA 31520 • 17,605
Brunswick, ME 04011 • 10,990
Brunswick, MD 21716 • 4,572
Brunswick, MO 65236 • 1,272
Brunswick, OH 44212 • 28,104
Brunswick □, NC • 35,777
Brunswick □, VA • 15,632
Brush, CO 80723 • 4,082
Brusly, LA 70719 • 1,762
Bryan, OH 43506 • 7,879
Bryan, TX 77801–06 • 44,337
Bryan □, GA • 10,175
Bryan □, OK • 30,535
Bryans Road, MD 20616 • 3,739
Bryant, AR 72022 • 2,682
Bryantville, MA 02327 • 1,500
Bryn Mawr, PA 19010 • 9,500
Bryn Mawr, WA 98178 • 2,100
Bryson City, NC 28713 • 1,556
Buchanan, GA 30113 • 1,019
Buchanan, MI 49107 • 5,142
Buchanan, VA 24066 • 1,205
Buchanan □, IA • 22,900
Buchanan □, MO • 87,888
Buchanan □, VA • 37,989
Buckatunna, MS 39322 • 700
Buckeye, AZ 85326 • 3,434
Buckeye Lake, OH 43008 • 2,521
Buckhannon, WV 26201 • 6,820
Buckhorn, AZ 85205 • 4,000
Buckingham □, VA • 11,751
Buckley, IL 60918 • 604
Buckley, WA 98321 • 3,143
Bucklin, KS 67834 • 786
Bucklin, MO 64631 • 713
Bucknell Manor, VA 22307 • 2,350
Buckner, MO 64016 • 2,848
Bucks □, PA • 479,211
Bucksport, ME 04416 • 2,853
Bucksport, SC 29527 • 1,125
Bucyrus, OH 44820 • 13,433
Buda, IL 61314 • 668
Bude, MS 39630 • 1,092
Buechel, KY 40218 • 6,912
Buena, NJ 08310 • 3,642
Buena, WA 98921 • 800
Buena Park, CA 90620–24 • 64,165
Buena Vista, CO 81211 • 2,075
Buena Vista, FL 33589 • 3,000
Buena Vista, GA 31803 • 1,544
Buena Vista, VA 24416 • 6,717
Buena Vista □, IA • 20,774
Buffalo, IA 52728 • 1,569
Buffalo, MN 55313 • 4,560
Buffalo, MO 65622 • 2,217
Buffalo, NY 14201–99 • 357,870
Buffalo, OH 43722 • 800
Buffalo, OK 73834 • 1,381
Buffalo, SC 29321 • 1,641
Buffalo, TX 75831 • 1,507
Buffalo, WV 25033 • 1,034
Buffalo, WI 54622 • 894
Buffalo, WY 82834 • 3,799
Buffalo □, NE • 34,797
Buffalo □, SD • 1,795
Buffalo □, WI • 14,309
Buffalo Center, IA 50424 • 1,233
Buffalo Grove, IL 60089 • 22,230
Buffalo Lake, MN 55314 • 782
Buford, GA 30518 • 6,578
Buhl, ID 83316 • 3,629
Buhl, MN 55713 • 1,284
Buhler, KS 67522 • 1,188
Buies Creek, NC 27506 • 1,939
Bullhead City, AZ 86430 • 5,000
Bullitt □, KY • 43,346
Bulloch □, GA • 35,785
Bullock □, AL • 10,596
Bullock Creek, MI 48640 • 900
Bulls Gap, TN 37711 • 821
Bull Shoals, AR 72619 • 1,312
Buna, TX 77612 • 1,900
Bunche Park, FL 33054 • 4,000
Buncombe □, NC • 160,934
Bunker, MO 63629 • 673
Bunker Hill, IL 62014 • 1,700
Bunker Hill, IN 46914 • 984
Bunker Hill, OR 97420 • 1,555
Bunker Hill, WV 25309 • 800
Bunkie, LA 71322 • 5,364
Bunnell, FL 32010 • 1,816
Buras, LA 70041 • 2,600
Burbank, CA 91501–99 • 84,625
Burbank, IL 60459 • 28,462
Burbank, WA 99323 • 700
Bureau □, IL • 39,114
Burgaw, NC 28425 • 1,738
Burgettstown, PA 15021 • 1,867
Burgin, KY 40310 • 1,008
Burien, WA 98166 • 14,250
Burkburnett, TX 76354 • 10,668
Burke, SD 57523 • 859
Burke, VA 22015 • 1,500
Burke □, GA • 19,349
Burke □, NC • 72,504
Burke □, ND • 3,822
Burke City, MO 63135 • 2,600
Burkesville, KY 42717 • 2,051
Burkeville, VA 23922 • 606
Burleigh □, ND • 54,811
Burleson, TX 76028 • 11,734
Burleson □, TX • 12,313
Burley, ID 83318 • 8,761
Burlingame, CA 94010 • 26,173
Burlingame, KS 66413 • 1,239
Burlington, CO 80807 • 3,107
Burlington, IN 46915 • 680
Burlington, IA 52601 • 29,529
Burlington, KS 66839 • 2,901
Burlington, MA 01803 • 23,486
Burlington, NJ 08016 • 10,246
Burlington, NC 27215 • 37,266
Burlington, ND 58722 • 762
Burlington, VT 05401 • 37,712
Burlington, WA 98233 • 3,894
Burlington, WI 53105 • 8,385
Burlington □, NJ • 362,542
Burlington Beach, IN 46383 • 900
Burlington Junction, MO 64428 • 657
Burnet, TX 78611 • 3,410
Burnet □, TX • 17,803
Burnett □, WI • 12,340
Burney, CA 96013 • 3,187
Burnham, PA 17009 • 2,457
Burns, OR 97720 • 3,579
Burns, TN 37029 • 777
Burns Flat, OK 73624 • 2,431
Burnside, KY 42519 • 775
Burnsville, MN 55337 • 35,674
Burnsville, MS 38833 • 889
Burnsville, NC 28714 • 1,452
Burnt Hills, NY 12027 • 2,000
Burr Oak, MI 49030 • 853
Burrton, KS 67020 • 976
Burt, IA 50522 • 689
Burt □, NE • 8,813
Burton, MI 48509 • 29,976
Burton, OH 44021 • 1,401
Burwell, NE 68823 • 1,383
Bushnell, FL 33513 • 983
Bushnell, IL 61422 • 3,811
Butler, AL 36904 • 1,882
Butler, GA 31006 • 1,959
Butler, IN 46721 • 2,509
Butler, KY 41006 • 663
Butler, MO 64730 • 4,107
Butler, NJ 07405 • 7,616
Butler, OH 44822 • 991
Butler, PA 16001 • 17,026
Butler, WI 53007 • 2,059
Butler □, AL • 21,680
Butler □, IA • 17,668
Butler □, KS • 44,782
Butler □, KY • 11,064
Butler □, MO • 37,693
Butler □, NE • 9,330
Butler □, OH • 258,787
Butler □, PA • 147,912
Butner, NC 27509 • 4,240
Butte, MT 59701 • 37,205
Butte □, CA • 143,851
Butte □, ID • 3,342
Butte □, SD • 8,372
Butterfield, MN 56120 • 634
Buttonwillow, CA 93206 • 1,350
Butts □, GA • 13,665
Buxton, NC 27920 • 700

Buzzards Bay, MA 02532 • *3,375*
Byers, CO 80103 • *1,100*
Byesville, OH 43723 • *2,572*
Byfield, MA 01922 • *950*
Byhalia, MS 38611 • *757*
Bylas, AZ 85530 • *1,175*
Byng, OK 74820 • *833*
Byrdstown, TN 38549 • *884*
Byron, CA 94514 • *900*
Byron, GA 31008 • *1,661*
Byron, IL 61010 • *2,035*
Byron, MN 55920 • *1,715*
Byron, WY 82412 • *633*

C

Cabarrus □, NC • *85,895*
Cabell □, WV • *106,835*
Cabin Creek, WV 25035 • *900*
Cabin John, MD 20818 • *1,500*
Cabool, MO 65689 • *2,090*
Cabot, AR 72023 • *4,806*
Cache, OK 73527 • *1,661*
Cache □, UT • *57,176*
Caddo, OK 74729 • *923*
Caddo □, LA • *252,358*
Caddo □, OK • *30,905*
Cadillac, MI 49601 • *10,199*
Cadiz, KY 42211 • *1,661*
Cadiz, OH 43907 • *4,058*
Cadott, WI 54727 • *1,247*
Cahaba Heights, AL 35243 • *3,800*
Cahokia, IL 62206 • *18,904*
Cairnbrook, PA 15924 • *800*
Cairo, GA 31728 • *8,777*
Cairo, IL 62914 • *5,931*
Cairo, NE 68824 • *737*
Cairo, NY 12413 • *725*
Calabasas, CA 91302 • *900*
Calais, ME 04619 • *4,262*
Calaveras □, CA • *20,710*
Calavo Gardens, CA 92041 • *6,100*
Calcasieu □, LA • *167,223*
Calcutta, OH 43920 • *1,121*
Caldwell, ID 83605 • *17,699*
Caldwell, KS 67022 • *1,401*
Caldwell, NJ 07006 • *7,624*
Caldwell, OH 43724 • *1,935*
Caldwell, TX 77836 • *2,953*
Caldwell □, KY • *13,473*
Caldwell □, LA • *10,761*
Caldwell □, MO • *8,660*
Caldwell □, NC • *67,746*
Caldwell □, TX • *23,637*
Caledonia, MI 49316 • *722*
Caledonia, MN 55921 • *2,691*
Caledonia, NY 14423 • *2,188*
Caledonia, OH 43314 • *759*
Caledonia □, VT • *25,808*
Calera, AL 35040 • *2,035*
Calera, OK 74730 • *1,390*
Calexico, CA 92231 • *14,412*
Calhoun, GA 30701 • *5,563*
Calhoun, KY 42327 • *1,080*
Calhoun □, AL • *119,761*
Calhoun □, AR • *6,079*
Calhoun □, FL • *9,294*
Calhoun □, GA • *5,717*
Calhoun □, IL • *5,867*
Calhoun □, IA • *13,542*
Calhoun □, MI • *141,557*
Calhoun □, MS • *15,664*
Calhoun □, SC • *12,206*
Calhoun □, TX • *19,574*
Calhoun □, WV • *8,250*
Calhoun City, MS 38916 • *2,033*
Calhoun Falls, SC 29628 • *2,491*
Calico Rock, AR 72519 • *1,046*
Caliente, NV 89008 • *982*
Califon, NJ 07830 • *1,023*
California, MO 65018 • *3,381*
California, PA 15419 • *5,703*
Calion, AR 71724 • *638*
Calipatria, CA 92233 • *2,636*
Calistoga, CA 94515 • *3,879*
Callahan, FL 32011 • *869*
Callahan, KS 67209 • *900*
Callahan □, TX • *10,992*
Callaway, FL 32401 • *7,154*
Callaway □, MO • *32,252*
Calloway □, KY • *30,031*
Calmar, IA 52132 • *1,053*
Calumet, MI 49913 • *1,013*
Calumet □, WI • *30,867*
Calumet City, IL 60409 • *39,697*
Calumet Park, IL 60643 • *8,788*
Calvert, TX 77837 • *1,732*
Calvert □, MD • *34,638*
Calvert City, KY 42029 • *2,388*
Calverton, MD 20705 • *7,649*
Calverton Park, MO 63136 • *1,717*
Calwa, CA 93725 • *6,640*
Calypso, NC 28325 • *689*
Camanche, IA 52730 • *4,725*
Camarillo, CA 93010 • *37,797*
Camas, WA 98607 • *5,681*
Camas □, ID • *818*
Cambria, CA 93428 • *3,061*
Cambria, WI 53923 • *680*
Cambria □, PA • *183,263*
Cambrian Park, CA 95124 • *4,000*
Cambridge, IL 61238 • *2,217*
Cambridge, IA 50046 • *732*
Cambridge, MD 21613 • *11,703*
Cambridge, MA 02138 • *95,322*
Cambridge, MN 55008 • *3,287*
Cambridge, NE 69022 • *1,206*
Cambridge, NY 12816 • *1,820*
Cambridge, OH 43725 • *13,573*
Cambridge, WI 53523 • *844*
Cambridge City, IN 47327 • *2,407*
Cambridge Springs, PA 16403 • *2,102*
Camden, AL 36726 • *2,406*
Camden, AR 71701 • *15,356*
Camden, DE 19934 • *1,757*
Camden, IN 46917 • *618*
Camden, ME 04843 • *3,743*
Camden, NJ 08101–99 • *84,910*
Camden, NY 13316 • *2,667*
Camden, OH 45311 • *1,971*
Camden, SC 29020 • *7,462*
Camden, TN 38320 • *3,279*
Camden □, GA • *13,371*
Camden □, MO • *20,017*
Camden □, NJ • *471,650*
Camden □, NC • *5,829*
Camdenton, MO 65020 • *2,303*
Cameron, LA 70631 • *1,736*
Cameron, MO 64429 • *4,519*
Cameron, TX 76520 • *5,721*
Cameron, WV 26033 • *1,474*
Cameron, WI 54822 • *1,115*
Cameron □, LA • *9,336*
Cameron □, PA • *6,674*
Cameron □, TX • *209,727*
Camilla, GA 31730 • *5,414*
Camino, CA 95709 • *900*
Cammack Village, AR 72207 • *920*
Camp □, TX • *9,275*
Campbell, CA 95008 • *26,910*
Campbell, FL 32741 • *2,941*
Campbell, MO 63933 • *2,134*
Campbell, OH 44405 • *11,619*
Campbell □, KY • *83,317*
Campbell □, SD • *2,243*
Campbell □, TN • *34,923*
Campbell □, VA • *45,424*
Campbell □, WY • *24,367*
Campbellsburg, IN 47108 • *695*
Campbellsburg, KY 40011 • *714*
Campbellsport, WI 53010 • *1,740*
Campbellsville, KY 42718 • *8,715*
Camp Hill, AL 36850 • *1,628*
Camp Hill, PA 17011 • *8,422*
Camp Point, IL 62320 • *1,285*
Camp Springs, MD 20748 • *2,500*
Campti, LA 71411 • *1,069*
Camp Verde, AZ 86322 • *1,125*
Camp Wood, TX 78833 • *728*
Canaan, CT 06018 • *1,160*
Canadensis, PA 18325 • *800*
Canadian, TX 79014 • *3,491*
Canadian □, OK • *56,452*
Canajoharie, NY 13317 • *2,412*
Canal Fulton, OH 44614 • *3,481*
Canal Point, FL 33438 • *950*
Canal Winchester, OH 43110 • *2,749*
Canandaigua, NY 14424 • *10,419*
Canaseraga, NY 14822 • *700*
Canastota, NY 13032 • *4,773*
Canby, MN 56220 • *2,143*
Canby, OR 97013 • *7,659*
Candler □, GA • *7,518*
Candlewood Isle, CT 06812 • *750*
Candlewood Shores, CT 06804 • *1,950*
Cando, ND 58324 • *1,496*
Candor, NC 27229 • *868*
Candor, NY 13743 • *917*
Caney, KS 67333 • *2,284*
Caneyville, KY 42721 • *642*
Canfield, OH 44406 • *5,535*
Canisteo, NY 14823 • *2,679*
Canistota, SD 57012 • *626*
Cannelton, IN 47520 • *2,373*
Cannelton, WV 25036 • *750*
Cannon □, TN • *10,234*
Cannon Beach, OR 97110 • *1,187*
Cannondale, CT 06897 • *1,300*
Cannon Falls, MN 55009 • *2,653*
Canon, GA 30520 • *704*
Canon City, CO 81212 • *13,037*
Canonsburg, PA 15317 • *10,459*
Canton, CT 06019 • *1,680*
Canton, GA 30114 • *3,601*
Canton, IL 61520 • *14,626*
Canton, KS 67428 • *926*
Canton, MA 02021 • *18,182*
Canton, MI 48187 • *5,000*
Canton, MS 39046 • *11,116*
Canton, MO 63435 • *2,435*
Canton, NC 28716 • *4,631*
Canton, NY 13617 • *7,055*
Canton, OH 44701–99 • *93,077*
Canton, OK 73724 • *854*
Canton, PA 17724 • *1,959*
Canton, SD 57013 • *2,886*
Canton, TX 75103 • *2,845*
Cantonment, FL 32533 • *3,200*
Canute, OK 73626 • *676*
Canutillo, TX 79835 • *2,000*
Canyon, TX 79015 • *10,724*
Canyon □, ID • *83,756*
Canyon City, OR 97820 • *639*
Canyon Lake, TX 78130 • *6,000*
Canyonville, OR 97417 • *1,288*
Capac, MI 48014 • *1,377*
Cape Canaveral, FL 32920 • *5,733*
Cape Charles, VA 23310 • *1,512*
Cape Coral, FL 33904 • *32,103*
Cape Elizabeth, ME 04107 • *7,838*
Cape Girardeau, MO 63701 • *34,361*
Cape Girardeau □, MO • *58,837*
Cape May, NJ 08204 • *4,853*
Cape May □, NJ • *82,266*
Cape May Court House, NJ 08210 • *3,597*
Cape Vincent, NY 13618 • *785*
Capitan, NM 88316 • *762*
Capitola, CA 95010 • *9,095*
Capitol Heights, IA 50317 • *815*
Capitol Heights, MD 20743 • *3,271*
Capron, IL 61012 • *678*
Captain Cook, HI 96704 • *2,008*
Captiva, FL 33924 • *1,200*
Caraway, AR 72419 • *1,165*
Carbon □, MT • *8,099*
Carbon □, PA • *53,285*
Carbon □, UT • *22,179*
Carbon □, WY • *21,896*
Carbondale, CO 81623 • *2,084*
Carbondale, IL 62901 • *26,414*
Carbondale, KS 66414 • *1,518*
Carbondale, PA 18407 • *11,255*
Carbon Hill, AL 35549 • *2,452*
Cardiff-By-The-Sea, CA 92007 • *10,054*
Cardington, OH 43315 • *1,665*
Cardwell, MO 63829 • *831*
Carencro, LA 70520 • *3,712*
Caretta, WV 24821 • *950*
Carey, OH 43316 • *3,674*
Caribou, ME 04736 • *9,916*
Caribou □, ID • *8,695*
Carle Place, NY 11514 • *6,300*
Carleton, MI 48117 • *2,786*
Carlin, NV 89822 • *1,232*
Carlinville, IL 62626 • *5,439*
Carlisle, AR 72024 • *2,567*
Carlisle, IN 47838 • *717*
Carlisle, IA 50047 • *3,073*
Carlisle, KY 40311 • *1,757*
Carlisle, OH 45005 • *4,276*
Carlisle, PA 17013 • *18,314*
Carlisle □, KY • *5,487*
Carl Junction, MO 64834 • *3,937*
Carlsbad, CA 92008 • *35,490*
Carlsbad, NM 88220 • *25,496*
Carlstadt, NJ 07072 • *6,166*
Carlton, MN 55718 • *862*
Carlton, OR 97111 • *1,302*
Carlton □, MN • *29,936*
Carlyle, IL 62231 • *3,388*
Carmel, CA 93923 • *4,707*
Carmel, IN 46032 • *18,272*
Carmel, NY 10512 • *3,395*
Carmi, IL 62821 • *6,264*
Carmichael, CA 95608 • *43,108*
Carmichaels, PA 15320 • *630*
Carnation, WA 98014 • *913*
Carnegie, OK 73015 • *2,016*
Carnegie, PA 15106 • *10,099*
Carney, OK 74832 • *622*
Carneys Point, NJ 08069 • *7,574*
Carnot, PA 15108 • *5,400*
Caro, MI 48723 • *4,317*
Carol City, FL 33055 • *47,349*
Caroleen, NC 28019 • *1,000*
Carolina, WV 26563 • *650*
Carolina Beach, NC 28428 • *2,000*
Caroline □, MD • *23,143*
Caroline □, VA • *17,904*
Carol Stream, IL 60188 • *15,472*
Carpentersville, IL 60110 • *23,272*
Carpinteria, CA 93013 • *10,835*
Carrabelle, FL 32322 • *1,304*
Carrboro, NC 27510 • *7,336*
Carrier Mills, IL 62917 • *2,268*
Carrington, ND 58421 • *2,641*
Carrizo Springs, TX 78834 • *6,886*
Carrizozo, NM 88301 • *1,222*
Carroll, IA 51401 • *9,705*
Carroll, OH 43112 • *641*
Carroll □, AR • *16,203*
Carroll □, GA • *56,346*
Carroll □, IL • *18,779*
Carroll □, IN • *19,722*
Carroll □, IA • *22,951*
Carroll □, KY • *9,270*
Carroll □, MD • *96,356*
Carroll □, MS • *9,776*
Carroll □, MO • *12,131*
Carroll □, NH • *27,931*
Carroll □, OH • *25,598*
Carroll □, TN • *28,285*
Carroll □, VA • *27,270*
Carrollton, AL 35447 • *1,104*
Carrollton, GA 30117 • *14,078*
Carrollton, IL 62016 • *2,816*
Carrollton, KY 41008 • *3,967*
Carrollton, MI 48724 • *7,482*
Carrollton, MO 64633 • *4,700*
Carrollton, OH 44615 • *3,065*
Carrollton, TX 75006–08 • *40,595*
Carrolltown, PA 15722 • *1,395*
Carrville, AL 36023 • *820*
Carson, CA 90745 • *81,221*
Carson, IA 51525 • *716*
Carson, WA 98610 • *950*
Carson □, TX • *6,672*
Carson City, MI 48811 • *1,229*
Carson City, NV 89701 • *32,022*
Carsonville, MI 48419 • *622*
Carter □, KY • *25,060*
Carter □, MO • *5,428*
Carter □, MT • *1,799*
Carter □, OK • *43,610*
Carter □, TN • *50,205*
Carteret, NJ 07008 • *20,598*
Carteret □, NC • *41,092*
Carter Lake, IA 51510 • *3,438*
Cartersville, GA 30120 • *9,247*
Carterville, IL 62918 • *3,445*
Carterville, MO 64835 • *1,973*
Carthage, IL 62321 • *2,978*
Carthage, IN 46115 • *886*
Carthage, MS 39051 • *3,453*
Carthage, MO 64836 • *11,104*
Carthage, NC 28327 • *925*
Carthage, NY 13619 • *3,643*
Carthage, TN 37030 • *2,672*
Carthage, TX 75633 • *6,447*
Caruthersville, MO 63830 • *7,958*
Carver, MA 02330 • *650*
Carver, MN 55315 • *642*
Carver □, MN • *37,046*
Carver Ranch Estates, FL 33023 • *5,600*
Carville, LA 70721 • *1,037*
Cary, IL 60013 • *6,640*
Cary, NC 27511 • *21,763*
Caryville, FL 32427 • *633*
Caryville, TN 37714 • *2,039*
Casa Grande, AZ 85222 • *14,971*
Casas Adobes, AZ 85704 • *5,300*
Cascade, ID 83611 • *945*
Cascade, IA 52033 • *1,912*
Cascade, MT 59421 • *773*
Cascade, WI 53011 • *615*
Cascade □, MT • *80,696*
Cascade Locks, OR 97014 • *838*
Caseville, MI 48725 • *851*
Casey, IL 62420 • *3,026*
Casey □, KY • *14,818*
Cashion, AZ 85329 • *3,014*
Cashmere, WA 98815 • *2,240*
Cashton, WI 54619 • *827*
Casper, WY 82601–15 • *51,016*
Caspian, MI 49915 • *1,038*
Cass □, IL • *15,084*
Cass □, IN • *40,936*
Cass □, IA • *16,932*
Cass □, MI • *49,499*
Cass □, MN • *21,050*
Cass □, MO • *51,029*
Cass □, NE • *20,297*
Cass □, ND • *88,247*
Cass □, TX • *29,430*
Cassadaga, NY 14718 • *821*
Cass City, MI 48726 • *2,258*
Casselberry, FL 32707–08 • *15,247*
Casselton, ND 58012 • *1,661*
Cassia □, ID • *19,427*
Cass Lake, MN 56633 • *1,001*
Cassopolis, MI 49031 • *1,933*
Cassville, MO 65625 • *2,091*
Cassville, WI 53806 • *1,270*
Castalia, OH 44824 • *973*
Castanea, PA 17726 • *1,204*
Castile, NY 14427 • *1,135*
Castleberry, AL 36432 • *847*
Castle Dale, UT 84513 • *1,910*
Castle Hayne, NC 28429 • *1,087*
Castle Hills, DE 19720 • *1,950*
Castle Park, CA 92011 • *6,300*
Castle Point, MO 63136 • *6,500*
Castle Rock, CO 80104 • *3,921*
Castle Rock, WA 98611 • *2,162*
Castle Shannon, PA 15234 • *10,164*
Castleton on Hudson, NY 12033 • *1,627*
Castro □, TX • *10,556*
Castro Valley, CA 94546 • *44,011*
Castroville, CA 95012 • *4,396*
Castroville, TX 78009 • *1,821*
Caswell □, NC • *20,705*
Catahoula □, LA • *12,287*
Catalina Foothills, AZ 85718 • *1,500*
Catasauqua, PA 18032 • *6,711*
Cataumet, MA 02534 • *800*
Catawba □, NC • *105,208*
Catawissa, PA 17820 • *1,568*
Cathedral City, CA 92234 • *4,130*
Cathlamet, WA 98612 • *635*
Catlettsburg, KY 41129 • *3,005*
Catlin, IL 61817 • *2,226*
Catonsville, MD 21228 • *33,208*
Catoosa, OK 74015 • *1,561*
Catoosa □, GA • *36,991*
Catron □, NM • *2,720*
Catskill, NY 12414 • *4,718*
Cattaraugus, NY 14719 • *1,200*
Cattaraugus □, NY • *85,697*
Cavalier, ND 58220 • *1,505*
Cavalier □, ND • *7,636*
Cave City, AR 72521 • *1,634*
Cave City, KY 42127 • *2,098*
Cave Creek, AZ 85331 • *1,589*
Cave Junction, OR 97523 • *1,023*
Cave Spring, GA 30124 • *883*
Cave Spring, VA 24018 • *6,300*
Cavetown, MD 21720 • *1,533*
Cawker City, KS 67430 • *640*
Cawood, KY 40815 • *800*
Cayce, SC 29033 • *11,701*
Cayuga, IN 47928 • *1,258*
Cayuga □, NY • *79,894*
Cayuga Heights, NY 14850 • *3,170*
Cazenovia, NY 13035 • *2,599*
Cecil, PA 15321 • *900*
Cecil □, MD • *60,430*
Cedar □, IA • *18,635*
Cedar □, MO • *11,894*
Cedar □, NE • *11,375*
Cedar Bluff, AL 35959 • *1,129*
Cedar Bluff, TN 37722 • *1,200*
Cedar Bluffs, NE 68015 • *632*
Cedarburg, WI 53012 • *9,005*
Cedar City, UT 84720 • *10,972*
Cedar Crest, NM 87008 • *900*
Cedaredge, CO 81413 • *1,184*
Cedar Falls, IA 50613 • *36,322*
Cedar Grove, NJ 07009 • *12,600*
Cedar Grove, WV 25039 • *1,479*
Cedar Grove, WI 53013 • *1,420*
Cedar Hill, MO 63016 • *1,512*
Cedar Hill, TX 75104 • *6,849*
Cedar Hills, OR 97225 • *8,000*
Cedarhurst, NY 11516 • *6,162*
Cedar Key, FL 32625 • *700*
Cedar Knolls, NJ 07927 • *3,000*
Cedar Lake, IN 46303 • *8,754*
Cedar Rapids, IA 52401–99 • *110,243*
Cedar Springs, MI 49319 • *2,615*
Cedartown, GA 30125 • *8,619*
Cedar Vale, KS 67024 • *848*
Cedarville, CA 96104 • *950*
Cedarville, IL 61013 • *766*
Cedarville, NJ 08311 • *990*
Cedarville, OH 45314 • *2,799*
Celina, OH 45822 • *9,137*
Celina, TN 38551 • *1,580*
Celina, TX 75009 • *1,520*
Celoron, NY 14720 • *1,405*
Cement, OK 73017 • *884*
Cementon, PA 18052 • *1,200*
Center, CO 81125 • *1,630*
Center, MO 63436 • *669*
Center, ND 58530 • *900*
Center, TX 75935 • *5,827*
Centerbrook, CT 06409 • *900*
Centerburg, OH 43011 • *1,275*
Centereach, NY 11720 • *34,600*
Centerfield, UT 84622 • *653*
Center Hill, FL 34254 • *751*
Center Line, MI 48015 • *9,293*
Center Moriches, NY 11934 • *4,000*
Center Point, AL 35215 • *23,317*
Center Point, IA 52213 • *1,591*
Centerville, IN 47330 • *2,284*
Centerville, IA 52544 • *6,558*
Centerville, MA 02632 • *3,640*
Centerville, OH 45459 • *18,886*
Centerville, PA 15417 • *4,207*
Centerville, SD 57014 • *892*
Centerville, TN 37033 • *2,824*
Centerville, TX 75833 • *799*
Centerville, UT 84014 • *8,069*
Central, NM 88026 • *1,968*
Central, SC 29630 • *1,914*
Central City, IL 62801 • *1,505*
Central City, IA 52214 • *1,067*
Central City, KY 42330 • *5,214*
Central City, NE 68826 • *3,083*
Central City, PA 15926 • *1,496*
Central Falls, RI 02863 • *16,995*
Central Heights, AZ 85501 • *1,500*
Centralia, IL 62801 • *15,126*
Centralia, MO 65240 • *3,537*
Centralia, WA 98531 • *11,555*
Central Islip, NY 11722 • *26,000*
Central Lake, MI 49622 • *895*
Central Park, WA 98520 • *2,900*
Central Point, OR 97502 • *6,357*
Central Square, NY 13036 • *1,418*
Central Valley, CA 96019 • *3,424*
Central Valley, NY 10917 • *1,200*
Central Village, CT 06332 • *1,200*
Centre, AL 35960 • *2,351*
Centre □, PA • *112,760*
Centre City, NJ 08051 • *2,500*
Centre Hall, PA 16828 • *1,233*
Centreville, AL 35042 • *2,504*
Centreville, IL 62207 • *9,747*
Centreville, MD 21617 • *2,018*
Centreville, MI 49032 • *1,202*
Centreville, MS 39631 • *1,844*
Centreville, VA 22020 • *950*
Centuria, WI 54824 • *711*
Century, FL 32535 • *1,805*
Ceredo, WV 25507 • *2,255*
Ceres, CA 95307 • *13,281*
Ceresco, NE 68017 • *836*
Cerritos, CA 90701 • *53,020*
Cerro Gordo, IL 61818 • *1,553*
Cerro Gordo □, IA • *48,458*
Chadbourn, NC 28431 • *1,975*
Chadron, NE 69337 • *5,933*
Chadwick, IL 61014 • *631*
Chadwicks, NY 13319 • *1,500*
Chaffee, MO 63740 • *3,241*
Chaffee □, CO • *13,227*
Chaffin, MA 01520 • *3,700*
Chagrin Falls, OH 44022 • *4,335*
Chalfonte, DE 19810 • *2,200*
Challis, ID 83226 • *758*
Chalmette, LA 70043 • *33,847*
Chama, NM 87520 • *1,090*
Chamberlain, SD 57325 • *2,258*
Chambers □, AL • *39,191*
Chambers □, TX • *18,538*
Chambersburg, PA 17201 • *16,174*
Chamblee, GA 30341 • *7,137*
Champaign, IL 61820–21 • *58,133*
Champaign □, IL • *168,392*
Champaign □, OH • *33,649*
Champion, OH 44481 • *5,270*
Champlain, NY 12919 • *1,410*

Champlin, MN 55316 • 9,006
Chandler, AZ 85224 • 29,673
Chandler, IN 47610 • 3,043
Chandler, OK 74834 • 2,926
Chandler, TX 75758 • 1,308
Chandler Heights, AZ 85227 • 750
Chandlerville, IL 62627 • 842
Chanhassen, MN 55317 • 6,359
Channahon, IL 60410 • 3,734
Channel Lake, IL 60002 • 1,613
Channelview, TX 77530 • 16,000
Chantilly, VA 22021 • 950
Chanute, KS 66720 • 10,506
Chapel Hill, NC 27514 • 32,421
Chapel Hill, TN 37034 • 861
Chapel Square, VA 22003 • 2,000
Chapin, IL 62628 • 648
Chapman, KS 67431 • 1,255
Chapmanville, WV 25508 • 1,164
Chappaqua, NY 10514 • 5,100
Chappell, NE 69129 • 1,095
Chardon, OH 44024 • 4,434
Charenton, LA 70523 • 950
Chariton, IA 50049 • 4,987
Chariton □, MO • 10,489
Charleroi, PA 15022 • 5,717
Charles □, MD • 72,751
Charles City, IA 50616 • 8,778
Charles City □, VA • 6,692
Charles Mix □, SD • 9,680
Charleston, AR 72933 • 1,748
Charleston, IL 61920 • 19,355
Charleston, MS 38921 • 2,878
Charleston, MO 63834 • 5,230
Charleston, OR 97420 • 700
Charleston, SC 29401–25 • 69,510
Charleston, TN 37310 • 756
Charleston, WV 25301–99 • 63,968
Charleston □, SC • 276,974
Charlestown, IN 47111 • 5,596
Charlestown, MD 21914 • 720
Charlestown, NH 03603 • 1,294
Charlestown, RI 02813 • 1,200
Charles Town, WV 25414 • 2,857
Charlevoix, MI 49720 • 3,296
Charlevoix □, MI • 19,907
Charlotte, MI 48813 • 8,251
Charlotte, NC 28201–99 • 314,447
Charlotte, TN 37036 • 788
Charlotte, TX 78011 • 1,443
Charlotte □, FL • 58,460
Charlotte □, VA • 12,266
Charlotte Hall, MD 20622 • 1,000
Charlotte Harbor, FL 33950 • 2,084
Charlottesville, VA 22901–10 • 39,916
Charlton □, GA • 7,343
Charlton City, MA 01508 • 1,100
Charmco, WV 25958 • 800
Charter Oak, IA 51439 • 615
Chase, KS 67524 • 753
Chase, MD 21027 • 700
Chase □, KS • 3,309
Chase □, NE • 4,758
Chase City, VA 23924 • 2,749
Chaska, MN 55318 • 8,346
Chassell, MI 49916 • 700
Chateaugay, NY 12920 • 869
Chatfield, MN 55923 • 2,055
Chatham, IL 62629 • 5,597
Chatham, LA 71226 • 714
Chatham, MA 02633 • 1,922
Chatham, NJ 07928 • 8,537
Chatham, NY 12037 • 2,001
Chatham, VA 24531 • 1,390
Chatham □, GA • 202,226
Chatham □, NC • 33,415
Chatom, AL 36518 • 1,122
Chatsworth, GA 30705 • 2,493
Chatsworth, IL 60921 • 1,187
Chattahoochee, FL 32324 • 5,332
Chattahoochee □, GA • 21,732
Chattanooga, TN 37401–99 • 169,558
Chattaroy, WV 25667 • 1,200
Chattooga □, GA • 21,856
Chaumont, NY 13622 • 620
Chauncey, OH 45719 • 1,050
Chautauqua □, KS • 5,016
Chautauqua □, NY • 146,925
Chauvin, LA 70344 • 3,338
Chaves □, NM • 51,103
Chazy, NY 12921 • 800
Cheatham □, TN • 21,616
Chebanse, IL 60922 • 1,191
Cheboygan, MI 49721 • 5,106
Cheboygan □, MI • 20,649
Checotah, OK 74426 • 3,454
Cheektowaga, NY 14225 • 100,400
Chehalis, WA 98532 • 6,100
Chelan, WA 98816 • 2,802
Chelan □, WA • 45,061
Chelmsford, MA 01824 • 31,174
Chelsea, MA 02150 • 25,431
Chelsea, MI 48118 • 3,816
Chelsea, OK 74016 • 1,754
Chelsea Estates, DE 19720 • 1,500
Cheltenham, PA 19012 • 7,700
Chelyan, WV 25035 • 800
Chemung □, NY • 97,656
Chenango □, NY • 49,344
Chenango Bridge, NY 13745 • 2,600
Cheney, KS 67025 • 1,404
Cheney, WA 99004 • 7,630
Cheneyville, LA 71325 • 865
Chenoa, IL 61726 • 1,847
Chenoweth, OR 97058 • 2,820
Chepachet, RI 02814 • 900
Cheraw, SC 29520 • 5,654
Cheriton, VA 23316 • 695
Cherokee, AL 35616 • 1,589
Cherokee, IA 51012 • 7,004
Cherokee, KS 66724 • 775
Cherokee, OK 73728 • 2,105
Cherokee □, AL • 18,760
Cherokee □, GA • 51,699
Cherokee □, IA • 16,238
Cherokee □, KS • 22,304
Cherokee □, NC • 18,933
Cherokee □, OK • 30,684
Cherokee □, SC • 40,983
Cherokee □, TX • 38,127
Cherokee Village, AR 72525 • 3,200
Cherry □, NE • 6,758
Cherry Creek, NY 14723 • 677
Cherry Hill, NJ 08002–03 • 68,785
Cherry Hills Village, CO 80110 • 5,127
Cherryvale, KS 67335 • 2,769
Cherry Valley, AR 72324 • 729
Cherry Valley, IL 61016 • 946
Cherry Valley, MA 01611 • 1,400
Cherry Valley, NY 13320 • 684
Cherryville, NC 28021 • 4,844
Chesaning, MI 48616 • 2,656
Chesapeake, OH 45619 • 1,370
Chesapeake, VA 23320–25 • 114,486
Chesapeake, WV 25315 • 2,364
Chesapeake Beach, MD 20732 • 1,408
Chesapeake City, MD 21915 • 899
Cheshire, CT 06410 • 5,722
Cheshire, MA 01225 • 1,100
Cheshire □, NH • 62,116
Chesilhurst, NJ 08089 • 1,590
Chesnee, SC 29323 • 1,069
Chester, CA 96020 • 1,756
Chester, CT 06412 • 1,388
Chester, IL 62233 • 8,401
Chester, MA 01011 • 750
Chester, MT 59522 • 963
Chester, NJ 07930 • 1,433
Chester, NY 10918 • 1,910
Chester, PA 19013–16 • 45,794
Chester, SC 29706 • 6,820
Chester, VA 23831 • 7,000
Chester, WV 26034 • 3,297
Chester □, PA • 316,660
Chester □, SC • 30,148
Chester □, TN • 12,727
Chesterfield, IN 46017 • 2,701
Chesterfield, SC 29709 • 1,432
Chesterfield □, SC • 38,161
Chesterfield □, VA • 141,372
Chesterton, IN 46304 • 8,531
Chestertown, MD 21620 • 3,300
Chestertown, NY 12817 • 750
Chester Township, PA 19013 • 5,687
Chestnut Hill Estates, DE 19713 • 2,000
Cheswick, PA 15024 • 2,336
Chetek, WI 54728 • 1,931
Chetopa, KS 67336 • 1,751
Cheverly, MD 20785 • 5,751
Cheviot, OH 45211 • 9,888
Chevy Chase, MD 20815 • 12,232
Chewelah, WA 99109 • 1,888
Cheyenne, OK 73628 • 1,207
Cheyenne, WY 82001–09 • 47,283
Cheyenne □, CO • 2,153
Cheyenne □, KS • 3,678
Cheyenne □, NE • 10,057
Cheyenne Canon, CO 80907 • 1,100
Cheyenne Wells, CO 80810 • 950
Chicago, IL 60601–99 • 3,005,072
Chicago Heights, IL 60411 • 37,026
Chicago Ridge, IL 60415 • 13,473
Chickamauga, GA 30707 • 2,232
Chickasaw, AL 36611 • 7,402
Chickasaw □, IA • 15,437
Chickasaw □, MS • 17,853
Chickasha, OK 73018 • 15,828
Chico, CA 95926 • 26,603
Chico, TX 76030 • 890
Chico, WA 98310 • 750
Chicopee, GA 30501 • 900
Chicopee, MA 01013–22 • 55,112
Chicora, PA 16025 • 1,192
Chicot □, AR • 17,793
Chiefland, FL 32626 • 1,986
Childersburg, AL 35044 • 5,084
Childress, TX 79201 • 5,817
Childress □, TX • 6,950
Chilhowie, VA 24319 • 1,269
Chili Center, NY 14624 • 5,300
Chillicothe, IL 61523 • 6,176
Chillicothe, MO 64601 • 9,089
Chillicothe, OH 45601 • 23,420
Chillicothe, TX 79225 • 1,052
Chillum, MD 20783 • 14,900
Chiloquin, OR 97624 • 778
Chilton, WI 53014 • 2,965
Chilton □, AL • 30,612
Chimayo, NM 87522 • 1,993
China Grove, NC 28023 • 2,081
Chincoteague, VA 23336 • 1,607
Chinle, AZ 86503 • 2,815
Chino, CA 91710 • 40,165
Chinook, MT 59523 • 1,660
Chinook, WA 98614 • 650
Chino Valley, AZ 86323 • 2,858
Chipley, FL 32428 • 3,330
Chippewa □, MI • 29,029
Chippewa □, MN • 14,941
Chippewa □, WI • 52,127
Chippewa Falls, WI 54729 • 12,270
Chisago □, MN • 25,717
Chisago City, MN 55013 • 1,634
Chisholm, ME 04239 • 1,796
Chisholm, MN 55719 • 5,930
Chittenango, NY 13037 • 4,290
Chittenden □, VT • 115,534
Chocowinity, NC 27817 • 644
Choctaw, OK 73020 • 7,520
Choctaw □, AL • 16,839
Choctaw □, MS • 8,996
Choctaw □, OK • 17,203
Choteau, MT 59422 • 1,798
Choudrant, LA 71227 • 809
Chouteau, OK 74337 • 1,559
Chouteau □, MT • 6,092
Chowan □, NC • 12,558
Chowchilla, CA 93610 • 5,122
Chrisman, IL 61924 • 1,413
Christian □, IL • 36,446
Christian □, KY • 66,878
Christian □, MO • 22,402
Christiana, PA 17509 • 1,183
Christiansburg, VA 24073 • 10,345
Christmas, FL 32709 • 1,200
Christopher, IL 62822 • 3,086
Christoval, TX 76935 • 700
Chubbuck, ID 83202 • 7,052
Chula Vista, CA 92010–12 • 83,927
Church Hill, TN 37642 • 4,110
Churchill, OH 44505 • 7,700
Churchill □, NV • 13,917
Church Point, LA 70525 • 4,599
Churchton, MD 20733 • 800
Churchville, NY 14428 • 1,399
Churubusco, IN 46723 • 1,638
Cibecue, AZ 85911 • 950
Cibola □, NM • 30,102
Cicero, IL 60650 • 61,232
Cicero, IN 46034 • 2,557
Cimarron, KS 67835 • 1,491
Cimarron, NM 87714 • 888
Cimarron □, OK • 3,648
Cincinnati, OH 45201–99 • 385,457
Cinnaminson, NJ 08077 • 16,072
Circle, MT 59215 • 931
Circle Pines, MN 55014 • 3,321
Circleville, OH 43113 • 11,700
Cisco, TX 76437 • 4,517
Cisne, IL 62823 • 705
Cissna Park, IL 60924 • 825
Citra, FL 32627 • 1,500
Citronelle, AL 36522 • 2,841
Citrus □, FL • 54,703
Citrus Heights, CA 95610 • 85,911
City of Commerce, CA 90040 • 10,509
City View, SC 29611 • 1,662
Clackamas, OR 97015 • 3,250
Clackamas □, OR • 241,911
Claflin, KS 67525 • 764
Claiborne, LA 71291 • 2,000
Claiborne □, LA • 17,095
Claiborne □, MS • 12,279
Claiborne □, TN • 24,595
Clair-Mel City, FL 33619 • 7,000
Clairton, PA 15025 • 12,188
Clallam □, WA • 51,648
Clanton, AL 35045 • 5,832
Clara City, MN 56222 • 1,574
Clare, MI 48617 • 3,300
Clare □, MI • 23,822
Claremont, CA 91711 • 30,950
Claremont, NH 03743 • 14,557
Claremont, NC 28610 • 880
Claremore, OK 74017 • 12,085
Clarence, IA 52216 • 1,001
Clarence, LA 71414 • 612
Clarence, MO 63437 • 1,147
Clarendon, AR 72029 • 2,361
Clarendon, PA 16313 • 776
Clarendon, TX 79226 • 2,220
Clarendon □, SC • 27,464
Clarendon Hills, IL 60514 • 6,870
Clarinda, IA 51632 • 5,458
Clarion, IA 50525 • 3,060
Clarion, PA 16214 • 6,198
Clarion □, PA • 43,362
Clarissa, MN 56440 • 663
Clark, NJ 07066 • 16,699
Clark, SD 57225 • 1,351
Clark □, AR • 23,326
Clark □, ID • 798
Clark □, IL • 16,913
Clark □, IN • 88,838
Clark □, KS • 2,599
Clark □, KY • 28,322
Clark □, MO • 8,493
Clark □, NV • 463,087
Clark □, OH • 150,236
Clark □, SD • 4,894
Clark □, WA • 192,227
Clark □, WI • 32,910
Clarkdale, AZ 86324 • 1,512
Clarke □, AL • 27,702
Clarke □, GA • 74,498
Clarke □, IA • 8,612
Clarke □, MS • 16,945
Clarke □, VA • 9,965
Clarkesville, GA 30523 • 1,348
Clarkfield, MN 56223 • 1,171
Clarks, LA 71415 • 931
Clarksboro, NJ 08020 • 800
Clarksburg, WV 26301 • 22,371
Clarksdale, MS 38614 • 21,137
Clarks Grove, MN 56016 • 620
Clarks Hill, IN 47930 • 653
Clarkson, KY 42726 • 666
Clarkson, NE 68629 • 817
Clarks Summit, PA 18411 • 5,272
Clarkston, GA 30021 • 4,539
Clarkston, MI 48016 • 968
Clarkston, WA 99403 • 6,903
Clarksville, AR 72830 • 5,237
Clarksville, IN 47130 • 15,164
Clarksville, IA 50619 • 1,424
Clarksville, TN 37040–43 • 54,777
Clarksville, TX 75426 • 4,917
Clarksville, VA 23927 • 1,468
Clarkton, MO 63837 • 1,228
Clarkton, NC 28433 • 664
Clatskanie, OR 97016 • 1,648
Clatsop □, OR • 32,489
Claude, TX 79019 • 1,112
Clawson, MI 48017 • 15,103
Claxton, GA 30417 • 2,694
Clay, KY 42404 • 1,356
Clay, WV 25043 • 940
Clay □, AL • 13,703
Clay □, AR • 20,616
Clay □, FL • 67,052
Clay □, GA • 3,553
Clay □, IL • 15,283
Clay □, IN • 24,862
Clay □, IA • 19,576
Clay □, KS • 9,802
Clay □, KY • 22,752
Clay □, MN • 49,327
Clay □, MS • 21,082
Clay □, MO • 136,488
Clay □, NE • 8,106
Clay □, NC • 6,619
Clay □, SD • 13,689
Clay □, TN • 7,676
Clay □, TX • 9,582
Clay □, WV • 11,265
Clay Center, KS 67432 • 4,948
Clay Center, NE 68933 • 962
Clay City, IL 62824 • 1,038
Clay City, IN 47841 • 883
Clay City, KY 40312 • 1,276
Claymont, DE 19702 • 10,022
Claypool, AZ 85532 • 2,362
Claysburg, PA 16625 • 1,516
Claysville, PA 15323 • 1,029
Clayton, AL 36016 • 1,589
Clayton, DE 19938 • 1,216
Clayton, GA 30525 • 1,838
Clayton, IL 62324 • 889
Clayton, IN 46118 • 703
Clayton, LA 71326 • 1,204
Clayton, MO 63105 • 14,273
Clayton, NJ 08312 • 6,013
Clayton, NM 88415 • 2,968
Clayton, NC 27520 • 4,091
Clayton, NY 13624 • 1,816
Clayton, OK 74536 • 833
Clayton □, GA • 150,357
Clayton □, IA • 21,098
Clear Creek □, CO • 7,308
Clearfield, KY 40313 • 1,250
Clearfield, PA 16830 • 7,580
Clearfield, UT 84015 • 17,982
Clearfield □, PA • 83,578
Clearlake, CA 95422 • 13,300
Clear Lake, IA 50428 • 7,458
Clear Lake, SD 57226 • 1,310
Clearlake, WA 98235 • 900
Clear Lake, WI 54005 • 899
Clear Lake City, TX 77062 • 8,700
Clear Lake Shores, TX 77565 • 755
Clearwater, FL 33515–20 • 85,528
Clearwater, KS 67026 • 1,684
Clearwater, SC 29822 • 3,967
Clearwater □, ID • 10,390
Clearwater □, MN • 8,761
Cleburne, TX 76031 • 19,218
Cleburne □, AL • 12,595
Cleburne □, AR • 16,909
Cle Elum, WA 98922 • 1,773
Cleland Heights, DE 19805 • 1,500
Clementon, NJ 08021 • 5,764
Clemmons, NC 27012 • 7,401
Clemson, SC 29631 • 8,118
Clendenin, WV 25045 • 1,373
Cleona, PA 17042 • 2,003
Clermont, FL 32711 • 5,461
Clermont, IA 52135 • 602
Clermont □, OH • 128,483
Cleveland, GA 30528 • 1,578
Cleveland, MN 56017 • 699
Cleveland, MS 38732 • 14,524
Cleveland, NY 13042 • 855
Cleveland, OH 44101–99 • 573,822
Cleveland, OK 74020 • 2,972
Cleveland, TN 37311–12 • 26,415
Cleveland, TX 77327 • 5,977
Cleveland, WI 53015 • 1,270
Cleveland □, AR • 7,868
Cleveland □, NC • 83,435
Cleveland □, OK • 133,173
Cleveland Heights, OH 44118 • 56,438
Cleves, OH 45002 • 2,094
Clewiston, FL 33440 • 5,219
Cliffside Park, NJ 07010 • 21,464
Cliffwood Beach, NJ 07735 • 6,300
Clifton, AZ 85533 • 4,245
Clifton, CO 81520 • 5,223
Clifton, IL 60927 • 1,390
Clifton, KS 66937 • 695
Clifton, NJ 07011–15 • 74,388
Clifton, SC 29324 • 800
Clifton, TN 38425 • 773
Clifton, TX 76634 • 3,063
Clifton Forge, VA 24422 • 5,046
Clifton Heights, PA 19018 • 7,320
Clifton Knolls, NY 12065 • 4,000
Clifton Springs, NY 14432 • 2,039
Climax, MI 49034 • 619
Clinch □, GA • 6,660
Clinchco, VA 24226 • 1,000
Clint, TX 79836 • 1,314
Clinton, AR 72031 • 1,284
Clinton, CT 06413 • 11,195
Clinton, IL 61727 • 8,014
Clinton, IN 47842 • 5,267
Clinton, IA 52732 • 32,828
Clinton, KY 42031 • 1,720
Clinton, LA 70722 • 1,919
Clinton, ME 04927 • 1,305
Clinton, MD 20735 • 16,438
Clinton, MA 01510 • 12,771
Clinton, MI 49236 • 2,342
Clinton, MN 56225 • 622
Clinton, MS 39056 • 14,660
Clinton, MO 64735 • 8,366
Clinton, NJ 08809 • 1,910
Clinton, NC 28328 • 7,552
Clinton, NY 13323 • 2,107
Clinton, OK 73601 • 8,796
Clinton, SC 29325 • 8,596
Clinton, TN 37716 • 5,245
Clinton, UT 84015 • 5,777
Clinton, WA 98236 • 2,000
Clinton, WI 53525 • 1,751
Clinton □, IL • 32,617
Clinton □, IN • 31,545
Clinton □, IA • 57,122
Clinton □, KY • 9,321
Clinton □, MI • 55,893
Clinton □, MO • 15,916
Clinton □, NY • 80,750
Clinton □, OH • 34,603
Clinton □, PA • 38,971
Clinton Township, MI 48043 • 72,400
Clintonville, WI 54929 • 4,567
Clintwood, VA 24228 • 1,369
Clio, AL 36017 • 1,224
Clio, MI 48420 • 2,669
Clio, SC 29525 • 1,031
Clive, IA 50053 • 6,064
Cloquet, MN 55720 • 11,142
Closter, NJ 07624 • 8,164
Cloud □, KS • 12,494
Clover, SC 29710 • 3,451
Cloverdale, CA 95425 • 3,989
Cloverdale, IN 46120 • 1,357
Cloverdale, VA 24077 • 850
Cloverleaf, TX 77015 • 11,800
Cloverport, KY 40111 • 1,585
Clovis, CA 93612 • 33,021
Clovis, NM 88101 • 31,194
Clute, TX 77531 • 9,577
Clyde, KS 66938 • 909
Clyde, NC 28721 • 1,008
Clyde, NY 14433 • 2,491
Clyde, OH 43410 • 5,489
Clyde, TX 79510 • 2,562
Clymer, PA 15728 • 1,761
Coachella, CA 92236 • 9,129
Coahoma, TX 79511 • 1,069
Coahoma □, MS • 36,918
Coal □, OK • 6,041
Coal City, IL 60416 • 3,028
Coaldale, PA 18218 • 2,762
Coal Fork, WV 25306 • 900
Coalgate, OK 74538 • 2,001
Coal Grove, OH 45638 • 2,602
Coal Hill, AR 72832 • 859
Coalinga, CA 93210 • 6,593
Coalmont, TN 37313 • 625
Coalport, PA 16627 • 739
Coalton, OH 45621 • 639
Coalville, UT 84017 • 1,031
Coalwood, WV 24824 • 1,100
Coatesville, PA 19320 • 10,698
Coats, NC 27521 • 1,385
Cobb □, GA • 297,718
Cobden, IL 62920 • 1,210
Cobleskill, NY 12043 • 5,272
Coburg, OR 97401 • 699
Cochise □, AZ • 85,686
Cochituate, MA 01778 • 6,126
Cochran, GA 31014 • 5,121
Cochran □, TX • 4,825
Cochranton, PA 16314 • 1,240
Cocke □, TN • 28,792
Cockeysville, MD 21030 • 17,013
Cockrell Hill, TX 75211 • 3,262
Cocoa, FL 32922–27 • 16,096
Cocoa Beach, FL 32931 • 10,926
Cocoa West, FL 32922 • 6,432
Coconino □, AZ • 75,008
Coconut Creek, FL 33060 • 6,288
Codington □, SD • 20,885
Cody, WY 82414 • 6,790
Coeburn, VA 24230 • 2,625
Coeur d'Alene, ID 83814 • 20,054
Coffee □, AL • 38,533
Coffee □, GA • 26,894
Coffee □, TN • 38,311

Coffeen, IL 62017 • *842*
Coffeeville, MS 38922 • *1,129*
Coffey □, KS • *9,370*
Coffeyville, KS 67337 • *15,185*
Coggon, IA 52218 • *639*
Cohasset, MA 02025 • *5,300*
Cohocton, NY 14826 • *902*
Cohoes, NY 12047 • *18,144*
Cokato, MN 55321 • *2,056*
Coke □, TX • *3,196*
Colbert, OK 74733 • *1,122*
Colbert □, AL • *54,519*
Colby, KS 67701 • *5,544*
Colby, WI 54421 • *1,496*
Colchester, CT 06415 • *3,190*
Colchester, IL 62326 • *1,729*
Cold Spring, KY 41076 • *2,117*
Cold Spring, MN 56320 • *2,294*
Cold Spring, NJ 08204 • *850*
Cold Spring Harbor, NY 11724 • *5,490*
Coldwater, KS 67029 • *989*
Coldwater, MI 49036 • *9,461*
Coldwater, MS 38618 • *1,505*
Coldwater, OH 45828 • *4,220*
Cole □, MO • *56,663*
Colebrook, NH 03576 • *1,131*
Cole Camp, MO 65325 • *1,022*
Coleman, FL 34255 • *1,022*
Coleman, MI 48618 • *1,429*
Coleman, TX 76834 • *5,960*
Coleman, WI 54112 • *852*
Coleman □, TX • *10,439*
Coleraine, MN 55722 • *1,116*
Coleridge, NE 68727 • *673*
Coles □, IL • *52,260*
Colfax, CA 95713 • *981*
Colfax, IL 61728 • *920*
Colfax, IN 46035 • *823*
Colfax, IA 50054 • *2,234*
Colfax, LA 71417 • *1,680*
Colfax, WA 99111 • *2,780*
Colfax, WI 54730 • *1,149*
Colfax □, NE • *9,890*
Colfax □, NM • *13,667*
College, AK 99701 • *800*
Collegedale, TN 37315 • *1,500*
College Park, GA 30337 • *24,632*
College Park, MD 20740 • *23,614*
College Place, WA 99324 • *5,771*
College Station, AR 72053 • *4,000*
College Station, TX 77840 • *37,272*
Collegeville, IN 47978 • *1,059*
Collegeville, PA 19426 • *3,406*
Colleton □, SC • *31,776*
Colleyville, TX 76034 • *6,700*
Collier □, FL • *85,971*
Collierville, TN 38017 • *7,839*
Collin □, TX • *144,576*
Collingdale, PA 19023 • *9,539*
Collingswood, NJ 08108 • *15,838*
Collingsworth □, TX • *4,648*
Collins, GA 30421 • *639*
Collins, MS 39428 • *2,131*
Collins Park, DE 19720 • *2,850*
Collinsville, AL 35961 • *1,383*
Collinsville, CT 06022 • *2,555*
Collinsville, IL 62234 • *19,613*
Collinsville, OK 74021 • *3,556*
Collinsville, VA 24078 • *7,400*
Collinwood, TN 38450 • *1,064*
Colmar Manor, MD 20722 • *1,286*
Colo, IA 50056 • *808*
Coloma, MI 49038 • *1,833*
Colon, MI 49040 • *1,190*
Colonia, NJ 07067 • *20,900*
Colonial Beach, VA 22443 • *2,474*
Colonial Heights, TN 37663 • *6,744*
Colonial Heights, VA 23834 • *16,509*
Colonial Park, PA 17109 • *10,000*
Colonie, NY 12212 • *8,869*
Colorado □, TX • *18,823*
Colorado City, CO 81019 • *950*
Colorado City, TX 79512 • *5,405*
Colorado Springs, CO 80901-99 • *214,821*
Colquitt, GA 31737 • *2,065*
Colquitt □, GA • *35,376*
Colstrip, MT 59323 • *1,476*
Colter Bay, WY 83001 • *2,000*
Colton, CA 92324 • *15,201*
Colton, SD 57018 • *757*
Columbia, AL 36319 • *881*
Columbia, CA 95310 • *950*
Columbia, IL 62236 • *4,269*
Columbia, KY 42728 • *3,710*
Columbia, LA 71418 • *687*
Columbia, MD 21045-46 • *52,518*
Columbia, MS 39429 • *7,733*
Columbia, MO 65201-18 • *62,061*
Columbia, NC 27925 • *758*
Columbia, PA 17512 • *10,466*
Columbia, SC 29201-99 • *100,385*
Columbia, TN 38401 • *26,571*
Columbia □, AR • *26,644*
Columbia □, FL • *35,399*
Columbia □, GA • *40,118*
Columbia □, NY • *59,487*
Columbia □, OR • *35,646*
Columbia □, PA • *61,967*
Columbia □, WA • *4,057*
Columbia □, WI • *43,222*
Columbia City, IN 46725 • *5,091*
Columbia City, OR 97018 • *678*
Columbia Falls, MT 59912 • *3,112*
Columbia Heights, MN 55421 • *20,029*
Columbiana, AL 35051 • *2,655*
Columbiana, OH 44408 • *4,987*
Columbiana □, OH • *113,572*
Columbiaville, MI 48421 • *953*
Columbus, GA 31901-99 • *169,441*
Columbus, IN 47201-03 • *30,614*
Columbus, KS 66725 • *3,426*
Columbus, MS 39701-04 • *27,383*
Columbus, MT 59019 • *1,439*
Columbus, NE 68601 • *17,328*
Columbus, NJ 08022 • *700*
Columbus, NC 28722 • *727*
Columbus, OH 43201-99 • *565,032*
Columbus, TX 78934 • *3,923*
Columbus, WI 53925 • *4,049*
Columbus □, NC • *51,037*
Columbus Grove, OH 45830 • *2,313*
Columbus Junction, IA 52738 • *1,429*
Colusa, CA 95932 • *4,075*
Colusa □, CA • *12,791*
Colver, PA 15927 • *1,175*
Colville, WA 99114 • *4,510*
Colwich, KS 67030 • *935*
Comal □, TX • *36,446*
Comanche, OK 73529 • *1,937*
Comanche, TX 76442 • *4,075*
Comanche □, KS • *2,554*
Comanche □, OK • *112,456*
Comanche □, TX • *12,617*
Combined Locks, WI 54113 • *2,573*
Combs, KY 41729 • *700*
Comer, GA 30629 • *930*
Comfort, TX 78013 • *950*
Commack, NY 11725 • *24,300*
Commerce, GA 30529 • *4,092*
Commerce, OK 74339 • *2,556*
Commerce, TX 75428 • *6,136*
Commerce City, CO 80022 • *16,234*
Common Fence Point, RI 02871 • *850*
Como, MS 38619 • *1,378*
Compton, CA 90220-24 • *81,286*
Comstock, MI 49041 • *5,310*
Concho □, TX • *2,915*
Concord, CA 94518-24 • *103,255*
Concord, MA 01742 • *6,400*
Concord, MI 49237 • *900*
Concord, MO 63851 • *20,896*
Concord, NH 03301-06 • *30,400*
Concord, NC 28025 • *16,942*
Concordia, KS 66901 • *6,847*
Concordia, MO 64020 • *2,129*
Concordia □, LA • *22,981*
Condon, OR 97823 • *783*
Conecuh □, AL • *15,884*
Conejos □, CO • *7,794*
Conemaugh, PA 15909 • *2,128*
Confluence, PA 15424 • *968*
Congers, NY 10920 • *5,000*
Conklin, NY 13748 • *1,900*
Conneaut, OH 44030 • *13,835*
Conneaut Lake, PA 16316 • *767*
Conneautville, PA 16406 • *971*
Connell, WA 99326 • *1,981*
Connellsville, PA 15425 • *10,319*
Connersville, IN 47331 • *17,023*
Conover, NC 28613 • *4,245*
Conrad, IA 50621 • *1,133*
Conrad, MT 59425 • *3,074*
Conroe, TX 77301-05 • *18,034*
Conshohocken, PA 19428 • *8,475*
Constantia, NY 13044 • *900*
Constantine, MI 49042 • *1,680*
Continental, OH 45831 • *1,179*
Contoocook, NH 03229 • *1,499*
Contra Costa □, CA • *656,380*
Converse, IN 46919 • *1,279*
Converse, SC 29329 • *1,173*
Converse □, WY • *14,069*
Convoy, OH 45832 • *1,140*
Conway, AR 72032 • *20,375*
Conway, FL 32809 • *16,000*
Conway, MO 65632 • *601*
Conway, NH 03818 • *1,781*
Conway, NC 27820 • *678*
Conway, PA 15027 • *2,747*
Conway, SC 29526 • *10,240*
Conway □, AR • *19,505*
Conway Springs, KS 67031 • *1,313*
Conyers, GA 30207-08 • *6,567*
Cook, MN 55723 • *800*
Cook □, GA • *13,490*
Cook □, IL • *5,253,655*
Cook □, MN • *4,092*
Cooke □, TX • *27,656*
Cookeville, TN 38501 • *20,535*
Cooleemee, NC 27014 • *1,448*
Coolidge, AZ 85228 • *6,851*
Coolidge, GA 31738 • *736*
Coolidge, TX 76635 • *810*
Coolville, OH 45723 • *649*
Coon Rapids, IA 50058 • *1,448*
Coon Rapids, MN 55433 • *35,826*
Coon Valley, WI 54623 • *758*
Cooper, TX 75432 • *2,338*
Cooper □, MO • *14,643*
Cooper City, FL 33328 • *10,140*
Cooper Road, LA 71107 • *10,000*
Coopersburg, PA 18036 • *2,595*
Cooperstown, ND 58425 • *1,308*
Cooperstown, NY 13326 • *2,342*
Cooperstown, PA 16317 • *644*
Coopersville, MI 49404 • *2,889*
Coos □, NH • *35,147*
Coos □, OR • *64,047*
Coosa □, AL • *11,377*
Coosada, AL 36020 • *980*
Coos Bay, OR 97420 • *14,424*
Copake, NY 12516 • *700*
Copalis Beach, WA 98535 • *800*
Copan, OK 74022 • *960*
Copeland, FL 33926 • *700*
Copenhagen, NY 13626 • *656*
Copiague, NY 11726 • *21,000*
Copiah □, MS • *26,503*
Coplay, PA 18037 • *3,130*
Copperas Cove, TX 76522 • *19,469*
Copperton, UT 84006 • *850*
Coquille, OR 97423 • *4,481*
Coral, PA 15731 • *700*
Coral Gables, FL 33134 • *43,241*
Coralville, IA 52241 • *7,687*
Coram, NY 11727 • *5,400*
Coraopolis, PA 15108 • *7,308*
Corbin, KY 40701 • *8,075*
Corcoran, CA 93212 • *6,454*
Corcoran, MN 55340 • *4,252*
Cordaville, MA 01772 • *1,384*
Cordele, GA 31015 • *11,184*
Cordell, OK 73632 • *3,301*
Cordova, AL 35550 • *3,123*
Cordova, AK 99574 • *1,879*
Cordova, IL 61242 • *697*
Cordova, NC 28330 • *1,200*
Corfu, NY 14036 • *689*
Corinna, ME 04928 • *950*
Corinth, MS 38834 • *13,839*
Corinth, NY 12822 • *2,702*
Cornelia, GA 30531 • *3,203*
Cornelius, NC 28031 • *1,460*
Cornelius, OR 97113 • *4,462*
Cornell, IL 61319 • *603*
Cornell, WI 54732 • *1,583*
Cornersville, TN 37047 • *722*
Corning, AR 72422 • *3,650*
Corning, CA 96021 • *4,745*
Corning, IA 50841 • *1,939*
Corning, NY 14830 • *12,953*
Corning, OH 43730 • *789*
Cornville, AZ 86325 • *800*
Cornwall, PA 17016 • *2,653*
Cornwall On Hudson, NY 12520 • *3,164*
Cornwells Heights, PA 19020 • *8,700*
Corona, CA 91720 • *37,791*
Coronado, CA 92118 • *18,790*
Corpus Christi, TX 78401-99 • *231,999*
Correctionville, IA 51016 • *935*
Corrigan, TX 75939 • *1,770*
Corriganville, MD 21524 • *1,020*
Corry, PA 16407 • *7,149*
Corsica, SD 57328 • *644*
Corsicana, TX 75110 • *21,712*
Corson □, SD • *5,196*
Corte Madera, CA 94925 • *8,074*
Cortez, CO 81321 • *7,095*
Cortez, FL 33522 • *1,450*
Cortland, IL 60112 • *1,019*
Cortland, NY 13045 • *20,138*
Cortland, OH 44410 • *5,011*
Cortland □, NY • *48,820*
Corunna, MI 48817 • *3,206*
Corvallis, OR 97330-33 • *40,960*
Corydon, IN 47112 • *2,724*
Corydon, IA 50060 • *1,818*
Corydon, KY 42406 • *874*
Coryell □, TX • *56,767*
Coshocton, OH 43812 • *13,405*
Coshocton □, OH • *36,024*
Cosmopolis, WA 98537 • *1,575*
Costa Mesa, CA 92626-27 • *82,562*
Costilla □, CO • *3,071*
Cottage Grove, MN 55016 • *18,994*
Cottage Grove, OR 97424 • *7,148*
Cotter, AR 72626 • *920*
Cottle □, TX • *2,947*
Cotton □, OK • *7,338*
Cottondale, AL 35453 • *2,300*
Cottondale, FL 32431 • *1,056*
Cotton Plant, AR 72036 • *1,323*
Cottonport, LA 71327 • *1,911*
Cotton Valley, LA 71018 • *1,445*
Cottonwood, AL 36320 • *1,352*
Cottonwood, AZ 86326 • *4,550*
Cottonwood, CA 96022 • *1,553*
Cottonwood, ID 83522 • *941*
Cottonwood, MN 56229 • *924*
Cottonwood, UT 84121 • *11,554*
Cottonwood □, MN • *14,854*
Cottonwood Falls, KS 66845 • *954*
Cottonwood Heights, UT 84121 • *18,000*
Cotuit, MA 02635 • *1,300*
Cotulla, TX 78014 • *3,912*
Coudersport, PA 16915 • *2,791*
Coulee Dam, WA 99116 • *1,412*
Coulterville, IL 62237 • *1,118*
Council, ID 83612 • *917*
Council Bluffs, IA 51501 • *56,449*
Council Grove, KS 66846 • *2,381*
Country Club Hills, IL 60477 • *14,676*
Country Homes, WA 99218 • *3,850*
Countryside, IL 60525 • *6,538*
Coupeville, WA 98239 • *1,006*
Courtland, VA 23837 • *976*
Coushatta, LA 71019 • *2,084*
Covedale, OH 45238 • *6,530*
Covelo, CA 95428 • *1,448*
Coventry, CT 06238 • *3,769*
Coventry, DE 19720 • *830*
Coventry, RI 02816 • *8,000*
Covina, CA 91722-24 • *33,751*
Covington, GA 30209 • *10,586*
Covington, IN 47932 • *2,883*
Covington, KY 41011-19 • *49,563*
Covington, LA 70433 • *7,892*
Covington, OH 45318 • *2,610*
Covington, OK 73730 • *715*
Covington, TN 38019 • *6,065*
Covington, VA 24426 • *9,063*
Covington □, AL • *36,850*
Covington □, MS • *15,927*
Cowan, TN 37318 • *1,790*
Cowden, IL 62422 • *623*
Cowen, WV 26206 • *723*
Coweta, OK 74429 • *4,554*
Coweta □, GA • *39,268*
Cowley □, KS • *36,824*
Cowlitz □, WA • *79,548*
Cowpens, SC 29330 • *2,023*
Coxsackie, NY 12051 • *2,786*
Cozad, NE 69130 • *4,453*
Crab Orchard, KY 40419 • *843*
Crab Orchard, TN 37723 • *1,065*
Crab Orchard, WV 25827 • *1,900*
Crabtree, PA 15624 • *1,021*
Crafton, PA 15205 • *7,623*
Craig, CO 81625 • *8,133*
Craig □, OK • *15,014*
Craig □, VA • *3,948*
Craighead □, AR • *63,239*
Craigmont, ID 83523 • *617*
Craigsville, VA 24430 • *845*
Craigsville, WV 26205 • *900*
Cramerton, NC 28032 • *1,869*
Cranbury, NJ 08512 • *1,255*
Crandall, TX 75114 • *831*
Crandon, WI 54520 • *1,969*
Crane, AZ 85364 • *2,400*
Crane, MO 65633 • *1,185*
Crane, TX 79731 • *3,622*
Crane □, TX • *4,600*
Cranesville, PA 16410 • *703*
Cranford, NJ 07016 • *24,573*
Cranston, RI 02910 • *71,992*
Craven □, NC • *71,043*
Crawford, NE 69339 • *1,315*
Crawford □, AR • *36,892*
Crawford □, GA • *7,684*
Crawford □, IL • *20,818*
Crawford □, IN • *9,820*
Crawford □, IA • *18,935*
Crawford □, KS • *37,916*
Crawford □, MI • *9,465*
Crawford □, MO • *18,300*
Crawford □, OH • *50,075*
Crawford □, PA • *88,869*
Crawford □, WI • *16,556*
Crawfordsville, AR 72327 • *685*
Crawfordsville, IN 47933 • *13,325*
Crawfordville, FL 32327 • *1,110*
Creal Springs, IL 62922 • *845*
Creede, CO 81130 • *610*
Creedmoor, NC 27522 • *1,641*
Creek □, OK • *59,016*
Creighton, NE 68729 • *1,341*
Creighton, PA 15030 • *1,658*
Crenshaw, MS 38621 • *1,019*
Crenshaw □, AL • *14,110*
Creola, AL 36525 • *1,652*
Cresaptown, MD 21502 • *4,645*
Crescent, OK 73028 • *1,651*
Crescent, OR 97733 • *700*
Crescent City, CA 95531 • *3,075*
Crescent City, FL 32012 • *1,722*
Crescent City, IL 60928 • *641*
Crescent Springs, KY 41016 • *1,951*
Cresco, IA 52136 • *3,860*
Cresskill, NJ 07626 • *7,609*
Cresson, PA 16630 • *2,184*
Cressona, PA 17929 • *1,810*
Crested Butte, CO 81224 • *959*
Cresthaven, FL 33064 • *2,400*
Crest Hill, IL 60435 • *9,252*
Crestline, OH 44827 • *5,406*
Creston, IA 50801 • *8,429*
Creston, OH 44217 • *1,828*
Crestview, FL 32536 • *7,617*
Crestview, HI 96797 • *1,000*
Crestwood, IL 60445 • *10,852*
Crestwood, MO 63126 • *12,815*
Crestwood Village, NJ 08759 • *7,965*
Creswell, OR 97426 • *1,770*
Crete, IL 60417 • *5,417*
Crete, NE 68333 • *4,872*
Creve Coeur, IL 61611 • *6,851*
Creve Coeur, MO 63141 • *11,757*
Crewe, VA 23930 • *2,325*
Cricket, NC 28659 • *2,307*
Cridersville, OH 45806 • *1,843*
Cripple Creek, CO 80813 • *655*
Crisfield, MD 21817 • *2,924*
Crisp □, GA • *19,489*
Crittenden □, AR • *49,499*
Crittenden □, KY • *9,207*
Crivitz, WI 54114 • *1,041*
Crocker, MO 65452 • *979*
Crockett, CA 94525 • *2,900*
Crockett, TX 75835 • *7,405*
Crockett □, TN • *14,941*
Crockett □, TX • *4,608*
Crofton, KY 42217 • *823*
Crofton, MD 21114 • *12,009*
Crofton, NE 68730 • *948*
Croghan, NY 13327 • *703*
Cromona, KY 41810 • *700*
Cromwell, CT 06416 • *10,100*
Crook □, OR • *13,091*
Crook □, WY • *5,308*
Crookston, MN 56716 • *8,628*
Crooksville, OH 43731 • *2,766*
Crosby, MN 56441 • *2,218*
Crosby, ND 58730 • *1,469*
Crosby, TX 77532 • *1,450*
Crosby □, TX • *8,859*
Crosbyton, TX 79322 • *2,289*
Cross □, AR • *20,434*
Cross City, FL 32628 • *2,154*
Crossett, AR 71635 • *6,706*
Cross Hill, SC 29332 • *604*
Crosslake, MN 56442 • *1,064*
Cross Lanes, WV 25313 • *3,500*
Cross Mill, NC 28752 • *1,200*
Cross Plains, TN 37049 • *655*
Cross Plains, TX 76443 • *1,240*
Cross Plains, WI 53528 • *2,156*
Crossville, AL 35962 • *1,222*
Crossville, IL 62827 • *944*
Crossville, TN 38555 • *6,394*
Croswell, MI 48422 • *2,073*
Crothersville, IN 47229 • *1,747*
Croton-on-Hudson, NY 10520 • *6,889*
Crouse, NC 28033 • *900*
Crow Agency, MT 59022 • *750*
Crowder, MS 38622 • *789*
Crowell, TX 79227 • *1,509*
Crowley, LA 70526 • *16,036*
Crowley, TX 76036 • *5,852*
Crowley □, CO • *2,988*
Crown Point, IN 46307 • *16,455*
Crown Point, LA 70072 • *1,016*
Crown Point, NE 68122 • *700*
Crownpoint, NM 87313 • *1,134*
Crown Point, NY 12928 • *900*
Crow Wing □, MN • *41,722*
Croydon, PA 19020 • *10,000*
Crozet, VA 22932 • *1,433*
Crucible, PA 15325 • *800*
Crystal, MN 55428 • *25,543*
Crystal Bay, NV 89402 • *1,200*
Crystal Beach, FL 34256 • *1,450*
Crystal City, MO 63019 • *3,618*
Crystal City, TX 78839 • *8,334*
Crystal Falls, MI 49920 • *1,965*
Crystal Lake, FL 33803 • *6,827*
Crystal Lake, IL 60014 • *18,590*
Crystal Lawns, IL 60435 • *2,800*
Crystal Manor, IL 60014 • *750*
Crystal River, FL 32629 • *2,778*
Crystal Springs, FL 34257 • *800*
Crystal Springs, MS 39059 • *4,902*
Cuba, IL 61427 • *1,648*
Cuba, MO 65453 • *2,120*
Cuba, NM 87013 • *609*
Cuba, NY 14727 • *1,739*
Cuba City, WI 53807 • *2,129*
Cucamonga, CA 91730 • *55,250*
Cudahy, CA 90201 • *17,984*
Cudahy, WI 53110 • *19,547*
Cuero, TX 77954 • *7,124*
Culberson □, TX • *3,315*
Culbertson, MT 59218 • *887*
Culbertson, NE 69024 • *767*
Cullen, LA 71021 • *1,869*
Cullman, AL 35055 • *13,084*
Cullman □, AL • *61,642*
Culloden, WV 25510 • *1,500*
Cullom, IL 60929 • *608*
Cullowhee, NC 28723 • *2,000*
Culpeper, VA 22701 • *6,621*
Culpeper □, VA • *22,620*
Culver, IN 46511 • *1,601*
Culver City, CA 90230-32 • *38,139*
Cumberland, KY 40823 • *3,712*
Cumberland, MD 21502 • *25,933*
Cumberland, NC 28331 • *900*
Cumberland, WI 54829 • *1,983*
Cumberland □, IL • *11,062*
Cumberland □, KY • *7,289*
Cumberland □, ME • *215,789*
Cumberland □, NJ • *132,866*
Cumberland □, NC • *247,160*
Cumberland □, PA • *178,541*
Cumberland □, TN • *28,676*
Cumberland □, VA • *7,881*
Cumberland Center, ME 04021 • *2,015*
Cumberland Foreside, ME 04110 • *1,000*
Cumberland Hill, RI 02864 • *5,421*
Cuming □, NE • *11,664*
Cumming, GA 30130 • *2,094*
Cupertino, CA 95014 • *34,265*
Currituck □, NC • *11,089*
Curry □, NM • *42,019*
Curry □, OR • *16,992*
Curtice, OH 43412 • *800*
Curtis, NE 69025 • *1,014*
Curtisville, PA 15032 • *1,337*
Curwensville, PA 16833 • *3,116*
Cushing, OK 74023 • *7,720*
Cusseta, GA 31805 • *1,218*
Custer, SD 57730 • *1,830*
Custer □, CO • *1,528*
Custer □, ID • *3,385*
Custer □, MT • *13,109*
Custer □, NE • *13,877*

Custer □, OK • *25,995*
Custer □, SD • *6,000*
Cut Bank, MT 59427 • *3,688*
Cutchogue, NY 11935 • *1,000*
Cuthbert, GA 31740 • *4,340*
Cutler Ridge, FL 33157 • *20,886*
Cutlerville, MI 49508 • *8,256*
Cut Off, LA 70345 • *5,049*
Cuyahoga □, OH • *1,498,400*
Cuyahoga Falls, OH 44221-24 • *43,890*
Cygnet, OH 43413 • *646*
Cynthiana, IN 47612 • *874*
Cynthiana, KY 41031 • *5,881*
Cypress, CA 90630 • *40,391*
Cypress, TX 77429 • *700*
Cypress Quarters, FL 33472 • *1,479*
Cyril, OK 73029 • *1,220*

D

Dacono, CO 80514 • *2,321*
Dacula, GA 30211 • *1,577*
Dade □, FL • *1,625,781*
Dade □, GA • *12,318*
Dade □, MO • *7,383*
Dade City, FL 33525 • *4,923*
Dadeville, AL 36853 • *3,263*
Daggett, CA 92327 • *650*
Daggett □, UT • *769*
Dahlonega, GA 30533 • *2,844*
Daingerfield, TX 75638 • *3,030*
Daisetta, TX 77533 • *1,177*
Dakota □, MN • *194,279*
Dakota □, NE • *16,573*
Dakota City, IA 50529 • *1,072*
Dakota City, NE 68731 • *1,440*
Dale, IN 47523 • *1,693*
Dale □, AL • *47,821*
Dale City, VA 22193 • *23,000*
Daleville, AL 36322 • *4,250*
Daleville, IN 47334 • *2,000*
Dalhart, TX 79022 • *6,854*
Dallam □, TX • *6,531*
Dallas, GA 30132 • *2,508*
Dallas, NC 28034 • *3,340*
Dallas, OR 97338 • *8,530*
Dallas, PA 18612 • *2,679*
Dallas, TX 75201-99 • *904,078*
Dallas □, AL • *53,981*
Dallas □, AR • *10,515*
Dallas □, IA • *29,513*
Dallas □, MO • *12,096*
Dallas □, TX • *1,556,390*
Dallas Center, IA 50063 • *1,360*
Dallas City, IL 62330 • *1,408*
Dallastown, PA 17313 • *3,949*
Dalton, GA 30720 • *20,939*
Dalton, MA 01226 • *6,797*
Dalton, OH 44618 • *1,357*
Dalton, PA 18414 • *1,383*
Dalton Gardens, ID 83814 • *1,795*
Daly City, CA 94014-17 • *78,519*
Dalzell, IL 61320 • *824*
Damariscotta, ME 04543 • *950*
Damascus, MD 20872 • *4,129*
Damascus, VA 24236 • *1,330*
Damon, TX 77430 • *700*
Dana, IN 47847 • *803*
Danbury, CT 06810-17 • *60,470*
Danbury, TX 77534 • *1,357*
Dandridge, TN 37725 • *1,383*
Dane □, WI • *323,545*
Dania, FL 33004 • *11,811*
Daniels □, MT • *2,835*
Danielson, CT 06239 • *4,553*
Dannemora, NY 12929 • *3,770*
Dansville, NY 14437 • *4,979*
Dante, VA 24237 • *1,200*
Danvers, IL 61732 • *921*
Danvers, MA 01923 • *24,100*
Danville, AR 72833 • *1,698*
Danville, CA 94526 • *26,000*
Danville, IL 61832-33 • *38,985*
Danville, IN 46122 • *4,220*
Danville, IA 52623 • *994*
Danville, KY 40422 • *12,942*
Danville, OH 43014 • *1,127*
Danville, PA 17821 • *5,239*
Danville, VA 24541-43 • *45,642*
Danville, WV 25053 • *727*
Daphne, AL 36526 • *3,406*
Darby, PA 19023 • *11,513*
Darbydale, OH 43123 • *825*
Dardanelle, AR 72834 • *3,621*
Dare □, NC • *13,377*
Darien, CT 06820 • *18,892*
Darien, GA 31305 • *1,731*
Darien, IL 60559 • *14,536*
Darien, WI 53114 • *1,152*
Darke □, OH • *55,096*
Darley Woods, DE 19810 • *1,400*
Darlington, IN 47940 • *811*
Darlington, SC 29532 • *7,989*
Darlington, WI 53530 • *2,300*
Darlington □, SC • *62,717*
Darrington, WA 98241 • *1,064*
Dassel, MN 55325 • *1,066*
Dauphin, PA 17018 • *901*
Dauphin □, PA • *232,317*
Davenport, FL 33837 • *1,509*
Davenport, IA 52801-99 • *103,264*
Davenport, OK 74026 • *974*
Davenport, WA 99122 • *1,559*
David City, NE 68632 • *2,514*
Davidson, NC 28036 • *3,241*
Davidson □, NC • *113,162*
Davidson □, TN • *477,811*
Davidsville, PA 15928 • *900*
Davie, FL 33329 • *20,877*
Davie □, NC • *24,599*
Daviess □, IN • *27,836*
Daviess □, KY • *85,949*
Daviess □, MO • *8,905*
Davis, CA 95616 • *36,640*
Davis, OK 73030 • *2,782*
Davis, WV 26260 • *979*
Davis □, IA • *9,104*
Davis □, UT • *146,540*
Davison, MI 48423 • *6,087*
Davison □, SD • *17,820*
Davy, WV 24828 • *882*
Dawes □, NE • *9,609*
Dawson, GA 31742 • *5,699*
Dawson, MN 56232 • *1,901*
Dawson, PA 15428 • *661*
Dawson, TX 76639 • *747*
Dawson □, GA • *4,774*
Dawson □, MT • *11,805*
Dawson □, NE • *22,304*
Dawson □, TX • *16,184*
Dawson Springs, KY 42408 • *3,275*
Day □, SD • *8,133*
Dayton, IN 47941 • *781*
Dayton, IA 50530 • *941*
Dayton, KY 41074 • *6,979*
Dayton, MD 21036 • *700*
Dayton, MN 55327 • *4,070*
Dayton, NJ 08810 • *900*
Dayton, OH 45401-99 • *193,444*
Dayton, OR 97114 • *1,409*
Dayton, PA 16222 • *648*
Dayton, TN 37321 • *5,913*
Dayton, TX 77535 • *4,908*
Dayton, VA 22821 • *1,017*
Dayton, WA 99328 • *2,565*
Dayton, WY 82836 • *701*
Daytona Beach, FL 32014-23 • *54,176*
Dayville, CT 06241 • *1,100*
Deadwood, SD 57732 • *2,035*
Deaf Smith □, TX • *21,165*
Deal, NJ 07723 • *1,952*
Deale, MD 20751 • *3,008*
Dearborn, MI 48120-26 • *90,660*
Dearborn □, IN • *34,291*
Dearborn Heights, MI 48127 • *67,706*
De Baca □, NM • *2,454*
De Bary, FL 32713 • *4,980*
Debolt, NE 68152 • *800*
Decatur, AL 35601-03 • *42,002*
Decatur, AR 72722 • *1,013*
Decatur, GA 30030-38 • *18,404*
Decatur, IL 62521-26 • *94,081*
Decatur, IN 46733 • *8,649*
Decatur, MI 49045 • *1,915*
Decatur, MS 39327 • *1,148*
Decatur, NE 68020 • *723*
Decatur, TN 37322 • *1,069*
Decatur, TX 76234 • *4,104*
Decatur □, GA • *25,495*
Decatur □, IN • *23,841*
Decatur □, IA • *9,794*
Decatur □, KS • *4,509*
Decatur □, TN • *10,857*
Decaturville, TN 38329 • *1,004*
Decherd, TN 37324 • *2,233*
Deckerville, MI 48427 • *887*
Decorah, IA 52101 • *7,991*
Dedham, MA 02026 • *25,298*
Deep River, CT 06417 • *2,495*
Deepwater, NJ 08023 • *650*
Deer Creek, IL 61733 • *688*
Deerfield, IL 60015 • *17,430*
Deerfield, MI 49238 • *957*
Deerfield, WI 53531 • *1,466*
Deerfield Beach, FL 33441 • *39,193*
Deer Lodge, MT 59722 • *4,023*
Deer Lodge □, MT • *12,518*
Deer Park, NY 11729 • *33,400*
Deer Park, OH 45236 • *6,745*
Deer Park, TX 77536 • *22,648*
Deer Park, WA 99006 • *2,140*
Deer River, MN 56636 • *907*
Defiance, OH 43512 • *16,810*
Defiance □, OH • *39,987*
De Forest, WI 53532 • *3,367*
De Funiak Springs, FL 32433 • *5,563*
De Graff, OH 43318 • *1,358*
De Kalb, IL 60115 • *33,099*
De Kalb, MS 39328 • *1,159*
De Kalb, TX 75559 • *2,217*
De Kalb □, AL • *53,658*
De Kalb □, GA • *483,024*
De Kalb □, IL • *74,624*
De Kalb □, IN • *33,606*
De Kalb □, MO • *8,222*
De Kalb □, TN • *13,589*
Delafield, WI 53018 • *4,083*
Del Aire, CA 90250 • *3,900*
Delanco, NJ 08075 • *3,730*
De Land, FL 32720-24 • *15,354*
Delano, CA 93215 • *16,491*
Delano, MN 55328 • *2,480*
Delavan, IL 61734 • *1,973*
Delavan, WI 53115 • *5,684*
Delavan Lake, WI 53115 • *2,124*
Delaware, OH 43015 • *18,780*
Delaware □, IN • *128,587*
Delaware □, IA • *18,933*
Delaware □, NY • *46,824*
Delaware □, OH • *53,840*
Delaware □, OK • *23,946*
Delaware □, PA • *555,007*
Delaware City, DE 19706 • *1,858*
Delbarton, WV 25670 • *981*
Delcambre, LA 70528 • *2,216*
Del City, OK 73115 • *28,523*
De Leon, TX 76444 • *2,478*
De Leon Springs, FL 32028 • *1,669*
Delevan, NY 14042 • *1,113*
Delhi, LA 71232 • *3,290*
Delhi, NY 13753 • *3,374*
Delhi Hills, OH 45238 • *7,650*
Dell Rapids, SD 57022 • *2,389*
Dellslow, WV 26531 • *700*
Dellwood, MO 63136 • *6,200*
Del Mar, CA 92014 • *5,017*
Delmar, DE 19940 • *948*
Delmar, IA 52037 • *633*
Delmar, MD 21875 • *1,232*
Delmar, NY 12054 • *8,900*
Del Norte, CO 81132 • *1,709*
Del Norte □, CA • *18,217*
Del Park Manor, DE 19808 • *1,700*
Delphi, IN 46923 • *3,042*
Delphos, OH 45833 • *7,314*
Delran, NJ 08075 • *10,065*
Delray Beach, FL 33444-47 • *34,325*
Del Rio, TX 78840 • *30,034*
Delta, CO 81416 • *3,931*
Delta, OH 43515 • *2,831*
Delta, PA 17314 • *692*
Delta, UT 84624 • *1,930*
Delta □, CO • *21,225*
Delta □, MI • *38,947*
Delta □, TX • *4,839*
Delta Junction, AK 99737 • *945*
Deltona, FL 32725 • *4,868*
Demarest, NJ 07627 • *4,963*
Deming, NM 88030 • *9,964*
Demopolis, AL 36732 • *7,678*
Demorest, GA 30535 • *1,130*
Demotte, IN 46310 • *2,559*
Denham Springs, LA 70726 • *8,563*
Denison, IA 51442 • *6,675*
Denison, TX 75020 • *23,884*
Denmark, SC 29042 • *4,434*
Denmark, WI 54208 • *1,475*
Dennis, MA 02638 • *900*
Dennison, OH 44621 • *3,398*
Dennis Port, MA 02639 • *2,570*
Denny Terrace, SC 29203 • *1,885*
Dent □, MO • *14,517*
Denton, MD 21629 • *1,927*
Denton, NC 27239 • *949*
Denton, TX 76201-06 • *48,063*
Denton □, TX • *143,126*
Dentsville, SC 29204 • *5,000*
Denver, CO 80201-99 • *492,365*
Denver, IA 50622 • *1,647*
Denver, PA 17517 • *2,018*
Denver □, CO • *492,365*
Denver City, TX 79323 • *4,704*
Denville, NJ 07834 • *14,045*
De Pere, WI 54115 • *14,892*
Depew, NY 14043 • *19,819*
Depew, OK 74028 • *682*
Depoe Bay, OR 97341 • *723*
Deport, TX 75435 • *724*
Deposit, NY 13754 • *1,897*
Depue, IL 61322 • *1,873*
De Queen, AR 71832 • *4,594*
De Quincy, LA 70633 • *3,966*
Derby, CT 06418 • *12,346*
Derby, KS 67037 • *9,786*
Derby, NY 14047 • *1,200*
Derby Line, VT 05830 • *874*
De Ridder, LA 70634 • *11,057*
Derma, MS 38839 • *793*
Dermott, AR 71638 • *4,731*
Derry, NH 03038 • *12,248*
Derry, PA 15627 • *3,072*
Des Allemands, LA 70030 • *2,920*
Des Arc, AR 72040 • *2,001*
Deschutes □, OR • *62,142*
Desert Hot Springs, CA 92240 • *5,941*
Desha, AR 72527 • *750*
Desha □, AR • *19,760*
Deshler, NE 68340 • *997*
Deshler, OH 43516 • *1,870*
Desloge, MO 63601 • *2,934*
De Smet, SD 57231 • *1,237*
Des Moines, IA 50301-99 • *191,003*
Des Moines, WA 98188 • *7,378*
Des Moines □, IA • *46,203*
De Soto, IL 62924 • *1,589*
De Soto, IA 50069 • *1,035*
De Soto, KS 66018 • *2,061*
De Soto, MO 63020 • *5,993*
De Soto, TX 75115 • *15,538*
De Soto □, FL • *19,039*
De Soto □, LA • *25,727*
De Soto □, MS • *53,930*
Despard, WV 26301 • *1,200*
Des Peres, MO 63131 • *8,254*
Des Plaines, IL 60016-18 • *53,568*
Destin, FL 32541 • *3,672*
Destrehan, LA 70047 • *2,382*
Detroit, MI 48201-99 • *1,203,339*
Detroit, TX 75436 • *805*
Detroit Lakes, MN 56501 • *7,106*
Deuel □, NE • *2,462*
Deuel □, SD • *5,289*
De Valls Bluff, AR 72041 • *738*
Devils Lake, ND 58301 • *7,442*
Devine, TX 78016 • *3,756*
Devola, OH 45750 • *2,708*
Devon, PA 19333 • *6,700*
Devonshire, DE 19810 • *1,800*
Dewar, OK 74431 • *1,048*
Dewey, OK 74029 • *3,545*
Dewey □, OK • *5,922*
Dewey □, SD • *5,366*
Dewey Beach, DE 19971 • *1,500*
Deweyville, TX 77614 • *950*
De Witt, AR 72042 • *3,928*
De Witt, IA 52742 • *4,512*
De Witt, MI 48820 • *3,165*
De Witt, NE 68341 • *642*
De Witt, NY 13214 • *10,032*
De Witt □, IL • *18,108*
De Witt □, TX • *18,903*
Dexter, IA 50070 • *678*
Dexter, ME 04930 • *3,118*
Dexter, MI 48130 • *1,524*
Dexter, MO 63841 • *7,043*
Dexter, NM 88230 • *882*
Dexter, NY 13634 • *1,053*
Diamond Bar, CA 91765 • *28,045*
Diamond Hill, RI 02864 • *1,150*
Diamond Lake, IL 60060 • *1,503*
Diamond Springs, CA 95619 • *2,287*
Diamondville, WY 83116 • *1,000*
Diaz, AR 72043 • *1,192*
D'Iberville, MS 39532 • *9,000*
Diboll, TX 75941 • *5,227*
Dickens □, TX • *3,539*
Dickenson □, VA • *19,806*
Dickey □, ND • *7,207*
Dickeyville, WI 53808 • *1,156*
Dickinson, ND 58601 • *15,924*
Dickinson, TX 77539 • *7,505*
Dickinson □, IA • *15,629*
Dickinson □, KS • *20,175*
Dickinson □, MI • *25,341*
Dickson, OK 73401 • *996*
Dickson, TN 37055 • *7,040*
Dickson □, TN • *30,037*
Dickson City, PA 18519 • *6,699*
Dierks, AR 71833 • *1,249*
Dieterich, IL 62424 • *633*
Dighton, KS 67839 • *1,390*
Dighton, MA 02715 • *900*
Dike, IA 50624 • *987*
Dillard, OR 97432 • *1,000*
Dill City, OK 73641 • *649*
Dilley, TX 78017 • *2,579*
Dillingham, AK 99576 • *914*
Dillon, MT 59725 • *3,976*
Dillon, SC 29536 • *7,060*
Dillon □, SC • *31,083*
Dillonvale, OH 43917 • *912*
Dillsboro, IN 47018 • *1,038*
Dillsburg, PA 17019 • *1,733*
Dillwyn, VA 23936 • *637*
Dilworth, MN 56529 • *2,585*
Dimmit □, TX • *11,367*
Dimmitt, TX 79027 • *5,019*
Dimondale, MI 48821 • *1,008*
Dinuba, CA 93618 • *9,907*
Dinwiddie □, VA • *22,602*
Dishman, WA 99213 • *9,900*
District Heights-Forestville, MD 20747 • *6,799*
Divernon, IL 62530 • *1,081*
Divide □, ND • *3,494*
Dix, IL 62830 • *3,198*
Dixfield, ME 04224 • *1,725*
Dix Hills, NY 11746 • *10,500*
Dixie □, FL • *7,751*
Dixon, CA 95620 • *7,541*
Dixon, IL 61021 • *15,701*
Dixon, MO 65459 • *1,402*
Dixon □, NE • *7,137*
Dixonville, PA 15734 • *900*
Dobbs Ferry, NY 10522 • *10,053*
Dobson, NC 27017 • *1,222*
Docena, AL 35060 • *1,140*
Dock Junction, GA 31520 • *6,189*
Doddridge □, WV • *7,433*
Dodge, NE 68633 • *815*
Dodge □, GA • *16,955*
Dodge □, MN • *14,773*
Dodge □, NE • *35,847*
Dodge □, WI • *75,064*
Dodge Center, MN 55927 • *1,816*
Dodge City, KS 67801 • *18,001*
Dodgeville, WI 53533 • *3,458*
Doerun, GA 31744 • *1,062*
Doe Run, MO 63637 • *900*
Dolgeville, NY 13329 • *2,602*
Dollar Bay, MI 49922 • *900*
Dolomite, AL 35061 • *2,400*
Dolores, CO 81323 • *802*
Dolores □, CO • *1,658*
Dolton, IL 60419 • *24,766*
Dona Ana □, NM • *96,340*
Donaldsonville, LA 70346 • *7,901*
Donalsonville, GA 31745 • *3,320*
Doneraile, SC 29532 • *1,276*
Dongola, IL 62926 • *886*
Doniphan, MO 63935 • *1,921*
Doniphan, NE 68832 • *696*
Doniphan □, KS • *9,268*
Donley □, TX • *4,075*
Donna, TX 78537 • *9,952*
Donnellson, IA 52625 • *972*
Donora, PA 15033 • *7,524*
Doolittle, MO 65401 • *701*
Dooly □, GA • *10,826*
Door □, WI • *25,029*
Dora, AL 35062 • *2,327*
Doraville, GA 30340 • *7,414*
Dorchester, NE 68343 • *611*
Dorchester, WI 54425 • *613*
Dorchester □, MD • *30,623*
Dorchester □, SC • *58,761*
Dormont, PA 15216 • *11,275*
Dorothy Pond, MA 01527 • *1,900*
Dorris, CA 96023 • *836*
Dorsey, MD 21227 • *1,186*
Dothan, AL 36301-03 • *48,750*
Double Springs, AL 35553 • *1,057*
Dougherty □, GA • *100,718*
Douglas, AZ 85607 • *13,058*
Douglas, GA 31533 • *10,980*
Douglas, MI 49406 • *948*
Douglas, WY 82633 • *6,030*
Douglas □, CO • *25,153*
Douglas □, GA • *54,573*
Douglas □, IL • *19,774*
Douglas □, KS • *67,640*
Douglas □, MN • *27,839*
Douglas □, MO • *11,594*
Douglas □, NE • *397,038*
Douglas □, NV • *19,421*
Douglas □, OR • *93,748*
Douglas □, SD • *4,181*
Douglas □, WA • *22,144*
Douglas □, WI • *44,421*
Douglass, KS 67039 • *1,450*
Douglasville, GA 30133-35 • *7,641*
Dousman, WI 53118 • *1,153*
Dove Creek, CO 81324 • *826*
Dover, AR 72837 • *948*
Dover, DE 19901 • *23,507*
Dover, FL 33527 • *2,354*
Dover, MA 02030 • *2,051*
Dover, NH 03820 • *22,377*
Dover, NJ 07801 • *14,681*
Dover, OH 44622 • *11,782*
Dover, PA 17315 • *1,910*
Dover, TN 37058 • *1,197*
Dover-Foxcroft, ME 04426 • *2,974*
Dover Plains, NY 12522 • *800*
Dowagiac, MI 49047 • *6,307*
Dow City, IA 51528 • *616*
Downers Grove, IL 60515-17 • *42,572*
Downey, CA 90240-42 • *82,602*
Downey, ID 83234 • *645*
Downieville, CA 95936 • *950*
Downingtown, PA 19335 • *7,650*
Downs, KS 67437 • *1,324*
Downsville, NY 13755 • *950*
Dows, IA 50071 • *771*
Doyle, CA 96109 • *900*
Doylestown, OH 44230 • *2,493*
Doylestown, PA 18901 • *8,717*
Doyline, LA 71023 • *801*
Dracut, MA 01826 • *21,249*
Drain, OR 97435 • *1,148*
Drakesboro, KY 42337 • *798*
Drakes Branch, VA 23937 • *617*
Draper, UT 84020 • *5,521*
Drayton, ND 58225 • *1,082*
Drayton, SC 29333 • *1,443*
Drayton Plains, MI 48020 • *18,000*
Dreamland Villa, AZ 85205 • *3,200*
Dresden, OH 43821 • *1,646*
Dresden, TN 38225 • *2,256*
Dresser, WI 54009 • *670*
Drew, MS 38737 • *2,528*
Drew □, AR • *17,910*
Drexel, MO 64742 • *908*
Drexel, NC 28619 • *1,392*
Drexel, OH 45427 • *2,250*
Drexel Hill, PA 19026 • *29,600*
Driggs, ID 83422 • *727*
Dripping Springs, TX 78620 • *606*
Driscoll, TX 78351 • *648*
Drumright, OK 74030 • *3,162*
Drybranch, WV 25061 • *700*
Dryden, MI 48428 • *650*
Dryden, NY 13053 • *1,761*
Dry Ridge, KY 41035 • *1,250*
Duarte, CA 91010 • *16,766*
Dubach, LA 71235 • *1,161*
Dublin, CA 94568 • *19,000*
Dublin, GA 31021 • *16,083*
Dublin, IN 47335 • *979*
Dublin, OH 43017 • *3,855*
Dublin, PA 18917 • *1,565*
Dublin, TX 76446 • *2,723*
Dublin, VA 24084 • *2,368*
Du Bois, PA 15801 • *9,290*
Dubois, WY 82513 • *1,067*
Dubois □, IN • *34,238*
Duboistown, PA 17701 • *1,218*
Dubuque, IA 52001 • *62,321*
Dubuque □, IA • *93,745*
Duchesne, UT 84021 • *1,677*
Duchesne □, UT • *12,565*
Duck Hill, MS 38925 • *706*
Dudley, MA 01570 • *3,700*
Duenweg, MO 64841 • *703*
Due West, SC 29639 • *1,366*
Dugger, IN 47848 • *1,118*
Duke Center, PA 16729 • *900*
Dukes □, MA • *8,942*
Dulce, NM 87528 • *1,648*
Duluth, GA 30136 • *2,956*
Duluth, MN 55801-99 • *92,811*
Dumas, AR 71639 • *6,091*
Dumas, TX 79029 • *12,194*
Dumfries, VA 22026 • *3,214*

Dumont, IA 50625 • 815
Dumont, NJ 07628 • 18,334
Dunaire, GA 30032 • 5,400
Dunbar, PA 15431 • 1,369
Dunbar, WV 25064 • 9,285
Duncan, AZ 85534 • 603
Duncan, OK 73533 • 22,517
Duncan, SC 29334 • 1,259
Duncan Falls, OH 43734 • 1,200
Duncannon, PA 17020 • 1,645
Duncansville, PA 16635 • 1,355
Duncanville, TX 75116 • 27,781
Dundalk, MD 21222 • 71,293
Dundee, FL 33838 • 2,227
Dundee, IL 60118 • 3,551
Dundee, MI 48131 • 2,575
Dundee, NY 14837 • 1,556
Dundee, OR 97115 • 1,223
Dundy □, NE • 2,861
Dunedin, FL 33528 • 30,203
Dunellen, NJ 08812 • 6,593
Dunkerton, IA 50626 • 718
Dunkirk, IN 47336 • 3,180
Dunkirk, NY 14048 • 15,310
Dunkirk, OH 45836 • 954
Dunklin □, MO • 36,324
Dunlap, IL 61525 • 824
Dunlap, IN 46514 • 2,500
Dunlap, IA 51529 • 1,374
Dunlap, TN 37327 • 3,681
Dunleith, DE 19801 • 2,700
Dunlo, PA 15930 • 950
Dunmore, PA 18512 • 16,781
Dunn, NC 28334 • 8,962
Dunn □, ND • 4,627
Dunn □, WI • 34,314
Dunnellon, FL 32630 • 1,427
Dunn Loring Woods, VA 22180 • 2,800
Dunseith, ND 58329 • 625
Dunsmuir, CA 96025 • 2,253
Dunstable, MA 01827 • 900
Dunwoody, GA 30338 • 5,100
Du Page □, IL • 658,829
Duplin □, NC • 40,952
Dupont, CO 80024 • 2,000
Dupont, PA 18641 • 3,460
Dupont City, WV 25015 • 900
Dupont Manor, DE 19901 • 1,059
Duquesne, PA 15110 • 10,094
Du Quoin, IL 62832 • 6,594
Durand, IL 61024 • 1,073
Durand, MI 48429 • 4,241
Durand, WI 54736 • 2,047
Durango, CO 81301 • 11,649
Durant, IA 52747 • 1,583
Durant, MS 39063 • 2,889
Durant, OK 74701 • 11,972
Durham, CA 95938 • 950
Durham, CT 06422 • 2,641
Durham, NH 03824 • 8,448
Durham, NC 27701-99 • 100,538
Durham □, NC • 152,785
Duryea, PA 18642 • 5,415
Dushore, PA 18614 • 692
Duson, LA 70529 • 1,253
Dutchess □, NY • 245,055
Duval □, FL • 571,003
Duval □, TX • 12,517
Duxbury, MA 02332 • 1,685
Dwight, IL 60420 • 4,146
Dyer, AR 72935 • 608
Dyer, IN 46311 • 9,555
Dyer, TN 38330 • 2,419
Dyer □, TN • 34,663
Dyersburg, TN 38024 • 15,856
Dyersville, IA 52040 • 3,825
Dysart, IA 52224 • 1,355

E

Eads, CO 81036 • 878
Eagan, MN 55121 • 20,700
Eagar, AZ 85925 • 2,791
Eagle, CO 81631 • 950
Eagle, ID 83616 • 2,620
Eagle, NE 68347 • 832
Eagle, WI 53119 • 1,008
Eagle □, CO • 13,320
Eagle Grove, IA 50533 • 4,324
Eagle Lake, MN 56024 • 1,470
Eagle Lake, TX 77434 • 3,921
Eagle Lake, WI 53139 • 1,000
Eagle Pass, TX 78852 • 21,407
Eagle Point, OR 97524 • 2,764
Eagle River, WI 54521 • 1,326
Earle, AR 72331 • 3,517
Earlham, IA 50072 • 1,140
Earlimart, CA 93219 • 4,578
Earlington, KY 42410 • 2,011
Earlville, IL 60518 • 1,382
Earlville, IA 52041 • 844
Earlville, NY 13332 • 985
Early, IA 50535 • 670
Early □, GA • 13,158
Earth, TX 79031 • 1,512
Easley, SC 29640 • 14,264
East Acton, MA 01720 • 1,200
East Alton, IL 62024 • 7,096
East Aurora, NY 14052 • 6,803
East Bangor, PA 18013 • 955
East Bank, WV 25067 • 1,155
East Barre, VT 05649 • 900
East Baton Rouge □, LA • 366,191
East Bend, NC 27018 • 602
East Berlin, CT 06023 • 900
East Berlin, PA 17316 • 1,054
East Bernard, TX 77435 • 1,700
East Bernstadt, KY 40729 • 700
East Bethel, MN 55005 • 6,626
East Billerica, MA 01821 • 2,900
Eastborough, KS 67206 • 854
East Brady, PA 16028 • 1,153
East Brewster, MA 02631 • 700
East Brewton, AL 36426 • 3,012
East Bridgewater, MA 02333 • 3,300
East Brookfield, MA 01515 • 1,443
East Brooklyn, CT 06239 • 1,251
East Brunswick, NJ 08816 • 37,711
East Butler, PA 16029 • 799
East Canaan, CT 06024 • 800
East Carbon, UT 84520 • 1,942
East Carroll □, LA • 11,772
East Chelmsford, MA 01824 • 2,900
Eastchester, NY 10709 • 22,600
East Chicago, IN 46312 • 39,786
East Chicago Heights, IL 60411 • 5,347
East Cleveland, OH 44112 • 36,957
East Dennis, MA 02641 • 800
East Detroit, MI 48021 • 38,280
East Douglas, MA 01516 • 1,683
East Dubuque, IL 61025 • 2,194
East Falmouth, MA 02536 • 5,181
East Feliciana □, LA • 19,015
East Flat Rock, NC 28726 • 3,365
East Fultonham, OH 43735 • 650
East Gaffney, SC 29340 • 4,092
East Galesburg, IL 61430 • 928
Eastgate, WA 98004 • 5,300
East Glenville, NY 12302 • 11,800
East Grand Forks, MN 56721 • 8,537
East Grand Rapids, MI 49506 • 10,914
East Greenville, PA 18041 • 2,456
East Greenwich, RI 02818 • 10,211
East Half Hollow Hills, NY 11746 • 9,691
Eastham, MA 02642 • 1,100
East Hampden, ME 04401 • 950
East Hampstead, NH 03826 • 900
East Hampton, CT 06424 • 2,600
Easthampton, MA 01027 • 15,580
East Hampton, NY 11937 • 1,886
East Hanover, NJ 07936 • 9,319
East Hartford, CT 06108 • 52,563
East Haven, CT 06512 • 25,028
East Helena, MT 59635 • 1,647
East Hills, NY 11576 • 7,160
East Islip, NY 11730 • 13,700
East Jordan, MI 49727 • 2,185
Eastlake, OH 44094 • 22,104
Eastland, TX 76448 • 3,747
Eastland □, TX • 19,480
East Lansing, MI 48823 • 51,392
East Las Vegas, NV 89112 • 6,449
East Liverpool, OH 43920 • 16,687
East Longmeadow, MA 01028 • 12,905
East Los Angeles, CA 90022 • 110,017
East Lyme, CT 06333 • 700
Eastman, GA 31023 • 5,330
East Marion, NY 11939 • 900
East Meadow, NY 11554 • 47,300
East Millbury, MA 01527 • 1,000
East Millinocket, ME 04430 • 2,361
East Moline, IL 61244 • 20,907
East Naples, FL 33940 • 9,000
East Newark, NJ 07029 • 1,923
East Newnan, GA 30263 • 1,499
East Norriton, PA 19401 • 12,711
East Northport, NY 11731 • 22,200
East Olympia, WA 98540 • 700
Easton, MD 21601 • 7,536
Easton, PA 18042 • 26,027
Eastondale, MA 02375 • 900
East Orange, NJ 07017-19 • 77,690
East Orleans, MA 02643 • 1,200
Eastover, SC 29044 • 899
East Palatka, FL 32031 • 1,613
East Palestine, OH 44413 • 5,306
East Palo Alto, CA 94303 • 18,191
East Patchogue, NY 11772 • 8,300
East Pea Ridge, WV 25705 • 1,900
East Peoria, IL 61611 • 22,385
East Pepperell, MA 01463 • 2,212
East Petersburg, PA 17520 • 3,600
East Pittsburgh, PA 15112 • 2,493
Eastpoint, FL 32328 • 1,246
East Point, GA 30344 • 37,486
Eastport, ME 04631 • 1,982
Eastport, NY 11941 • 1,308
East Prairie, MO 63845 • 3,713
East Providence, RI 02914 • 50,980
East Quogue, NY 11942 • 1,200
East Randolph, NY 14730 • 655
East Ridge, TN 37412 • 21,236
East River, CT 06443 • 1,800
East Rochester, NY 14445 • 7,596
East Rockaway, NY 11518 • 10,917
East Rockingham, NC 28379 • 5,190
East Rutherford, NJ 07073 • 7,849
East Saint Louis, IL 62201-08 • 55,200
Eastside, OR 97420 • 1,601
Eastsound, WA 98245 • 900
East Sparta, OH 44626 • 868
East Spencer, NC 28039 • 2,150
East Stroudsburg, PA 18301 • 8,039
East Sudbury, MA 01776 • 1,500
East Tawas, MI 48730 • 2,584
East Templeton, MA 01438 • 980
East Troy, WI 53120 • 2,385
East Tustin, CA 92705 • 10,000
East Vestal, NY 13902 • 5,300
East View, WV 26301 • 1,618
East Walpole, MA 02032 • 4,900
East Wareham, MA 02538 • 1,000
East Washington, PA 15301 • 2,241
East Wenatchee, WA 98801 • 1,640
East Windsor, NJ 08520 • 15,000
Eastwood, MI 49001 • 7,186
Eastwood Hills, UT 84106 • 1,200
Eaton, CO 80615 • 1,932
Eaton, IN 47338 • 1,804
Eaton, OH 45320 • 6,839
Eaton □, MI • 88,337
Eaton Rapids, MI 48827 • 4,510
Eatonton, GA 31024 • 4,833
Eatontown, NJ 07724 • 12,703
Eatonville, WA 98328 • 998
Eau Claire, WI 54701-03 • 51,509
Eau Claire □, WI • 78,805
Ebensburg, PA 15931 • 4,096
Eccles, WV 25836 • 1,100
Echo, OR 97826 • 624
Echols □, GA • 2,297
Eckhart Mines, MD 21528 • 1,333
Eckman, WV 24829 • 700
Eclectic, AL 36024 • 1,124
Economy, PA 15005 • 9,538
Ecorse, MI 48229 • 14,447
Ecru, MS 38841 • 687
Ector □, TX • 115,374
Edcouch, TX 78538 • 3,092
Eddy □, NM • 47,855
Eddy □, ND • 3,554
Eddystone, PA 19013 • 2,555
Eddyville, IA 52553 • 1,116
Eddyville, KY 42038 • 1,949
Eden, NC 27288 • 15,672
Eden, NY 14057 • 3,000
Eden, TX 76837 • 1,294
Eden Prairie, MN 55344 • 16,263
Edenton, NC 27932 • 5,357
Eden Valley, MN 55329 • 763
Edgar, NE 68935 • 705
Edgar, WI 54426 • 1,194
Edgar □, IL • 21,725
Edgard, LA 70049 • 680
Edgartown, MA 02539 • 1,138
Edgecombe □, NC • 55,988
Edgefield, SC 29824 • 2,713
Edgefield □, SC • 17,528
Edgeley, ND 58433 • 843
Edgemere, MD 21222 • 7,800
Edgemont, SD 57735 • 1,468
Edgemoor, DE 19802 • 7,397
Edgerton, KS 66021 • 1,214
Edgerton, MN 56128 • 1,123
Edgerton, OH 43517 • 1,813
Edgerton, WI 53534 • 4,335
Edgewater, AL 35224 • 1,400
Edgewater, CO 80214 • 4,766
Edgewater, FL 32032 • 6,726
Edgewater, MD 21037 • 800
Edgewater, NJ 07020 • 4,628
Edgewater Park, NJ 08010 • 9,273
Edgewood, IN 46011 • 2,215
Edgewood, IA 52042 • 900
Edgewood, KY 41017 • 7,230
Edgewood, MD 21040 • 19,455
Edgewood, OH 44004 • 3,099
Edgewood, PA 15218 • 4,382
Edgewood, WA 98371 • 1,800
Edgeworth, PA 15143 • 1,738
Edina, MN 55424 • 46,073
Edina, MO 63537 • 1,520
Edinboro, PA 16412 • 6,324
Edinburg, IL 62531 • 1,231
Edinburg, TX 78539 • 24,075
Edinburg, VA 22824 • 752
Edinburgh, IN 46124 • 4,856
Edison, GA 31746 • 1,128
Edison, NJ 08817-20 • 70,193
Edmond, OK 73034 • 34,637
Edmonds, WA 98020 • 27,679
Edmondson Heights, MD 21207 • 5,000
Edmonson □, KY • 9,962
Edmonton, KY 42129 • 1,401
Edmore, MI 48829 • 1,176
Edmunds □, SD • 5,159
Edna, TX 77957 • 5,650
Edon, OH 43518 • 947
Edwards, MS 39066 • 1,515
Edwards □, IL • 7,961
Edwards □, KS • 4,271
Edwards □, TX • 2,033
Edwardsburg, MI 49112 • 1,135
Edwardsville, IL 62025 • 12,480
Edwardsville, KS 66113 • 3,364
Edwardsville, PA 18704 • 5,729
Effingham, IL 62401 • 11,270
Effingham, KS 66023 • 634
Effingham □, GA • 18,327
Effingham □, IL • 30,944
Egg Harbor City, NJ 08215 • 4,618
Egypt, MA 02066 • 1,100
Ehrenberg, AZ 85334 • 900
Ekalaka, MT 59324 • 620
Elaine, AR 72333 • 991
Elba, AL 36323 • 4,355
Elba, NY 14058 • 750
Elberfeld, IN 47613 • 640
Elbert □, CO • 6,850
Elbert □, GA • 18,758
Elberton, GA 30635 • 5,686
Elbow Lake, MN 56531 • 1,358
Elburn, IL 60119 • 1,224
El Cajon, CA 92020-22 • 73,892
El Campo, TX 77437 • 10,462
El Centro, CA 92243 • 23,996
El Cerrito, CA 94530 • 22,731
Eldon, IA 52554 • 1,255
Eldon, MO 65026 • 4,342
Eldora, IA 50627 • 3,063
El Dorado, AR 71730 • 25,270
Eldorado, GA 31794 • 1,000
Eldorado, IL 62930 • 5,198
El Dorado, KS 67042 • 10,510
Eldorado, OK 73537 • 688
Eldorado, TX 76936 • 2,061
El Dorado □, CA • 85,812
El Dorado Springs, MO 64744 • 3,868
Eldred, PA 16731 • 965
Eldridge, IA 52748 • 3,279
Eleanor, WV 25070 • 1,282
Electra, TX 76360 • 3,755
El Encanto Heights, CA 93117 • 7,700
Elgin, IL 60120 • 63,981
Elgin, IA 52141 • 702
Elgin, MN 55932 • 667
Elgin, NE 68636 • 807
Elgin, ND 58533 • 930
Elgin, OK 73538 • 1,003
Elgin, OR 97827 • 1,701
Elgin, SC 29720 • 900
Elgin, TX 78621 • 4,535
Elida, OH 45807 • 1,349
Eliot, ME 03903 • 2,450
Elizabeth, CO 80107 • 789
Elizabeth, GA 30060 • 1,700
Elizabeth, IL 61028 • 772
Elizabeth, NJ 07201-99 • 106,201
Elizabeth, WV 26143 • 856
Elizabeth City, NC 27909 • 13,784
Elizabethton, TN 37643 • 12,431
Elizabethtown, IN 47232 • 603
Elizabethtown, KY 42701 • 15,380
Elizabethtown, NC 28337 • 3,551
Elizabethtown, NY 12932 • 650
Elizabethtown, PA 17022 • 8,233
Elizabethville, PA 17023 • 1,531
El Jebel, CO 81628 • 900
Elk □, KS • 3,918
Elk □, PA • 38,338
Elkader, IA 52043 • 1,688
Elk City, ID 83525 • 670
Elk City, OK 73644 • 9,579
Elk Grove, CA 95624 • 10,059
Elk Grove Village, IL 60007 • 28,907
Elkhart, IN 46514-17 • 41,305
Elkhart, KS 67950 • 2,243
Elkhart, TX 75839 • 1,317
Elkhart □, IN • 137,330
Elkhart Lake, WI 53020 • 1,054
Elk Horn, IA 51531 • 746
Elkhorn, NE 68022 • 1,344
Elkhorn, WV 24831 • 700
Elkhorn, WI 53121 • 4,605
Elkhorn City, KY 41522 • 1,446
Elkin, NC 28621 • 2,858
Elkins, WV 26241 • 8,536
Elkins Park, PA 19117 • 14,000
Elkland, PA 16920 • 1,974
Elk Mound, WI 54739 • 737
Elko, NV 89801 • 8,758
Elko □, NV • 17,269
Elk Point, SD 57025 • 1,661
Elk Rapids, MI 49629 • 1,504
Elkridge, MD 21227 • 2,100
Elk River, MN 55330 • 6,785
Elkton, KY 42220 • 1,815
Elkton, MD 21921 • 6,468
Elkton, MI 48731 • 953
Elkton, SD 57026 • 632
Elkton, VA 22827 • 1,520
Elkview, WV 25071 • 1,486
Elkville, IL 62932 • 973
Ellaville, GA 31806 • 1,684
Ellendale, ND 58436 • 1,967
Ellensburg, WA 98926 • 11,752
Ellenton, FL 33532 • 1,561
Ellenville, NY 12428 • 4,405
Ellerbe, NC 28338 • 1,415
Ellerslie, MD 21529 • 1,150
Ellettsville, IN 47429 • 3,328
Ellicott City, MD 21043 • 4,000
Ellicottville, NY 14731 • 713
Ellijay, GA 30540 • 1,507
Ellington, CT 06029 • 1,000
Ellington, MO 63638 • 1,215
Ellinwood, KS 67526 • 2,508
Elliott, MS 38926 • 1,200
Elliott □, KY • 6,908
Ellis, KS 67637 • 2,062
Ellis □, KS • 26,098
Ellis □, OK • 5,596
Ellis □, TX • 59,743
Elliston, VA 24087 • 750
Ellisville, MS 39437 • 4,652
Ellisville, MO 63011 • 6,233
Elloree, SC 29047 • 909
Ellport, PA 16117 • 1,290
Ellsworth, KS 67439 • 2,465
Ellsworth, ME 04605 • 5,179
Ellsworth, MN 56129 • 629
Ellsworth, PA 15331 • 1,228
Ellsworth, WI 54011 • 2,143
Ellsworth □, KS • 6,640
Ellwood City, PA 16117 • 9,998
Elma, IA 50628 • 714
Elma, WA 98541 • 2,720
Elm City, NC 27822 • 1,561
Elm Creek, NE 68836 • 862
Elmer, NJ 08318 • 1,569
Elm Grove, WI 53122 • 6,735
Elmhurst, IL 60126 • 44,276
Elmhurst, PA 18416 • 953
Elmira, NY 14901-99 • 35,327
El Mirage, AZ 85335 • 4,307
Elmira Heights, NY 14903 • 4,279
Elmont, NY 11003 • 30,000
El Monte, CA 91731-35 • 79,494
Elmora, PA 15737 • 950
Elmore, MN 56027 • 882
Elmore, OH 43416 • 1,271
Elmore □, AL • 43,390
Elmore □, ID • 21,565
Elm Springs, AR 72728 • 781
Elmwood, IL 61529 • 2,117
Elmwood, MA 02337 • 750
Elmwood, WI 54740 • 885
Elmwood Park, IL 60635 • 24,016
Elmwood Park, NJ 07407 • 18,377
Elmwood Place, OH 45216 • 2,840
Elnora, IN 47529 • 756
Eloise, FL 33880 • 1,408
Elon College, NC 27244 • 2,873
Eloy, AZ 85231 • 6,240
El Paso, IL 61738 • 2,676
El Paso, TX 79901-99 • 425,259
El Paso □, CO • 309,424
El Paso □, TX • 479,899
El Portal, CA 95318 • 850
El Portal, FL 33138 • 2,055
El Prado, NM 87529 • 700
Elrama, PA 15038 • 800
El Reno, OK 73036 • 15,486
El Rio, CA 93030 • 5,674
Elroy, WI 53929 • 1,504
Elsa, TX 78543 • 5,061
Elsah, IL 62028 • 990
Elsberry, MO 63343 • 1,272
El Segundo, CA 90245 • 13,752
Elsie, MI 48831 • 1,022
Elsinore, UT 84724 • 612
Elsmere, DE 19805 • 6,493
Elsmere, KY 41018 • 7,203
Elsmere, NY 12054 • 5,500
El Sobrante, CA 94803 • 10,535
Elton, LA 70532 • 1,450
El Toro, CA 92630 • 38,153
Elvins, MO 63601 • 1,548
Elwood, IN 46036 • 10,867
Elwood, KS 66024 • 1,275
Elwood, NE 68937 • 716
Elwood, NJ 08217 • 900
Elwood, NY 11731 • 15,400
Ely, MN 55731 • 4,820
Ely, NV 89301 • 4,882
Elyria, OH 44035-39 • 57,538
Elysburg, PA 17824 • 1,337
Emanuel □, GA • 20,795
Emerson, GA 30137 • 1,110
Emerson, NE 68733 • 874
Emerson, NJ 07630 • 7,793
Emery □, UT • 11,451
Eminence, KY 40019 • 2,260
Eminence, MO 65466 • 614
Emlenton, PA 16373 • 807
Emmaus, PA 18049 • 11,001
Emmet □, IA • 13,336
Emmet □, MI • 22,992
Emmetsburg, IA 50536 • 4,621
Emmett, ID 83617 • 4,605
Emmitsburg, MD 21727 • 1,552
Emmons □, ND • 5,877
Emory, TX 75440 • 813
Empire, LA 70050 • 630
Emporia, KS 66801 • 25,287
Emporia, VA 23847 • 4,840
Emporium, PA 15834 • 2,837
Emsworth, PA 15202 • 3,074
Encampment, WY 82325 • 611
Encinal, TX 78019 • 704
Encinitas, CA 92024 • 10,796
Enderlin, ND 58027 • 1,151
Endicott, NY 13760 • 14,457
Endwell, NY 13760 • 15,999
Enfield, CT 06082 • 8,151
Enfield, IL 62835 • 890
Enfield, NH 03748 • 1,581
Enfield, NC 27823 • 2,995
England, AR 72046 • 3,081
Engleside, VA 22309 • 21,400
Englewood, CO 80110-12 • 30,021
Englewood, FL 33533 • 10,242
Englewood, NJ 07631-32 • 23,701
Englewood, OH 45322 • 11,329
Englewood, TN 37329 • 1,840
Englewood Cliffs, NJ 07632 • 5,698
English, IN 47118 • 633
Englishtown, NJ 07726 • 976
Enid, OK 73701 • 50,363
Enka, NC 28728 • 5,567
Ennis, MT 59729 • 660
Ennis, TX 75119 • 12,110
Enoch, UT 84720 • 678
Enola, PA 17025 • 3,600
Enon, OH 45323 • 2,597
Enoree, SC 29335 • 1,107
Enosburg Falls, VT 05450 • 1,207
Ensley, FL 32504 • 2,200
Enterprise, AL 36330 • 18,033

Enterprise, KS 67441 • 839
Enterprise, MS 39330 • 607
Enterprise, OR 97828 • 2,003
Enterprise, UT 84725 • 905
Enterprise, WV 26568 • 950
Enumclaw, WA 98022 • 5,427
Ephraim, UT 84627 • 2,810
Ephrata, PA 17522 • 11,095
Ephrata, WA 98823 • 5,359
Epping, NH 03042 • 1,384
Epps, LA 71237 • 672
Epworth, IA 52045 • 1,380
Equality, IL 62934 • 831
Erath, LA 70533 • 2,133
Erath □, TX • 22,560
Erdenheim, PA 19118 • 3,300
Erial, NJ 08081 • 900
Erick, OK 73645 • 1,375
Erie, CO 80516 • 1,254
Erie, IL 61250 • 1,725
Erie, KS 66733 • 1,415
Erie, MI 48133 • 700
Erie, PA 16501-99 • 119,123
Erie □, NY • 1,015,472
Erie □, OH • 79,655
Erie □, PA • 279,780
Erin, TN 37061 • 1,614
Erlanger, KY 41018 • 14,433
Erma, NJ 08204 • 1,200
Errol Heights, OR 97266 • 7,800
Erwin, NC 28339 • 2,828
Erwin, TN 37650 • 4,739
Escalante, UT 84726 • 652
Escalon, CA 95320 • 3,127
Escambia □, AL • 38,440
Escambia □, FL • 233,794
Escanaba, MI 49829 • 14,355
Escatawpa, MS 39552 • 5,367
Escondido, CA 92025-27 • 64,355
Eskridge, KS 66423 • 603
Esmeralda □, NV • 777
Esmond, RI 02917 • 3,500
Espanola, NM 87532 • 6,803
Esparto, CA 95627 • 1,303
Espy, PA 17815 • 1,652
Essex, CT 06426 • 2,501
Essex, IA 51638 • 1,001
Essex, MD 21221 • 39,614
Essex, MA 01929 • 1,490
Essex, VT 05451 • 800
Essex □, MA • 633,632
Essex □, NJ • 851,116
Essex □, NY • 36,176
Essex □, VT • 6,313
Essex □, VA • 8,864
Essex Fells, NJ 07021 • 2,363
Essex Junction, VT 05452 • 7,033
Essexville, MI 48732 • 4,378
Estacada, OR 97023 • 1,419
Estancia, NM 87016 • 830
Estelline, SD 57234 • 719
Estell Manor, NJ 08319 • 848
Estero, FL 33928 • 950
Estes Park, CO 80517 • 2,703
Estherville, IA 51334 • 7,518
Estherwood, LA 70534 • 691
Estill, SC 29918 • 2,308
Estill □, KY • 14,495
Estill Springs, TN 37330 • 1,324
Etna, CA 96027 • 754
Etna, PA 15223 • 4,534
Etowah, TN 37331 • 3,758
Etowah □, AL • 103,057
Ettrick, VA 23803 • 4,000
Euclid, OH 44117 • 59,999
Eudora, AR 71640 • 3,840
Eudora, KS 66025 • 2,934
Eufaula, AL 36027 • 12,097
Eufaula, OK 74432 • 3,159
Eugene, OR 97401-05 • 105,624
Eulaton, AL 36201 • 1,869
Euless, TX 76039-40 • 24,002
Eunice, LA 70535 • 12,479
Eunice, NM 88231 • 2,970
Eupora, MS 39744 • 2,048
Eureka, CA 95501 • 24,153
Eureka, IL 61530 • 4,306
Eureka, KS 67045 • 3,425
Eureka, MO 63025 • 3,862
Eureka, MT 59917 • 1,119
Eureka, SC 29706 • 1,627
Eureka, SD 57437 • 1,360
Eureka, UT 84628 • 670
Eureka □, NV • 1,198
Eureka Springs, AR 72632 • 1,989
Eustis, FL 32726 • 9,453
Eutaw, AL 35462 • 2,444
Eutawville, SC 29048 • 615
Evangeline □, LA • 33,343
Evans, CO 80620 • 5,063
Evans, GA 30809 • 800
Evans □, GA • 8,428
Evans City, PA 16033 • 2,299
Evansdale, IA 50707 • 4,798
Evans Mills, NY 13637 • 651
Evanston, IL 60201-99 • 73,706
Evanston, WY 82930 • 6,421
Evansville, IL 62242 • 863
Evansville, IN 47701-99 • 130,496
Evansville, WI 53536 • 2,835
Evansville, WY 82636 • 2,335
Evart, MI 49631 • 1,945
Evarts, KY 40828 • 1,234
Eveleth, MN 55734 • 5,042
Everett, MA 02149 • 37,195
Everett, PA 15537 • 1,828
Everett, WA 98201-07 • 54,413
Evergreen, AL 36401 • 4,171
Evergreen, CO 80439 • 6,376
Evergreen Park, IL 60642 • 22,260
Everly, IA 51338 • 796
Everman, TX 76140 • 5,387
Everson, PA 15631 • 1,032
Everson, WA 98247 • 898
Ewa, HI 96706 • 2,637
Ewa Beach, HI 96706-07 • 14,369
Ewing Township, NJ 08618 • 34,842
Excelsior Springs, MO 64024 • 10,424
Exeter, CA 93221 • 5,606
Exeter, NE 68351 • 807
Exeter, NH 03833 • 8,947
Exeter, PA 18643 • 5,493
Exira, IA 50076 • 978
Exmore, VA 23350 • 1,300
Experiment, GA 30212 • 3,000
Export, PA 15632 • 1,143
Eyota, MN 55934 • 1,244

F

Fabens, TX 79838 • 3,500
Factoryville, PA 18419 • 924
Fairbank, IA 50629 • 980
Fairbanks, AK 99701 • 22,645
Fair Bluff, NC 28439 • 1,095
Fairborn, OH 45324 • 29,702
Fairburn, GA 30213 • 3,466
Fairbury, IL 61739 • 3,544
Fairbury, NE 68352 • 5,265
Fairchance, PA 15436 • 2,106
Fairdale, KY 40118 • 7,315
Fairfax, AL 36854 • 3,776
Fairfax, CA 94930 • 7,391
Fairfax, DE 19803 • 2,850
Fairfax, IA 52228 • 683
Fairfax, MN 55332 • 1,405
Fairfax, MO 64446 • 835
Fairfax, OK 74637 • 1,949
Fairfax, SC 29827 • 2,154
Fairfax, VA 22030-39 • 19,390
Fairfax □, VA • 596,901
Fairfield, AL 35064 • 13,242
Fairfield, CA 94533 • 58,099
Fairfield, CT 06430 • 54,849
Fairfield, IL 62837 • 5,954
Fairfield, IA 52556 • 9,428
Fairfield, ME 04937 • 3,169
Fairfield, MT 59436 • 650
Fairfield, NJ 07006 • 7,987
Fairfield, OH 45014 • 30,777
Fairfield, TX 75840 • 3,505
Fairfield □, CT • 807,143
Fairfield □, OH • 93,678
Fairfield □, SC • 20,700
Fairfield Bay, AR 72088 • 1,000
Fairgrove, MI 48733 • 691
Fair Grove, MO 65648 • 863
Fair Grove, NC 27360 • 1,500
Fairhaven, MA 02719 • 15,759
Fair Haven, MI 48023 • 900
Fair Haven, NJ 07701 • 5,679
Fair Haven, NY 13064 • 976
Fair Haven, VT 05743 • 2,819
Fairhope, AL 36532 • 7,286
Fairland, IN 46126 • 900
Fairland, OK 74343 • 1,073
Fair Lawn, NJ 07410 • 32,229
Fairlawn, OH 44313 • 6,100
Fairlawn, VA 24141 • 2,000
Fairlea, WV 24902 • 1,200
Fairless Hills, PA 19030 • 12,500
Fairmont, IL 60441 • 2,600
Fairmont, MN 56031 • 11,506
Fairmont, NE 68354 • 767
Fairmont, NC 28340 • 2,658
Fairmont, WV 26554 • 23,863
Fairmount, GA 30139 • 842
Fairmount, IL 61841 • 851
Fairmount, IN 46928 • 3,286
Fairmount, NY 13219 • 8,700
Fairmount Heights, MD 20743 • 1,616
Fair Oaks, CA 95628 • 20,235
Fair Oaks, GA 30060 • 8,486
Fairoaks, PA 15003 • 1,854
Fair Plain, MI 49022 • 8,289
Fairport, NY 14450 • 5,970
Fairport Harbor, OH 44077 • 3,357
Fairton, NJ 08320 • 1,107
Fairview, MT 59221 • 1,366
Fairview, NJ 07022 • 10,519
Fairview, NY 12601 • 8,517
Fairview, OK 73737 • 3,370
Fairview, OR 97024 • 1,749
Fairview, PA 16415 • 1,855
Fairview, TN 37062 • 3,648
Fairview, UT 84629 • 916
Fairview, WV 26570 • 759
Fairview Heights, IL 62208 • 12,414
Fairview Park, IN 47842 • 1,545
Fairview Park, OH 44126 • 19,311
Fairview Shores, FL 32804 • 6,100
Fairway, KS 66205 • 4,619
Faison, NC 28341 • 636
Falconer, NY 14733 • 2,778
Falcon Heights, MN 55113 • 5,291
Falcon Heights, OR 97601 • 1,389
Falfurrias, TX 78355 • 6,103
Falkville, AL 35622 • 1,310
Fall Branch, TN 37656 • 1,340
Fallbrook, CA 92028 • 14,041
Fall City, WA 98024 • 1,600
Fall Creek, WI 54742 • 1,148
Fall Mountain Lake, CT 06786 • 730
Fallon, NV 89406 • 4,262
Fallon □, MT • 3,763
Fall River, MA 02720-26 • 92,574
Fall River, WI 53932 • 850
Fall River □, SD • 8,439
Fall River Mills, CA 96028 • 900
Falls □, TX • 17,946
Falls Church, VA 22040-48 • 9,515
Falls City, NE 68355 • 5,374
Falls City, OR 97344 • 804
Falls Creek, PA 15840 • 1,208
Fallston, MD 21047 • 5,572
Fallston, NC 28042 • 614
Falmouth, KY 41040 • 2,482
Falmouth, ME 04105 • 6,853
Falmouth, MA 02540-41 • 4,200
Falmouth, VA 22403 • 970
Fannin □, GA • 14,748
Fannin □, TX • 24,285
Fanwood, NJ 07023 • 7,767
Fargo, ND 58102-99 • 61,383
Far Hills, NJ 07931 • 677
Faribault, MN 55021 • 16,241
Faribault □, MN • 19,714
Farley, IA 52046 • 1,287
Farmer City, IL 61842 • 2,252
Farmers Branch, TX 75234 • 24,863
Farmersburg, IN 47850 • 1,240
Farmersville, CA 93223 • 5,544
Farmersville, IL 62533 • 686
Farmersville, TX 75031 • 2,360
Farmerville, LA 71241 • 3,768
Farmingdale, ME 04345 • 2,014
Farmingdale, NJ 07727 • 1,348
Farmingdale, NY 11735 • 7,946
Farmington, AR 72730 • 1,283
Farmington, CT 06032 • 2,000
Farmington, IL 61531 • 3,118
Farmington, IA 52626 • 869
Farmington, ME 04938 • 3,583
Farmington, MI 48024 • 11,022
Farmington, MN 55024 • 4,370
Farmington, MO 63640 • 8,270
Farmington, NH 03835 • 3,284
Farmington, NM 87401 • 31,222
Farmington, UT 84025 • 4,691
Farmington Hills, MI 48018 • 58,056
Farmingville, NY 11738 • 5,700
Farmland, IN 47340 • 1,560
Farmville, NC 27828 • 4,707
Farmville, VA 23901 • 6,067
Farragut, IA 51639 • 603
Farrell, PA 16121 • 8,645
Farwell, MI 48622 • 804
Farwell, TX 79325 • 1,354
Faulk □, SD • 3,327
Faulkland Heights, DE 19808 • 1,650
Faulkner □, AR • 46,192
Faulkton, SD 57438 • 981
Fauquier □, VA • 35,889
Fayette, AL 35555 • 5,287
Fayette, IA 52142 • 1,515
Fayette, MS 39069 • 2,033
Fayette, MO 65248 • 2,983
Fayette, OH 43521 • 1,222
Fayette □, AL • 18,809
Fayette □, GA • 29,043
Fayette □, IL • 22,167
Fayette □, IN • 28,272
Fayette □, IA • 25,488
Fayette □, KY • 204,165
Fayette □, OH • 27,467
Fayette □, PA • 159,417
Fayette □, TN • 25,305
Fayette □, TX • 18,832
Fayette □, WV • 57,863
Fayetteville, AR 72701-03 • 36,608
Fayetteville, GA 30214 • 2,715
Fayetteville, NC 28301-08 • 59,507
Fayetteville, PA 17222 • 2,449
Fayetteville, TN 37334 • 7,559
Fayetteville, WV 25840 • 2,366
Fayville, MA 01745 • 1,000
Feasterville, PA 19047 • 6,900
Federal Heights, CO 80221 • 7,846
Federalsburg, MD 21632 • 1,952
Federal Way, WA 98003 • 17,850
Feeding Hills, MA 01030 • 8,500
Felicity, OH 45120 • 929
Fellowship, NJ 08057 • 1,900
Fellsmere, FL 32948 • 1,161
Felton, CA 95018 • 4,000
Fennimore, WI 53809 • 2,212
Fennville, MI 49408 • 934
Fenton, MI 48430 • 8,098
Fentress □, TN • 14,826
Ferdinand, IN 47532 • 2,192
Fergus □, MT • 13,076
Fergus Falls, MN 56537 • 12,519
Ferguson, KY 42533 • 1,009
Ferguson, MO 63135 • 24,740
Fernandina Beach, FL 32034 • 7,224
Fern Creek, KY 40291 • 16,866
Ferndale, CA 95536 • 1,367
Ferndale, MD 21061 • 2,600
Ferndale, MI 48220 • 26,227
Ferndale, PA 15905 • 2,204
Ferndale, WA 98248 • 3,855
Fernley, NV 89408 • 1,200
Fernwood, ID 83830 • 680
Ferriday, LA 71334 • 4,472
Ferris, TX 75125 • 2,228
Ferron, UT 84523 • 1,718
Ferry □, WA • 5,811
Ferry Farms, VA 22401 • 1,300
Fertile, MN 56540 • 869
Fessenden, ND 58438 • 761
Festus, MO 63028 • 7,574
Fieldale, VA 24089 • 1,400
Field Crest Estates, CT 06355 • 1,200
Fig Garden, CA 93704 • 9,000
Filer, ID 83328 • 1,645
Fillmore, CA 93015 • 9,602
Fillmore, UT 84631 • 2,083
Fillmore □, MN • 21,930
Fillmore □, NE • 7,920
Findlay, IL 62534 • 868
Findlay, OH 45840 • 35,594
Finley, ND 58230 • 718
Finley, TN 38030 • 1,014
Finney □, KS • 23,825
Fircrest, WA 98466 • 5,477
Firebaugh, CA 93622 • 3,740
Firestone, CO 80520 • 1,204
Fisher, IL 61843 • 1,572
Fisher □, TX • 5,891
Fishers, IN 46038 • 2,008
Fishersville, VA 22939 • 700
Fishing Creek, MD 21634 • 650
Fishkill, NY 12524 • 1,555
Fiskdale, MA 01518 • 1,859
Fitchburg, MA 01420 • 39,580
Fitzgerald, GA 31750 • 10,187
Five Points, NM 87105 • 5,500
Flagler □, FL • 10,913
Flagler Beach, FL 32036 • 2,208
Flagtown, NJ 08821 • 800
Flanagan, IL 61740 • 978
Flanders, NJ 07836 • 6,000
Flandreau, SD 57028 • 2,114
Flathead □, MT • 51,966
Flat Lick, KY 40935 • 700
Flatonia, TX 78941 • 1,070
Flat River, MO 63601 • 4,443
Flat Rock, MI 48134 • 6,853
Flat Rock, NC 28731 • 1,200
Flatwoods, KY 41139 • 8,354
Fleetwood, PA 19522 • 3,422
Fleming □, KY • 12,323
Fleming-Neon, KY 41816 • 1,195
Flemingsburg, KY 41041 • 2,835
Flemington, NJ 08822 • 4,132
Flemington, PA 17745 • 1,416
Fletcher, NC 28732 • 700
Fletcher, OK 73541 • 1,074
Flint, MI 48501-99 • 159,611
Flint City, AL 35601 • 673
Flippin, AR 72634 • 1,072
Flomaton, AL 36441 • 1,882
Floodwood, MN 55736 • 648
Flora, IL 62839 • 5,379
Flora, IN 46929 • 2,303
Flora, MS 39071 • 1,507
Florala, AL 36442 • 2,165
Floral City, FL 32636 • 1,181
Floral Park, NY 11001-05 • 16,805
Florence, AL 35630-33 • 37,029
Florence, AZ 85232 • 3,391
Florence, CA 90001 • 38,000
Florence, CO 81226 • 2,987
Florence, KS 66851 • 729
Florence, KY 41042 • 15,586
Florence, MS 39073 • 1,111
Florence, NJ 08518 • 5,000
Florence, OR 97439 • 4,411
Florence, SC 29501-03 • 29,176
Florence, TX 76527 • 744
Florence □, SC • 110,163
Florence □, WI • 4,172
Floresville, TX 78114 • 4,381
Florham Park, NJ 07932 • 9,359
Florida, NY 10921 • 1,947
Florida City, FL 33034 • 6,174
Florien, LA 71429 • 964
Florin, CA 95828 • 16,523
Florissant, MO 63031-34 • 55,372
Flossmoor, IL 60422 • 8,423
Flourtown, PA 19031 • 5,200
Flower Hill, NY 11050 • 4,558
Flowery Branch, GA 30542 • 755
Flowood, MS 39208 • 943
Floyd □, GA • 79,800
Floyd □, IN • 61,205
Floyd □, IA • 19,597
Floyd □, KY • 48,764
Floyd □, TX • 9,834
Floyd □, VA • 11,563
Floydada, TX 79235 • 4,193
Flushing, MI 48433 • 8,624
Flushing, OH 43977 • 1,266
Fluvanna □, VA • 10,244
Foard □, TX • 2,158
Folcroft, PA 19032 • 8,231
Foley, AL 36535 • 4,003
Foley, MN 56329 • 1,606
Folkston, GA 31537 • 2,243
Follansbee, WV 26037 • 3,994
Folly Beach, SC 29439 • 1,478
Folsom, CA 95630 • 11,003
Folsom, NJ 08037 • 1,892
Folsom, PA 19033 • 7,600
Fonda, IA 50540 • 863
Fonda, NY 12068 • 1,006
Fond du Lac, WI 54935 • 35,863
Fond du Lac □, WI • 88,964
Fontana, CA 92335 • 37,107
Fontana, WI 53125 • 1,764
Fontanelle, IA 50846 • 805
Foothill Farms, CA 95841 • 13,700
Footville, WI 53537 • 794
Ford □, IL • 15,265
Ford □, KS • 24,315
Ford City, CA 93268 • 3,392
Ford City, PA 16226 • 3,923
Fordoche, LA 70732 • 676
Fords, NJ 08863 • 12,600
Fords Prairie, WA 98531 • 2,000
Fordyce, AR 71742 • 5,175
Foreman, AR 71836 • 1,377
Forest, MS 39074 • 5,229
Forest, OH 45843 • 1,633
Forest □, PA • 5,072
Forest □, WI • 9,044
Forest Acres, SC 29206 • 6,071
Forest City, IA 50436 • 4,270
Forest City, NC 28043 • 7,688
Forest City, PA 18421 • 1,924
Forest Grove, OR 97116 • 11,499
Forest Hill, TX 76119 • 11,684
Forest Hills, PA 15221 • 8,198
Forest Knolls, CA 94933 • 2,000
Forest Lake, MN 55025 • 4,596
Forest Park, GA 30050 • 18,782
Forest Park, IL 60130 • 15,177
Forest Park, LA 71291 • 1,500
Forest Park, OH 45240 • 18,675
Forestville, MD 20747 • 16,401
Forestville, NY 14062 • 804
Forgan, OK 73938 • 611
Forge Village, MA 01886 • 1,400
Forked River, NJ 08731 • 1,422
Forks, WA 98331 • 3,060
Forman, ND 58032 • 629
Forney, TX 75126 • 2,483
Forrest, IL 61741 • 1,246
Forrest □, MS • 66,018
Forrest City, AR 72335 • 13,803
Forreston, IL 61030 • 1,384
Forsyth, GA 31029 • 4,624
Forsyth, IL 62535 • 1,072
Forsyth, MO 65653 • 1,010
Forsyth, MT 59327 • 2,553
Forsyth □, GA • 27,958
Forsyth □, NC • 243,683
Fort Ashby, WV 26719 • 1,200
Fort Atkinson, WI 53538 • 9,785
Fort Bend □, TX • 130,846
Fort Benton, MT 59442 • 1,693
Fort Bragg, CA 95437 • 5,019
Fort Branch, IN 47648 • 2,504
Fort Calhoun, NE 68023 • 641
Fort Cobb, OK 73038 • 760
Fort Collins, CO 80521-26 • 65,092
Fort Covington, NY 12937 • 1,200
Fort Davis, TX 79734 • 850
Fort Defiance, AZ 86504 • 3,431
Fort Deposit, AL 36032 • 1,519
Fort Dodge, IA 50501 • 29,423
Fort Edward, NY 12828 • 3,561
Fort Fairfield, ME 04742 • 2,282
Fort Gaines, GA 31751 • 1,260
Fort Gay, WV 25514 • 886
Fort Gibson, OK 74434 • 2,477
Fort Hall, ID 83203 • 900
Fort Howard, MD 21052 • 1,050
Fort Kent, ME 04743 • 2,375
Fort Lauderdale, FL 33301-99 • 153,279
Fort Lee, NJ 07024 • 32,449
Fort Loramie, OH 45845 • 977
Fort Loudon, PA 17224 • 900
Fort Lupton, CO 80621 • 4,251
Fort Madison, IA 52627 • 13,520
Fort McKinley, OH 45426 • 11,536
Fort Meade, FL 33841 • 5,546
Fort Mill, SC 29715 • 4,162
Fort Mitchell, KY 41017 • 7,297
Fort Morgan, CO 80701 • 8,768
Fort Myers, FL 33901-14 • 36,638
Fort Myers Beach, FL 33931 • 5,753
Fort Ogden, FL 33842 • 900
Fort Oglethorpe, GA 30742 • 5,443
Fort Payne, AL 35967 • 11,485
Fort Pierce, FL 33450-54 • 33,802
Fort Pierre, SD 57532 • 1,789
Fort Plain, NY 13339 • 2,555
Fort Recovery, OH 45846 • 1,370
Fort Scott, KS 66701 • 8,893
Fort Shawnee, OH 45806 • 4,541
Fort Smith, AR 72901-16 • 71,626
Fort Stockton, TX 79735 • 8,688
Fort Sumner, NM 88119 • 1,421
Fort Thomas, KY 41075 • 16,012
Fort Totten, ND 58335 • 750
Fort Towson, OK 74735 • 789
Fortuna, CA 95540 • 7,591
Fort Valley, GA 31030 • 9,000
Fortville, IN 46040 • 2,787
Fort Walton Beach, FL 32548 • 20,829
Fort Washington, PA 19034 • 4,500
Fort Washington Forest, MD 20744 • 1,800
Fort Wayne, IN 46801-99 • 172,028
Fort Wingate, NM 87316 • 900
Fort Worth, TX 76101-99 • 385,164
Fort Wright, KY 41011 • 4,481
Fort Yates, ND 58538 • 771
Forty Fort, PA 18704 • 5,590
Fort Yukon, AK 99740 • 619
Fosston, MN 56542 • 1,599
Foster □, ND • 4,611
Foster Brook, PA 16701 • 950
Foster City, CA 94404 • 23,287

Foster Village, HI 96818 • *3,700*
Fostoria, OH 44830 • *15,743*
Fouke, AR 71837 • *614*
Fountain, CO 80817 • *8,324*
Fountain □, IN • *19,033*
Fountain City, IN 47341 • *839*
Fountain City, WI 54629 • *963*
Fountain Hill, PA 18015 • *4,805*
Fountain Inn, SC 29644 • *4,226*
Fountain Place, LA 70811 • *9,200*
Fountain Valley, CA 92708 • *55,080*
Four Corners, OR 97301 • *11,331*
Four Oaks, NC 27524 • *1,049*
Fowler, CA 93625 • *2,496*
Fowler, CO 81039 • *1,227*
Fowler, IN 47944 • *2,319*
Fowler, MI 48835 • *1,021*
Fowlerville, MI 48836 • *2,289*
Foxboro, MA 02035 • *5,697*
Fox Chapel, PA 15238 • *5,049*
Fox Lake, IL 60020 • *6,831*
Fox Lake, WI 53933 • *1,373*
Fox Point, WI 53217 • *7,649*
Fox River Grove, IL 60021 • *2,515*
Foxworth, MS 39483 • *1,000*
Frackville, PA 17931 • *5,308*
Framingham, MA 01701 • *65,113*
Francesville, IN 47946 • *944*
Francisco, IN 47649 • *612*
Frankenmuth, MI 48734 • *3,753*
Frankford, DE 19945 • *828*
Frankfort, IL 60423 • *4,357*
Frankfort, IN 46041 • *15,168*
Frankfort, KS 66427 • *1,038*
Frankfort, KY 40601 • *25,973*
Frankfort, MI 49635 • *1,603*
Frankfort, NY 13340 • *2,995*
Frankfort, OH 45628 • *1,008*
Franklin, GA 30217 • *711*
Franklin, IL 62638 • *645*
Franklin, IN 46131 • *11,563*
Franklin, KY 42134 • *7,738*
Franklin, LA 70538 • *9,584*
Franklin, MA 02038 • *18,217*
Franklin, NE 68939 • *1,167*
Franklin, NH 03235 • *7,901*
Franklin, NJ 07416 • *4,486*
Franklin, NC 28734 • *2,640*
Franklin, OH 45005 • *10,711*
Franklin, PA 16323 • *8,146*
Franklin, TN 37064 • *12,407*
Franklin, TX 77856 • *1,349*
Franklin, VA 23851 • *7,308*
Franklin, WV 26807 • *780*
Franklin, WI 53132 • *16,871*
Franklin □, AL • *28,350*
Franklin □, AR • *14,705*
Franklin □, FL • *7,661*
Franklin □, GA • *15,185*
Franklin □, ID • *8,895*
Franklin □, IL • *43,201*
Franklin □, IN • *19,612*
Franklin □, IA • *13,036*
Franklin □, KS • *22,062*
Franklin □, KY • *41,830*
Franklin □, LA • *24,141*
Franklin □, ME • *27,447*
Franklin □, MA • *64,317*
Franklin □, MS • *8,208*
Franklin □, MO • *71,233*
Franklin □, NE • *4,377*
Franklin □, NC • *30,055*
Franklin □, NY • *44,929*
Franklin □, OH • *869,126*
Franklin □, PA • *113,629*
Franklin □, TN • *31,983*
Franklin □, TX • *6,893*
Franklin □, VT • *34,788*
Franklin □, VA • *35,740*
Franklin □, WA • *35,025*
Franklin Grove, IL 61031 • *965*
Franklin Lakes, NJ 07417 • *8,769*
Franklin Park, IL 60131 • *17,507*
Franklin Park, PA 15143 • *6,135*
Franklin Square, NY 11010 • *32,800*
Franklinton, LA 70438 • *4,119*
Franklinton, NC 27525 • *1,394*
Franklinville, NJ 08322 • *900*
Franklinville, NC 27248 • *607*
Franklinville, NY 14737 • *1,887*
Frankston, TX 75763 • *1,255*
Frankton, IN 46044 • *2,080*
Fraser, MI 48026 • *14,560*
Frazee, MN 56544 • *1,284*
Frazeysburg, OH 43822 • *1,025*
Frazier Park, CA 93225 • *1,444*
Frederic, WI 54837 • *1,039*
Frederica, DE 19946 • *864*
Frederick, CO 80530 • *855*
Frederick, MD 21701 • *28,086*
Frederick, OK 73542 • *6,153*
Frederick □, MD • *114,792*
Frederick □, VA • *34,150*
Fredericksburg, IA 50630 • *1,075*
Fredericksburg, PA 17026 • *750*
Fredericksburg, TX 78624 • *6,412*
Fredericksburg, VA 22401–05 • *15,322*
Fredericktown, MO 63645 • *4,036*
Fredericktown, OH 43019 • *2,299*
Fredericktown, PA 15333 • *1,067*
Fredonia, AZ 86022 • *1,040*
Fredonia, KS 66736 • *3,047*
Fredonia, NY 14063 • *11,126*
Fredonia, PA 16124 • *712*
Fredonia, WI 53021 • *1,437*
Freeborn □, MN • *36,329*
Freeburg, IL 62243 • *2,989*
Freeburg, PA 17827 • *643*
Freedom, CA 95019 • *6,416*
Freedom, PA 15042 • *2,272*
Freehold, NJ 07728 • *10,020*
Freeland, MI 48623 • *1,364*
Freeland, PA 18224 • *4,285*
Freelandville, IN 47535 • *680*
Freeman, SD 57029 • *1,462*
Freemansburg, PA 18017 • *1,879*
Freeport, FL 32439 • *669*
Freeport, IL 61032 • *26,266*
Freeport, ME 04032 • *1,906*
Freeport, NY 11520 • *38,272*
Freeport, PA 16229 • *2,381*
Freeport, TX 77541 • *13,444*
Freer, TX 78357 • *3,213*
Freestone □, TX • *14,830*
Fremont, CA 94536–39 • *131,945*
Fremont, IN 46737 • *1,180*
Fremont, IA 52561 • *730*
Fremont, MI 49412 • *3,672*
Fremont, NE 68025 • *23,979*
Fremont, NC 27830 • *1,736*
Fremont, OH 43420 • *17,834*
Fremont □, CO • *28,676*
Fremont □, ID • *10,813*
Fremont □, IA • *9,401*
Fremont □, WY • *38,992*
French Island, WI 54601 • *3,000*
French Lick, IN 47432 • *2,265*
French Settlement, LA 70733 • *761*
Frenchtown, NJ 08825 • *1,573*
Frenchville, ME 04745 • *615*
Fresno, CA 93701–99 • *217,289*
Fresno □, CA • *514,229*
Frewsburg, NY 14738 • *2,000*
Friars Point, MS 38631 • *1,400*
Friday Harbor, WA 98250 • *1,200*
Fridley, MN 55432 • *30,228*
Friedens, PA 18080 • *900*
Friend, NE 68359 • *1,079*
Friendship, NY 14739 • *1,285*
Friendship, TN 38034 • *763*
Friendship, WI 53934 • *744*
Friendsville, TN 37737 • *694*
Friendswood, TX 77546 • *10,719*
Fries, VA 24330 • *758*
Frio □, TX • *13,785*
Friona, TX 79035 • *3,809*
Frisco, CO 80443 • *1,221*
Frisco City, AL 36445 • *1,424*
Fritch, TX 79036 • *2,299*
Frontenac, KS 66762 • *2,586*
Frontier □, NE • *3,647*
Front Royal, VA 22630 • *11,126*
Frostburg, MD 21532 • *7,715*
Frostproof, FL 33843 • *2,995*
Fruita, CO 81521 • *2,810*
Fruit Heights, UT 84037 • *2,728*
Fruitland, ID 83619 • *2,559*
Fruitland, MD 21826 • *2,694*
Fruitland, NM 87416 • *700*
Fruitland Park, FL 32731 • *2,259*
Fruitport, MI 49415 • *1,143*
Fruitvale, WA 98902 • *3,600*
Fruitville, FL 33582 • *3,070*
Fryeburg, ME 04037 • *1,644*
Fulda, MN 56131 • *1,308*
Fullerton, CA 92631–35 • *102,034*
Fullerton, NE 68638 • *1,506*
Fulton, AL 36446 • *606*
Fulton, IL 61252 • *3,936*
Fulton, KY 42041 • *3,137*
Fulton, MI 49052 • *750*
Fulton, MS 38843 • *3,238*
Fulton, MO 65251 • *11,046*
Fulton, NY 13069 • *13,312*
Fulton □, AR • *9,975*
Fulton □, GA • *589,904*
Fulton □, IL • *43,687*
Fulton □, IN • *19,335*
Fulton □, KY • *8,971*
Fulton □, NY • *55,153*
Fulton □, OH • *37,751*
Fulton □, PA • *12,842*
Fultondale, AL 35068 • *6,217*
Funkstown, MD 21734 • *1,103*
Fuquay-Varina, NC 27526 • *3,110*
Furnas □, NE • *6,486*
Fyffe, AL 35971 • *1,305*

G

Gabbs, NV 89409 • *811*
Gadsden, AL 35901–05 • *47,565*
Gadsden, TN 38337 • *683*
Gadsden □, FL • *41,565*
Gaffney, SC 29340 • *13,453*
Gage, OK 73843 • *667*
Gage □, NE • *24,456*
Gahanna, OH 43230 • *18,001*
Gaines □, TX • *13,150*
Gainesboro, TN 38562 • *1,119*
Gainesville, FL 32601–14 • *81,371*
Gainesville, GA 30501–06 • *15,280*
Gainesville, MO 65655 • *707*
Gainesville, TX 76240 • *14,081*
Gaithersburg, MD 20877–79 • *26,424*
Galatia, IL 62935 • *1,042*
Galax, VA 24333 • *6,524*
Galena, AK 99741 • *765*
Galena, IL 61036 • *3,876*
Galena, KS 66739 • *3,587*
Galena Park, TX 77547 • *9,879*
Galesburg, IL 61401 • *35,305*
Galesburg, MI 49053 • *1,822*
Gales Ferry, CT 06335 • *1,191*
Galesville, WI 54630 • *1,239*
Galeton, PA 16922 • *1,462*
Galeville, NY 13088 • *5,600*
Galien, MI 49113 • *692*
Galion, OH 44833 • *12,391*
Gallatin, MO 64640 • *2,063*
Gallatin, TN 37066 • *17,191*
Gallatin □, IL • *7,590*
Gallatin □, KY • *4,842*
Gallatin □, MT • *42,865*
Gallaway, TN 38036 • *804*
Gallia □, OH • *30,098*
Galliano, LA 70354 • *5,159*
Gallipolis, OH 45631 • *5,576*
Gallitzin, PA 16641 • *2,315*
Gallup, NM 87301 • *18,167*
Galt, CA 95632 • *5,514*
Galva, IL 61434 • *3,185*
Galva, KS 67443 • *651*
Galveston, IN 46932 • *1,822*
Galveston, TX 77550–53 • *61,902*
Galveston □, TX • *195,940*
Gambier, OH 43022 • *2,056*
Gambrills, MD 21054 • *650*
Ganado, AZ 86505 • *1,200*
Ganado, TX 77962 • *1,770*
Gang Mills, NY 14870 • *1,258*
Gantt, SC 29605 • *1,600*
Gap, PA 17527 • *1,022*
Garber, OK 73738 • *1,215*
Garberville, CA 95440 • *1,200*
Garden □, NE • *2,802*
Gardena, CA 90247–49 • *45,165*
Garden City, AL 35070 • *655*
Garden City, GA 31408 • *6,895*
Garden City, ID 83704 • *4,571*
Garden City, KS 67846 • *18,256*
Garden City, MI 48135 • *35,640*
Garden City, MO 64747 • *1,021*
Garden City, NY 11530 • *22,927*
Garden City Park, NY 11040 • *5,200*
Gardendale, AL 35071 • *7,928*
Garden Grove, CA 92640–45 • *123,307*
Garden Home, OR 97223 • *5,500*
Garden Plain, KS 67050 • *775*
Gardiner, ME 04345 • *6,485*
Gardner, IL 60424 • *1,322*
Gardner, KS 66030 • *2,392*
Gardner, MA 01440 • *17,900*
Gardnerville, NV 89410 • *2,800*
Garfield, NJ 07026 • *26,803*
Garfield □, CO • *22,514*
Garfield □, MT • *1,656*
Garfield □, NE • *2,363*
Garfield □, OK • *62,820*
Garfield □, UT • *3,673*
Garfield □, WA • *2,468*
Garfield Heights, OH 44125 • *34,938*
Garfield Park, DE 19720 • *1,000*
Garibaldi, OR 97118 • *999*
Garland, AR 71839 • *660*
Garland, NC 28441 • *885*
Garland, TX 75040–43 • *138,857*
Garland, UT 84312 • *1,405*
Garland □, AR • *70,531*
Garnavillo, IA 52049 • *723*
Garner, IA 50438 • *2,908*
Garner, NC 27529 • *10,073*
Garnett, KS 66032 • *3,310*
Garrard □, KY • *10,853*
Garretson, SD 57030 • *963*
Garrett, IN 46738 • *4,751*
Garrett □, MD • *26,498*
Garrett Park, MD 20896 • *2,800*
Garrettsville, OH 44231 • *1,769*
Garrison, KY 41141 • *650*
Garrison, MD 21055 • *750*
Garrison, ND 58540 • *1,830*
Garrison, NY 10524 • *650*
Garrison, TX 75946 • *1,059*
Garvin □, OK • *27,856*
Garwin, IA 50632 • *626*
Garwood, NJ 07027 • *4,752*
Gary, IN 46401–99 • *151,953*
Gary, WV 24836 • *2,233*
Garysburg, NC 27831 • *1,434*
Garyville, LA 70051 • *2,856*
Garza □, TX • *5,336*
Gas City, IN 46933 • *6,370*
Gasconade □, MO • *13,181*
Gasport, NY 14067 • *950*
Gassaway, WV 26624 • *1,225*
Gassville, AR 72635 • *859*
Gaston, IN 47342 • *1,150*
Gaston, NC 27832 • *883*
Gaston, SC 29053 • *960*
Gaston □, NC • *162,568*
Gastonia, NC 28052–54 • *47,333*
Gate City, VA 24251 • *2,494*
Gates, NY 14624 • *29,756*
Gates, TN 38037 • *729*
Gates □, NC • *8,875*
Gatesville, TX 76528 • *6,260*
Gatlinburg, TN 37738 • *3,210*
Gauley Bridge, WV 25085 • *1,177*
Gautier, MS 39553 • *8,917*
Gaylord, MI 49735 • *3,011*
Gaylord, MN 55334 • *1,933*
Gays Mills, WI 54631 • *627*
Gearhart, OR 97138 • *967*
Geary, OK 73040 • *1,700*
Geary □, KS • *29,852*
Geauga □, OH • *74,474*
Geistown, PA 15904 • *3,304*
Gem □, ID • *11,972*
Genesee, ID 83832 • *791*
Genesee, MI 48437 • *950*
Genesee □, MI • *450,449*
Genesee □, NY • *59,400*
Geneseo, IL 61254 • *6,373*
Geneseo, NY 14454 • *6,746*
Geneva, AL 36340 • *4,866*
Geneva, IL 60134 • *9,881*
Geneva, IN 46740 • *1,430*
Geneva, NE 68361 • *2,400*
Geneva, NY 14456 • *15,133*
Geneva, OH 44041 • *6,655*
Geneva □, AL • *24,253*
Geneva-on-the-Lake, OH 44041 • *1,634*
Genoa, IL 60135 • *3,276*
Genoa, NE 68640 • *1,090*
Genoa, OH 43430 • *2,213*
Genoa City, WI 53128 • *1,202*
Genola, UT 84655 • *630*
Gentry, AR 72734 • *1,468*
Gentry □, MO • *7,887*
George, IA 51237 • *1,241*
George □, MS • *15,297*
Georgetown, CA 95634 • *2,000*
Georgetown, CO 80444 • *830*
Georgetown, CT 06829 • *1,834*
Georgetown, DE 19947 • *1,710*
Georgetown, GA 31754 • *935*
Georgetown, IL 61846 • *4,220*
Georgetown, IN 47122 • *1,494*
Georgetown, KY 40324 • *10,972*
Georgetown, MA 01833 • *2,600*
Georgetown, OH 45121 • *3,467*
Georgetown, SC 29440 • *10,144*
Georgetown, TX 78626 • *9,468*
Georgetown □, SC • *42,461*
George West, TX 78022 • *2,627*
Georgiana, AL 36033 • *1,993*
Gerald, MO 63037 • *921*
Geraldine, AL 35974 • *911*
Gerber, CA 96035 • *950*
Gering, NE 69341 • *7,760*
Germantown, IL 62245 • *1,191*
Germantown, MD 20874 • *9,721*
Germantown, OH 45327 • *5,015*
Germantown, TN 38138 • *21,482*
Germantown, WI 53022 • *10,729*
Geronimo, OK 73543 • *726*
Gervais, OR 97026 • *799*
Gettysburg, PA 17325 • *7,194*
Gettysburg, SD 57442 • *1,623*
Geyserville, CA 95441 • *950*
Giants Neck, CT 06357 • *1,150*
Gibbon, MN 55335 • *787*
Gibbon, NE 68840 • *1,531*
Gibbstown, NJ 08027 • *5,676*
Gibsland, LA 71028 • *1,354*
Gibson, GA 30810 • *730*
Gibson □, IN • *33,156*
Gibson □, TN • *49,467*
Gibsonburg, OH 43431 • *2,479*
Gibson City, IL 60936 • *3,498*
Gibsonia, PA 15044 • *2,065*
Gibsonton, FL 33534 • *3,700*
Gibsonville, NC 27249 • *2,865*
Giddings, TX 78942 • *3,950*
Gideon, MO 63848 • *1,240*
Gifford, FL 32960 • *6,240*
Gifford, IL 61847 • *848*
Gig Harbor, WA 98335 • *2,429*
Gila □, AZ • *37,080*
Gila Bend, AZ 85337 • *1,585*
Gilbert, AZ 85234 • *5,717*
Gilbert, IA 50105 • *805*
Gilbert, LA 71336 • *800*
Gilbert, MN 55741 • *2,721*
Gilbert, OR 97266 • *4,000*
Gilbert, WV 25621 • *757*
Gilbertsville, PA 19525 • *900*
Gilbertville, IA 50634 • *740*
Gilbertville, MA 01031 • *1,029*
Gilchrist □, FL • *5,767*
Gilcrest, CO 80623 • *1,025*
Giles □, TN • *24,625*
Giles □, VA • *17,810*
Gillespie, IL 62033 • *3,740*
Gillespie □, TX • *13,532*
Gillett, AR 72055 • *927*
Gillett, WI 54124 • *1,356*
Gillette, WY 82716 • *12,134*
Gilliam □, OR • *2,057*
Gilman, IL 60938 • *1,913*
Gilman, IA 50106 • *642*
Gilmer, TX 75644 • *5,167*
Gilmer □, GA • *11,110*
Gilmer □, WV • *8,334*
Gilmore City, IA 50541 • *626*
Gilpin □, CO • *2,441*
Gilroy, CA 95020 • *21,641*
Girard, IL 62640 • *2,246*
Girard, KS 66743 • *2,888*
Girard, OH 44420 • *12,517*
Girard, PA 16417 • *2,615*
Girardville, PA 17935 • *2,268*
Glacier □, MT • *10,628*
Gladbrook, IA 50635 • *970*
Glades □, FL • *5,992*
Glade Spring, VA 24340 • *1,722*
Gladewater, TX 75647 • *6,548*
Gladstone, MI 49837 • *4,533*
Gladstone, MO 64118 • *24,990*
Gladstone, NJ 07934 • *2,038*
Gladstone, OR 97027 • *9,500*
Gladwin, MI 48624 • *2,479*
Gladwin □, MI • *19,957*
Glandorf, OH 45848 • *746*
Glasco, KS 67445 • *710*
Glasco, NY 12432 • *1,169*
Glascock □, GA • *2,382*
Glasford, IL 61533 • *1,201*
Glasgow, KY 42141 • *12,958*
Glasgow, MO 65254 • *1,336*
Glasgow, MT 59230 • *4,455*
Glasgow, VA 24555 • *1,259*
Glasgow, WV 25086 • *1,031*
Glasgow Village, MO 63137 • *7,200*
Glassboro, NJ 08028 • *14,574*
Glasscock □, TX • *1,304*
Glassport, PA 15045 • *6,242*
Glastonbury, CT 06033 • *7,049*
Gleason, TN 38229 • *1,335*
Glen Allen, VA 23060 • *1,100*
Glen Alpine, NC 28628 • *645*
Glen Avon, CA 92509 • *8,444*
Glen Burnie, MD 21061 • *30,000*
Glen Carbon, IL 62034 • *5,197*
Glencoe, AL 35905 • *4,648*
Glencoe, IL 60022 • *9,200*
Glencoe, MN 55336 • *4,396*
Glen Cove, NY 11542 • *24,618*
Glendale, AZ 85301–11 • *97,172*
Glendale, CA 91201–99 • *139,060*
Glendale, CO 80222 • *2,496*
Glendale, MS 39401 • *1,329*
Glendale, MO 63122 • *6,035*
Glendale, OH 45246 • *2,368*
Glendale, OR 97442 • *712*
Glendale, SC 29346 • *1,049*
Glen Dale, WV 26038 • *1,875*
Glendale, WI 53209 • *13,882*
Glendale Heights, IL 60139 • *23,163*
Glendale Heights, WV 26038 • *700*
Glendive, MT 59330 • *5,978*
Glendola, NJ 07719 • *2,300*
Glendora, CA 91740 • *38,500*
Glendora, NJ 08029 • *5,632*
Glen Ellyn, IL 60137 • *23,717*
Glen Gardner, NJ 08826 • *834*
Glenham, NY 12527 • *2,720*
Glen Head, NY 11545 • *6,800*
Glen Lyon, PA 18617 • *3,408*
Glenmora, LA 71433 • *1,479*
Glenn □, CA • *21,350*
Glenns Ferry, ID 83623 • *1,374*
Glennville, GA 30427 • *4,144*
Glenolden, PA 19036 • *7,633*
Glenpool, OK 74033 • *2,706*
Glen Raven, NC 27215 • *2,755*
Glen Ridge, NJ 07028 • *7,855*
Glen Rock, NJ 07452 • *11,497*
Glen Rock, PA 17327 • *1,662*
Glenrock, WY 82637 • *2,736*
Glen Rose, TX 76043 • *2,075*
Glens Falls, NY 12801 • *15,897*
Glenshaw, PA 15116 • *14,000*
Glenside, PA 19038 • *17,400*
Glen Ullin, ND 58631 • *1,125*
Glenview, IL 60025 • *32,060*
Glenville, MN 56036 • *851*
Glenville, WV 26351 • *2,155*
Glenwood, AR 71943 • *1,402*
Glenwood, FL 32722 • *950*
Glenwood, GA 30428 • *824*
Glenwood, IL 60425 • *10,538*
Glenwood, IA 51534 • *5,280*
Glenwood, MN 56334 • *2,523*
Glenwood, VA 24541 • *1,000*
Glenwood City, WI 54013 • *950*
Glenwood Farms, VA 23223 • *3,200*
Glenwood Springs, CO 81601 • *4,637*
Glidden, IA 51443 • *1,076*
Glide, OR 97443 • *900*
Globe, AZ 85501 • *6,886*
Gloster, MS 39638 • *1,726*
Gloucester, MA 01930 • *27,768*
Gloucester, VA 23061 • *900*
Gloucester □, NJ • *199,917*
Gloucester □, VA • *20,107*
Gloucester City, NJ 08030 • *13,121*
Gloucester Point, VA 23062 • *850*
Glouster, OH 45732 • *2,211*
Gloversville, NY 12078 • *17,836*
Gloverville, SC 29828 • *2,619*
Gluck, SC 29621 • *650*
Glyndon, MD 21071 • *1,100*
Glyndon, MN 56547 • *882*
Glynn □, GA • *54,981*
Gnadenhutten, OH 44629 • *1,320*
Gobles, MI 49055 • *816*
Goddard, KS 67052 • *1,427*
Godfrey, IL 62035 • *2,600*
Godley, TX 76044 • *614*
Goffstown, NH 03045 • *2,500*
Gogebic □, MI • *19,686*
Golconda, IL 62938 • *960*
Gold Bar, WA 98251 • *794*
Gold Beach, OR 97444 • *1,515*
Golden, CO 80401–19 • *12,237*
Golden Beach, FL 33160 • *612*
Golden City, MO 64748 • *900*
Goldendale, WA 98620 • *3,575*
Golden Meadow, LA 70357 • *2,282*
Golden Valley, MN 55427 • *22,775*
Golden Valley □, MT • *1,026*
Golden Valley □, ND • *2,391*
Goldfield, IA 50542 • *789*

Hamtramck, MI 48212 • 21,300
Hana, HI 96713 • 643
Hanahan, SC 29410 • 13,224
Hanamaulu, HI 96715 • 3,227
Hanapepe, HI 96716 • 1,417
Hanceville, AL 35077 • 2,220
Hancock, MD 21750 • 1,887
Hancock, MI 49930 • 5,122
Hancock, MN 56244 • 877
Hancock, NY 13783 • 1,526
Hancock □, GA • 9,466
Hancock □, IL • 23,877
Hancock □, IN • 43,939
Hancock □, IA • 13,833
Hancock □, KY • 7,742
Hancock □, ME • 41,781
Hancock □, MS • 24,537
Hancock □, OH • 64,581
Hancock □, TN • 6,887
Hancock □, WV • 41,053
Hand □, SD • 4,948
Handley, WV 25102 • 633
Hanford, CA 93230 • 20,958
Hankinson, ND 58041 • 1,158
Hanna, WY 82327 • 2,288
Hanna City, IL 61536 • 1,361
Hannibal, MO 63401 • 18,811
Hannibal, NY 13074 • 680
Hannibal, OH 43931 • 650
Hanover, IL 61041 • 1,069
Hanover, IN 47243 • 4,054
Hanover, KS 66945 • 802
Hanover, MA 02339 • 2,500
Hanover, MN 55341 • 647
Hanover, NH 03755 • 6,861
Hanover Township, NJ • 11,846
Hanover, OH 43055 • 926
Hanover, PA 17331 • 14,890
Hanover □, VA • 50,398
Hanover Center, MA 02339 • 1,000
Hanover Park, IL 60103 • 28,850
Hansen, ID 83334 • 1,078
Hansford □, TX • 6,209
Hanson, MA 02341 • 2,120
Hanson □, SD • 3,415
Hapeville, GA 30354 • 6,166
Happy, TX 79042 • 674
Happy Camp, CA 96039 • 1,110
Happy Valley, NM 88220 • 630
Happy Valley, OR 97236 • 1,499
Harahan, LA 70123 • 11,384
Haralson □, GA • 18,422
Harbor, OR 97415 • 2,856
Harbor Beach, MI 48441 • 2,000
Harborcreek, PA 16421 • 800
Harbor Springs, MI 49740 • 1,567
Hardee □, FL • 19,379
Hardeeville, SC 29927 • 1,250
Hardeman □, TN • 23,873
Hardeman □, TX • 6,368
Hardin, IL 62047 • 1,107
Hardin, MO 64035 • 688
Hardin, MT 59034 • 3,300
Hardin □, IL • 5,383
Hardin □, IA • 21,776
Hardin □, KY • 88,917
Hardin □, OH • 32,719
Hardin □, TN • 22,280
Hardin □, TX • 40,721
Harding, MA 02052 • 950
Harding □, NM • 1,090
Harding □, SD • 1,700
Hardinsburg, KY 40143 • 2,211
Hardwick, GA 31034 • 6,000
Hardwick, VT 05843 • 1,476
Hardy, AR 72542 • 643
Hardy □, WV • 10,030
Harford □, MD • 145,930
Hargill, TX 78549 • 800
Harker Heights, TX 76543 • 7,345
Harkers Island, NC 28531 • 1,901
Harlan, IN 46743 • 1,000
Harlan, IA 51537 • 5,357
Harlan, KY 40831 • 3,024
Harlan □, KY • 41,889
Harlan □, NE • 4,292
Harlem, FL 33440 • 2,669
Harlem, GA 30814 • 1,485
Harlem, MT 59526 • 1,023
Harleyville, SC 29448 • 606
Harlingen, TX 78550–52 • 43,543
Harlowton, MT 59036 • 1,181
Harmon □, OK • 4,519
Harmony, IN 47853 • 613
Harmony, MN 55939 • 1,133
Harmony, PA 16037 • 1,334
Harmony, RI 02829 • 800
Harmony Hills, DE 19711 • 1,350
Harnett □, NC • 59,570
Harney □, OR • 8,314
Harper, KS 67058 • 1,823
Harper □, KS • 7,778
Harper □, OK • 4,715
Harpersville, AL 35078 • 934
Harper Woods, MI 48225 • 16,361
Harrah, OK 73045 • 2,897
Harriman, TN 37748 • 8,303
Harrington, DE 19952 • 2,405
Harrington Park, NJ 07640 • 4,532
Harris, MN 55032 • 678
Harris, RI 02816 • 1,000
Harris □, GA • 15,464
Harris □, TX • 2,409,547
Harrisburg, AR 72432 • 1,921
Harrisburg, IL 62946 • 10,410
Harrisburg, OR 97446 • 1,881
Harrisburg, PA 17101–99 • 53,264
Harrison, AR 72601 • 9,567
Harrison, MI 48625 • 1,700
Harrison, NJ 07029 • 12,242
Harrison, NY 10528 • 23,046
Harrison, OH 45030 • 5,855
Harrison, TN 37341 • 6,206
Harrison □, IN • 27,276
Harrison □, IA • 16,348
Harrison □, KY • 15,166
Harrison □, MS • 157,665
Harrison □, MO • 9,890
Harrison □, OH • 18,152
Harrison □, TX • 52,265
Harrison □, WV • 77,710
Harrisonburg, LA 71340 • 610
Harrisonburg, VA 22801 • 19,671
Harrisonville, MO 64701 • 6,372
Harristown, IL 62537 • 1,456
Harrisville, NY 13648 • 937
Harrisville, PA 16038 • 1,033
Harrisville, RI 02830 • 1,224
Harrisville, UT 84404 • 1,371
Harrisville, WV 26362 • 1,673
Harrodsburg, KY 40330 • 7,265
Hart, MI 49420 • 1,888
Hart, TX 79043 • 1,008
Hart □, GA • 18,585
Hart □, KY • 15,402
Hartford, AL 36344 • 2,647
Hartford, AR 72938 • 613
Hartford, CT 06101–99 • 136,392
Hartford, IL 62048 • 1,887
Hartford, IA 50118 • 761
Hartford, KY 42347 • 2,512
Hartford, MI 49057 • 2,493
Hartford, SD 57033 • 1,207
Hartford, WI 53027 • 7,046
Hartford □, CT • 807,766
Hartford City, IN 47348 • 7,622
Hartington, NE 68739 • 1,730
Hartland, ME 04943 • 1,041
Hartland, WI 53029 • 5,559
Hartley, IA 51346 • 1,700
Hartley □, TX • 3,987
Hartsdale, NY 10530 • 12,226
Hartselle, AL 35640 • 8,858
Hartshorne, OK 74547 • 2,380
Hartsville, SC 29550 • 7,631
Hartsville, TN 37074 • 2,674
Hartville, OH 44632 • 1,772
Hartwell, GA 30643 • 4,855
Harvard, IL 60033 • 5,126
Harvard, MA 01451 • 900
Harvard, NE 68944 • 1,217
Harvey, IL 60426 • 35,810
Harvey, LA 70058 • 15,000
Harvey, MI 49855 • 1,341
Harvey, ND 58341 • 2,527
Harvey □, KS • 30,531
Harwich, MA 02645 • 1,000
Harwich Port, MA 02646 • 1,900
Harwinton, CT 06791 • 3,293
Harwood, MA 01460 • 900
Harwood Heights, IL 60656 • 8,228
Hasbrouck Heights, NJ 07604 • 12,166
Haskell, AR 72015 • 1,074
Haskell, OK 74436 • 1,953
Haskell, TX 79521 • 3,782
Haskell □, KS • 3,814
Haskell □, OK • 11,010
Haskell □, TX • 7,725
Haslett, MI 48840 • 7,025
Hastings, FL 32045 • 636
Hastings, MI 49058 • 6,418
Hastings, MN 55033 • 12,827
Hastings, NE 68901 • 23,045
Hastings, PA 16646 • 1,574
Hastings-On-Hudson, NY 10706 • 8,573
Hatboro, PA 19040 • 7,579
Hatch, NM 87937 • 1,028
Hatfield, MA 01038 • 1,251
Hatfield, PA 19440 • 2,533
Hatteras, NC 27943 • 700
Hattiesburg, MS 39401–02 • 40,829
Hatton, ND 58240 • 787
Haubstadt, IN 47639 • 1,389
Haughton, LA 71037 • 1,510
Hauppauge, NY 11788 • 14,200
Hauser, OR 97459 • 630
Hauula, HI 96717 • 2,997
Havana, FL 32333 • 2,782
Havana, IL 62644 • 4,277
Havelock, NC 28532 • 17,718
Haven, KS 67543 • 1,125
Haverford Township, PA 19041 • 5,800
Haverhill, MA 01830 • 46,865
Haverstraw, NY 10927 • 8,800
Havertown, PA 19083 • 36,000
Haviland, KS 67059 • 770
Havre, MT 59501 • 10,891
Havre de Grace, MD 21078 • 8,763
Havre North, MT 59501 • 1,073
Hawaii □, HI • 92,053
Hawaiian Gardens, CA 90716 • 10,548
Hawarden, IA 51023 • 2,722
Hawesville, KY 42348 • 1,036
Hawi, HI 96719 • 795
Hawkins □, TN • 43,751
Hawkinsville, GA 31036 • 4,372
Hawk Run, PA 16840 • 750
Hawley, MN 56549 • 1,634
Hawley, PA 18428 • 1,181
Hawley, TX 79525 • 679
Haworth, NJ 07641 • 3,509
Haw River, NC 27258 • 1,858
Hawthorne, CA 90250 • 56,447
Hawthorne, FL 32640 • 1,303
Hawthorne, NV 89415 • 3,741
Hawthorne, NJ 07506 • 18,200
Hawthorne, NY 10532 • 4,900
Haxtun, CO 80731 • 1,014
Hayden, AZ 85235 • 1,205
Hayden, CO 81639 • 1,720
Hayden, ID 83835 • 2,586
Haydenville, MA 01039 • 900
Hayes, LA 70646 • 830
Hayes □, NE • 1,356
Hayesville, OR 97303 • 9,213
Hayfield, MN 55940 • 1,243
Hayfield, VA 22310 • 2,200
Hayfork, CA 96041 • 1,788
Haynesville, LA 71038 • 3,454
Hays, KS 67601 • 16,301
Hays, NC 28635 • 900
Hays □, TX • 40,594
Hay Springs, NE 69347 • 794
Haysville, KS 67060 • 8,006
Hayti, MO 63851 • 3,964
Hayti Heights, MO 63851 • 1,023
Hayward, CA 94540–46 • 94,342
Hayward, WI 54843 • 1,698
Hayward Addition, SD 57106 • 725
Haywood □, NC • 46,495
Haywood □, TN • 20,318
Hazard, KY 41701 • 5,371
Hazardville, CT 06082 • 5,436
Hazel Crest, IL 60429 • 13,973
Hazel Dell, WA 98665 • 6,000
Hazel Green, AL 35750 • 1,503
Hazel Green, WI 53811 • 1,282
Hazel Park, MI 48030 • 20,914
Hazelwood, MO 63042–45 • 12,935
Hazelwood, NC 28738 • 1,811
Hazen, AR 72064 • 1,636
Hazen, ND 58545 • 2,365
Hazlehurst, GA 31539 • 4,249
Hazlehurst, MS 39083 • 4,437
Hazlet, NJ 07730 • 28,013
Hazleton, IA 50641 • 877
Hazleton, PA 18201 • 27,318
Headland, AL 36345 • 3,327
Healdsburg, CA 95448 • 7,217
Healdton, OK 73438 • 3,769
Heard □, GA • 6,520
Hearne, TX 77859 • 5,418
Heath, OH 43056 • 6,969
Heath Springs, SC 29058 • 979
Hebbronville, TX 78361 • 4,079
Heber City, UT 84032 • 4,362
Heber Springs, AR 72543 • 4,589
Hebron, IL 60034 • 786
Hebron, IN 46341 • 2,696
Hebron, MD 21830 • 714
Hebron, NE 68370 • 1,906
Hebron, ND 58638 • 1,078
Hebron, OH 43025 • 2,035
Hector, MN 55342 • 1,252
Hedges, FL 32097 • 900
Hedrick, IA 52563 • 847
Heflin, AL 36264 • 3,014
Hegins, PA 17938 • 900
Heidelberg, MS 39439 • 1,098
Heilwood, PA 15745 • 700
Helena, AL 35080 • 2,130
Helena, AR 72342 • 9,598
Helena, GA 31037 • 1,390
Helena, MT 59601 • 23,938
Helena, OK 73741 • 710
Hellam, PA 17406 • 1,428
Hellertown, PA 18055 • 6,025
Helmetta, NJ 08828 • 955
Helotes, TX 78023 • 1,409
Helper, UT 84526 • 2,724
Hemet, CA 92343–44 • 22,454
Hemingford, NE 69348 • 1,023
Hemingway, SC 29554 • 853
Hemlock, MI 48626 • 1,362
Hemphill, TX 75948 • 1,353
Hemphill □, TX • 5,304
Hempstead, NY 11550–54 • 40,404
Hempstead, TX 77445 • 3,456
Hempstead □, AR • 23,635
Henagar, AL 35978 • 1,188
Henderson, KY 42420 • 24,834
Henderson, LA 70517 • 1,560
Henderson, MN 56044 • 739
Henderson, NE 68371 • 1,072
Henderson, NV 89015 • 24,363
Henderson, NC 27536 • 13,522
Henderson, TN 38340 • 4,449
Henderson, TX 75652 • 11,473
Henderson, WV 25106 • 604
Henderson □, IL • 9,114
Henderson □, KY • 40,849
Henderson □, NC • 58,580
Henderson □, TN • 21,390
Henderson □, TX • 42,606
Henderson's Point, MS 39571 • 1,114
Hendersonville, NC 28739 • 6,862
Hendersonville, TN 37075 • 26,561
Hendricks, MN 56136 • 737
Hendricks □, IN • 69,804
Hendry □, FL • 18,599
Henlawson, WV 25624 • 950
Hennepin, IL 61327 • 716
Hennepin □, MN • 941,411
Hennessey, OK 73742 • 2,287
Henniker, NH 03242 • 1,538
Henning, MN 56551 • 832
Henning, TN 38041 • 638
Henrico □, VA • 180,735
Henrietta, NC 28076 • 1,412
Henrietta, NY 14467 • 1,200
Henrietta, TX 76365 • 3,149
Henry, IL 61537 • 2,740
Henry □, AL • 15,302
Henry □, GA • 36,309
Henry □, IL • 57,968
Henry □, IN • 53,336
Henry □, IA • 18,890
Henry □, KY • 12,740
Henry □, MO • 19,672
Henry □, OH • 28,383
Henry □, TN • 28,656
Henry □, VA • 57,654
Henryetta, OK 74437 • 6,432
Henryville, IN 47126 • 1,132
Hephzibah, GA 30815 • 1,452
Heppner, OR 97836 • 1,498
Herculaneum, MO 63048 • 2,293
Hercules, CA 94547 • 5,963
Hereford, TX 79045 • 15,853
Herington, KS 67449 • 2,930
Heritage Village, CT 06488 • 5,200
Herkimer, NY 13350 • 8,383
Herkimer □, NY • 66,714
Hermann, MO 65041 • 2,695
Hermansville, MI 49847 • 700
Hermantown, MN 55811 • 6,759
Herminie, PA 15637 • 1,100
Hermiston, OR 97838 • 9,408
Hermitage, PA 16148 • 16,365
Hermosa Beach, CA 90254 • 18,070
Hernando, FL 32642 • 1,653
Hernando, MS 38632 • 2,969
Hernando □, FL • 44,469
Herndon, VA 22070–71 • 11,449
Heron Lake, MN 56137 • 783
Herrin, IL 62948 • 10,708
Herscher, IL 60941 • 1,214
Hershey, NE 69143 • 633
Hershey, PA 17033 • 9,000
Hertford, NC 27944 • 1,941
Hertford □, NC • 23,368
Hesperia, CA 92345 • 13,540
Hesperia, MI 49421 • 876
Hessmer, LA 71341 • 743
Hesston, KS 67062 • 3,013
Hettinger, ND 58639 • 1,739
Hettinger □, ND • 4,275
Heuvelton, NY 13654 • 777
Hewitt, TX 76643 • 5,247
Hewlett, NY 11557 • 6,880
Heyburn, ID 83336 • 2,889
Heyworth, IL 61745 • 1,598
Hialeah, FL 33010–16 • 145,254
Hiawatha, IA 52233 • 4,825
Hiawatha, KS 66434 • 3,702
Hibbing, MN 55746 • 21,193
Hickman, KY 42050 • 2,894
Hickman, NE 68372 • 687
Hickman □, KY • 6,065
Hickman □, TN • 15,151
Hickory, MS 39332 • 670
Hickory, NC 28601 • 20,757
Hickory □, MO • 6,367
Hickory Hills, IL 60457 • 13,778
Hicksville, NY 11801–99 • 43,245
Hicksville, OH 43526 • 3,929
Hico, TX 76457 • 1,375
Hico, WV 25854 • 700
Hidalgo, TX 78557 • 2,288
Hidalgo □, NM • 6,049
Hidalgo □, TX • 283,323
Hiddenite, NC 28636 • 800
Higbee, MO 65257 • 817
Higganum, CT 06441 • 1,660
Higgins, TX 79046 • 702
Higginsville, MO 64037 • 4,595
High Bridge, NJ 08829 • 3,435
Highland, CA 92346 • 10,400
Highland, IL 62249 • 7,122
Highland, IN 46322 • 25,935
Highland, KS 66035 • 954
Highland, MI 48031 • 1,000
Highland, NY 12528 • 2,184
Highland, WI 53543 • 860
Highland □, OH • 33,477
Highland □, VA • 2,937
Highland Falls, NY 10928 • 4,187
Highland Heights, OH 44124 • 5,739
Highland Lakes, NJ 07422 • 2,888
Highland Park, IL 60035 • 30,611
Highland Park, MI 48203 • 27,909
Highland Park, NJ 08904 • 13,396
Highland Park, TX 75205 • 8,909
Highlands, NJ 07732 • 5,187
Highlands, NC 28741 • 653
Highlands, TX 77562 • 4,450
Highlands □, FL • 47,526
Highland Springs, VA 23075 • 7,500
Highmore, SD 57345 • 1,055
High Point, NC 27260–64 • 63,808
High Ridge, MO 63049 • 900
High Rolls Mountain Park, NM 88325 • 650
High Spire, PA 17034 • 2,959
High Springs, FL 32643 • 2,491
Hightstown, NJ 08520 • 4,581
Highview, KY 40228 • 13,286
Highwood, IL 60040 • 5,452
Hilbert, WI 54129 • 1,176
Hildale, UT 86021 • 1,009
Hill □, MT • 17,985
Hill □, TX • 25,024
Hill City, KS 67642 • 2,028
Hillcrest, IL 61068 • 818
Hillcrest, NY 10977 • 5,357
Hillcrest Center, CA 93306 • 30,000
Hillcrest Heights, MD 20748 • 17,021
Hilliard, FL 32046 • 1,869
Hilliard, OH 43026 • 8,008
Hillsboro, IL 62049 • 4,408
Hillsboro, KS 67063 • 2,717
Hillsboro, MO 63050 • 1,508
Hillsboro, NH 03244 • 1,797
Hillsboro, ND 58045 • 1,600
Hillsboro, OH 45133 • 6,356
Hillsboro, OR 97123–24 • 27,664
Hillsboro, TX 76645 • 7,397
Hillsboro, WI 54634 • 1,263
Hillsborough, CA 94010 • 10,372
Hillsborough, NC 27278 • 3,019
Hillsborough □, FL • 646,960
Hillsborough □, NH • 276,608
Hillsdale, IL 61257 • 731
Hillsdale, MI 49242 • 7,432
Hillsdale, NJ 07642 • 10,495
Hillsdale □, MI • 42,071
Hillside, IL 60162 • 8,279
Hillside, NJ 07205 • 21,440
Hillside Heights, DE 19711 • 800
Hillsville, PA 16132 • 915
Hillsville, VA 24343 • 2,123
Hillview, KY 40229 • 5,196
Hilo, HI 96720 • 35,269
Hilton, NY 14468 • 4,151
Hilton Head Island, SC 29928 • 11,344
Hima, KY 40951 • 700
Hinckley, IL 60520 • 1,447
Hinckley, MN 55037 • 963
Hindman, KY 41822 • 876
Hinds □, MS • 250,998
Hines, OR 97738 • 1,632
Hinesville, GA 31313 • 11,309
Hingham, MA 02043 • 12,800
Hinkley, CA 92347 • 700
Hinsdale, IL 60521 • 16,726
Hinsdale, MA 01235 • 950
Hinsdale, NH 03451 • 1,546
Hinsdale □, CO • 408
Hinton, IA 51024 • 659
Hinton, OK 73047 • 1,432
Hinton, WV 25951 • 4,622
Hiram, GA 30141 • 1,030
Hiram, OH 44234 • 1,360
Hitchcock, TX 77563 • 6,655
Hitchcock □, NE • 4,079
Hitchcock Lake, CT 06716 • 1,600
Hitchins, KY 41146 • 700
Hoagland, IN 46745 • 650
Hobart, IN 46342 • 22,987
Hobart, OK 73651 • 4,735
Hobbs, NM 88240 • 29,153
Hobe Sound, FL 33455 • 6,822
Hoboken, NJ 07030 • 42,460
Hockessin, DE 19707 • 950
Hocking □, OH • 24,304
Hockley □, TX • 23,230
Hodge, LA 71247 • 708
Hodgeman □, KS • 2,269
Hodgenville, KY 42748 • 2,531
Hoffman, MN 56339 • 631
Hoffman Estates, IL 60195 • 37,272
Hogansville, GA 30230 • 3,362
Hohenwald, TN 38462 • 3,922
Ho-Ho-Kus, NJ 07423 • 4,129
Hoisington, KS 67544 • 3,678
Hokah, MN 55941 • 686
Hoke □, NC • 20,383
Hokes Bluff, AL 35903 • 3,216
Holbrook, AZ 86025 • 5,785
Holbrook, MA 02343 • 11,140
Holbrook, NY 11741 • 12,800
Holcomb, KS 67851 • 816
Holcomb, MO 63852 • 632
Holden, MA 01520 • 3,900
Holden, MO 64040 • 2,195
Holden, WV 25625 • 1,600
Holden Heights, FL 32805 • 8,000
Holdenville, OK 74848 • 5,469
Holdingford, MN 56340 • 635
Holdrege, NE 68949 • 5,624
Holgate, OH 43527 • 1,315
Holiday, FL 33590 • 15,400
Holladay, UT 84117 • 22,189
Holland, IN 47541 • 683
Holland, MI 49423 • 26,281
Holland, NY 14080 • 1,000
Holland, OH 43528 • 1,048
Holland, TX 76534 • 863
Hollandale, MS 38748 • 4,336
Holley, NY 14470 • 1,882
Holliday, TX 76366 • 1,349
Hollidaysburg, PA 16648 • 5,892
Hollins, VA 24019 • 11,000
Hollis, OK 73550 • 2,958
Hollister, CA 95023 • 11,488
Hollister, MO 65672 • 1,439
Holliston, MA 01746 • 12,622
Holloway Terrace, DE 19720 • 1,000
Hollow Rock, TN 38342 • 955
Hollsopple, PA 15935 • 900
Holly, CO 81047 • 969
Holly, MI 48442 • 4,874
Holly Grove, AR 72069 • 754

Lexington Park, MD 20653 • 10,361
Libby, MT 59923 • 2,748
Liberal, KS 67901 • 14,911
Liberal, MO 64762 • 701
Liberty, IN 47353 • 1,844
Liberty, KY 42539 • 2,206
Liberty, MS 39645 • 669
Liberty, MO 64068 • 16,251
Liberty, NC 27298 • 1,997
Liberty, NY 12754 • 4,293
Liberty, SC 29657 • 3,167
Liberty, TX 77575 • 7,945
Liberty □, FL • 4,260
Liberty □, GA • 37,583
Liberty □, MT • 2,329
Liberty □, TX • 47,088
Liberty Acres, CA 90250 • 4,600
Liberty Center, OH 43532 • 1,111
Liberty Corner, NJ 07938 • 800
Liberty Lake, WA 99019 • 900
Libertyville, IL 60048 • 16,520
Libuse, LA 71348 • 700
Licking, MO 65542 • 1,272
Licking □, OH • 120,981
Lidgerwood, ND 58053 • 971
Liftwood, DE 19803 • 800
Lighthouse Point, FL 33064 • 11,488
Ligonier, IN 46767 • 3,134
Ligonier, PA 15658 • 1,917
Lihue, HI 96766 • 4,000
Lilbourn, MO 63862 • 1,463
Lilburn, GA 30247 • 3,765
Lillington, NC 27546 • 1,948
Lilly, PA 15938 • 1,462
Lilly Grove, WV 24740 • 1,700
Lima, NY 14485 • 2,025
Lima, OH 45801-09 • 47,381
Limestone, ME 04750 • 1,334
Limestone □, AL • 46,005
Limestone □, TX • 20,224
Limon, CO 80828 • 1,805
Lincoln, AL 35096 • 2,081
Lincoln, AR 72744 • 1,422
Lincoln, CA 95648 • 4,132
Lincoln, ID 83401 • 700
Lincoln, IL 62656 • 16,327
Lincoln, KS 67455 • 1,599
Lincoln, ME 04457 • 3,524
Lincoln, MA 01773 • 3,300
Lincoln, MO 65338 • 819
Lincoln, NE 68501-99 • 171,932
Lincoln □, AR • 13,369
Lincoln □, CO • 4,663
Lincoln □, GA • 6,716
Lincoln □, ID • 3,436
Lincoln □, KS • 4,145
Lincoln □, KY • 19,053
Lincoln □, LA • 39,763
Lincoln □, ME • 25,691
Lincoln □, MN • 8,207
Lincoln □, MS • 30,174
Lincoln □, MO • 22,193
Lincoln □, MT • 17,752
Lincoln □, NE • 36,455
Lincoln □, NV • 3,732
Lincoln □, NM • 10,997
Lincoln □, NC • 42,372
Lincoln □, OK • 26,601
Lincoln □, OR • 35,264
Lincoln □, SD • 13,942
Lincoln □, TN • 26,483
Lincoln □, WA • 9,604
Lincoln □, WV • 23,675
Lincoln □, WI • 26,555
Lincoln □, WY • 12,177
Lincoln Acres, CA 92047 • 1,800
Lincoln City, OR 97367 • 5,469
Lincoln Heights, OH 45215 • 5,259
Lincoln Park, CO 81212 • 3,426
Lincoln Park, GA 30286 • 1,755
Lincoln Park, MI 48146 • 45,105
Lincoln Park, NJ 07035 • 8,806
Lincolnshire, IL 60069 • 4,151
Lincolnton, GA 30817 • 1,406
Lincolnton, NC 28092 • 4,879
Lincoln Village, CA 95207 • 6,476
Lincoln Village, OH 43228 • 10,548
Lincolnville, SC 29483 • 808
Lincolnwood, IL 60645 • 11,921
Lincroft, NJ 07738 • 4,100
Linda, CA 95901 • 10,225
Lindale, GA 30147 • 2,958
Lindale, TX 75771 • 2,180
Linden, AL 36748 • 2,773
Linden, IN 47955 • 700
Linden, MI 48451 • 2,174
Linden, NJ 07036 • 37,836
Linden, TN 37096 • 1,087
Linden, TX 75563 • 2,443
Lindenhurst, IL 60046 • 6,220
Lindenhurst, NY 11757 • 26,919
Lindenwold, NJ 08021 • 18,196
Lindon, UT 84062 • 2,796
Lindsay, CA 93247 • 6,924
Lindsay, OK 73052 • 3,454
Lindsborg, KS 67456 • 3,155
Lindstrom, MN 55045 • 1,972
Linesville, PA 16424 • 1,198
Lineville, AL 36266 • 2,257
Linglestown, PA 17112 • 3,000
Linn, MO 65051 • 1,211
Linn □, IA • 169,775
Linn □, KS • 8,234
Linn □, MO • 15,495
Linn □, OR • 89,495
Lino Lakes, MN 55014 • 4,966
Linthicum Heights, MD 21090 • 7,457
Linton, IN 47441 • 6,315
Linton, ND 58552 • 1,561
Linwood, MA 01525 • 1,100
Linwood, NJ 08221 • 6,144
Linworth, OH 43085 • 650
Lipscomb, AL 35020 • 3,741
Lipscomb □, TX • 3,766
Lisbon, IA 52253 • 1,458
Lisbon, ME 04250 • 1,200
Lisbon, NH 03585 • 1,151
Lisbon, ND 58054 • 2,283
Lisbon, OH 44432 • 3,159
Lisbon Center, ME 04251 • 625
Lisbon Falls, ME 04252 • 4,370
Lisle, IL 60532 • 13,625
Lisman, AL 36912 • 638
Litchfield, CT 06759 • 1,489
Litchfield, IL 62056 • 7,204
Litchfield, MI 49252 • 1,353
Litchfield, MN 55355 • 5,904
Litchfield □, CT • 156,769
Litchfield Park, AZ 85340 • 3,657
Lithia Springs, GA 30057 • 9,145
Lithonia, GA 30058 • 2,637
Lititz, PA 17543 • 7,590
Little Canada, MN 55110 • 7,102
Little Chute, WI 54140 • 7,907
Little Falls, MN 56345 • 7,250
Little Falls, NJ 07424 • 11,496
Little Falls, NY 13365 • 6,156
Little Ferry, NJ 07643 • 9,399
Littlefield, TX 79339 • 7,409
Littlefork, MN 56653 • 918
Little Hocking, OH 45742 • 800
Little Lake, MI 49833 • 900
Little River □, AR • 13,952
Little Rock, AR 72201-99 • 158,461
Little Silver, NJ 07739 • 5,548
Littlestown, PA 17340 • 2,870
Littleton, CO 80120-27 • 28,631
Littleton, MA 01460 • 3,109
Littleton, NH 03561 • 4,480
Littleton, NC 27850 • 820
Little Valley, NY 14755 • 1,203
Littleville, AL 35653 • 1,262
Live Oak, CA 95953 • 3,103
Live Oak, FL 32060 • 6,732
Live Oak, TX 78233 • 8,183
Live Oak □, TX • 9,606
Live Oak Manor, LA 70094 • 1,500
Livermore, CA 94550 • 48,349
Livermore, KY 42352 • 1,672
Livermore Falls, ME 04254 • 2,441
Liverpool, PA 17045 • 809
Liverpool, TX 77577 • 602
Livingston, AL 35470 • 3,187
Livingston, CA 95334 • 5,326
Livingston, IL 62058 • 949
Livingston, LA 70754 • 1,260
Livingston, MT 59047 • 6,994
Livingston, NJ 07039 • 28,040
Livingston, TN 38570 • 3,372
Livingston, TX 77351 • 4,928
Livingston, WI 53554 • 642
Livingston □, IL • 41,381
Livingston □, KY • 9,219
Livingston □, LA • 58,806
Livingston □, MI • 100,289
Livingston □, MO • 15,739
Livingston □, NY • 57,006
Livingston Manor, NY 12758 • 1,522
Livonia, LA 70755 • 980
Livonia, MI 48150-54 • 104,814
Livonia, NY 14487 • 1,238
Llangollen Estates, DE 19720 • 870
Llano, TX 78643 • 3,071
Llano □, TX • 10,144
Lloyd Harbor, NY 11743 • 3,405
Loami, IL 62661 • 770
Lobelville, TN 37097 • 993
Loch Lomond, VA 22110 • 2,300
Lockesburg, AR 71846 • 616
Lockhart, FL 32810 • 10,571
Lockhart, TX 78644 • 7,953
Lock Haven, PA 17745 • 9,617
Lockland, OH 45215 • 4,292
Lockney, TX 79241 • 2,334
Lockport, IL 60441 • 9,170
Lockport, LA 70374 • 2,424
Lockport, NY 14094 • 24,844
Lockwood, MO 65682 • 971
Lockwood, MT 59101 • 1,600
Locust, NJ 07760 • 700
Locust, NC 28097 • 1,590
Locust Grove, GA 30248 • 1,479
Locust Grove, NY 11791 • 11,648
Locust Grove, OK 74352 • 1,179
Lodge Grass, MT 59050 • 771
Lodi, CA 95240 • 35,221
Lodi, NJ 07644 • 23,956
Lodi, OH 44254 • 2,942
Lodi, WI 53555 • 1,959
Logan, IA 51546 • 1,540
Logan, KS 67646 • 720
Logan, NM 88426 • 735
Logan, OH 43138 • 6,557
Logan, UT 84321 • 26,844
Logan, WV 25601 • 3,029
Logan □, AR • 20,144
Logan □, CO • 19,800
Logan □, IL • 31,802
Logan □, KS • 3,478
Logan □, KY • 24,138
Logan □, NE • 983
Logan □, ND • 3,493
Logan □, OH • 39,155
Logan □, OK • 26,881
Logan □, WV • 50,679
Logansport, IN 46947 • 17,731
Logansport, LA 71049 • 1,565
Loganville, GA 30249 • 1,841
Loganville, PA 17342 • 1,020
Log Lane Village, CO 80701 • 709
Lolo, MT 59847 • 2,418
Loma Linda, CA 92354 • 10,694
Lomax, IL 61454 • 601
Lombard, IL 60148 • 36,897
Lometa, TX 76853 • 666
Lomira, WI 53048 • 1,446
Lomita, CA 90717 • 18,807
Lompoc, CA 93436 • 26,267
Lonaconing, MD 21539 • 1,420
London, AR 72847 • 859
London, KY 40741 • 4,002
London, OH 43140 • 6,958
Londonderry, NH 03053 • 950
Londontowne, MD 21037 • 3,500
Lone Grove, OK 73443 • 3,369
Lone Pine, CA 93545 • 1,684
Lone Tree, IA 52755 • 1,014
Lone Wolf, OK 73655 • 613
Long □, GA • 4,524
Long Bar Harbor, MD 21009 • 700
Long Beach, CA 90801-99 • 361,334
Long Beach, IN 46360 • 2,262
Long Beach, MD 20685 • 900
Long Beach, MS 39560 • 7,967
Long Beach, NY 11561 • 34,073
Long Beach, WA 98631 • 1,199
Longboat Key, FL 33548 • 4,843
Long Branch, NJ 07740 • 29,819
Longbranch, WA 98351 • 900
Long Lake, IL 60041 • 2,201
Longmeadow, MA 01106 • 16,301
Longmont, CO 80501 • 42,942
Longport, NJ 08403 • 1,249
Long Prairie, MN 56347 • 2,859
Long Valley, NJ 07853 • 1,682
Long View, KY 42701 • 650
Long View, NC 28601 • 3,587
Longview, TX 75601-08 • 62,762
Longview, WA 98632 • 31,052
Longwood, FL 32750 • 10,029
Lonoke, AR 72086 • 4,128
Lonoke □, AR • 34,518
Lonsdale, MN 55046 • 1,160
Lonsdale, RI 02865 • 4,100
Loogootee, IN 47553 • 3,100
Lookout Mountain, TN 37350 • 1,886
Loon Lake, WA 99148 • 650
Lorain, OH 44052-55 • 75,416
Lorain □, OH • 274,909
Loraine, TX 79532 • 929
Lordsburg, NM 88045 • 3,195
Loreauville, LA 70552 • 860
Lorenzo, TX 79343 • 1,394
Loretto, KY 40037 • 954
Loretto, PA 15940 • 1,395
Loretto, TN 38469 • 1,612
Lorida, FL 33857 • 620
Loris, SC 29569 • 2,193
Lorman, MS 39096 • 650
Los Alamitos, CA 90720 • 11,529
Los Alamos, CA 93440 • 950
Los Alamos, NM 87544 • 11,039
Los Alamos □, NM • 17,599
Los Altos, CA 94022 • 25,769
Los Altos Hills, CA 94022 • 7,421
Los Angeles, CA 90001-99 • 2,966,850
Los Angeles □, CA • 7,477,503
Los Banos, CA 93635 • 10,341
Los Fresnos, TX 78566 • 2,173
Los Gatos, CA 95030 • 26,906
Los Lunas, NM 87031 • 3,525
Los Molinos, CA 96055 • 1,241
Los Nietos, CA 90606 • 7,100
Los Padillas, NM 87105 • 2,500
Los Ranchos de Albuquerque, NM 87107 • 2,702
Lost Creek, WV 26385 • 604
Lost Hills, CA 93249 • 800
Lott, TX 76656 • 865
Loudon, TN 37774 • 3,943
Loudon □, TN • 28,553
Loudonville, NY 12211 • 9,000
Loudonville, OH 44842 • 2,945
Loudoun □, VA • 57,427
Loughman, FL 33858 • 800
Louisa, KY 41230 • 1,832
Louisa, VA 23093 • 932
Louisa □, IA • 12,055
Louisa □, VA • 17,825
Louisburg, KS 66053 • 1,744
Louisburg, NC 27549 • 3,238
Louise, TX 77455 • 900
Louisiana, MO 63353 • 4,261
Louisville, AL 36048 • 791
Louisville, CO 80027 • 5,593
Louisville, GA 30434 • 2,823
Louisville, IL 62858 • 1,166
Louisville, KY 40201-99 • 298,840
Louisville, MS 39339 • 7,323
Louisville, NE 68037 • 1,022
Louisville, OH 44641 • 7,996
Loup □, NE • 859
Loup City, NE 68853 • 1,368
Love □, OK • 7,469
Loveland, CO 80537 • 30,244
Loveland, OH 45140 • 9,106
Loveland Park, OH 45140 • 1,653
Lovell, WY 82431 • 2,447
Lovelock, NV 89419 • 1,680
Lovely, KY 41231 • 700
Loves Park, IL 61111 • 13,192
Lovettsville, VA 22080 • 613
Lovilia, IA 50150 • 637
Loving, NM 88256 • 1,355
Loving □, TX • 91
Lovington, IL 61937 • 1,313
Lovington, IA 50322 • 850
Lovington, NM 88260 • 9,727
Lowden, IA 52255 • 717
Lowell, AR 72745 • 1,078
Lowell, IN 46356 • 5,827
Lowell, MA 01850-54 • 92,418
Lowell, MI 49331 • 3,707
Lowell, NC 28098 • 2,917
Lowell, OH 45744 • 729
Lowell, OR 97452 • 661
Lowellville, OH 44436 • 1,558
Lower Burrell, PA 15068 • 13,200
Lower Paia, HI 96779 • 1,500
Lowmoor, VA 24457 • 700
Lowndes □, AL • 13,253
Lowndes □, GA • 67,972
Lowndes □, MS • 57,304
Lowry City, MO 64763 • 676
Lowville, NY 13367 • 3,364
Loxley, AL 36551 • 804
Loyal, WI 54446 • 1,252
Loyall, KY 40854 • 1,210
Loyalton, CA 96118 • 1,030
Lubbock, TX 79401-99 • 173,979
Lubbock □, TX • 211,651
Lubec, ME 04652 • 990
Lucama, NC 27851 • 1,070
Lucas, OH 44843 • 753
Lucas □, IA • 10,313
Lucas □, OH • 471,741
Lucasville, OH 45648 • 3,349
Luce □, MI • 6,659
Lucedale, MS 39452 • 2,429
Lucerne, CA 95458 • 1,767
Lucernemines, PA 15754 • 1,380
Lucerne Valley, CA 92356 • 1,300
Luck, WI 54853 • 997
Luckey, OH 43443 • 895
Ludington, MI 49431 • 8,937
Ludlow, KY 41016 • 4,959
Ludlow, MA 01056 • 18,150
Ludlow, PA 16333 • 800
Ludlow, VT 05149 • 1,352
Ludowici, GA 31316 • 1,286
Lufkin, TX 75901 • 28,562
Lugoff, SC 29078 • 2,909
Lukachukai, AZ 86507 • 1,049
Lula, GA 30554 • 857
Luling, LA 70070 • 4,006
Luling, TX 78648 • 5,039
Lumber City, GA 31549 • 1,426
Lumberport, WV 26386 • 939
Lumberton, MS 39455 • 2,217
Lumberton, NJ 08048 • 700
Lumberton, NC 28358 • 18,241
Lumpkin, GA 31815 • 1,335
Lumpkin □, GA • 10,762
Luna □, NM • 15,585
Luna Pier, MI 48157 • 1,443
Lunenburg, MA 01462 • 1,789
Lunenburg □, VA • 12,124
Luray, VA 22835 • 3,584
Lusk, WY 82225 • 1,650
Lutcher, LA 70071 • 4,730
Lutesville, MO 63762 • 865
Luther, OK 73054 • 1,159
Lutherville-Timonium, MD 21093 • 17,854
Luttrell, TN 37779 • 962
Lutz, FL 33549 • 5,555
Luverne, AL 36049 • 2,639
Luverne, MN 56156 • 4,568
Luxemburg, WI 54217 • 1,040
Luxora, AR 72358 • 1,739
Luzerne, PA 18709 • 3,703
Luzerne □, PA • 343,079
Lycoming □, PA • 118,416
Lyford, TX 78569 • 1,618
Lykens, PA 17048 • 2,181
Lyle, WA 98635 • 700
Lyman, SC 29365 • 1,067
Lyman, WY 82937 • 2,284
Lyman □, SD • 3,864
Lynch, KY 40855 • 1,614
Lynchburg, OH 45142 • 1,205
Lynchburg, TN 37352 • 668
Lynchburg, VA 24501-15 • 66,743
Lynden, WA 98264 • 4,022
Lyndhurst, NJ 07071 • 20,326
Lyndhurst, OH 44124 • 18,092
Lyndon, IL 61261 • 777
Lyndon, KS 66451 • 1,132
Lyndon, KY 40222 • 1,553
Lyndonville, NY 14098 • 916
Lyndonville, VT 05851 • 1,401
Lyndora, PA 16045 • 1,900
Lynn, IN 47355 • 1,250
Lynn, MA 01901-10 • 78,471
Lynn □, TX • 8,605
Lynne Acres, MD 21207 • 7,700
Lynnfield, MA 01940 • 11,267
Lynn Garden, TN 37665 • 7,213
Lynn Haven, FL 32444 • 6,239
Lynnwood, WA 98036-37 • 22,641
Lynwood, CA 90262 • 48,548
Lyon □, IA • 12,896
Lyon □, KS • 35,108
Lyon □, KY • 6,490
Lyon □, MN • 25,207
Lyon □, NV • 13,594
Lyon Mountain, NY 12952 • 950
Lyons, CO 80540 • 1,137
Lyons, GA 30436 • 4,203
Lyons, IL 60534 • 9,925
Lyons, IN 47443 • 782
Lyons, KS 67554 • 4,134
Lyons, MI 48851 • 708
Lyons, NE 68038 • 1,214
Lyons, NY 14489 • 4,160
Lyons, OR 97358 • 877
Lyons Falls, NY 13368 • 755
Lytle, TX 78052 • 1,920

M

Mabank, TX 75147 • 1,443
Mabel, MN 55954 • 861
Maben, MS 39750 • 855
Mableton, GA 30059 • 20,200
Mabscott, WV 25871 • 1,668
Mabton, WA 98935 • 1,248
McAdoo, PA 18237 • 2,940
McAlester, OK 74501 • 17,255
McAlisterville, PA 17049 • 650
McAllen, TX 78501-04 • 66,281
McAlmont, AR 72117 • 1,600
McAlpine, MD 21043 • 2,500
McArthur, OH 45651 • 1,912
McBee, SC 29101 • 774
McCall, ID 83638 • 2,188
McCamey, TX 79752 • 2,436
McCammon, ID 83250 • 770
McCandless, PA 15237 • 26,250
McCaysville, GA 30555 • 1,219
McClain □, OK • 20,291
McCleary, WA 98557 • 1,419
MacClenny, FL 32063 • 3,851
McCloud, CA 96057 • 1,656
McClure, IL 62957 • 700
McClure, OH 43534 • 694
McClure, PA 17841 • 1,024
McClusky, ND 58463 • 658
McColl, SC 29570 • 2,677
McComas, WV 24735 • 800
McComb, MS 39648 • 12,331
McComb, OH 45858 • 1,608
McCone □, MT • 2,702
McConnellsburg, PA 17233 • 1,178
McConnelsville, OH 43756 • 2,018
McCook, NE 69001 • 8,404
McCook □, SD • 6,444
McCormick, SC 29835 • 1,725
McCormick □, SC • 7,797
McCracken □, KY • 61,310
McCreary □, KY • 15,634
McCrory, AR 72101 • 1,942
McCulloch □, TX • 8,735
McCurtain □, OK • 36,151
McDonald □, MO • 14,917
McDonough, GA 30253 • 2,778
McDonough □, IL • 37,467
McDowell □, NC • 35,135
McDowell □, WV • 49,899
McDuffie □, GA • 18,546
Macedon, NY 14502 • 1,400
Macedonia, OH 44056 • 6,571
McEwen, TN 37101 • 1,352
McFarland, CA 93250 • 5,151
McFarland, WI 53558 • 3,783
McGehee, AR 71654 • 5,671
McGill, NV 89318 • 1,419
McGraw, NY 13101 • 1,188
McGregor, IA 52157 • 945
McGregor, TX 76657 • 4,513
McGuffey, OH 45859 • 646
McHenry, IL 60050 • 11,949
McHenry □, IL • 147,897
McHenry □, ND • 7,858
Machias, ME 04654 • 1,277
Machias, NY 14101 • 700
McIntosh, MN 56556 • 681
McIntosh □, GA • 8,046
McIntosh □, ND • 4,800
McIntosh □, OK • 15,562
McKean □, PA • 50,635
McKee, KY 40447 • 759
McKeesport, PA 15130-35 • 31,012
McKees Rocks, PA 15136 • 8,742
McKenzie, AL 36456 • 605
McKenzie, TN 38201 • 5,405
McKenzie □, ND • 7,132
Mackinac □, MI • 10,178
Mackinaw, IL 61755 • 1,354
Mackinaw City, MI 49701 • 820
McKinley □, NM • 56,536
McKinleyville, CA 95521 • 7,772
McKinney, TX 75069 • 16,256
McLain, MS 39456 • 688
McLaughlin, SD 57642 • 754
McLean, IL 61754 • 836
McLean, TX 79057 • 1,160
McLean, VA 22101-03 • 22,000
McLean □, IL • 119,149
McLean □, KY • 10,090
McLean □, ND • 12,383
McLeansboro, IL 62859 • 2,960
McLennan □, TX • 170,755
McLeod □, MN • 29,657
McLoud, OK 74851 • 4,061
McLouth, KS 66054 • 700

McMechen, WV 26040 • *2,402*
McMinn □, TN • *41,878*
McMinnville, OR 97128 • *14,080*
McMinnville, TN 37110 • *10,683*
McMullen □, TX • *789*
McNairy □, TN • *22,525*
McNary, AZ 85930 • *1,320*
McNeil, AR 71752 • *725*
McNulty, OR 97051 • *1,805*
Macomb, IL 61455 • *19,863*
Macomb □, MI • *694,600*
Macon, GA 31201–99 • *116,896*
Macon, IL 62544 • *1,300*
Macon, MS 39341 • *2,396*
Macon, MO 63552 • *5,680*
Macon □, AL • *26,829*
Macon □, GA • *14,003*
Macon □, IL • *131,375*
Macon □, MO • *16,313*
Macon □, NC • *20,178*
Macon □, TN • *15,700*
Macoupin □, IL • *49,384*
McPherson, KS 67460 • *11,753*
McPherson □, KS • *26,855*
McPherson □, NE • *593*
McPherson □, SD • *4,027*
McQueeney, TX 78123 • *950*
McRae, AR 72102 • *641*
McRae, GA 31055 • *3,409*
McRoberts, KY 41835 • *1,106*
McSherrystown, PA 17344 • *2,764*
Macungie, PA 18062 • *1,899*
McVeigh, KY 41546 • *800*
McVille, ND 58254 • *626*
Madawaska, ME 04756 • *4,165*
Maddock, ND 58348 • *677*
Madeira, OH 45243 • *9,341*
Madelia, MN 56062 • *2,130*
Madera, CA 93637–39 • *21,732*
Madera, PA 16661 • *900*
Madera □, CA • *63,116*
Madill, OK 73446 • *3,173*
Madison, AL 35758 • *4,057*
Madison, AR 72359 • *1,238*
Madison, CT 06443 • *2,069*
Madison, FL 32340 • *3,487*
Madison, GA 30650 • *2,954*
Madison, IL 62060 • *5,915*
Madison, IN 47250 • *12,472*
Madison, KS 66860 • *1,099*
Madison, ME 04950 • *2,788*
Madison, MN 56256 • *2,212*
Madison, MS 39110 • *2,241*
Madison, MO 65263 • *656*
Madison, NE 68748 • *1,950*
Madison, NJ 07940 • *15,357*
Madison, NC 27025 • *2,806*
Madison, OH 44057 • *2,291*
Madison, SD 57042 • *6,210*
Madison, WV 25130 • *3,228*
Madison, WI 53701–99 • *170,616*
Madison □, AL • *196,966*
Madison □, AR • *11,373*
Madison □, FL • *14,894*
Madison □, GA • *17,747*
Madison □, ID • *19,480*
Madison □, IL • *247,661*
Madison □, IN • *139,336*
Madison □, IA • *12,597*
Madison □, KY • *53,352*
Madison □, LA • *15,975*
Madison □, MS • *41,613*
Madison □, MO • *10,725*
Madison □, MT • *5,448*
Madison □, NE • *31,382*
Madison □, NC • *16,827*
Madison □, NY • *65,150*
Madison □, OH • *33,004*
Madison □, TN • *74,546*
Madison □, TX • *10,649*
Madison □, VA • *10,232*
Madison Heights, MI 48071 • *35,375*
Madison Heights, VA 24572 • *3,500*
Madisonville, KY 42431 • *16,979*
Madisonville, LA 70447 • *799*
Madisonville, TN 37354 • *2,884*
Madisonville, TX 77864 • *3,660*
Madras, OR 97741 • *2,235*
Madrid, IA 50156 • *2,281*
Madrid, NY 13660 • *800*
Maeser, UT 84078 • *2,216*
Magalia, CA 95954 • *950*
Magazine, AR 72943 • *799*
Magdalena, NM 87825 • *1,022*
Magee, MS 39111 • *3,497*
Magna, UT 84044 • *13,138*
Magnolia, AR 71753 • *11,909*
Magnolia, MS 39652 • *2,461*
Magnolia, NJ 08049 • *4,881*
Magnolia, OH 44643 • *986*
Magnolia, TX 77355 • *867*
Magoffin □, KY • *13,515*
Mahanoy City, PA 17948 • *6,167*
Mahaska □, IA • *22,867*
Mahnomen, MN 56557 • *1,283*
Mahnomen □, MN • *5,535*
Mahomet, IL 61853 • *1,986*
Mahoning □, OH • *289,487*
Mahopac, NY 10541 • *5,265*
Mahwah, NJ 07430 • *7,500*
Maiden, NC 28650 • *2,574*
Maili, HI 96792 • *5,026*
Maine, NY 13802 • *700*
Maitland, FL 32751 • *8,763*
Maize, KS 67101 • *1,294*
Major □, OK • *8,772*

Makaha, HI 96792 • *7,905*
Makakilo City, HI 96706 • *7,691*
Makawao, HI 96788 • *1,066*
Makaweli, HI 96769 • *700*
Malabar, FL 32950 • *1,118*
Malad City, ID 83252 • *1,915*
Malaga, NJ 08328 • *950*
Malakoff, TX 75148 • *2,082*
Malden, MA 02148 • *53,386*
Malden, MO 63863 • *6,096*
Malden, WV 25306 • *950*
Malheur □, OR • *26,896*
Malibu, CA 90265 • *10,000*
Malone, FL 32445 • *897*
Malone, NY 12953 • *7,668*
Malta, IL 60150 • *995*
Malta, MT 59538 • *2,367*
Malta, OH 43758 • *956*
Malvern, AR 72104 • *10,163*
Malvern, IA 51551 • *1,244*
Malvern, OH 44644 • *1,032*
Malvern, PA 19355 • *2,999*
Malverne, NY 11565 • *9,262*
Mamaroneck, NY 10543 • *17,616*
Mammoth, AZ 85618 • *1,906*
Mammoth, WV 25132 • *750*
Mammoth Lakes, CA 93546 • *3,000*
Mammoth Spring, AR 72554 • *1,158*
Mamou, LA 70554 • *3,194*
Man, WV 25635 • *1,333*
Manahawkin, NJ 08050 • *1,467*
Manasquan, NJ 08736 • *5,354*
Manassa, CO 81141 • *945*
Manassas, VA 22110–11 • *15,438*
Manassas Park, VA 22111 • *6,524*
Manatee □, FL • *148,442*
Manawa, WI 54949 • *1,205*
Mancelona, MI 49659 • *1,432*
Manchaug, MA 01526 • *1,000*
Manchester, CT 06040 • *49,761*
Manchester, GA 31816 • *4,796*
Manchester, IA 52057 • *4,942*
Manchester, KY 40962 • *1,838*
Manchester, MD 21102 • *1,830*
Manchester, MA 01944 • *5,424*
Manchester, MI 48158 • *1,686*
Manchester, MO 63011 • *6,191*
Manchester, NH 03101–99 • *90,936*
Manchester, NY 14504 • *1,698*
Manchester, OH 45144 • *2,313*
Manchester, PA 17345 • *2,027*
Manchester, TN 37355 • *7,250*
Manchester Center, VT 05255 • *1,719*
Mancos, CO 81328 • *870*
Mandan, ND 58554 • *15,513*
Mandeville, AR 75501 • *700*
Mandeville, LA 70448 • *6,076*
Mangham, LA 71259 • *867*
Mangum, OK 73554 • *3,833*
Manhasset, NY 11030 • *8,530*
Manhattan, KS 66502 • *32,644*
Manhattan, MT 59741 • *988*
Manhattan Beach, CA 90266 • *31,542*
Manheim, PA 17545 • *5,015*
Manila, AR 72442 • *2,553*
Manilla, IA 51454 • *1,020*
Manistee, MI 49660 • *7,566*
Manistee □, MI • *23,019*
Manistique, MI 49854 • *3,962*
Manito, IL 61546 • *1,869*
Manitou Beach, MI 49779 • *4,500*
Manitou Springs, CO 80829 • *4,475*
Manitowoc, WI 54220 • *32,547*
Manitowoc □, WI • *82,918*
Mankato, KS 66956 • *1,205*
Mankato, MN 56001 • *28,651*
Manlius, NY 13104 • *5,241*
Manly, IA 50456 • *1,496*
Mannford, OK 74044 • *1,610*
Manning, IA 51455 • *1,609*
Manning, SC 29102 • *4,746*
Mannington, WV 26582 • *3,036*
Manomet, MA 02345 • *950*
Manor, TX 78653 • *1,044*
Manorhaven, NY 11050 • *5,384*
Mansfield, AR 72944 • *1,000*
Mansfield, IL 61854 • *921*
Mansfield, LA 71052 • *6,485*
Mansfield, MA 02048 • *6,786*
Mansfield, MO 65704 • *1,423*
Mansfield, OH 44901–99 • *53,927*
Mansfield, PA 16933 • *3,322*
Mansfield, TX 76063 • *8,102*
Mansfield Center, CT 06250 • *1,043*
Manson, IA 50563 • *1,924*
Mansura, LA 71350 • *2,074*
Mantachie, MS 38855 • *732*
Manteca, CA 95336 • *24,925*
Manteno, IL 60950 • *3,155*
Manteo, NC 27954 • *902*
Manti, UT 84642 • *2,080*
Manton, MI 49663 • *1,212*
Mantorville, MN 55955 • *705*
Mantua, NJ 08051 • *1,900*
Mantua, OH 44255 • *1,041*
Mantua Hills, VA 22030 • *1,550*
Manvel, TX 77578 • *3,549*
Manville, NJ 08835 • *11,278*
Manville, RI 02838 • *3,100*
Many, LA 71449 • *3,988*
Many Farms, AZ 86538 • *1,364*
Maple Bluff, WI 53704 • *1,351*
Maple Grove, MN 55369 • *20,525*
Maple Heights, OH 44137 • *29,735*

Maple Lake, MN 55358 • *1,132*
Maple Plain, MN 55359 • *1,421*
Maple Rapids, MI 48853 • *683*
Maple Shade, NJ 08052 • *20,525*
Maplesville, AL 36750 • *754*
Mapleton, IA 51034 • *1,495*
Mapleton, MN 56065 • *1,516*
Mapleton, OR 97453 • *900*
Mapleton, UT 84663 • *2,726*
Maple Valley, WA 98038 • *900*
Mapleville, RI 02839 • *900*
Maplewood, MN 55109 • *26,990*
Maplewood, MO 63143 • *10,960*
Maplewood, NJ 07040 • *22,950*
Maquoketa, IA 52060 • *6,313*
Marana, AZ 85653 • *1,674*
Marathon, FL 33050 • *7,508*
Marathon, NY 13803 • *1,046*
Marathon, TX 79842 • *750*
Marathon, WI 54448 • *1,552*
Marathon □, WI • *111,270*
Marble, MN 55764 • *757*
Marble, NC 28905 • *700*
Marble Cliff, OH 43212 • *630*
Marble Falls, TX 78654 • *3,252*
Marblehead, MA 01945 • *20,126*
Marblehead, OH 43440 • *679*
Marble Hill, MO 63764 • *601*
Marbury, MD 20658 • *1,189*
Marceline, MO 64658 • *2,938*
Marcellus, MI 49067 • *1,134*
Marco, FL 33937 • *4,679*
Marcus, IA 51035 • *1,206*
Marcus Hook, PA 19061 • *2,638*
Marengo, IL 60152 • *4,361*
Marengo, IN 47140 • *892*
Marengo, IA 52301 • *2,308*
Marengo □, AL • *25,047*
Marfa, TX 79843 • *2,466*
Margaret, AL 35112 • *757*
Margaretville, NY 12455 • *755*
Margate, FL 33063 • *35,900*
Margate, MD 21061 • *4,800*
Margate City, NJ 08402 • *9,179*
Marianna, AR 72360 • *6,220*
Marianna, FL 32446 • *7,006*
Maricopa, AZ 85239 • *900*
Maricopa, CA 93252 • *946*
Maricopa □, AZ • *1,509,262*
Mariemont, OH 45227 • *3,295*
Marienville, PA 16239 • *900*
Maries □, MO • *7,551*
Marietta, GA 30060–69 • *30,829*
Marietta, OH 45750 • *16,467*
Marietta, OK 73448 • *2,494*
Marietta, SC 29661 • *900*
Marin □, CA • *222,592*
Marina, CA 93933 • *20,647*
Marina del Rey, CA 90292 • *8,065*
Marine, IL 62061 • *957*
Marine City, MI 48039 • *4,414*
Marinette, WI 54143 • *11,965*
Marinette □, WI • *39,314*
Maringouin, LA 70757 • *1,291*
Marion, AL 36756 • *4,467*
Marion, AR 72364 • *2,996*
Marion, CT 06444 • *800*
Marion, IL 62959 • *14,031*
Marion, IN 46952–53 • *35,874*
Marion, IA 52302 • *19,474*
Marion, KS 66861 • *1,951*
Marion, KY 42064 • *3,392*
Marion, LA 71260 • *989*
Marion, MA 02738 • *1,438*
Marion, MI 49665 • *816*
Marion, MS 39342 • *771*
Marion, NC 28752 • *3,684*
Marion, NY 14505 • *950*
Marion, OH 43302 • *37,040*
Marion, PA 17235 • *900*
Marion, SC 29571 • *7,700*
Marion, SD 57043 • *830*
Marion, VA 24354 • *7,029*
Marion, WI 54950 • *1,348*
Marion □, AL • *30,041*
Marion □, AR • *11,334*
Marion □, FL • *122,488*
Marion □, GA • *5,297*
Marion □, IL • *43,523*
Marion □, IN • *765,233*
Marion □, IA • *29,669*
Marion □, KS • *13,522*
Marion □, KY • *17,910*
Marion □, MS • *25,708*
Marion □, MO • *28,638*
Marion □, OH • *67,974*
Marion □, OR • *204,692*
Marion □, SC • *34,179*
Marion □, TN • *24,416*
Marion □, TX • *10,360*
Marion □, WV • *65,789*
Marionville, MO 65705 • *1,920*
Mariposa, CA 95338 • *1,150*
Mariposa □, CA • *11,108*
Marissa, IL 62257 • *2,568*
Marked Tree, AR 72365 • *3,201*
Markesan, WI 53946 • *1,446*
Markham, IL 60426 • *15,172*
Markham, TX 77456 • *1,100*
Markle, IN 46770 • *975*
Marks, MS 38646 • *2,260*
Marksville, LA 71351 • *5,113*
Marlboro, NJ 07746 • *5,700*
Marlboro, NY 12542 • *1,580*
Marlboro, VA 23224 • *950*
Marlboro □, SC • *31,634*

Marlborough, CT 06447 • *1,039*
Marlborough, MA 01752 • *30,617*
Marlborough, NH 03455 • *1,231*
Marlene Village, OR 97005 • *1,500*
Marlette, MI 48453 • *1,761*
Marley, MD 21061 • *4,800*
Marlin, TX 76661 • *7,099*
Marlinton, WV 24954 • *1,352*
Marlow, OK 73055 • *5,017*
Marlowe, WV 25419 • *700*
Marlton, NJ 08053 • *9,411*
Marmaduke, AR 72443 • *1,168*
Marmet, WV 25315 • *2,196*
Maroa, IL 61756 • *1,760*
Marquette, KS 67464 • *639*
Marquette, MI 49855 • *23,288*
Marquette □, MI • *74,101*
Marquette □, WI • *11,672*
Marquette Heights, IL 61554 • *3,386*
Marrero, LA 70072 • *36,548*
Marrtown, WV 26101 • *900*
Mars, PA 16046 • *1,803*
Marseilles, IL 61341 • *4,766*
Marshall, AR 72650 • *1,595*
Marshall, IL 62441 • *3,655*
Marshall, MI 49068 • *7,201*
Marshall, MN 56258 • *11,161*
Marshall, MO 65340 • *12,781*
Marshall, NC 28753 • *809*
Marshall, TX 75670 • *24,921*
Marshall, WI 53559 • *2,363*
Marshall □, AL • *65,622*
Marshall □, IL • *14,479*
Marshall □, IN • *39,155*
Marshall □, IA • *41,652*
Marshall □, KS • *12,787*
Marshall □, KY • *25,637*
Marshall □, MN • *13,027*
Marshall □, MS • *29,296*
Marshall □, OK • *10,550*
Marshall □, SD • *5,404*
Marshall □, TN • *19,698*
Marshall □, WV • *41,608*
Marshallton, DE 19808 • *3,950*
Marshalltown, IA 50158 • *26,938*
Marshallville, GA 31057 • *1,540*
Marshallville, OH 44645 • *788*
Marshfield, MA 02050 • *4,421*
Marshfield, MO 65706 • *3,871*
Marshfield, WI 54449 • *18,290*
Marshfield Hills, MA 02051 • *2,308*
Mars Hill, ME 04758 • *1,500*
Mars Hill, NC 28754 • *2,126*
Marshville, NC 28103 • *2,011*
Marsing, ID 83639 • *786*
Marston, MO 63866 • *742*
Mart, TX 76664 • *2,324*
Martin, KY 41649 • *827*
Martin, SD 57551 • *1,018*
Martin, TN 38237 • *8,898*
Martin □, FL • *64,014*
Martin □, IN • *11,001*
Martin □, KY • *13,925*
Martin □, MN • *24,687*
Martin □, NC • *25,948*
Martin □, TX • *4,684*
Martinez, CA 94553 • *22,582*
Martinez, GA 30907 • *16,472*
Martinsburg, PA 16662 • *2,231*
Martinsburg, WV 25401 • *13,063*
Martins Ferry, OH 43935 • *9,331*
Martinsville, IL 62442 • *1,298*
Martinsville, IN 46151 • *11,311*
Martinsville, VA 24112 • *18,149*
Marvell, AR 72366 • *1,724*
Maryland City, MD 20707 • *6,250*
Maryland Heights, MO 63043 • *5,676*
Marysville, CA 95901 • *9,898*
Marysville, KS 66508 • *3,670*
Marysville, MI 48040 • *7,345*
Marysville, OH 43040 • *7,414*
Marysville, PA 17053 • *2,452*
Marysville, WA 98270 • *5,080*
Maryville, KY 40229 • *6,000*
Maryville, MO 64468 • *9,558*
Maryville, TN 37801 • *17,480*
Masaryktown, FL 33512 • *800*
Mascot, TN 37806 • *2,203*
Mascoutah, IL 62258 • *4,962*
Mason, MI 48854 • *6,019*
Mason, OH 45040 • *8,692*
Mason, TX 76856 • *2,153*
Mason, WV 25260 • *1,432*
Mason □, IL • *19,492*
Mason □, KY • *17,765*
Mason □, MI • *26,365*
Mason □, TX • *3,683*
Mason □, WA • *31,184*
Mason □, WV • *27,045*
Mason City, IL 62664 • *2,719*
Mason City, IA 50401 • *30,144*
Masontown, PA 15461 • *4,909*
Masontown, WV 26542 • *1,052*
Massac □, IL • *14,990*
Massapequa, NY 11758 • *27,500*
Massapequa Park, NY 11762 • *19,779*
Massena, NY 13662 • *12,851*
Massillon, OH 44646 • *30,557*
Mastic, NY 11950 • *5,200*
Mastic Beach, NY 11951 • *5,200*
Masury, OH 44438 • *1,836*
Matador, TX 79244 • *1,052*
Matagorda, TX 77457 • *850*
Matagorda □, TX • *37,828*

Matamoras, PA 18336 • *2,111*
Matawan, NJ 07747 • *8,837*
Matewan, WV 25678 • *822*
Matfield, MA 02379 • *700*
Mather, PA 15346 • *860*
Matherville, IL 61263 • *793*
Mathews, LA 70375 • *900*
Mathews, VA 23109 • *650*
Mathews □, VA • *7,995*
Mathis, TX 78368 • *5,667*
Mathiston, MS 39752 • *632*
Matoaca, VA 23803 • *2,000*
Matoaka, WV 24736 • *613*
Mattapoisett, MA 02739 • *3,159*
Mattawamkeag, ME 04459 • *750*
Matteson, IL 60443 • *10,223*
Matthews, IN 46957 • *745*
Matthews, NC 28105 • *1,648*
Mattituck, NY 11952 • *1,200*
Mattoon, IL 61938 • *19,055*
Mattydale, NY 13211 • *8,292*
Maud, OK 74854 • *1,444*
Maugansville, MD 21767 • *1,707*
Maui □, HI • *70,847*
Mauldin, SC 29662 • *8,143*
Maumee, OH 43537 • *15,747*
Maunaloa, HI 96770 • *633*
Maunawili, HI 96734 • *2,200*
Maury □, TN • *51,095*
Maury City, TN 38050 • *989*
Mauston, WI 53948 • *3,284*
Maverick □, TX • *31,398*
Maxton, NC 28364 • *2,711*
Maxwell, CA 95955 • *800*
Maxwell, IA 50161 • *783*
Maxwell Acres, WV 26041 • *1,000*
Maybeury, WV 24861 • *700*
Mayer, AZ 86333 • *950*
Mayes □, OK • *32,261*
Mayesville, SC 29104 • *663*
Mayfield, KY 42066 • *10,705*
Mayfield, NY 12117 • *944*
Mayfield, PA 18433 • *1,812*
Mayfield Heights, OH 44124 • *21,550*
Mayflower, AR 72106 • *1,381*
Maynard, MA 01754 • *9,590*
Maynardville, TN 37807 • *924*
Mayo, FL 32066 • *891*
Mayo, MD 21106 • *1,500*
Mayo, SC 29368 • *900*
Mayodan, NC 27027 • *2,627*
May Park, OR 97850 • *1,466*
Mays Landing, NJ 08330 • *2,054*
Maysville, GA 30558 • *619*
Maysville, KY 41056 • *7,983*
Maysville, MO 64469 • *1,187*
Maysville, NC 28555 • *877*
Maysville, OK 73057 • *1,396*
Mayville, MI 48744 • *958*
Mayville, ND 58257 • *2,255*
Mayville, NY 14757 • *1,626*
Mayville, WI 53050 • *4,333*
Maywood, CA 90270 • *21,810*
Maywood, IL 60153 • *27,998*
Maywood, NJ 07607 • *9,895*
Maywood Park, OR 97220 • *1,083*
Mazeppa, MN 55956 • *680*
Mazomanie, WI 53560 • *1,248*
Mazon, IL 60444 • *828*
Mead, WA 99021 • *1,400*
Meade, KS 67864 • *1,777*
Meade □, KS • *4,788*
Meade □, KY • *22,854*
Meade □, SD • *20,717*
Meadow Lands, PA 15347 • *1,200*
Meadowood, DE 19711 • *2,260*
Meadville, PA 16335 • *15,544*
Meagher □, MT • *2,154*
Mebane, NC 27302 • *2,782*
Mecca, CA 92254 • *1,698*
Mechanic Falls, ME 04256 • *2,616*
Mechanicsburg, OH 43044 • *1,792*
Mechanicsburg, PA 17055 • *9,487*
Mechanicsville, IA 52306 • *1,166*
Mechanicsville, VA 23111 • *9,000*
Mechanicville, NY 12118 • *5,500*
Mecklenburg □, NC • *404,270*
Mecklenburg □, VA • *29,444*
Mecosta □, MI • *36,961*
Medaryville, IN 47957 • *731*
Medfield, MA 02052 • *6,108*
Medford, MA 02155 • *58,076*
Medford, MN 55049 • *775*
Medford, NJ 08055 • *1,448*
Medford, NY 11763 • *5,000*
Medford, OK 73759 • *1,419*
Medford, OR 97501–04 • *39,603*
Medford, WI 54451 • *4,035*
Medford Lakes, NJ 08055 • *4,958*
Media, PA 19063–65 • *6,119*
Mediapolis, IA 52637 • *1,685*
Medical Lake, WA 99022 • *3,600*
Medicine Bow, WY 82329 • *953*
Medicine Lodge, KS 67104 • *2,384*
Medina, NY 14103 • *6,392*
Medina, OH 44256 • *15,268*
Medina, TN 38355 • *687*
Medina, WA 98039 • *3,220*
Medina □, OH • *113,150*
Medina □, TX • *23,164*
Medora, IN 47260 • *853*
Medway, MA 02053 • *4,300*
Meeker, CO 81641 • *2,356*
Meeker, OK 74855 • *1,032*
Meeker □, MN • *20,594*

Mehlville, MO 63129 • 22,900
Meigs, GA 31765 • 1,231
Meigs □, OH • 23,641
Meigs □, TN • 7,431
Meiners Oaks, CA 93023 • 5,600
Melbourne, AR 72556 • 1,619
Melbourne, FL 32901–19 • 46,536
Melbourne, IA 50162 • 732
Melbourne, KY 41059 • 628
Melbourne Beach, FL 32951 • 2,713
Melcher, IA 50163 • 953
Mellen, WI 54546 • 1,046
Mellette □, SD • 2,249
Melrose, FL 32666 • 1,700
Melrose, MA 02176 • 30,055
Melrose, MN 56352 • 2,409
Melrose, NM 88124 • 649
Melrose Park, FL 33312 • 5,725
Melrose Park, IL 60160–65 • 20,735
Melville, LA 71353 • 1,764
Melville, NY 11747 • 10,250
Melvin, KY 41650 • 700
Melvindale, MI 48122 • 12,322
Memphis, FL 33561 • 5,501
Memphis, MI 48041 • 1,171
Memphis, MO 63555 • 2,105
Memphis, TN 38101–99 • 646,174
Memphis, TX 79245 • 3,352
Mena, AR 71953 • 5,154
Menahga, MN 56464 • 980
Menan, ID 83434 • 605
Menands, NY 12204 • 4,012
Menard, TX 76859 • 1,697
Menard □, IL • 11,700
Menard □, TX • 2,346
Menasha, WI 54952 • 14,728
Mendenhall, MS 39114 • 2,533
Mendham, NJ 07945 • 4,899
Mendocino, CA 95460 • 1,008
Mendocino □, CA • 66,738
Mendon, IL 62351 • 979
Mendon, MA 01756 • 900
Mendon, MI 49072 • 951
Mendon, OH 45862 • 749
Mendon, UT 84325 • 663
Mendota, CA 93640 • 5,038
Mendota, IL 61342 • 7,134
Mendota Heights, MN 55118 • 7,288
Menifee □, KY • 5,117
Menlo, GA 30731 • 611
Menlo Park, CA 94025 • 26,369
Menno, SD 57045 • 793
Menominee, MI 49858 • 10,099
Menominee □, MI • 26,201
Menominee □, WI • 3,373
Menomonee Falls, WI 53051
• 27,845
Menomonie, WI 54751 • 12,769
Mentone, IN 46539 • 973
Mentor, OH 44060 • 42,065
Mentor-on-the-Lake, OH 44060
• 7,919
Mequon, WI 53092 • 16,193
Meraux, LA 70075 • 4,100
Merced, CA 95340 • 36,499
Merced □, CA • 134,558
Mercedes, TX 78570 • 11,851
Mercer, PA 16137 • 2,532
Mercer, WI 54547 • 1,250
Mercer □, IL • 19,286
Mercer □, KY • 19,011
Mercer □, MO • 4,685
Mercer □, NJ • 307,863
Mercer □, ND • 9,404
Mercer □, OH • 38,334
Mercer □, PA • 128,299
Mercer □, WV • 73,942
Mercer Island, WA 98040 • 21,522
Mercersburg, PA 17236 • 1,617
Mercerville, NJ 08619 • 15,500
Merchantville, NJ 08109 • 3,972
Meredith, NH 03253 • 1,202
Meredosia, IL 62665 • 1,272
Meriden, CT 06450 • 57,118
Meriden, KS 66512 • 707
Meridian, ID 83642 • 6,658
Meridian, MS 39301–05 • 46,577
Meridian, PA 16001 • 2,400
Meridian, TX 76665 • 1,330
Meridian Hills, IN 46260 • 1,801
Meridianville, AL 35759 • 1,403
Merion Station, PA 19066 • 7,400
Meriwether □, GA • 21,229
Merkel, TX 79536 • 2,493
Mermentau, LA 70556 • 771
Merriam, KS 66203 • 10,794
Merrick, NY 11566 • 26,400
Merrick □, NE • 8,945
Merrifield, VA 22116 • 2,100
Merrill, IA 51038 • 737
Merrill, MI 48637 • 851
Merrill, OR 97633 • 809
Merrill, WI 54452 • 9,578
Merrillville, IN 46410 • 27,677
Merrimac, MA 01860 • 2,300
Merrimack, NH 03054 • 1,200
Merrimack □, NH • 98,302
Merritt Island, FL 32952–54 • 30,708
Mer Rouge, LA 71261 • 802
Merryville, LA 70653 • 1,286
Merton, WI 53056 • 1,045
Mertzon, TX 76941 • 687
Mesa, AZ 85201–08 • 152,453
Mesa □, CO • 81,530
Mescalero, NM 88340 • 1,259
Mesilla, NM 88046 • 2,029
Mesquite, NV 89024 • 700
Mesquite, TX 75149–50 • 67,053
Metairie, LA 70001–11 • 164,160
Metamora, IL 61548 • 2,482
Metcalfe, MS 38760 • 952
Metcalfe □, KY • 9,484
Methuen, MA 01844 • 36,701
Metlakatla, AK 99926 • 1,056
Metropolis, IL 62960 • 7,171
Metter, GA 30439 • 3,531
Metuchen, NJ 08840 • 13,762
Metzger, OR 97223 • 5,544
Mexia, TX 76667 • 7,094
Mexico, IN 46958 • 850
Mexico, ME 04257 • 3,207
Mexico, MO 65265 • 12,276
Mexico, NY 13114 • 1,621
Meyersdale, PA 15552 • 2,581
Miami, AZ 85539 • 2,716
Miami, FL 33101–99 • 346,865
Miami, OK 74354 • 14,237
Miami, TX 79059 • 813
Miami □, IN • 39,820
Miami □, KS • 21,618
Miami □, OH • 90,381
Miami Beach, FL 33139 • 96,298
Miamisburg, OH 45342 • 15,304
Miami Shores, FL 33153 • 9,244
Miami Springs, FL 33166 • 12,350
Miamitown, OH 45041 • 650
Micanopy, FL 32667 • 737
Micco, FL 32958 • 3,585
Michigan Center, MI 49254 • 5,244
Michigan City, IN 46360 • 36,850
Middleboro, MA 02346 • 7,012
Middlebourne, WV 26149 • 941
Middleburg, FL 32068 • 2,500
Middleburg, NY 12122 • 1,358
Middleburg, PA 17842 • 1,357
Middleburg, VA 22117 • 619
Middleburgh, NY 12122 • 1,358
Middleburg Heights, OH 44130
• 16,218
Middlebury, CT 06762 • 3,900
Middlebury, IN 46540 • 1,665
Middlebury, VT 05753 • 5,591
Middlefield, OH 44062 • 1,997
Middle Point, OH 45863 • 709
Middleport, NY 14105 • 1,995
Middleport, OH 45760 • 2,971
Middle River, MD 21220 • 26,756
Middlesboro, KY 40965 • 12,251
Middlesex, NJ 08846 • 13,480
Middlesex, NC 27557 • 837
Middlesex □, CT • 129,017
Middlesex □, MA • 1,367,034
Middlesex □, NJ • 595,893
Middlesex □, VA • 7,719
Middleton, ID 83644 • 1,901
Middleton, MA 01949 • 4,135
Middleton, WI 53562 • 11,848
Middletown, CA 95461 • 2,000
Middletown, CT 06457 • 39,040
Middletown, DE 19709 • 2,946
Middletown, IN 47356 • 2,978
Middletown, MD 21769 • 1,748
Middletown, NJ 07718 • 61,615
Middletown, NY 10940 • 21,454
Middletown, OH 45042–43 • 43,719
Middletown, PA 17057 • 10,122
Middletown, RI 02840 • 3,350
Middletown, VA 22645 • 841
Middleville, MI 49333 • 1,797
Middleville, NY 13406 • 647
Midfield, AL 35228 • 6,203
Midland, MD 21542 • 601
Midland, MI 48640 • 37,250
Midland, PA 15059 • 4,310
Midland, TX 79701–11 • 70,525
Midland □, MI • 73,578
Midland □, TX • 82,636
Midland City, AL 36350 • 1,903
Midland Park, KS 67216 • 1,350
Midland Park, NJ 07432 • 7,381
Midland Park, SC 29405 • 1,300
Midlothian, IL 60445 • 14,274
Midlothian, TX 76065 • 3,219
Midlothian, VA 23113 • 1,000
Midvale, OH 44653 • 654
Midvale, UT 84047 • 10,146
Midville, GA 30441 • 670
Midway, KY 40347 • 1,445
Midway, OR 97233 • 19,000
Midway, PA 15060 • 1,187
Midway, UT 84049 • 1,194
Midwest, WY 82643 • 638
Midwest City, OK 73110 • 49,559
Mifflin, PA 17058 • 648
Mifflin □, PA • 46,908
Mifflinburg, PA 17844 • 3,151
Mifflintown, PA 17059 • 783
Mifflinville, PA 18631 • 1,074
Milaca, MN 56353 • 2,104
Milam □, TX • 22,732
Milan, GA 31060 • 1,115
Milan, IL 61264 • 6,264
Milan, IN 47031 • 1,566
Milan, MI 48160 • 4,182
Milan, MO 63556 • 1,947
Milan, NM 87021 • 3,747
Milan, OH 44846 • 1,569
Milan, TN 38358 • 8,083
Milbank, SD 57252 • 4,120
Mildred, PA 18632 • 800
Miles, TX 76861 • 720
Milesburg, PA 16853 • 1,309
Miles City, MT 59301 • 9,602
Milford, CT 06460 • 49,101
Milford, DE 19963 • 5,366
Milford, IL 60953 • 1,716
Milford, IN 46542 • 1,153
Milford, IA 51351 • 2,076
Milford, ME 04461 • 1,688
Milford, MA 01757 • 23,390
Milford, MI 48042 • 5,041
Milford, NE 68405 • 2,108
Milford, NH 03055 • 6,289
Milford, NJ 08848 • 1,368
Milford, OH 45150 • 5,232
Milford, PA 18337 • 1,143
Milford, UT 84751 • 1,293
Milford Center, OH 43045 • 764
Mililani Town, HI 96789 • 20,351
Millard □, UT • 8,970
Millbrae, CA 94030 • 20,058
Millbrook, AL 36054 • 3,101
Millbrook, NY 12545 • 1,343
Millburn, NJ 07041 • 19,543
Millbury, MA 01527 • 5,700
Millbury, OH 43447 • 955
Mill City, OR 97360 • 1,565
Millcreek, UT 84109 • 24,150
Mill Creek, WV 26280 • 801
Millcreek Township, PA 16505
• 44,303
Milldale, CT 06467 • 1,100
Milledgeville, GA 31061 • 12,176
Milledgeville, IL 61051 • 1,209
Mille Lacs □, MN • 18,430
Millen, GA 30442 • 3,988
Miller, SD 57362 • 1,931
Miller □, AR • 37,766
Miller □, GA • 7,038
Miller □, MO • 18,532
Millersburg, IN 46543 • 809
Millersburg, KY 40348 • 987
Millersburg, OH 44654 • 3,247
Millersburg, PA 17061 • 2,770
Millers Falls, MA 01349 • 1,101
Millersport, OH 43046 • 844
Millersville, PA 17551 • 7,668
Millerton, NY 12546 • 1,013
Mill Grove, MO 64673 • 850
Mill Hall, PA 17751 • 1,744
Millheim, PA 16854 • 800
Milligan College, TN 37682 • 1,200
Milliken, CO 80543 • 1,506
Millington, MI 48746 • 1,237
Millington, TN 38053 • 20,236
Millinocket, ME 04462 • 7,567
Millis, MA 02054 • 3,777
Millport, AL 35576 • 1,287
Millry, AL 36558 • 956
Mills, WY 82644 • 2,139
Mills □, IA • 13,406
Mills □, TX • 4,477
Millsboro, DE 19966 • 1,233
Millsboro, PA 15348 • 900
Millstadt, IL 62260 • 2,736
Milltown, IN 47145 • 1,006
Milltown, NJ 08850 • 7,136
Milltown, WI 54858 • 732
Millvale, PA 15209 • 4,772
Mill Valley, CA 94941 • 12,967
Millville, MA 01529 • 1,764
Millville, NJ 08332 • 24,815
Millville, OH 45013 • 809
Millville, PA 17846 • 975
Millville, UT 84326 • 848
Millwood, WA 99212 • 1,717
Milnor, ND 58060 • 716
Milo, IA 50166 • 778
Milo, ME 04463 • 2,255
Milpitas, CA 95035 • 37,820
Milroy, IN 46156 • 900
Milroy, PA 17063 • 1,575
Milstead, GA 30207 • 1,157
Milton, DE 19968 • 1,359
Milton, FL 32570 • 7,206
Milton, IN 47357 • 729
Milton, KY 40045 • 718
Milton, MA 02186 • 25,860
Milton, NH 03851 • 1,000
Milton, PA 17847 • 6,730
Milton, VT 05468 • 1,411
Milton, WA 98354 • 3,162
Milton, WV 25541 • 2,178
Milton, WI 53563 • 4,092
Milton-Freewater, OR 97862 • 5,086
Milwaukee, WI 53201–99 • 636,236
Milwaukee □, WI • 964,988
Milwaukie, OR 97222 • 17,931
Mimosa Park, LA 70070 • 3,737
Mims, FL 32754 • 7,583
Minatare, NE 69356 • 969
Minco, OK 73059 • 1,489
Minden, LA 71055 • 15,084
Minden, NE 68959 • 2,939
Minden, NV 89423 • 1,300
Minden, WV 25879 • 800
Mine Hill, NJ 07801 • 3,250
Mineola, NY 11501 • 20,757
Mineola, TX 75773 • 4,346
Miner, MO 63801 • 1,182
Miner □, SD • 3,739
Mineral □, CO • 804
Mineral □, MT • 3,675
Mineral □, NV • 6,217
Mineral □, WV • 27,234
Mineral City, OH 44656 • 884
Mineral Point, WI 53565 • 2,259
Mineral Springs, AR 71851 • 936
Mineral Wells, TX 76067 • 14,468
Minersville, PA 17954 • 5,635
Minerva, OH 44657 • 4,549
Minetto, NY 13115 • 900
Mineville, NY 12956 • 1,000
Mingo □, WV • 37,336
Mingo Junction, OH 43938 • 4,834
Minidoka □, ID • 19,718
Minier, IL 61759 • 1,261
Minneapolis, KS 67467 • 2,075
Minneapolis, MN 55401–99
• 370,951
Minnehaha □, SD • 109,435
Minneola, KS 67865 • 712
Minneota, MN 56264 • 1,470
Minnesota Lake, MN 56068 • 744
Minnetonka, MN 55345 • 38,683
Minocqua, WI 54548 • 900
Minonk, IL 61760 • 2,039
Minooka, IL 60447 • 1,565
Minot, MA 02055 • 800
Minot, ND 58701 • 32,843
Minquadale, DE 19720 • 1,700
Minster, OH 45865 • 2,557
Mint Hill, NC 28212 • 7,915
Minturn, CO 81645 • 1,060
Mio, MI 48647 • 1,500
Mira Loma, CA 91752 • 8,707
Miramar, FL 33023 • 32,813
Misenheimer, NC 28109 • 1,250
Mishawaka, IN 46544–45 • 40,201
Mishicot, WI 54228 • 1,503
Missaukee □, MI • 10,009
Mission, KS 66222 • 8,643
Mission, SD 57555 • 748
Mission, TX 78572 • 22,653
Mission Hills, KS 66205 • 3,904
Mission Viejo, CA 92691 • 50,666
Mississippi □, AR • 59,517
Mississippi □, MO • 15,726
Mississippi State, MS 39762 • 4,595
Missoula, MT 59801–12 • 33,388
Missoula □, MT • 76,016
Missouri City, TX 77459 • 24,533
Missouri Valley, IA 51555 • 3,107
Mitchell, IL 62040 • 1,500
Mitchell, IN 47446 • 4,641
Mitchell, NE 69357 • 1,956
Mitchell, SD 57301 • 13,916
Mitchell □, GA • 21,114
Mitchell □, IA • 12,329
Mitchell □, KS • 8,117
Mitchell □, NC • 14,428
Mitchell □, TX • 9,088
Mitchellville, IA 50169 • 1,530
Moab, UT 84532 • 5,333
Moberly, MO 65270 • 13,418
Mobile, AL 36601–99 • 200,452
Mobile □, AL • 364,980
Mobridge, SD 57601 • 4,174
Mocanaqua, PA 18655 • 990
Mocksville, NC 27028 • 2,637
Moclips, WA 98562 • 700
Modesto, CA 95350–56 • 106,602
Modoc □, CA • 8,610
Moenkopi, AZ 86045 • 900
Moffat □, CO • 13,133
Mogadore, OH 44260 • 4,190
Mohall, ND 58761 • 1,049
Mohave □, AZ • 55,865
Mohave Valley, AZ 86440 • 750
Mohawk, MI 49950 • 950
Mohawk, NY 13407 • 2,956
Mohnton, PA 19540 • 2,156
Mojave, CA 93501 • 2,886
Mokelumne Hill, CA 95245 • 950
Mokena, IL 60448 • 4,578
Molalla, OR 97038 • 2,992
Moline, IL 61265 • 46,278
Moline, MI 49335 • 800
Molino, FL 32577 • 1,456
Momence, IL 60954 • 3,297
Monaca, PA 15061 • 7,661
Monahans, TX 79756 • 8,397
Monarch Mills, SC 29379 • 2,353
Moncks Corner, SC 29461 • 3,699
Mondovi, WI 54755 • 2,545
Monee, IL 60449 • 993
Monessen, PA 15062 • 11,928
Monett, MO 65708 • 6,148
Monette, AR 72447 • 1,165
Monfort Heights, OH 45239 • 9,745
Moniteau □, MO • 12,068
Monmouth, IL 61462 • 10,706
Monmouth, OR 97361 • 5,594
Monmouth □, NJ • 503,173
Monmouth Beach, NJ 07750 • 3,318
Monmouth Junction, NJ 08852
• 2,579
Mono □, CA • 8,577
Monon, IN 47959 • 1,540
Monona, IA 52159 • 1,530
Monona, WI 53716 • 8,809
Monona □, IA • 11,692
Monongah, WV 26554 • 1,132
Monongahela, PA 15063 • 5,950
Monongalia □, WV • 75,024
Monroe, CT 06468 • 760
Monroe, GA 30655 • 8,854
Monroe, IN 46772 • 739
Monroe, IA 50170 • 1,875
Monroe, LA 71201–12 • 57,597
Monroe, MI 48161 • 23,531
Monroe, NC 28110 • 12,639
Monroe, NY 10950 • 5,996
Monroe, OH 45050 • 4,256
Monroe, UT 84754 • 1,476
Monroe, WA 98272 • 2,869
Monroe, WI 53566 • 10,027
Monroe □, AL • 22,651
Monroe □, AR • 14,052
Monroe □, FL • 63,188
Monroe □, GA • 14,610
Monroe □, IL • 20,117
Monroe □, IN • 98,785
Monroe □, IA • 9,209
Monroe □, KY • 12,353
Monroe □, MI • 134,659
Monroe □, MS • 36,404
Monroe □, MO • 9,716
Monroe □, NY • 702,238
Monroe □, OH • 17,382
Monroe □, PA • 69,409
Monroe □, TN • 28,700
Monroe □, WV • 12,873
Monroe □, WI • 35,074
Monroe Center, CT 06468 • 6,950
Monroe City, MO 63456 • 2,557
Monroe Park, DE 19807 • 1,250
Monroeton, PA 18832 • 677
Monroeville, AL 36460 • 5,674
Monroeville, IN 46773 • 1,372
Monroeville, OH 44847 • 1,329
Monroeville, PA 15146 • 30,977
Monrovia, CA 91016 • 30,531
Monsey, NY 10952 • 7,400
Monson, MA 01057 • 2,167
Montague, CA 96064 • 1,285
Montague, MA 01351 • 900
Montague, MI 49437 • 2,332
Montague □, TX • 17,410
Mont Alto, PA 17237 • 1,592
Montandon, PA 17850 • 650
Montauk, NY 11954 • 1,300
Mont Belvieu, TX 77580 • 1,730
Montcalm □, MI • 47,555
Montclair, CA 91763 • 22,628
Montclair, NJ 07042–44 • 38,321
Mont Clare, PA 19453 • 1,274
Monteagle, TN 37356 • 1,126
Montebello, CA 90640 • 52,929
Montecito, CA 93108 • 9,300
Montegut, LA 70377 • 800
Montello, WI 53949 • 1,273
Monterey, CA 93940 • 27,558
Monterey, TN 38574 • 2,610
Monterey □, CA • 290,444
Monterey Park, CA 91754 • 54,338
Montesano, WA 98563 • 3,247
Montevallo, AL 35115 • 3,965
Montevideo, MN 56265 • 5,845
Monte Vista, CO 81144 • 3,902
Montezuma, GA 31063 • 4,830
Montezuma, IN 47862 • 1,352
Montezuma, IA 50171 • 1,485
Montezuma, KS 67867 • 730
Montezuma □, CO • 16,510
Montfort, WI 53569 • 616
Montgomery, AL 36101–99
• 177,857
Montgomery, IL 60538 • 3,369
Montgomery, LA 71454 • 843
Montgomery, MN 56069 • 2,349
Montgomery, NY 12549 • 2,316
Montgomery, OH 45242 • 10,088
Montgomery, PA 17752 • 1,653
Montgomery, WV 25136 • 3,104
Montgomery □, AL • 197,038
Montgomery □, AR • 7,771
Montgomery □, GA • 7,011
Montgomery □, IL • 31,686
Montgomery □, IN • 35,501
Montgomery □, IA • 13,413
Montgomery □, KS • 42,281
Montgomery □, KY • 20,046
Montgomery □, MD • 579,053
Montgomery □, MS • 13,366
Montgomery □, MO • 11,537
Montgomery □, NC • 22,469
Montgomery □, NY • 53,439
Montgomery □, OH • 571,697
Montgomery □, PA • 643,621
Montgomery □, TN • 83,342
Montgomery □, TX • 128,487
Montgomery □, VA • 63,516
Montgomery City, MO 63361 • 2,101
Montgomery Creek, CA 96065 • 800
Montgomery Village, MD 20879
• 16,600
Monticello, AR 71655 • 8,259
Monticello, FL 32344 • 2,994
Monticello, GA 31064 • 2,382
Monticello, IL 61856 • 4,753
Monticello, IN 47960 • 5,162
Monticello, IA 52310 • 3,641
Monticello, KY 42633 • 5,677
Monticello, MN 55362 • 2,830
Monticello, MS 39654 • 1,834
Monticello, NY 12701 • 6,306
Monticello, UT 84535 • 1,929
Monticello, WI 53570 • 1,021
Montmorenci, SC 29839 • 900
Montmorency □, MI • 7,492
Montour □, PA • 16,675
Montour Falls, NY 14865 • 1,791
Montoursville, PA 17754 • 5,403
Montpelier, ID 83254 • 3,107
Montpelier, IN 47359 • 1,995
Montpelier, OH 43543 • 4,431
Montpelier, VT 05602 • 8,241
Montreal, WI 54550 • 887
Montreat, NC 28757 • 741

Newkirk, OK 74647 • 2,413
New Knoxville, OH 45871 • 760
New Washoe City, NV 89701 • 2,543

North Bend, OR 97459 • 9,779
North Oaks, CA 91350 • 5,800
Nutter Fort, WV 26301 • 2,078

135

O'Donnell, TX 79351 • 1,200
Oelwein, IA 50662 • 7,564
O'Fallon, IL 62269 • 12,241
O'Fallon, MO 63366 • 8,677
Ogallala, NE 69153 • 5,638
Ogden, IL 61859 • 818
Ogden, IA 50212 • 1,953
Ogden, KS 66517 • 1,804
Ogden, UT 84401-99 • 64,407
Ogdensburg, NJ 07439 • 2,737
Ogdensburg, NY 13669 • 12,375
Ogemaw □, MI • 16,436
Ogle □, IL • 46,338
Oglesby, IL 61348 • 3,979
Oglethorpe, GA 31068 • 1,305
Oglethorpe □, GA • 8,929
Ogunquit, ME 03907 • 1,492
Ohatchee, AL 36271 • 860
Ohio □, IN • 5,114
Ohio □, KY • 21,765
Ohio □, WV • 61,389
Ohio City, OH 45874 • 881
Ohioville, PA 15059 • 4,217
Oil City, LA 71061 • 1,323
Oil City, PA 16301 • 13,881
Oildale, CA 93308 • 23,382
Oilton, OK 74052 • 1,244
Ojai, CA 93023 • 6,816
Okaloosa □, FL • 109,920
Okanogan, WA 98840 • 2,302
Okanogan □, WA • 30,639
Okarche, OK 73762 • 1,064
Okauchee, WI 53069 • 1,800
Okauchee Lake, WI 53058 • 1,400
Okawville, IL 62271 • 1,337
Okeechobee, FL 33472 • 4,225
Okeechobee □, FL • 20,264
Okeene, OK 73763 • 1,601
Okemah, OK 74859 • 3,381
Okemos, MI 48864 • 8,882
Okfuskee □, OK • 11,125
Oklahoma □, OK • 568,933
Oklahoma City, OK 73101-99 • 403,136
Oklawaha, FL 32679 • 1,200
Okmulgee, OK 74447 • 16,263
Okmulgee □, OK • 39,169
Okolona, KY 40219 • 20,039
Okolona, MS 38860 • 3,409
Oktibbeha □, MS • 36,018
Ola, AR 72853 • 1,121
Olanta, SC 29114 • 699
Olathe, CO 81425 • 1,262
Olathe, KS 66061-62 • 37,258
Olcott, NY 14126 • 1,650
Old Bethpage, NY 11804 • 7,160
Old Bridge, NJ 08857 • 12,500
Oldenburg, IN 47036 • 770
Old Forge, NY 13420 • 950
Old Forge, PA 18518 • 9,304
Old Fort, NC 28762 • 752
Oldham □, KY • 27,795
Oldham □, TX • 2,283
Oldham Village, MA 02359 • 900
Old Orchard Beach, ME 04064 • 6,291
Old Saybrook, CT 06475 • 1,857
Oldsmar, FL 33557 • 2,608
Old Tappan, NJ 07675 • 4,168
Old Town, ME 04468 • 8,422
Olean, NY 14760 • 18,207
Oley, PA 19547 • 700
Olin, IA 52320 • 735
Olive Branch, MS 38654 • 2,067
Olive Hill, KY 41164 • 2,539
Olivehurst, CA 95961 • 8,929
Oliver, PA 15472 • 1,500
Oliver □, ND • 2,495
Oliver Springs, TN 37840 • 3,659
Olivet, MI 49076 • 1,604
Olivette, MO 63132 • 7,985
Olivia, MN 56277 • 2,802
Olla, LA 71465 • 1,603
Olmito, TX 78575 • 1,500
Olmos Park, TX 78212 • 2,069
Olmsted □, MN • 92,006
Olmsted Falls, OH 44138 • 5,868
Olney, IL 62450 • 9,026
Olney, MD 20832 • 10,000
Olney, TX 76374 • 4,060
Olton, TX 79064 • 2,235
Olustee, OK 73560 • 721
Olympia, WA 98501-07 • 27,447
Olympia Heights, FL 33165 • 33,112
Olyphant, PA 18447 • 5,204
Omaha, NE 68101-99 • 313,911
Omak, WA 98841 • 4,007
Omar, WV 25638 • 950
Omega, GA 31775 • 996
Omro, WI 54963 • 2,763
Onaga, KS 66521 • 752
Onalaska, WI 54650 • 9,249
Onamia, MN 56359 • 691
Onancock, VA 23417 • 1,461
Onarga, IL 60955 • 1,269
Onawa, IA 51040 • 3,283
Onaway, MI 49765 • 1,084
Oneco, FL 34264 • 6,417
Oneida, IL 61467 • 765
Oneida, NY 13421 • 10,810
Oneida, OH 45042 • 1,650
Oneida, TN 37841 • 3,717
Oneida □, ID • 3,258
Oneida □, NY • 253,466
Oneida □, WI • 31,216
O'Neill, NE 68763 • 4,049
Oneonta, AL 35121 • 4,824
Oneonta, NY 13820 • 14,933
Onida, SD 57564 • 851
Onondaga □, NY • 463,920
Onset, MA 02558 • 1,493
Onslow □, NC • 112,784
Onsted, MI 49265 • 670
Ontario, CA 91761-62 • 88,820
Ontario, NY 14519 • 750
Ontario, OH 44862 • 4,123
Ontario, OR 97914 • 8,814
Ontario □, NY • 88,909
Ontonagon, MI 49953 • 2,182
Ontonagon □, MI • 9,861
Oolitic, IN 47451 • 1,495
Oologah, OK 74053 • 798
Ooltewah, TN 37363 • 900
Oostburg, WI 53070 • 1,647
Opal Cliffs, CA 95062 • 5,041
Opa-Locka, FL 33054-56 • 14,460
Opelika, AL 36801 • 21,896
Opelousas, LA 70570 • 18,903
Opp, AL 36467 • 7,204
Opportunity, WA 99214 • 17,600
Oquawka, IL 61469 • 1,533
Oracle, AZ 85623 • 2,484
Oradell, NJ 07649 • 8,658
Oran, MO 63771 • 1,266
Orange, CA 92667-69 • 91,450
Orange, CT 06477 • 13,237
Orange, MA 01364 • 3,942
Orange, NJ 07050-52 • 31,136
Orange, TX 77630 • 23,628
Orange, VA 22960 • 2,631
Orange □, CA • 1,932,709
Orange □, FL • 471,016
Orange □, IN • 18,677
Orange □, NC • 77,055
Orange □, NY • 259,603
Orange □, TX • 83,838
Orange □, VT • 22,739
Orange □, VA • 18,063
Orangeburg, SC 29115 • 14,933
Orangeburg □, SC • 82,276
Orange City, FL 32763 • 2,795
Orange City, IA 51041 • 4,588
Orange Grove, MS 39501 • 2,700
Orange Grove, TX 78372 • 1,212
Orange Lake, FL 32681 • 950
Orangevale, CA 95662 • 20,585
Orangeville, UT 84537 • 1,309
Orchard City, CO 81410 • 1,914
Orchard Homes, MT 59801 • 4,000
Orchard Mesa, CO 81501 • 4,876
Orchard Park, NY 14127 • 3,671
Orchards, WA 98662 • 3,950
Orchard Valley, WY 82001 • 800
Orcutt, CA 93455 • 1,500
Ord, NE 68862 • 2,658
Ordway, CO 81063 • 1,135
Oreana, IL 62554 • 999
Ore City, TX 75683 • 1,050
Oregon, IL 61061 • 3,559
Oregon, MO 64473 • 901
Oregon, OH 43616 • 18,675
Oregon, WI 53575 • 3,876
Oregon □, MO • 10,238
Oregon City, OR 97045 • 14,673
Oreland, PA 19075 • 9,000
Orem, UT 84057-59 • 52,399
Orfordville, WI 53576 • 1,143
Orient, NY 11957 • 800
Orinda, CA 94563 • 16,825
Orion, IL 61273 • 2,013
Oriskany, NY 13424 • 1,680
Oriskany Falls, NY 13425 • 802
Orland, CA 95963 • 4,031
Orlando, FL 32801-99 • 128,291
Orland Park, IL 60462 • 23,045
Orleans, CA 95556 • 900
Orleans, IN 47452 • 2,161
Orleans, MA 02653 • 1,811
Orleans, VT 05860 • 983
Orleans □, LA • 557,927
Orleans □, NY • 38,496
Orleans □, VT • 23,440
Ormond Beach, FL 32074 • 21,378
Ormond By The Sea, FL 32074 • 7,665
Orofino, ID 83544 • 3,711
Oro Grande, CA 92368 • 900
Orono, ME 04473 • 10,578
Orono, MN 55323 • 6,845
Oroville, CA 95965 • 8,683
Oroville, WA 98844 • 1,483
Orrick, MO 64077 • 922
Orrville, OH 44667 • 7,511
Orting, WA 98360 • 1,787
Ortonville, MI 48462 • 1,190
Ortonville, MN 56278 • 2,550
Orwell, OH 44076 • 1,067
Orwigsburg, PA 17961 • 2,700
Osage, IA 50461 • 3,718
Osage □, KS • 15,319
Osage □, MO • 12,014
Osage □, OK • 39,327
Osage Beach, MO 65065 • 1,992
Osage City, KS 66523 • 2,667
Osakis, MN 56360 • 1,355
Osawatomie, KS 66064 • 4,459
Osborne, KS 67473 • 2,120
Osborne □, KS • 5,959
Osbornsville, NJ 08723 • 800
Osburn, ID 83849 • 2,220
Osceola, AR 72370 • 8,881
Osceola, IN 46561 • 1,990
Osceola, IA 50213 • 3,750
Osceola, MO 64776 • 841
Osceola, NE 68651 • 975
Osceola, WI 54020 • 1,581
Osceola □, FL • 49,287
Osceola □, IA • 8,371
Osceola □, MI • 18,928
Osceola Mills, PA 16666 • 1,466
Oscoda, MI 48750 • 2,431
Oscoda □, MI • 6,858
Osgood, IN 47037 • 1,554
Oshkosh, NE 69154 • 1,057
Oshkosh, WI 54901-04 • 50,016
Oskaloosa, IA 52577 • 10,989
Oskaloosa, KS 66066 • 1,092
Osmond, NE 68765 • 871
Osprey, FL 33559 • 1,660
Osseo, MN 55369 • 2,974
Osseo, WI 54758 • 1,474
Ossian, IN 46777 • 1,945
Ossian, IA 52161 • 829
Ossining, NY 10562 • 20,196
Osteen, FL 32764 • 900
Osterville, MA 02655 • 1,799
Oswego, IL 60543 • 3,021
Oswego, KS 67356 • 2,218
Oswego, NY 13126 • 19,793
Oswego □, NY • 113,901
Otay, CA 92010 • 6,400
Oteen, NC 28805 • 2,200
Otego, NY 13825 • 1,089
Otero □, CO • 22,567
Otero □, NM • 44,665
Othello, WA 99344 • 4,454
Otho, IA 50569 • 692
Otis Orchards, WA 99027 • 1,000
Otisville, MI 48463 • 682
Otoe □, NE • 15,183
Otsego, MI 49078 • 3,802
Otsego □, MI • 14,993
Otsego □, NY • 59,075
Ottawa, IL 61350 • 18,166
Ottawa, KS 66067 • 11,016
Ottawa, OH 45875 • 3,874
Ottawa □, KS • 5,971
Ottawa □, MI • 157,174
Ottawa □, OH • 40,076
Ottawa □, OK • 32,870
Ottawa Hills, OH 43606 • 4,065
Otterbein, IN 47970 • 1,118
Otter Tail □, MN • 51,937
Ottoville, OH 45876 • 833
Ottumwa, IA 52501 • 27,381
Ouachita □, AR • 30,541
Ouachita □, LA • 139,241
Ouray, CO 81427 • 684
Ouray □, CO • 1,925
Outagamie □, WI • 128,730
Overbrook, KS 66524 • 930
Overland, MO 63114 • 19,620
Overland Park, KS 66204 • 81,784
Overlea, MD 21206 • 6,200
Overton, NE 68863 • 633
Overton, NV 89040 • 1,111
Overton, TX 75684 • 2,430
Overton □, TN • 17,575
Ovid, MI 48866 • 1,712
Ovid, NY 14521 • 666
Owasso, OK 74055 • 6,149
Owatonna, MN 55060 • 18,632
Owego, NY 13827 • 4,364
Owen, WI 54460 • 998
Owen □, IN • 15,841
Owen □, KY • 8,924
Owensboro, KY 42301 • 54,450
Owens Cross Roads, AL 35763 • 804
Owensville, IN 47665 • 1,261
Owensville, MO 65066 • 2,241
Owensville, OH 45160 • 858
Owenton, KY 40359 • 1,341
Owings Mills, MD 21117 • 9,526
Owingsville, KY 40360 • 1,419
Owosso, MI 48867 • 16,455
Owsley □, KY • 5,709
Owyhee, NV 89832 • 700
Owyhee □, ID • 8,272
Oxford, AL 36203 • 8,939
Oxford, CT 06483 • 900
Oxford, GA 30267 • 1,750
Oxford, IN 47971 • 1,327
Oxford, IA 52322 • 676
Oxford, KS 67119 • 1,125
Oxford, ME 04270 • 625
Oxford, MD 21654 • 754
Oxford, MA 01540 • 6,369
Oxford, MI 48051 • 2,746
Oxford, MS 38655 • 9,882
Oxford, NE 68967 • 1,109
Oxford, NJ 07863 • 1,587
Oxford, NC 27565 • 7,603
Oxford, NY 13830 • 1,765
Oxford, OH 45056 • 17,655
Oxford, PA 19363 • 3,633
Oxford □, ME • 48,968
Oxnard, CA 93030-39 • 108,195
Oxon Hill, MD 20745 • 8,100
Oyster Bay, NY 11771 • 7,200
Ozark, AL 36360 • 13,188
Ozark, AR 72949 • 3,597
Ozark, MO 65721 • 2,980
Ozark □, MO • 7,961
Ozaukee □, WI • 66,981
Ozona, FL 34265 • 1,200
Ozona, TX 76943 • 2,864

P

Paauilo, HI 96776 • 755
96776 • 755
Pace, FL 32570 • 5,006
Pacific, MO 63069 • 4,410
Pacific, WA 98047 • 2,261
Pacific □, WA • 17,237
Pacifica, CA 94044 • 36,866
Pacific Beach, WA 98571 • 1,000
Pacific City, OR 97135 • 1,500
Pacific Grove, CA 93950 • 15,755
Pacific Palisades, HI 96782 • 9,500
Packwood, WA 98361 • 1,150
Pacolet, SC 29372 • 1,556
Pacolet Mills, SC 29373 • 1,051
Paddock Lake, WI 53168 • 2,207
Paden City, WV 26159 • 3,671
Paducah, KY 42001 • 29,315
Paducah, TX 79248 • 2,216
Page, AZ 86040 • 4,907
Page □, IA • 19,063
Page □, VA • 19,401
Pageland, SC 29728 • 2,720
Page Manor, OH 45431 • 9,300
Pagosa Springs, CO 81147 • 1,331
Pahala, HI 96777 • 1,619
Pahoa, HI 96778 • 923
Pahokee, FL 33476 • 6,346
Pahrump, NV 89041 • 1,000
Paia, HI 96779 • 1,000
Paincourtville, LA 70391 • 2,004
Painesdale, MI 49955 • 650
Painesville, OH 44077 • 16,391
Painted Post, NY 14870 • 2,196
Paintsville, KY 41240 • 3,815
Pajarito, NM 87105 • 2,000
Palacios, TX 77465 • 4,667
Palatine, IL 60067 • 32,166
Palatka, FL 32077 • 10,175
Palestine, AR 72372 • 976
Palestine, IL 62451 • 1,718
Palestine, TX 75801 • 15,948
Palisade, CO 81526 • 1,551
Palisades Park, NJ 07650 • 13,732
Palm Bay, FL 32905 • 18,560
Palm Beach, FL 33480 • 9,729
Palm Beach □, FL • 576,863
Palm Beach Gardens, FL 33410 • 6,102
Palmdale, CA 93550 • 12,277
Palm Desert, CA 92260 • 11,801
Palmer, AK 99645 • 2,141
Palmer, MA 01069 • 3,854
Palmer, MI 49871 • 900
Palmer, MS 39401 • 2,765
Palmer, TN 37365 • 1,027
Palmer, TX 75152 • 1,187
Palmer Lake, CO 80133 • 1,130
Palmer Park, MD 20785 • 7,986
Palmerton, PA 18071 • 5,455
Palmetto, FL 33561 • 8,637
Palmetto, GA 30268 • 2,086
Palm Harbor, FL 33563 • 5,215
Palm Springs, CA 92262-64 • 32,366
Palm Springs, FL 33460 • 8,166
Palmyra, IL 62674 • 864
Palmyra, IN 47164 • 692
Palmyra, MO 63461 • 3,469
Palmyra, NJ 08065 • 7,085
Palmyra, NY 14522 • 3,729
Palmyra, PA 17078 • 7,228
Palmyra, WI 53156 • 1,515
Palo Alto, CA 94301-99 • 55,225
Palo Alto □, IA • 12,721
Palo Pinto □, TX • 24,062
Palos Heights, IL 60463 • 11,096
Palos Hills, IL 60465 • 16,654
Palos Park, IL 60464 • 3,150
Palos Verdes Estates, CA 90274 • 14,376
Palouse, WA 99161 • 1,005
Pamlico □, NC • 10,398
Pampa, TX 79065 • 21,396
Pamplico, SC 29583 • 1,213
Pana, IL 62557 • 6,040
Panacea, FL 32346 • 950
Panama, IL 62077 • 637
Panama, OK 74951 • 1,425
Panama City, FL 32401-10 • 33,346
Panama City Beach, FL 32407 • 2,148
Pandora, OH 45877 • 977
Pangburn, AR 72121 • 673
Panguitch, UT 84759 • 1,343
Panhandle, TX 79068 • 2,226
Panola □, MS • 28,164
Panola □, TX • 20,724
Panora, IA 50216 • 1,211
Panthersville, GA 30032 • 11,366
Paola, KS 66071 • 4,557
Paoli, IN 47454 • 3,637
Paoli, PA 19301 • 6,100
Paonia, CO 81428 • 1,425
Papaikou, HI 96781 • 1,567
Papillion, NE 68046 • 6,399
Paradis, LA 70080 • 800
Paradise, CA 95969 • 22,571
Paradise, NV 89109 • 45,000
Paradise, PA 17963 • 900
Paradise Hills, NM 87114 • 5,096
Paradise Valley, AZ 85253 • 11,085
Paradise Valley, WY 82601 • 2,300
Paragould, AR 72450 • 15,248
Paramount, CA 90723 • 36,407
Paramount, MD 21740 • 1,878
Paramus, NJ 07652 • 26,474
Parchment, MI 49004 • 1,817
Pardeeville, WI 53954 • 1,594
Paris, AR 72855 • 3,991
Paris, ID 83261 • 707
Paris, IL 61944 • 9,885
Paris, KY 40361 • 7,935
Paris, MO 65275 • 1,598
Paris, TN 38242 • 10,728
Paris, TX 75460 • 25,498
Park □, CO • 5,333
Park □, MT • 12,869
Park □, WY • 21,639
Park City, KS 67219 • 3,778
Park City, KY 42160 • 614
Park City, UT 84060 • 2,823
Parke □, IN • 16,372
Parker, AZ 85344 • 2,542
Parker, FL 32401 • 4,298
Parker, PA 16049 • 808
Parker, SD 57053 • 999
Parker □, TX • 44,609
Parker City, IN 47368 • 1,414
Parkersburg, IA 50665 • 1,968
Parkersburg, WV 26101-05 • 39,967
Parkers Prairie, MN 56361 • 917
Parkesburg, PA 19365 • 2,578
Park Falls, WI 54552 • 3,192
Park Forest, IL 60466 • 26,222
Park Forest South, IL 60466 • 6,245
Park Hills, KY 41015 • 3,500
Parkin, AR 72373 • 2,035
Parkland, WA 98444 • 22,300
Park Layne, OH 45431 • 5,372
Park Rapids, MN 56470 • 2,976
Park Ridge, IL 60068 • 38,704
Park Ridge, NJ 07656 • 8,515
Park River, ND 58270 • 1,844
Parkrose, OR 97230 • 21,103
Parksley, VA 23421 • 979
Parkston, SD 57366 • 1,545
Parkville, MD 21234 • 35,159
Parkville, MO 64152 • 1,997
Parkwater, WA 99211 • 4,850
Parkway, CA 95823 • 12,000
Parkwood, NC 27707 • 3,420
Parlier, CA 93648 • 2,902
Parma, ID 83660 • 1,820
Parma, MI 49269 • 873
Parma, MO 63870 • 1,081
Parma, OH 44129 • 92,548
Parma Heights, OH 44130 • 23,112
Parmer □, TX • 11,038
Parowan, UT 84761 • 1,836
Parrish, AL 35580 • 1,583
Parrish, FL 33564 • 950
Parshall, ND 58770 • 1,059
Parsippany, NJ 07054 • 8,000
Parsons, KS 67357 • 12,898
Parsons, TN 38363 • 2,422
Parsons, WV 26287 • 1,937
Pasadena, CA 91101-99 • 118,072
Pasadena, MD 21122 • 3,900
Pasadena, TX 77501-07 • 112,560
Pascagoula, MS 39567 • 29,318
Pasco, WA 99301 • 18,425
Pasco □, FL • 193,661
Pascoag, RI 02859 • 3,807
Paso Robles, CA 93446 • 9,163
Pasquotank □, NC • 28,462
Passaic, NJ 07055 • 52,463
Passaic □, NJ • 447,585
Pass Christian, MS 39571 • 5,014
Patagonia, AZ 85624 • 980
Pataskala, OH 43062 • 2,284
Patchogue, NY 11772 • 11,291
Paterson, NJ 07501-99 • 137,970
Patoka, IL 62875 • 662
Patoka, IN 47666 • 832
Patrick □, VA • 17,647
Patten, ME 04765 • 1,057
Patterson, GA 31557 • 763
Patterson, LA 70392 • 4,693
Patterson, NY 12563 • 950
Patton, PA 16668 • 2,441
Paul, ID 83347 • 940
Paulding, OH 45879 • 2,754
Paulding □, GA • 26,110
Paulding □, OH • 21,302
Paulina, LA 70763 • 980
Paullina, IA 51046 • 1,224
Paulsboro, NJ 08066 • 6,944
Pauls Valley, OK 73075 • 5,664
Pavo, GA 31778 • 830
Pawcatuck, CT 06379 • 5,216
Paw Creek, NC 28130 • 1,700
Pawhuska, OK 74056 • 4,771
Pawleys Island, SC 29585 • 2,200
Pawling, NY 12564 • 1,996
Pawnee, IL 62558 • 2,577
Pawnee, OK 74058 • 1,688
Pawnee □, KS • 8,065
Pawnee □, NE • 3,937
Pawnee □, OK • 15,310
Pawnee City, NE 68420 • 1,156
Pawpaw, IL 61353 • 839
Paw Paw, MI 49079 • 3,211
Paw Paw, WV 25434 • 644
Pawtucket, RI 02860-65 • 71,204
Paxton, FL 32538 • 659
Paxton, IL 60957 • 4,258
Paxton, MA 01612 • 1,800
Payette, ID 83661 • 5,448
Payette □, ID • 15,825
Payne, OH 45880 • 1,399

Porter, TX 77365 • *5,000*
Porter □, IN • *119,816*
Porterdale, GA 30270 • *1,451*
Porterville, CA 93257 • *19,707*
Port Ewen, NY 12466 • *2,600*
Port Gibson, MS 39150 • *2,371*
Port Henry, NY 12974 • *1,450*
Port Hueneme, CA 93041 • *17,803*
Port Huron, MI 48060 • *33,981*
Port Isabel, TX 78578 • *3,769*
Port Jefferson, NY 11777 • *6,731*
Port Jefferson Station, NY 11776 • *7,500*
Port Jervis, NY 12771 • *8,699*
Portland, AR 71663 • *701*
Portland, CT 06480 • *8,383*
Portland, IN 47371 • *7,074*
Portland, ME 04101–99 • *61,572*
Portland, MI 48875 • *3,963*
Portland, ND 58274 • *627*
Portland, OR 97201–99 • *366,383*
Portland, TN 37148 • *4,030*
Portland, TX 78374 • *12,023*
Port Lavaca, TX 77979 • *10,911*
Port Leyden, NY 13433 • *740*
Port Matilda, PA 16870 • *647*
Port Monmouth, NJ 07758 • *3,600*
Port Neches, TX 77651 • *13,944*
Port Norris, NJ 08349 • *1,730*
Port O'Connor, TX 77982 • *1,500*
Portola, CA 96122 • *1,885*
Port Orange, FL 32019 • *18,756*
Port Orchard, WA 98366 • *4,787*
Port Orford, OR 97465 • *1,061*
Port Reading, NJ 07064 • *4,300*
Port Republic, NJ 08241 • *837*
Port Richey, FL 33568 • *2,165*
Port Royal, PA 17082 • *835*
Port Royal, SC 29935 • *2,977*
Port Saint Joe, FL 32456 • *4,027*
Port Saint Lucie, FL 33450 • *14,690*
Port Salerno, FL 33492 • *4,511*
Portsmouth, NH 03801 • *26,254*
Portsmouth, OH 45662 • *25,943*
Portsmouth, RI 02871 • *4,300*
Portsmouth, VA 23701–99 • *104,577*
Port Sulphur, LA 70083 • *3,318*
Port Townsend, WA 98368 • *6,067*
Portville, NY 14770 • *1,136*
Port Vue, PA 15133 • *5,316*
Port Washington, NY 11050 • *15,923*
Port Washington, OH 43837 • *622*
Port Washington, WI 53074 • *8,612*
Port Wentworth, GA 31407 • *3,947*
Porum, OK 74455 • *668*
Posen, IL 60469 • *4,642*
Posey □, IN • *26,414*
Poseyville, IN 47633 • *1,247*
Post, TX 79356 • *3,961*
Post Falls, ID 83854 • *5,736*
Postville, IA 52162 • *1,475*
Poteau, OK 74953 • *7,089*
Poteet, TX 78065 • *3,086*
Poth, TX 78147 • *1,461*
Potlatch, ID 83855 • *819*
Potomac, IL 61865 • *874*
Potomac, MD 20854 • *22,800*
Potomac Heights, MD 20640 • *2,456*
Potomac Park, MD 21502 • *1,250*
Potosi, MO 63664 • *2,528*
Potosi, WI 53820 • *736*
Potsdam, NY 13676 • *10,635*
Pottawatomie □, KS • *14,782*
Pottawatomie □, OK • *55,239*
Pottawattamie □, IA • *86,561*
Potter □, PA • *17,726*
Potter □, SD • *3,674*
Potter □, TX • *98,637*
Potter Valley, CA 95469 • *1,500*
Pottstown, PA 19464 • *22,729*
Pottsville, PA 17901 • *18,195*
Poughkeepsie, NY 12601–99 • *29,757*
Poulan, GA 31781 • *818*
Poulsbo, WA 98370 • *3,453*
Poultney, VT 05764 • *1,554*
Pound, VA 24279 • *1,086*
Poway, CA 92064 • *33,300*
Powder River □, MT • *2,520*
Powder Springs, GA 30073 • *3,381*
Powell, WY 82435 • *5,310*
Powell □, KY • *11,101*
Powell □, MT • *6,958*
Powellhurst, OR 97236 • *9,000*
Powellton, WV 25161 • *1,200*
Power □, ID • *6,844*
Powers, OR 97466 • *819*
Poweshiek □, IA • *19,306*
Powhatan □, VA • *13,062*
Powhatan Point, OH 43942 • *2,181*
Poynette, WI 53955 • *1,447*
Prague, OK 74864 • *2,208*
Prairie □, AR • *10,140*
Prairie □, MT • *1,836*
Prairie City, IA 50228 • *1,278*
Prairie City, OR 97869 • *1,106*
Prairie du Chien, WI 53821 • *5,859*
Prairie Du Rocher, IL 62277 • *701*
Prairie du Sac, WI 53578 • *2,145*
Prairie Grove, AR 72753 • *1,708*
Prairie View, TX 77446 • *3,993*
Prairie Village, KS 66208 • *24,657*
Pratt, KS 67124 • *6,885*
Pratt, WV 25162 • *821*
Pratt □, KS • *10,275*
Prattsburg, NY 14873 • *750*
Prattville, AL 36067 • *18,647*
Preble □, OH • *38,223*
Premont, TX 78375 • *2,984*
Prentice, WI 54556 • *605*
Prentiss, MS 39474 • *1,465*
Prentiss □, MS • *24,025*
Prescott, AZ 86301 • *20,055*
Prescott, AR 71857 • *4,103*
Prescott, WI 54021 • *2,654*
Presho, SD 57568 • *760*
Presidio, TX 79845 • *1,100*
Presidio □, TX • *5,188*
Presque Isle, ME 04769 • *11,172*
Presque Isle □, MI • *14,267*
Preston, ID 83263 • *3,759*
Preston, IA 52069 • *1,120*
Preston, MN 55965 • *1,478*
Preston □, WV • *30,460*
Prestonsburg, KY 41653 • *4,011*
Pretty Prairie, KS 67570 • *655*
Price, TX 75687 • *650*
Price, UT 84501 • *9,086*
Price □, WI • *15,788*
Prichard, AL 36610 • *39,541*
Priest River, ID 83856 • *1,639*
Primghar, IA 51245 • *1,050*
Prince Edward □, VA • *16,456*
Prince Frederick, MD 20678 • *1,805*
Prince George □, VA • *25,733*
Prince Georges □, MD • *665,071*
Princes Lakes, IN 46164 • *937*
Princess Anne, MD 21853 • *1,499*
Princeton, FL 33032 • *5,300*
Princeton, IL 61356 • *7,342*
Princeton, IN 47670 • *8,976*
Princeton, IA 52768 • *965*
Princeton, KY 42445 • *7,073*
Princeton, ME 04668 • *800*
Princeton, MN 55371 • *3,146*
Princeton, MO 64673 • *1,264*
Princeton, NJ 08540 • *12,035*
Princeton, NC 27569 • *1,034*
Princeton, WV 24740 • *7,493*
Princeton, WI 54968 • *1,479*
Princeton Junction, NJ 08550 • *2,419*
Princeville, IL 61559 • *1,712*
Princeville, NC 27886 • *1,508*
Prince William □, VA • *144,703*
Prineville, OR 97754 • *5,276*
Prior Lake, MN 55372 • *7,284*
Proctor, MN 55810 • *3,180*
Proctor, VT 05765 • *1,998*
Proctorville, OH 45669 • *975*
Prophetstown, IL 61277 • *2,141*
Prospect, CT 06712 • *6,807*
Prospect, KY 40059 • *1,981*
Prospect, OH 43342 • *1,159*
Prospect, OR 97536 • *1,200*
Prospect, PA 16052 • *1,016*
Prospect Heights, IL 60070 • *11,808*
Prospect Park, NJ 07508 • *5,142*
Prospect Park, PA 19076 • *6,593*
Prosperity, SC 29127 • *803*
Prosperity, WV 25909 • *1,000*
Prosser, WA 99350 • *3,896*
Protection, KS 67127 • *684*
Provencal, LA 71468 • *695*
Providence, KY 42450 • *4,434*
Providence, RI 02901–99 • *156,804*
Providence, UT 84332 • *2,675*
Providence □, RI • *571,349*
Provincetown, MA 02657 • *3,536*
Provo, UT 84601–04 • *74,108*
Prowers □, CO • *13,070*
Prudenville, MI 48651 • *1,000*
Pryor, OK 74361 • *8,483*
Pueblo, CO 81001–19 • *101,686*
Pueblo □, CO • *125,972*
Puhi, HI 96766 • *991*
Pukalani, HI 96788 • *3,950*
Pulaski, NY 13142 • *2,415*
Pulaski, TN 38478 • *7,184*
Pulaski, VA 24301 • *10,106*
Pulaski, WI 54162 • *1,875*
Pulaski □, AR • *340,613*
Pulaski □, GA • *8,950*
Pulaski □, IL • *8,840*
Pulaski □, IN • *13,258*
Pulaski □, KY • *45,803*
Pulaski □, MO • *42,011*
Pulaski □, VA • *35,229*
Pullman, WA 99163 • *23,579*
Pumphrey, MD 21227 • *3,300*
Punta Gorda, FL 33950–55 • *6,797*
Punxsutawney, PA 15767 • *7,479*
Purcell, OK 73080 • *4,638*
Purcellville, VA 22132 • *1,567*
Purdy, MO 65734 • *928*
Purvis, MS 39475 • *2,256*
Puryear, TN 38251 • *624*
Pushmataha □, OK • *11,773*
Putnam, CT 06260 • *6,855*
Putnam □, FL • *50,549*
Putnam □, GA • *10,295*
Putnam □, IL • *6,085*
Putnam □, IN • *29,163*
Putnam □, MO • *6,092*
Putnam □, NY • *77,193*
Putnam □, OH • *32,991*
Putnam □, TN • *47,690*
Putnam □, WV • *38,181*
Putney, GA 31782 • *650*
Putney, VT 05346 • *1,100*
Puxico, MO 63960 • *833*
Puyallup, WA 98371–73 • *18,251*

Q

Quail Oaks, VA 23234 • *1,700*
Quaker City, OH 43773 • *698*
Quaker Hill, CT 06375 • *2,052*
Quakertown, PA 18951 • *8,867*
Quanah, TX 79252 • *3,890*
Quantico, VA 22134 • *621*
Quapaw, OK 74363 • *1,097*
Quarryville, PA 17566 • *1,558*
Quay □, NM • *10,577*
Queen Annes □, MD • *25,508*
Queen City, MO 63561 • *783*
Queen City, TX 75572 • *1,748*
Queen Creek, AZ 85242 • *900*
Queens □, NY • *1,891,325*
Questa, NM 87556 • *1,202*
Quidnessett, RI 02852 • *3,300*
Quidnick, RI 02816 • *2,300*
Quilcene, WA 98376 • *950*
Quincy, CA 95971 • *2,700*
Quincy, FL 32351 • *8,591*
Quincy, IL 62301 • *42,554*
Quincy, MA 02169 • *84,743*
Quincy, MI 49082 • *1,569*
Quincy, OH 43343 • *633*
Quincy, WA 98848 • *3,525*
Quinebaug, CT 06262 • *1,088*
Quinlan, TX 75474 • *1,002*
Quinnesec, MI 49876 • *900*
Quinter, KS 67752 • *951*
Quinton, OK 74561 • *1,228*
Quitaque, TX 79255 • *696*
Quitman, GA 31643 • *5,188*
Quitman, MS 39355 • *2,632*
Quitman, TX 75783 • *1,893*
Quitman □, GA • *2,357*
Quitman □, MS • *12,636*
Quonochontaug, RI 02808 • *1,000*

R

Rabun □, GA • *10,466*
Raceland, KY 41169 • *1,970*
Raceland, LA 70394 • *6,302*
Racine, OH 45771 • *908*
Racine, WV 25165 • *650*
Racine, WI 53401–99 • *85,725*
Racine □, WI • *173,132*
Radcliff, KY 40160 • *14,519*
Radford, VA 24141 • *13,225*
Raeford, NC 28376 • *3,630*
Ragland, AL 35131 • *1,860*
Rahway, NJ 07065–67 • *26,723*
Rainbow City, AL 35901 • *6,299*
Rainelle, WV 25962 • *1,983*
Rainier, OR 97048 • *1,655*
Rainier, WA 98576 • *891*
Rains □, TX • *4,839*
Rainsville, AL 35986 • *3,907*
Raleigh, MS 39153 • *998*
Raleigh, NC 27601–99 • *150,255*
Raleigh, WV 25911 • *900*
Raleigh □, WV • *86,821*
Raleigh Hills, OR 97225 • *6,500*
Ralls, TX 79357 • *2,422*
Ralls □, MO • *8,984*
Ralston, NE 68127 • *5,143*
Rambleton Acres, DE 19720 • *1,500*
Ramblewood, NJ 08054 • *6,475*
Ramona, CA 92065 • *8,173*
Ramsay, MI 49959 • *1,068*
Ramseur, NC 27316 • *1,162*
Ramsey, IL 62080 • *1,058*
Ramsey, MN 55303 • *10,093*
Ramsey, NJ 07446 • *12,899*
Ramsey □, MN • *459,784*
Ramsey □, ND • *13,048*
Ranchester, WY 82839 • *655*
Rancho Cordova, CA 95670 • *42,881*
Rancho Mirage, CA 92270 • *6,281*
Rancho Palos Verdes, CA 90274 • *36,577*
Rancho Rinconado, CA 95014 • *5,100*
Rancho Santa Fe, CA 92067 • *4,014*
Ranchos de Taos, NM 87557 • *1,411*
Rancocas Woods, NJ 08060 • *1,400*
Rand, WV 25306 • *2,500*
Randall □, TX • *75,062*
Randallstown, MD 21133 • *20,500*
Randleman, NC 27317 • *2,156*
Randolph, ME 04345 • *1,834*
Randolph, MA 02368 • *22,218*
Randolph, NE 68771 • *1,106*
Randolph, NY 14772 • *1,398*
Randolph, OH 44265 • *800*
Randolph, UT 84064 • *659*
Randolph, VT 05060 • *2,217*
Randolph, WI 53956 • *1,691*
Randolph □, AL • *20,075*
Randolph □, AR • *16,834*
Randolph □, GA • *9,599*
Randolph □, IL • *35,652*
Randolph □, IN • *29,997*
Randolph □, MO • *25,460*
Randolph □, NC • *91,728*
Randolph □, WV • *28,734*
Random Lake, WI 53075 • *1,287*
Rangeley, ME 04970 • *700*
Rangely, CO 81648 • *2,113*
Ranger, TX 76470 • *3,142*
Rankin, IL 60960 • *727*
Rankin, PA 15104 • *2,892*
Rankin, TX 79778 • *1,216*
Rankin □, MS • *69,427*
Ransom □, ND • *6,698*
Ransomville, NY 14131 • *1,500*
Ranson, WV 25438 • *2,471*
Rantoul, IL 61866 • *20,161*
Raoul, GA 30510 • *1,400*
Rapid City, SD 57701–08 • *46,492*
Rapides □, LA • *135,282*
Rapid River, MI 49878 • *700*
Rapids City, IL 61278 • *1,058*
Rappahannock □, VA • *6,093*
Raritan, NJ 08869 • *6,128*
Rathdrum, ID 83858 • *1,369*
Raton, NM 87740 • *8,225*
Ravalli □, MT • *22,493*
Raven, VA 24639 • *1,880*
Ravena, NY 12143 • *3,091*
Ravenel, SC 29470 • *1,655*
Ravenna, KY 40472 • *793*
Ravenna, MI 49451 • *951*
Ravenna, NE 68869 • *1,296*
Ravenna, OH 44266 • *11,987*
Ravenswood, WV 26164 • *4,126*
Rawlins, WY 82301 • *11,547*
Rawlins □, KS • *4,105*
Ray, ND 58849 • *766*
Ray □, MO • *21,378*
Ray City, GA 31645 • *658*
Raymond, IL 62560 • *957*
Raymond, MN 56282 • *723*
Raymond, MS 39154 • *1,967*
Raymond, NH 03077 • *1,192*
Raymond, WA 98577 • *2,991*
Raymondville, TX 78580 • *9,493*
Raymore, MO 64083 • *3,154*
Rayne, LA 70578 • *9,066*
Raynham, MA 02767 • *2,124*
Raynham Center, MA 02768 • *3,776*
Raytown, MO 64133 • *31,759*
Rayville, LA 71269 • *4,610*
Reader, WV 26167 • *700*
Reading, MA 01867 • *22,678*
Reading, MI 49274 • *1,203*
Reading, OH 45215 • *12,843*
Reading, PA 19601–99 • *78,686*
Readlyn, IA 50668 • *858*
Reagan □, TX • *4,135*
Real □, TX • *2,469*
Reamstown, PA 17567 • *1,050*
Rector, AR 72461 • *2,336*
Red Bank, NJ 07701 • *12,031*
Red Bank, TN 37415 • *13,299*
Red Bay, AL 35582 • *3,232*
Redbird, OH 44057 • *1,600*
Red Bluff, CA 96080 • *9,490*
Red Boiling Springs, TN 37150 • *1,173*
Red Bud, IL 62278 • *2,850*
Red Cloud, NE 68970 • *1,300*
Red Creek, NY 13143 • *645*
Reddick, FL 32686 • *657*
Redding, CA 96001–03 • *41,995*
Redding, CT 06875 • *950*
Redfield, AR 72132 • *745*
Redfield, IA 50233 • *959*
Redfield, SD 57469 • *3,027*
Redford, MI 48239 • *58,441*
Redgranite, WI 54970 • *976*
Red Hook, NY 12571 • *1,692*
Red Jacket, WV 25692 • *1,000*
Redkey, IN 47373 • *1,537*
Red Lake □, MN • *5,471*
Red Lake Falls, MN 56750 • *1,732*
Redlands, CA 92373–74 • *43,619*
Red Lion, PA 17356 • *5,824*
Red Lodge, MT 59068 • *1,896*
Redmond, OR 97756 • *6,452*
Redmond, UT 84652 • *619*
Redmond, WA 98052–53 • *23,318*
Red Oak, GA 30272 • *1,200*
Red Oak, IA 51566 • *6,810*
Red Oak, OK 74563 • *676*
Red Oak, TX 75154 • *1,882*
Red Oaks, LA 70815 • *2,000*
Redondo Beach, CA 90277–78 • *57,102*
Red River □, LA • *10,433*
Red River □, TX • *16,101*
Red Springs, NC 28377 • *3,607*
Red Willow □, NE • *12,615*
Red Wing, MN 55066 • *13,736*
Redwood, UT 84119 • *2,000*
Redwood □, MN • *19,341*
Redwood City, CA 94061–65 • *54,951*
Redwood Falls, MN 56283 • *5,210*
Redwood Valley, CA 95470 • *1,300*
Reece City, AL 35954 • *718*
Reed City, MI 49677 • *2,221*
Reedley, CA 93654 • *11,071*
Reedsburg, WI 53959 • *5,038*
Reedsport, OR 97467 • *4,984*
Reedsville, PA 17084 • *950*
Reedsville, WI 54230 • *1,134*
Reedurban, OH 44710 • *6,650*
Reese, MI 48757 • *1,645*
Reeseville, WI 53579 • *649*
Reeves □, TX • *15,801*
Reform, AL 35481 • *2,245*
Refugio, TX 78377 • *3,898*
Refugio □, TX • *9,289*
Rehoboth Beach, DE 19971 • *1,730*
Reidland, KY 42001 • *3,730*
Reidsville, GA 30453 • *2,296*
Reidsville, NC 27320 • *12,492*
Reinbeck, IA 50669 • *1,808*
Reisterstown, MD 21136 • *19,385*
Remington, IN 47977 • *1,268*
Remsen, IA 51050 • *1,592*
Remsen, NY 13438 • *621*
Reno, NV 89501–99 • *100,756*
Reno, OH 45773 • *850*
Reno □, KS • *64,983*
Renovo, PA 17764 • *1,812*
Rensselaer, IN 47978 • *4,944*
Rensselaer, NY 12144 • *9,047*
Rensselaer □, NY • *151,966*
Renton, WA 98055–57 • *30,612*
Renville, MN 56284 • *1,493*
Renville □, MN • *20,401*
Renville □, ND • *3,608*
Republic, MI 49879 • *1,000*
Republic, MO 65738 • *4,485*
Republic, OH 44867 • *656*
Republic, PA 15475 • *1,500*
Republic, WA 99166 • *1,018*
Republic □, KS • *7,569*
Reserve, LA 70084 • *7,288*
Reston, VA 22090 • *32,000*
Revere, MA 02151 • *42,423*
Revloc, PA 15948 • *800*
Rex, GA 30273 • *700*
Rexburg, ID 83440 • *11,559*
Reynolds, GA 31076 • *1,298*
Reynolds, IL 61279 • *701*
Reynolds, IN 47980 • *632*
Reynolds □, MO • *7,230*
Reynoldsburg, OH 43068 • *20,661*
Reynoldsville, PA 15851 • *3,016*
Rhea □, TN • *24,235*
Rhinebeck, NY 12572 • *2,542*
Rhinelander, WI 54501 • *7,873*
Rhodhiss, NC 28667 • *727*
Rialto, CA 92376 • *37,474*
Rib Lake, WI 54470 • *945*
Rice □, KS • *11,900*
Rice □, MN • *46,087*
Rice Lake, WI 54868 • *7,691*
Riceville, IA 50466 • *919*
Rich □, UT • *2,100*
Richardson, TX 75080–85 • *72,496*
Richardson □, NE • *11,315*
Richardton, ND 58652 • *699*
Rich Creek, VA 24147 • *746*
Richfield, MN 55423 • *37,851*
Richfield, UT 84701 • *5,482*
Richfield Springs, NY 13439 • *1,561*
Richford, VT 05476 • *1,471*
Rich Hill, MO 64779 • *1,471*
Richland, GA 31825 • *1,802*
Richland, MO 65556 • *1,922*
Richland, NJ 08350 • *800*
Richland, WA 99352 • *33,578*
Richland □, IL • *17,587*
Richland □, LA • *22,187*
Richland □, MT • *12,243*
Richland □, ND • *19,207*
Richland □, OH • *131,205*
Richland □, SC • *269,735*
Richland □, WI • *17,476*
Richland Center, WI 53581 • *4,997*
Richlands, NC 28574 • *825*
Richlands, VA 24641 • *5,796*
Richlandtown, PA 18955 • *1,180*
Richmond, CA 94801–99 • *74,676*
Richmond, IL 60071 • *1,068*
Richmond, IN 47374 • *41,349*
Richmond, KY 40475 • *21,705*
Richmond, ME 04357 • *1,578*
Richmond, MI 48062 • *3,536*
Richmond, MN 56368 • *867*
Richmond, MO 64085 • *5,499*
Richmond, TX 77469 • *9,692*
Richmond, UT 84333 • *1,705*
Richmond, VT 05477 • *865*
Richmond, VA 23201–99 • *219,214*
Richmond □, GA • *181,629*
Richmond □, NC • *45,481*
Richmond □, NY • *352,121*
Richmond □, VA • *6,952*
Richmond Beach, WA 98160 • *8,000*
Richmond Dale, OH 45673 • *650*
Richmond Heights, FL 33156 • *8,577*
Richmond Heights, MO 63117 • *11,516*
Richmond Heights, OH 44143 • *10,095*
Richmond Highlands, WA 98133 • *20,300*
Richmond Hill, GA 31324 • *1,177*
Richmondville, NY 12149 • *792*
Rich Square, NC 27869 • *1,057*
Richton, MS 39476 • *1,205*
Richton Park, IL 60471 • *9,403*
Richwood, OH 43344 • *2,181*
Richwood, WV 26261 • *3,568*
Riddle, OR 97469 • *1,265*
Ridgecrest, CA 93555 • *15,929*
Ridgecrest, WA 98155 • *7,000*
Ridge Farm, IL 61870 • *1,096*
Ridgefield, CT 06877 • *6,066*
Ridgefield, NJ 07657 • *10,294*
Ridgefield, WA 98642 • *1,062*
Ridgefield Park, NJ 07660 • *12,738*
Ridgeland, MS 39157 • *5,461*
Ridgeland, SC 29936 • *1,143*
Ridgeley, WV 26753 • *994*
Ridgely, MD 21660 • *933*
Ridgely, TN 38080 • *1,932*
Ridgemont, NY 14626 • *8,500*

Stanleyville, NC 27045 • 5,039
Stanly □, NC • 48,517
Stanton, CA 90680 • 23,723
Stanton, IA 51573 • 747
Stanton, KY 40380 • 2,691
Stanton, MI 48888 • 1,315
Stanton, NE 68779 • 1,603
Stanton, ND 58571 • 623
Stanton, TX 79782 • 2,314
Stanton □, KS • 2,339
Stanton □, NE • 6,549
Stantonsburg, NC 27883 • 920
Stanwood, IA 52337 • 705
Stanwood, WA 98292 • 1,646
Staples, MN 56479 • 2,887
Stapleton, AL 36578 • 900
Star, NC 27356 • 816
Starbuck, MN 56381 • 1,224
Star City, AR 71667 • 2,066
Star City, WV 26505 • 1,464
Stargo, AZ 85540 • 1,038
Stark □, IL • 7,389
Stark □, ND • 23,697
Stark □, OH • 378,823
Starke, FL 32091 • 5,306
Starke □, IN • 21,997
Starks, LA 70661 • 780
Starkville, MS 39759 • 15,169
Starr □, TX • 27,266
Startex, SC 29377 • 1,006
State Center, IA 50247 • 1,292
State College, PA 16801–05 • 36,130
Stateline, NV 89449 • 1,500
State Line, PA 17263 • 700
Statenville, GA 31648 • 650
State Road, NC 28676 • 800
Statesboro, GA 30458 • 14,866
Statesville, NC 28677 • 18,622
Statham, GA 30666 • 1,101
Staunton, IL 62088 • 4,744
Staunton, IN 47881 • 607
Staunton, VA 24401 • 21,857
Stayton, OR 97383 • 4,396
Steamboat Springs, CO 80487 • 5,098
Stearns, KY 42647 • 1,557
Stearns □, MN • 108,161
Steele, AL 35987 • 795
Steele, MO 63877 • 2,419
Steele, ND 58482 • 796
Steele □, MN • 30,328
Steele □, ND • 3,106
Steeleville, IL 62288 • 2,240
Steelton, PA 17113 • 6,484
Steelville, MO 65565 • 1,470
Steger, IL 60475 • 9,269
Steilacoom, WA 98388 • 4,886
Steinhatchee, FL 32359 • 800
Stephen, MN 56757 • 898
Stephens, AR 71764 • 1,366
Stephens □, GA • 21,763
Stephens □, OK • 43,419
Stephens □, TX • 9,926
Stephens City, VA 22655 • 1,179
Stephenson, MI 49887 • 967
Stephenson □, IL • 49,536
Stephenville, TX 76401 • 11,881
Sterling, AK 99672 • 919
Sterling, CO 80751 • 11,385
Sterling, IL 61081 • 16,281
Sterling, KS 67579 • 2,312
Sterling, MA 01564 • 1,200
Sterling, OK 73567 • 702
Sterling, VA 22170 • 12,000
Sterling □, TX • 1,206
Sterling City, TX 76951 • 915
Sterling Heights, MI 48077 • 108,999
Sterlington, LA 71280 • 1,400
Steuben □, IN • 24,694
Steuben □, NY • 99,217
Steubenville, OH 43952 • 26,400
Stevens □, KS • 4,736
Stevens □, MN • 11,322
Stevens □, WA • 28,979
Stevenson, AL 35772 • 2,568
Stevenson, WA 98648 • 1,172
Stevens Point, WI 54481 • 22,970
Stevensville, MI 49127 • 1,268
Stevensville, MT 59870 • 1,207
Stewardson, IL 62463 • 745
Stewart, MN 55385 • 616
Stewart □, GA • 5,896
Stewart □, TN • 8,665
Stewartstown, PA 17363 • 1,072
Stewartsville, MO 64490 • 832
Stewartsville, NJ 08886 • 900
Stewartville, MN 55976 • 3,925
Stickney, IL 60402 • 5,893
Stigler, OK 74462 • 2,630
Stillman Valley, IL 61084 • 961
Stillwater, MN 55082 • 12,290
Stillwater, NY 12170 • 1,572
Stillwater, OK 74074–78 • 38,268
Stillwater □, MT • 5,598
Stilwell, OK 74960 • 2,369
74960 • 2,369
Stinnett, TX 79083 • 2,222
Stirling, NJ 07980 • 2,000
Stockbridge, GA 30281 • 2,103
Stockbridge, MA 01262 • 1,109
Stockbridge, MI 49285 • 1,213
Stockdale, TX 78160 • 1,265
Stockertown, PA 18083 • 661
Stockton, CA 95201–12 • 149,779
Stockton, IL 61085 • 1,872

Stockton, KS 67669 • 1,825
Stockton, MO 65785 • 1,432
Stockton, NJ 08559 • 643
Stoddard, WI 54658 • 762
Stoddard □, MO • 29,009
Stokes □, NC • 33,086
Stokesdale, NC 27357 • 1,070
Stollings, WV 25646 • 900
Stone □, AR • 9,022
Stone □, MS • 9,716
Stone □, MO • 15,587
Stoneboro, PA 16153 • 1,177
Stoneham, MA 02180 • 21,424
Stone Harbor, NJ 08247 • 1,187
Stone Mountain, GA 30086–88 • 4,867
Stoneville, NC 27048 • 1,054
Stonewall, LA 71078 • 1,175
Stonewall, MS 39363 • 1,345
Stonewall, OK 74871 • 672
Stonewall □, TX • 2,406
Stonewood, WV 26301 • 2,058
Stonington, CT 06378 • 1,228
Stonington, IL 62567 • 1,184
Stonington, ME 04681 • 700
Stony Brook, NY 11790 • 6,600
Stony Creek, CT 06405 • 700
Stony Point, NC 28678 • 1,150
Stony Point, NY 10980 • 8,270
Storey □, NV • 1,503
Storm Lake, IA 50588 • 8,814
Storrs, CT 06268 • 11,394
Story, WY 82842 • 700
Story □, IA • 72,326
Story City, IA 50248 • 2,762
Stottville, NY 12172 • 1,300
Stoughton, MA 02072 • 26,710
Stoughton, WI 53589 • 7,589
Stover, MO 65078 • 1,041
Stow, MA 01775 • 1,100
Stow, OH 44224 • 25,303
Stowe, PA 19464 • 4,038
Stowe Township, PA 15136 • 10,119
Strabane, PA 15363 • 1,900
Strafford, MO 65757 • 1,121
Strafford □, NH • 85,408
Strasburg, CO 80136 • 1,105
Strasburg, ND 58573 • 623
Strasburg, OH 44680 • 2,091
Strasburg, PA 17579 • 1,999
Strasburg, VA 22657 • 2,311
Stratford, CA 93266 • 850
Stratford, CT 06497 • 50,541
Stratford, IA 50249 • 806
Stratford, NJ 08084 • 8,005
Stratford, OK 74872 • 1,459
Stratford, TX 79084 • 1,917
Stratford, WI 54484 • 1,385
Stratford Landing, VA 22308 • 2,650
Strathmore, CA 93267 • 1,221
Strathmore, NJ 07747 • 7,674
Stratton, CO 80836 • 705
Stratton Meadows, CO 80906 • 6,223
Strawberry Point, IA 52076 • 1,463
Strawn, TX 76475 • 694
Streamwood, IL 60103 • 23,456
Streator, IL 61364 • 14,795
Streetsboro, OH 44241 • 9,055
Stringtown, OK 74569 • 1,047
Stromsburg, NE 68666 • 1,290
Strong, AR 71765 • 785
Strong, ME 04983 • 700
Strong City, KS 66869 • 675
Stronghurst, IL 61480 • 865
Strongsville, OH 44136 • 28,577
Stroud, OK 74079 • 3,148
Stroudsburg, PA 18360 • 5,148
Strum, WI 54770 • 944
Struthers, OH 44471 • 13,624
Stryker, OH 43557 • 1,423
Stuart, FL 33494–97 • 9,467
Stuart, IA 50250 • 1,650
Stuart, NE 68780 • 641
Stuart, VA 24171 • 1,131
Stuarts Draft, VA 24477 • 950
Sturbridge, MA 01566 • 1,891
Sturgeon, MO 65284 • 901
Sturgeon Bay, WI 54235 • 8,847
Sturgis, KY 42459 • 2,293
Sturgis, MI 49091 • 9,468
Sturgis, SD 57785 • 5,184
Sturtevant, WI 53177 • 4,130
Stutsman □, ND • 24,154
Stuttgart, AR 72160 • 10,941
Subiaco, AR 72865 • 744
Sublette, KS 67877 • 1,293
Sublette □, WY • 4,548
Sublimity, OR 97385 • 1,077
Succasunna, NJ 07876 • 9,000
Sudan, TX 79371 • 1,091
Sudbury, MA 01776 • 2,200
Sudbury Center, MA 01776 • 2,900
Suffern, NY 10901 • 10,794
Suffield, CT 06078 • 1,122
Suffolk, VA 23434–38 • 47,621
Suffolk □, MA • 650,142
Suffolk □, NY • 1,284,231
Sugar City, ID 83448 • 1,022
Sugar Creek, MO 64054 • 4,305
Sugarcreek, PA 16323 • 5,954
Sugargrove, PA 16350 • 630
Sugar Hill, GA 30518 • 2,473
Sugar Land, TX 77478–79 • 8,826
Sugarland Run, VA 22170 • 4,500
Sugar Loaf, VA 24018 • 6,000

Sugar Notch, PA 18706 • 1,191
Suisun City, CA 94585 • 11,087
Suitland, MD 20746 • 24,800
Sulligent, AL 35586 • 2,130
Sullivan, IL 61951 • 4,526
Sullivan, IN 47882 • 4,774
Sullivan, MO 63080 • 5,461
Sullivan □, IN • 21,107
Sullivan □, MO • 7,434
Sullivan □, NH • 36,063
Sullivan □, NY • 65,155
Sullivan □, PA • 6,349
Sullivan □, TN • 143,968
Sullivans Island, SC 29482 • 1,867
Sully, IA 50251 • 828
Sully □, SD • 1,990
Sulphur, LA 70663 • 19,709
Sulphur, OK 73086 • 5,516
Sulphur Springs, TX 75482 • 12,804
Sultan, WA 98294 • 1,578
Sumas, WA 98295 • 712
Sumiton, AL 35148 • 2,815
Summerfield, NC 27358 • 1,680
Summers □, WV • 15,875
Summersville, WV 26651 • 2,972
Summerton, SC 29148 • 1,173
Summerville, GA 30747 • 4,878
Summerville, PA 15864 • 830
Summerville, SC 29483 • 6,706
Summit, IL 60501 • 10,110
Summit, MS 39666 • 1,753
Summit, NJ 07901 • 21,071
Summit, TN 37363 • 1,500
Summit □, CO • 8,848
Summit □, OH • 524,472
Summit □, UT • 10,198
Summit Hill, PA 18250 • 3,418
Summitville, IN 46070 • 1,085
Sumner, IL 62466 • 1,238
Sumner, IA 50674 • 2,335
Sumner, WA 98390 • 4,936
Sumner □, KS • 24,928
Sumner □, TN • 85,790
Sumrall, MS 39482 • 1,197
Sumter, SC 29150–52 • 24,890
Sumter □, AL • 16,908
Sumter □, FL • 24,272
Sumter □, GA • 29,360
Sumter □, SC • 88,243
Sunapee, NH 03782 • 900
Sunbury, OH 43074 • 2,101
Sunbury, PA 17801 • 12,292
Sun City, AZ 85351 • 40,505
Sun City, CA 92381 • 6,500
Sun City, FL 34268 • 700
Suncook, NH 03275 • 4,698
Sundance, WY 82729 • 1,087
Sundown, TX 79372 • 1,511
Sunflower, MS 38778 • 1,027
Sunflower □, MS • 34,844
Sunland Park, NM 88063 • 3,377
Sunman, IN 47041 • 924
Sunnyland, FL 33583 • 650
Sunnymead, CA 92388 • 11,554
Sunnyside, UT 84539 • 611
Sunnyside, WA 98944 • 9,225
Sunnyvale, CA 94086–88 • 106,618
Sunol, CA 94586 • 750
Sun Prairie, WI 53590 • 12,931
Sunray, TX 79086 • 1,952
Sunrise, FL 33313 • 39,681
Sunrise Manor, NV 89110 • 44,155
Sunset, LA 70584 • 2,300
Sunset, UT 84015 • 5,733
Sunset Beach, HI 96712 • 800
Sunset Park, KS 67217 • 1,050
Sun Valley, NV 89433 • 8,822
Superior, AZ 85273 • 4,600
Superior, MT 59872 • 1,054
Superior, NE 68978 • 2,502
Superior, WI 54880 • 29,571
Suquamish, WA 98392 • 1,500
Surf City, NJ 08008 • 1,571
Surfside, FL 33154 • 3,763
Surfside Beach, SC 29577 • 2,522
Surgoinsville, TN 37873 • 1,536
Surprise, AZ 85345 • 3,723
Surrey, ND 58785 • 999
Surry □, NC • 59,449
Surry □, VA • 6,046
Susanville, CA 96130 • 6,520
Susquehanna, PA 18847 • 1,994
Susquehanna □, PA • 37,876
Sussex, NJ 07461 • 2,418
Sussex, WI 53089 • 3,482
Sussex □, DE • 97,983
Sussex □, NJ • 116,119
Sussex □, VA • 10,874
Sutherland, IA 51058 • 897
Sutherland, NE 69165 • 1,238
Sutherlin, OR 97479 • 4,560
Sutter □, CA • 52,246
Sutter Creek, CA 95685 • 1,705
Sutton, NE 68979 • 1,416
Sutton, WV 26601 • 1,192
Sutton □, TX • 5,130
Sutton Park, NJ 07836 • 2,500
Suwanee, GA 30174 • 1,026
Suwannee □, FL • 22,287
Svensen, OR 97103 • 650
Swain □, NC • 10,283
Swainsboro, GA 30401 • 7,602
Swampscott, MA 01907 • 13,837
Swannanoa, NC 28778 • 5,586
Swansboro, NC 28584 • 976
Swansea, IL 62221 • 5,347

Swansea, MA 02777 • 750
Swansea, SC 29160 • 888
Swanton, OH 43558 • 3,424
Swanton, VT 05488 • 2,520
Swanwyck Estates, DE 19720 • 1,700
Swanzey Center, NH 03431 • 700
Swarthmore, PA 19081 • 5,950
Swartz Creek, MI 48473 • 5,013
Swayzee, IN 46986 • 1,127
Swea City, IA 50590 • 813
Swedesboro, NJ 08085 • 2,031
Sweeny, TX 77480 • 3,538
Sweet Briar, VA 24595 • 900
Sweet Grass □, MT • 3,216
Sweet Home, AR 72164 • 1,100
Sweet Home, OR 97386 • 6,921
Sweetser, IN 46987 • 944
Sweet Springs, MO 65351 • 1,694
Sweetwater, TN 37874 • 4,725
Sweetwater, TX 79556 • 12,242
Sweetwater □, WY • 41,723
Sweetwater Creek, FL 33614 • 18,000
Swepsonville, NC 27359 • 900
Swift □, MN • 12,920
Swifton, AR 72471 • 859
Swink, CO 81077 • 668
Swisher, IA 52338 • 654
Swisher □, TX • 9,723
Swissvale, PA 15218 • 11,345
Switzer, WV 25647 • 1,000
Switzerland, FL 32043 • 2,400
Switzerland □, IN • 7,153
Swoyerville, PA 18704 • 5,795
Sycamore, AL 35149 • 900
Sycamore, IL 60178 • 9,219
Sycamore, OH 44882 • 1,059
Sykesville, MD 21784 • 1,712
Sykesville, PA 15865 • 1,537
Sylacauga, AL 35150 • 12,708
Sylva, NC 28779 • 1,699
Sylvan Beach, NY 13157 • 1,243
Sylvan Hills, AR 72116 • 2,900
Sylvania, AL 35988 • 1,156
Sylvania, GA 30467 • 3,352
Sylvania, OH 43560 • 15,527
Sylvan Lake, MI 48053 • 1,949
Sylvester, GA 31791 • 5,860
Syosset, NY 11791 • 10,200
Syracuse, IN 46567 • 2,579
Syracuse, KS 67878 • 1,654
Syracuse, NE 68446 • 1,638
Syracuse, NY 13201–99 • 170,105
Syracuse, OH 45779 • 946
Syracuse, UT 84041 • 3,702

T

Tabor, IA 51653 • 1,088
Tabor City, NC 28463 • 2,710
Tacoma, WA 98401–99 • 158,501
Taft, CA 93268 • 5,316
Taft, TX 78390 • 3,686
Tahlequah, OK 74464 • 9,708
Tahoe City, CA 95730 • 1,300
Tahoka, TX 79373 • 3,262
Taholah, WA 98587 • 800
Takoma Park, MD 20912 • 16,231
Talbot □, GA • 6,536
Talbot □, MD • 25,604
Talbotton, GA 31827 • 1,140
Talco, TX 75487 • 751
Talent, OR 97540 • 2,577
Taliaferro □, GA • 2,032
Talihina, OK 74571 • 1,387
Talladega, AL 35160 • 19,128
Talladega □, AL • 73,826
Tallahassee, FL 32301–17 • 81,548
Tallahatchie □, MS • 17,157
Tallapoosa, GA 30176 • 2,647
Tallapoosa □, AL • 38,676
Tallassee, AL 36078 • 4,763
Talleyville, DE 19803 • 6,880
Tallmadge, OH 44278 • 15,269
Tallula, IL 62688 • 681
Tallulah, LA 71282 • 11,634
Tama, IA 52339 • 2,968
Tama □, IA • 19,533
Tamaqua, PA 18252 • 8,843
Tamarac, FL 33321 • 29,376
Tamaroa, IL 62888 • 885
Tamina, TX 77302 • 900
Tamms, IL 62988 • 826
Tampa, FL 33601–99 • 271,523
Tampico, IL 61283 • 966
Taney □, MO • 20,467
Taneytown, MD 21787 • 2,618
Tangier, VA 23440 • 771
Tangipahoa □, LA • 80,698
Tannersville, NY 12485 • 685
Taos, MO 65101 • 759
Taos, NM 87571 • 3,369
Taos □, NM • 19,456
Taos Pueblo, NM 87571 • 1,030
Tappahannock, VA 22560 • 1,821
Tappan, NY 10983 • 6,100
Tara Hills, CA 94564 • 6,000
Tarboro, NC 27886 • 8,634
Tarentum, PA 15084 • 6,419
Tariffville, CT 06081 • 1,324
Tarkio, MO 64491 • 2,375
Tarpey, CA 93727 • 4,000
Tarpon Springs, FL 33589–90 • 13,251
Tarrant □, TX • 860,880

Tarrant City, AL 35217 • 8,148
Tarrytown, NY 10591 • 10,648
Tate, GA 30177 • 900
Tate □, MS • 20,119
Tateville, KY 42558 • 725
Tattnall □, GA • 18,134
Tatum, NM 88267 • 896
Taunton, MA 02780 • 45,001
Tavares, FL 32778 • 4,103
Tavernier, FL 33070 • 1,834
Tawas City, MI 48763 • 1,967
Taylor, AZ 85939 • 1,915
Taylor, AR 71861 • 657
Taylor, MI 48180 • 77,568
Taylor, PA 18517 • 7,246
Taylor, TX 76574 • 10,619
Taylor □, FL • 16,532
Taylor □, GA • 7,902
Taylor □, IA • 8,353
Taylor □, KY • 21,178
Taylor □, TX • 110,932
Taylor □, WV • 16,584
Taylor □, WI • 18,817
Taylor Mill, KY 41015 • 4,509
Taylors, SC 29687 • 12,100
Taylors Falls, MN 55084 • 623
Taylor Springs, IL 62089 • 671
Taylorsville, IN 47280 • 1,247
Taylorsville, KY 40071 • 801
Taylorsville, MS 39168 • 1,387
Taylorsville, NC 28681 • 1,103
Taylorsville, UT 84107 • 17,448
Taylorville, IL 62568 • 11,386
Tazewell, TN 37879 • 2,090
Tazewell, VA 24651 • 4,468
Tazewell □, IL • 132,078
Tazewell □, VA • 50,511
Tchula, MS 39169 • 1,931
Tea, SD 57064 • 729
Teague, TX 75860 • 3,390
Teaneck, NJ 07666 • 39,007
Teaticket, MA 02536 • 2,000
Tecumseh, MI 49286 • 7,320
Tecumseh, NE 68450 • 1,926
Tecumseh, OK 74873 • 5,123
Tehachapi, CA 93561 • 4,126
Tehama □, CA • 38,888
Tekamah, NE 68061 • 1,886
Tekoa, WA 99033 • 854
Tekonsha, MI 49092 • 755
Telfair □, GA • 11,445
Telford, PA 18969 • 3,507
Tell City, IN 47586 • 8,704
Teller □, CO • 8,034
Tellico Plains, TN 37385 • 698
Telluride, CO 81435 • 1,047
Temecula, CA 92390 • 1,783
Tempe, AZ 85281–89 • 106,743
Temperance, MI 48182 • 3,500
Temple, GA 30179 • 1,520
Temple, OK 73568 • 1,339
Temple, PA 19560 • 1,486
Temple, TX 76501–08 • 42,354
Temple City, CA 91780 • 28,972
Temple Terrace, FL 33617 • 11,097
Templeton, MA 01468 • 900
Templeton, PA 16259 • 700
Tenafly, NJ 07670 • 13,552
Tenaha, TX 75974 • 1,005
Tenino, WA 98589 • 1,280
Tennessee Ridge, TN 37178 • 1,325
Tennille, GA 31089 • 1,709
Tensas □, LA • 8,525
Terra Alta, WV 26764 • 1,946
Terral, OK 73569 • 604
Terrebonne, OR 97760 • 900
Terrebonne □, LA • 94,393
Terre Haute, IN 47801–12 • 61,125
Terre Hill, PA 17581 • 1,217
Terrell, TX 75160 • 13,269
Terrell □, GA • 12,017
Terrell □, TX • 1,595
Terrell Hills, TX 78209 • 4,644
Terry, MS 39170 • 655
Terry, MT 59349 • 929
Terry □, TX • 14,581
Terrytown, NE 69341 • 727
Terryville, CT 06786 • 5,234
Terryville, NY 11776 • 5,900
Tesuque, NM 87574 • 1,014
Teton □, ID • 2,897
Teton □, MT • 6,491
Teton □, WY • 9,355
Teutopolis, IL 62467 • 1,414
Tewksbury, MA 01876 • 11,500
Texarkana, AR 75502 • 21,459
Texarkana, TX 75501–07 • 31,271
Texas □, MO • 21,070
Texas □, OK • 17,727
Texas City, TX 77590–91 • 41,403
Texhoma, OK 73949 • 785
Texico, NM 88135 • 958
Thatcher, AZ 85552 • 3,374
Thayer, IL 62689 • 759
Thayer, MO 65791 • 2,211
Thayer □, NE • 7,582
The Colony, TX 75056 • 11,586
The Dalles, OR 97058 • 10,820
Theodore, AL 36582 • 6,392
The Plains, OH 45780 • 2,044
Theresa, NY 13691 • 827
Theresa, WI 53091 • 766
Thermopolis, WY 82443 • 3,852
The Village, OK 73120 • 11,049
Thibodaux, LA 70301–02 • 15,810
Thief River Falls, MN 56701 • 9,105

Venice, IL 62090 • 3,480
Ventnor City, NJ 08406 • 11,704
Ventura (San Buenaventura), CA 93001-09 • 74,393
Ventura, IA 50482 • 614
Ventura □, CA • 529,174
Verda, KY 40828 • 1,132
Verden, OK 73092 • 625
Verdi, NV 89439 • 800
Verdigre, NE 68783 • 617
Verdunville, WV 25649 • 950
Vergennes, VT 05491 • 2,273
Vermilion, OH 44089 • 11,012
Vermilion □, IL • 95,222
Vermilion □, LA • 48,458
Vermillion, SD 57069 • 10,136
Vermillion □, IN • 18,229
Vermont, IL 61484 • 885
Vermontville, MI 49096 • 832
Vernal, UT 84078 • 6,600
Vernon, AL 35592 • 2,609
Vernon, CT 06066 • 27,974
Vernon, FL 32462 • 885
Vernon, TX 76384 • 12,695
Vernon □, LA • 53,475
Vernon □, MO • 19,806
Vernon □, WI • 25,642
Vernon Hills, IL 60061 • 9,827
Vernonia, OR 97064 • 1,785
Vero Beach, FL 32960-64 • 16,176
Verona, MS 38879 • 2,497
Verona, NJ 07044 • 14,166
Verona, PA 15147 • 3,179
Verona, WI 53593 • 3,336
Versailles, IN 47042 • 1,560
Versailles, KY 40383 • 6,427
Versailles, MO 65084 • 2,406
Versailles, OH 45380 • 2,384
Vestal, NY 13850 • 6,000
Vestal Center, NY 13850 • 900
Vestavia Hills, AL 35216 • 15,722
Vevay, IN 47043 • 1,343
Vian, OK 74962 • 1,521
Viborg, SD 57070 • 812
Viburnum, MO 65566 • 836
Vici, OK 73859 • 845
Vicksburg, MI 49097 • 2,224
Vicksburg, MS 39180 • 25,434
Victor, IA 52347 • 1,046
Victor, NY 14564 • 2,370
Victoria, KS 67671 • 1,328
Victoria, MS 38679 • 950
Victoria, TX 77901-04 • 50,695
Victoria, VA 23974 • 2,004
Victoria □, TX • 68,807
Victorville, CA 92392 • 14,220
Vidalia, GA 30474 • 10,393
Vidalia, LA 71373 • 5,936
Vidor, TX 77662 • 11,834
Vidor, TX 77662 • 12,117
Vienna, GA 31092 • 2,886
Vienna, IL 62995 • 1,420
Vienna, VA 22180 • 15,469
Vienna, WV 26105 • 11,618
View Park, CA 90043 • 5,900
Vigo □, IN • 112,385
Vilas □, WI • 16,535
Villa Grove, IL 61956 • 2,707
Villanova, PA 19085 • 6,600
Villa Park, CA 92667 • 7,137
Villa Park, IL 60181 • 23,185
Villa Rica, GA 30180 • 3,420
Villas, NJ 08251 • 5,909
Ville Platte, LA 70586 • 9,201
Villisca, IA 50864 • 1,434
Vilonia, AR 72173 • 736
Vinalhaven, ME 04863 • 900
Vincennes, IN 47591 • 20,857
Vincent, AL 35178 • 1,652
Vincentown, NJ 08088 • 800
Vine Grove, KY 40175 • 3,583
Vineland, NJ 08360 • 53,753
Vinemont, AL 35179 • 615
Vineyard Haven, MA 02568 • 1,704
Vinita, OK 74301 • 6,740
Vinton, IA 52349 • 5,040
Vinton, LA 70668 • 3,631
Vinton, VA 24179 • 8,027
Vinton □, OH • 11,584
Vintondale, PA 15961 • 697
Viola, IL 61486 • 1,144
Viola, WI 54664 • 696
Violet, LA 70092 • 6,000
Virden, IL 62690 • 3,899
Virginia, AL 35020 • 700
Virginia, IL 62691 • 1,825
Virginia, MN 55792 • 11,056
Virginia Beach, VA 23450-65 • 262,199
Viroqua, WI 54665 • 3,716
Visalia, CA 93277-79 • 49,729
Vista, CA 92083-84 • 35,834
Vivian, LA 71082 • 4,146
Volcano, HI 96785 • 900
Volga, SD 57071 • 1,221
Volusia □, FL • 258,762

W

Wabash, IN 46992 • 12,985
Wabash □, IL • 13,713
Wabash □, IN • 36,640
Wabasha, MN 55981 • 2,372
Wabasha □, MN • 19,335
Wabasso, FL 32970 • 2,157
Wabasso, MN 56293 • 745
Wabaunsee □, KS • 6,867
Wabeno, WI 54566 • 700
Waco, TX 76701-99 • 101,261
Waconia, MN 55387 • 2,638
Waddington, NY 13694 • 980
Wadena, MN 56482 • 4,699
Wadena □, MN • 14,192
Wadesboro, NC 28170 • 4,206
Wading River, NY 11792 • 2,500
Wadley, GA 30477 • 2,438
Wadsworth, IL 60083 • 1,104
Wadsworth, OH 44281 • 15,166
Waelder, TX 78959 • 942
Wagener, SC 29164 • 903
Wagner, SD 57380 • 1,453
Wagoner, OK 74467 • 6,191
Wagoner □, OK • 41,801
Wagram, NC 28396 • 617
Wahiawa, HI 96786 • 16,911
Wahkiakum □, WA • 3,832
Wahoo, NE 68066 • 3,555
Wahpeton, ND 58075 • 9,064
Waialua, HI 96791 • 4,051
Waianae, HI 96792 • 5,000
Waikapu, HI 96793 • 698
Wailua, HI 96746 • 1,587
Wailuku, HI 96793 • 10,260
Waimanalo, HI 96795 • 3,562
Waimea, HI 96796 • 1,569
Waipahu, HI 96797 • 29,139
Waipio Acres, HI 96786 • 4,091
Waite Park, MN 56387 • 3,496
Waitsburg, WA 99361 • 1,035
Wakarusa, IN 46573 • 1,281
Wake □, NC • 301,327
Wa Keeney, KS 67672 • 2,388
Wakefield, KS 67487 • 803
Wakefield, MA 01880 • 24,895
Wakefield, MI 49968 • 2,591
Wakefield, NE 68784 • 1,125
Wakefield, RI 02879-83 • 3,400
Wakefield, VA 23888 • 1,355
Wake Forest, NC 27587 • 3,780
Wakeman, OH 44889 • 906
Wakulla □, FL • 10,887
Walbridge, OH 43465 • 2,900
Walcott, IA 52773 • 1,425
Walden, CO 80480 • 947
Walden, NY 12586 • 5,659
Waldo, AR 71770 • 1,685
Waldo, FL 32694 • 993
Waldo □, ME • 28,414
Waldoboro, ME 04572 • 1,195
Waldorf, MD 20601 • 9,782
Waldport, OR 97394 • 1,274
Waldron, AR 72958 • 2,642
Waldron, IN 46182 • 800
Waldwick, NJ 07463 • 10,802
Walhalla, ND 58282 • 1,429
Walhalla, SC 29691 • 3,977
Walker, IA 52352 • 733
Walker, LA 70785 • 2,957
Walker, MI 49504 • 15,088
Walker, MN 56484 • 970
Walker □, AL • 68,660
Walker □, GA • 56,470
Walker □, TX • 41,789
Walkersville, MD 21793 • 2,212
Walkerton, IN 46574 • 2,051
Walkertown, NC 27051 • 2,100
Walkerville, MT 59701 • 887
Wall, SD 57790 • 770
Wallace, ID 83873 • 1,736
Wallace, NC 28466 • 2,903
Wallace, WV 26448 • 900
Wallace □, KS • 2,045
Walla Walla, WA 99362 • 25,618
Walla Walla □, WA • 47,435
Walled Lake, MI 48088 • 4,748
Wallen, IN 46806 • 1,200
Waller, TX 77484 • 1,241
Waller □, TX • 19,798
Wallingford, CT 06492 • 37,274
Wallingford, VT 05773 • 1,141
Wallington, NJ 07057 • 10,741
Wallis, TX 77485 • 1,138
Wallkill, NY 12589 • 1,849
Wall Lake, IA 51466 • 892
Wallowa, OR 97885 • 847
Wallowa □, OR • 7,273
Walnut, CA 91789 • 12,478
Walnut, IL 61376 • 1,513
Walnut, IA 51577 • 897
Walnut Cove, NC 27052 • 1,147
Walnut Creek, CA 94595-98 • 53,643
Walnut Grove, MN 56180 • 753
Walnut Park, CA 90255 • 11,811
Walnutport, PA 18088 • 2,007
Walnut Ridge, AR 72476 • 4,152
Walpole, MA 02081 • 5,274
Walpole, NH 03608 • 700
Walsenburg, CO 81089 • 3,945
Walsh, CO 81090 • 884
Walsh □, ND • 15,371
Walterboro, SC 29488 • 6,209
Walters, OK 73572 • 2,778
Walthall □, MS • 13,761
Waltham, MA 02154 • 58,200
Walthill, NE 68067 • 847
Walthourville, GA 31333 • 905
Walton, IN 46994 • 1,202
Walton, KY 41094 • 1,651
Walton, NY 13856 • 3,329
Walton □, FL • 21,300
Walton □, GA • 31,211
Walworth, WI 53184 • 1,607
Walworth □, SD • 7,011
Walworth □, WI • 71,507
Wamac, IL 62801 • 1,665
Wamego, KS 66547 • 3,159
Wamesit, MA 01876 • 2,700
Wampum, PA 16157 • 851
Wamsutter, WY 82336 • 681
Wanamingo, MN 55983 • 717
Wanaque, NJ 07465 • 10,025
Wanatah, IN 46390 • 879
Wanchese, NC 27981 • 1,105
Wando Woods, SC 29405 • 5,253
Wantagh, NY 11793 • 22,300
Wapakoneta, OH 45895 • 8,402
Wapato, WA 98951 • 3,307
Wapella, IL 61777 • 768
Wapello, IA 52653 • 2,011
Wapello □, IA • 40,241
Wappingers Falls, NY 12590 • 5,110
War, WV 24892 • 2,158
Ward, AR 72176 • 981
Ward □, ND • 58,392
Ward □, TX • 13,976
Warden, WA 98857 • 1,479
Ware, MA 01082 • 6,806
Ware □, GA • 37,180
Wareham, MA 02571 • 2,473
Warehouse Point, CT 06088 • 1,850
Ware Shoals, SC 29692 • 2,370
Waretown, NJ 08758 • 1,175
Warminster, PA 18974 • 35,543
Warner, NH 03278 • 700
Warner, OK 74469 • 1,310
Warner Robins, GA 31093 • 39,893
Warr Acres, OK 73132 • 9,940
Warren, AR 71671 • 7,646
Warren, IL 61087 • 1,595
Warren, IN 46792 • 1,254
Warren, MA 01083 • 1,548
Warren, MI 48089-93 • 161,134
Warren, MN 56762 • 2,105
Warren, OH 44481-86 • 56,629
Warren, OR 97053 • 800
Warren, PA 16365 • 12,146
Warren, RI 02885 • 10,640
Warren □, GA • 6,583
Warren □, IL • 21,943
Warren □, IN • 8,976
Warren □, IA • 34,878
Warren □, KY • 71,828
Warren □, MS • 51,627
Warren □, MO • 14,900
Warren □, NJ • 84,429
Warren □, NC • 16,232
Warren □, NY • 54,854
Warren □, OH • 99,276
Warren □, PA • 47,449
Warren □, TN • 32,653
Warren □, VA • 21,200
Warrendale, PA 15086 • 800
Warren Park, IN 46219 • 1,803
Warrensburg, IL 62573 • 1,372
Warrensburg, MO 64093 • 13,807
Warrensburg, NY 12885 • 2,743
Warrensville Heights, OH 44122 • 16,565
Warrenton, GA 30828 • 2,172
Warrenton, MO 63383 • 3,219
Warrenton, NC 27589 • 908
Warrenton, OR 97146 • 2,493
Warrenton, VA 22186 • 3,907
Warrenville, IL 60555 • 7,519
Warrenville, SC 29851 • 1,029
Warrick □, IN • 41,474
Warrington, FL 32507 • 15,792
Warrior, AL 35180 • 3,260
Warroad, MN 56763 • 1,216
Warsaw, IL 62379 • 1,842
Warsaw, IN 46580 • 10,647
Warsaw, KY 41095 • 1,328
Warsaw, MO 65355 • 1,494
Warsaw, NC 28398 • 2,910
Warsaw, NY 14569 • 3,619
Warsaw, OH 43844 • 765
Warsaw, VA 22572 • 771
Wartburg, TN 37887 • 761
Warwick, NY 10990 • 4,320
Warwick, RI 02886-89 • 87,123
Wasatch □, UT • 8,523
Wasco, CA 93280 • 9,613
Wasco □, OR • 21,732
Waseca, MN 56093 • 8,219
Waseca □, MN • 18,448
Washakie □, WY • 9,496
Washburn, IL 61570 • 1,206
Washburn, IA 50706 • 1,400
Washburn, ME 04786 • 1,221
Washburn, ND 58577 • 1,767
Washburn, WI 54891 • 2,080
Washburn □, WI • 13,174
Washington, DC 20001-99 • 638,432
Washington, GA 30673 • 4,662
Washington, IL 61571 • 10,364
Washington, IN 47501 • 11,325
Washington, IA 52353 • 6,584
Washington, KS 66968 • 1,488
Washington, KY 41096 • 624
Washington, LA 70589 • 1,266
Washington, MS 39190 • 900
Washington, MO 63090 • 9,251
Washington, NJ 07882 • 6,429
Washington, NC 27889 • 8,418
Washington, PA 15301 • 18,363
Washington, UT 84780 • 3,092
Washington □, AL • 16,821
Washington □, AR • 100,494
Washington □, CO • 5,304
Washington □, FL • 14,509
Washington □, GA • 18,842
Washington □, ID • 8,803
Washington □, IL • 15,472
Washington □, IN • 21,932
Washington □, IA • 20,141
Washington □, KS • 8,543
Washington □, KY • 10,764
Washington □, LA • 44,207
Washington □, ME • 34,963
Washington □, MD • 113,086
Washington □, MN • 113,571
Washington □, MS • 72,344
Washington □, MO • 17,983
Washington □, NE • 15,508
Washington □, NC • 14,801
Washington □, NY • 54,795
Washington □, OH • 64,266
Washington □, OK • 48,113
Washington □, OR • 245,860
Washington □, PA • 217,074
Washington □, RI • 93,317
Washington □, TN • 88,755
Washington □, TX • 21,998
Washington □, UT • 26,065
Washington □, VT • 52,393
Washington □, VA • 46,487
Washington □, WI • 84,848
Washington Court House, OH 43160 • 12,682
Washington Park, IL 62204 • 8,223
Washington Terrace, UT 84403 • 8,212
Washington Township, NJ 07675 • 9,550
Washita □, OK • 13,798
Washoe □, NV • 193,623
Washougal, WA 98671 • 3,834
Washtenaw □, MI • 264,748
Wasilla, AK 99687 • 1,559
Waskom, TX 75692 • 1,821
Wataga, IL 61488 • 996
Watauga, TX 76148 • 10,284
Watauga □, NC • 31,666
Watchung, NJ 07060 • 5,290
Waterbury, CT 06701-49 • 103,266
Waterbury, VT 05676 • 1,892
Waterford, CT 06385 • 2,736
Waterford, MI 48095 • 64,250
Waterford, NY 12188 • 2,405
Waterford, PA 16441 • 1,568
Waterford, WI 53185 • 2,051
Waterloo, IL 62298 • 4,646
Waterloo, IN 46793 • 1,951
Waterloo, IA 50701-99 • 75,985
Waterloo, NY 13165 • 5,303
Waterloo, WI 53594 • 2,393
Waterman, IL 60556 • 943
Waterproof, LA 71375 • 1,339
Watersmeet, MI 49969 • 700
Watertown, CT 06795 • 6,000
Watertown, MA 02172 • 34,384
Watertown, NY 13601 • 27,861
Watertown, SD 57201 • 15,649
Watertown, TN 37184 • 1,300
Watertown, WI 53094 • 18,113
Water Valley, MS 38965 • 4,147
Waterville, KS 66548 • 694
Waterville, ME 04901 • 17,779
Waterville, MN 56096 • 1,717
Waterville, NY 13480 • 1,672
Waterville, OH 43566 • 3,884
Waterville, WA 98858 • 908
Watervliet, MI 49098 • 1,867
Watervliet, NY 12189 • 11,354
Watford City, ND 58854 • 2,119
Wathena, KS 66090 • 1,418
Watkins, MN 55389 • 757
Watkins Glen, NY 14891 • 2,440
Watkinsville, GA 30677 • 1,240
Watonga, OK 73772 • 4,139
Watonwan □, MN • 12,361
Watseka, IL 60970 • 5,543
Watson Chapel, AR 71601 • 900
Watsontown, PA 17777 • 2,366
Watsonville, CA 95076 • 23,663
Wattsville, SC 29360 • 1,324
Waubay, SD 57273 • 675
Wauchula, FL 33873 • 2,986
Wauconda, IL 60084 • 5,688
Waukee, IA 50263 • 2,227
Waukegan, IL 60085-87 • 67,653
Waukesha, WI 53186-88 • 50,365
Waukesha □, WI • 280,080
Waukomis, OK 73773 • 1,551
Waukon, IA 52172 • 3,983
Waunakee, WI 53597 • 3,866
Wauneta, NE 69045 • 746
Waupaca, WI 54981 • 4,472
Waupaca □, WI • 42,831
Waupun, WI 53963 • 8,132
Wauregan, CT 06387 • 900
Waurika, OK 73573 • 2,258
Wausa, NE 68786 • 647
Wausau, WI 54401 • 32,426
Wausaukee, WI 54177 • 648
Wauseon, OH 43567 • 6,173
Waushara □, WI • 18,526
Wautoma, WI 54982 • 1,629
Wauwatosa, WI 53213 • 51,308
Waveland, MS 39576 • 4,186
Waverly, IL 62692 • 1,537
Waverly, IA 50677 • 8,444
Waverly, KS 66871 • 671
Waverly, MO 64096 • 941
Waverly, NE 68462 • 1,726
Waverly, NY 14892 • 4,738
Waverly, OH 45690 • 4,603
Waverly, TN 37185 • 4,405
Waverly, VA 23890 • 2,284
Waverly Hall, GA 31831 • 913
Waxahachie, TX 75165 • 14,624
Waxhaw, NC 28173 • 1,208
Waycross, GA 31501 • 19,371
Wayland, IA 52654 • 720
Wayland, KY 41666 • 601
Wayland, MA 01778 • 5,500
Wayland, MI 49348 • 2,023
Wayland, NY 14572 • 1,846
Waylyn, SC 29405 • 2,400
Waymart, PA 18472 • 1,248
Wayne, MI 48184 • 21,159
Wayne, NE 68787 • 5,240
Wayne, NJ 07470 • 46,474
Wayne, OH 43466 • 894
Wayne, OK 73095 • 621
Wayne, PA 19087 • 8,900
Wayne, WV 25570 • 1,495
Wayne □, GA • 20,750
Wayne □, IL • 18,059
Wayne □, IN • 76,058
Wayne □, IA • 8,199
Wayne □, KY • 17,022
Wayne □, MI • 2,337,891
Wayne □, MS • 19,135
Wayne □, MO • 11,277
Wayne □, NE • 9,858
Wayne □, NC • 97,054
Wayne □, NY • 84,581
Wayne □, OH • 97,408
Wayne □, PA • 35,237
Wayne □, TN • 13,946
Wayne □, UT • 1,911
Wayne □, WV • 46,021
Wayne City, IL 62895 • 1,132
Waynesboro, GA 30830 • 5,760
Waynesboro, MS 39367 • 5,349
Waynesboro, PA 17268 • 9,726
Waynesboro, TN 38485 • 2,109
Waynesboro, VA 22980 • 15,329
Waynesburg, OH 44688 • 1,160
Waynesburg, PA 15370 • 4,482
Waynesville, MO 65583 • 2,879
Waynesville, NC 28786 • 6,765
Waynesville, OH 45068 • 1,796
Waynetown, IN 47990 • 915
Waynewood, VA 22308 • 4,500
Waynoka, OK 73860 • 1,377
Wayzata, MN 55391 • 3,621
Weakley □, TN • 32,896
Weatherford, OK 73096 • 9,640
Weatherford, TX 76086 • 12,049
Weatherly, PA 18255 • 2,891
Weatogue, CT 06089 • 2,249
Weaver, AL 36277 • 2,765
Weaverville, CA 96093 • 2,787
Weaverville, NC 28787 • 1,495
Webb, MS 38966 • 782
Webb □, TX • 99,258
Webb City, MO 64870 • 7,309
Webberville, MI 48892 • 1,535
Weber □, UT • 144,616
Weber City, VA 24251 • 1,543
Webster, FL 33597 • 856
Webster, MA 01570 • 14,480
Webster, NY 14580 • 5,499
Webster, PA 15087 • 800
Webster, SD 57274 • 2,417
Webster, TX 77598 • 2,405
Webster, WI 54893 • 610
Webster □, GA • 2,341
Webster □, IA • 45,953
Webster □, KY • 14,832
Webster □, LA • 43,631
Webster □, MS • 10,300
Webster □, MO • 20,414
Webster □, NE • 4,858
Webster □, WV • 12,245
Webster City, IA 50595 • 8,572
Webster Groves, MO 63119 • 23,097
Webster Springs, WV 26288 • 939
Wedgewood, MO 63031 • 5,700
Wedowee, AL 36278 • 908
Weed, CA 96094 • 2,879
Weed Heights, NV 89447 • 650
Weedsport, NY 13166 • 1,952
Weehawken, NJ 07087 • 13,168
Weeksbury, KY 41667 • 700
Weeping Water, NE 68463 • 1,109
Weimar, TX 78962 • 2,128
Weiner, AR 72479 • 750
Weippe, ID 83553 • 828
Weir, KS 66781 • 705
Weirsdale, FL 32695 • 1,500
Weirton, WV 26062 • 25,371
Weiser, ID 83672 • 4,771
Welch, OK 74369 • 697
Welch, WV 24801 • 3,885
Welcome, MN 56181 • 855
Welcome, SC 29611 • 6,922
Weld □, CO • 123,438
Weldon, NC 27890 • 1,844
Weleetka, OK 74880 • 1,195
Wellesley, MA 02181 • 27,209
Wellfleet, MA 02667 • 950
Wellford, SC 29385 • 2,143
Wellington, CO 80549 • 1,215
Wellington, KS 67152 • 8,212
Wellington, MO 64097 • 780
Wellington, OH 44090 • 4,146

Wellington, TX 79095 • *3,043*
Wellington, UT 84542 • *1,406*
Wellman, IA 52356 • *1,125*
Wells, ME 04090 • *850*
Wells, MI 49894 • *1,100*
Wells, MN 56097 • *2,777*
Wells, NV 89835 • *1,218*
Wells, TX 75976 • *926*
Wells □, IN • *25,401*
Wells □, ND • *6,979*
Wellsboro, PA 16901 • *3,805*
Wellsburg, IA 50680 • *761*
Wellsburg, NY 14894 • *647*
Wellsburg, WV 26070 • *3,963*
Wellston, OH 45692 • *6,016*
Wellston, OK 74881 • *802*
Wellsville, KS 66092 • *1,612*
Wellsville, MO 63384 • *1,546*
Wellsville, NY 14895 • *5,769*
Wellsville, OH 43968 • *5,095*
Wellsville, UT 84339 • *1,952*
Wellton, AZ 85356 • *911*
Welsh, LA 70591 • *3,515*
Wenatchee, WA 98801 • *17,257*
Wendell, ID 83355 • *1,974*
Wendell, NC 27591 • *2,222*
Wendover, UT 84083 • *1,099*
Wenham, MA 01984 • *3,897*
Wenona, IL 61377 • *1,025*
Wenonah, NJ 08090 • *2,303*
Wentzville, MO 63385 • *3,193*
Wequetequock, CT 02891 • *800*
Weslaco, TX 78596 • *19,331*
Wesleyville, PA 16510 • *3,998*
Wessington Springs, SD 57382 • *1,203*
Wesson, MS 39191 • *1,313*
West, TX 76691 • *2,485*
West Abington, MA 02351 • *2,000*
West Acton, MA 01720 • *5,800*
West Alexandria, OH 45381 • *1,313*
West Allis, WI 53214 • *63,982*
West Amityville, NY 11758 • *6,470*
West Andover, MA 01810 • *3,700*
West Athens, CA 90247 • *8,531*
West Babylon, NY 11704 • *32,500*
West Baden Springs, IN 47469 • *796*
West Barrington, RI 02806 • *3,700*
West Baton Rouge □, LA • *19,086*
West Bay Shore, NY 11706 • *8,900*
West Bend, IA 50597 • *941*
West Bend, WI 53095 • *21,484*
West Berlin, NJ 08091 • *3,300*
West Billerica, MA 01862 • *2,000*
West Blocton, AL 35184 • *1,147*
Westborough, MA 01581 • *13,619*
West Bountiful, UT 84087 • *3,556*
West Boylston, MA 01583 • *3,500*
West Branch, IA 52358 • *1,867*
West Branch, MI 48661 • *1,785*
West Bridgewater, MA 02379 • *2,100*
Westbrook, CT 06498 • *2,035*
Westbrook, ME 04092 • *14,976*
Westbrook, MN 56183 • *978*
West Brookfield, MA 01585 • *1,423*
West Burlington, IA 52655 • *3,371*
Westbury, NY 11590 • *13,871*
Westby, WI 54667 • *1,797*
West Caldwell, NJ 07006 • *11,407*
West Cape May, NJ 08204 • *1,091*
West Carroll □, LA • *12,922*
West Carrollton, OH 45449 • *13,148*
West Carson, CA 90502 • *17,997*
West Carthage, NY 13619 • *1,824*
West Chatham, MA 02669 • *1,398*
West Chazy, NY 12992 • *700*
Westchester, FL 33144 • *20,000*
Westchester, IL 60153 • *17,730*
West Chester, PA 19380–82 • *17,435*
Westchester □, NY • *866,599*
West Chicago, IL 60185 • *12,550*
West City, IL 62812 • *886*
West College Corner, IN 45003 • *614*
West Columbia, SC 29169 • *10,409*
West Columbia, TX 77486 • *4,109*
West Concord, MA 01742 • *5,331*
West Concord, MN 55985 • *762*
West Concord, NC 28025 • *3,200*
West Covina, CA 91790–93 • *80,291*
West Crossett, AR 71635 • *1,466*
West Cumberland, ME 04021 • *800*
West Dennis, MA 02670 • *2,030*
West Des Moines, IA 50265 • *21,894*
West Elmira, NY 14905 • *5,901*
West End, NC 27376 • *900*
Westerly, RI 02891 • *14,093*
Western Hills, CO 80221 • *6,000*
Westernport, MD 21562 • *2,706*
Western Springs, IL 60558 • *12,876*
Westerville, OH 43081 • *23,414*
West Fairview, PA 17025 • *1,426*
West Falmouth, MA 02574 • *1,200*
West Fargo, ND 58078 • *10,099*
West Feliciana □, LA • *12,186*
Westfield, IL 62474 • *733*
Westfield, IN 46074 • *2,783*
Westfield, MA 01085 • *36,465*
Westfield, NJ 07090–92 • *30,447*
Westfield, NY 14787 • *3,446*
Westfield, PA 16950 • *1,268*
Westfield, WI 53964 • *1,033*
Westfield Center, OH 44251 • *791*
Westford, MA 01886 • *1,000*
West Fork, AR 72774 • *1,526*
West Frankfort, IL 62896 • *9,437*
Westgate, FL 33401 • *2,100*
West Groton, MA 01472 • *950*
West Grove, PA 19390 • *1,820*
Westham, VA 23229 • *3,600*
West Hamlin, WV 25571 • *643*
West Hanover, MA 02339 • *1,600*
West Hartford, CT 06107 • *61,306*
West Haven, CT 06516 • *53,184*
West Haven, OR 97225 • *3,400*
West Haverstraw, NY 10993 • *9,181*
West Hazleton, PA 18201 • *4,871*
West Helena, AR 72390 • *11,367*
West Hempstead, NY 11552 • *26,500*
West Hollywood, CA 90069 • *35,703*
Westhope, ND 58793 • *741*
West Huntington, NY 11743 • *6,170*
West Hyannisport, MA 02672 • *1,200*
West Islip, NY 11795 • *29,533*
West Jefferson, NC 28694 • *822*
West Jefferson, OH 43162 • *4,448*
West Jordan, UT 84084 • *27,192*
West Kingston, RI 02892 • *700*
West Lafayette, IN 47906 • *21,247*
West Lafayette, OH 43845 • *2,225*
Westlake, LA 70669 • *5,246*
Westlake, OH 44145 • *19,483*
Westland, MI 48185 • *84,603*
West Laramie, WY 82070 • *2,000*
West Lawn, PA 19609 • *1,686*
West Lebanon, IN 47991 • *946*
West Leisenring, PA 15489 • *700*
West Liberty, IA 52776 • *2,723*
West Liberty, KY 41472 • *1,381*
West Liberty, OH 43357 • *1,653*
West Liberty, WV 26074 • *744*
West Linn, OR 97068 • *12,956*
West Long Branch, NJ 07764 • *7,380*
West Mansfield, OH 43358 • *716*
West Marion, NC 28752 • *1,596*
West Medway, MA 02053 • *2,269*
West Melbourne, FL 32901 • *5,078*
West Memphis, AR 72301 • *28,138*
Westmere, NY 12203 • *5,500*
West Miami, FL 33174 • *6,076*
West Middlesex, PA 16159 • *1,064*
West Mifflin, PA 15122 • *26,552*
West Milford, NJ 07480 • *1,600*
West Milton, OH 45383 • *4,119*
West Milton, PA 17886 • *775*
West Milwaukee, WI 53214 • *3,535*
Westminster, CA 92683 • *71,133*
Westminster, CO 80030 • *50,211*
Westminster, MD 21157 • *8,808*
Westminster, MA 01473 • *950*
Westminster, SC 29693 • *3,114*
West Modesto, CA 95351 • *6,135*
West Monroe, LA 71291 • *14,993*
Westmont, CA 90044 • *27,916*
Westmont, IL 60559 • *16,718*
Westmont, NJ 08108 • *5,700*
Westmont, PA 15905 • *6,113*
Westmoreland, TN 37186 • *1,754*
Westmoreland □, PA • *392,294*
Westmoreland □, VA • *14,041*
Westmorland, CA 92281 • *1,590*
West Mystic, CT 06388 • *3,364*
West Newbury, MA 01985 • *950*
West Newton, PA 15089 • *3,387*
West New York, NJ 07093 • *39,194*
West Norriton, PA 19401 • *14,034*
Weston, CT 06883 • *1,200*
Weston, MA 02193 • *11,169*
Weston, MO 64098 • *1,440*
Weston, OH 43569 • *1,708*
Weston, OR 97886 • *719*
Weston, WV 26452 • *6,250*
Weston, WI 54476 • *3,400*
Weston □, WY • *7,106*
West Orange, NJ 07052 • *39,400*
Westover, WV 26505 • *4,884*
West Palm Beach, FL 33401–18 • *63,305*
West Park, NY 12493 • *700*
West Paterson, NJ 07424 • *11,293*
West Pelzer, SC 29669 • *944*
West Pensacola, FL 32505 • *24,571*
West Peoria, IL 61604 • *5,219*
Westphalia, MI 48894 • *896*
West Pittsburg, CA 94565 • *6,000*
West Pittsburg, PA 16160 • *950*
West Pittston, PA 18643 • *5,980*
West Plains, MO 65775 • *7,741*
West Point, CA 95255 • *1,500*
West Point, GA 31833 • *4,294*
West Point, IA 52656 • *1,133*
West Point, KY 40177 • *1,339*
West Point, MS 39773 • *8,811*
West Point, NE 68788 • *3,609*
West Point, NY 10996 • *8,000*
West Point, UT 84015 • *2,170*
West Point, VA 23181 • *2,726*
Westport, CT 06880 • *25,290*
Westport, IN 47283 • *1,450*
47283 • *1,450*
Westport, MA 02790 • *1,850*
Westport, NY 12993 • *613*
Westport, WA 98595 • *1,954*
West Portsmouth, OH 45662 • *4,095*
West Puente Valley, CA 91744 • *20,445*
West Reading, PA 19611 • *4,507*
West Rutland, VT 05777 • *2,351*
West Sacramento, CA 95691 • *10,875*
West Saint Paul, MN 55118 • *18,527*
West Salem, IL 62476 • *1,145*
West Salem, OH 44287 • *1,357*
West Salem, WI 54669 • *3,276*
West Sayville, NY 11796 • *5,000*
West Scarborough, ME 04074 • *700*
West Seneca, NY 14224 • *51,210*
West Simsbury, CT 06092 • *2,140*
West Slope, OR 97225 • *5,364*
West Springfield, MA 01089 • *27,042*
West Springfield, VA 22152 • *16,000*
West Stockbridge, MA 01266 • *800*
West Swanzey, NH 03469 • *1,022*
West Terre Haute, IN 47885 • *2,806*
West Townsend, MA 01474 • *700*
West Union, IA 52175 • *2,783*
West Union, OH 45693 • *2,791*
West Union, WV 26456 • *1,090*
West Unity, OH 43570 • *1,639*
West University Place, TX 77005 • *12,010*
West Upton, MA 01587 • *1,000*
Westvale, NY 13219 • *7,300*
West Valley City, UT 84120 • *72,511*
West Van Lear, KY 41268 • *900*
West View, PA 15229 • *7,648*
Westville, IL 61883 • *3,573*
Westville, IN 46391 • *2,887*
Westville, NH 03865 • *700*
Westville, NJ 08093 • *4,786*
Westville, OK 74965 • *1,049*
West Wareham, MA 02576 • *1,837*
West Warren, MA 01092 • *1,200*
West Warwick, RI 02893 • *27,026*
West Webster, NY 14580 • *10,600*
Westwego, LA 70094 • *12,663*
West Whittier, CA 90606 • *13,800*
West Winfield, NY 13491 • *979*
Westwood, CA 96137 • *2,081*
Westwood, KS 66205 • *1,783*
Westwood, KY 41101 • *5,973*
Westwood, MA 02090 • *6,500*
Westwood, MI 49007 • *8,519*
Westwood, NJ 07675 • *10,714*
Westwood Lakes, FL 33165 • *11,478*
West Wyoming, PA 18644 • *3,288*
West Yarmouth, MA 02673 • *3,882*
West Yellowstone, MT 59758 • *735*
West York, PA 17404 • *4,526*
Wethersfield, CT 06109 • *26,013*
Wetumka, OK 74883 • *1,725*
Wetumpka, AL 36092 • *4,341*
Wetzel □, WV • *21,874*
Wewahitchka, FL 32465 • *1,742*
Wewoka, OK 74884 • *5,480*
Wexford □, MI • *25,102*
Weyauwega, WI 54983 • *1,549*
Weymouth, MA 02188 • *55,601*
Whalom, MA 01420 • *1,400*
Wharton, NJ 07885 • *5,485*
Wharton, TX 77488 • *9,033*
Wharton □, TX • *40,242*
What Cheer, IA 50268 • *803*
Whatcom □, WA • *106,701*
Wheatfield, IN 46392 • *755*
Wheatland, CA 95692 • *1,474*
Wheatland, IA 52777 • *840*
Wheatland, PA 16161 • *1,132*
Wheatland, WY 82201 • *5,816*
Wheatland □, MT • *2,359*
Wheaton, IL 60187–89 • *43,043*
Wheaton, MD 20902 • *48,600*
Wheaton, MN 56296 • *1,969*
Wheat Ridge, CO 80033 • *30,293*
Wheeler, TX 79096 • *1,584*
Wheeler □, GA • *5,155*
Wheeler □, NE • *1,060*
Wheeler □, OR • *1,513*
Wheeler □, TX • *7,137*
Wheelersburg, OH 45694 • *4,796*
Wheeling, IL 60090 • *23,266*
Wheeling, WV 26003 • *43,070*
Wheelwright, KY 41669 • *865*
Whitacres, CT 06082 • *2,500*
Whitakers, NC 27891 • *924*
White □, AR • *50,835*
White □, GA • *10,120*
White □, IL • *17,864*
White □, IN • *23,867*
White □, TN • *19,567*
White Bear Lake, MN 55110 • *22,538*
White Bluff, TN 37187 • *2,055*
White Castle, LA 70788 • *2,160*
White Center, WA 98126 • *19,700*
White City, FL 32465 • *725*
White City, OR 97503 • *5,445*
White City, UT 84070 • *1,180*
White Cloud, MI 49349 • *1,101*
White Deer, TX 79097 • *1,210*
Whitefield, NH 03598 • *1,005*
Whitefish, MT 59937 • *3,703*
Whitefish Bay, WI 53217 • *14,930*
White Hall, AR 71602 • *2,214*
White Hall, IL 62092 • *2,935*
Whitehall, MI 49461 • *2,856*
Whitehall, MT 59759 • *1,030*
Whitehall, NY 12887 • *3,241*
Whitehall, OH 43213 • *21,299*
Whitehall, PA 15227 • *15,143*
Whitehall, WI 54773 • *1,530*
White Haven, PA 18661 • *1,921*
White Horse, NJ 08610 • *10,098*
White Horse Beach, MA 02381 • *800*
Whitehouse, OH 43571 • *2,137*
White House, TN 37188 • *2,225*
White House Station, NJ 08889 • *1,019*
White Island Shores, MA 02538 • *950*
Whitelaw, WI 54247 • *649*
White Meadow Lake, NJ 07866 • *8,429*
White Oak, OH 45239 • *4,900*
White Oak, PA 15131 • *9,480*
White Pigeon, MI 49099 • *1,478*
White Pine, MI 49971 • *1,400*
White Pine, TN 37890 • *1,900*
White Pine □, NV • *8,167*
White Plains, KY 42464 • *859*
White Plains, MD 20695 • *5,167*
White Plains, NY 10601–99 • *46,999*
Whiteriver, AZ 85941 • *1,400*
White River Junction, VT 05001 • *2,582*
White Salmon, WA 98672 • *1,853*
Whitesboro, NJ 08252 • *900*
Whitesboro, NY 13492 • *4,460*
Whitesboro, TX 76273 • *3,197*
Whitesburg, GA 30185 • *775*
Whitesburg, KY 41858 • *1,525*
White Settlement, TX 76108 • *13,508*
Whiteside □, IL • *65,970*
White Springs, FL 32096 • *781*
White Sulphur Springs, MT 59645 • *1,302*
White Sulphur Springs, WV 24986 • *3,371*
Whitesville, KY 42378 • *788*
Whitesville, WV 25209 • *689*
Whiteville, NC 28472 • *5,565*
Whiteville, TN 38075 • *1,270*
Whitewater, KS 67154 • *751*
Whitewater, WI 53190 • *11,520*
Whitewood, SD 57793 • *821*
Whitewright, TX 75491 • *1,760*
Whitfield □, GA • *65,789*
Whitfield Estates, FL 33580 • *3,000*
Whiting, IN 46394 • *5,630*
Whiting, IA 51063 • *734*
Whiting, NJ 08759 • *700*
Whiting, WI 54481 • *2,050*
Whitinsville, MA 01588 • *5,379*
Whitley □, IN • *26,215*
Whitley □, KY • *33,396*
Whitley City, KY 42653 • *1,683*
Whitman, MA 02382 • *13,534*
Whitman, WV 25652 • *950*
Whitman □, WA • *40,103*
Whitman Square, NJ 08012 • *2,600*
Whitmire, SC 29178 • *2,038*
Whitmore Lake, MI 48189 • *2,920*
Whitmore Village, HI 96786 • *2,318*
Whitney, SC 29303 • *1,800*
Whitney, TX 76692 • *1,631*
Whitney Point, NY 13862 • *1,093*
Whittemore, IA 50598 • *647*
Whittier, CA 90601–12 • *69,717*
Whitwell, TN 37397 • *1,783*
Wibaux, MT 59353 • *782*
Wibaux □, MT • *1,476*
Wichita, KS 67201–99 • *279,835*
Wichita □, KS • *3,041*
Wichita □, TX • *121,082*
Wichita Falls, TX 76301–11 • *94,201*
Wickenburg, AZ 85358 • *3,535*
Wickett, TX 79788 • *689*
Wickliffe, KY 42087 • *1,034*
Wickliffe, OH 44515 • *8,800*
Wicomico □, MD • *64,540*
Wiconisco, PA 17097 • *1,236*
Widefield, CO 80911 • *7,500*
Wiggins, MS 39577 • *3,205*
Wilbarger □, TX • *15,931*
Wilber, NE 68465 • *1,624*
Wilberforce, OH 45384 • *2,512*
Wilbraham, MA 01095 • *3,379*
Wilbur, WA 99185 • *1,122*
Wilburton, OK 74578 • *2,996*
Wilcox, PA 15870 • *900*
Wilcox □, AL • *14,755*
Wilcox □, GA • *7,682*
Wilder, ID 83676 • *1,260*
Wilder, VT 05088 • *1,461*
Wild Rose, WI 54984 • *741*
Wildwood, FL 32785 • *2,665*
Wildwood, NJ 08260 • *4,913*
Wildwood Crest, NJ 08260 • *4,149*
Wilkes □, GA • *10,951*
Wilkes □, NC • *58,657*
Wilkes-Barre, PA 18701–99 • *51,551*
Wilkesboro, NC 28697 • *2,335*
Wilkin □, MN • *8,454*
Wilkinsburg, PA 15221 • *23,669*
Wilkinson, WV 25653 • *700*
Wilkinson □, GA • *10,368*
Wilkinson □, MS • *10,021*
Will □, IL • *324,460*
Willacoochee, GA 31650 • *1,166*
Willacy □, TX • *17,495*
Willamina, OR 97396 • *1,749*
Willard, MO 65781 • *1,799*
Willard, NY 14588 • *700*
Willard, OH 44890 • *5,720*
Willard, UT 84340 • *1,241*
Willcox, AZ 85643 • *3,243*
Williams, AZ 86046 • *2,266*
Williams, CA 95987 • *1,655*
Williams □, ND • *22,237*
Williams □, OH • *36,369*
Williams Bay, WI 53191 • *1,763*
Williamsburg, IA 52361 • *2,033*
Williamsburg, KY 40769 • *5,560*
Williamsburg, MA 01096 • *950*
Williamsburg, OH 45176 • *1,952*
Williamsburg, PA 16693 • *1,400*
Williamsburg, VA 23185 • *9,870*
Williamsburg □, SC • *38,226*
Williamson, NY 14589 • *1,991*
Williamson, WV 25661 • *5,219*
Williamson □, IL • *56,538*
Williamson □, TN • *58,108*
Williamson □, TX • *76,507*
Williamsport, IN 47993 • *1,747*
Williamsport, MD 21795 • *2,153*
Williamsport, OH 43164 • *792*
Williamsport, PA 17701 • *33,401*
Williamston, MI 48895 • *2,981*
Williamston, NC 27892 • *6,159*
Williamston, SC 29697 • *4,310*
Williamstown, KY 41097 • *2,502*
Williamstown, MA 01267 • *4,798*
Williamstown, NJ 08094 • *5,768*
Williamstown, PA 17098 • *1,664*
Williamstown, VT 05679 • *650*
Williamstown, WV 26187 • *3,095*
Williamsville, IL 62693 • *996*
Williamsville, NY 14221 • *6,017*
Willimantic, CT 06226 • *14,652*
Willingboro, NJ 08046 • *39,912*
Willis, TX 77378 • *1,674*
Williston, FL 32696 • *2,240*
Williston, ND 58801 • *13,336*
Williston, SC 29853 • *3,173*
Williston Park, NY 11596 • *8,216*
Willisville, IL 62997 • *628*
Willits, CA 95490 • *4,008*
Willmar, MN 56201 • *15,895*
Willoughby, OH 44094 • *19,329*
Willoughby Hills, OH 44092 • *8,612*
Willow Brook, CA 90222 • *30,845*
Willow Grove, PA 19090 • *21,300*
Willowick, OH 44094 • *17,834*
Willow Run, DE 19805 • *1,950*
Willow Run, MI 48197 • *6,400*
Willows, CA 95988 • *4,777*
Willow Springs, IL 60480 • *4,147*
Willow Springs, MO 65793 • *2,215*
Willsboro, NY 12996 • *950*
Willston, VA 22044 • *2,500*
Wilmar, AR 71675 • *747*
Wilmer, TX 75172 • *2,367*
Wilmerding, PA 15148 • *2,421*
Wilmette, IL 60091 • *28,229*
Wilmington, DE 19801–99 • *70,195*
Wilmington, IL 60481 • *4,424*
Wilmington, MA 01887 • *17,471*
Wilmington, NC 28401–06 • *44,000*
Wilmington, OH 45177 • *10,431*
Wilmington Manor, DE 19720 • *2,000*
Wilmington Manor Gardens, DE 19720 • *1,600*
Wilmore, KY 40390 • *3,787*
Wilmot, AR 71676 • *1,227*
Wilson, AR 72395 • *1,115*
Wilson, KS 67490 • *978*
Wilson, LA 70789 • *656*
Wilson, NC 27893 • *34,424*
Wilson, NY 14172 • *1,259*
Wilson, OK 73463 • *1,585*
Wilson, PA 18042 • *7,564*
Wilson □, KS • *12,128*
Wilson □, NC • *63,132*
Wilson □, TN • *56,064*
Wilson □, TX • *16,756*
Wilsonville, AL 35186 • *914*
Wilsonville, IL 62093 • *608*
Wilsonville, OR 97070 • *2,920*
Wilton, AL 35187 • *642*
Wilton, CT 06897 • *6,500*
Wilton, IA 52778 • *2,502*
Wilton, ME 04294 • *2,262*
Wilton, NH 03086 • *1,310*
Wilton, ND 58579 • *950*
Wilton Manors, FL 33334 • *12,742*
Wimauma, FL 33598 • *1,477*
Winamac, IN 46996 • *2,370*
Winburne, PA 16879 • *650*
Winchendon, MA 01475 • *4,030*
Winchester, IL 62694 • *1,716*
Winchester, IN 47394 • *5,659*
Winchester, KY 40391 • *15,216*
Winchester, MA 01890 • *20,701*
Winchester, NV 89101 • *19,728*
Winchester, NH 03470 • *1,732*
Winchester, OH 45697 • *1,080*
Winchester, TN 37398 • *5,821*
Winchester, VA 22601 • *20,217*
Winchester Bay, OR 97467 • *900*
Windber, PA 15963 • *5,585*
Windcrest, TX 78239 • *5,332*
Winder, GA 30680 • *6,705*
Windfall, IN 46076 • *911*
Windgap, PA 18091 • *2,651*
Windham, CT 06280 • *700*
Windham, OH 44288 • *3,721*
Windham □, CT • *92,312*
Windham □, VT • *36,933*

Wind Lake, WI 53185 • *2,400*
Windom, MN 56101 • *4,666*
Window Rock, AZ 86515 • *2,230*
Wind Point, WI 53402 • *1,695*
Windsor, CO 80550 • *4,277*
Windsor, CT 06095 • *17,517*
Windsor, IL 61957 • *1,228*
Windsor, MO 65360 • *3,058*
Windsor, NC 27983 • *2,126*
Windsor, PA 17366 • *1,205*
Windsor, VT 05089 • *4,084*
Windsor, VA 23487 • *985*
Windsor ☐, VT • *51,030*
Windsor Forest, GA 31406 • *7,288*
Windsor Heights, IA 50311 • *5,474*
Windsor Hills, CA 90052 • *6,200*
Windsor Locks, CT 06096 • *12,190*
Windy Hill, SC 29501 • *1,605*
Windy Hills, DE 19711 • *1,300*
Winfall, NC 27985 • *634*
Winfield, AL 35594 • *3,781*
Winfield, IA 52659 • *1,042*
Winfield, KS 67156 • *10,736*
Winfield, NJ 07036 • *1,785*
Wingate, NC 28174 • *2,615*
Wingo, KY 42088 • *606*
Winifrede, WV 25214 • *800*
Wink, TX 79789 • *1,182*
Winkelman, AZ 85292 • *1,060*
Winkler ☐, TX • *9,944*
Winlock, WA 98596 • *1,052*
Winn ☐, LA • *17,253*
Winnebago, IL 61088 • *1,644*
Winnebago, MN 56098 • *1,869*
Winnebago, NE 68071 • *902*
Winnebago ☐, IL • *250,884*
Winnebago ☐, IA • *13,010*
Winnebago ☐, WI • *131,772*
Winneconne, WI 54986 • *1,935*
Winnemucca, NV 89445 • *4,140*
Winner, SD 57580 • *3,472*
Winneshiek ☐, IA • *21,876*
Winnetka, IL 60093 • *12,772*
Winnfield, LA 71483 • *7,311*
Winnsboro, LA 71295 • *5,921*
Winnsboro, SC 29180 • *2,919*
Winnsboro, TX 75494 • *3,458*
Winnsboro Mills, SC 29180 • *1,890*
Winona, MN 55987 • *25,075*
Winona, MS 38967 • *6,177*
Winona, MO 65588 • *1,050*
Winona ☐, MN • *46,256*
Winona Lake, IN 46590 • *2,827*
Winooski, VT 05404 • *6,318*
Winslow, AZ 86047 • *7,921*
Winslow, IN 47598 • *1,017*
Winslow, ME 04901 • *5,903*
Winslow, WA 98110 • *2,196*
Winsted, CT 06098 • *8,092*
Winsted, MN 55395 • *1,522*
Winston, FL 33803 • *5,500*
Winston, OR 97496 • *3,359*
Winston ☐, AL • *21,953*
Winston ☐, MS • *19,474*
Winston-Salem, NC 27101–99
 • *131,885*
Winter Beach, FL 32971 • *700*
Winter Garden, FL 32787 • *6,789*
Winter Harbor, ME 04693 • *900*
Winter Haven, FL 33880–88 • *21,119*
Winter Park, FL 32789–93 • *22,339*
Winter Park, NC 28401 • *4,504*
Winterport, ME 04496 • *1,126*
Winters, CA 95694 • *2,652*
Winters, TX 79567 • *3,061*
Winterset, IA 50273 • *4,021*
Winter Springs, FL 32708 • *10,475*

Wintersville, OH 43952 • *4,724*
Winterville, GA 30683 • *621*
Winterville, NC 28590 • *2,052*
Winthrop, IA 50682 • *767*
Winthrop, ME 04364 • *3,264*
Winthrop, MA 02152 • *19,294*
Winthrop, MN 55396 • *1,376*
Winthrop Harbor, IL 60096 • *5,431*
Winton, NC 27986 • *825*
Wirt ☐, WV • *4,922*
Wiscasset, ME 04578 • *1,350*
Wisconsin Dells, WI 53965 • *2,521*
Wisconsin Rapids, WI 54494
 • *17,995*
Wise, VA 24293 • *3,894*
Wise ☐, TX • *26,575*
Wise ☐, VA • *43,863*
Wishek, ND 58495 • *1,345*
Wishram, WA 98673 • *675*
Wisner, LA 71378 • *1,424*
Wisner, NE 68791 • *1,335*
Withamsville, OH 45245 • *3,650*
Witherbee, NY 12998 • *1,000*
Witt, IL 62094 • *1,205*
Wittenberg, WI 54499 • *997*
Wittmann, AZ 85361 • *700*
Wixom, MI 48096 • *6,705*
Woburn, MA 01801 • *36,626*
Wolcott, CT 06716 • *5,500*
Wolcott, IN 47995 • *923*
Wolcott, NY 14590 • *1,496*
Wolcottville, IN 46795 • *890*
Wolfe ☐, KY • *6,698*
Wolfeboro, NH 03894 • *1,800*
Wolfe City, TX 75496 • *1,594*
Wolf Lake, MI 49442 • *3,876*
Wolf Point, MT 59201 • *3,074*
Womelsdorf, PA 19567 • *1,827*
Wonder Lake, IL 60097 • *752*
Wonewoc, WI 53968 • *842*
Wood ☐, OH • *107,372*
Wood ☐, TX • *24,697*
Wood ☐, WV • *93,648*
Wood ☐, WI • *72,799*
Woodbine, GA 31569 • *910*
Woodbine, IA 51579 • *1,463*
Woodbine, NJ 08270 • *2,809*
Woodbourne, NY 12788 • *1,155*
Woodbridge, CT 06525 • *7,600*
Woodbridge, NJ 07095 • *16,400*
Woodbridge, VA 22191–99 • *35,000*
Woodburn, IN 46797 • *1,002*
Woodburn, OR 97071 • *11,196*
Woodbury, CT 06798 • *1,290*
Woodbury, GA 30293 • *1,738*
Woodbury, MN 55119 • *10,297*
Woodbury, NJ 08096 • *10,353*
Woodbury, TN 37190 • *2,160*
Woodbury ☐, IA • *100,884*
Woodcliff Lake, NJ 07675 • *5,644*
Wood Dale, IL 60191 • *11,251*
Woodfield, SC 29206 • *9,588*
Woodford ☐, IL • *33,320*
Woodford ☐, KY • *19,778*
Woodhaven, MI 48183 • *10,902*
Woodhull, IL 61490 • *901*
Woodlake, CA 93286 • *4,343*
Woodland, CA 95695 • *30,235*
Woodland, GA 31836 • *664*
Woodland, ME 04694 • *1,363*
Woodland, NC 27897 • *861*
Woodland, WA 98674 • *2,341*
Woodland Acres, CO 81069 • *800*
Woodland Park, CO 80863 • *2,634*
Woodlawn, KY 42001 • *1,200*
Woodlawn, MD 21207 • *8,000*
Woodlawn, OH 45215 • *2,715*

Woodlyn, PA 19094 • *6,000*
Woodlynne, NJ 08107 • *2,578*
Woodmere, NY 11598 • *19,700*
Woodmont, CT 06460 • *1,797*
Woodmoor, MD 21207 • *7,600*
Wood-Ridge, NJ 07075 • *7,929*
Wood River, IL 62095 • *12,446*
Wood River, NE 68883 • *1,334*
Woodruff, SC 29388 • *5,171*
Woodruff, WI 54568 • *900*
Woodruff ☐, AR • *11,222*
Woods ☐, OK • *10,923*
Woodsboro, TX 78393 • *1,974*
Woods Cross, UT 84087 • *4,263*
Woodsfield, OH 43793 • *3,145*
Woods Hole, MA 02543 • *1,080*
Woodside, CA 94062 • *5,291*
Woodson ☐, KS • *4,600*
Woodstock, GA 30188 • *2,699*
Woodstock, IL 60098 • *11,725*
Woodstock, MD 21163 • *700*
Woodstock, NY 12498 • *1,073*
Woodstock, VT 05091 • *1,178*
Woodstock, VA 22664 • *2,627*
Woodstown, NJ 08098 • *3,250*
Woodsville, NH 03785 • *1,195*
Woodville, FL 32362 • *1,768*
Woodville, MS 39669 • *1,512*
Woodville, OH 43469 • *2,050*
Woodville, TX 75979 • *2,821*
Woodville, WI 54028 • *725*
Woodward, IA 50276 • *1,212*
Woodward, OK 73801 • *13,610*
Woodward ☐, OK • *21,172*
Woodway, TX 76710 • *7,091*
Woolmarket, MS 39532 • *670*
Woolrich, PA 17779 • *700*
Woonsocket, RI 02895 • *45,914*
Woonsocket, SD 57385 • *799*
Wooster, OH 44691 • *19,289*
Worcester, MA 01601–99 • *161,799*
Worcester, NY 12197 • *950*
Worcester ☐, MD • *30,889*
Worcester ☐, MA • *646,352*
Worden, IL 62097 • *953*
Worland, WY 82401 • *6,391*
Worth, IL 60482 • *11,592*
Worth ☐, GA • *18,064*
Worth ☐, IA • *9,075*
Worth ☐, MO • *3,008*
Wortham, TX 76693 • *1,187*
Worthington, IN 47471 • *1,574*
Worthington, KY 41183 • *1,948*
Worthington, MN 56187 • *10,243*
Worthington, OH 43085 • *15,016*
Worthington, PA 16262 • *760*
Wrangell, AK 99929 • *2,184*
Wray, CO 80758 • *2,131*
Wrens, GA 30833 • *2,415*
Wrentham, MA 02093 • *1,400*
Wright ☐, IA • *16,319*
Wright ☐, MN • *58,681*
Wright ☐, MO • *16,188*
Wright City, MO 63390 • *1,179*
Wright City, OK 74766 • *1,168*
Wrightstown, NJ 08562 • *3,031*
Wrightstown, WI 54180 • *1,169*
Wrightsville, AR 72183 • *1,100*
Wrightsville, GA 31096 • *2,526*
Wrightsville, PA 17368 • *2,365*
Wrightsville Beach, NC 28480
 • *2,910*
Wrightwood, CA 92397 • *2,511*
Wurtsboro, NY 12790 • *1,128*
Wyalusing, PA 18853 • *716*
Wyandanch, NY 11798 • *17,900*

Wyandot ☐, OH • *22,651*
Wyandotte, MI 48192 • *34,006*
Wyandotte ☐, KS • *172,335*
Wyanet, IL 61379 • *1,069*
Wyckoff, NJ 07481 • *15,500*
Wymore, NE 68466 • *1,841*
Wyncote, PA 19095 • *5,300*
Wyndmoor, PA 19118 • *5,800*
Wynne, AR 72396 • *7,805*
Wynnewood, OK 73098 • *2,615*
Wynnewood, PA 19096 • *7,700*
Wynona, OK 74084 • *780*
Wyoming, DE 19934 • *960*
Wyoming, IL 61491 • *1,614*
Wyoming, IA 52362 • *702*
Wyoming, MI 49509 • *59,616*
Wyoming, MN 55092 • *1,559*
Wyoming, OH 45215 • *8,282*
Wyoming, PA 18644 • *3,655*
Wyoming ☐, NY • *39,895*
Wyoming ☐, PA • *26,433*
Wyoming ☐, WV • *35,993*
Wyomissing, PA 19610 • *6,551*
Wythe ☐, VA • *25,522*
Wytheville, VA 24382 • *7,135*

X

Xenia, OH 45385 • *24,653*

Y

Yadkin ☐, NC • *28,439*
Yadkinville, NC 27055 • *2,216*
Yakima, WA 98901–09 • *49,826*
Yakima ☐, WA • *172,508*
Yalaha, FL 32797 • *950*
Yale, MI 48097 • *1,814*
Yale, OK 74085 • *1,652*
Yalobusha ☐, MS • *13,139*
Yamhill, OR 97148 • *690*
Yamhill ☐, OR • *55,332*
Yancey ☐, NC • *14,934*
Yanceyville, NC 27379 • *1,511*
Yankton, SD 57078 • *12,011*
Yankton ☐, SD • *18,952*
Yardley, PA 19067 • *2,533*
Yardville, NJ 08620 • *8,400*
Yarmouth, ME 04096 • *2,421*
Yarmouth, MA 02675 • *900*
Yarmouth Port, MA 02675 • *2,490*
Yarnell, AZ 85362 • *950*
Yates ☐, NY • *21,459*
Yatesboro, PA 16263 • *700*
Yates Center, KS 66783 • *1,998*
Yates City, IL 61572 • *860*
Yavapai ☐, AZ • *68,145*
Yazoo ☐, MS • *27,349*
Yazoo City, MS 39194 • *12,092*
Yeadon, PA 19050 • *11,727*
Yeagertown, PA 17099 • *1,363*
Yell ☐, AR • *17,026*
Yellow Medicine ☐, MN • *13,653*
Yellow Springs, OH 45387 • *4,077*
Yellowstone ☐, MT • *108,035*
Yellowstone National Park ☐, MT
 • *275*
Yellville, AR 72687 • *1,044*
Yelm, WA 98597 • *1,294*
Yemassee, SC 29945 • *789*
Yerington, NV 89447 • *2,021*
Yermo, CA 92398 • *1,092*
Yoakum, TX 77995 • *6,148*
Yoakum ☐, TX • *8,299*
Yolo ☐, CA • *113,374*

Yoncalla, OR 97499 • *805*
Yonkers, NY 10701–99 • *195,351*
Yorba Linda, CA 92686 • *28,254*
York, AL 36925 • *3,392*
York, ME 03909 • *3,130*
York, NE 68467 • *7,723*
York, PA 17401–99 • *44,619*
York, SC 29745 • *6,412*
York ☐, ME • *139,666*
York ☐, NE • *14,798*
York ☐, PA • *312,963*
York ☐, SC • *106,720*
York ☐, VA • *35,463*
York Beach, ME 03910 • *860*
York Harbor, ME 03911 • *1,400*
York Haven, PA 17370 • *746*
Yorkshire, NY 14173 • *850*
Yorktown, IN 47396 • *3,945*
Yorktown, NY 10598 • *5,400*
Yorktown, TX 78164 • *2,498*
Yorktown Heights, NY 10598 • *5,900*
Yorktown Manor, RI 02852 • *1,300*
Yorkville, IL 60560 • *3,422*
Yorkville, NY 13495 • *3,115*
Yorkville, OH 43971 • *1,447*
Yosemite National Park, CA 95389
 • *1,073*
Young ☐, TX • *19,083*
Young Harris, GA 30582 • *687*
Youngstown, NY 14174 • *2,191*
Youngstown, OH 44501–99
 • *115,436*
Youngsville, LA 70592 • *1,053*
Youngsville, PA 16371 • *2,006*
Youngtown, AZ 85363 • *2,254*
Youngwood, PA 15697 • *3,749*
Ypsilanti, MI 48197 • *24,031*
Yreka, CA 96097 • *5,916*
Yuba ☐, CA • *49,733*
Yuba City, CA 95991 • *18,736*
Yucaipa, CA 92399 • *20,000*
Yukon, OK 73099 • *17,112*
Yulee, FL 32097 • *3,168*
Yuma, AZ 85364–69 • *42,481*
Yuma, CO 80759 • *2,824*
Yuma ☐, AZ • *78,054*
Yuma ☐, CO • *9,682*
Yutan, NE 68073 • *631*

Z

Zachary, LA 70791 • *7,297*
Zanesville, OH 43701 • *28,655*
Zapata, TX 78076 • *2,500*
Zapata ☐, TX • *6,628*
Zavala, TX 11,666
Zavalla, TX 75980 • *762*
Zearing, IA 50278 • *630*
Zebulon, GA 30295 • *995*
Zebulon, NC 27597 • *2,055*
Zeeland, MI 49464 • *4,764*
Zeigler, IL 62999 • *1,858*
Zelienople, PA 16063 • *3,502*
Zephyr Cove, NV 89448 • *1,300*
Zephyrhills, FL 34248–49 • *5,742*
Ziebach ☐, SD • *2,308*
Zillah, WA 98953 • *1,599*
Zilwaukee, MI 48604 • *2,201*
Zimmerman, MN 55398 • *1,074*
Zion, IL 60099 • *17,861*
Zionsville, IN 46077 • *3,948*
Zolfo Springs, FL 33890 • *1,495*
Zumbrota, MN 55992 • *2,129*
Zuni, NM 87327 • *5,551*
Zwolle, LA 71486 • *2,602*

Geographical Facts about the United States

ELEVATION

The highest elevation in the United States is Mount McKinley, Alaska, 20,320 feet.
The lowest elevation in the United States is in Death Valley, California, 282 feet below sea level.
The average elevation of the United States is 2,500 feet.

EXTREMITIES

Direction	Location	Latitude	Longitude
North	Point Barrow, Alaska	71°23′N.	156°29′W.
South	Ka Lae (point) Hawaii	18°56′N.	155°41′W.
East	West Quoddy Head, Maine	44°49′N.	66°57′W.
West	Cape Wrangell, Alaska	52°55′N.	172°27′E.

The two places in the United States separated by the greatest distance are Kure Island, Hawaii, and Mangrove Point, Florida. These points are 5,848 miles apart.

LENGTH OF BOUNDARIES

The total length of the Canadian boundary of the United States is 5,525 miles.
The total length of the Mexican boundary of the United States is 1,933 miles.

The total length of the Atlantic coastline of the United States is 2,069 miles.
The total length of the Pacific and Arctic coastline of the United States is 8,683 miles.
The total length of the Gulf of Mexico coastline of the United States is 1,631 miles.
The total length of all coastlines and land boundaries of the United States is 19,841 miles.
The total length of the tidal shoreline and land boundaries of the United States is 96,091 miles.

GEOGRAPHIC CENTERS

The geographic center of the United States (including Alaska and Hawaii) is in Butte County, South Dakota at 44°58′N., 103°46′W.
The geographic center of North America is in North Dakota, a few miles west of Devils Lake, at 48°10′N., 100°10′W.

EXTREMES OF TEMPERATURE

The highest temperature ever recorded in the United States was 134°F., at Greenland Ranch, Death Valley, California, on July 10, 1913.

The lowest temperature ever recorded in the United States was —76°F., at Tanana, Alaska, in January, 1886.

PRECIPITATION

The average annual precipitation for the United States is approximately 29 inches.
Hawaii is the wettest state, with an average annual rainfall of 82.48 inches. Nevada, with an average annual rainfall of 8.81 inches, is the driest state.
The greatest local average annual rainfall in the United States is at Mt. Waialeale, Kauai, Hawaii, 460 inches.
Greatest 24-hour rainfall in the United States, 23.22 inches at New Smyrna, Florida, October 10–11, 1924.
Extreme minimum rainfall records in the United States include a total fall of only 3.93 inches at Bagdad, California, for a period of 5 years, 1909–13, and an annual average of 1.78 inches at Death Valley, California.
Heavy snowfall records include 76 inches at Silver Lake, Colorado, in 1 day; 42 inches at Angola, New York, in 2 days; 87 inches at Giant Forest, California, in 3 days; and 108 inches at Tahoe, California, in 4 days.
Greatest seasonal snowfall, 1,000.3 inches, more than 83 feet, at Paradise Ranger Station, Washington, during the winter of 1955–56.

Historical Facts about the United States

TERRITORIAL ACQUISITIONS

Accession	Date	Area (sq. mi.)	Cost in Dollars
Original territory of the Thirteen States	1790	888,685	
Purchase of Louisiana Territory, from France	1803	827,192	$11,250,000.00
By treaty with Spain: Florida	1819	58,560	$ 5,000,000.00
Other areas	1819	13,443	
Annexation of Texas	1845	390,144	
Oregon Territory, by treaty with Great Britain	1846	285,580	
Mexican Cession	1848	529,017	$15,000,000.00
Gadsden Purchase, from Mexico	1853	29,640	$10,000,000.00
Purchase of Alaska, from Russia	1867	586,412	7,200,000.00
Annexation of Hawaiian Islands	1898	6,450	
Puerto Rico, by treaty with Spain	1899	3,435	
Guam, by treaty with Spain	1899	212	
American Samoa, by treaty with Great Britain and Germany	1900	76	
Virgin Islands, by purchase from Denmark	1917	133	$25,000,000.00
Total		3,618,979	$73,450,000.00

Note: The Philippines, ceded by Spain in 1898 for $20,000,000.00, were a territorial possession of the United States from 1898 to 1946. On July 4, 1946 they became the independent republic of the Philippines.

Note. The Canal Zone, ceded by Panama in 1903 for $10,000,000.00, was a territory of the United States from 1903 to 1979. As a result of treaties signed in 1977, sovereignty over the Canal Zone reverted to Panama in 1979.

WESTWARD MOVEMENT OF CENTER OF POPULATION

Year	U.S. Population Total at Census	Approximate Location
1790	3,929,214	23 miles east of Baltimore, Md.
1800	5,308,483	18 miles west of Baltimore, Md.
1810	7,239,881	40 miles northwest of Washington, D.C.
1820	9,638,453	16 miles east of Moorefield, W. Va.
1830	12,866,020	19 miles southwest of Moorefield, W. Va.
1840	17,069,453	16 miles south of Clarksburg, W. Va.
1850	23,191,876	23 miles southeast of Parkersburg, W. Va.
1860	31,443,321	20 miles southeast of Chillicothe, Ohio
1870	39,818,449	48 miles northeast of Cincinnati, Ohio
1880	50,155,783	8 miles southwest of Cincinnati, Ohio
1890	62,947,714	20 miles east of Columbus, Ind.
1900	75,994,575	6 miles southeast of Columbus, Ind.
1910	91,972,266	Bloomington, Ind.
1920	105,710,620	8 miles southeast of Spencer, Ind.
1930	122,775,046	3 miles northeast of Linton, Ind.
1940	131,669,275	2 miles southeast of Carlisle, Ind.
1950	150,697,361	8 miles northwest of Olney, Ill.
1960	179,323,175	6 miles northwest of Centralia, Ill.
1970	204,816,296	5 miles southeast of Mascoutah, Ill.
1980	226,504,825	Near DeSoto, Mo.

State Areas and Populations

STATE	Land Area square miles	Water Area* square miles	Total Area* square miles	Area Rank land area	1980 Resident Population	1980 Population per square mile	1970 Population	1960 Population	1950 Population	1980	1970	1960
Alabama	50,766	938	51,704	28	3,893,978	77	3,444,165	3,266,740	3,061,743	22	21	19
Alaska	570,833	20,171	591,004	1	401,851	0.7	302,173	226,167	128,643	50	50	50
Arizona	113,510	492	114,002	6	2,718,425	24	1,772,482	1,302,161	749,587	29	33	35
Arkansas	52,082	1,109	53,191	27	2,286,419	44	1,923,295	1,786,272	1,909,511	33	32	31
California	156,297	2,407	158,704	3	23,667,837	151	19,953,134	15,717,204	10,586,223	1	1	2
Colorado	103,598	496	104,094	8	2,889,735	28	2,207,259	1,753,947	1,325,089	28	30	33
Connecticut	4,872	147	5,019	48	3,107,576	638	3,032,217	2,535,234	2,007,280	25	24	25
Delaware	1,933	112	2,045	49	594,317	307	548,104	446,292	318,085	47	46	46
District of Columbia	63	6	69	..	638,432	10,134	756,510	763,956	802,178	..	..	..
Florida	54,157	4,511	58,668	26	9,746,421	180	6,789,443	4,951,560	2,771,305	7	9	10
Georgia	58,060	854	58,914	21	5,463,087	94	4,589,575	3,943,116	3,444,578	13	15	16
Hawaii	6,427	46	6,473	47	964,691	150	769,913	632,772	499,794	39	40	43
Idaho	82,413	1,153	83,566	11	944,038	11	713,008	667,191	588,637	41	42	42
Illinois	55,646	2,226	57,872	24	11,427,414	205	11,113,976	10,081,158	8,712,176	5	5	4
Indiana	35,936	481	36,417	38	5,490,260	153	5,193,669	4,662,498	3,934,224	12	11	11
Iowa	55,965	310	56,275	23	2,913,808	52	2,825,041	2,757,537	2,621,073	27	25	24
Kansas	81,783	499	82,282	13	2,364,236	29	2,249,071	2,178,611	1,905,299	32	28	28
Kentucky	39,674	740	40,414	37	3,660,257	92	3,219,311	3,038,156	2,944,806	23	23	22
Louisiana	44,520	3,230	47,750	33	4,206,098	94	3,643,180	3,257,022	2,683,516	19	20	20
Maine	30,995	2,270	33,265	39	1,125,030	36	993,663	969,265	913,774	38	38	36
Maryland	9,838	623	10,461	42	4,216,941	429	3,922,399	3,100,689	2,343,001	18	18	21
Massachusetts	7,826	460	8,286	45	5,737,081	733	5,689,170	5,148,578	4,690,514	11	10	9
Michigan	56,959	40,148	97,107	22	9,262,070	163	8,875,083	7,823,194	6,371,766	8	7	7
Minnesota	79,548	7,066	86,614	14	4,075,970	51	3,805,069	3,413,864	2,982,483	21	19	18
Mississippi	47,234	457	47,691	31	2,520,631	53	2,216,912	2,178,141	2,178,914	31	29	29
Missouri	68,945	752	69,697	18	4,916,759	71	4,677,399	4,319,813	3,954,653	15	13	13
Montana	145,388	1,657	147,045	4	786,690	5.4	694,409	674,767	591,024	44	43	41
Nebraska	76,639	711	77,350	15	1,569,825	20	1,483,791	1,411,330	1,325,510	35	35	34
Nevada	109,895	667	110,562	7	800,493	7.3	488,738	285,278	160,083	43	47	49
New Hampshire	8,992	286	9,278	44	920,610	102	737,681	606,921	533,242	42	41	45
New Jersey	7,468	319	7,787	46	7,365,011	986	7,168,164	6,066,782	4,835,329	9	8	8
New Mexico	121,336	258	121,594	5	1,303,445	11	1,016,000	951,023	681,187	37	37	37
New York	47,379	5,358	52,737	30	17,558,072	371	18,241,266	16,782,304	14,830,192	2	2	1
North Carolina	48,843	3,826	52,669	29	5,881,385	120	5,082,059	4,556,155	4,061,929	10	12	12
North Dakota	69,299	1,403	70,702	17	652,717	9.4	617,761	632,446	619,636	46	45	44
Ohio	41,004	3,782	44,786	35	10,797,624	263	10,652,017	9,706,397	7,946,627	6	6	5
Oklahoma	68,656	1,301	69,957	19	3,025,495	44	2,559,253	2,328,284	2,233,351	26	27	27
Oregon	96,187	889	97,076	10	2,633,149	27	2,091,385	1,768,687	1,521,341	30	31	32
Pennsylvania	44,892	1,155	46,047	32	11,864,751	264	11,793,909	11,319,366	10,498,012	4	3	3
Rhode Island	1,054	158	1,212	50	947,154	899	949,723	859,488	791,896	40	39	39
South Carolina	30,207	909	31,116	40	3,122,814	103	2,590,516	2,382,594	2,117,027	24	26	26
South Dakota	75,956	1,164	77,120	16	690,768	9.1	666,257	680,514	652,740	45	44	40
Tennessee	41,154	989	42,143	34	4,591,120	112	3,924,164	3,567,089	3,291,718	17	17	17
Texas	262,015	4,790	266,805	2	14,227,574	54	11,196,730	9,579,677	7,711,194	3	4	6
Utah	82,076	2,826	84,902	12	1,461,037	18	1,059,273	890,627	688,862	36	36	38
Vermont	9,273	341	9,614	43	511,456	55	444,732	389,881	377,747	48	48	47
Virginia	39,700	1,063	40,763	36	5,346,797	135	4,648,494	3,966,949	3,318,680	14	14	14
Washington	66,512	1,627	68,139	20	4,132,204	62	3,409,169	2,853,214	2,378,963	20	22	23
West Virginia	24,124	112	24,236	41	1,950,258	81	1,744,237	1,860,421	2,005,552	34	34	30
Wisconsin	54,424	11,789	66,213	25	4,705,642	86	4,417,933	3,951,777	3,434,575	16	16	15
Wyoming	96,988	820	97,808	9	469,557	4.8	332,416	330,066	290,529	49	49	48
United States	3,539,341	139,904	3,679,245	..	226,549,010	64	203,235,298	179,323,175	151,325,798	..	..	..

*Includes the United States area of the Great Lakes.

U.S. State General Information

148

STATE	CAPITAL	LARGEST CITY	ENTERED UNION AS STATE Date of Entry	Rank of Entry	Greatest N-S Measurement (miles)	Greatest E-W Measurement (miles)	HIGHEST POINT Location	Altitude (feet)	STATE FLOWER	STATE BIRD	STATE NICKNAME
Alabama	Montgomery	Birmingham	Dec. 14, 1819	22	330	200	Cheaha Mountain	2,407	Camellia	Yellowhammer	Yellowhammer
Alaska	Juneau	Anchorage	Jan. 3, 1959	49	1,332	2,250	Mt. McKinley	20,320	Forget-me-not	Willow Ptarmigan	Last Frontier
Arizona	Phoenix	Phoenix	Feb. 14, 1912	48	390	335	Humphreys Peak	12,633	Saguaro Cactus	Cactus Wren	Grand Canyon
Arkansas	Little Rock	Little Rock	June 15, 1836	25	240	275	Magazine Mtn.	2,753	Apple Blossom	Mockingbird	Land of Opportunity
California	Sacramento	Los Angeles	Sept. 9, 1850	31	800	375	Mt. Whitney	14,494	Golden Poppy	California Valley Quail	Golden
Colorado	Denver	Denver	Aug. 1, 1876	38	270	380	Mt. Elbert	14,433	Rocky Mountain Columbine	Lark Bunting	Centennial
Connecticut*	Hartford	Hartford	Jan. 9, 1788	5	75	90	S. slope of Mt. Frissell	2,380	Mountain Laurel	Robin	Constitution
Delaware*	Dover	Wilmington	Dec. 7, 1787	1	95	35	Ebright Road, New Castle Co.	442	Peach Blossom	Blue Hen Chicken	First
District of Columbia	Washington	Washington	March 3, 1791	..	15	15	Tenleytown	410	American Beauty Rose	Wood Thrush	......
Florida	Tallahassee	Jacksonville	March 3, 1845	27	460	400	N. boundary, Walton Co.	345	Orange Blossom	Mockingbird	Sunshine
Georgia*	Atlanta	Atlanta	Jan. 2, 1788	4	315	250	Brasstown Bald (mtn.)	4,784	Cherokee Rose	Brown Thrasher	Peach
Hawaii	Honolulu	Honolulu	Aug. 21, 1959	50	...	1,600	Mauna Kea	13,796	Red Hibiscus	Nene (Hawaiian Goose)	Aloha
Idaho	Boise	Boise	July 3, 1890	43	480	305	Borah Peak	12,662	Syringa	Mountain Bluebird	Gem
Illinois	Springfield	Chicago	Dec. 3, 1818	21	380	205	Charles Mound	1,235	Violet	Cardinal	Prairie
Indiana	Indianapolis	Indianapolis	Dec. 11, 1816	19	265	160	Near Spartanburg	1,257	Peony	Cardinal	Hoosier
Iowa	Des Moines	Des Moines	Dec. 28, 1846	29	205	310	N. W. corner Osceola Co.	1,670	Wild Rose	Eastern Goldfinch	Hawkeye
Kansas	Topeka	Wichita	Jan. 29, 1861	34	205	410	Mt. Sunflower	4,039	Sunflower	Western Meadowlark	Sunflower
Kentucky	Frankfort	Louisville	June 1, 1792	15	175	350	Black Mountain	4,145	Goldenrod	Kentucky Cardinal	Bluegrass
Louisiana	Baton Rouge	New Orleans	April 30, 1812	18	275	300	Driskill Mountain	535	Magnolia	Pelican	Pelican
Maine	Augusta	Portland	March 15, 1820	23	310	210	Mt. Katahdin	5,268	White Pine	Chickadee	Pine Tree
Maryland*	Annapolis	Baltimore	April 28, 1788	7	120	200	Backbone Mountain	3,360	Black-eyed Susan	Baltimore Oriole	Old Free
Massachusetts*	Boston	Boston	Feb. 6, 1788	6	110	190	Mt. Greylock	3,491	Mayflower	Chickadee	Old Bay
Michigan	Lansing	Detroit	Jan. 26, 1837	26	400	310	Mt. Curwood	1,980	Apple Blossom	Robin	Wolverine
Minnesota	St. Paul	Minneapolis	May 11, 1858	32	400	350	Eagle Mtn.	2,301	Showy Lady's-slipper	Loon	Gopher
Mississippi	Jackson	Jackson	Dec. 10, 1817	20	340	180	Woodall Mountain	806	Magnolia	Mockingbird	Magnolia
Missouri	Jefferson City	St. Louis	Aug. 10, 1821	24	280	300	Taum Sauk Mountain	1,772	Hawthorne	Bluebird	Show Me
Montana	Helena	Billings	Nov. 8, 1889	41	315	570	Granite Peak	12,799	Bitterroot	Western Meadowlark	Big Sky
Nebraska	Lincoln	Omaha	March 1, 1867	37	210	415	S.W. corner Kimball Co.	5,426	Goldenrod	Western Meadowlark	Cornhusker
Nevada	Carson City	Las Vegas	Oct. 31, 1864	36	485	315	Boundary Peak	13,143	Shrub Sagebrush	Mountain Bluebird	Silver
New Hampshire*	Concord	Manchester	June 21, 1788	9	185	90	Mt. Washington	6,288	Purple Lilac	Purple Finch	Granite
New Jersey*	Trenton	Newark	Dec. 18, 1787	3	166	70	High Point	1,803	Purple Violet	Eastern Goldfinch	Garden
New Mexico	Santa Fe	Albuquerque	Jan. 6, 1912	47	390	350	Wheeler Peak	13,161	Yucca	Roadrunner	Land of Enchantment
New York*	Albany	New York	July 26, 1788	11	310	330	Mt. Marcy	5,344	Rose	Bluebird	Empire
North Carolina*	Raleigh	Charlotte	Nov. 21, 1789	12	200	520	Mt. Mitchell	6,684	Dogwood	Cardinal	Tar Heel
North Dakota	Bismarck	Fargo	Nov. 2, 1889	39	210	360	White Butte	3,506	Wild Prairie Rose	Western Meadowlark	Flickertail
Ohio	Columbus	Cleveland	March 1, 1803	17	230	205	Campbell Hill	1,550	Scarlet Carnation	Cardinal	Buckeye
Oklahoma	Oklahoma City	Oklahoma City	Nov. 16, 1907	46	210	460	Black Mesa	4,973	Mistletoe	Scissor-tailed Flycatcher	Sooner
Oregon	Salem	Portland	Feb. 14, 1859	33	290	375	Mt. Hood	11,239	Oregon Grape	Western Meadowlark	Beaver
Pennsylvania*	Harrisburg	Philadelphia	Dec. 12, 1787	2	180	310	Mt. Davis	3,213	Mountain Laurel	Ruffed Grouse	Keystone
Rhode Island*	Providence	Providence	May 29, 1790	13	50	35	Jerimoth Hill	812	Violet	Rhode Island Red	Little Rhody
South Carolina*	Columbia	Columbia	May 23, 1788	8	215	285	Sassafras Mountain	3,560	Carolina Jessamine	Carolina Wren	Palmetto
South Dakota	Pierre	Sioux Falls	Nov. 2, 1889	40	240	360	Harney Peak	7,242	Pasque	Ringnecked Pheasant	Coyote
Tennessee	Nashville	Memphis	June 1, 1796	16	120	430	Clingmans Dome	6,643	Iris	Mockingbird	Volunteer
Texas	Austin	Houston	Dec. 29, 1845	28	710	760	Guadalupe Peak	8,751	Bluebonnet	Mockingbird	Lone Star
Utah	Salt Lake City	Salt Lake City	Jan. 4, 1896	45	345	275	Kings Peak	13,528	Sego Lily	Seagull	Beehive
Vermont	Montpelier	Burlington	March 4, 1791	14	155	90	Mt. Mansfield	4,393	Red Clover	Hermit Thrush	Green Mountain
Virginia*	Richmond	Norfolk	June 25, 1788	10	205	425	Mt. Rogers	5,729	Flowering Dogwood	Cardinal	Old Dominion
Washington	Olympia	Seattle	Nov. 11, 1889	42	230	340	Mt. Rainier	14,410	Rhododendron	Willow Goldfinch	Evergreen
West Virginia	Charleston	Huntington	June 20, 1863	35	200	225	Spruce Knob	4,862	Rhododendron	Cardinal	Mountain
Wisconsin	Madison	Milwaukee	May 29, 1848	30	300	290	Timms Hill	1,952	Violet	Robin	Badger
Wyoming	Cheyenne	Cheyenne	July 10, 1890	44	275	365	Gannett Peak	13,804	Indian Paint Brush	Meadowlark	Equality
United States	Washington, D.C.	New York	...	..	275	...	Mt. McKinley, Alaska	20,320	......	Bald Eagle	......

*One of the Thirteen Original States.

Abbreviations

admin	administered
Afg	Afghanistan
Afr	Africa
Ala	Alabama
Alb	Albania
Alg	Algeria
Alsk	Alaska
Alta	Alberta
Am	American
Am. Sam	American Samoa
And	Andorra
Ang	Angola
Ant	Antarctica
Arc	Arctic
arch	archipelago
Arg	Argentina
Ariz	Arizona
Ark	Arkansas
Atl. O	Atlantic Ocean
Aus	Austria
Austl	Australia, Australian
auton	autonomous
Az. Is	Azores Islands
Ba	Bahamas
Barb	Barbados
B. C.	British Columbia
Bel	Belgium, Belgian
Bhu	Bhutan
Bis. Arch	Bismarck Archipelago
Bngl	Bangladesh
Bol	Bolivia
Bots	Botswana
Br	British
Braz	Brazil
Bru	Brunei
Bul	Bulgaria
Bur	Burma
Calif	California
Cam	Cameroon
Can	Canada
Can. Is	Canary Islands
Cen. Afr. Rep	Central African Republic
Cen. Am	Central America
co	county
Col	Colombia
Colo	Colorado
Con	Congo
Conn	Connecticut
cont	continent
C. R.	Costa Rica
C. V.	Cape Verde
Cyp	Cyprus
Czech	Czechoslovakia
D.C.	District of Columbia
Del	Delaware
Den	Denmark
dep	dependency, dependencies
dept	department
dist	district
div	division
Dji	Djibouti
Dom. Rep	Dominican Republic
Ec	Ecuador
Eg	Egypt
Eng	England
Equat. Gui	Equatorial Guinea
Eth	Ethiopia
Eur	Europe
Falk. Is	Falkland Islands
Fed	Federation
Fin	Finland
Fla	Florida
Fr	France, French
Fr. Gu	French Guiana
Ga	Georgia
Gam	Gambia
Ger., Fed. Rep. of	Federal Republic of Germany
Ger. Dem. Rep	German Democratic Republic
Gib	Gibraltar
Grc	Greece
Grnld	Greenland
Guad	Guadeloupe
Guat	Guatemala
Guy	Guyana
Hai	Haiti
Haw	Hawaii
Hond	Honduras
Hung	Hungary
I.	Island
I.C.	Ivory Coast
Ice	Iceland
Ill	Illinois
incl	includes, including
Ind	Indiana
Indian res	Indian reservation
Indon	Indonesia
I. of Man	Isle of Man
Ire	Ireland
is	islands
isl	island
Isr	Israel
It	Italy
Jam	Jamaica
Jap	Japan
Kam	Kampuchea
Kans	Kansas
Ken	Kenya
Kor	Korea
Kuw	Kuwait
Ky	Kentucky
La	Louisiana
Leb	Lebanon
Le. Is	Leeward Islands
Leso	Lesotho
Lib	Liberia
Liech	Liechtenstein
Lux	Luxembourg
Mad	Madagascar
Mad. Is	Madeira Islands
Mala	Malaysia
Man	Manitoba
Mart	Martinique
Mass	Massachusetts
Maur	Mauritania
Md	Maryland
Medit	Mediterranean
Mex	Mexico
Mich	Michigan
Minn	Minnesota
Miss	Mississippi
Mo	Missouri
Mong	Mongolia
Mont	Montana
Mor	Morocco
Moz	Mozambique
mtn	mount, mountain
mts	mountains
mun	municipality
N.A.	North America
nat. mon	national monument
nat. park	national park
N.B	New Brunswick
N.C	North Carolina
N. Cal	New Caledonia
N. Dak	North Dakota
Nebr	Nebraska
Nep	Nepal
Neth	Netherlands
Nev	Nevada
Newf	Newfoundland
N.H	New Hampshire
Nic	Nicaragua
Nig	Nigeria
N. Ire	Northern Ireland
N.J	New Jersey
N. Mex	New Mexico
Nor	Norway, Norwegian
N.S	Nova Scotia
N.W. Ter	Northwest Territories
N.Y	New York
N.Z	New Zealand
occ	occupied area
Okla	Oklahoma
Om	Oman
Ont	Ontario
Oreg	Oregon
Pa	Pennsylvania
Pac. O	Pacific Ocean
Pak	Pakistan
Pan	Panama
Pap. N. Gui	Papua New Guinea
Par	Paraguay
par	parish
P.D.R. of Yem	Yemen, People's Democratic Republic of
P.E.I	Prince Edward Island
pen	peninsula
Phil	Philippines
Pol	Poland
pol. dist	political district
pop	population
Port.	Portugal, Portuguese
poss	possession
P.R	Puerto Rico
pref	prefecture
prot	protectorate
prov	province, provincial
pt	point
Que	Quebec
reg	region
rep	republic
res	reservation, reservoir
R.I	Rhode Island
riv	river
Rom	Romania
S. A	South America
S. Afr	South Africa
Sal	El Salvador
Sask	Saskatchewan
Sau. Ar	Saudi Arabia
S.C	South Carolina
Scot	Scotland
S. Dak	South Dakota
Sen	Senegal
S.L	Sierra Leone
Sol. Is	Solomon Islands
Som	Somalia
Sov. Un	Soviet Union
Sp	Spain, Spanish
St., Ste	Saint, Sainte
Sud	Sudan
Sur	Suriname
Swaz	Swaziland
Swe	Sweden
Switz	Switzerland
Syr	Syria
Tan	Tanzania
Tenn	Tennessee
ter	territories, territory
Tex	Texas
Thai	Thailand
Trin	Trinidad & Tobago
trust	trusteeship
Tun	Tunisia
Tur	Turkey
U.A.E	United Arab Emirates
Ug	Uganda
U.K	United Kingdom
Ur	Uruguay
U.S	United States
Va	Virginia
Ven	Venezuela
Viet	Vietnam
Vir. Is	Virgin Islands
vol	volcano
Vt	Vermont
Wash	Washington
W.I	West Indies
Win. Is	Windward Islands
Wis	Wisconsin
W. Sah	Western Sahara
W. Sam	Western Samoa
W. Va	West Virginia
Wyo	Wyoming
Yugo	Yugoslavia
Zimb	Zimbabwe

Index

This universal index includes in a single alphabetical list all important names that appear on the reference maps. Each place name is followed by its location, the map index key, and the page number of the map.

State locations are given for all places in the United States. Province and country locations are given for all places in Canada. All other place name entries show only country locations.

The index reference key, always a letter and figure combination, and the map page number are the last items in each entry. Because some places are shown on both a main map and an inset map, more than one index key may be given for a single map page number. Reference also may be made to more than a single map. In each case, however, the index key *letter and figure* precede the map page number to which reference is made. A lowercase key letter indicates reference to an inset map which has been keyed separately.

Each major and minor political division is followed both by a descriptive term (co., dist., region, prov.; dept.; state, etc.) indicating political status, and by the name of the country in which it is located. United States counties are listed with state locations; all other divisions are given with country references.

The more important physical names that are shown on the maps are listed in the index. Each entry is followed by a descriptive term (bay, hill, range, riv., mtn., isl., etc.), to indicate its nature.

Country locations are given for all names except features entirely within a state of the United States or a province of Canada, in which case this division is given.

Some names included in the index were omitted from the maps because of scale size or lack of space. These entries are identified by an asterisk (*), and reference is given to the approximate location on the map.

A long name may appear on the map in a shortened form, with the full name given in the index. The part of the name not on the map then appears in italics, thus: St. Gabriel-*de-Brandon.*

The system of alphabetizing used in the index is standard. When more than one name with the same spelling is shown, place names are listed *first* and political divisions *second.*

A

Aachen, Ger., Fed. Rep. of	C3	6
Aalen, Ger., Fed. Rep. of	D5	6
Aalst, Bel.	B6	5
Äänekoski, Fin.	F11	11
Aarau, Switz.	E4	6
Aargau, canton, Switz.	*E3	6
Aba, China	E5	17
Aba, Nig.	G6	22
Ābādān, Iran	B7	23
Abaetetuba, Braz.	*D6	27
Abakan, Sov. Un.	D12	13
Abancay, Peru	D3	31
Abashiri, Jap.	D12	18
Abbeville, Ala.	D4	46
Abbeville, Fr.	B4	5
Abbeville, La.	E3	63
Abbeville, S.C.	C3	82
Abbeville, co., S.C.	C2	82
Abbiategrasso, It.	C2	82
Abbotsford, B.C., Can.	f13	37
Abbotsford, Wis.	D3	88
Åbenrå, co., Den.	*J3	11
Abeokuta, Nig.	G5	22
Aberdare, Wales	E5	4
Aberdeen, Idaho	G6	57
Aberdeen, Md.	A5	53
Aberdeen, Miss.	B5	68
Aberdeen, N.C.	B3	76
Aberdeen, Scot.	B5	4
Aberdeen, S. Dak.	E7	77
Aberdeen, Wash.	C2	86
Aberdeen, co., Scot.	*B5	4
Abergavenny, Wales	E5	4
Abernathy, Tex.	C2	84
Aberystwyth, Wales	D4	4
Abidjan, I.C.	G4	22
Abilene, Kans.	D6	61
Abilene, Tex.	C3	84
Abingdon, Ill.	C3	58
Abingdon, Va.	f10	85
Abington, Mass.	B6, h12	65
Abington, Pa.	o12	81
Abitibi, co., Que., Can.	*h12	42
Åbo, see Turku, Fin.		
Abomey, Benin	G5	22
Abony, Hung.	B5	10
Abra, prov., Phil.	*B6	19
Abruzzi, reg., It.	C4	9
Abruzzi e Molise, pol. dist., It.	C4	9
Absecon, N.J.	E3	74
Abu Dhabi (Abū Zaby)	E5	15
Abū Kamāl, Syr.	E13	14
Aby, Swe.	u34	11
Acadia, par., La.	D3	63
Acámbaro, Mex.	C4, m13	34
Acaponeta, Mex.	C4	34
Acapulco *de Juárez,* Mex.	D5	34
Acarigua, Ven.	B4	32
Acatlán *de Osorio,* Mex.	D5, m14	34
Acayucan, Mex.	D6	34
Accomack, co., Va.	C7	85
Accoville, W. Va.	D3, n12	87
Accra, Ghana	G4	22
Achinsk, Sov. Un.	D12	13
Acireale, It.	F5	9
Ackerman, Miss.	B4	68
Ackley, Iowa	B4	60
Acmetonia, Pa.	*E1	81
Aconcagua, prov., Chile	A2	28

Aconcagua, peak, Arg.	A3	28
Acqui, It.	B2	9
Acre, state, Braz.	C3	31
Acre, riv., Braz.	D4	31
Acton, Ont., Can.	D4	41
Acton Vale, Que., Can.	D5	42
Açu, Braz.	*D7	27
Acushnet, Mass.	C6	65
Acworth, Ga.	B2	55
Ada, Minn.	C2	67
Ada, Ohio	B2	78
Ada, Okla.	C5	79
Ada, Yugo.	C5	10
Ada, co., Idaho	F2	57
Adair, co., Iowa	C3	60
Adair, co., Ky.	C4	62
Adiar, co., Mo.	A5	69
Adair, co., Okla.	B7	79
Adairsville, Ga.	B2	55
Adam, mtn., Wash.	C4	86
Adamantina, Braz.	C2	30
Adams, Mass.	A1	65
Adams, Minn.	G6	67
Adams, N.Y.	B4	75
Adams, Wis.	E4	88
Adams, co., Colo.	B6	51
Adams, co., Idaho	E2	57
Adams, co., Ill.	D2	58
Adams, co., Ind.	C8	59
Adams, co., Iowa	C3	60
Adams, co., Miss.	D2	68
Adams, co., Nebr.	D7	71
Adams, co., N. Dak.	D7	77
Adams, co., Ohio	D2	78
Adams, co., Pa.	G7	81
Adams, co., Wash.	B7	86
Adams, co., Wis.	D4	88
Adams, mtn., Mass.	A2	65
Adams, mtn, Wash.	C4	86
Adams Center, N.Y.	B5	75
Adamston, N.J.	C4	74
Adamstown, Pa.	F9	81
Adamsville, Ala.	f7	46
Adamsville, Tenn.	B3	83
Adana, Tur.	D10	14
Adapazari, Tur.	B8	14
Ad Dāmir, Sud.	E4	23
Addis Ababa, Eth.	G5	23
Addison, Ill.	k9	58
Addison, co., Vt.	C1	73
Ad Dīwānīyah, Iraq	C3	15
Ad Duwaym, Sud.	F4	23
Addyston, Ohio	o12	78
Adel, Ga.	E3	55
Adel, Iowa	C3	60
Adelaide, Austl.	F6	25
Adelphi, Md.	*C4	53
Aden, P.D.R. of Yem.	G4	15
Adena, Ohio	B5	78
Adigrat, Eth.	F5	23
Adirondack, mts., N.Y.	A6, f10	75
Adi Ugri, Eth.	F5	23
Adiyaman, Tur.	C12	14
Adjuntas, P.R.	*G11	35
Admiralty, is., Pap. N. Gui.	h12	25
Ado-Ekiti, Nig.	*E6	22
Adrano, It.	F5	9
Adria, It.	B4	9
Adrian, Mich.	G6	66

Adrian, Minn.	G3	67
Adrian, Mo.	C3	69
Adrianople, see Edirne, Tur.		
Adwā, Eth.	F5	23
Afars & Issas, see Djibouti, country, Fr.		
Affton, Mo.	C7	69
Afghanistan, country, Asia	B4	20
Africa, cont.		21
Afton, Iowa	C3	60
Afton, N.Y.	C5	75
Afton, Okla.	A7	79
Afton, Wyo.	D2	89
'Afula, Isr.	B3	15
Afyon, Tur.	C8	14
Agadèz, Niger	E6	22
Agadir, Mor.	B3	22
Agana, Guam	*F6	2
Agartala, India	D9	20
Agate Beach, Oreg.	C2	80
Agawam, Mass.	B2	65
Agboville, I.C.	G4	22
Agde, Fr.	F5	5
Agemastu, Jap.	n16	18
Agen, Fr.	E4	5
Agira, It.	F5	9
Agnone, It.	D5	9
Āgra, India	C6	20
Agrícola Oriental, Mex.	*D5	34
Agrigento, It.	F4	9
Agrínion, Grc.	C3	14
Aguada, P.R.	*G11	35
Aguadas, Col.	B2	32
Aguadilla, P.R.	G11	35
Aguascalientes, Mex.	C4, m12	34
Aguascalientes, state, Mex.	C4, k12	34
Aguilar, Colo.	D6	51
Aguita, Mex.	*B4	34
Agusan, prov., Phil.	*D7	19
Ahlen, Ger., Fed. Rep. of	C3	6
Ahmadabad, India	D5	20
Ahmadnagar, India	E5	20
Ahmadpur East, Pak.	C5	20
Ahoskie, N.C.	A6	76
Ahrweiler, Ger., Fed. Rep. of	C3	6
Ahuachapan, Sal.	E7	34
Ahualulco de Mercado, Mex.	m12	34
Ahvāz, Iran	B7	23
Ahvenanmaa (Åland), prov. Fin.	G8	11
Aibonito, P.R.	*G11	35
Aichi, pref., Jap.	*I8	18
Aiea, Haw.	B4, g10	56
Aihui, China	A10	17
Aikawa, Jap.	G9	18
Aiken, S.C.	D4	82
Aiken, co., S.C.	D4	82
Aiken West, S.C.	*D4	82
Aimorés, Braz.	B4	30
Aïn, dept., Fr.	*D6	5
Aïn Sefna, Alg.	B4	22
Aire-sur-la-Lys, Fr.	B5	5
Aisén, prov., Chile	D2	28
Aitkin, Minn.	D5	67
Aitkin, co., Minn.	D5	67
Aitolía kai Akarnanía	*C3	14
Aitolikón, Grc.	C3	14
Aiud, Rom.	B6	10
Aix-en-Provence, Fr.	F6	5

Aix-la-Chapelle, see Aachen, Ger., Fed. Rep. of		
Aix-les-Bains, Fr.	E6	5
Aiyina, Grc.	D4	14
Aiyion, Grc.	C4	14
Aizu-wakamatsu, Jap.	H9	18
Ajaccio, Fr.	D2	9
Ajax, Ont. Can.	D6	41
Ajmer, India	C5	20
Ajo, Ariz.	C2	48
Akashi, Jap.	I7	18
Akcaabat, Tur.	B12	14
Akershus, co., Nor.	*H4	11
Aketi, Zaire	H2	23
Akhaía (Achaea), prov., Grc.	*C3	14
Akharnaí, Grc.	g11	14
Akhisar, Tur.	C6	14
Akhtyrka, Sov. Un.	F10	12
Aki, Jap.	J6	18
Akita, Jap.	G10	18
Akita, pref., Jap.	*G1	18
Akkeshi, Jap.	E12	18
'Akko (Acre), Isr.	B3, g5	15
Akola, India	D6	20
Akron, Colo.	A7	51
Akron, Ind.	B5	59
Akron, Iowa	B1	60
Akron, N.Y.	B2	75
Akron, Ohio	A4	78
Akron, Pa.	F9	81
Aksaray, Tur.	C10	14
Akşehir, Tur.	C8	14
Aksenovo-Zilovskove, Sov. Un.	D14	13
Aktyubinsk, Sov. Un.	D8	13
Akureyri, Ice.	n23	11
Alabama, state, U.S.		46
Alabaster, Ala.	B3	46
Alachua, Fla.	C4	54
Alachua, co., Fla.	C4	54
Alagôa Grande, Braz.	*D7	27
Alagôas, state, Braz.	*D7	27
Alagoinhas, Braz.	*E7	27
Alajuela, C.R.	E8	34
Al 'Alamayn (El Alamein), Eg.	G7	14
Alamance, co. N.C.	B3	76
Alameda, Calif.	h8	50
Alameda, N. Mex.	B5, D5	48
Alameda, co. Calif.	D3	50
Alamo, Calif.	*D3	50
Alamo, Tenn.	B2	83
Alamo, Tex.	F3	84
Alamogordo, N. Mex.	C6	48
Alamo Heights, Tex.	E3, k7	84
Alamosa, Colo.	D5	51
Alamosa, co., Colo.	D5	51
Alanya, Tur.	D9	14
Alaşehir, Tur.	C7	14
Alaska, State, U.S.		47
Alassio, It.	C2	9
Alatyr, Sov. Un.	D16	12
Alava prov., Sp.	*A4	8
Alba, It.	B2	9
Albacete, Sp.	C5	8
Alba Iulia, Rom.	B6	10
Albania, country, Eur.	B2	14
Albano Laziale, It.	D4, h9	9
Albany, Ga.	E2	55
Albany, Ind.	D7	59
Albany, Ky.	D4	62

B

C

Creston, B.C., Can. E9 37
Creston, Newf., Can. E4 44
Creston, Iowa C3 60
Creston, Ohio B4 78
Crestview, Fla. u15 54
Crestwood, Ill. *B6 58
Crestwood, Mo. *C7 69
Crete, Ill. B6, m9 58
Crete, Nebr. D9 71
Crete, isl., Grc. E5 14
Crete, sea, Grc. E5 14
Creuse, dept., Fr. *D4 5
Creutzwald, Fr. C7 5
Creve Coeur, Ill. C4 58
Creve Coeur, Mo. *C7 69
Crevillente, Sp. C5 8
Crewe, Eng. D5 4
Crewe, Va. C4 85
Cricket, N.C. A1 76
Cridersville, Ohio B1 78
Crieff, Scot. B5 4
Crimmitschau, Ger. Dem. Rep. C6 6
Crisana, reg., Rom. B6 10
Crisfield, Md. E6 53
Crisp, co, Ga. E3 55
Cristóbal Colón, mtn., Col. A3 32
Crittenden, co., Ark. B5 49
Crittenden, co., Ky. e9 62
Croatia, reg. Yugo. *C2 10
Croatia, rep., Yugo. C2 10
Crocker, Mo. D5 69
Crockett, Calif. g8 50
Crockett, Tex. D5 84
Crockett, co., Tenn. B2 83
Crockett, co., Tex. B2 84
Croghan, N.Y. B5 75
Cromona, Ky. C7 62
Cromwell, Conn. C6 52
Crook, co., Oreg. C6 80
Crook, co., Wyo. B8 89
Crookston, Minn. C2 67
Crooksville, Ohio C3 78
Crosby, Minn. D5 67
Crosby, Miss. D2 68
Crosby, N. Dak. A2 77
Crosby, Tex. r14 84
Crosby, co., Tex. C2 84
Crosby, mtn., Wyo. C3 89
Crosbyton, Tex. C2 84
Cross, co., Ark. B5 49
Cross City, Fla. C3 54
Crossett, Ark. D4 49
Cross Mill, N.C. f10 76
Cross Plains, Tex. C3 84
Cross Plains, Wis. E4 88
Crossville, Ill. E5 58
Crossville, Tenn. D8 83
Croswell, Mich. E8 66
Crothersville, Ind. G6 59
Crotone, It. E6 9
Croton-on-Hudson, N.Y. D7, m15 75
Crouse, N.C. B1 76
Crow, peak, Mont. D5 70
Crow Agency, Mont. E9 70
Crowell, Tex. C3 84
Crowley, La. D3 63
Crowley, co., Colo. C7 51
Crown Point, Ind. B3 59
Crown Point, N.Y. B7 75
Crow Wing, co., Minn. D4 67
Croydon, Pa. F12 81
Crozet, Va. B4 85
Cruces, Cuba C3 35
Crucible, Pa. G1 81
Cruden Bay, Scot. B6 4
Crum Lynne, Pa. *E1 81
Cruz Alta, Braz. D2 10
Cruz del Eje, Arg. A4 28
Cruzeiro, Braz. C4 30
Crystal, Minn. m12 67
Crystal Beach, Fla. D4 54
Crystal City, Mo. C7, g13 69
Crystal City, Tex. E3 84
Crystal Falls, Mich. B2 66
Crystal Lake, Fla. u16 54
Crystal Lake, Ill. A5, h8 58
Crystal Lakes, Ohio C1 78
Crystal River, Fla. D4 54
Crystal Springs, Miss. D3 68
Csongrád, Hung. B5 10
Csongrád, co., Hung. *B5 10
Csorna, Hung. B3 10
Cuajimalpa, Mex. h9 34
Cuauhtémoc, Mex. B3 34
Cuautepec, Mex. g9 34
Cuautla, Mex. n14 34
Cuba, Ill. C3 58
Cuba, Mo. C6 69
Cuba, N.Y. C2 75
Cuba, country, N.A. C3 35
Cuba City, Wis. F3 88
Cucamonga, Calif. *E5 50
Cúcuta, Col. B3 32
Cudahy, Calif. *F4 50
Cudahy, Wis. F6, n12 88
Cuddalore, India F6 20
Cuddapah, India F6 20
Cuddy, Pa. *B5 81
Cuenca, Ec. B2 31
Cuenca, Sp. B4 8
Cuenca, prov. Sp. *B4 8
Cuencamé *de Ceniceros*, Mex. C4 34
Cuernavaca, Mex. D5, n14 34
Cuero, Tex E4 84
Cuetzalan, Mex. m15 34
Cuevas, Sp. D5 8
Cuiabá, Braz. B1 30
Cuicatlán, Mex. o15 34
Culberson, co., Tex. o12 84
Culbertson, Mont. B12 70
Culbertson, Nebr. D5 71
Culhuacán, Mex. h9 34
Culiacán, Mex. C3 34
Cúllar de Baza, Sp. D4 8
Cullen, La. B2 63
Cullera, Sp. C5 8
Cullman, Ala. A3 46
Cullman, co., Ala. A3 46
Culloden, W. Va. *C2 87
Cullowhee, N.C. f9 76
Culmore, Va. *B5 85
Culpeper, Va. B4 85
Culpeper, co., Va. B5 85
Culver, Ind. B5 59
Culver City, Calif. m12 50
Cumaná, Ven. A5 32
Cumberland, B.C., Can. E5 37
Cumberland, Ind. E6, k11 59
Cumberland, Ky. D7 62
Cumberland, Md. k13 53
Cumberland, Wis. C2 88
Cumberland, co., N.S., Can. D5 43
Cumberland, co., Eng. *C5 4
Cumberland, co., Ill. D5 58
Cumberland, co., Ky. D4 62
Cumberland, co., Maine E2 64
Cumberland, co., N.J. E2 74
Cumberland, co., N.C. C4 76
Cumberland, co., Pa. F7 81
Cumberland, co., Tenn. D8 83
Cumberland, co., Va. C4 85
Cumberland, mtn., Ky., Tenn. C9 83
Cumberland, riv., U.S. C10 45
Cuming, co., Nebr. C9 71
Cumming, Ga. B2 55
Cumpas, Mex. A3 34
Çumra, Tur. D9 14
Cundinamarca, dept., Col. C3 32
Cuneo, It. B1 9
Cunnamulla, Austl. E8 25
Cupertino, Calif. *D2 50
Curaçao, isl., Neth. Antilles A4 32
Curacautín, Chile B2 28
Curicó, Chile B2 28
Curicó, prov., Chile A2 28
Curitiba, Braz. D3 30
Currais Novos, Braz. *D7 27
Currituck, co., N.C. A6 76
Curry, co., N. Mex. B7 48
Curry, co., Oreg. E2 80
Curtea-de-Arges, Rom. C7 10
Curtici, Rom. B5 10
Curtis, Nebr. D5 71
Curtisville, Pa. E1, h14 81
Curug, Yugo. C5 10
Curuzú Cuatia, Arg. E4 29
Curvelo, Braz. B4 30
Curwensville, Pa. E4 81
Cushing, Okla. B5 79
Cusset, Fr. D5 5
Custer, S. Dak. G2 77
Custer, co., Colo. C5 51
Custer, co., Idaho E4 57
Custer, co., Mont. D11 70
Custer, co., Nebr. C6 79
Custer, co., Okla. B2 71
Custer, co., S. Dak. G2 77
Cut Bank, Mont. B4 70
Cutchogue, N.Y. m16 75
Cutervo, Peru C2 31
Cuthbert, Ga. E2 55
Cutler, Calif. *D4 50
Cutler Ridge, Fla. *G6 54
Cutack, India D8 20
Cutten, Calif. *B1 50
Cuxhaven, Ger., Fed. Rep. of B4 6
Cuyahoga, co., Ohio A4 78
Cuyahoga Falls, Ohio A4 78
Cuzco, Peru D3 31
Cuzco, dept., Peru D3 31
Cynthiana, Ky. B5 62
Cypress, Calif. *F4 50
Cypress Quarters, Fla. E6 54
Cyprus, country, Asia E9 14
Cyprus, isl., Asia E9 14
Cyrenaica, prov., Libya B2 23
Cyril, Okla. C3 79
Czechoslovakia, country, Eur. D4 7
Czersk, Pol. B4 7
Częstochowa, Pol. C5 7

D

Da'an, China D2 18
Dab, Pol., (part of Katowice) g9 7
Dab, Pol., (part of Szczecin) B3 7
Dabeiba, Col. B2 32
Dablice, Czech. n18 7
Dąbrowa, Pol. C6 7
Dąbrowa Gornicza, Pol. C5, g10 7
Dacca, Bngl. D9 20
Dachau, Ger., Fed. Rep. of D5 6
Dade, co., Fla. G6 54
Dade, co., Ga. B1 55
Dade, co., Mo. D4 69
Dade City, Fla. D4 54
Dadeville, Ala. C4 46
Dadra and Nagar Haveli, ter., India *D5 20
Dadu, Pak. C4 20
Daet, Phil. *C6 19
Daggett, co., Utah A7 72
Dagupan, Phil n13 19
Dahlgren, Va. B5 85
Dahlonega, Ga. B3 55
Dailey, W. Va. C5 87
Daimiel, Sp. C4 8
Daingerfield, Tex. C5 84
Daio, Jap. o15 18
Dairen, see Lüda, China
Dairy Valley, Calif. *F4 50
Daisetta, Tex. D5 84
Daisytown, Pa. *F1 81
Dajabon, Dom. Rep. E8 35
Dakar, Sen. F1 22
Dakota, co., Minn. F5 67
Dakota, co., Nebr. B9 71
Dakota City, Nebr. B9 71
Da Lat, Viet. C3 19
D'Albertis Dome, mtn., Pap. N. Gui. h11 25
Dalby, Austl. E9 25
Dale, Ind. H4 59
Dale, Pa. *E4 81
Dale, co., Ala. D4 46
Daleville, Ind. D6 59
Dalhart, Tex. A1 84
Dalhousie, N.B., Can. A3 43
Dall, mtn., Alsk. f15 47
Dallam, co., Tex. A1 84
Dallas, Ga. C2 55
Dallas, N.C. B1 76
Dallas, Oreg. C3 80
Dallas, Pa. D10, m17 81
Dallas, Tex. C4, n10 84
Dallas, co., Ala. C2 46
Dallas, co., Ark. D3 49
Dallas, co., Iowa C3 60
Dallas, co., Mo. D4 69
Dallas, co., Tex. C4 84
Dallas Center, Iowa C4 60
Dallas City, Ill. C2 58
Dallastown, Pa. G8 81
Dalmatia, reg., Yugo D3 10
Dalmellington, Scot. C4 4
Dalnerechensk, Sov. Un. E16 13
Dalnyaya, Sov. Un. D11 18
Dalrymple, mtn., Austl. D8 25
Dalton, Ga. B2 55
Dalton, Mass. B1 65
Dalton, Ohio B4 78
Dalton, Pa. C10 81
Daltonganj, India D7 20
Dalton Gardens, Idaho B2 57
Daly City, Calif. h8 50
Damān, India D5 20
Damanhūr, Eg. G8 14
Damariscotta, Maine D3 64
Damascus, Md. B3 53
Damascus, Va. f10 85
Damascus (Dimashq), Syr. F11 14
Da Nang, Viet. B3 19
Dana Point, Calif. *F5 50
Danbury, Conn. D3 52
Dandong, China C9 17
Dane, co., Wis. E4 88
Dania, Fla. F6, r13 54

E

F

Fayetteville, N.Y. ... B5 75
Fayetteville, N.C. ... B4 76
Fayetteville, Pa. ... G6 81
Fayetteville, Tenn. ... B5 83
Fayetteville, W.Va. ... C3,m13 87
Fayville, Mass. ... g9 65
Feasterville, Pa. ... o21 81
Feather Falls, Calif. ... C3 50
Fécamp, Fr. ... C4 5
Federalsburg, Md. ... C6 53
Federal Way, Wash. ... *B3 86
Fedscreek, Ky. ... C7 62
Feeding Hills, Mass. ... B2 65
Feilding, N.Z. ... N15 26
Feira de Santana, Braz. ... *E7 27
Fejér, co., Hung. ... *B4 10
Felanitx, Sp. ... C7 8
Feldkirch, Aus. ... E4 6
Felicity, Ohio ... D1 78
Felipe Carrillo Puerto, Mex. ... D7 34
Fellsmere, Fla. ... E6 54
Felton, Calif. ... D2 50
Feltre, It. ... A3 9
Fenelon Falls, Ont., Can. ... C6 41
Fengshan, Taiwan ... *G9 17
Fennimore, Wis. ... F3 88
Fennville, Mich. ... F4 66
Fenton, Mich. ... F7 66
Fenton, Mo. ... f13 69
Fentress, co., Tenn. ... C9 83
Fenyang, China ... D7 17
Fedosiya, Sov. Un. ... I10 12
Ferdinand, Ind. ... H4 59
Ferentino, It. ... D4 9
Fergana, Sov. Un. ... *E10 13
Fergus, Ont., Can. ... D4 41
Fergus, co., Mont. ... C7 70
Fergus Falls, Minn. ... D2 67
Ferguson, Mo. ... C7, f13 69
Fermanagh, co., N.Ire. ... *C3 4
Ferme-Neuve, Que., Can. ... C2 42
Fermo, It. ... C4 9
Fernandina Beach, Fla. ... B5, k9 54
Fern Creek, Ky. ... g11 62
Ferndale, Calif. ... B1 50
Ferndale, Md. ... B4 53
Ferndale, Mich. ... *F7 66
Ferndale, Pa. ... F4 81
Ferndale, Wash. ... A3 86
Fernie, B.C., Can. ... E10 37
Fern Park, Fla. ... D5 54
Fernwood, N.Y. ... B4 75
Ferrara, It. ... B3 9
Ferreñafe, Peru ... C2 31
Ferriday, La. ... C4 63
Ferris, Ont., Can. ... *A5 41
Ferris, Tex. ... C4, n10 84
Ferris, mts., Wyo ... D5 89
Ferry, co., Wash. ... A7 86
Ferryland, Newf., Can. ... E5 44
Ferrysburg, Mich. ... *E4 66
Ferryville, Tun. ... F2 9
Fertile, Minn. ... C2 67
Fès, Mor. ... B3 22
Fessenden, N. Dak. ... C6 77
Festus, Mo. ... C7, g13 69
Fetesti, Rom. ... C8 10
Fetters Hot Springs, Calif. ... *C2 50
Ffestiniog, Wales ... D5 4
Fianarantsoa, Malag. ... E9 24
Fidenza, It. ... B3 9
Fieldale, Va. ... D3 85
Fier, Alb. ... *B2 14
Fierro Urco, vol., Peru ... B2 31
Fife, co., Sask., Can. ... *B5 4
Fife, Wash. ... *B3 86
Figeac, Fr. ... E4 5
Figueira da Foz, Port. ... B1 8
Figueras, Sp. ... A7 8
Fiji, country, Oceania ... H8 2
Filer, Idaho ... G4 57
Filiatra, Grc. ... D3 14
Fillmore, Calif. ... E4 50
Fillmore, Utah ... B5 72
Fillmore, co., Minn. ... G6 67
Fillmore, co., Nebr. ... D8 71
Finderne, N.J. ... *B3 74
Findlay, Ohio ... A2 78
Findlay, Ill. ... D5 58
Findlay, mtn., B.C., Can. ... D9 37
Finistère, dept., Fr. ... *C2 5
Finland, country, Eur. ... E12 11
Finney, co., Kans. ... D3 61
Finneytown, Ohio ... *C1 78
Finnmark, co., Nor. ... *B13 11
Finspång, Swe. ... u33 11
Finsterwalde, Ger. Dem. Rep. ... C6 6
Firat (Euphrates) riv.,
   Asia ... D12 14
Fircrest, Wash. ... f10 86
Firebaugh, Calif. ... D3 50
Firenze, see Florence, It.

Firenzuola, It. ... B3 9
Firminy, Fr. ... E6 5
Firozabad, India ... *C6 20
Firozpur, India ... B5 20
Fisher, Ill. ... C5 58
Fisher, co., Tex. ... C2 84
Fisher, peak, Va. ... D2 85
Fishersville, Va. ... B4 85
Fishguard, Wales ... E4 4
Fishing Creek, Md. ... D5 53
Fishkill, N.Y. ... D7 75
Fiskdale, Mass. ... D3 65
Fitchburg, Mass. ... A4 65
Fitzgerald, Ga. ... E3 55
Fitz Roy, mtn., Arg. ... D2 28
Fiume, see Rijeka, Yugo.
Five Points, N.Mex. ... *B3 48
Flagler, co., Fla. ... C5 54
Flagler Beach, Fla. ... C5 54
Flagstaff, Ariz. ... B3 48
Flagtown, N.J. ... B3 74
Flanagan, Ill. ... C5 58
Flanders, N.Y. ... *n16 75
Flandreau, S.Dak. ... F9 77
Flat Creek, Ala. ... B2, f6 46
Flathead, co., Mont. ... B2 70
Flathead, mts., Mont. ... B2 70
Flatonia, Tex. ... E4 84
Flat River, Mo. ... D7 69
Flat Rock, Newf., Can. ... *E5 44
Flat Rock, Mich. ... F7 66
Flat Rock, N.C. ... f10 76
Flatwoods, Ky. ... B7 62
Fleetwing Estates, Pa. ... *F11 81
Fleetwood, Pa. ... F10 81
Fleming, co., Ky. ... B6 62
Flemingsburg, Ky. ... B6 62
Flemington, N.J. ... B3 74
Flemington, Pa. ... D7 81
Flensburg, Ger., Fed. Rep. of ... A4 6
Flers, Fr. ... C3 5
Fletcher, N.C. ... f10 76
Fletcher, Okla. ... C4 79
Flin Flon, Man., Can. ... B1, g7 40
Flint, Mich. ... F7 66
Flint, co., Wales ... *D5 4
Flintridge, Calif. ... *F4 50
Flomaton, Ala. ... D2 46
Floodwood, Minn. ... D6 67
Flora, Ill. ... E5 58
Flora, Ind. ... C4 59
Florala, Ala. ... D3 46
Floral City, Fla. ... D4 54
Floral Park, Mont. ... *D4 70
Floral Park, N.Y. ... k13 75
Flordell Hills, Mo. ... *C7 69
Florence, Ala. ... A2 46
Florence, Ariz. ... C3, D2 48
Florence, Calif. ... *E4 50
Florence, Colo. ... C5 51
Florence (Firenze), It. ... C3 9
Florence, Kans. ... D7 61
Florence, KY. ... B5, k13 62
Florence, N.J. ... C3 74
Florence, Oreg. ... D2 80
Florence, S.C. ... C8 82
Florence, Wis. ... C5 88
Florence, co., S.C. ... C8 82
Florence, co., Wis. ... C5 88
Florence (Firenze), It. ... C3 9
Florencia, Col. ... C2 32
Flores, Guat. ... H12 33
Flores, isl., Indon. ... G6 19
Flores, dept., Ur. ... *E1 30
Floresville, Tex. ... E3, k7 84
Florham Park, N.J. ... B4 74
Floriano, Braz. ... D6 27
Florianópolis, Braz. ... D3 30
Florida, Cuba ... D6, m14 35
Florida, N.Y. ... *E1 30
Florida, Ur. ... *E1 30
Florida, dept., Ur. ... *E1 30
Florida, state, U.S. ... E10 45
Florida, bay, Fla. ... E10 54
Florida City, Fla. ... G6, t13 54
Florida Keys, is., Fla. ... H6 54
Florina, Grc. ... E5 10
Flórina, prov., Grc. ... *B3 14
Florissant, Mo. ... f13 69
Flossmoor, Ill. ... k9 58
Flourtown, Pa. ... o21 81
Flower Hill, N.Y. ... *E7 75
Floyd, co., Ga. ... B1 55
Floyd, co., Ind. ... H6 59
Floyd, co., Iowa ... A5 60
Floyd, co., Ky. ... C7 62
Floyd, co., Tex. ... B2 84
Floyd, co., Va. ... D2 85
Floydada, Tex. ... B2 84
Flushing, Mich. ... E7 66
Flushing, Ohio ... B4 78
Fluvanna, co., Va. ... C4 85
Foam Lake, Sask., Can. ... F4 39

Foard, co., Tex. ... B3 84
Focșani, Rom. ... C8 10
Foggia, It. ... D5 9
Fogo, Newf., Can. ... D4 44
Fohnsdorf, Aus. ... E7 6
Foix, Fr. ... F4 5
Folcroft, Pa. ... *G11 81
Foley, Ala. ... E2 46
Foley, Minn. ... E5 67
Foligno, It. ... C4 9
Folkestone, Eng. ... E7 4
Folkston, Ga. ... F4 55
Follansbee, W. Va. ... A4, f8 87
Follonica, It. ... C3 9
Folly Beach, S.C. ... F8, k12 82
Folsom, Calif. ... *C3 50
Folsom, Pa. ... *G11 81
Fomento, Cuba ... C4 35
Fonda, Iowa ... B3 60
Fonda, N.Y. ... C6 75
Fond du Lac, Wis. ... E5, k9 88
Fond du Lac, co., Wis. ... E5 88
Fondi, It. ... D4 9
Fonsagrada, Sp. ... A2 8
Fontainebleau, Fr. ... C5 5
Fontana, Calif. ... m14 50
Fontana, Wis. ... F5 88
Fontanelle, Iowa ... C3 60
Fontenay-le-Comte, Fr. ... D3 5
Fontenay -sous-Bois, Fr. ... g10 5
Foochow, see Fuzhou, China
Footville, Wis. ... F4 88
Forbach, Fr. ... C7 5
Forbes, Austl. ... F8 25
Forbes, mtn., Alta., Can. ... D2 38
Forchheim, Ger., Fed. Rep. of ... D5 6
Ford, co., Ill. ... C5 58
Ford, co., Kans. ... E4 61
Ford City, Calif. ... E4 50
Ford City, Pa. ... E2 81
Fords, N.J. ... *B4 74
Fords Prairie, Wash. ... *C3 86
Fordyce, Ark. ... D3 49
Foreman, Ark. ... D1 49
Forest, Bel. ... B6 5
Forest, Ont., Can. ... D2 41
Forest, Miss. ... C4 68
Forest, Ohio ... B2 78
Forest, co., Pa. ... C3 81
Forest, co., Wis. ... C5 88
Forest Acres, S.C. ... C6 82
Forestburg, Alta., Can. ... C4 38
Forest City, Iowa ... A4 60
Forest City, N.C. ... B1, f11 76
Forest City, Pa. ... C11 81
Forest Grove, Oreg. ... B3, g11 80
Forest Heights, Md. ... *C4 53
Forest Hills, N.B., Can. ... *D4 43
Forest Hill, Tex. ... *C4 84
Forest Hills, Pa. ... k14 81
Forest Homes, Ill. ... *E3 58
Forest Knolls, Calif. ... g7 50
Forest Lake, Minn. ... E6 67
Forest Park, Ga. ... h8 55
Forest Park, Ill. ... k9 58
Forestview, Ill. ... *B6 58
Forestville, Md. ... *C4 53
Forestville, N.Y. ... C1 75
Forfar, Scot. ... B5 4
Forge Village, Mass. ... A5, f10 65
Forked River, N.J. ... D4 74
Forks, Wash. ... B1 86
Forli, It. ... B4 9
Formiga, Braz. ... C3 30
Formosa, Arg. ... E4 29
Formosa, prov., Arg. ... E4 29
Formosa, see Taiwan, Asia
Forney, Tex. ... C4, n10 84
Forres, Scot. ... B5 4
Forrest, Ill. ... C5 58
Forrest, co., Miss. ... D4 68
Forrest City, Ark. ... B5 49
Forreston, Ill. ... A4 58
Forst, Ger. Dem. Rep. ... C7 6
Forster-Tuncurry,
   Austl. ... F9 26
Forsyth, Ga. ... C3 55
Forsyth, Mont. ... D10 70
Forsyth, co., Ga. ... B2 55
Forsyth, co., N.C. ... A2 76
Fortaleza, Braz. ... D7 27
Fort Atkinson, Wis. ... F5 88
Fort Bend, co., Tex. ... E5 84
Fort Benton, Mont. ... C6 70
Fort Bragg, Calif. ... C2 50
Fort Branch, Ind. ... H2 59
Fort Chipewyan, Alta., Can. ... f8 38
Fort Cobb, Okla. ... B3 79
Fort Collins, Colo. ... A5 51
Fort Collins West, Colo. ... *A5 51
Fort Coulonge, Que., Can. ... B8 41
Fort Covington, N.Y. ... f10 75
Fort Davis, Tex. ... o13 84

Fort-de France, Mart. ... I14 35
Fort Deposit, Ala. ... D3 46
Fort Dodge, Iowa ... B3 60
Fort Edward, N.Y. ... B7 75
Fort Erie, Ont., Can. ... E6 41
Fort Fairfield, Maine ... B7 64
Fort Frances, Ont., Can. ... o16 41
Fort Gaines, Ga. ... E1 55
Fort-George, Que., Can. ... h11 42
Fort Gibson, Okla. ... B6 79
Fort Hall, Idaho ... F6 57
Fort Hancock, Tex. ... o12 84
Fort Howard, Md. ... B5 53
Fort Johnson, N.Y. ... *C6 75
Fort Kent, Maine ... A4 64
Fort-Lamy, see Ndjamena, Chad
Fort Langley, B.C., Can. ... f13 37
Fort Lauderdale, Fla. ... F6, r13 54
Fort Lee, N.J. ... h9 74
Fort Levenworth, Kans. ... C8, k15 61
Fort-Liberté, Hai. ... E8 35
Fort Loramie, Ohio ... B1 78
Fort Lupton, Colo. ... A6 51
Fort Macleod, Alta., Can. ... E4 38
Fort Madison, Iowa ... D6 60
Fort McKinley, Ohio ... *C1 78
Fort Meade, Fla. ... E5 54
Fort Mill, S.C. ... A6 82
Fort Morgan, Colo. ... A7 51
Fort Myers, Fla. ... F5 54
Fort Myers Beach, Fla. ... F5 54
Fort Nelson, B.C., Can. ... m18 37
Fort Oglethorpe, Ga. ... B1 55
Fort Payne, Ala. ... A4 46
Fort Peck, Mont. ... B10 70
Fort Pierce, Fla. ... E6 54
Fort Pierre, S. Dak. ... F5 77
Fort Plain, N.Y. ... C6 75
Fort Qu'Appelle, Sask., Can. ... G4 39
Fort Recovery, Ohio ... B1 78
Fort Riley, Kans. ... C7 61
Fort St. James, B.C., Can. ... B5 37
Fort St. John, B.C., Can. ... A7, m18 37
Fort Saskatchewan, Alta., Can. ... C4 38
Fort Scott, Kans. ... E9 61
Fort Shawnee, Ohio ... B1 78
Fort Smith, Ark. ... B1 49
Fort St. John, B.C., Can. ... A7, m18 37
Fort Stockton, Tex. ... D1 84
Fort Sumner, N. Mex. ... B6 48
Fort Thomas, Ky. ... h14 62
Fortuna, Calif. ... B1 50
Fortune, Newf., Can. ... E4 44
Fort Valley, Ga. ... D3 55
Fort Vermilion, Alta., Can. ... f7 38
Fortville, Ind. ... D6 59
Fort Walton Beach, Fla. ... u15 54
Fort Washington, Pa. ... o21 81
Fort Washington Forest,
   Md. ... C4 53
Fort Wayne, Ind. ... B7 59
Fort William, Scot. ... B4 4
Fort Worth, Tex. ... C4, n9 84
Fort Wright, Ky. ... h13 62
Fort Yates, N. Dak. ... D5 77
Forty Fort, Pa. ... D10, n17 81
Fossano, It. ... B1 9
Fossil, Oreg. ... B6 80
Fossombrone, It. ... C4 9
Fosston, Minn. ... C3 67
Foster, co., N. Dak. ... C7 77
Foster Brook, Pa. ... C4 81
Foster Village, Haw. ... g10 56
Fostoria, Ohio ... A2 78
Fougères, Fr. ... C3 5
Foumban, Cam. ... G7 22
Fountain, Colo. ... C6 51
Fountain, co., Ind. ... D3 59
Fountain, peak, Calif. ... E6 50
Fountain City, Ind. ... E8 59
Fountain City, Wis. ... D2 88
Fountain Green, Utah ... B6 72
Fountain Hill, Pa. ... E11 81
Fountain Inn, S.C. ... B3 82
Fountain Place, La. ... *D4 63
Fountain Valley, Calif. ... *F5 50
Four Corners, Oreg. ... *C4 80
Fourmies, Fr. ... B6 5
Four Oaks, N.C. ... B4 76
Fowler, Calif. ... D4 50
Fowler, Colo. ... C6 51
Fowler, Ind. ... C3 59
Fowler, Kans. ... E3 61
Fowler, Mich. ... E6 66
Fowlerville, Mich. ... F6 66
Foxboro, Mass. ... B5 65
Fox Chapel, Pa. ... *E1 81
Fox Farm, Wyo ... *E8 89
Fox Harbour, Newf., Can. ... E5 44
Fox Lake, Ill. ... A5, h8 58
Fox Lake, Wis. ... E5 88
Fox Point, Wis. ... E5, m12 88
Fox River Grove, Ill. ... h8 58

Foxworth, Miss. ... D4 68
Frackville, Pa. ... E9 81
Fraga, Sp. ... B6 8
Framingham, Mass. ... B5, g10 65
Franca, Braz. ... C3 30
Francavilla Fontana, It. ... D6 9
France, country, Eur. ... 5
Francesville, Ind. ... C4 9
Franche-Comté reg., Fr. ... D6 5
Francistown, Bots. ... E5 24
Franconville, Fr. ... g9 5
Frankenberg, Ger., Fed. Rep. of ... C4 6
Frankenmuth, Mich. ... E7 66
Frankenthal, Ger., Fed. Rep. of ... D4 6
Frankford, Ont., Can. ... C7 41
Frankfort, Ill. ... m9 58
Frankfort, Ind. ... D4 59
Frankfort, Kans. ... C7 61
Frankfort, Ky. ... B5 62
Frankfort, Mich. ... D4 66
Frankfort, N.Y. ... B5 75
Frankfurt *am Main*, Ger., Fed. Rep. of ... C4 6
Frankfurt *an der Oder*, Ger. Dem. Rep ... B7 6
Franklin, Idaho ... *F2 57
Franklin, Ind. ... F5 59
Franklin, Kans. ... E9 61
Franklin, Ky. ... D3 62
Franklin, La. ... E4 63
Franklin, Mass. ... B5 65
Franklin, Mich. ... *F7 66
Franklin, Nebr. ... D7 71
Franklin, N.H. ... E4 73
Franklin, N.J. ... A3 74
Franklin, N.C. ... f9 76
Franklin, Ohio ... C1 78
Franklin, Pa. ... *E4 81
Franklin, Pa. ... D2 81
Franklin, Tenn. ... B5 83
Franklin, Tex. ... D4 84
Franklin (Independent City) Va. ... D6 85
Franklin, Wis. ... n11 88
Franklin, co., Ala. ... A2 46
Franklin, co., Ark. ... B2 49
Franklin, co., Fla. ... C2 54
Franklin, co., Ga. ... B3 55
Franklin, co., Idaho ... G7 57
Franklin, co., Ill. ... E5 58
Franklin, co., Ind. ... F7 59
Franklin, co., Iowa ... B4 60
Franklin, co., Kans. ... D8 61
Franklin, co., Ky. ... B5 62
Franklin, co., Maine ... C2 64
Franklin, co., Mass. ... A2 65
Franklin, co., Miss. ... D3 68
Franklin, co., Mo. ... C6 69
Franklin, co., Nebr. ... D7 71
Franklin, co., N.Y. ... A6 75
Franklin, co., N.C. ... A4 76
Franklin, co., Ohio ... B2 78
Franklin, co., Pa. ... G6 81
Franklin, co., Tenn. ... B5 83
Franklin, co., Tex. ... C5 84
Franklin, co., Vt. ... B2 73
Franklin, co., Va. ... D3 85
Franklin, co., Wash. ... C6 86
Franklin, dist., N. W. Ter., Can. ... B13 36
Franklin, par.,La. ... B4 63
Franklin Furnace, Ohio ... D3 78
Franklin Grove, Ill. ... B4 58
Franklin Lakes, N.J. ... *B4 74

Franklin Park, Ill. ... k9 58
Franklin Park, N.J. ... C3 74
Franklin Park, Va. ... *B5 85
Franklin Square, N.Y. ... G2 52
Franklinton La. ... D5 63
Franklinton, N.C. ... A4 76
Franklinville, N.J. ... D2 74
Franklinville, N.Y. ... C2 75
Franklinville, N.C. ... B3 76
Frankston, Tex. ... C5 84
Frankton, Ind. ... D6 59
Frascati, It. ... D4, h9 9
Fraser, Mich. ... *F8 66
Fraser, riv., B.C., Can. ... C6 37
Fraser, mtn., B.C., Can. ... C8 37
Fraserburgh, Scot. ... B6 4
Frauenfeld, Switz. ... E4 6
Fray Bentos, Ur. ... E1 30
Frazee, Minn. ... D3 67
Frazeyburg, Ohio ... B3 78
Frazier Park, Calif. ... E4 50
Frederic, Wis. ... C1 88
Fredericia, Den. ... J3 11
Frederick, Md. ... B3 53
Frederick, Okla. ... C2 79
Frederick, co., Md. ... B3 53
Frederick, co., Va. ... A4 85
Fredericksburg, Iowa ... B5 60
Fredericksburg, Pa. ... *F9 81
Fredericksburg, Tex. ... D3 84
Fredericksburg (Independent City), Va. ... B5 85
Fredericktown, Mo. ... D7 69
Fredericktown, Ohio ... B3 78
Fredericktown, Pa. ... F1 81
Fredericton, N.B., Can. ... D3 43
Frederiksborg, co., Den. ... *J5 11
Frederikshavn, Den. ... I4 11
Frederiksted, Vir. Is., (U.S.) ... H12 35
Fredonia, Kans. ... E8 61
Fredonia, N.Y. ... C1 75
Fredonia, Pa. ... D1 81
Fredonia, Wis. ... E6 88
Fredrikstad, Nor. ... H4, p28 11
Freeborn, co., Minn. ... G5 67
Freeburg, Ill. ... E4 58
Freedom, Calif. ... *D3 50
Freedom, Pa. ... E1 81
Freehold, N.J. ... C4 74
Freel, peak, Calif. ... C4 50
Freeland, Mich. ... E6 66
Freeland, Pa. ... D10 81
Freelandville, Ind. ... G3 59
Freeman, S. Dak. ... G8 77
Freemansburg, Pa. ... E11 81
Freeport, Fla. ... u15 54
Freeport, Ill. ... A4 58
Freeport, Maine ... E2, g7 64
Freeport ,Minn. ... E4 67
Freeport, N.Y. ... G2 52
Freeport, Pa. ... E2 81
Freeport, Tex. ... E5, s14 84
Freer, Tex. ... F3 84
Freestone, co., Tex. ... D4 84
Freetown, N.Y. ... *m16 75
Freetown, S.L. ... G2 22
Fregenal de la Sierra, Sp. ... C2 8
Freiberg, Ger. Dem. Rep ... C6 6
Freiburg *im Breisgau*, Ger., Fed. Rep. of ... D3 6
Freising, Ger., Fed. Rep. of ... D5 6
Freistadt, Aus. ... D7 6
Fréjus, Fr. ... F3 5

Fremantle, Austl. ... F2 25
Fremont, Calif. ... D2, h9 50
Fremont, Ind. ... A8 59
Fremont, Mich. ... E5 66
Fremont, Nebr. ... C9, g11 71
Fremont, N.C. ... B5 76
Fremont, Ohio ... A2 78
Fremont, co., Colo. ... C5 51
Fremont, co., Idaho ... E7 57
Fremont, co., Iowa ... D2 60
Fremont, co., Wyo. ... C4 89
French Camp, Calif. ... *D3 50
French Guiana, dep., S.A. ... C5 27
French Lick, Ind. ... G4 59
French Polynesia, Fr. dep., Oceania ... *H11 2
Frenchtown, N.J. ... B2 74
Frenchville, Maine ... A4 64
Freshfield, mtn., Alta., Can. ... D9 37
Freshwater, Newf., Can. ... *f9 44
Fresnillo de González Echeverría, Mex. ... C4 34
Fresno, Calif. ... D4 50
Fresno, co., Calif. ... D4 50
Freudenstadt, Ger., Fed. Rep. of ... D4 6
Frewsburg, N.Y. ... C1 75
Friant, Calif. ... D4 50
Friars Point, Miss. ... A3 68
Frias, Arg. ... E2 29
Fribourg, Switz. ... E8 6
Fribourg, canton, Switz. ... *E3 6
Friday Harbor, Wash. ... A2 86
Fridley, Minn. ... m12 67
Friedberg, Ger., Fed. Rep. of ... B6 6
Friedens, Pa. ... F4 81
Friedland, Ger. Dem. Rep. ... B6 6
Friedrichshafen, Ger., Fed. Rep. of ... E4 6
Friend, Nebr. ... D8 71
Friendship, N.Y. ... C2 75
Friern Barnet, Eng. ... k12 4
Fries, Va. ... D2 85
Friesland, prov., Neth. ... *A6 5
Frio, co., Tex. ... E3 84
Friona, Tex. ... B1 84
Frisco, Pa. ... *E1 81
Frisco, Tex. ... *C4 84
Frisco City, Ala. ... D2 46
Fritch, Tex. ... B2 84
Fritzlar, Ger., Fed. Rep. of ... C4 6
Friuli-Venezia Giulia, reg., It. ... *B4 9
Frontenac, Kans. ... E9 61
Frontenac, Mo. ... *C7 69
Frontenac, co., Ont., Can. ... C8 41
Frontenac, co., Que., Can. ... D7 42
Frontera, Mex. ... D6 34
Frontier, co., Nebr. ... D5 71
Frontignan, Fr. ... F5 5
Frontino, peak, Col. ... B2 32
Front Royal, Va. ... B4 85
Frosinone, It. ... D4 9
Frostburg, Md. ... k13 53
Frostproof, Fla. ... E5 54
Frouard, Fr. ... C7 4
Fruita, Colo. ... B2 51
Fruitdale, Oreg. ... *E3 80
Fruitland, Idaho ... F2 57
Fruitland, Ill. ... *B3 58
Fruitland, Md. ... D6 53
Fruitland Park, Fla. ... D5 54
Fruitport, Mich. ... E4 66
Fruitvale, Wash. ... *C5 86

Fruitville, Fla. ... E4, q11 54
Frunze, Sov. Un. ... E10 13
Frýdek-Místek,Czech. ... D5 7
Fryeburg, Maine ... D2 64
Fthiotis (Phthiotis), prov., Grc. ... *C4 14
Fuchou see Fuzhou, China
Fuchu, Jap. ... *I9 18
Fuente Alamo, Sp. ... D5 8
Fuente de Cantos, Sp. ... C2 8
Fuenteovejuna, Sp. ... C3 8
Fuhai, China ... B2 17
Fuji, Jap. ... n17 18
Fuji, vol., Jap. ... I9, n17 18
Fujian, prov., China ... F8 17
Fujieda, Jap. ... o17 18
Fujimi, Jap. ... n17 18
Fujin, China ... B11 17
Fujinomiya, Jap. ... n17 18
Fujisawa, Jap. ... *I9 18
Fuji-yoshida, Jap. ... n17 18
Fukagawa, Jap. ... E10 18
Fukuchiyama, Jap. ... I7, n14 18
Fukui, Jap. ... H8 18
Fukui, pref., Jap. ... *H8 18
Fukuoka, Jap. ... F10 18
Fukuoka, Jap. ... J5 18
Fukuoka, pref., Jap. ... *J5 18
Fukushima, Jap. ... I8, n16 18
Fukushima, Jap. ... H10 18
Fukushima, pref., Jap. ... *H10 18
Fukuyama, Jap. ... I6 18
Fulda, Ger., Fed. Rep. of ... C4 6
Fulda, Minn. ... G3 67
Fullerton, Calif. ... n13 50
Fullerton, Ky. ... B7 62
Fullerton, Nebr. ... C8 71
Fulton, Ill. ... B3 58
Fulton, Ky. ... f9 62
Fulton, Miss. ... A5 68
Fulton, Mo. ... C6 69
Fulton, N.Y. ... B4 75
Fulton, co., Ark. ... A4 49
Fulton, co., Ga. ... C2 55
Fulton, co., Ill. ... C3 58
Fulton, co., Ind. ... B5 59
Fulton, co., Ky. ... B2 62
Fulton, co., N.Y. ... B6 75
Fulton, co., Ohio ... A1 78
Fulton, co., Pa. ... G5 81
Fultondale, Ala. ... f7 46
Fumay, Fr. ... C6 5
Funabashi, Jap. ... n19 18
Funchal, Port. ... h12 8
Fundación, Col. ... A3 32
Funkstown, Md. ... A2 53
Fuquay-Varina, N.C. ... *B4 76
Furano, Jap. ... E11 18
Furman University,S.C. ... *B3 82
Furnas, co., Nebr. ... D6 71
Fürstenfeld, Aus. ... E8 6
Fürstenwalde, Ger. Dem. Rep. ... B7 6
Fürth, Ger., Fed. Rep. of ... D5 6
Furukawa, Jap. ... H8, m16 18
Fusagasugá, Col. ... C3 32
Fushun, China ... C9 17
Fusong, China ... E3 18
Füssen, Ger., Fed. Rep. of ... E5 6
Fuxin, China ... C9 17
Fuyang, China ... E8 17
Fuyu, China ... B9 17
Fuyuan, China ... B7 18
Fuzhou, China ... F8 17

G

Gabès, Tun. ... B7 22
Gabin, Pol. ... B5 7
Gabon (Gabun),country, Afr. ... I7 22
Gaborone, Bots. ... E5 24
Gabrovo, Bul. ... D7 10
Gadag, India ... E6 20
Gadsden, Ala. ... A3 46
Gadsden, co., Fla. ... B2 54
Gadyach, Sov.Un. ... F9 12
Gǎesti, Rom. ... C7 10
Gaeta, It. ... D4 9
Gaffney, S.C. ... A4 82
Gafsa, Tun. ... B6 22
Gage, co., Nebr. ... D9 71
Gages Lake, Ill. ... *A5 58

Gagnon, Que., Can. ... h13 42
Gagny, Fr. ... g11 5
Gahanna, Ohio ... k11 78
Gaillac, Fr. ... F4 5
Gaines, co., Tex. ... C1 84
Gainesboro, Tenn. ... C8 83
Gainesville, Fla. ... C4 54
Gainesville, Ga. ... B3 55
Gainesville, Tex. ... C4 84
Gainsborough, Eng. ... D6 4
Gairdner, lake, Austl. ... F6 25
Gairloch, Scot. ... B4 4
Gaithersburg, Md. ... B3 53
Gaixian, China ... C9 17
Galacz, see Galati, Rom.

Galápagos, prov., Ec. ... g5 31
Galashiels, Scot. ... C5 4
Galati, Rom. ... C8 10
Galatia, Ill. ... F5 58
Galatina, It. ... D7 9
Galax (Independent City), Va. ... D2 85
Gáldar, Sp. ... m14 8
Galeana, Mex. ... A3 34
Galena, Ill. ... A3 58
Galena, Kans. ... E9 61
Galena Park, Tex. ... r14 84
Gales, peak, Oreg. ... g11 80
Galesburg, Ill. ... C3 58
Galesburg, Mich. ... F5 66
Galesville, Md. ... C4 53

Galesville, Wis. ... D2 88
Galeton, Pa. ... C6 81
Galeville, N.Y. ... *B4 75
Galicia, reg., Pol., Sov. Un. ... D6 7
Galicia, reg., Sp. ... A1 8
Galien, Mich. ... G4 66
Galion, Ohio ... B3 78
Gallarate, It. ... B1 9
Gallatin, Mo. ... B4 69
Gallatin, Tenn. ... A5 83
Gallatin, co., Ill. ... F5 58
Gallatin, co., Ky. ... B5 62
Gallatin, co., Mont. ... E5 70
Galle, Sri Lanka ... G7 20
Gallia, co., Ohio ... D3 78

H

Hillsdale, Mo. ...*C7 69
Hillsdale, N.J. ...g8 74
Hillsdale, co., Mich. ...G6 66
Hillside, Ill. ...*B6 58
Hillside, N.J. ...k8 74
Hillside Manor, N.Y. ...*G2 52
Hillsville, Pa. ...D1 81
Hillsville, Va. ...D2 85
Hilltop, N.J. ...*D2 74
Hillwood, Va. ...*B5 85
Hilo, Haw. ...D6, n16 56
Hilton, N.Y. ...B3 75
Hilversum, Neth. ...A6 5
Himachal Pradesh, state, India ...*B6 20
Himalayas, mts., India ...C7 20
Himeji, Jap. ...I7 18
Himi, Jap. ...H8 18
Hims, (Homs), Syr. ...B5 23
Hinche, Hai ...E7 35
Hinckley, Ill. ...B5 58
Hinckley, Minn. ...D6 67
Hindenburg, see Zabrze, Pol.
Hinds, co., Miss. ...C3 68
Hines, Oreg. ...D7 80
Hinesville, Ga. ...D5 55
Hingham, Mass. ...B6, h12 65
Hinojosa del Duque, Sp. ...C3 8
Hinsdale, Ill. ...k9 58
Hinsdale, Mass. ...B1 65
Hinsdale, N.H. ...F3 73
Hinsdale, co., Colo. ...D3 51
Hinton, Alta., Can. ...C2 38
Hinton, Okla. ...B3 79
Hinton, W. Va. ...D4 87
Hirakata, Jap. ...*I7 18
Hiram, Ohio ...A4 78
Hiratsuka, Jap. ...n17 18
Hiroo, Jap. ...E11 18
Hirosaki, Jap. ...F10 18
Hiroshima, Jap ...I6 18
Hiroshima, pref., Jap. ...*I6 18
Hirson, Fr. ...C5 5
Hisãr, India ...C6 20
Hispaniola, isl., N.A. ...D8 35
Hita, Jap. ...*J5 18
Hitachi, Jap. ...H10 18
Hitchcock, Tex. ...r14 84
Hitchcock, co., Nebr. ...D4 71
Hitchins, Ky. ...B7 62
Hitoyoshi, Jap. ...J5 18
Hixon, Tenn. ...D8, h11 83
Hjørring, Den. ...I3 11
Hjørring, co., Den. ...*I3 11
Hlohovec, Czech. ...D4 7
Hlomsak, Thai. ...*E11 20
Hoa Binh, Viet. ...*A3 19
Hobart, Austl. ...o15 25
Hobart, Ind. ...A3 59
Hobart, Okla. ...B2 79
Hobbs, N. Mex. ...C7 48
Hoboken, Bel. ...B6 5
Hoboken, N.J. ...k8 74
Ho Chi Minh City
(Saigon), Viet. ...C3 19
Hocking, co., Ohio ...C3 78
Hockley, co., Tex. ...C1 84
Hoddesdon, Eng. ...k13 4
Hodeida, Yemen ...F6 23
Hodgeman, co., Kans. ...D4 61
Hodgenville, Ky. ...C4 62
Hodgkins, Il. ...*B6 58
Hódmezővásárhely, Hung. ...B5 10
Hodonín, Czech. ...D4 7
Hoeryong, Kor. ...E4 18
Hof, Ger., Fed.,Rep of ...C5 6
Hoffman, Minn. ...E3 67
Hoffman Estates, Ill. ...h8 58
Hofu, Jap. ...I5 18
Hogansville, Ga. ...C2 55
Hogback, mtn., S.C. ...A3 82
Hohenwald, Tenn. ...B4 83
Hohhot, China ...C7 17
Ho-Ho-Kus (Hohokus) N.J. ...h8 74
Hoisington, Kans. ...D5 61
Hokah, Minn. ...G7 67
Hoke, co.,N.C. ...B3 76
Hokendauqua, Pa. ...*E10 81
Hokes Bluff, Ala. ...B4 46
Hokkaido, pref., Jap. ...*E10 18
Hokkaido, isl., Jap. ...E10 18
Holbaek, co., Den. ...*J4 11
Holbrook, Ariz. ...B3 48
Holbrook, Mass. ...B5, h11 65
Holbrook N.Y. ...*n15 75
Holden, Mass. ...B4 65
Holden, Mo. ...C4 69
Holden, W. Va. ...D2 87
Holdenville, Okla. ...B5 79
Holdrege, Nebr. ...D6 71
Holgate, Ohio ...A1 78
Holguín, Cuba ...D5 35
Hollabrunn, Aus. ...D8 6
Holladay, Utah ...*C3 72

Holland, Mich. ...F4 66
Holland, N.Y. ...C2 75
Holland, Ohio ...A2, e6 78
Hollandale, Miss. ...B3 68
Holley, N.Y. ...B2 75
Holliday, Tex. ...C3 84
Hollidaysburg, Pa. ...F5 81
Hollins, Va. ...C3 85
Hollis, Alsk. ...n23 47
Hollis, Okla. ...C2 79
Hollister, Calif. ...D3 50
Hollister, Mo. ...E4 69
Holliston, Mass. ...h10 65
Holloway Terrace, Del. ...*A6 53
Hollsopple, Pa. ...F4 81
Holly, Colo. ...C8 51
Holly, Mich. ...F7 66
Holly Hill, Fla. ...C5 54
Holly Hill, S.C. ...E7 82
Holly Oak, Del. ...A7 53
Holly Ridge, N.C. ...C5 76
Holly Springs, Miss. ...A4 68
Hollywood, Fla. ...f6, r13 54
Hollywood, La. ...*D2 63
Hollywood, Pa. ...*F11 81
Hollywood Heights, Ill. ...*E3 58
Holmdel Gardens, Kans. ...*D6 61
Holmen, Wis. ...E2 88
Holmes, Pa. ...*G11 81
Holmes, co., Fla. ...u16 54
Holmes, co., Miss. ...B3 68
Holmes, co., Ohio ...B4 78
Holmes, mtn., Wyo. ...B2 89
Holmes Beach, Fla. ...*E4 54
Holmes Run Acres, Va. ...*B5 85
Holmes Run Park, Va. ...*B5 85
Holon, Isr. ...B2 15
Holopaw, Fla. ...D5 54
Holstebro, Den. ...I3 11
Holstein, Iowa ...B2 60
Holt, Ala. ...B2 46
Holt, Mich. ...F6 66
Holt, co., Mo. ...A2 69
Holt, co., Nebr. ...B7 71
Holton, Kans. ...C8 61
Holtville, Calif. ...F6 50
Holyhead, Wales ...D4 4
Holyoke, Colo. ...A8 51
Holyoke, Mass. ...B2 65
Holyoke, range, Mass. ...B2 65
Holyrood, Kans. ...D5 61
Holzminden, Ger., Fed. Rep of ...C4 6
Homalin, Bur. ...D9 20
Homeacre, Pa. ...*E2 81
Home Corner, Ind. ...C6 59
Homécourt, Fr. ...C6 5
Homedale, Idaho ...F2 57
Homedale, Ohio ...*B2 78
Home Gardens, Calif. ...*F5 50
Home Hill, Austl. ...C8 25
Homer, Alsk. ...D6, h16 47
Homer, Ill. ...C6 58
Homer, La. ...B2 63
Homer, Mich. ...F6 66
Homer, N.Y. ...C4 75
Homer City, Pa. ...E3 81
Homerville, Ga. ...E4 55
Homestead, Fla. ...G6, t13 54
Homestead, Pa. ...k14 81
Homestead Valley, Calif. ...*C2 50
Hometown, Ill. ...*B6 58
Homewood, Ala. ...g7 46
Homewood, Calif. ...C3 50
Homewood, Ill. ...B6, k9 58
Homeworth, Ohio ...B4 78
Hominy, Okla. ...A5 79
Honaker, Va. ...e10 85
Honan, see Henan, China
Honda, Col. ...B3 32
Hondo, Tex. ...E3 84
Honduras, country, N.A. ...D7 34
Honea Path, S.C. ...C3 82
Honeoye Falls, N.Y. ...C3 75
Honesdale, Pa. ...C11 81
Honey Brook, Pa. ...F10 81
Honey Grove, Tex. ...C5 84
Honfleur, Fr. ...C4 5
Hon Gai, Viet. ...*A3 19
Hongwon, Kor. ...G3 18
Hong Kong, Br. dep.,Asia ...G7 17
Honokaa, Haw. ...C6 56
Honolulu, Haw. ...B4, g10 56
Honolulu, co., Haw. ...B3 56
Honshu, isl., Jap. ...H8 18
Honto, see Nevelsk, Sov. Un.
Hood, co., Tex. ...C4 84
Hood, mtn., Oreg. ...B5 80
Hoodoo, peak, Wash. ...A5 86
Hood River, Oreg. ...B5 80
Hood River, co., Oreg. ...B5 80
Hoodsport, Wash. ...B2 86
Hooghly-Chinsura, India ...*D8 20
Hooker, Okla. ...e9 79
Hooker, co., Nebr. ...C4 71

Hooker, mtn., B.C., Can. ...C8 37
Hooks, Tex. ...*C5 84
Hooksett, N.H. ...E5 73
Hoolehua, Haw. ...B4 56
Hooper, Nebr. ...C9 71
Hooper, Utah ...A5, C2 72
Hooper Bay, Alsk. ...C6 47
Hoopeston, Ill. ...C6 58
Hoorn, Neth. ...A6 5
Hoosac, range, Mass. ...A1 65
Hoosick Falls, N.Y. ...C7 75
Hooversville, Pa. ...F4 81
Hopatcong, N.J. ...B3 74
Hope, Ark. ...D2 49
Hope, B.C., Can. ...E7 37
Hope, Ind. ...F6 59
Hopedale, Ill. ...C4 58
Hopedale, La. ...E6 63
Hopedale, Mass. ...B4, h9 65
Hopedale, Ohio ...B5 78
Hopelawn, N.J. ...*B4 74
Hope Mills, N.C. ...C4 76
Hope Ranch, Calif. ...*E4 50
Hope Valley, R.I. ...C10 52
Hopewell, N.J. ...C3 74
Hopewell
(Independent City), Va. ...C5, n18 85
Hopewell Junction, N.Y. ...D7 75
Hopkins, Minn. ...n12 67
Hopkins, Mo. ...A3 69
Hopkins, co., Ky. ...C2 62
Hopkins, co., Tex. ...C5 84
Hopkinsville, Ky. ...D2 62
Hopkinton, Iowa ...B6 60
Hopkinton, Mass. ...B4, h9 65
Hopland, Calif. ...C2 50
Hopwood, Pa. ...G2 81
Hoquiam, Wash. ...B2 86
Hordaland, co., Nor. ...*G1 11
Horicon, Wis. ...E5 88
Hornell, N.Y. ...C3 75
Hornersville, Mo. ...E7 69
Horní Počernice, Czech. ...n18 7
Hornsea, Eng. ...D6 4
Hornsey, Eng. ...k12 4
Horqueta, Par. ...D4 29
Horry, co., S.C. ...D9 82
Horseback Knob, hill, Ohio ...C2 78
Horse Cave, Ky. ...C4 62
Horseheads, N.Y. ...C4 75
Horsens,Den. ...J3 11
Horsham, Austl. ...G7 25
Horsham, Pa. ...*F11 81
Horta, Port. (Azores) ...k9 22
Horten, Nor. ...H4, p28 11
Horton, Kans. ...C8 61
Hortonville, Wis. ...D5 88
Hoshiãrpur, India ...B6 20
Hospers, Iowa ...A2 60
Hospitalet, Sp. ...B7 8
Hotan, China ...A6 20
Hot Springs, N.C. ...f10 76
Hot Springs, S. Dak. ...G2 77
Hot Springs, co., Ark. ...C2 49
Hot Springs, co., Wyo. ...C4 89
Hot Springs, see Truth or
Consequences, N. Mex.
Hot Springs *National Park*, Ark. ...C2, f7 49
Houghton, Mich. ...A2 66
Houghton, N.Y. ...C2 75
Houghton, Wash. ...e11 86
Houghston, co., Mich. ...B2 66
Houghton Lake, Mich. ...D6 66
Houghton Lake Heights, Mich. ...D6 66
Houilles, Fr. ...g9 5
Houlton, Maine ...B5 64
Houma, La. ...E5, k10 63
Housatonic, Mass. ...B1 65
Houston, B.C., Can. ...B4 37
Houston, Minn. ...G7 67
Houston, Miss. ...B4 68
Houston, Mo. ...D6 69
Houston, Pa. ...F1 81
Houston, Tex. ...E5, r14 84
Houston, co., Ala. ...D4 46
Houston, co., Ga. ...D3 55
Houston, co., Minn. ...G7 67
Houston, co., Tenn. ...A4 83
Houston, co., Tex. ...D5 84
Houtzdale,Pa. ...E5 81
Hove, Eng. ...E6 4
Howard, Kans. ...E7 61
Howard, S. Dak. ...F8 77
Howard, Wis. ...D5, g9 88
Howard, co., Ark. ...C2 49
Howard, co., Ind. ...C5 59
Howard, co., Iowa ...A5 60
Howard, co., Md. ...B4 53
Howard, co., Mo. ...B5 69
Howard, co., Nebr. ...C7 71
Howard, co., Tex. ...C2 84
Howard City, Mich. ...E5 66
Howard Lake, Minn. ...E4 67

Howe, Ind. ...A7 59
Howell, Mich. ...F7 66
Howell, co., Mo. ...E6 69
Howells, Nebr. ...C8 71
Howick, Que., Can. ...D4 42
Howland, Maine ...C4 64
Howland, peak, Newf., Can. ...D2 44
Howrah, India ...D8 20
Howson, peak, B.C., Can. ...B4, n17 37
Hoxie, Ark. ...A5 49
Hoxie, Kans. ...C3 61
Hoya, Ger., Fed. Rep. of ...B4 6
Hoyerswerda, Ger. Dem Rep. ...C7 6
Hoyt Lakes, Minn. ...C6 67
Hradec Králové, Czech. ...C3 7
Hranice, Czech. ...D4 7
Hriňová, Czech. ...D5 7
Hrubieszów, Pol. ...C7 7
Hsinchu, Taiwan ...G9 17
Hsinkao, mtn., Taiwan ...G9 17
Hsipaw, Bur. ...*D10 20
Huacho, Peru ...D2 31
Huadian, China ...C10 17
Huaide, China ...E2 18
Huailley, Peru ...D2 31
Huainan, China ...E8 17
Hualgayoc, Peru ...C2 3
Hualien,Taiwan ...G9 17
Huamachuco, Peru ...C2 31
Huamantla, Mex. ...n15 34
Huambo, Ang. ...C3 24
Huancabamba, Peru ...C2 31
Huancané, Peru ...E4 31
Huancavelica, Peru ...D2 31
Huancavelica, dept., Peru ...D2 31
Huancayo, Peru ...D2 31
Huang He (Yellow), riv., China ...F13 16
Huangshi, China ...E8 17
Huanta, Peru ...D3 31
Huánuco, Peru ...C2 31
Huánuco, dept., Peru ...C2 31
Huaral, Peru ...D2 31
Huaráz, Peru ...C2 31
Huariaca, Peru ...C2 31
Huascaran, mtn., Peru ...C2 31
Huatabampo, Mex. ...B3 34
Huatusco de Chicuellar, Mex. ...n15 34
Huauchinango, Mex. ...m14 34
Huaytará, Peru ...D2 31
Hubbard, Iowa ...B4 60
Hubbard, Ohio ...A5 78
Hubbard, Tex. ...D4 84
Hubbard, co., Minn. ...C3 67
Hubbell, Mich. ...A2 66
Hubei, prov., China ...E7 17
Huberdeau, Que., Can. ...D3 42
Huber Heights, Ohio ...*C1 78
Hubli, India ...E6 20
Huddersfield, Eng. ...D6 4
Hudiksvall, Swe. ...G7 11
Hudson, Que., Can. ...D3, q18 42
Hudson, Iowa ...B5 60
Hudson, Mass. ...B4, g9 65
Hudson, Mich. ...g6 66
Hudson, N.H. ...F5 73
Hudson, N.Y. ...C7 75
Hudson, N.C. ...B1 76
Hudson, Ohio ...A4 78
Hudson, Pa. ...*D9 81
Hudson, Wis. ...D1 88
Hudson, co., N.J. ...B4 74
Hudson, bay, Can. ...D16 36
Hudson, mtn., Maine ...B3 64
Hudson Bay, Sask., Can. ...E4 39
Hudson Falls, N.Y. ...B7 75
Hudsonville, Mich. ...F5 66
Hudspeth, co.,Tex. ...o12 84
Hue, Viet. ...B3 19
Hueco, mts., Tex. ...o11 84
Huedin, Rom. ...B6 10
Huehuetenango, Guat. ...*D6 34
Huelma, Sp. ...D4 8
Huelva, Sp. ...D2 8
Huelva, prov., Sp. ...*D2 8
Huércal-Overa, Sp. ...D5 8
Huerfano, co., Colo. ...C6 51
Huesca, Sp. ...A5 8
Huesca, prov., Sp. ...*A5 8
Huéscar, Sp. ...D4 8
Hueytown, Ala. ...g6 46
Hughes, Ark. ...C5 49
Hughes, co., Okla. ...B5 79
Hughes, co., S. Dak. ...F6 77
Hughes Springs, Tex. ...*C5 84
Hughestown, Pa. ...*D9 81
Hughesville, Pa. ...D8 81
Hughson, Calif. ...*D3 50
Hugo, Colo. ...B7 51
Hugo, Okla. ...C6 79
Hugoton, Kans. ...E2 61
Huguley, Ala. ...*C4 6
Huichon, Kor. ...F3 18
Huila, dept., Col. ...C2 32

I

Inverness, Miss. ... B3 68
Inverness, Scot. ... B4 4
Inverness, co., N.S., Can. ... C8 43
Inverness, co., Scot. ... *B4 4
Invisible, mtn.,Idaho ... F5 57
Inwood, Iowa ... A1 60
Inwood, N.Y. ... k13 75
Inyan Kara, mtn., Wyo. ... B8 89
Inyo,co., Calif. ... D5 50
Inyokern, Calif. ... E5 50
Ioánnina, Grc. ... C3 14
Ioannina, prov.,Grc. ... *C3 14
Iola, Kans. ... E8 61
Iola, Wis. ... D4 88
Iona, Idaho ... F7 57
Ione, Calif. ... D3 50
Ionia, Mich. ... F5 66
Ionia, co., Mich. ... F5 66
Iosco, co., Mich. ... D7 66
Iota, La. ... D3 63
Iowa, La. ... D2 63
Iowa, co.,Iowa ... C5 60
Iowa, co., Wis. ... E3 88
Iowa, state, U.S. ... 60
Iowa City, Iowa ... C6 60
Iowa Falls, Iowa ... B4 60
Iowa Park, Tex. ... C3 84
Ipameri, Braz. ... B3 30
Ipava, Ill. ... C3 58
Ipiales, Col. ... C2 32
Ipin, China ... F5 17
Ipoh, Mala. ... E2 19
Ipswich, Austl. ... E9 25
Ipswich, Eng. ... D7 4
Ipswich, Mass. ... A6 55
Ipswich, S. Dak. ... E6 77
Iquique, Chile ... D2 29
Iquitos, Peru ... B3 31
Iraan, Tex. ... D2 84
Iraklion (Candia), Grc. ... E5 14
Iraklion, prov., Grc. ... *E5 14
Iran, (Persia), country, Asia ... F8 16
Irapuato, Mex. ... C4, m13 34
Iraq, country, Asia ... C3 15
Irbid, Jordan ... B3, g5 15
Irbil, Iraq ... D15 14
Iredell, co., N.C. ... B2 76
Ireland (Eire), country, Eur. ... D3 4
Ireton, Iowa ... B1 60
Iri, Kor. ... I3 18
Iringa, Tan. ... B7 24
Irion, co.,Tex. ... D2 84
Irkutsk, Sov. Un. ... D13 13
Iron, co., Mich. ... B2 66
Iron, co., Mo. ... D7 69
Iron, co., Utah ... C5 72
Iron, co., Wis. ... B3 88
Iron, mts., Va. ... f10 85

Irondale, Ala. ... f7 46
Irondale, Ohio ... B5 78
Irondequoit, N.Y. ... B3 75
Ironia, N.J. ... B3 74
Iron Mountain, Mich. ... C2 66
Iron River, Mich. ... B2 66
Iron River, Wis. ... B2 88
Ironton, Minn. ... D5 67
Ironton, Mo. ... D7 69
Ironton, Ohio ... D3 78
Ironwood, Mich. ... nII 66
Iroquois, N.B., Can. ... *B1 43
Iroquois, Ont., Can. ... C9 41
Iroquois, co., Ill. ... C6 58
Iroquois Falls, Ont., Can. ... *o19 41
Irosin, Phil. ... *C6 19
Irrawaddy, riv., Bur. ... D10 20
Irtysh, riv., Sov. Un. ... D10 13
Irún, Sp. ... A5 8
Irvine, Ky. ... C6 62
Irvine, Scot. ... C4 4
Irving, Tex. ... n10 84
Irvington, Ky. ... C3 62
Irvington, N.J. ... k8 74
Irvington, N.Y. ... g13 75
Irvona, Pa. ... E4 81
Irwin, Pa. ... F2 81
Irwin, S.C. ... *B6 82
Irwin, co., Ga. ... E3 55
Irwindale, Calif. ... *E4 50
Isabell, mtn., Wyo. ... D2 89
Isabela, P.R. ... *G11 35
Isabela, prov.,Phil. ... *D6 19
Isabella, Pa. ... G2 81
Isabella, Tenn. ... D9 83
Isabella, co., Mich. ... E6 66
Isahaya, Jap. ... J5 18
Isanti, Minn. ... E5 67
Isanti,co., Minn. ... E5 67
Ise (Uji-yamada), Jap. ... I8, o15 18
Iselin, N.J. ... B4 74
Iselin, Pa. ... E3 81
Isère, dept., Fr. ... *E6 5
Iserlohn, Ger., Fed. Rep. of ... *C3 6
Isernia, It. ... D5 9
Isesaki, Jap. ... H9, m18 18
Iseyin, Nig. ... G5 22
Ishikawa, pref., Jap. ... *H8 18
Ishim, Sov. Un. ... D9 13
Ishimbay, Sov. Un. ... *D8 13
Ishinomaki, Jap. ... G10 18
Ishioka, Jap. ... m19 18
Ishpeming, Mich. ... B3 66
Isigny-sur-Mer, Fr. ... C3 5
Isiro (Paulis), Zaire ... H3 23
Iskenderun (Alexandretta), Tur. ... D11 14
Iskilip, Tur. ... B10 14
Isla Cristina, Sp. ... D2 8

Islâmâbâd, Pak. ... B5 20
Islamorado,Fla. ... H6 54
Island, co., Wash. ... A3 86
Island Falls, Maine ... B4 64
Island Heights, N.J. ... D4 74
Island Lake, Ill. ... *E2 58
Island Park, N.Y. ... *E7 75
Island Pond, Vt. ... B4 73
Islav, isl. U.K. ... C3 4
Isle, Minn. ... D5 67
Isle-aux-Morts, Newf. Can. ... E2 44
Isle, of Ely, co., Eng. ... *D7 4
Isle of Man, Br. dep; Eur. ... *C4 4
Isle of Man, isl., U.K. ... C4 4
Isle of Palms, S.C. ... k12 82
Isle of Wight, co., Eng. ... *E6 4
Isle of Wight, co., Va. ... D6 85
Isle of Wight, isl.U.K. ... E6 4
Isle Royale, isl., Mich. ... h9 66
Isleton, Calif. ... C3 50
Isle-Verte, Que., Can. ... A8 42
Islington, Mass. ... h11 65
Islip, N.Y. ... n15 75
Islip Terrace, N.Y. ... *n15 75
Isola Capo Rizzuto, It. ... E6 9
Isparta, Tur. ... D8 14
Israel, country, Asia ... C2 15
Issaquah, Wash. ... e11 86
Issaquena, co., Miss. ... C2 68
Issoire, Fr. ... E5 5
Issoudun, Fr. ... D4 5
Issyk-kul, lake, Sov. Un. ... E10 13
Issy les-Moulineaux, Fr. ... g10 5
Istanbul (Constantinople),
Tur. ... B7 14
Istmina, Col. ... B2 32
Itá, Par. ... E4 29
Itabaiana, Braz. ... *E7 27
Itabaiana, Braz. ... *D7 27
Itaberaba, Braz. ... *E6 27
Itabira, Braz. ... B4 30
Itabuna, Braz. ... E7 27
Itajaí, Braz. ... D3 30
Itajubá, Braz. ... C3 30
Italy, Tex. ... C4 84
Italy, country, Eur. ... 9
Itami, Jap. ... o14 18
Itaperuna, Braz. ... C4 30
Itapetininga, Braz. ... C3, m7 30
Itapeva, Braz. ... C3 30
Itápolis, Braz. ... k7 30
Itapúa, dept., Par. ... E4 29
Itaqui, Braz. ... D1 30
Itararé, Braz. ... C3 30
Itasca, Ill. ... k8 58
Itasca, Tex. ... C4 84
Itasca, co., Minn. ... C5 67
Itatiba, Braz. ... m8 30

Itaúna, Braz. ... C4 30
Itawamba, co., Miss. ... A5 68
Ithaca, Mich. ... E6 66
Ithaca, N.Y. ... C4 75
Itô, Jap. ... o18 18
Itoigawa, Jap. ... H8 18
Itta Bena, Miss. ... B3 68
Itu, Braz. ... C3, m8 30
Ituango, Col. ... B2 32
Ituiutaba, Braz. ... B3 30
Ituna, Sask. Can. ... F4 39
Itzehoe, Ger.Fed. Rep. of ... B4 6
Iuka, Miss. ... A4 68
Iva, S.C. ... C2 82
Ivanhoe, Calif. ... *D4 50
Ivanhoe, Minn. ... F2 67
Ivanhoe, Va. ... D2 85
Ivano-Frankovsk, Sov. Un. ... G5 12
Ivanovka, Sov. Un. ... q21 12
Ivanovo, Sov. Un. ... C13 12
Ivanteyevka, Sov. Un. ... n17 12
Ivory Coast, country, Afr. ... G3 22
Ivoryton, Conn. ... D7 52
Ivrea, It. ... B1 9
Ivry-sur-Seine, Fr. ... g10 5
Ivywild, Colo. ... C6 51
Iwaki (Tairi), Jap. ... H10 18
Iwaki-yama, mtn., Jap. ... F10 18
Iwakuni, Jap. ... I6 18
Iwamizawa, Jap. ... E10 18
Iwanai, Jap. ... E10 18
Iwate, pref., Jap. ... *G10 18
Iwate-yama, mtn., Jap. ... G10 18
Iwo, Nig. ... G5 22
Ixmiquilpan, Mex. ... m14 34
Ixtacalco, Mex. ... h9 34
Ixtacihuatl, mtn., Mex. ... n14 34
Ixtapalapa, Mex. ... h9 34
Ixtlán de Juárez, Mex. ... o15 34
Ixtlán del Rio, Mex. ... C4, m11 34
Izamal, Mex. ... C7 34
Izard, co., Ark. ... A4 49
Izhevsk, see Ustinov, Sov. Un.
Izmail, Sov. Un. ... I7 12
Izmir (Smyrna), Tur. ... C6 14
Izmit (Kocaeli), Tur. ... B7 14
Izúcar de Matamoros, Mex. ... n14 34
Izuhara, Jap. ... I4 18
Izumo, Jap. ... I6 18
Izyum, Sov. Un. ... G11 12

J

Jabalpur (Jubbulpore), India ... D6 20
Jaboatão, Braz. ... *D7 27
Jaboticabal, Braz. ... C3, k7 30
Jaca, Sp. ... A5 8
Jacala de Ledesma, Mex. ... m14 34
Jacareí, Braz. ... m9 30
Jacarèzinho, Braz. ... C3 30
Jáchymov, Czech. ... C2 7
Jacinto City, Tex. ... r14 84
Jack, co., Tex. ... C3 84
Jack, mtn., Mont. ... D4 70
Jack, mtn., Wash. ... B3 85
Jackfork, mtn., Okla. ... C6 79
Jacks, mtn., Pa. ... E6 81
Jacksboro, Tex. ... C3 84
Jackson, Ala. ... D2 46
Jackson, Calif. ... C3 50
Jackson, Ga. ... C3 55
Jackson, Ky. ... C6 62
Jackson, La. ... D4 63
Jackson, Mich. ... F6 66
Jackson, Minn. ... G3 67
Jackson, Miss. ... C3 68
Jackson, Mo. ... D8 69
Jackson, N.C. ... A5 76
Jackson, Ohio ... C3 78
Jackson, S.C. ... E4 82
Jackson, Tenn. ... B3 83
Jackson, Wyo. ... C2 89
Jackson, co., Ala. ... A3 46
Jackson, co., Ark. ... B4 49

Jackson, co., Colo. ... A4 51
Jackson, co., Fla. ... B1 54
Jackson, co., Ga. ... B3 55
Jackson, co., Ill. ... F4 58
Jackson, co., Ind. ... G5 59
Jackson, co., Iowa ... B7 60
Jackson, co., Kans. ... C8 61
Jackson, co., Ky. ... C5 62
Jackson, co., Mich. ... F6 66
Jackson, co., Minn. ... G3 67
Jackson, co., Miss. ... E5 68
Jackson, co., Mo. ... C3 69
Jackson, co., N.C. ... f9 76
Jackson, co., Ohio ... C3 78
Jackson, co., Okla. ... C2 79
Jackson, co., Oreg. ... E3 80
Jackson, co., S. Dak. ... G4 77
Jackson, co., Tenn. ... C8 83
Jackson, co., Tex. ... E4 84
Jackson, co., W. Va. ... C3 87
Jackson, co., Wis. ... D3 88
Jackson, par., La. ... B3 63
Jackson, mtn., Maine ... D2 64
Jackson Center, Ohio ... B1 78
Jacksonville, Ala. ... B4 46
Jacksonville, Ark. ... C3, h10 49
Jacksonville, Fla. ... B5, m8 54
Jacksonville, Ill. ... D3 58
Jacksonville, N.C. ... C5 76
Jacksonville, Oreg. ... E4 80
Jacksonville, Tex. ... D5 84

Jacksonville Beach, Fla. ... B5, m9 54
Jacmel, Hai. ... E7 35
Jacobábad, Pak. ... C4 20
Jacobina, Braz. ... *E6 27
Jacomino, Cuba. ... *C2 35
Jacques Cartier, mtn.,
Que., Can. ... k13 42
Jaén, Sp. ... D4 8
Jaén, prov., Sp. ... *D4 8
Jaffna, Sri Lanka ... G7 20
Jaffrey, N.H. ... F3 73
Jaguarão, Braz. ... E2 30
Jagüey Grande, Cuba ... C3 35
Jaipur, India ... C6 20
Jaisalmer, India ... C5 20
Jajce, Yugo. ... C3 10
Jâjpur, India ... D8 20
Jakarta (Djakarta), Indon. ... G3 19
Jakobstad (Pietersaari), Fin. ... F10 11
Jal, N. Mex. ... C7 48
Jalalabad, Afg. ... B5 20
Jalapa, Guat. ... *F6 34
Jalapa Enriquez, Mex. ... D5, n15 34
Jalca Grande, Peru ... C2 31
Jâlgaon, India ... D6 20
Jalisco,state, Mex. ... C4, m12 34
Jâlna, India ... E6 20
Jalpa, Mex. ... C4, m12 34
Jalpan, Mex. ... C5, m14 34
Jamaica, country, N.A. ... E5 35
Jambi, Indon. ... F2 19

James, riv., S. Dak. ... F7 77
Jamesburg, N.J. ... C4 74
James City, N.C. ... B5 76
James City, co., Va. ... C6 85
Jamesport, Mo. ... B4 69
Jamestown, Calif. ... D3 50
Jamestown, Ind. ... E4 59
Jamestown, Ky. ... D4 62
Jamestown, N.Y. ... C1 75
Jamestown, N.C. ... B3 76
Jamestown, N. Dak. ... D7 77
Jamestown, Ohio ... C2 78
Jamestown, Pa. ... D1 81
Jamestown, R.I. ... D11 52
Jamestown, Tenn. ... C9 83
Jamesville, N.Y. ... *C4 75
Jamiltepec, Mex. ... D5 34
Jammu, India ... B5 20
Jammu and Kashmir, Disputed reg.,
India, Pak. ... B6 20
Jâmnagar, India ... D5 20
Jamshedpur, India ... D8 20
Jämtland, co., Swe. ... *F6 11
Janesville, Iowa ... B5 60
Janesville, Minn. ... F5 67
Janesville, Wis. ... F4 88
Janin, Jordan ... B3 15
Janos, Mex. ... A3 34
Jánoshalma, Hung. ... B4 10
Janów, Lubelski, Pol. ... C7 7
Januária, Braz. ... B4 30

K

L

M

Mahbūbnagar, India E6 20
Mahe, India F6 20
Mahnomen, Minn. C3 67
Mahnomen, co., Minn. C2 67
Mahogany, mtn., Oreg. D9 80
Mahomet, Ill. C5 58
Mahón, Sp. C8 8
Mahone Bay, N.S., Can. E5 43
Mahoning, co., Ohio B5 78
Mahopac, N.Y. D7, m15 75
Mahtomedi, Minn. E7 67
Mahwah, N.J. A4 74
Maiden, N.C. B1 76
Maidstone, Sask., Can. D1 39
Maidstone, Eng. E7 4
Maiduguri, Nig. F7 22
Maimana, Afg. A3 20
Maine, former prov., Fr. C3 5
Maine, state, U.S. 64
Maine-et-Loire, dept., Fr. *D3 5
Maintirano, Mad. D8 24
Main Topsail, mtn., Newf., Can. D3 44
Mainz, Ger., Fed. Rep. of C4 6
Maipú, Arg. B5 28
Maiquetía, Ven. A4 32
Maisonette, N.B., Can. B4 43
Maisons-Alfort, Fr. g10 5
Maisons-Laffitte, Fr. g9 5
Maitland, Austl. F9 25
Maitland (Lake Maitland), Fla. *D5 54
Maize, Kans. g12 61
Maizuru, Jap. I7, n14 18
Majagual, Col. B3 32
Majestic, Ky. C7 62
Major, co., Okla. A3 79
Makaha, Haw. g9 56
Makajanga, Mad. D9 24
Makarov Shirutoru, Sov. Un. B11 18
Makarska, Yugo. D3 10
Makasar, see Ujung Pandang, Indon.
Makati, Phil. *o3 19
Makawao, Haw. C5 56
Makaweli, Haw. B2 56
Makeyevka, Sov. Un. G11, q20 12
Makhachkala, Sov. Un. E7 13
Makhlata, Bul. D7 10
Makurazaki, Jap. K5 18
Makurdi, Nig. G6 22
Malabar, Fla. D6 54
Malabo, Equat. Gui. H6 22
Malacca, state, Mala. E2 19
Malad City, Idaho G6 57
Málaga, Col. B3 32
Malaga, N.J. D2 74
Málaga, Sp. D3 8
Málaga, prov., Sp. *D3 8
Malagasy Republic, see
Madagascar, country, Afr.
Malakāl, Sud. G4 23
Malakoff, Fr. g10 5
Malakoff, Tex. C4 84
Malang, Indon. G4 19
Malanje, Ang. B3 24
Malartic, Que., Can. k11 42
Malatya, Tur. C12 14
Malawi, country, Afr. C6 24
Malaya Vishera, Sov. Un. B9 12
Malaybalay, Phil. D7 19
Malaysia, country, Asia E4 19
Malbork, Pol. A5 7
Malchin, Ger. Dem. Rep. B6 6
Malden, Mass. B5, g11 65
Malden, Mo. E8 69
Malden, W. Va. m12 87
Maldives, country, Asia G5 20
Maldonado, Ur. E2 30
Maldonado, dept., Ur. *E2 30
Malegaon, India *D5 20
Māler Kotla, India B6 20
Malheur, co., Oreg. D9 80
Mali, country, Afr. F3 22
Malibu, Calif. m11 50
Malin, Oreg. E5 80
Malinec, Czech. D5 7
Malita, Phil. *D7 19
Malkara, Tur. B6 14
Mallawī, Eg. C4 23
Malleco, prov., Chile B2 28
Mallory, W. Va. *D3 87
Mallow, Ire. D2 4
Malmédy, Bel. B7 5
Malmö, Swe. J5 11
Malmöhus, co., Swe. *J5 11
Maloarkhangelsk, Sov. Un. E11 12
Malolos, Phil. o13 19
Malone, Fla. B1 54
Malone, N.Y. f10 75
Maloyaroslavets, Sov. Un. D11 12
Malta, Mont. B9 70
Malta, Ohio C4 78
Malta, country, Eur. A7 22
Malton, Eng. C6 4
Malvern, Ark. C3, g8 49
Malvern, Iowa D2 60
Malvern, Ohio B4 78
Malvern, Pa. F10, o19 81
Malverne, N.Y. *G2 52
Mamanguape, Braz. *D7 27
Mamaroneck, N.Y. h13 75
Mamba, Jap. m17 18
Mamers, Fr. C4 5
Mammoth, Ariz. C3 48
Mammoth, W. Va. C3, m13 87
Mamou, Guinea F2 22
Mamou, La. D3 63
Man, W. Va. D3, n12 87
Man, Isle of, see Isle of
Man, Br. dep., Eur.
Manabi, prov., Ec. B1 31
Manacor, Sp. C7 8
Manado, Indon. E6 19
Managua, Nic. E7 34
Manahawkin, N.J. D4 74
Manakara, Mad. E9 24
Manama, Bahrain D5 15
Mananjary, Mad. E9 24
Manasquan, N.J. C4 74
Manassas, Va. B5, g12 85
Manassas Park, Va. *B5 85
Manatee, co., Fla. E4 54
Manatí, P.R. *G11 35
Manaus, Braz. D4 27
Manawa, Wis. D5 88
Mancelona, Mich. D5 66
Mancha, reg., Sp. C4 8
Mancha Real, Sp. D4 8
Manchaug, Mass. B4 65
Manche, dept., Fr. *C3 5
Manchester, Conn. B6 52
Manchester, Eng. D5 4
Manchester, Ga. D2 55
Manchester, Iowa B6 60
Manchester, Ky. C6 62
Manchester, Md. A4 53
Manchester, Mass. A6, f12 65
Manchester, Mich. F6 66
Manchester, Mo. f12 69
Manchester, N.H. F5 73
Manchester, N.Y. C3 75
Manchester, Ohio D2 78
Manchester, Pa. F8 81
Manchester, Tenn. B5 83
Manchester Depot, Vt. E1 73
Manchuria, reg., China B10 17
Mandalay, Bur. D10 20
Mandan, N. Dak. D5 77
Mandasor, India D6 20
Manderson, Wyo. B5 89
Mandeville, Jam. E5 35
Mandeville, La. D5, h11 63
Mandurah, Austl. F2 25
Manduria, It. D6 9
Māndvi, India D4 20
Manfalūţ, Eg. C4 23
Manfredonia, It. D5 9
Mangalore, India F5 20
Mangham, La. B4 63
Mangum, Okla. C2 79
Manhasset, N.Y. F2 52
Manhattan, Ill. *B6 58
Manhattan, Kans. C7 61
Manhattan, N.Y. *B5 75
Manhattan Beach, Calif. n12 50
Manheim, Pa. F9 81
Manhuaçu, Braz. C4 30
Manila, Ark. B5 49
Manila, Phil. o13 19
Manilla, Iowa C2 60
Manipur, state, India D9 20
Manisa, Tur. C6 14
Manistee, Mich. D4 66
Manistee, co., Mich. D4 66
Manistique, Mich. C4 66
Manito, Ill. C4 58
Manitoba, prov., Can. 40
Manitoba, lake, Man., Can. D2 40
Manitou, Man., Can. E2 40
Manitou Beach, Mich. *G6 66
Manitoulin, dist., Ont., Can. B2 41
Manitou Springs, Colo. C6 51
Manitowoc, Wis. D6, h10 88
Manitowac, co., Wis. D6 88
Maniwaki, Que., Can. C2 42
Manizales, col. B2 32
Manjimup, Austl. F2 25
Mankato, Kans. C5 61
Mankato, Minn. F5 67
Manlius, N.Y. C5 75
Manlléu, Sp. A7 8
Manly, Iowa A4 60
Mannar, Sri Lanka G6 20
Mannheim, Ger., Fed. Rep. of D4 6
Manning, Alta., Can. A2 38
Manning, Iowa C2 60
Manning, S.C. D7 82
Mannington, W. Va. B4, h10 87
Mannum, Austl. G2 26
Mannville, Alta., Can. C5 38
Manomet, Mass. C6 65
Manomet, hill, Mass. C6 65
Manono, Zaire B5 24
Manor, Pa. *F2 81
Manorhaven, N.Y. *E7 75
Manosque, Fr. F6 5
Manresa, Sp. B6 8
Manseau, Que., Can. C5 42
Mansfield, Eng. D6 4
Mansfield Ill. C5 58
Mansfield, La. B2 63
Mansfield, Mass. B5 65
Mansfield, Ohio B3 78
Mansfield, Pa. C7 81
Mansfield, Tex. n9 84
Mansfield, mtn., Vt. B2 73
Mansfield Southeast, Ohio *B3 78
Manson, Iowa B3 60
Mansura, La. C3 63
Manta, Ec. B1 31
Manteca, Calif. D3 50
Manteno, Ill. B6 58
Mantes *la-Jolie*, Fr. C4 5
Manti, Utah B6 72
Manton, Mich. D5 66
Mantova, It. B3 9
Mantua, N.J. D2 74
Mantua, Ohio A4 78
Manuel Benavides, Mex. B4 34
Manuels, Newf., Can. *E5 44
Manukau, N.Z. *L15 26
Manville, N.J. B3 74
Manville, R.I. B11 52
Many, La. C2 63
Manzanares, Sp. C4 8
Manzanillo, Cuba D5 35
Manzanillo, Mex. D4, n11 34
Manzhouli, China B8 17
Maoming, China G7 17
Mapastepec, Mex. D6 34
Maple, Ont., Can. k14 41
Maple Bluff, Wis. E4 88
Maple Creek, Sask., Can. H1 39
Maple Heights, Ohio h9 78
Maple Lake, Minn. E4 67
Maple Lane, Ind. *A5 59
Maple Mount, Ky. C2 62
Maple Plain, Minn. m11 67
Maple Rapids, Mich. E6 66
Maple Shade, N.J. D2 74
Mapleton, Iowa B2 60
Mapleton, Maine B4 64
Mapleton, Minn. G5 67
Mapleton, Oreg. C3 80
Mapleton, Utah D2 72
Maplewood, La. D2 63
Maplewood, Minn. m12 67
Maplewood, Mo. f13 69
Maplewood, N.J. B4 74
Maplewood, N.Y. *C7 75
Maplewood Park, Pa. *G11 81
Maputo, Moz. F6 24
Maquoketa, Iowa B7 60
Marabá, Braz. D6 27
Maracaibo, Ven. A3 32
Maracaju, Braz. F5 27
Maracay, Ven. A4 32
Maradi, Niger F6 22
Marāgheh, Iran B4 15
Maragogipe, Braz. *E7 27
Marana, Ariz. C3 48
Maranguape, Braz. *D7 27
Maranhão, state, Braz. *D6 27
Marañón, riv., Peru B2 31
Maraş, Tur. D11 14
Marathon, Ont., Can. o18 41
Marathon, Fla. H5 54
Marathon, Iowa B3 60
Marathon, N.Y. C4 75
Marathon, Tex. D1, o13 84
Marathon, Wis. D4 88
Marathon, co., Wis. D4 88
Maravatío de Ocampo, Mex. n13 34
Mara Vista, Mass. C6 65
Marawi, Sud. E4 23
Marbella, Sp. D3 8
Marble, Minn. C5 67
Marble Cliff, Ohio m10 78
Marble Falls, Tex. D3 84
Marblehead, Mass. B6, f12 65
Marblehead, Ohio A3 78
Marbleton, Que., Can. D6 42
Marburg, Ger., Fed. Rep. of C4 6
Marbury, Md. C3 53
Marceline, Mo. B5 69
Marcellus, Mich. F5 66
Marcellus, N.Y. C4 75
Marche, former prov., Fr. D4 5
Marche, pol. dist., It. *C4 9
Marchena, Sp. D3 8
Marches, reg., It. C4 9
Marcola, Oreg. C4 80
Marcos Juarez, Arg. A4 28
Marcus, Iowa B2 60
Marcus Hook, Pa. G11 81
Marcy, mtn., N.Y. A7 75
Mardān, Pak. B5 20
Mar Del Plata, Arg. B5 28
Mardin, Tur. D13 14
Marechal Deodoro, Braz. *D7 27
Marengo, Ill. A5 58
Marengo, Ind. H5 59
Marengo, Iowa C5 60
Marengo, co., Ala. C2 46
Marenisco, Mich. n12 66
Marfa, Tex. o12 84
Margaret, Ala. B3 46
Margaretville, N.Y. C6 75
Margate, Eng. E7 4
Margate, Fla. *F6 54
Margate City, N.J. E3 74
Margelan, Sov. Un. E10 13
Margherita, mtn., Ug. H3 23
Maria la Baja, col. A2 32
Mariana, is., Pac. O. E6 2
Marianna, Ark. C5 49
Marianna, Fla. B1 54
Marianna, Pa. *F1 81
Mariánské Lázně, Czech. D2 7
Maribo, co., Den. *J4 11
Maribor, Yugo. B2 10
Maricopa, Calif. E4 50
Maricopa, co., Ariz. C2 48
Mariemont, Ohio o13 78
Marienville, Pa. D3 81
Maries, co., Mo. C6 69
Mariestad, Swe. H5 11
Marietta, Ga. C2, h7 55
Marietta, Ohio C4 78
Marietta, Okla. D4 79
Marietta, Pa. F8 81
Marietta, S.C. A2 82
Marieville, Que., Can. D4 42
Marília, Braz. C3 30
Marín, Sp. A1 8
Marin, co., Calif. C2 50
Marin City, Calif. *C2 50
Marinduque, prov., Phil. *C6 19
Marine, Ill. E4 58
Marine City, Mich. F8 66
Marinette, Wis. C6 88
Marinette, co., Wis. C5 88
Maringouin, La. D4 63
Marinha Grande, Port. C1 8
Marino, It. H9 9
Marion, Ala. C2 46
Marion, Ill. F5 58
Marion, Ind. C6 59
Marion, Iowa B6 60
Marion, Kans. D6 61
Marion, Ky. e9 62
Marion, La. B3 63
Marion, Mass. C6 65
Marion, Mich. D5 66
Marion, N.Y. B3 75
Marion, N.C. B1, f10 76
Marion, Ohio B2 78
Marion, S.C. C9 82
Marion, Va. f10 85
Marion, Wis. D5 88
Marion, co., Ala. A2 46
Marion, co., Ark. A3 49
Marion, co., Fla. C4 54
Marion, co., Ga. D2 55
Marion, co., Ill. E5 58
Marion, co., Ind. E5 59
Marion, co., Iowa C4 60
Marion, co., Kans. D6 61
Marion, co., Ky. C4 62
Marion, co., Miss. D4 68
Marion, co., Mo. B6 69
Marion, co., Ohio B2 78
Marion, co., Oreg. C4 80
Marion, co., S.C. C9 82
Marion, co., Tenn. D8 83
Marion, co., Tex. C5 84
Marion, co., W. Va. B4 87
Marion Heights, Pa. *D8 81
Marionville, Mo. D4 69
Mariposa, Calif. D4 50
Mariposa, co., Calif. D3 50
Marissa, Ill. E4 58
Maris Town, Miss. C3 68
Mariupol, see Zhdanov, Sov. Un.
Marka, Som. H6 23
Markdale, Ont., Can. C4 41
Marked Tree, Ark. B5 49
Markesan, Wis. E5 88
Markham, Ont., Can. D5, k15 41
Markham, Ill. k9 58
Markham, mtn., Ant. L7 2
Markle, Ind. C7 59
Markovka, Sov. Un. G12 12
Marks, Miss. A3 68

Mar-Mei 191

Marksville, La. C3 63
Marktredwitz, Ger., Fed. Rep. of C6 6
Marlbank, Ont., Can. C7 41
Marlboro, Mass. B4, g9 65
Marlboro, N.J. C4 74
Marlboro, N.Y. D6 75
Marlboro, co., S.C. B8 82
Marlborough, N.H. F3 73
Marlette, Mich. E7 66
Marley, Md. B4 53
Marlin, Tex. D4 84
Marlinton, W. Va. C4 87
Marlow, Okla. C4 79
Marlowe, W.Va. B7 87
Marlton, N.J. D3 74
Marmande, Fr. E4 5
Marmet, W. Va. C3, m12 87
Marmora, Ont., Can. C7 41
Marmora, N.J. E3 74
Marmora, peak, It. D2 9
Marne, Mich. E5 66
Marne, dept., Fr. *C6 5
Maroa, Ill. C5 58
Maroantsetra, Mad. D9 24
Maromokotro, mtn., Mad. C9 24
Maroochydore-Mooloolaba, Austl. C9 26
Maroua, Cam. F7 22
Marovoay, Mad. D9 24
Marquesas, is., Fr. Polynesia G11 2
Marquette, Kans. D6 61
Marquette, Mich. B3 66
Marquette, co., Mich. B3 66
Marquette, co., Wis. E4 88
Marquette Heights, Ill. C4 58
Marrakech, Mor. B3 22
Marrero, La. k11 63
Marromeu, Moz. D7 24
Mars, Pa. E1 81
Mars, hill, Maine g7 64
Marsala, It. F4 9
Marsa Matruh, Eg. B3 23
Marseille, Fr. F6 5
Marseilles, Ill. B5 58
Marshall, Ark. B3 49
Marshall, Ill. D6 58
Marshall, Mich. F6 66
Marshall, Minn. F3 67
Marshall, Mo. B4 69
Marshall, N.C. F10 76
Marshall, Tex. C5 84
Marshall, Va. B5 85
Marshall, Wis. E4 88
Marshall, co., Ala. A3 46
Marshall, co., Ill. B4 58
Marshall, co., Ind. B5 59
Marshall, co., Iowa C4 60
Marshall, co., Kans. C7 61
Marshall, co., Ky. f9 62
Marshall, co., Minn. B2 67
Marshall, co., Miss. A4 68
Marshall, co., Okla. C5 79
Marshall, co., S. Dak. E8 77
Marshall, co., Tenn. B5 83
Marshall, co., W. Va. B4 87
Marshallberg, N.C. C6 76
Marshall Northeast, Tex. *C5 84
Marshallton, Del. A6 35
Marshallton, Pa. *D8 81
Marshalltown, Iowa B5 60
Marshallville, Ga. D3 55
Marshallville, Ohio B4 78
Marshfield, Mass. B6, h13 65
Marshfield, Mo. D5 69
Marshfield, Wis. D3 88
Marshfield Hills, Mass. B6, h13 65
Mars Hill, Ind. E5, m10 59
Mars Hill, Maine B5 64
Mars Hill, N.C. f10 76
Marshville, N.C. C2 76
Marsing, Idaho F2 57
Marston, Mo. E8 69
Mart, Tex. D4 84
Martel, Que., Can. A6 42
Martí, Cuba D5 35
Martigues, Fr. F6 5
Martin, Ky. C7 62
Martin, Mich. F5 66
Martin, S. Dak. G4 77
Martin, Tenn. A3 83
Martin, co., Fla. E6 54
Martin, co., Ind. G4 59
Martin, co., Ky. C7 62
Martin, co., Minn. G4 67
Martin, co., N.C. B5 76
Martin, co., Tex. C2 84
Martina *Franca*, It. D6 9
Martinez, Calif. C2, h8 50
Martinez, Ga. C4 55
Martinique, Fr. dep., N.A. I14 35
Martinsburg, Pa. F5 81
Martinsburg, W. Va. B7 87
Martins Creek, Pa. B2 81
Martins Ferry, Ohio B5 78
Martinsville, Ill. D6 58
Martinsville, Ind. F5 59
Martinsville, N.J. B3 74
Martinsville (Independent City), Va. D3 85
Martos, Sp. D4 8
Marudi, Mala. E5 19
Maruf, Afg. B4 20
Marugame, Jap. I6 18
Marvell, Ark. C5 49
Mary, Sov. Un. F9 13
Maryborough, Austl. E9 25
Maryborough, Austl. G7 25
Maryfield, Sask., Can. H5 39
Maryland, state, U.S. 53
Maryland Heights, Mo. f13 69
Maryport, Eng. C5 4
Marys, peak, Oreg. C3 80
Mary's Harbour, Newf., Can. B4 44
Marystown, Newf., Can. E4 44
Marysville, Calif. C3 50
Marysville, B.C., Can. E10 37
Marysville, Kans. C7 61
Marysville, Mich. F8 66
Marysville, Ohio B2 78
Marysville, Pa. F8 81
Marysville, Wash. A3 86
Maryvale, Ariz. *C2 48
Maryville, Mo. A3 69
Maryville, Tenn. D10, n14 83
Masan, Kor. I4 18
Masaya, Nic. E7 34
Masbate, Phil. C6 19
Masbate, prov., Phil. *H7 19
Mascot, Tenn. C10, m14 83
Mascota, Mex. m11 34
Mascouche, Que., Can. D4 42
Mascoutah, Ill. E4 58
Mashhad (Meshed), Iran B6 15
Masindi, Ug. H4 23
Masisea, Peru C3 31
Masjed, Soleyman, Iran C4 15
Maskinongé, Que., Can. C4 42
Maskinongé, co., Que., Can. C4 42
Mason, Mich. F6 66
Mason, Ohio C1, n13 78
Mason, Tex. D3 84
Mason, W. Va. B2 87
Mason, co., Ill. C4 58
Mason, co., Ky. B6 62
Mason, co., Mich. D4 66
Mason, co., Tex. D3 84
Mason, co., Wash. B2 86
Mason, co., W. Va. C3 87
Mason City, Ill. C4 58
Mason City, Iowa A4 60
Masontown, Pa. G2 81
Masontown, W. Va. B5 87
Mass, Mich. B1, m12 66
Massa, It. B3 9
Massac, co., Ill. F5 58
Massachusetts, state, U.S. 65
Massaemett, mtn., Mass. A2 65
Massafra, It. D6 9
Massa Marittima, It. C3 9
Massanutten, mtn., Va. B4 85
Massapequa, N.Y. G3 52
Massapequa Park, N.Y. *E7 75
Massawa, Eth. E5 23
Massena, N.Y. f10 75
Masset, B.C., Can. C1 37
Massey, Ont., Can. A2 41
Massillon, Ohio B4 78
Massive, mtn., Colo. B4 51
Masson, Que., Can. D2 42
Masterton, N.Z. N15 26
Mastic, N.Y. *n15 75
Mastic Beach, N.Y. *F4 52
Mastung, Pak. C4 20
Masuda, Jap. I5 18
Masuria, reg., Pol. B6 7
Masury, Ohio. A5 78
Masvingo, Zimb. E6 24
Matachewan, Ont. Can. p19 41
Matadi, Zaire B2 24
Matador, Tex. C2 84
Matagalpa, Nic. E7 34
Matagorda, co., Tex. E5 84
Matamoras, Pa. D12 81
Matamoros, Mex. B5 34
Matamoros *de la Laguna*, Mex. B4 34
Matane, Que., Can. G20 36
Matane, co., Que., Can. *G20 36
Matanzas, Cuba C3 35
Matanzas, prov., Cuba C3 35
Matapedia, co., Que., Can. *G20 36
Matara, Sri Lanka G7 20
Mataram, Indon. G5 19
Mataró, Sp. B7 8
Matawan, N.J. C4 74
Matehuala, Mex. C4 34
Matera, It. D6 9
Mátészalka, Hung. B6 10
Mateur, Tun. F2 9
Matewan, W. Va. D2 87
Matfield, Mass. B6 65
Mather, Pa. G1 81
Mather, peak, Wyo. B5 89
Mathews, co., Va. C6 85
Mathis, Tex. E4 84
Mathura, India C6 20
Matoaca, Va. n18 85
Matoaka, W. Va. D3 87
Mato Grosso, state, Braz. B1 30
Matozinhos, Port. B1 8
Maṭrāḥ, Om. E6 15
Matsudo, Jap. *I9 18
Matsue, Jap. I6 18
Matsuida, Jap. m17 18
Matsumae, Jap. F10 18
Matsumoto, Jap. H9, m16 18
Matsuyama, Jap. J6 18
Matsuzaka, Jap. I8, o15 18
Matsuzaki, Jap. o17 18
Mattapoisett, Mass. C6 65
Mattawa, Ont., Can. A6, p20 41
Mattawamkeag, Maine C4 64
Matterhorn, mtn., Switz. E3 6
Matteson, Ill. k9 58
Matthews, Ind. D7 59
Matthews, N.C. B2 76
Matthews, mtn. Mo. D7 69
Matthew Town, Ba. D7 35
Mattituck, N.Y. n16 75
Mattoon, Ill. D5 58
Mattydale, N.Y. *B4 75
Matucana, Peru D2 31
Matun, Afg. B4 20
Maturín, Ven. B5 32
Maubeuge, Fr. B5 5
Maubin, Bur. *E10 20
Mauch Chunk, see Jim Thorpe, Pa.
Maud, Ohio C1, n13 78
Maud, Okla. B5 79
Maud, Tex. C5 84
Maugansville, Md. A2 52
Maugerville, N.B., Can. D3 43
Maui (incl. Kalawao), co., Haw. B6 56
Maui, isl., Haw. C6 56
Mauldin, S.C. *B3 82
Maule, prov., Chile B2 28
Maumee, Ohio A2, e6 78
Mauna Kea, vol., Haw. D6 56
Maunaloa, Haw. B4 56
Mauna Loa, vol., Haw. D6 56
Mauritania, country, Afr. E2 22
Mauritius, country, Afr. *H24 2
Maury, co., Tenn. B4 83
Mauston, Wis. E3 88
Maverick, co., Tex. E2 84
Maxcanú, Mex. C7 34
Max Meadows, Va. D2 85
Maxton, N.C. C3 76
Maxwell, Iowa C4, e9 60
May, mtn., Alta., Can. B1 38
Mayagüez, P.R. G11 35
Mayarí, Cuba D6 35
Maybee, Mich. F7 66
Maybeury, W.Va. *D3 87
Maybole, Scot. C4 4
Maybrook, N.Y. D6 75
Mayen, Ger., Fed. Rep of C3 6
Mayenne, Fr. C3 5
Mayenne, dept., Fr. *C3 5
Mayer, Ariz. B2 48
Mayerthorpe, Alta., Can. C3 38
Mayes, co., Okla. A6 79
Mayesville, S.C. D7 82
Mayfield, Ky. f9 62
Mayfield, N.Y. B6 75
Mayfield, Ohio *A4 78
Mayfield, Pa. C11 81
Mayfield Heights, Ohio A4 78
Mayking, Ky. C7 62
Maykop, Sov. Un. *E7 13
Maymyo, Bur. D10 20
Maynard, Iowa B6 60
Maynard, Mass. B5, g10 65
Mayo, Yukon, Can. D6 36
Mayo, Fla. B3 54
Mayo, Md. C4 53
Mayo, S.C. A4 82
Mayo, co., Ire. *D2 4
Mayodan, N.C. A3 76
Mayon, vol., Phil. C6 19
Mayotte, Fr. ter., Afr. C9 24
May Pen, Jam. F5 35
Mays Landing, N.J. E3 74
Maysville, Ky. B6 62
Maysville, Mo. B3 69
Maysville, N.C. C5 76
Maysville, Okla. C4 79
Mayville, Mich. E7 66
Mayville, N.J. E3 74
Mayville, N.Y. C1 75
Mayville, N. Dak. C8 77
Mayville, Wis. E5 88
Maywood, Calif. *F4 50
Maywood, Ill. k9 58
Maywood, N.J. h8 74
Maywood, N.Y. *C7 75
Mazamet, Fr. F5 5
Mazapil, Mex. C4 34
Mazara Del Vallo, It. F4 9
Mazar-I-Sharif, Afg. A4 20
Mazarrón, Sp. D5 8
Mazatenango, Guat. E6 34
Mazatlán, Mex. C3 34
Mazomanie, Wis. E4 88
Mazon, Ill. B5 58
Mazzarino, It. F5 9
Mbabane, Swaz. F6 24
Mbala, Zambia B6 24
Mbalmayo, Cam. H7 22
Mbandaka, Zaïre H1 23
Mbanza-Ngungu, Zaire B2 24
Mbeya, Tan. B6 24
Mead, Wash. B8, g14 86
Meade, Kans. E3 61
Meade, co., Kans. E3 61
Meade, co., Ky. C3 62
Meade, co., S. Dak. F3 77
Meade, peak, Idaho G7 57
Meaderville, Mont. *D4 70
Meadowbrook, Ind. *B7 59
Meadowbrook, W. Va. k10 87
Meadow Lake, Sask., Can. n7 39
Meadow Lands, Pa. F1 81
Meadow Park, Fla. F6 54
Meadowview, Va. f10 85
Meadville, Pa. C1 81
Meaford, Ont., Can. C4 41
Meagher, co., Mont. D6 70
Meath, co., Ire. *D3 4
Meaux, Fr. C5 5
Mebane, N.C. A3 76
Mecca, Ind. E3 59
Mecca (Makkah), Sau. Ar. E2 15
Mechanic Falls, Maine D2 64
Mechanicsburg, Ohio B2 78
Mechanicsburg, Pa. F7 81
Mechanicsville, Iowa C6 60
Mechanicsville, Va. C5 85
Mechanicville, N.Y. C7 75
Mechelen, Bel. B6 5
Mecklenburg, co., N.C. B2 76
Mecklenburg, co., Va. D4 85
Mecklenburg, state, Ger. Dem. Rep. *B6 6
Mecosta, co., Mich. E5 66
Medan, Indon. E1, m11 19
Medaryville, Ind. B4 59
Medéa, Alg. A5 22
Medellín, Col. B2 32
Medfield, Mass. h10 65
Medford, Mass. B5, g11 65
Medford, N.J. D3 74
Medford, Okla. A4 79
Medford, Oreg. E4 80
Medford, Wis. C3 88
Medford Lakes, N.J. D3 74
Medgidia, Rom. C9 10
Media, Pa. G11, p20 81
Mediapolis, Iowa C6 60
Medias, Rom. B7 10
Medical Lake, Wash. B8, g13 86
Medicine Bow, peak, Wyo. E6 89
Medicine Hat, Alta., Can. D5, g8 38
Medicine Lodge, Kans. E5 61
Medicine Park, Okla. C3 79
Medina, N.Y. B2 75
Medina, Ohio A4 78
Medina (Al Madīnah), Sau. Ar. E2 15
Medina, Wash. e11 86
Medina, co., Ohio A4 78
Medina, co., Tex. E3 84
Medina del Campo, Sp. B3 8
Medina Sidonia, Sp. D3 8
Mediterranean, sea D21 2
Medora, Ind. G5 59
Medvezhegorsk, Sov. Un. F16 11
Medway, Mass. B5, h10 65
Medzhibozh, Sov. Un. G6 12
Meekatharra, Austl. E2 25
Meeker, Colo. A3 51
Meeker, Okla. B5 79
Meeker, co., Minn. E4 67
Meerane, Ger. Dem. Rep. C6 6
Meerut, India C6 20
Mégantic, co., Que., Can. C6 42
Mégantic, mtn., Que., Can. D6 42
Megara, Grc. C4 14
Meggett, S.C. F7, k11 82
Meghalaya, state, India C9 20
Megunticook, mtn., Maine D3 64
Mehun-sur-Yèvre, Fr. D5 5
Meigs, Ga. E2 55

Mil-Mon 193

Mill City, Oreg. C4 80
Milldale, Conn. C4 52
Milledgeville, Ga. C3 55
Milledgeville, Ill. B4 58
Mille Lacs, co., Minn. E5 67
Mille Lacs, lake, Minn. D5 67
Millen, Ga. D5 55
Miller, S. Dak. F7 77
Miller, co., Ark. D2 49
Miller, co., Ga. E2 55
Miller, co., Mo. C5 69
Millerovo, Sov. Un. G13 12
Millersburg, Ky. B5 62
Millersburg, Ohio B4 78
Millersburg, Pa. E8 81
Millers Falls, Mass. A3 65
Millersport, Ohio C3 78
Millersville, Pa. F9 81
Millerton, N.Y. D7 75
Mill Hall, Pa. D7 81
Millicent, Austl. G7 25
Milligan, Fla. u15 54
Millington, Mich. E7 66
Millington, N.J. *B3 74
Millington, Tenn. B2 83
Millinocket, Maine C4 64
Millis, Mass. B5, h10 65
Millport, Ala. B1 46
Mills, Wyo. D6 89
Mills, co., Iowa C2 60
Mills, co., Tex. D3 84
Millsboro, Del. C2 53
Millsboro, Pa. G1 81
Millside, Del. *A6 53
Millstadt, Ill. E3 58
Milltown, N.B., Can. D2 43
Milltown, Ind. H5 59
Milltown, Mont. D3 70
Milltown, N.J. C4 74
Milltown, Wis. C1 88
Millvale, Pa. k14 81
Mill Valley, Calif. D2, h7 50
Millville, Mass. B4 65
Millville, N.J. E2 74
Millville, Ohio n12 78
Millville, Pa. D9 81
Millwood, Wash. g14 86
Milmont Park, Pa. *G11 81
Milo, Maine C4 64
Milpitas, Calif. *D3 50
Milroy, Ind. F7 59
Milroy, Pa. E6 81
Milstead, Ga. C3, h8 55
Milton, N.S., Can. E5 43
Milton, Ont., Can. D5 41
Milton, Del. C7 53
Milton, Fla. u14 54
Milton, Ind. E7 59
Milton, Iowa D5 60
Milton, Mass. B5, g11 65
Milton, N.H. D5 73
Milton, N.J. A3 74
Milton, N.Y. D7 75
Milton, Pa. D8 81
Milton, Wash. f11 86
Milton, W. Va. C2 87
Milton, Wis. F5 88
Milton-Freewater, Oreg. B8 80
Milton Junction, Wis. F5 88
Miltonvale, Kans. C6 61
Milverton, Ont., Can. D4 41
Milwaukee, Wis. E6, m12 88
Milwaukee, co., Wis. E6 88
Milwaukie, Oreg. B4, h12 80
Mims, Fla. D6 54
Minamata, Jap. J5 18
Minas, Ur. E1 30
Minas de Riotinto, Sp. D2 8
Minas Gerais, state, Braz. B4 30
Minatare, Nebr. C2 71
Minatitlán, Mex. D6 34
Minato, Jap. m19 18
Minbu, Bur. D9 20
Minco, Okla. B4 79
Mindanao, isl., Phil. D6 19
Minden, Ont., Can. C6 41
Minden, Ger., Fed. Rep. of B4 6
Minden, La. B2 63
Minden, Nebr. D7 71
Minden, W. Va. D3, n13 87
Mindoro, isl., Phil. C6 19
Minechoag, mtn.,Mass. B3 65
Minehead, Eng. E5 4
Mine Hill, N.J. *B3 74
Mineola, N.Y. E7, n15 75
Mineola, Tex. C5 84
Miner, Mo. E8 69
Miner, co., S. Dak. G8 77
Mineral, co., Colo. D4 51
Mineral, co., Mont. C1 70
Mineral, co., Nev. B2 72
Mineral, co., W. Va. B6 87
Mineral City, Ohio B4 78
Mineral del Oro, Mex. n13 34
Mineral Point, Wis. F3 88
Mineral Ridge, Ohio *A5 78
Mineral Wells, Tex. C3 84
Minersville, Pa. E9 81
Minerva, Ohio B4 78
Minerva Park, Ohio *C3 78
Minervino Murge, It. D6 9
Minetto, N.Y. B4 75
Mineville, N.Y. A7 75
Mingenew, Austl. E2 25
Mingo, co., W. Va. D2 87
Mingo Junction, Ohio B5 78
Mingshui, China C2 18
Minho, prov., Port. *B1 8
Minidoka, co., Idaho G5 57
Minier, Ill. C4 58
Minitonas, Man., Can. C1 40
Minna, Nig. G6 22
Minneapolis, Kans. C6 61
Minneapolis, Minn. F5, n12 67
Minnedosa, Man., Can. D2 40
Minnehaha, Wash. *D3 86
Minnehaha, co., S. Dak. G9 77
Minneola, Kans. E3 61
Minneota, Minn. F3 67
Minnesota, state, U.S. 67
Minnesota, riv., Minn. F3 67
Minnesota Lake, Minn. G5 67
Minnetonka, Minn. *F5 67
Minnetrista, Minn. *E5 67
Mino, Jap. n15 18
Minoa, N.Y. *B4 75
Minocqua, Wis. C4 88
Minokamo, Jap. n15 18
Minonk, Ill. C4 58
Minot, N. Dak. B4 77
Minquadale, Del. *A6 53
Minsk, Sov. Un. E6 12
Minster, Ohio B1 78
Minturno, It. D4 9
Minūf, Eg. *G8 14
Minusinsk, Sov. Un. D12 13
Miraflores, Col. C3 32
Miraflores, Peru A3 31
Miraj, Indai E5 20
Mira Loma, Calif. *E5 50
Miramar, Fla. s13 54
Miranda, state, Ven. A4 32
Miranda de Ebro, Sp. A4 8
Mirassol, Braz. C3 30
Mirebalais, Hai. E7 35
Mirecourt, Fr. C7 5
Mirgorod, Sov. Un. G9 12
Miri, Mala. E4 19
Mirpur-Khas, Pak. *C4 20
Mirror, Alta., Can. C4 38
Mirzāpur, India C7 20
Misakubo, Jap. n16 18
Misamis Occidental, prov., Phil. *D6 19
Misamis Oriental, prov., Phil. *D7 19
Misantla, Mex. D5, h15 34
Misenheimer, N.C. B2 76
Mishan, China D6 18
Mishawaka, Ind. A5 59
Mishicot, Wis. D6, h10 88
Mishima, Jap. I9, h17 18
Misiones, dept., Par. E4 19
Misiones, prov., Arg. E4 29
Miskolc, Hung. A5 10
Misrātah, Libya B8 22
Missaukee, co., Mich. D5 66
Mission, Kans. *B9 61
Mission, Tex. F3 84
Mission City, B.C., Can. E6, f13 37
Mission Hills, Kans. B9 61
Missisquoi, co., Que., Can. D4 42
Mississauga, Ont., Can. D5, m14 41
Mississippi, co., Ark. B5 49
Mississippi, co., Mo. E8 69
Mississippi, state, U.S. 68
Mississippi, riv., U.S. D8 45
Mississippi City, Miss. E4, f7 68
Missoula, Mont. D2 70
Missoula, co., Mont. D2 70
Missoula Southwest, Mont. *D2 70
Missouri, state, U.S. 69
Missouri, riv., U.S. B7 45
Missouri Valley, Iowa C2 60
Mistelbach *an der Zaya*, Aus. D8 6
Misti, vol., Peru E3 31
Mistretta, It. F5 9
Mitaka, Jap. *I9 18
Mitake, Jap. I8, n16 18
Mitchell, Austl. E8 25
Mitchell, Ont., Can. D3 41
Mitchell, Ind. G5 59
Mitchell, Nebr. C2 71
Mitchell, S. Dak. G7 77
Mitchell, co., Ga. E2 55
Mitchell, co., Iowa A5 60
Mitchell, co., Kans. C5 61
Mitchell, co., N.C. e10 76
Mitchell, co., Tex. C2 84
Mitchell, mtn., N.C. f10 76
Mitchellsberg, Ky. C5 62
Mitchellville, Iowa C4 60
Mitilini (Mytilene), Grc. C6 14
Mito, Jap. H10, m19 18
Mittagong, Austl. *F9 25
Mitterteich, Ger., Fed. Rep. of C6 6
Mittweida, Ger. Dem. Rep. C6 6
Mitú, Col. C3 32
Miura, Jap. n18 18
Mixquiahuala, Mex. m13 34
Miyagi, pref., Jap. *G10 18
Miyako, Jap. G10 18
Miyakonojo, Jap. K5 18
Miyazaki, Jap. K5 18
Miyazaki, pref., Jap. *K5 18
Miyazu, Jap. n14 18
Mizil, Rom C8 10
Mizoram, ter., India D9 20
Mjölby, Swe H6 11
Mlada Boleslav, Czech. C3, n18 7
Mława, Pol. B6 7
Moab, Utah B7 72
Mobara, Jap. n19 18
Moberly, Mo. B5 69
Mobile, Ala. E1 46
Mobile, co., Ala. E1 46
Mobridge, S. Dak. E5 77
Moca, mun., P.R. E8 35
Moçambique, Moz. D8 24
Moçâmedes, Ang. D2 24
Mocanaqua, Pa. D9 81
Mochudi, Bots. E5 24
Mocksville, N.C. B2 76
Moclips, Wash. B1 86
Mocoa, Col. C2 32
Mococa, Braz. C3, k8 30
Mocorito, Mex. B3 34
Moctezuma, Mex. B3 34
Modena, It. B3 9
Modesto, Calif. D3 50
Modica, It. F5 9
Modjokerto, Indon. *G4 19
Modlin, Pol. B6, k13 7
Mödling, Aus. D8 6
Modoc, co.,Calif. B3 50
Modřany, Czech. o17 7
Moeo-Yallourn, Austl. I6 26
Moffat, co., Colo. A2 51
Mogadishu, Som. H7 23
Mogadore, Ohio A4 78
Mogaung, Bur. C10 20
Mogi das Cruzes, Braz. C3, m8 30
Mogilev, Sov. Un. E8 12
Mogilev-Podolskiy, Sov. Un. G6 12
Mogilno, Pol. B4 7
Mogi Mirim, Braz. C3, m8 30
Mogocha, Sov. Un. D14 13
Mogok, Bur. D10 20
Moguer, Sp. D2 8
Mohács, Hung. C4 10
Mohall, N. Dak. B4 77
Mohammedia, Mor. B3 22
Mohave, co., Ariz. B1 48
Mohawk, Mich. A2 66
Mohawk, N.Y. C5 75
Mohnton, Pa. F10 81
Moinesti, Rom. B8 10
Moissac, Fr. E4 5
Mojave, Calif. E4 50
Mokleumne Hill, Calif. C3 50
Mokena, Ill. k9 58
Mokpo, Kor I3 18
Mol, Yugo C5 10
Mola *de Bari*, It. D6 9
Molalla, Oreg. B4 80
Mold, Wales *D5 4
Moldavia, reg., Rom. B8 10
Moldavia (S.S.R.), rep., Sov. Un. H7 12
Molepolole, Bots. E5 24
Molfetta, It. D6 9
Molina, Chile B2 28
Molina de Segura, Sp. C5 8
Moline, Ill. B3 58
Moline, Kans. E7 61
Moline, Mich. F5 66
Moline Acres, Mo. *C7 69
Molino, Fla. u14 54
Molino de Rosas, Mex. h9 34
Moliterno, It. D5 9
Mollendo, Peru E3 31
Mölndal, Swe I5 11
Molodechno, Sov. Un. D6 12
Molotovsk, Sov. Un. E18 11
Molotovskoye, Sov. Un. I13 12
Molus, Ky. D6 62
Mombasa, Ken. I5 23
Mombetsu, Jap. D11 18
Momence, Ill. B6 58
Momostenango, Guat. *D6 34
Mompós, Col. B3 32
Monaca, Pa. E1 81
Monaco, country, Eur. F7 5
Monagas, state, Ven. B5 32
Monaghan, S.C. B5 82
Monaghan, co., Ire. *C3 4
Monahans, Tex. D1 84
Monarch, S.C. B4 82
Monarch, mtn., B.C., Can. D5, n17 37
Monashee, mts., B.C., Can. D8 37
Monastir, Tur. A7 22
Monchegorsk, Sov. Un. D15 11
Mönchengladbach, Ger., Fed. Rep. of C3 6
Moncks Corner, S.C. E7 82
Monclova, Mex. B4 34
Moncton, N.B., Can. C5 43
Mondoñedo, Sp. A2 8
Mondovì, It. B1 9
Mondovi, Wis. D2 88
Monessen, Pa. F2 81
Monett, Mo. E4 69
Monette, Ark. B4 49
Monfalcone, It. B4 9
Monforte de Lemos, Sp. A2 8
Monfort Heights, Ohio *C1 78
Monghyr, India C8 20
Mong Mit, Bur. D10 20
Mongolia, country, Asia B4 17
Moniquirá, Col. B3 32
Moniteau, co., Mo. C5 69
Monmouth, Ill. C3 58
Monmouth, Oreg. C3, k11 80
Monmouth, co., N.J. C4 74
Monmouth, co., Wales *E5 4
Monmouth, mtn., B.C., Can. D6 37
Monmouth Beach, N.J. C5 74
Monmouth Junction, N.J. C3 74
Mono, co., Calif. D4 50
Monon, Ind. C4 59
Monona, Iowa A6 60
Monona, Wis. E4 88
Monona, co., Iowa B1 60
Monongah, W. Va. B4, k10 87
Monongahela, Pa. F2 81
Monongahela, riv., Pa. G2 81
Monongalia, co., W. Va. B4 87
Monopoli, It. D6 9
Monor, Hung. B4 10
Monóvar, Sp. C5 8
Monponsett, Mass. B9 65
Monreale, It. E4 9
Monroe, Conn. D3 52
Monroe, Ga. C3 55
Monroe, Iowa C4 60
Monroe, La. B3 63
Monroe, Mich. G7 66
Monroe, N.Y. D6, m14 75
Monroe, N.C. C2 76
Monroe, Ohio *C1 78
Monroe, Utah B5 72
Monroe, Va. C3 85
Monroe, Wash. B4 86
Monroe, Wis. F4 88
Monroe, co., Ala. D2 46
Monroe, co., Ark. C4 49
Monroe, co., Fla. G5 54
Monroe, co., Ga. D3 55
Monroe, co., Ill. E3 58
Monroe, co., Ind. F4 59
Monroe, co., Iowa D5 60
Monroe, co., Ky. D4 62
Monroe, co., Mich. G7 66
Monroe, co., Miss. B5 68
Monroe, co., Mo. B5 69
Monroe, co., N.Y. B3 75
Monroe, co., Ohio C4 78
Monroe, co., Pa. D11 81
Monroe, co., Tenn. D9 83
Monroe, co., W. Va. D4 87
Monroe, co., Wis. E3 88
Monroe City, Mo. B6 69
Monroeville, Ala. D2 46
Monroeville, Ind. C8 59
Monroeville, Ohio A3 78
Monroeville, Pa. *E1 81
Monrovia, Calif. m13 50
Monrovia, Lib. G2 22
Mons, Bel. B5 5
Monson, Maine C3 64
Monson, Mass. B2 65
Montague, Calif. B2 50
Montague, P.E.I., Can. C7 43
Montague, Mass. A2 65
Montague, Mich. E4 66
Montague, co., Tex. C4 84
Montague City, Mass. A2 65
Mont Alto, Pa. G6 81
Montalvo, Calif. *E4 50
Montana, state, U.S. 70
Montánchez, Sp. C2 8
Montargis, Fr. D5 5
Montauban, Que., Can. C5 42
Montauban, Fr. E4 5
Montauk, N.Y. m17 75

N

O

P

Q

Qamdo, China	E4	17
Qāna, Leb.	A3	15
Qaṣr al Farāfirah, Eg.	C3	23
Qatar, country, Asia	D5	15
Qazvin, Iran	B5	15
Qiemo, China	A8	20
Qina, Eg.	C4	23
Qingdao, China	D9	17
Qinghai, prov., China	D4	17
Qinghai, lake, China	D4	17
Qingjiang, China	E8	20
Qinhuangdao, China	D8	17
Qiqihar, China	B9	17
Qitai, China	C2	17
Qiryat Shemona, Isr.	A3	15
Qiryat Yam, Isr.	B3	15
Qom, Iran	C5	15
Quakenbruck, Ger., Fed. Rep. of	B3	6
Quaker Hill, Conn.	D8	52
Quakertown, Pa.	F11	81
Quanah, Tex.	B3	84
Quang Ngai, Viet.	B3	19
Quang Tri, Viet.	B3	19
Quantico, Va.	B5	85
Quanzhou, China	G8	17
Quapaw, Okla.	A7	79
Quaraí, Braz.	E1	30
Quarryville, Pa.	G9	81
Quartu Sant' Elena, It.	E2	9
Quartz Hill, Calif.	*E4	50
Quay, co., N. Mex.	B7	48
Québec, Que., Can.	C6, n17	42
Québec, co., Que., Can.	B5	42
Québec, prov., Can.		42
Québec-Quest, Que., Can.	*C6	42
Quedlinburg, Ger. Dem. Rep.	C5	6
Queen Annes, co., Md.	B5	53
Queen Bess, mtn., B.C., Can.	D5	37
Queen City, Tex.	*C5	84
Queen Elizabeth is., N.W. Ter., Can.	m31	36
Queens, borough and co., N.Y.	E7	75
Queens, co., N.B., Can.	D4	43
Queens, co., N.S., Can.	E4	43
Queens, co., P.E.I., Can.	C6	43
Queensland, state, Austl.	D7	25
Queenstown, S. Afr.	G5	24
Quelimane, Moz.	D7	24
Querétaro, Mex.	C4, m13	34
Querétaro, state, Mex.	C4, m13	34
Quesada, Sp.	D4	8
Quesnel, B.C., Can.	C6	37
Questa, N. Mex.	A6	48
Quetta, Pak.	B4	20
Quezaltenango, Guat.	E6	34
Quezaltepeque, Sal.	*E7	34
Quezon, prov., Phil.	*C6	19
Quezon City, Phil.	C6	19
Quibdó, Col.	B2	32
Quidnessett, R.I.	C11	52
Quidnick, R.I.	C10	52
Quiindy, Par.	E4	29
Quilá, Mex.	C3	34
Quillota, Chile	A2	28
Quilmes, Arg	g7	28
Quilon, India	G6	20
Quilpie, Austl.	E7	25
Quilpué, Chile	A2	28
Quimper, Fr.	C2	5
Quimperlé, Fr.	D2	5
Quincy, Calif.	C3	50
Quincy, Fla.	B2	54
Quincy, Ill.	D2	58
Quincy, Mass.	h11	65
Quincy, Mich.	G6	66
Quincy, Wash.	B6	86
Qui Nhon, Viet.	C3	19
Quinnville, R.I.	B11	52
Quintana de la Serena, Sp.	C3	8
Quintanar, Sp.	C4	8
Quintana Roo, state, Mex.	D7	34
Quinter, Kans.	C3	61
Quinton, Okla.	B6	79
Quiroga, Sp.	A2	8
Quitman, Ga.	F3	55
Quitman, Miss.	C5	68
Quitman, Tex.	C5	84
Quitman, co., Ga.	E1	55
Quitman, co., Miss.	A3	68
Quito, Ec.	B2	31
Quixadá, Braz.	*D7	27
Quxian, China	F8	17

R

Raba, Indon.	G5	19
Rabat, Mor.	B3	22
Rabaul, Pap. N. Gui.	h13	25
Rabun, Ala.	D2	46
Rabun, co., Ga.	B3	55
Raceland, Ky.	B7	62
Raceland, La.	E5, k10	63
Rach Gia, Viet.	*C2	19
Racibórz, Pol.	C5	7
Racine, Wis.	F6, n12	88
Racine, co., Wis.	F5	88
Radauti, Rom.	B7	10
Radcliff, Ky.	C4	62
Radeberg, Ger. Dem. Rep.	C6	6
Radford (Independent City), Va.	C2	85
Radiant Valley, Md.	C4	53
Radnor, Pa.	*G11	81
Radnor, co., Wales	*D5	4
Radom, Pol.	C6	7
Radomir, Bul.	D6	10
Radomsko, Pol.	C5	7
Radville, Sask., Can.	H3	39
Radzionków, Pol.	g9	7
Rãe Bareli, India	C7	20
Raeford, N.C.	C3	76
Rafaela, Arg.	A4	28
Rafah, Gaza Strip	C2	15
Ragland, Ala.	B3	46
Ragusa, It.	F5	9
Rahīmyár-Khān, Pak.	C5	20
Rahway, N.J.	B4, k7	74
Rāichūr, India	E6	20
Raigarh, India	D7	20
Rainbow City, Ala.	*A3	46
Rainbow City, Pan.	*B2	32
Rainier, Oreg.	A4	80
Rainier, mtn., Wash.	C4	86
Rains, co., Tex.	C5	84
Rainsville, Ala.	A4	46
Rainy River, Ont., Can.	*o16	41
Rainy River, dist., Ont., Can.	o16	41
Raipur, India	D7	20
Rãjahmundry, India	E7	20
Rajapalaiyam, India	*G6	20
Rãjasthãn, state, India	C5	20
Rãjkot, India	D5	20
Rãjshãhi, Bngl.	D8	20
Rakovník, Czech.	C2	7
Rakvere, Sov. Un.	B6	12
Raleigh, N.C.	B4	76
Raleigh, W. Va.	n13	87
Raleigh, co., W. Va.	D3	87
Ralls, Tex.	C2	84
Ralls, co., Mo.	B6	69
Ralston, Nebr.	g12	71
Rãm Allãh, Jordan	C3	15
Ramat Gan, Isr.	B2	15
Ramat HaSharon, Isr.	*B2	15
Rambervillers, Fr.	C7	5
Ramea, Newf., Can.	E3	44
Ramenskoye, Sov. Un.	D12, n18	12
Ramla, Isr.	C2	15
Ramleh, Eg.	*G8	14
Ramona, Calif.	F5	50
Rãmpur, India	C6	20
Ramsay, Mich.	n12	66
Ramseur, N.C.	B3	76
Ramsey, N.J.	A4	74
Ramsey, co. Minn.	E5	67
Ramsey, co., N. Dak.	B7	77
Ramsgate, Eng.	E7	4
Rancagua, Chile	A2	28
Ranches of Taos, N. Mex.	A6	48
Rãnchī, India	D8	20
Rancho Cordova, Calif.	*C3	50
Rand, W. Va.	m12	87
Randall, co., Tex.	B2	84
Randallstown, Md.	B4	53
Randers, Den.	I4	11
Randers, co., Den.	*I4	11
Randleman, N.C.	B3	76
Randolph, Maine	D3	64
Randolph, Mass.	B5, h11	65
Randolph, Nebr.	B8	71
Randolph, Vt.	D2	73
Randolph, Wis.	E4	88
Randolph, co., Ala.	B4	46
Randolph, co., Ark.	A4	49
Randolph, co., Ga.	E2	55
Randolph, co., Ill.	E4	58
Randolph, co., Ind.	D7	59
Randolph, co., Mo.	B5	69
Randolph, co., N.C.	B3	76
Randolph, co., W. Va.	C5	87
Randolph Hills, Md.	*B3	53
Rangely, Colo.	A2	51
Ranger, Tex.	C3	84
Rangoon, Bur.	E10	20
Rangpur, Bngl.	C8	20
Rãnīganj, India	D8	20
Rankin, Pa.	k14	81
Rankin, Tex.	D2	84
Rankin, co., Miss.	C4	68
Ranlo, N.C.	*B1	76
Ranshaw, Pa.	*E9	81
Ransom, co., N. Dak.	D8	77
Ranson, W. Va.	B7	87
Rantoul, Ill.	C5	58
Rapallo, It.	B2	9
Rapid City, S. Dak.	F2	77
Rapides, par., La.	C3	63
Rappahannock, co., Va.	B4	85
Raritan, N.J.	B3	74
Raseiniai, Sov. Un.	A7	77
Rashīd (Rosetta), Eg.	G8	14
Rasht, Iran	A7	23
Rasskazovo, Sov. Un.	E13	12
Rastatt, Ger. Dem. Rep. of	D4	6
Rat Buri, Thai.	C1	19
Rathenow, Ger. Dem. Rep.	B6	6
Ratibor, see Raciborz, Pol.		
Ratlãm, India	*D6	20
Ratnãgiri, India	E5	20
Raton, N. Mex.	A6	48
Rauch, Arg.	B5	28
Rauma, Fin.	G9	11
Raurkela, India	*D7	20
Ravalli, co., Mont.	D2	70
Rava-Russkaya, Sov. Un.	F4	12
Raven, Va.	e10	85
Ravena, N.Y.	C7	75
Ravenna, It.	B4	9
Ravenna, Ky.	C6	62
Ravenna, Nebr.	C7	71
Ravenna, Ohio	A4	78
Ravensburg, Ger., Fed. Rep. of	E4	6
Ravenswood, W. Va.	C3	87
Rãwalpindi, Pak.	B5	20
Rawa Mazowiecka, Pol.	C6	7
Rawdon, Que., Can.	C4	42
Rawicz, Pol.	C4	7
Rawlins, Wyo.	E5	89
Rawlins, co.,Kans.	C2	61
Rawlins, co., Kan.	C2	61
Ray, Ariz.	C3, D3	48
Ray, N. Dak.	B2	77
Ray, co., Mo.	B3	69
Raybon, Ga.	E5	55
Raychikhinsk, Sov. Un.	B4	18
Raymond, Alta, Can.	E4	38
Raymond, Miss.	C3	68
Raymond, Wash.	C2	86
Raymond Terrace, Austl.	F8	26
Raymondville, Tex.	F4	84
Rayne, La.	D3	63
Raynham Center, Mass.	C5	65
Rayong, Thai.	*C2	19
Raytown, Ga.	C4	55
Raytown, Mo.	h11	69
Rayville, La.	B4	63
Razgrad, Bul.	D8	10
Razlog, Bul.	E6	10
Reading, Eng.	E6	4
Reading, Mass.	A5, f11	65
Reading, Mich.	G6	66
Reading, Ohio	C1, o13	78
Reading, Pa.	F10	81
Reagan, co., Tex.	D2	84
Real, co., Tex.	E3	84
Ream, Camb.	*C2	19
Ream, W. Va.	*D3	87
Reamstown, Pa.	F9	81
Recanati, It.	C4	9
Rechitsa, Sov. Un.	E8	12
Recife (Pernambuco), Braz.	D7	27
Recklinghausen, Ger., Fed. Rep. of	C3	6
Reconquista, Arg.	E4	29
Rector, Ark.	A5	49
Red, riv., U.S.	D8	45
Red, sea, Afr.	D9	21
Red, sea, Asia	D9	21
Red Bank, N.J.	C4	74
Red Bank, Tenn.	D8	83
Red Bay, Ala.	A1	46
Red Bluff, Calif.	B2	50
Red Boiling Springs, Tenn.	C8	83
Red Bud, Ill.	E4	58

S

T

U

V

W

X

Xánthi, Grc. ... B5 14
Xavier, Kans. ... B8 61
Xenia, Ohio ... C2 78
Xiamen, China ... G8 17
Xi'an, China ... E6 17
Xiangtan, China ... F7 17

Xianyang, China ... E6 17
Xichang, China ... F5 17
Xigazê, China ... C8 20
Xi Jiang, riv., China ... G7 17
Xilitla, Mex. ... m14 34
Xingú, riv., Braz. ... D5 27

Xining, China ... D5 17
Xinjiang Uygur, auton. reg. China ... F11 13
Xinmin, China ... C9 17
Xinxiang, China ... D7 17
Xinyang, China ... E7 17

Xixabangma, mtn., China ... C8 20
Xochimilco, Mex. ... h9 34
Xuanhua, China ... C8 17
Xuchang, China ... E7 17
Xuzhou, China ... E8 17

Y

Ya'an, China ... F5 17
Yadkin, co., N.C. ... A2 76
Yadkinville, N.C. ... A2 76
Yaizu, Jap. ... o17 18
Yakima, Wash. ... C5 86
Yakima, co., Wash. ... C5 86
Yakutsk, Sov. Un. ... C15 13
Yalobusha, co., Miss. ... A4 68
Yalta, Sov. Un. ... I10 12
Yalu, China ... B9 17
Yalvaç, Tur. ... C8 14
Yamachiche, Que., Can. ... C5 42
Yamagata, Jap. ... G10 18
Yamagata, pref.,Jap. ... *G10 18
Yamaguchi, Jap. ... I5 18
Yamaguchi, pref., Jap. ... *I5 18
Yamanashi, pref., Jap. ... *I9 18
Yamaska, co., Que., Can. ... C5 42
Yambol, Bul. ... D8 10
Yamethin, Bur. ... D10 20
Yamhill, co., Oreg. ... B3 80
Yamoussoukro, I.C. ... G3 22
Yanam, India ... E7 20
Yanbu', Sau. Ar. ... E2 15
Yancey, co., N.C. ... f10 76
Yanceyville, N.C. ... A3 76
Yangquan, China ... D7 17
Yangtze, riv., China ... E8 17
Yangzhou, China ... E8 17
Yankton, S. Dak. ... H8 77
Yankton, co., S. Dak. ... G8 77
Yanji, China ... C10 17
Yanqi, China ... C2 17
Yantai, China ... D9 17
Yao, Jap. ... *I7 18
Yaoundé, Cam. ... H7 22
Yaracuy, state, Ven. ... A4 32
Yardley, Pa. ... F12 81
Yarīm, Yemen ... G3 15
Yarmouth, N.S., Can. ... F3 43
Yarmouth, Maine ... E2, g7 64
Yarmouth, co., N.S., Can. ... F4 43
Yaroslavl, Sov. Un. ... C12 12
Yartsevo, Sov. Un. ... D9 12
Yarumal, Col. ... B2 32

Yasinovataya, Sov. Un. ... q20 12
Yass, Austl. ... G7 26
Yates, co., N.Y. ... C3 75
Yates Center, Kans. ... E8 61
Yatsushiro, Jap. ... J5 18
Yauco, P.R. ... *G11 35
Yavapai, co., Ariz. ... B2 48
Yavorov, Sov. Un. ... G4 12
Yawatahama, Jap. ... J6 18
Yazd (Yezd), Iran ... B8 23
Yazoo, co., Miss. ... C3 68
Yazoo City, Mis. ... C3 68
Yeadon, Pa. ... q20 81
Yeagertown, Pa. ... E6 81
Yecla, Sp. ... C5 8
Yefremov, Sov. Un. ... E12 12
Yegoryevsk, Sov. Un. ... D12, n19 12
Yelan, Sov. Un. ... F14 12
Yelets, Sov. Un. ... E12 12
Yell, co.,Ark. ... B2 49
Yellow, see Huang He, riv., China
Yellow, sea, China ... D9 17
Yellowknife, N.W. Ter. Can. ... D11 36
Yellow Medicine, co., Minn. ... F2 67
Yellow Springs, Ohio ... C2 78
Yellowstone, co., Mont. ... D8 70
Yellowstone, riv., U.S. ... B2 89
Yellowstone National Park (part), co., Wyo. ... B2 89
Yemen, country, Asia ... F3 15
Yemen, People's Democratic Republic of, country, Asia ... H7 16
Yenakiyevo, Sov. Un. ... q20 12
Yenangyaung, Bur. ... *G4 17
Yenisey, riv., Sov. Un. ... C11 16
Yeniseysk, Sov. Un. ... D12 13
Yeovil, Eng. ... E5 4
Yeppoon, Austl. ... D9 25
Yerevan, Sov. Un. ... E7 13
Yerupaja, mtn., Peru ... D2 31
Yessey, Sov. Un. ... C13 13
Yevpatoriya, Sov. Un. ... I9 12
Yeysk, Sov. Un. ... H12 12
Yiannitsá, Grc. ... *B4 14
Yibin, China ... F5 17

Yichang, China ... E7 17
Yichun, China ... C4 18
Yilan, China ... B10 17
Yiliang, China ... G5 17
Yinchuan, China ... D6 17
Yingkou, China ... C9 17
Yiyang, China ... F7 17
Yoakum, Tex. ... E4 84
Yoakum, co., Tex. ... C1 84
Yogyakarta, Indon. ... G4 9
Yoichi, Jap. ... E10 18
Yokkaichi, Jap. ... I8, o15 18
Yokohama, Jap. ... I9, n18 18
Yokosuka, Jap. ... I9, n18 18
Yokote, Jap. ... G10 18
Yolo, co., Calif. ... C2 50
Yolyn, W. Va. ... D5 87
Yonago, Jap. ... I6 18
Yonezawa, Jap. ... H10 18
Yonghung, Kor. ... G3 18
Yonkers, N.Y. ... E7, n15 75
Yonne, dept., Fr. ... *D5 5
Yorba Linda, Calif. ... *F5 50
York, Ala. ... C1 46
York, Ont., Can. ... *m15 41
York, Eng. ... D6 4
York, Maine ... E1 64
York, Nebr. ... D8 71
York, Pa. ... G8 81
York, S.C. ... B5 82
York, co., N.B., Can. ... C3 43
York, co., Ont., Can. ... D5 43
York, co., Eng. ... *D6 4
York, co., Maine ... E2 64
York, co., Nebr. ... D8 71
York, co., Pa. ... G8 81
York, co., S.C. ... A5 82
York, co., Va. ... C6 85
Yorkshire, N.Y. ... C2 75
Yorkton, Sask.,Can. ... F4, n8 39
Yorktown, Ind. ... D6 59
Yorktown, N.Y. ... *D7 75
Yorktown, Tex. ... E4 84
Yorktown Heights, N.Y. ... *D7 75
Yorktown Manor, R.I. ... C11 52

Yorkville, Ill. ... B5 58
Yorkville, N.Y. ... B5 75
Yorkville, Ohio ... B5 78
Yoshkar-Ola, Sov. Un. ... *D7 13
Yōsu, Kor. ... I3 18
Young, Austl. ... *F8 25
Young, co., Tex. ... C3 84
Youngstown, N.Y. ... B2 75
Youngstown, Ohio ... A5 78
Youngsville, La. ... D3 63
Youngsville, Pa. ... C3 81
Youngtown, Ariz. ... D1 48
Youngwood, Pa. ... F2 81
Yozgat, Tur. ... C10 14
Ypacaraí, Par. ... E4 29
Ypsilanti, Mich. ... F7, p4 66
Yreka, Calif. ... B2 50
Ystad, Swe. ... J5 11
Yuanling, China ... F7 17
Yuba, co., Calif. ... C3 50
Yuba City, Calif. ... C3 50
Yuba City South, Calif. ... *C3 50
Yūbari, Jap. ... E10 18
Yucatán, state, Mex. ... C7 34
Yueyang, China ... F7 17
Yugoslavia, country, Eur. ... C3 10
Yukon, Okla. ... B4 79
Yukon, ter., Can. ... D6 36
Yukon, riv., N.A. ... C9 47
Yuma, Ariz. ... C1 48
Yuma, Colo. ... A8 51
Yuma, co., Ariz. ... C2 48
Yuma, co., Colo. ... A8 51
Yumen, China ... D4 17
Yumenzhen, China ... C4 17
Yunnan, prov., China ... G5 17
Yurécuaro, Mex. ... m12 34
Yuryevets, Sov. Un. ... C14 12
Yuryev-Polskiy, Sov. Un. ... C12 12
Yuty, Par. ... E4 29
Yuzha, Sov. Un. ... C13 12
Yuzhno-Sakhalinsk, Sov. Un. ... E17 13
Yverdon, Switz. ... E3 6

Z

Zabkowice, Pol. ... C4 7
Zabrze, Pol. ... C5, g9 7
Zacatecas, Mex. ... C4 34
Zacatecas, state, Mex. ... C4, m12 34
Zachary, La. ... D4 63
Zadar, Yugo. ... C2 10
Zagorsk, Sov. Un. ... C12 12
Zagreb, Yugo. ... C2 10
Zāhedān, Iran ... G9 16
Zaḥlah, Leb. ... F10 14
Zaire, country, Afr. ... B4 24
Zaječar, Yugo. ... D6 10
Zákinthos, Grc. ... D3 14
Zákinthos (Zante), prov., Grc. ... *D3 14
Zakopane, Pol. ... D5 7
Zala, co., Hung. ... *B3 10
Zalaegerszeg, Hung. ... B3 10
Zalău, Rom. ... B6 10
Zambales, prov., Phil. ... *B5 19
Zambezi, riv., Afr. ... H8 21
Zambia (Northern Rhodesia), country, Afr. ... D5 24
Zamboanga, Phil. ... D6 19
Zamboanga del Norte, prov., Phil. ... *D6 19
Zamboanga del Sur., prov., Phil. ... *D6 19
Zamora, Sp. ... B3 8
Zamora, prov., Sp. ... *B3 8
Zamora de Hidalgo, Mex. ... C4, n12 34
Zamość, Pol. ... C7 7

Zanesville, Ohio ... C4 78
Zanjān, Iran ... A7 23
Zanzibar, Tan. ... B7 24
Zapata, Tex. ... F3 84
Zapata, co., Tex. ... F3 84
Zaporozhye, Sov. Un. ... H10 12
Zaragoza, Sp. ... B5 8
Zaragoza, prov., Sp. ... *B5 8
Zárate, Arg. ... A5, g7 28
Zaraysk, Sov. Un. ... D12 12
Zaria, Nig. ... F6 22
Zashiversk, Sov. Un. ... C17 13
Zatec, Czech. ... C2 7
Zavala, co., Tex. ... E3 84
Zavitaya, Sov. Un. ... D15 13
Zawiercie, Pol. ... C5, g10 7
Zaysan, Sov. Un. ... E11 13
Zdolbunov, Sov. Un. ... F6 12
Zduńska Wola, Pol. ... C5 7
Zebulon, N.C. ... B4 76
Zeeland, Mich. ... F5 66
Zeeland, prov., Neth. ... B5 5
Zefat (Safad), Isr. ... B3, g5 15
Zehdenick, Ger. Dem. Rep. ... B6 6
Zeigler, Ill. ... F4 58
Zeist, Neth. ... A6 5
Zeitz, Ger. Dem. Rep. ... C6 6
Zelienople, Pa. ... E1 81
Zella-Mehlis, Ger. Dem. Rep. ... C5 6
Zemetchino, Sov. Un. ... E14 12
Zenica, Yugo. ... C3 10

Zephyrhills, Fla. ... D4 54
Zerbst, Ger. Dem. Rep. ... C6 6
Zeya, Sov. Un. ... D15 13
Zgierz, Pol. ... C5 7
Zhangjiakou, China ... C7 17
Zhangzhou, China ... G8 17
Zhanjiang, China ... G7 17
Zhaoqing, China ... G7 17
Zhaoxing, China ... C5 18
Zhaozhou, China ... D2 18
Zhdanov, Sov. Un. ... H11 12
Zhejiang, prov., China ... F9 17
Zhengzhou, China ... E7 17
Zhenjiang, China ... E8 17
Zhitomir, Sov. Un. ... F7 12
Zhizdra, Sov. Un. ... E10 12
Zhmerinka, Sov. Un. ... G7 12
Zhongba, China ... C7 20
Zhuzhou, China ... F7 17
Zibo, China ... D8 17
Ziebach, co., S. Dak. ... F4 77
Zielona Gora, Pol. ... C3 7
Zigong, China ... F5 17
Ziguinchor, Sen. ... F1 22
Zile, Tur. ... B10 14
Zilina, Czech. ... D5 7
Zilwaukee, Mich. ... E7 66
Zimbabwe, country, Afr. ... D6 24
Zimnicea, Rom. ... D7 10
Zinder, Niger. ... F6 22
Zion, Ill. ... A6, h9 58

Zionsville, Ind. ... E5, k9 59
Zipaquirá, Col. ... B3 32
Zitácuaro, Mex. ... n13 34
Zittau, Ger. Dem. Rep. ... C7 6
Zlatoust, Sov. Un. ... D8 13
Zlynka, Sov. Un. ... E8 12
Znamenka, Sov. Un. ... G9 12
Znojmo, Czech. ... D4 7
Zolochev, Sov. Un. ... G5 12
Zolotonosha, Sov. Un. ... G9 12
Zomba, Malawi ... D7 24
Zonguldak, Tur. ... B8 14
Zrejanin (Petrovgrad), Yugo. ... C5 10
Zug, Switz. ... E4 6
Zug, canton, Switz. ... *E4 6
Zulia, state, Ven. ... B3 32
Zumbrota, Minn. ... F6 67
Zuni, N. Mex. ... B4 48
Zunyi, China ... F6 17
Zürich, Switz. ... *E4 6
Zürich, canton, Switz. ... *E4 6
Zutphen, Neth. ... A7 5
Zvenigorodka, Sov. Un. ... G8 12
Zvolen, Czech. ... D5 7
Zweibrücken, Ger., Fed. Rep. of ... D3 6
Zwickau, Ger. Dem. Rep. ... C6 6
Zwolle, La. ... C2 63
Zwolle, Neth. ... A7 5
Zyrardów, Pol. ... B6, m12 7